6-13

TATLIN

TATLIN

Edited by Larissa Alekseevna Zhadova

(Frontispiece) Tatlin, 1930s. Taken by M. Nappelbaum. Photograph: Collection M. Nappelbaum's family, Leningrad

Title of the Hungarian original: Tatlin, published by Corvina Kiadó, Budapest, 1984

This book is based on a Russian manuscript that was written for Corvina, Budapest, by the following authors:
Larissa Alekseevna Zhadova †, editor
Vladimir Ivanovich Kostin
Aleksandr Efimovich Parnis
Dmitrii Vladimirovich Sarab'ianov
Konstantin Mikhailovich Simonov †
Anatolii Anatol'evich Strigalev
Flora Iakovlevna Syrkina

The text was prepared for publication by **Éva Körner**
English translation by Paul Filotas, Mária Julian, Eugenia Lockwood, Doris Macknight, Éva Polgár, Colin Wright

Translation revised by Colin Wright

Designed by Simon Koppány

Published in the United States of America in 1988 by
RIZZOLI INTERNATIONAL PUBLICATIONS, INC.
597 Fifth Avenue, New York, NY 10017

Original edition published in Hungary by Corvina Kiadó, Budapest
This edition for sale in the USA only

Library of Congress Cataloging-in-Publication Data

Tatlin.
  Includes writings of Tatlin.
  Bibliography: p. 514
  Includes index.
  1. Tatlin, Vladimir Evgrafovich, 1885—1953 —
Criticism and interpretation. 2. Constructivism
(Art) — Russian S.F.S.R.I. Tatlin, Vladimir
Evgrafovich, 1885—1953. Il. Zhadova, L. (Larissa)
N6999.T39T38 1987 709'.2'4 86—31605
ISBN 0—8478—0827—0

Printed and bound in Hungary

Contents

Preface 8

Foreword: An Extraordinary Man, K.M. Simonov (Translated by Mária Julian) 10

Part One: Studies on Tatlin

From Painting to the Construction of Matter, A.A. Strigalev 13
(Translated by Mária Julian)

Tatlin's Painting, D.V. Sarab'ianov 44
(Translated by Paul Filotas)

'Composition-Analysis', or a New Synthesis?, L.A. Zhadova 63
(Translated by Paul Filotas)

Tatlin's Drawings, V.I. Kostin 67
(Translated by Doris Macknight)

Tatlin, the Illustrator and Designer of Books, L.A. Zhadova 129
(Translated by Paul Filotas)

Tatlin, the Organizer of Material into Objects, L.A. Zhadova 134
(Translated by Doris Macknight and Éva Polgár)

Tatlin's Theatre, F.I. Syrkina 155
(Translated by Mária Julian)

Part Two: Documents
1 Tatlin's Writings (Translated by Colin Wright)
Selection and Commentaries by A.A. Strigalev and L.A. Zhadova

Letter to the Editor [Studiia] (1911) 181

[Letter about a Trip Abroad] (1914) 181

[Letter to Shkol'nik] (1913) 182

[Letter to Benois] (1913) 182

[Letter to Anna Darmolatova] (1914) 184

On the Organization of an 'Artistic Society' on New Principles (1914) 184

My Answer to 'Letter to the Futurists' (1918) 185

Memorandum of the Moscow Artistic Collegium of the People's Commissariat
  of Education to the Council of People's Commissars, on the Erection of
  50 Monuments to Outstanding Figures (1918) 185

[Letter to Lunacharskii] (1918) 187

[Report on a Museum of Contemporary Art] (1918) 237

The Initiative Individual in the Creativity of the Collective (1919) 237

[Letter to Neradovskii] (1919)   **238**

The Work Ahead of Us (1920)   **239**

List of Works (1921)   **240**

To the Museums Department of the Petrograd Directorate of the Institutions of the Academic Centre (1922)   **241**

Programme for the Exhibition 'A Survey of New Tendencies in Art' (1922)   **242**

[Tatlin's Slogans] (1920–23)   **244**

[Letter to Miturich] (1922)   **245**

[Letter to Maiakovskii] (1922)   **245**

To the Head of the Petrograd Directorate of Scientific and Artistic Institutions, Kristi (1923)   **246**

[Letter to Matiushin] (1923)   **247**

On 'Zangezi' (1923)   **248**

Summary of the Programme of the Section for Research on the Construction of the Object (Material Culture) (1923)   **249**

[Extracts from Tugendkhol'd's Article 'On the Discussion of a Memorial to C[omrade] Lenin'] (1924)   **250**

Report of the Section for Material Culture under the Museum of Artistic Culture to the Leningrad Division of the Main Directorate of Scientific Institutions (1924)   **250**

To the Leningrad Division of Glavnauka (1924)   **252**

[Letter to Spandikov] (1924)   **253**

Research Plan of the Section for Material Culture under the Museum of Artistic Culture for 1924 and 1925 (1924)   **254**

Report of the Section for Material Culture's Work for 1923–1924 (1924)   **254**

Report of the Section for Material Culture's Research Work for 1924 (1924)   **256**

To the Leningrad Division of Glavnauka (1924)   **257**

To the Director of the Leningrad Division of Glavnauka, Kristi (1924)   **259**

To the Committee for the USSR Section of the International Exhibition in Paris (1925)   **259**

[Letter to Novitskii] (1927)   **260**

[Letter to Neradovskii] (1927)   **261**

Questionnaire (1928)   **262**

Autobiography (1929)   **264**

The Artist as an Organizer of Everyday Life (1929)   **266**

The Problem of the Relationship between Man and Object (1930)   **267**

[From Zelinskii's Interview 'Letatlin'] (1932)   **309**

[From Rakhtanov's Essay 'Letatlin – an Aerial Bicycle'] (1932)   **309**

Art into Technology (1932)   **310**

[From Kut's Notes 'Return to Painting. At an Evening for the Artist Tatlin'] (1933)   **312**

[Speech at a 'Creative Evening' for Petrov-Vodkin] (1933)   **313**

[From the Article (Signed 'Sh.') 'Artist or Constructor. Tatlin Designs Ostrovskii'] (1934)   **314**

[From the Article 'Tatlin in the Theatre. A Conversation with the Artist'] (1935)   **315**

The Moon on Stage (1944)   **316**

[Speech at a Re-election Meeting of the Section of the Theatre Arts of the Moscow Branch of the Union of Soviet Artists] (1948)   **318**

[Speech at a Discussion of the Artist Shifrin's Works] (1949) 319

Curriculum Vitae of Honoured Art Worker Tatlin (1953) 320

[Letter about Work on Models] (1953) 329

2 Writings on Tatlin (Translated by Eugenia Lockwood)
Selection and Commentaries by L.A. Zhadova and A.E. Parnis

Vladimir Evgrafovich Tatlin (1915) 331

S.K. Isakov, On Tatlin's Counter-Reliefs (1915) 333

V. Khlebnikov, Tatlin (1916) 336

A Studio Headed by Tatlin (1918) 338

A New Art Teaching Studio (1919) 339

V. Shklovskii, On *Faktura* and Counter-Reliefs (1920) 341

V. Shklovskii, The Monument to the Third International (1921) 342

N. Punin, The Monument to the Third International (1921) 344

N. Punin, Tatlin (Against Cubism) (1921) 347

[Maiakovskii on Tatlin] (1923) 393

N. Punin, About 'Zangezi' (1923) 395

A.V. Tufanov, On the Stage Production of the Poem 'Zangezi' by Velemir Khlebnikov (1923) 400

N. Punin, Routine and Tatlin (1924) 403

The New Way of Life (1924) 407

K. Artseulov, About *Letatlin* (1932) 408

J. Mácza, About the Artist Tatlin (1934) 409

B. Alekseev, New Elements in the Art of V.E. Tatlin (1940) 411

Exhibition of Tatlin's Works in Moscow in 1977 and Related Materials 437

Appendices

Biographical Data (compiled by L.A. Zhadova) 445

Tatlin at Russian and Soviet Exhibitions (compiled by L.A. Zhadova) 489

List of Tatlin's Works for the Theatre (compiled by F.I. Syrkina) 503

Catalogue of Tatlin's Works Reproduced in this Book 505

Selected Bibliography 514

Picture Credits 518

Abbreviations 519

Subject Index (compiled by Katalin Bakos) 520

Index of Names 527

Preface

Tatlin is a legendary figure of the European avant-garde, but the true impact of his achievement is, paradoxically, little known. This publication is the first attempt to examine, collect and interpret whatever has been associated with Tatlin, to produce a sound monograph on Tatlin.

Vladimir Evgrafovich Tatlin was a painter and inventor, an architect and stage-designer. The richness of his hitherto little known *œuvre* determined the character of this publication and the editors' intention to present a storehouse of information dictated its novel arrangement. The work was undertaken by a team of authors whose fields of research cover Tatlin's entire output. The co-ordinator was Larissa Zhadova and the members were art historians Dmitrii Sarab'ianov, Vladimir Kostin and Anatolii Strigalev, theatre historian Flora Syrkina and literary historian Aleksandr Parnis.

The majority of documents and works of art connected with Tatlin are in Soviet museums, archives and libraries and in private collections. Most of this material has not been accessible to the public before. The authors therefore regarded the publication and analysis of this Russian and Soviet material as their priority.

The authors have divided Tatlin's various activities among them and each section is discussed in the greatest possible detail and depth. This does sometimes result in overlaps and repetitions, which we have – consciously – not eliminated. The reason for this is twofold. First, we did not wish to risk losing even the slightest shade of colour from an emerging portrait of Tatlin and, second, Tatlin's participation in the intellectual, artistic, literary and political life of Russia at that time can only be fully described by presenting an overall analysis of great variety and detail.

We also believe that in a work produced by a team of authors it is inevitable that there should be differences of opinion in the interpretation of certain issues, even data. We believe that a collective search for answers to questions still in dispute – polemics not excluded – could certainly prove fruitful. We hope that this collectively produced monograph will inspire further research into Tatlin and his work through the thought-provoking insights found in the articles and the numerous documents.

The manner in which this volume was compiled is justified not only by the difficulties of research for the above-mentioned reasons but also by the authors' wish (correct from the art-historical point of view) not to stick rigidly to opinions based solely on available documentation while the possibility remains of finding yet more details about Tatlin.

These were the circumstances which dictated the proportions of this publication – namely how the essays and documents should relate to one another in order to present the reader with as much previously unobtainable material as possible. The book contains a large number of documents, both written and pictorial, some of them previously unpublished. Among them are Tatlin's own writings, transcripts of his words and many other documents relating to him.

The section called Writings on Tatlin contains articles which appeared in the Russian–Soviet press between 1915 and 1940. Later, from 1940 to his death in 1953, Tatlin worked with almost no media coverage at all. As an appendix to that part we provide a selection of press reviews of the 1977 Moscow Tatlin Exhibition. Apart from this appendix, the section consists of articles that influenced his life and activities directly, these having been published in the Soviet press or such organs that could have a direct influence on the contemporary Soviet artistic scene. This is precisely why this publication does not contain writings published outside the Soviet Union, since these could in no way have affected the artist's fate and, moreover, they can be found in every library of international repute. There was no point in increasing the already lengthy back matter.

The never-ending process of research shows itself in the collection of documents in this book; even in the last minutes of editing, new documents came to light and were included. Despite all our efforts, in some of these cases we could not ensure full editorial precision.*

Art historian Larissa Zhadova, in addition to her contribution as an author, took over most of the co-ordination and without her devotion this book could never have been realized. She did not, unfortunately, live to see the completion of this volume, her *chef-d'œuvre,* as she unexpectedly died during the final stages of editing. Let this book perpetuate her memory also.

CORVINA, BUDAPEST

We dedicate this book to the memory of Konstantin Mikhailovich Simonov, who with tireless initiative, enthusiasm, energy and care, contributed to the publication of this book.

JANUARY 1980, MOSCOW   THE AUTHORS

*The edition of the original Hungarian version was completed in 1983. Relying on research done since then, the authors have altered some dates. The present book carries the revised dates without indicating where correction has been made.

Foreword
Konstantin Mikhailovich Simonov
AN EXTRAORDINARY MAN

A talented painter and graphic artist, Maiakovskii's first illustrator, outstanding stage and costume designer, creator of one of the most daring architectural projects, Tatlin has secured himself a place in every textbook on modern architecture. He is the inventor and producer of an extraordinary flying construction, designer and maker of novel utilitarian objects like modern working clothes and chairs – which could be placed alongside certain modern furniture designs half a century later. Tatlin is a man who works both in wood and metal, and the list of his activities over his lifetime is not complete even yet. He died in 1953 and rests in the Novodevichii Cemetery in Moscow. He was awarded the title Honoured Art Worker of the Russian Soviet Socialist Federal Republic in his lifetime.

He was also an accomplished musician and played the bandore. He played old Ukrainian ballads on instruments constructed by himself which are now on show at the Glinka Museum of Music History. Among his friends were airmen and glider pilots, musicians and poets. According to contemporary reports he excelled in reciting poems by Maiakovskii, Khlebnikov and Esenin.

One of his early paintings, **Sailor,** portrays the artist himself as a young man when, fascinated by the sea, he set off to travel to far-away places. An extraordinary man, indeed. He has a certain strange charisma that links him with our age and society where it is no longer unusual for someone to have two or more professional skills at the same time. During the year of the sixtieth anniversary of the Great October Socialist Revolution, it is indeed appropriate to show Tatlin's work at one of the exhibitions in honour of the Congress of Soviet Artists at the Writers' Hall.

Tatlin is a phenomenon in the history of Soviet culture, a man who cannot be ignored by us, men of letters. Extraordinary people will always retain their extraordinary qualities whether we meet them in person or in the pages of history books.

The artist's father was a railway engineer who went to the United States at about the turn of the century to study the achievements of American railway construction and subsequently wrote a book on his experience. I am almost certain that those who suggest that his father's influence did a great deal in awakening and stimulating the artist's interest in engineering, planning and design, are absolutely right. Tatlin's voyages as a young sailor cannot be explained by his romantic longing for the sea alone. We must also consider his great interest in the steamship as a technical phenomenon, and the very sight of the beautiful and logical rigging of large sailing ships.

Tatlin remained all his life one of those craftsmen who manage not only to design but also to execute projects with astonishing inventiveness. It is enough to look at his photographs – whether taken in his youth or in later years – to detect the real craftsman. He was a sturdy, muscular man with large, strong worker's hands. Quite a number of his creations prove that these hands managed to overcome the resistance of even the toughest of materials. One looks at old photographs, one looks at Tatlin and his comrades during the construction of the model for the **Monument to the Third International,** and one can see instantly that these are not merely engineers but committed people working feverishly, people who will shape the original design with their own hands into a model which, however complicated the structure, however tough the material, forms an integrated whole.

The idea of the **Monument,** or rather the beginning of the realization of the project, took shape at a time when Tatlin was working in the Fine Arts Department of the People's Commissariat of Education and it thus participated in the practical realization of monumental propaganda as set down by Lenin. The design for the **Monument to the Third International** was Tatlin's artistic contribution to the realization of that collective aim. His work was inspired by lofty revolutionary ideals and daring ideas in design. The tower-monument with its trellis-work façade and metallic glow, the proud tower of the Revolution, intended to be 400 metres high, could, however, never grow into the sky. But the model, executed with amazing technical brilliance, was exhibited first in Petrograd and later in Moscow at the House of Unions, where an exhibition was organized on the occasion of the Eighth Congress of Soviets, called together to discuss the GOELRO electrification plan for the Soviet Union.

The model of the tower provoked great controversy; it was praised by some, criticized by others: it would have been surprising indeed had such a daring idea left its contemporaries cold. But in spite of this great controversy, four years later, at one of the first international exhibitions with Soviet participation – the Paris Exhibition of Decorative and Industrial Arts of 1925 – a new model of Tatlin's work was awarded a gold medal. After that, Tatlin carried on working as hard as ever in the most varied fields. He painted, drew, designed for the stage, taught at various art schools (mostly in faculties of ceramics, wood and metal, as one would expect); he also worked at the Institute of Silicates and Building Materials. Finally, he conducted experiments on the construction of a gliding machine, **Letatlin.** During these experiments he worked with pilots, with people who were, like him, intrigued by the synthesis of optimum form and technical expediency. **Letatlin,** which was first exhibited at the Moscow Museum of Fine Arts, was later carefully reconstructed by our pilots and aviators and is now kept in the Museum of the Soviet Air Force. Its cleverly constructed, beautiful shape has lost nothing of its appeal.

Tatlin was accorded around this time the title Honoured Art Worker of the Russian Soviet Socialist Federal Republic. In 1932 an exhibition of his works was mounted at the Museum of Fine Arts in Moscow. The opening of the exhibition was marked by the publication of a small but very informative booklet written by Tatlin and the well-known military expert and glider pilot K. Artseulov. The booklet was mainly concerned with explaining the structure of the gliding machine, but the artist also took up a few other points he thought topical and relevant.

Tatlin, the committed Constructivist, criticized 'Constructivism' in inverted commas, the degradation of the term that meant so much to him to the level of a cheap fad, and called upon artists to concern themselves with what we would call today industrial design or technological aesthetics. 'Work in this area, which includes furniture and everyday objects, is still only beginning,' wrote Tatlin, 'while the birth of new cultural institutions for our everyday life – in which the working masses will live, think and reveal their talents – will demand of artists not only external decoration but above all will demand objects which correspond to the dialectics of the new everyday life.'

In Tatlin's life words and deeds were in perfect harmony. At the time of writing the above statement he was not only busy constructing his glider but also designing furniture and working clothes. There is a photograph in a magazine of the time, of a tall, skinny man dressed – well, I would say like our students when they go voluntary grape-picking. It is Tatlin himself, of course, trying to publicize one of his innovations by such demonstrative means. I do not know what others think of this – I find it very charming.

Tatlin did not stop painting and drawing in the years that followed while he was also working on several more practical projects such as a model for a pavilion for the All-Union Exhibition of Economic Achievement. But it was the theatre that moved more and more into the centre of his activities. Work for the theatre follows him through the thirties, the War, the first years after the War, right up to the last days of his life.

Tatlin was fifty-six at the beginning of the War, no longer young. Like most Soviet families the Tatlins too suffered a tragic loss. Having been wounded several times previously, his only son died at the front in 1943. The artist put all his energy into his work. His major theatre projects took place mostly during and just after the War. At the Moscow Art Theatre he worked on **Deep Reconnaissance** with Kedrov, at the Theatre of the Lenin Komsomol on **For Those at Sea** with Bersenev, on **Somewhere in Siberia** with the young Tovstonogov, as well as on a number of other productions, two of which received the State Award.

1953 was Vladimir Evgrafovich Tatlin's last year spent at work: the last year of his life of search, creative experiment and never decreasing hard work, the life of a man and artist who until the end remained a true son of his tempestuous time and his socialist fatherland.

Konstantin Mikhailovich Simonov
Константин Симонов:
'Какая интересная личность'.
Комсомольская правда, 13 February, 1977

Speech that opened Tatlin's exhibition in Moscow in 1977

PART ONE: STUDIES ON TATLIN

Anatolii Anatol'evich Strigalev
FROM PAINTING TO THE CONSTRUCTION OF MATTER

Tatlin regarded his artistic career as a single goal-oriented programme made up of a series of increasingly complicated tasks, and he expected others to look upon it the same way.

Indeed, the pursuit of a resolute programme was one of the main features of his working life. This was the solid basis on which a true unity of his professional, ethical commitment and his public statements could be achieved, being at the same time a logical consequence of his conviction about the importance of the artist's role in society. He regarded himself as having a special mission in the artistic scene of his country, which gave him an exceptional historical responsibility.

Devotion to his mission extended his influence over artists holding views different from or opposed to his own. His belief in his own vocation, however, did not make his life easy.

At the beginning of his career he was interested in figurative painting and the theatre. The ensuing period was characterized by abstract works of art, painterly reliefs and counter-reliefs, which bordered on painting and sculpture. Then he turned to architecture, and created the design for the **Monument to the Third International**. This was followed by 164–206 a long spell in industrial design, which ended with the construction of a flying apparatus. In the final period of his life he worked as a set designer and painted and drew again in the traditional way.

Such a pattern is revealed by examination of the facts and is underlined by all of his biographical statements.[1]

Although the pattern is more or less correct, it is in many ways incomplete as it restricts our idea of the whole œuvre, making the examination of his legacy rather difficult, first of all because it substantially reduces the number of his works within our field of vision.

Tatlin exhibited several dozen wide-ranging works even before the Revolution. But when he compiled a list of his works at about the beginning of 1921 he named for the monograph by Punin only a few examples of work in various genres and techniques.[2] He did so on principle. When he spoke of the counter-relief, for instance, he did not as a rule think of any particular creation, but of a whole new type of artistic work which he himself invented and of how he had arrived at it: that is, the 'system of the counter-relief', as it was referred to at that time.[3]

In every one of his exhibitions and in the catalogues, articles and curricula vitae Tatlin stressed the programmatic character of his creative method for which he considered his works merely as illustrations.[4] If we look at the single-mindedness in his life-work, we might get the impression that the artist drew up a detailed programme already in his youth, and all that remained for later years was the execution of those plans.

Khlebnikov's poem on Tatlin (1916) could be looked upon as prophecy regarding his later works like the **Monument to the Third International** (1919–20) or **Letatlin** 164–206 (1929–32).[5] There is no doubt that Tatlin started working out projects a long time before he 313–353 actually turned them into reality.

His creative activities came under a wide variety of influences, and each of them played a significant role.

He started working in art, namely painting, with an enormous amount of experience already behind him, which very few artists of his generation could match. In this were combined family traditions, an early independence, practice of a number of skills, and the hard, character-forming effect of having spent time at sea.

Various people who had 'seen the world' significantly enriched the culture of the time, but (until their number was increased by the First World War) they usually allowed their experiences to be mirrored in literature or drama rather than in the fine arts.

Tatlin's experiences were very different from those of other artists, who might have had just as hard a life, primarily because his world was outside that of the artistic, bohemian scene. Although as a young man he was obviously keen on adventures, his energies were dedicated to physical work, the crafts and a thirst for creation.

Productive work was for him a family tradition. In 1873 a certain F. Tatlin (from his age he could have been a brother or an uncle of the artist's father) published a carefully written book on bee-keeping. In its theme and character the book could almost be called a prime example of empirical science. In his preface the author comments: '...a truly knowledgeable and diligent person knows no obstacles. He will find a way to reach real wisdom.'[6] The artist's father, Evgraf Nikiforovich Tatlin, had to work very hard to start with. 'He started working on goods trains as a stoker before becoming an engine-driver.'[7] Later he graduated from the Practical Technological Institute in St Petersburg, which was the only institution in Russia at that time to train general engineers. In 1892, as an experienced engineer, he was sent to the United States to study the railway system. In his extensive report he pointed out the almost poetic beauty of technological progress together with the important role of creative initiative. He wrote:

...What has been achieved in America is due entirely to continuous experiments and practical experiences.
Who isn't an innovator in America?
Everyone knows that a successful invention, however insignificant, will bring in enough money to live comfortably, so the Americans are constantly experimenting – and it can be with the most banal things. They wouldn't dream of making fun of the inventor, on the contrary, they help him as much as they can. ...Simple, uneducated people (well, they might be able to write) involve themselves in experimenting and they can achieve, through practical experience, results that make scientists and great experts gasp with amazement.[8]

The significance of practical experience, combined with democracy, a search for new ways and the taking of risks, must have impressed the young V.E. Tatlin greatly. His father, although honoured for his services, sent him not to a classical school but a secondary school with technical emphasis (which Tatlin did not finish).

The young V.E. Tatlin moved back and forth from being a captain's boy on a ship, a sailor, an icon painter's assistant, and a prop-maker at the Solodovnikov Opera – with occasional courses at art schools.

The work of a sailor demands a close combination of initiative and discipline as well as the ability to adapt quickly a number of practical skills. Tatlin's youth spent at sea had a great influence on his whole life: on forming his character, on his health, his habits, the skill of his hands and, last but not least, his creativity.

The sea is one of the most obvious subjects in his early paintings and graphics.[9] It seems also to have determined what stage productions he would want to design[10] and which books to illustrate.[11] The reliability and thoroughness of the former sailor can be detected in all his designs, especially clothes. His skill as a boatswain is obvious from the way his suspended constructions are executed – ranging from the counter-relief to the moon on stage.[12] It must also have been during his life at sea that he acquired the habit of making his own furniture, workshop equipment, certain clothes, tools, a bandore, etc.

The basis for his working method is empiricism. His experiences influenced both his creative activities and his personality.

He regarded himself as one earning his living by manual work. This made him a democrat. He respected talent and skills. In the 'Order No. 1 for the Group of Material Culture' he was in charge of, he declared: 'Remove from our environment people who have displayed empty slogans not confirmed by their craft.'[13]

He had nothing even remotely bohemian about him, neither as a young man nor in his later years. He was always regarded as a craftsman and that is what he thought about himself. Art was not a 'job' or a 'vocation' for him, but an activity that came naturally. For him there was no division between art and non-art.

Like the majority of young artists of the period, he was spurred to constantly renewed activities through his close contact with the times he lived in. He had a lively interest in the age and the urge to participate actively in the shaping of the immediate future.

The young people of his time were sensitive to public issues and recognized their historical tasks. The formative experiences were the Japanese–Russian war, the first Russian Revolution of 1905–7, the loss of so many lives in the First World War and the premonition of yet more threatening revolutionary outbreaks to come. All this fuelled the conviction that the age they were born into differed basically from everything that happened before.

Another feature of the times, unique in history, was the development of science, technology and urbanization. The pace of everyday life was speeded up, transport and communications were developed. It seemed both impossible and unreasonable to carry on living in the old way.

In this climate it seemed inevitable for the arts to be contemporary. Artists turned with enthusiasm towards science, and names like Lobachevskii, Riemann, Mendeleev, Einstein, Röntgen, were on their lips. New technological discoveries filled them with delirious curiosity, and they were enthusiastic about aviation, film and radio.

Artists at that time, and not only in Russia, based their search for new ways of expression first of all on their fascination with 'all manifestations of modernity'. The speed of artistic development matched the speed of advance in other spheres of life: new tendencies came to life, issues like 'artistic discovery' and the 'creation of new ways' were put on the agenda. This provoked a feeling of 'solidarity with one's own generation' (taking the social structure into account of course): the poet Khlebnikov divided society into 'young people' and 'the older generation'. One of the most promising new groups called itself the Union of Youth.[14]

Characteristic of the era was the intense creative co-operation between young people working in different fields, the acquisition of multiple professional skills and the co-ordination of creative professional work and social activity.

The new generation of Russian artists found many faults in Marinetti's manifestos, while they appreciated the determination of the Italian Futurists to focus on the future.

Khlebnikov translated the word Futurists into Russian as *budetliane.* This term never became widely used, though, presumably because of its too obvious meaning.[15] The word Futurists (*futuristy*), on the other hand, gained wide currency and stood for representatives of the new art-form and was also used as a pejorative nickname. These characteristics of the age had a great influence on Tatlin's course and in many respects contributed to his development as an artist. Friend and foe saw him as an archetype of Russian Futurists.[16]

He was, in international terms too, among the first to try to build an organic unity between art and the age of unprecedented technological advancement, and in close harmony with this ideal he searched for new ways in what the called 'fine craft' (*izobrazitel'noe delo*).[17] He did not portray technology, technological mechanisms and the modern urban environment: his aim was to enrich art with certain technological methods and means, shaping them to accommodate artistic expression. One of the first scholars to investigate his work, Isakov, was right in pointing out that he did not 'glorify the machine' like, for instance, the Italian Futurists, but that he endeavoured to 'overcome the tyranny of the machine,... to liberate man from technological slavery'.[18]

It is more than likely that Tatlin started to get interested in aviation, and all the latest technical achievements which penetrated everyday life at the time, from a fairly early age.[19] His pioneering design work was also set to transform everyday life. He called upon artists 'to control the forms of the new life around us'.[20] The slogans 'art into life'[21] and 'art into technology' derive from him.[22]

He strove towards the renewal of art, disregarding all authority because he considered that to have new and fresh ideas was the duty of the artist, who himself was the 'initiative individual in the collective'.[23] At the same time, like the majority of Russian avant-garde artists at the turn of the century, he did not lean only on the experiences of his own time but incorporated tradition as well. He felt an especially close affinity with old Russian art and, to a somewhat lesser degree, with the manifestations of contemporary folk art which developed from that tradition.

He got in touch with this tradition in various ways. Before he took up studying art, and then between 1900 and 1910, he worked in icon-painting workshops where he learnt the idiom and techniques of Russian icon-painting.[24] When in his curriculum vitae he mentions that his teacher Afanas'ev painted frescoes with Riabushkin, he adds: 'Frescoes very much interested me then'.[25] There are quite a number of copies of old Russian frescoes painted by him. 'The Russian icon had a much more profound influence on him than Cézanne or Picasso,' Punin writes,[26] and this is a generally accepted view of his work as a painter.

He designed sets for five theatrical productions with Russian subjects and these were, without exception, important stages in his artistic career.[27]

He was also influenced by artistic traditions which were directly connected with living popular culture. He turned not only to icons but also to signboards, *lubki* (popular woodcuts) and folk crafts such as popular spectacles, entertainments in the market-place, the circus, sport, music and singing. He was familiar with Russian and Ukrainian folklore, old and new folk-songs, and he would sing beautifully to his own accompaniment on the bandore.[28]

36
104,105

The style of signboards left its mark on his series of abstract compositions with textual illustrations and occasional 'daubing' brushwork.[29] His illustrations and later graphics carry marks of the *lubki* and other similar prints.

Russian avant-garde artists were strongly attracted by Oriental art and other systems of artistic perception that differed from the European academic tradition. Artists very close to him at various times, like Larionov, Le Dantiu and Iakulov, were enthusiastic admirers of Oriental art, and its influence is presumably felt in his costume-designs for **Ivan Susanin**

137–155

(A Life for the Tsar) and a number of other works.

Resolute experiments to arrive at new forms of art and to blend these with forgotten, 'vulgar' artistic traditions (having found similar characteristics in them despite their inherent antagonism) evolved as one of the basic points of departure, a method even, for the new artistic culture in all branches of art: literature, the fine arts and the theatre.

Undoubtedly, this new culture gained expression in the deepest, most perfect and most original way in the personality and poetry of V. Khlebnikov. His exceptional perception of the times he lived in, and an almost prophetic intuition and vision of the future, were combined with an interest in history, ancient Russian and Slavic culture, and the Orient. In addition to the philosophy of history, he was intrigued by the laws of history, which he attempted to define through mathematical calculations. The old Russian, Slavic and Oriental culture offered him an inexhaustible mine of treasure. He turned his poetry into a unique research into grammar, phonetics, morphology and syntax.

Khlebnikov and Tatlin were of the same generation and are likely to have become acquainted no later than 1912. Khlebnikov died on 28 June 1922. In the last decade of his life he shared Tatlin's friendship, ideology and artistic aspirations. Tatlin regarded Khlebnikov's experiments in the renewal of language as an artistic effort which was very close to his own ideas.[30] He had the highest regard for Khlebnikov of all his fellow artists and he was more fond of him than of anyone else.

When analysing Tatlin's works one cannot overemphasize the importance of Khlebnikov's overall influence. On the other hand, the artist Tatlin's influence on the poet is also beyond doubt.[31] Their contemporaries saw in them analogous, almost 'symmetrical' figures of the same stature, working in different fields of art.[32]

Khlebnikov set against the harsh and inhuman reality his dream of a beautiful future, utopias based on a pantheistic relation with nature, and his belief in scientific and technological progress, as well as his own ethical maximalism.

In the years of the First World War he predicted that the year 1917 would bring a revolution. Out of the people who in his opinion possessed the highest moral authority he formed a coalition called 'the Government of the Presidents of the World'. During the first few days of the October Revolution he visited Tatlin in his studio in Moscow, offering him a post in the 'Government of the Presidents of the World'. The painter Dymshits-Tolstaia recalls this meeting in her memoirs as follows: 'They sat on the window-sill of the studio, behind them the orange sky of the late afternoon. Both skinny and long-nosed. Two Don Quixotes submerged in discussing the questions of universal art.'[33]

Tatlin did not receive a systematic professional training. As a young man he was taught by two young artists, one Levenets and one Kharchenko, who must have been students themselves. They prepared him for the entrance examination to the Moscow College of Painting, Sculpture and Architecture. He did not spend a lot of time there: he was expelled because of unsatisfactory results in his studies and a lack of discipline. He then transferred to the Sileverstov College of Art in Penza, a reputable provincial artistic institution in pre-Revolutionary Russia. His most important tutor in Penza was Afanas'ev. Later he included him, with Larionov and Picasso, in the list of three artists who had a hand in shaping his artistic profile.[34] In 1910 he graduated from the Painting Department of the Penza College of Art, which provided him with a 'draughtsman's diploma', meaning that he was now   6 qualified 'to teach drawing, geometry and handwriting' in institutions of secondary education.

Around the same time (according to his statement, during the years 1909–10), he again began to attend lectures at the Moscow College of Painting, Sculpture and Architecture, presumably as an auditor. It is also around this time that his name is mentioned among the visitors to Bernshtein's private studio in St Petersburg.[35]

Tatlin named two reasons when asked why he did not complete his studies: the pressing necessity of having to earn a living and his dissatisfaction with the teaching methods of official educational institutions. Both reasons were quite typical in the circle of young people Tatlin was surrounded by. To counterbalance this, a collective self-education emerged among young artists: collective studio work, the formation of independent societies of artists (Union of Youth in St Petersburg, Jack of Diamonds[36] in Moscow), the establishment of close contacts with young artists working in different fields of the arts, the organizing of independent exhibitions with the participation of representatives of the latest West European artistic tendencies, study trips abroad, etc. This movement was especially active in Moscow, where Larionov became the acknowledged leader of the young artistic avant-garde. Tatlin while still studying in Penza was part of the Moscow artistic scene and had been very close to Larionov to begin with.[37] In 1911 Tatlin opened a studio in Moscow (Ostozhenka Street),   68, 69 which he later reorganized into a collective studio and which was visited in the years to come by Aleksandr Vesnin, Popova, Udal'tsova, Khodasevich, Fal'k and others. The studio was run on a friendly basis and consisted of members with equal rights and status where, however, Tatlin's leading role was unanimously accepted. He also participated in the work of the Union of Youth in St Petersburg, making friends there with Le Dantiu, Shkol'nik, Zheverzheev and others.[38]

At the same time, he did not tolerate and was extremely suspicious of actual or assumed attempts to influence his activities or to limit his independence. This is why he fell out with Larionov[39] and also why his relationship with Malevich went through such difficult stages   96 and why it ended so unfortunately.[40]

An analysis of Tatlin's early painting and graphics, in which particular Constructivist tendencies had become more and more apparent, is offered by other essays in this volume.[41] Let us merely state here that Tatlin's first exhibits were unanimously described by the contemporary press as original, which proved the talent of the artist. This, however, cannot be said of the reception of his works to follow: these were rejected, even mocked at. Some called on him to carry on the old way. Tatlin himself regarded the years 1912, 1913 and 1914 as decisive in his work.

'Since 1912 I have been appealing to the members of my profession to improve their eyesight,' he wrote in 1918.[42] This presumably refers mainly to the first stages of activity at the Ostozhenka Street studio. Already in this period the tendency emerges in Tatlin's work which will be described by Punin a few years later as 'anti-Cubist',[43] although this tendency is hard to trace.

Tatlin was obviously attracted to the pictorial language of the old Russian icons, which tended to generalize. He was intrigued by the patch-like quality of that style, its contours and the relation of each patch to the other.

In 1913 he issued the slogan: 'Let us place the eye under the control of touch'.[44]

In the same context he started to become interested in 'non-painterly' materials (to use Khlebnikov's words, he created 'metal objects with his brush') and thus stepped out from the dimension of painting into real space.

85   In 1913 he participated in the exhibitions organized by the Jack of Diamonds group in Moscow and St Petersburg together with other artists of the Russian avant-garde and the most recent leading representatives of West European art, like Picasso, Braque, Derain, Van Dongen, Marquet and others.[45]

79   Tatlin's most significant piece in these exhibitions was **Nude Composition** (later known as **Nude**). This work had a programmatic importance to him and it preserved a significance in terms of principle in relation to the whole of his life's work.

91, 92   In 1914, after the opening of the St Petersburg exhibition, he spent some time in Berlin 90   and Paris. There is a funny story describing how he got into Picasso's studio.[46] Apart from the actual circumstances of that incident it was surely Picasso's work that represented the greatest single impression during the whole of his travels. He was already familiar with Picasso's work, having seen Shchukin's and Morozov's collections in Moscow and visited contemporary exhibitions. Picasso was regarded even at that time not merely as the generally acknowledged leader of the avant-garde, but the living symbol of the movement itself. Tatlin did have the opportunity – at places other than Picasso's studio – to get acquainted with the latest works of the artist.

107   Picasso was making novel sculptures at that time. The famous **Guitar** (early 1913), for instance, was constructed out of a metal sheet, other compositions were made of wood and paper and were either partly or completely covered in paint. Later he changed over to the traditional bronze moulds, some of which he also painted. He created three-dimensional Cubist still lifes and, as in his paintings, he sometimes used a collage technique.

Some of Picasso's works like the **Guitar** undoubtedly inspired Tatlin's later work, which does not suggest, however, that he became an epigone of the artist.

Tatlin believed that it was he himself who in 1914 based 'fine craft' on 'material, volume and construction', and he regarded this – together with the date – as something of principal significance in the development of art.[47]

108–112   Tatlin began to create novel works of art, which he called painterly reliefs. He held the first 113–121   exhibition of his reliefs 10–14 May 1914 in his Ostozhenka Street studio. The reliefs were followed by counter-reliefs. His new works embarrassed the public but the effect on artists close to his taste was that of true artistic relation. His works gave an energetic impulse to the development of tendencies dealing with the analysis of form in pre-Revolutionary Russian art, starting a wave of imitations.

Tatlin's work was, despite its novelty, a logical consequence of the natural development of contemporary Russian art. At the beginning of the 1910s the expressive deformation of realistic forms shifted towards extreme generalization in avant-garde art, the representational mode of expression was replaced by a language of non-figurative painterly 'signs' and 'formulas'. Various systems of abstract painting were established. Tatlin was very interested in analysing the construction and architectonics of the objective world. He arrived at a fundamental artistic discovery: non-figurative forms of various colours and textures *(fakturas)* were removed from the surface of the picture into the space in front of the picture, at first without divorcing them from the plain background. The represented relation in space of each of the components of the picture was thus turned into the real context of each component showing how they really relate in real space. These painterly reliefs produced a unique synthesis of painting and sculpting methods. Tatlin called these kinds of compositions selections of materials because the abstract picture that was turned into painterly relief was no longer painted with a brush but composed out of materials of various structural and painterly characteristics.

The next step was to break away from the surface of the picture. Now the composition was involved with real space (in front of the surface that served as a backdrop, or in between two surfaces perpendicular to each other) and was supported only by a wire or a stiffly bent pivot. This was the first 'sculpture without a pedestal', which at the same time inevitably showed architectural characteristics because of the real structural relations that developed between the various components of the composition. Tatlin called these creations counter-reliefs.

He regarded this method as a synthesis of painting, sculpture and architecture. He regarded material as of decisive value and therefore devoted great attention to the choice of materials for his projects, the process by which he created forms of space and structure depending on the characteristics of the materials chosen. This meant that the traditional methods of artistic approach had to be left behind.

With these creations Tatlin laid the foundation for Russian Constructivism.[48]

It might be worth discussing the question of Tatlin's new terminology in order to differentiate between the various kinds of works of this new type. He introduced a number of new terms partly acting as synonyms, partly characterizing differences in a whole 'class' of works.

If we compare the leaflet printed for The Last Futurist Exhibition, 0–10, enumerating Tatlin's work (end of 1915) with a list of his works compiled by the artist himself for the Punin monograph (1921), we will observe a certain gradual and parallel development in the evolution of these definitions. His earliest works are called selections (*podbor*) or reliefs – i.e. selections of material (*material'nyii podbor*) or painterly-reliefs (*zhivopisnyii rel'ef*), which means that these four definitions were regarded as synonyms by Tatlin. Next came the selections of a higher type, that is counter-reliefs. The latter term is fairly widely known, but the sense the author gave it is less known.[49]

The counter-relief is not a reverse or indented relief as one would imagine from its name, just the opposite. According to the artist a counter-relief has a much stronger impact than an ordinary relief. To the traditional classification of reliefs based on depth, low or high, Tatlin adds the 'highest possible (*sverkhvysokii*) relief' which he calls counter-relief. This latter breaks away from the wall surface that serves as its background, and hangs in the space in front of it. Tatlin made a distinction between central (*tsentrovoi*) and corner counter-relief (*uglovoi*). He placed the former in front of a surface that provided the background, the latter he fastened in between angled, flat surfaces.

The new term is formed by combining two already existing words in a new compound word to which Tatlin gave his own meaning. This method of creating new words was very common in Russian literature after the turn of the century.[50] The counter-relief came into use during the First World War (between 1914–15) and, according to the art historian Isakov, who was well acquainted with Tatlin, had been created along the same lines as the *kontrataka* (counter-attack). Just as the latter supposedly sounded more energetic than simply attack, so counter-relief sounded more expressive than simply relief.[51] It is also possible that Tatlin, who was also very musical, used the prefix 'counter' in a musical sense, where it does not mean a confrontation but a deviation in quality of a similar character, one octave down. In this sense the low, high and counter-relief would, to a certain extent, be equivalent to the octave – contraoctave – subcontraoctave line. Tatlin's term has, therefore, an associative character and as such, with its poetic, definitely subjective plasticity it is reminiscent of Khlebnikov's understanding of creation of language and of words.

If we compare Tatlin's reliefs and counter-reliefs with works of similar character by Picasso we might arrive at the following conclusion. Tatlin was susceptible to those of Picasso's picture and sculpture compositions which were close to his own Constructivist tendencies. Picasso portrayed the immediate environment but gave it a very subjective artistic interpreta-

107 tion (Cubist, Surrealist, etc.). Creations like the **Guitar** can be regarded, as already mentioned above, as specific, Cubist still-lifes in space. Tatlin, on the other hand, broke away from representation altogether in his works and did so on principle.

In these first creations he still needed some loose terms of reference. One of his compositions, consisting of a few bits of mouldering timber, was entitled **Tea-Room at Night** which was, according to the contemporary press reviews, in visual harmony with the theme of the title.[52] In the final analysis, however, his selections were special artistic *constructions.* While in Picasso's work the various materials interacted on the basis of a collage principle (the metal plate and wires were connected according to the rules of the body and the strings of a real guitar), in Tatlin's work the different materials were connected to one another as materials of different characteristics. The wires, the strings and the springs each had a definite structural function.

These characteristics were mentioned in the very first article on Tatlin's recent works, which stated that the artist was concerned through these objects with the 'problems of matter and tension', that in the corner counter-relief it was the 'tension... that was of primary interest' and that these works 'showed him to be an independent artist and not an imitator of Picasso'.[53]

108–121 The constructive character of the reliefs and counter-reliefs posed the question of Tatlin's concern with technicism early on, which, by the way, was never mentioned in connection with Picasso. Tatlin evolved a highly original graphic style which made a number of his drawings resemble geometrical drawings but preserved at the same time a visually expressive force and his own artistic vision. To a certain extent this was also true of his painterly technique.[54]

Experimenting with form is one of the objective conditions of artistic development. But the dominance of the formal element involves great contradictions. Such contradictions were fairly common among artistic endeavours in Russia at the beginning of the century.

These contradictions were to be found in the fundamental line of Tatlin's work before the Revolution. Let us just consider the self-contained nature of works like the counter-reliefs and their reception by the public, or the contradiction between their constructive meaning and their non-utilitarian character. Tatlin's works created in this period were subjective formulas and models, which came into being through a very high level of generalization of the impressions gained from his immediate environment. They were based on Tatlin's high visual culture, which became more and more refined and individual in the course of his career; for this reason meeting between artist and public was problematic both in theory and practice. Critics regarded Tatlin's works as incomprehensible, stating that they were incapable of making any artistic contact with the public.

His creations, which by nature commanded a concentrated and serious approach and a process of meditative identification – like all abstract reflections of reality, such as music or philosophy – provoked the critics' rejection and noisy scenes at exhibitions. He was accused of mystification and of lack of respect towards the public. Many pioneering creations of other contemporary artists were similarly received. The fact that the very art that set out to be the art of the epoch (as opposed to the traditional, old values) had been tempestuously rejected, bred a new set of conflicts. Thus one of the most difficult dilemmas for the new art became its very role in society: the dilemma of how to reunite art with the public.

The practitioners of the new art were generally conscious of the size of the problem and did not wish to underestimate it by trying to find easy solutions. They did not want to produce art for art's sake, neither did they wish to create for an élite in the traditional sense of the word. That is why these new artists – especially Maiakovskii, Khlebnikov, Kamenskii, Meierkhol'd, Malevich, Gastev, Shterenberg and many others – declared with so much zeal the important social relevance of the avant-garde art as something quite new and different from anything that went before.

The new artists proposed to solve the question of a wider accessibility of art in two ways: by mobilizing the spectator and by a revolutionary improvement in arts education. They believed that in order to achieve a proper appreciation of art one had to involve both the artist and the spectator (reader, listener, etc.), who had to have an incentive for a mutual approach in order to be able to meet half-way because there was no point whatsoever in the artist putting artistic creations of ultimate perfection as a *fait accompli* before an indifferent and passive spectator. Consequently, the difficulties arising from the understanding of new works of art and also the difficulties of coming to terms with the complicated forms were regarded as conditions of principle in the process of mobilizing the spectator. Maiakovskii spoke about this on many occasions and in numerous contexts, declaring in the name of avant-garde art that 'the appearance of new methods is necessitated not by artistic exuberance but by the fatal lack of vitality of the obsolete methods'.[55] Shklovskii referred to this statement later as the method of 'making things peculiar', and as a 'device of forms rendered more difficult'.[56]

The advocates of new art demanded basic changes in the professional training of artists and in the artistic education of the masses.[57] The educational tasks included the fight against academicism in all spheres, the removal of hierarchic value-judgments as to what is of 'lower' and 'higher' worth when differentiating between genres and the detailed study of traditions and all systems outside academic art, etc.

The circumstances described above make it easier to understand why it was so paramount for avant-garde artists to press for the mobilization of society, why prior to the Revolution they had intuitively sensed the social changes to come and why they took such an active part in such large numbers in the building of Soviet artistic culture in the first few years of the Revolution. The renewal of the social role of the arts was rightly paralleled by these artists with the cause of the great changes that took place in society as a whole.

Another contradiction regarding Tatlin's counter-reliefs and similar works had to do with their utility. This problem was not Tatlin's alone, but it was less general than the previous ones.

'What is this good for?' was a question asked more often in connection with Tatlin's 'artistic constructions' than in the context of 'conventional' abstract painting. By their very constructive character they seemed to provoke such questions.

The counter-reliefs did not aim at fulfilling any practical purpose. They served as forms expressing the visual and multi-dimensional exploration of the world as mediated by the subjective consciousness of an artist communicating something new to the spectator about this world. If we look at art in the traditional way as an almost immediate reproduction of reality, we could regard it also as the 'imitation of the machine',[58] that is, offering distorted and incomplete portraits of already discovered and functioning machinery, works of an artist who has no idea of the real function of these machines. Tatlin's works, however, were no mere imitations of already surpassed achievements by the projective and creative mind. Instead, they expanded the limitations of the former, creating a basis for exploration which had no direct practical value and yet had something in store for the future.

This specific quality in Tatlin's art of creating new forms was noted very early on by one of his most uncompromising adversaries, Radlov, who, not unwittingly, referred to Tatlin's reliefs and counter-reliefs as studio architecture (*stankovaia arkhitektura*).[59]

Even if Tatlin had done nothing but studio architecture, he would have influenced the architecture of his time. The modern object world that surrounds us is made up of the collective achievements of many artists, the individual search for an artistic route of each one of these being subtly interlinked with every other. Mondrian's paintings had an encouraging influence on architecture and industrial design although he was a painter throughout his career. Tatlin on the other hand made the journey himself from studio architecture to architecture as well as industrial design. Unlike Mondrian, he was one of the very rare artists who have consciously united in their work the three characteristic methods of the twentieth century for creating new forms: the presentation of reality; experiments towards constructing a model for the non-figurative artistic presentation of reality; as well as the construction of real objects which had a new function, both artistic and practical. Each period in Tatlin's work incorporated the experiences of the previous periods.

It was characteristic of Tatlin's generation that they strove for a synthesis in their professional and social activities. This social activity was connected first of all with organizational problems in the arts. From the very start, Tatlin took an active part in organizing exhibitions, editing publications, calling forums for discussions, etc.[60]

The young artists, working in different genres of the arts, had several leaders. After Larionov left for Paris, 'it was Tatlin and Malevich who enjoyed most authority and who established their own schools. The young artists were split into two antagonistic camps.'[61] But this antagonism developed considerably later. Malevich, the founder of Suprematism, and Tatlin, the creator of the counter-relief, were at first in alliance in their battle to establish the new art.

Tatlin was more of a leader than Malevich,[62] he exercised great influence on all sorts of people and enjoyed almost unconditional respect; even as an educator he was a leader and a master first and foremost, and a teacher second. Tatlin convinced others with his own beliefs and what he produced with his two hands. He was no theoretician, he hardly ever wrote for the press and he did not attempt to polish his speech. He wrote that since his childhood he had been interested in art which is perceived through the eye.[63]

Indeed, Tatlin's theoretical conception often lacked a detailed, clever and flexible argument. And yet, his conception was an example of topical thought in complete harmony with his own creative practice, which gave him enormous authority. The evolution of his views, and the analysis of these views in the secondary literature, are best followed in the writings of those contemporaries who were fascinated by Tatlin's ideas, principles, his creative practice or, for that matter, his personality.

In his most active years Tatlin's social activity went far beyond strictly professional matters. It reached a peak during the Revolution, between 1917 and 1919. This activity was more than characteristic of the then prevailing atmosphere, and it was also an obvious consequence of his personality.

Before the Revolution it was rare for young artists to maintain a direct contact with the revolutionary movement, despite the fact that most of them entertained progressive political views. Together with some of his fellow students at the College of Art in Penza, Tatlin was put under observation by the secret police because of his dubious political activity. The reason was that he was a member of the board of monitors at the school, which had been established in order to protect and fight for the rights of students. Even after he had settled in Moscow Tatlin was under police observation for a while.[64]

7–10

It would be unfair to underestimate the selfconsciousness, both professional and social, of those young avant-garde artists, who thought they supported the cause of the approaching Revolution even if this feeling was very vague, or because they ascribed the same significance to a social revolution as they did to a purely artistic revolution.[65]

The expectation of yet another revolution had a great influence on the intellectual life of Russia between 1905 and 1917: it enhanced the internal divisions of society. The young artists, inclined towards avant-garde concepts, were among those anxiously waiting for a new revolution: Khlebnikov, Maiakovskii and others were even keen to predict when exactly it might happen. The new art regarded itself as a revolutionary force and this had a strong basis: in their own way, young poets and artists revolutionized social consciousness, en-hancing the conviction that a fundamental transformation of life was needed. Both advocates and adversaries of the new tendencies agreed that the declared programme of the new art – whether it were realized or not – would bring an upheaval that could rightly be called 'revolutionary'.[66] In the consciousness of the artists, social problems were necessarily inter-twined with artistic and professional problems.

Following the overthrow of the tsarist regime, in February 1917, the proportion and character of Tatlin's activities were immediately transformed. During the February Revolution he stayed in Petrograd. He joined the 'Left Wing' of the newly established Union of Art Workers (SDI) and was sent to Moscow to help organize a whole new cultural life.[67]

In Moscow the newly formed Moscow Trade Union of Painters appointed Tatlin chairman of the Left-Wing Federation. (The organization had three wings: one for 'older artists', one for 'middle-aged artists' and one for the young, meaning 'left-wing'.)

During the summer and autumn of 1917 Tatlin worked as a member of a task force of artists under Iakulov on the interior decoration of the **Café Pittoresque**. Around this time Meierkhol'd proposed he should make sets for his film **Spectral Charms**. Khlebnikov, on the other hand, wanted to stage some of his writings, in a single production together with Tatlin. Nothing came of either of these plans.

132, 133

By the summer of 1917 the 'honeymoon' of the bourgeois Revolution had ended. By this time a large number of intellectuals – among them artists – got cold feet about the Revolution and were unable to recognize the full extent of the country's appalling social problems. The October Revolution was received by the Union of Art Workers with an organized and stubborn act of sabotage.[68] In November 1917 Tatlin, alongside a number of other members of the Left Wing, left the Union. On 21 November Tatlin was delegated by the Moscow Union of Painters to work in the Artistic Section of the Moscow Soviet of Workers' and Soldiers' Deputies.[69]

In his later years Tatlin wrote about himself in the third person: 'Tatlin was the first artist who went to work for Soviet power.'[70] Even if this was not exactly true, the gist of it was. Tatlin's example and authority influenced other artists. After the Revolution many artists regarded the organization of new forms for new artistic arrangements as their priority and social duty, putting it before their own artistic activities. At first, during 1917 and the winter of 1918, Tatlin worked on the Commission for Protecting Monuments of Art and Antiquity, which was a priority at that time. Tatlin took an active part in the work of the new organiza-tions brought to life under the People's Commissariat of Education (*Narkompros*), whose task was to assume control over the arts. After the establishment of the Moscow Artistic Col-legium, which served as part of the Narkompros Department of Fine Arts, he was made a member of this body and shortly after that he was appointed head of the Moscow Fine Arts Department and the Collegium closely linked to it.[71] At the same time, he became a member of the Museums Collegium of Narkompros.

168

It is worth considering that Lunacharskii, head of Narkompros, remained in Petrograd even after March 1918 when Moscow was declared the new capital, and moved permanently to Moscow only at the beginning of 1919: this meant that, so far as the administration of the arts was concerned, Tatlin must be regarded as one of Lunacharskii's most active collabora-tors during the year 1918. This was a period when artists themselves took part in handling the administrative, organizational, financial, technical and other aspects of the arts. This experiment was not without revolutionary precedents, however: it developed further the experiences of the French Revolution and the Paris Commune, related to the historical roles played by David and Courbet.

Tatlin was responsible, so far as the Commissariat of Education was concerned, for 'monumental propaganda' in Moscow;[72] he participated in compiling a platform, the or-ganization of planning, the distribution and acceptance of commissions for work, the festive decoration of towns, etc.

169

It was at this time that the foundation stones for Soviet museums were laid: Tatlin took an active part in preparing and carrying out nationalization of museums and in establishing new museums. He and his colleagues took special care to establish modern museums or, as Tatlin put it in one of his reports on the subject, the establishment of museums for 'living art'.[73] Such museums were set up as early as 1917, first in Moscow and Petrograd and later in Vitebsk, Nizhnii Novgorod (now Gor'kii), Kostroma and Barnaul – and were called Museums of Artistic Culture. These were the first specialized museums in the world dedicated to modern art, which were to serve the serious study of formal and technical specifics of fine art and their evolution. Tatlin was very active in organizing them. He helped in collecting the material to be exhibited and with the co-ordination of administration. Later he was involved directly with the work of the Petrograd Museum for Artistic Culture, the activities of which he co-ordinated practically single-handedly between 1921 and 1923.[74]

He was also actively involved in establishing contacts with progressive artists in the West and participated in the effort to establish a journal of the arts, **Internatsional Iskusstv**, in 1919.[75]

But more interesting than any other of his activities was his work in arts education, although it has not yet been looked at in a critical study. He was active in this field partly as an educator, partly as an organizer and co-ordinator. The academic year 1918/19 was the first in the life of the Free State Artistic Studios in Moscow, which were the amalgamation of the one-time Stroganov College of Applied Arts and the Moscow College of Painting, Sculpture and Architecture. According to the generally approved rules in the Studios, the leading tutors were chosen by the students themselves and the curriculum aimed 'at a balanced representation of the most significant artistic trends'. Tatlin was appointed to work in the Painting Section as a representative of Futurism together with Kandinsky, Iakulov, Dymshits-Tolstaia and Ivanov.[76]

Tatlin ran two teaching-workshops at the Moscow Free State Artistic Studios and from the spring of 1919 another one at the Petrograd Free State Artistic Teaching Studios (the former Academy of Arts), which was later generally referred to as the Studio of Material, Volume and Construction. In spite of the fact that he was appointed to work in the Painting Section, he did not teach his students painting. He himself referred to the new discipline which he invented as material culture.[77]

He was determined – even if he was not all that successful – to find an appropriate term for the new artistic genre he was working so hard to establish and which, according to his ideas, was aimed at renewing art as a whole.

Let us look at some of the phrases which are supposed to mean more or less the same according to Tatlin: 'Material, volume and construction' equals 'material culture' ('material artistic culture'), equals 'culture of materials', equals 'construction of materials', equals 'organization of material' ('organizing material into object'), equals 'constructing the object', equals 'material form'.

The first of these terms originate from 1919, the following from 1923 and the last few from just before 1929: Tatlin uses them synonymously. The term 'material culture' came into being presumably on the analogy of painterly culture, the two together forming an artistic culture.[78] It was presumably supposed to stress the role of material in creating forms, which were of fundamental importance to Tatlin, but it was not a sufficiently defined phrase – apart from the fact that it was already taken for a scientific principle of a different nature.[79] He therefore preferred the term 'culture of materials' to 'material culture'.

Because of the relatively few documents available, we know little about his actual achievements as a teacher. But even on the basis of the material available we can go so far as to say that his personality and the nature of his talent did not necessarily predestine him for a career as a teacher. Tatlin was a charismatic individual permeated by the fever of his art. One could not expect complete dedication and patience from him when teaching people of various talents and character, people he at first hardly knew. He was one of those artist-teachers who impress their pupils first and foremost by their own example: their art, ideology and human values – in a word, by their great personalities. Tatlin influenced a large number of people working in various fields of the arts but he had only a few disciples: owing perhaps to the lack of sufficient people around him whom he could regard as soul mates. And perhaps there were not many people who could match the genius of the teacher.

That said, he played a significant part in securing a new style of arts education which united the teaching of artistic subjects and how to adapt them to industry – the success of which was most apparent in the organization and activities of the renowned VKhUTEMAS 240–242 (Higher Artistic and Technical Studios).

But above everything else it was at his teaching workshops that training of this kind was first introduced after having been tried out earlier. His initiative was based entirely on his own methods. His workshop assistants were skilled workers coming from industry, and included a fairly small percentage of students. Nevertheless, this was the programme on the basis of which the Free State Artistic Studios (which had carried on with traditional arts training) could be transformed into the later famous VKhUTEMAS.

On the other hand, it is quite obvious that the programme proposals and plans put together by IZO Narkompros were fundamentally based on Tatlin's ideas, which they further developed.

The end of the Civil War in 1920 and the need to start the difficult task of rebuilding the country brought new problems for the socialist revolution: the reconstruction of the economy and its development on a socialist basis. Under such circumstances great priority had to be given to the pragmatic training of experts, the securing of the growth of technical and technological progress, production and productivity. The traditional arts training was in no way in the position to face new tasks. Only a certain percentage of graduates received training for the applied arts, and even that hardly offered anything more than the skill to decorate existing commodities. A reform in arts training could no longer be postponed.

It is no coincidence that Tatlin regarded himself as the creator of the slogan 'art into life'.[80] He rejected decorativism and sought a much stronger, closer relationship between artistic creation and creative activities in other areas of life.

VKhUTEMAS was officially established in December 1920. A little before that date an information bulletin was issued by IZO Narkompros, half of which dealt with arts training.[81] Among the official decrees, statutes, reports and information sheets we can read: 'Outline of a Curriculum for the Free State Artistic Studios', 'Problems of Art Education', 'Art and Education outside the School' or 'Programme for the Study of Art in a Comprehensive Working School'.[82] These texts, which deviate somewhat in style from the rest of the documents, are characterized by a careful, detailed, homogeneous pedagogical conception. It is a detailed programme, dealing with the combined training in artistic and industrial matters which was worked out by the Fine Arts Department prior to a corresponding reform in the area of higher education. The most significant aspect of this is that these texts are a further exposition of Tatlin's creative and pedagogical conceptions and reflect almost more than any other source the conception of the material culture.[83]

Especially important in this context was the 'Outline of a Curriculum for the Free State Artistic Studios' because the ideas inherent in this were first formulated by Tatlin very clearly. Neither he nor members of the following generation with similar ideas were able to realize them. The same applies to the long article entitled 'Problems of Art Education'.[84] This article is a critical analysis of the practice which had developed over several centuries and which makes a division between 'pure art' and 'artistic industry'. 'Technology had reached such a level of virtuosity that it was possible to manufacture anything at all out of anything at all; the constructibility of an article had been pushed into the background and its usefulness became a joke. This led to a state of affairs where the material as such lost its meaning from the point of view of its durability or appropriate treatment of it.' The article also criticizes the belief, widespread at that time, in the necessity of developing domestic production. 'The primitive organization of handicraftsmen of productive processes forces them to manufacture small-size objects in limited quantities; does not allow the construction of large productive plants, whereas the development of the industrial state demands the construction of plants on a considerable scale and manufactured articles in large numbers.'[85] The suggested solution is to unite art and production: 'The breaking down of the boundaries between pure and applied art is closely linked to the rehabilitation of material. It is finally time to get rid of the sharply romantic idea of the artist as a high priest carrying out a solemn rite in front of the altar of art; to fill in the ditch which until recently has sharply divided art from handicraft, production, industry. Production has not known artistic culture. Artistic culture has been managed outside of production, outside of practical life. The time has come to pour artistic culture into production and draw art away from a condition of aimless snobbishness closed in on itself: that is, to create production art.'[86] The article contains an exposition of new principles of art education.

We have new proof that Tatlin's views received widespread acclaim and recognition by 1919–20.[87] They anticipated and influenced such important phenomena of the artistic life of those years as the reform of art education in the direction of moving it closer to production, the conception of production art, the emergence of 'Constructivism' as a new artistic tendency. At the same time his views attracted the attention of foreign artists.

135, 136

164–206

The wide social response to Tatlin's conception naturally coincided in time with his work on his most important undertaking: the project of the **Monument to the Third International**.

Tatlin's proclamation of material as a leading factor in the development of new art corresponded in a particular way to the theoretical views which were being developed at about the same time in the other arts (literature). It had an effect on the formulation of these views and in its turn experienced their effect too, even if indirectly.

In the works of members of the Society for the Study of Poetic Language (OPOIaZ), 'the traditional division into form and content, distinguishing aesthetic and non-aesthetic moments in art, was opposed by another division into material and method'.[88] 'A literary work,' wrote Shklovskii in 1921, 'is pure form, it is not object, not material, but a relationship of materials. So the scale of the work, the arithmetical meaning of numerator and denominator is insignificant: it is their relationship which is important. Farcical, world-shakingly tragic, or one-room works, the contrasting of world to world or of a cat to a stone, all are equal to each other.'[89]

Of course the concept of material cannot in this case be identical for Shklovskii and for Tatlin. For Tatlin material is far more empirical, traditional, but even so for him it is not primarily a utilitarian means of embodying something, but an object to which an artist has to apply his creative impulses. And in this sense too the scale of the work is not the main thing: a relatively small counter-relief and the huge (as projected) building of the **Monument to the Third International** both have, as their creator sees it, a certain similarity in principle. Later Tatlin assigned to this the general term material form.[90]

It is necessary to indicate the main difference between Tatlin's and Shklovskii's concepts at that time. If a counter-relief could be considered as a kind of pure form, nevertheless, Tatlin – prompted by his principles – was by that time setting himself and art practical tasks, trying to resolve not only the form but the function too. In the evolution of this conception he as it were overtook Shklovskii, and this also corresponded to certain new trends in the theory of literature: within OPOIaZ itself questions were raised about the necessity of returning to an analysis of the contents of literary works, about the form's ability to show content.[91]

On the other hand, the gap grew between Tatlin's views and other recent trends in art, first of all between him and Suprematism. In the autumn of 1920, during the time of Tatlin's greatest artistic successes, Malevich found it necessary to declare that 'the concept of material of Suprematism is in contradiction with the ever growing agitation for material culture', which he called 'invitation to practise aesthetics', 'the idle decoration of the organism'.[92] Malevich too started to move towards the conception of production art in both his artistic and pedagogic activities at that time and not entirely independently from Tatlin's ideas. All the same, he found it necessary to stress the originality of his own approach, which was perfectly legitimate on his part, but he illustrated this with polemical attacks which deliberately misinterpreted Tatlin's basic positions. In August 1920 Pevsner and Gabo released their 'Realistic Manifesto'. The timing of the release of the manifesto coincided with the final stages in the work on the model for the **Monument to the Third International**. This was, of course, no coincidence. As their ideas touched at many points on Tatlin's, they were in a hurry to declare the independence of their aims and ideas.

Tatlin's main creation was the project for the **Monument to the Third International**.[93] The idea is supposed to have entered his mind approximately at the end of 1918 or the beginning of 1919. This was the period when monumental propaganda started to flourish, in the organization of which Tatlin took an active part. Circumstances were such that out of all the submitted large-scale projects for monumental propaganda, planned to be executed in various forms, most attention was devoted to erecting monuments of a portrait character honouring revolutionaries and other progressive personalities working in the cultures of various countries and epochs. Early in 1919, Tatlin became involved in the work of monumental propaganda no longer as an administrator but as a planner. His project was intended to challenge those small-scale, figurative monuments which were unable to alter the landscape of older towns. He planned a building-monument to honour the October Revolution. When work was in process he called this the **Monument to the Third International**.[94]

169

The idea of erecting a monument in the form of a building is rooted in old Russian tradition which until the eighteenth century, because of religious prohibitions, did not permit the erection of statues. Architecture on the other hand was regarded – given the historical circumstances of the period – as almost the most important artistic genre, symbolizing the establishment of a new society to which the new architecture should correspond.

The above-mentioned article, 'Problems of Art Education', proclaims: 'The time is near when the proletariat will need huge buildings which can accommodate tens of thousands of people. Minimum effort, minimum use of building material, maximum constructivity: these are the laws on the basis of which the proletariat will build. Only perfectly trained worker-artists will be able to realize these tasks with maximum co-ordination of work, the most effective usage of modern means of production incorporating the latest technological achievements.[95]

Tatlin planned a huge building-monument, 400 metres high, 'which will be built on the basis of entirely new architectural principles... and entirely new, hitherto unused architectural forms'.[96] The building was to become the headquarters of the main institutions of the future world-state. His project was unusual in every aspect. In fact, this was the plan for the first European skyscraper. And what a skyscraper it would have been! Buildings of that size were not built until a few years ago.[97]

Tatlin imagined the **Monument to the Third International** as an open spatial construction made of metal, inside which there would be four huge shapes made out of glass: a cube, a pyramid, a cylinder and half a sphere.[98] In reality these were to be four huge, independent buildings. (The planned diameter of the cube was 110 metres.) The supporting structure of the tower was to be two spirals, resembling springs fastened on each turning-point to a diagonal axle. A grill structure connecting the spiral shafts held the components together in a unified whole. Tatlin invented unbelievably complex and daring architectural forms, entirely different from any vertically constructed spiral building ever known. The spirals he used encompassed an unusual spatial form, but were not merely decorative and served as a huge support structure.

The use of suspended constructions made it possible to take the weight off the supporting structure and also allowed the use of suspended wall units as partition structures. This way there was no need to cramp the interiors of the suspended shapes with supporting pillars.

170, 171
On the sketches one can see clearly that these partitions or dividing panel structures were not supposed to function as supporting elements. Tatlin also wished to install air-conditioning systems inside the building, which he called a thermos.

To fix the internal structures to the supporting structure was extremely difficult as, according to his ideal, all four inner structures had to revolve around their own axes, each at a different speed. One would not have perceived the motion because of the low speed of rotation. But this was not the object anyway. What Tatlin wanted was that the basic elements of the monumental building should offer an ever-changing image through the continuous motion of the fixed and revolving parts.

His aim was to combine in architecture forms determined by structure and function, on the one hand, and on the other, artistic shapes with their own, independent power of expression.

The new forms thus created were given symbolic meanings by Tatlin, a concept which went back to ancient traditions in the history of architecture. The general function of the project was expressed by Tatlin through size, form and movement of the architectural mass which related the **Monument to the Third International** to the whole planet.

Thus the main construction was tilted in accordance with the angle of the Earth's axis. This symbol offers a clue to the rest: the revolving motion of the inner components of the tower around their own axes is associated with the Earth's rotation. The cube was supposed to take a full year to turn, the pyramid a month, the cylinder a day, whereas the half sphere would have turned presumably once in every hour. The size of the tower, 400 metres, was no coincidence either: it is equivalent to a one-hundred-thousandth part of the Earth's meridian.

To achieve maximum dynamism of the composition, it seemed extremely effective to make the basic support structure incline, and this was enhanced by the introduction of the double spiral shaft. As opposed to the traditional 'layer' or 'pyramid-shaped' vertical building, Tatlin's architectural composition seemed to 'throw gravity out of the window' and sought almost to reach into ethereal space. Finally, we should note the metaphorical character of the project, its likeness (which was noticed by many but was not always interpreted correctly) to the biblical Tower of Babel. Tatlin's Tower was derided by many as 'The Tower of Babel',[99] which was, according to the religious belief which had also infiltrated everyday life, the symbol of foolish presumption and its consequence, just retribution.

The similarity between the two towers was no coincidence and this meant not only a conscious similarity but also a conscious confrontation. Ever since ancient times, the myth about the building of the Tower of Babel has been interpreted in two entirely different ways: the Church saw it as a moral warning of the necessity for humility, while others interpreted it as a hymn to the creative potentialities of people united in a common effort, and as an expression (surely not without reason) of defiance towards God. Russian revolutionary culture adopted the myth of the Tower of Babel in this latter sense.[100] This was also the interpretation Tatlin adopted. The Tower of Babel was to reach the sky; it was never completed, but it was this daring dream that Tatlin tried to realize. The Tower of Babel divided humanity into peoples fighting each other. Tatlin's idea was that these antagonistic peoples would unite again under the aegis of the International. The story of the Tower of Babel symbolized the futility of fruitless ambition; the courage and daring of Tatlin's project on the other hand is staggering.

In spite of similarities in the outer forms, the two towers differ from one another fundamentally so far as structure and the division of space are concerned. The Babel ziggurat is a heavy, inert block of building material; Tatlin's trellis-work building is a kinetic construction.

During the last few years some Western critics have pointed out other works of art of universal impact which might also have inspired Tatlin – even though these artistic expressions might differ considerably from one another and are reminiscent of Tatlin's project only in some of their superficial characteristics: Brueghel's painting of the **Tower of Babel**; the **Eiffel Tower**; Rodin's **Tower of Labour**; Obrist's small model of a sculpture; Boccioni's **Bottle** and Borromini's **Sant'Ivo della Sapienza Tower**.[101] But it seems that Tatlin here, as in his painting, took the ancient Russian artistic tradition as a starting-point: seventeenth-century Russian frescoes and popular woodcuts which, in picturing the building of the Tower of Babel, imitated Piscator's engravings from Brueghel, but looked at their model through an entirely different aesthetic.

193
190, 201
200, 198

As we have mentioned earlier, Tatlin admired and had considerable knowledge of old Russian culture. He was familiar with the iconography of ancient Russian painting and had of course often seen on icons the portrayal of the Tower of Babel.[102]

We have also pointed out already how interested he was in the compositional conventions of icon painting. The effect of these conventions might not be immediately obvious in the plan of the tower but it is certainly there. Tatlin's plan in a way reinterprets the ancient icon theme not only in its basic conception but also in individual details.

The basic connection with ancient Russian art, although not obvious at first glance, is to be found in the spatial characteristics of Tatlin's project.

Looking at the **Monument to the Third International**, the eye immediately follows the line of the spirals, at times catching the logic of the form, confusing it at others; taking two spirals for one or confusing one with another. The composition of space in Tatlin's realistic architectural plan is very similar to those irrational space-constructions which cannot be described in terms of orthogonal projection and which one often encounters in iconic depictions of architecture.

164–206

197

Tatlin's Tower also carried on the tradition in ancient Russian art of trying to give an expressive silhouette to those buildings which dominated the landscape and, through this, to the town itself.

The **Monument to the Third International** would have played a dominant role in the silhouette of any town. But Tatlin, because of the strong manifesto character of the project, did not connect it to any definite environment.

In order to clarify the character and place of the **Monument to the Third International** in Tatlin's œuvre, let us briefly examine the history of its creation.

On the one hand, the idea of a building-monument was a logical development in Tatlin's search for artistic goals; on the other, it was his answer to the administrative and artistic drive for monuments which was being mounted at that time. It is very likely that it was the artist himself who put forward the suggestion for such a monument. The Moscow Branch of IZO Narkompros commissioned the project from him at a time when the results of the first and most powerful wave of practical work on monumental propaganda were being assessed.

Tatlin's records show the year 1918 as the starting date of the new project, but it is possible that this date is not correct. He wrote: 'this research into material, volume and construction allowed us in 1918 to begin creating an artistic form of a selection of materials like iron and glass, as materials belonging to modern classicism, equal to marble in the past in their austerity.'[103]

The first document on the basic idea of the project is to be found in Punin's article published on 9 March 1919.[104] Punin (contrary to his brochure of 1920 on the completion of the design) stressed in this article the originality of the functional programme which Tatlin suggested for the recreation of such an ancient type of structure as an architectural monument.

Describing the projected work Punin lists the principles of Tatlin's artistic programme, which are: the endeavour to arrive at a synthesis that bridges the various fields of the arts, 'the invention of new artistic forms' and 'their technical application', maximum exploitation of the latest technical possibilities, and the transformation of all technical and structural components into elements of artistic form in architecture. Tatlin set out to seek architectural solutions which would allow a dynamic functioning of the building. He describes the plastic dimensions of the future work: the enormous dimensions of the structure, the vertical construction, using also the possibilities of mechanical transport between the vertical sections; kinetics; the ways of connecting simple, geometrical spaces; the monolithic form that unites the different areas all serving a different function.

Tatlin started work in Moscow and carried on in Petrograd, to which he moved in the middle of 1919. Petrograd appeared attractive to him for two reasons: on the one hand he had more friends there sharing the same ideology (among them, first and foremost, the critic Punin), on the other, during those hard times the studios of the old Academy of Arts provided a more favourable working atmosphere for Tatlin's working methods as well as for designing and building the model.

The project matured gradually and it also changed during the working process, creating, in its half-completed form, great excitement among the artists.[105]

Public opinion was keenly concerned about where the monument should be erected: 'The monument is a grand building so it will have to be erected in the middle of an open space. There are some who feel it should be built in a working-class area amid workshops and factories. Moreover, it has not yet been decided whether it is to be in Petrograd or in Moscow.'[106]

By December 1919 the design was completed and an expert committee consisting of architects and engineers found that 'modern technology fully allows for the possibility of constructing such a building'.[107]

171
170, 182

This is the design which gives the two well-known views of the **Monument**: the vertical and the inclined (side) one, which Punin published in his booklet in 1920.[108] At that time, there were other sketches and drawings available as well – but we still do not know whether Tatlin completed the detailed blueprints or not.

The façade drawings are sketchy but the basic idea behind the plan is detectable. Both façades are presented in the orthogonal projection as customary for architectural projects. Yet: these are not conventional works of draughtsmanship but rather artistic free drawings, which aim at an increasingly expressive outline of the whole of the building and its individual parts.[109]

170

The façades do not correspond with one another exactly. These are not simply two projections but two variants of a form, different in detail. Because of these differences one cannot reconstruct the exact plan of the building on the basis of these two façade drawings. So far as the conception of the designer is concerned, we are reduced to making guesses which are always approximate and contentious. The same applies to some of the details which are fairly clear on the drawings. The pyramid and the cylinder, for example, as shown on the side view, could not possibly revolve inside the trellis support shell.

The peculiarities do not, however, lessen the value of the plan and can be explained very easily. During the process of making the sketches, trying to find the best conceivable solution, Tatlin concentrated on the main objective and not on detail.

182

At first he worked on the plan alone but as the work progressed he needed assistance. Punin says in an article dated June 1920 that after Tatlin received the commission from the Fine Arts Department he 'started work immediately and designed the project. Then the artists V.E. Tatlin, I.A. Meerzon, M.P. [*sic*] Vinogradov, T.M. Shapiro came together in an association, a "creative collective", developed the project in every detail and built the model for it.'[110]

172, 173

186, 187
313–353

The question of who were in fact Tatlin's assistants has recently been hotly debated, so let us examine it a little further.[111] As in the case of other works carried out with the help of assistants (the second model for the **Monument to the Third International**, a number of works from the early 1920s signed Tatlin's studio and **Letatlin**), Tatlin's authorship is beyond doubt. This was self-evident to all of Tatlin's contemporaries who knew him. Pokhomov, who was a student at that time and was looking for the most suitable training

workshop, convincingly describes what sort of tasks were required of Tatlin's assistants: 'I decided to change over from the Shtiglits Artistic College to the Academy, to quit Lebedev and join Tatlin. Tatlin had two pupils at that time: Shapiro and Meerzon. I went to see them for a friendly chat. They told me that Vladimir Evgrafovich did not teach them anything and that they were expected to perform only secondary tasks in the course of the building of the **Monument to the Third International** (like bending iron, sawing and riveting), and that it was their intention to transfer to the Faculty of Architecture.'[112] Tatlin started work on the model for the **Monument to the Third International** in March 1920[113] and finished it by   172, 173
the third anniversary of the October Revolution.[114] There was a mass-spectacle planned on this festive day in one of the squares of Petrograd similar to that of 'Liberated Labour' and 'Forward Towards the World-Commune' staged in May and June 1920. The theme of the festive performance had to be established and two months before the festival, presumably on the recommendation of the greatly respected Tatlin, the plan for the street mass-spectacle was approved of, its theme being 'The Building of the Monument to the Third International'.[115] Tatlin's plan was presumably to compile a programme of symbolic character based on improvisations, which was supposed to take place around the model, erected in the middle of the square. A mass-spectacle entitled 'The Building of the Monument to the Third International' offered the most varied possibilities for creating a theatrical opposite to the confusion of Babel.

The idea, although it was never realized, shows clearly the connection between Tatlin's individual works. One cannot help noticing, for instance, the similarity between photographs   172, 173
taken in his studio of the building of the model and the photographs of Khlebnikov's 1923 play **Zangezi**, directed by Tatlin. The scenes of the model-building seem theatrical, demon-   214
strating the importance of the process.

A model had to be built so that Tatlin could continue work on the design and so that a persuasive publicity campaign could be undertaken to make the project popular. For reasons beyond Tatlin's control he succeeded in achieving the latter rather than the former.

The model, as is often the case, went through a process of simplification during its building compared with the original designs. The basic principle of Tatlin's creativity is harmony between the form and function of the material used. The model was made of wood, plywood, cardboard, paper and wire, as well as special, home-made rivets. The model only approximated to a riveted metal construction and did not reflect all the constructive ideas of the original plan, depicting only its volumetric and spatial forms. The constructive nuclei of the plan and of the model are entirely different. The design referred to a new spatial structure consisting of curvilinear supporting elements (spirals), but with the materials and technical tools available it was possible to realize only a traditional beam-structure which did, however, result in an unusual form.[116] During the building process the spirals lost their supporting function and were taken over entirely by vertical and inclined components: the base structure formed by a girder beam and approximately twenty long poles which were put together as an inclined, truncated cone. Such a cone, which reduced the inside space, was a necessary structural basis in building a wooden model.

In the inside space of the structure there were four shapes one above the other but not on the same vertical axis: starting from the bottom, a cylinder, a pyramid, another cylinder, and a half sphere.

The bottom cylinder replaced the cube seen in the 1919 sketch. This was done presumably in order visually to stress the significance of the largest, lower shape and to make better use of the reduced inner space of the construction.

The finished model was exhibited in the Mosaics Workshop of the Academy of Arts from   165, 174
8 November until 1 December 1920. The opening of the exhibition was marked by a political   178, 179
rally during which the model provoked a lively exchange of opinions among architects, artists and engineers.[117] At the end of December the dismantled model was transported to Moscow and was put together again in the House of Unions for the exhibition dedicated to the Eighth   166, 181

Congress of Soviets, which discussed the plan for Russia's electrification (GOELRO). The dismantling, transportation to Moscow and reconstruction of the model there took less than a month, which means that no major changes could have been made on it. Although there are no surviving pictures of it in Moscow there is no reason to assume that two different versions were exhibited in Petrograd and Moscow in 1920.[118]

The actual building of the model took about eight months (from March until the beginning of November 1920). It was undertaken without preliminary sketches. The individual parts were executed as accurately as circumstances allowed, but it is striking that this was done by hand, without the help of machines. These factors brought the method of building the model close to that of sculpture, and the model itself close to a work of non-representational sculpture. This gave the model and its individual parts a lively sculptural effect which was fairly unusual in the case of metal constructions. Although the model was first produced to give an idea of the final project, it became a work of art in its own right along the lines of the original project. Of all the different variations, it was the 1920 model that displayed the most sculptural and least architectural characteristics. The structure of this model differentiated more strongly between the reduced inner space of the tower and the surrounding outer space. As a result, the role of the inner space and the shapes contained in it became less significant in the composition of the whole tower. The model impressed everyone greatly, but opinions varied considerably. Because of its great visual impact it was this version of the **Monument to the Third International** that became the most popular.[119]

Although this model, due to the circumstances, did not completely correspond to the particulars of the original plan (and therefore did not live up to the original sketches), for Tatlin the work on it (with its material form) was a most organic form of creative activity.

186, 187   He created another model of the **Monument to the Third International** for the 1925 Paris International Exhibition of Modern Decorative and Industrial Arts.

There is hardly any documentation about this model,[120] but one thing is certain: it differed considerably from the 1920 version. It is very likely that the experience Tatlin had gained during the building of the first model, and better technical conditions, made possible a more accomplished realization of the original plan.

Tatlin reduced considerably the number of supporting elements in the main structure and thus succeeded at last in achieving the special effect originally hoped for, namely, the impression of transparency which the first model did not give. In the model's inner space encompassed by two rising spirals, a cube, a pyramid, a cylinder and a half-sphere hung freely above one another.

How were these components fixed to the main structure though? With a vertical support axle as in 1920, or were they suspended? An old, very clear photograph shows some important detail: in the inner space of the model, apart from the four basic shapes, are clearly visible some horizontally suspended rings of various diameters. These rings probably served to hang the inner shapes onto the main structure of the model and to suggest that they were rotating around their own axes. Whether such rotation actually took place on the model, or whether this was only stated, is unknown. The spatial effect was definitely enhanced by the fact that the cube, the pyramid, the cylinder and the half-sphere were lit from the inside.
313–353   Some of these unique solutions produced ideas for the construction of Tatlin's flying-machine, **Letatlin**.

There are documents showing that Tatlin later also planned the building of a model twenty times reduced, 20 metres tall in other words.

He returned to the idea of a building-monument in 1924, when a large-scale debate took place in the Soviet press around the monument to Lenin. Tatlin's project must have contributed to the many suggestions to create building-monuments which could serve either as clubs, palaces of culture, a Lenin Museum, industrial plants, schools, or simply symbolic compositions. Tatlin envisaged the Lenin Monument as a large-scale project, a building entirely new in its form and with the latest technical equipment. He proposed that it should have a large conference room, an information centre, a radio station and so on. According to Tatlin's ideas the monument would consist of 'a large number of elements of a dynamic and utilitarian character'.[121]

The project for the **Monument to the Third International**, 'Tatlin's Tower', impressed contemporaries greatly, creating a never-ending controversy among both followers and adversaries, but it also deeply influenced many aspects of twentieth-century architecture.

Painting at the beginning of the twentieth century was forced by the questions it posed itself and the answers it received to step out of its dimensions, and thus it eventually arrived at architecture. This tendency was realized in Russia most thoroughly in Tatlin's work.

The symptoms of crisis that became apparent in Russian art at the turn of the century seemed also to arise from an increasing gap between the different genres of art, and it was thought that a solution to the crisis was to bring these genres together again. This might explain the sudden, growing interest of artists in architecture. However, architecture was interpreted in two very different ways: on the one hand in an abstract, idealistic way, as one of the most ancient, most basic of human activities, as 'the mother of the arts'; on the other hand, in a concretely historical evaluation, as an art that was thoroughly tied up in canonic rules which prevented any renewal.[122]

This had twofold consequences: the artists endeavoured either to create compositions in harmony with architecture or to take part in the planning of architecture. Their aim was not, however, to adopt the usual methods of architectural planning in order to arrive at traditional architectural results. Just the opposite, in fact. The reason artists wanted to move into this field was so as to change the methods of architectural planning and so renew architecture itself. This process took place between 1918 and 1925, in other words preceding by four years the first pioneering works in professional architectural planning, and started gradually to decline after the great upsurge of innovative Soviet architecture in the middle of the 1920s.

Tatlin obviously felt a great antipathy towards traditional architecture, which he set out to change completely. He saw the only possible way to achieve this in the radical redefinition of the creative methods of planning, although using of course some of the traditional achievements as well. He explained the decline of architecture as stemming from the fact that it removed itself, cut itself off, from the whole system of 'fine craft' (*izobrazitel'noe delo*), and this, in turn, had a negative influence on painting and sculpture: '... any connection between painting, sculpture and architecture was lost, as a result of which individualism appeared... and artists in their treatment of material reduced it to the level of being distorted in relation to one of the branches of fine art. So, at best, the artist decorated the walls of private dwellings... and left us a series of "Iaroslavl' stations" and a mass of forms which are comical now.'[123]

Tatlin made the point that there was a great difference between construction (*stroitel'stvo*) and architecture (*arkhitektura*). According to this conception, on the poster announcing the model for the **Monument to the Third International** he called the collective of workers working on the construction of the model 'builders'. He organized in 1922 A Survey of New Tendencies in Art in order to mobilize 'all the artistic forces of Petrograd working in the area of the new art in painting, theatre, music, sculpture and building (*stroitel'noe delo*)'.[124]

During the debate in 1924 about Lenin's monument, Tatlin 'is even against the participation of architects in the building project, allowing for only Constructivist artists and engineering technicians'.[125]

Tatlin described the reasons for his dissatisfaction with architecture as follows:

...existing forms in the art of building (in architecture) ... acquire a certain fixed and schematic character. Usually this is a combination of simple rectilinear forms and forms having the simplest curvature.
As for architecture, the use of curvature and forms of complex curvature... is still of a primitive character... this leads to monotony in the sense of a constructive-technical resolu-

tion and also locks the artist into a narrow range of ordinarily accepted building materials. This is clearly seen in projects for world-wide competitions in modern architecture.[126]

Tatlin penned these words in 1932, after a certain period of development had already passed, which means that he had continued to criticize the state of architecture as he had before the birth of the 'new architecture'. This is because he did not think the development of architecture radical enough and he regarded the results as still quite marginal. He noticed that the new movement got into a crisis and that the '"Constructivists" in inverted commas turned into decorators or took up graphic art'.[127]

The basis for Tatlin's architectural innovations was his own particular idea of the role of the modern artist. He believed that it was the vocation of the artist to uncover the laws of the dynamic relationship between material, its utilization and reactions, because without that no form defined by the necessities of life could be created. What sort of *modus operandi* did Tatlin propose, as opposed to the methods of traditional architecture? This is best described by his own slogan 'Painting + engineering − architecture = construction of materials $(a+v-o=k)$.'[128]

According to Tatlin the task of the artist is to 'invent' new form and the task of the engineer is to provide its technical realization. The fact that even in the process of architectural planning he envisaged co-operation between artists and engineers is proved by another slogan of his, the motto for the exhibition of his Tower: 'Engineers and bridge-builders, make calculations for an invented new form.'[129]

The conception of architectural planning as 'painting + engineering − architecture' will later become (to use a modern term) the principle of industrial design. For Tatlin this conception meant Constructivism.

The model for the **Monument to the Third International** was exhibited in Moscow at the House of Unions in the last few days of 1920, and visitors could be admitted until the end. Tatlin also travelled to Moscow. His work soon aroused great interest in the Moscow art world. His art became the 'latest sensation'. Punin's monograph was also published in 1921 under the title **Tatlin (Against Cubism)**.

166, 181

184

During the first few months of 1921 one regular item on the agenda at meetings of the Moscow Institute of Artistic Culture (INKhUK), with the participation of representatives from the various art genres, was the discussion (illustrated by works of art) of the problem of composition and construction. It is remarkable that this problem seemed so acute at the very time of Tatlin's presentation of the model. Still, Tatlin's art was always followed with interest in the Institute of Artistic Culture, and debates followed.[130] A little later Tatlin was elected the Petrograd corresponding member of INKhUK, and towards the end of 1921 he was charged with organizing and leading the Petrograd section of INKhUK.[131]

These circumstances greatly assisted in the establishment of a Moscow Constructivist group in close connection with INKhUK. The term Constructivist first appeared in 1921.[132] Its inventors gave it the same meaning as Tatlin gave the concept of culture of material. The term Constructivism was in total harmony both semantically and phonetically with Tatlin's concept and, since it was a much more fortunate linguistic term than culture of material or other expressions he had used previously, Tatlin adopted it without hesitation. The word was introduced by his Moscow followers and he never used it as his own invention. It was soon adopted by various branches of the arts but in the end it was mostly used in architecture, with a slightly different meaning.

Tatlin regarded himself as the leading figure of Constructivism but his ideas differed considerably from the Constructivism that became prevalent in the new architecture. According to Constructivist architects the form which has a practical function is at the same time a work of art, while according to Tatlin the consciously chosen artistic form must at the same time be functional.[133]

His aim was to introduce art into technology and into life, but he did not want art to dissolve in technology. In his mind, Constructivism always remained an artistic trend. A number of times he reached the border where art almost ended – but he was determined not to overstep that border. He was opposed both to the advocates of almighty rationalism and to imitators working in a 'Constructivist style'. He called both the former and the latter 'Constructivists in inverted commas'.[134] Tatlin was often misunderstood (even by people who respected and published his art) when his admiration for technology was taken out of context and exaggerated. His name became a symbol of avant-garde art. Soon he became famous, even abroad, especially in Germany.

135, 136
185

In spring 1920 in the Munich periodical **Der Ararat**, a young Russian journalist, Umansky, introduced Tatlin as the representative of the extreme technical viewpoint: '...for the new plans of monuments he borrows directly from the world of machines, he builds his works in a "machine-like" manner, he doesn't mind revealing his "machine-heart" and approaches the "monster of the cities" with an attitude of trust.' Umansky presented this method as the opposite of the Expressionism widely popular in Germany at that time. According to him, Tatlin regarded experiments with expressionistic modelling as an impotent escape of great spirits from their own age, which had become irresistibly mechanical and rational.[135]

Tatlin had such influence among German artists that his name was used as a slogan of a Dadaist exhibition in June 1920. There is a well-known photograph taken at the exhibition with John Heartfield and George Grosz and a sign with the following text: 'Art is dead. Long live the new machine-art of Tatlin.' Raoul Hausmann's collage **Tatlin at Home** was also exhibited there. One of the organizers of the exhibition was George Grosz, who during his visit to Russia in 1922 expressed the wish to be introduced to Tatlin and his work. The meeting disappointed him greatly: Tatlin did not at all fit the picture Grosz had made of him before he got to know him.[136]

This single event carries great significance because Tatlin was regarded by almost everyone as the spokesman for extreme technological tendencies in art, and this view was further spread by articles like Umansky's. This attitude was popular because many thought all problems of society would be solved by the achievements of scientific and especially technical and technological progress, determining the whole of intellectual life and the character of the new art.

In this context Hausmann's collage called **Tatlin at Home**, mentioned above, is revealing. It portrays Tatlin as an intellectual with a brain that functions like complicated, abstract pieces of machinery.

The truth lay elsewhere: Tatlin was not at all the man with a calculator-brain. The purpose of a second collage-portrait of Tatlin might have been to prove just that: it was done by El Lissitzky shortly after Hausmann's. Lissitzky lived in Germany at the time and knew Hausmann; but what is more important, he knew Tatlin better. His portrait is the extreme opposite of that by Hausmann, and perhaps that is why there is so much irony in it. Instead of the intellectual 'superman' he presents an 'ordinary' man, using one of Tatlin's original photographs, but replacing his eyes with compasses. In accordance with the artistic and social role he played at that time, Tatlin stands on a pedestal as if he were his own monument. The pedestal, however, is an ordinary kitchen stool – like the compasses: although accurately drawn, they are simple and traditional measuring instruments. One could argue that Lissitzky was out to lessen Tatlin's virtues in comparison with Hausmann.[137]

In Hausmann's portrait there is a man-machine surrounded by objects far more primitive than what he controls. In Lissitzky's portrait there is a simple man creating a new world for himself with the help of science and technology. This is without any doubt a more truthful interpretation of Tatlin's personality and artistic conception. Tatlin, who created the slogan 'Art into Technology' and who is known as the father of Constructivism, in fact made less use in his work of the methods and techniques of technology than he did of nature – unlike many representatives of technological and related conceptions. He probably regarded art as a significant non-formalistic method in the interest of humanizing technology. At the same time he had a great passion and curiosity for the laws and manifestations of nature.

In the process of solving the tasks he had set himself, Tatlin as it were re-evaluated the interconnection between man and nature and its individual elements: between the organic and the non-organic, the earthly and the cosmic. He interpreted man's constant desire to have an active contact with the whole of nature and all of its elements and spheres on a purely materialistic and anthropocentric basis and he came to the conclusion that this could only happen through the exploitation of the latest achievements of science and technology. His particular interest in the workings of nature can easily be proven on the basis of his creative methods (as an interaction between goals and means), as well as through the function of construction and objects (the aim) and also how he related to material on the whole (the means). He always defined his own chosen form in the given field, whether in architecture, industrial design or communication.

He ascribed great importance to the fact that the artist (the constructor) should not only develop his intellectual and physiological abilities but also the physical ones in order to try to reach perfection. He called upon his contemporaries to 'improve their eyesight' and to 'place the eye under the control of touch'. He believed that 'an artistic approach to technology can and must pour new life into outmoded methods'.[138]

Tatlin was interested in the most ancient roots of craftsmanship which he thought came to people almost as a 'natural gift' at one point in history. He regarded the artist as the depository of personal and universal human experiences which cannot be replaced. This is why he never stopped working on amalgamating the methods of modern technology with the empiricism of traditional craftsmanship. Tatlin approached the functional questions of architecture and industrial design in a most complex way, considering the level of information that was generally available at that time. The starting-point for architectural ideas – like the **Monument to the Third International** and the idea for **Lenin's Building-monument** – was that one must build huge public buildings of a new type to satisfy all sorts of requirements, but these must not be memorials in the traditional sense (this is why he excluded museums, libraries, etc. on principle). He saw it as the function of these new types of buildings to give enough space for the most active processes of modern life. Apart from communal needs, personal requirements had to be satisfied as well: an extremely highly developed information network could take care of intellectual needs; restaurants and gymnasiums, etc., of biological ones.

His idea was to offer all these functions under one roof through the 'synthetic form' (*ob'-emliushchaia forma*) of one single building as opposed to groups of buildings. The kinetic character of some of these parts of a building would make it look like a living organism: the mobile elements attached to them – cars and motorcycles – could be compared with biological 'families': as for instance with bees in their hive. Every object Tatlin made or designed in the style of his own 'industrial design' conception (clothes, stoves, dishes, furniture, a one-man flying-machine, a sort of aerial-bicycle, etc.)[139] was always arrived at with the human being in mind, in order to serve man's individual needs. It is characteristic of him that in a climate of blossoming technical utopias, when others turned their attention towards the air transport of the future and even spaceships, Tatlin regarded the exploration of the possibility of individual flying as his major task, so that people's natural abilities might be enhanced.

Tatlin, who was constantly looking for an organic relationship between 'material and its utilization and its reaction', considered that the basis for creating new forms should be a perfect knowledge of the characteristics of each and every material he used, together with a knowledge of what the combination of this and that material would result in. He felt that those who worked in the conservative traditions and the imitators of Constructivism – the 'Constructivists in inverted commas' – who would use materials in a superficial way, had

234–292
313–353

'locked the artist into a narrow range of ordinarily accepted building materials' and that this had reduced considerably further development in the exploration of new forms. He searched constantly for organic forms that would go with both new and traditional natural materials: iron, glass ('the classic materials of our age'), Duralumin, rubber – and he also often combined these with various kinds of wood (for instance with ash, lime, pine, palisander, wicker, cork, etc.), as well as with silk, cotton, fishbone, rope, and so on.

He worked out the form according to the specifics of the given material: for instance, parts which had to curve in a complicated way he made out of wood which had been previously steamed or soaked, with the help of a matrix. In other instances he did not saw the wood but tore it in order to preserve its natural structure. At the same time he attached great importance to the perceptible characteristics of the materials such as colour, *faktura*, texture, treatment and colouring.

Tatlin found it inevitable to use 'curvature in defining architectural forms...'.[140] Forms in his plans, such as a double spiral in space, a cross-linked grill-structure, functional spatial objects suspended on a supporting frame, could find more analogies in nature at that time than in architectural practice. 'A knot on a spider's web' – this was how Khlebnikov characterized those suspended structures which Tatlin had been using in his counter-reliefs. And lastly, the kinetic elements also reflect the connection with nature in Tatlin's architecture. His **Letatlin**, the one-man flying construction, is a classic example of how Tatlin used the 'bionic' method in his designing activity.[141]

Tatlin consciously endeavoured, on the one hand, to take account of and to utilize the laws and rules of nature in the process of creation and, on the other, to reconnect the object thus produced by the constructor with a natural environment. Natural environment meant for him the whole of nature: the cosmos, the organic and non-organic world surrounding the human being, as well as man's bio-social nature. In the bionic system of form-creation he gave a significant role to the natural gift and ability of the artist. He examined the bio-social factors which are indivisible parts of human nature, such as language, craftsmanship, etc., on the basis of how they relate to nature. To a certain extent, he himself benefited from the bionic traditions of craftsmanship. These creative aims and concrete professional skills fitted organically into the overall concept which Tatlin realized in his own working life and which he called material culture or, later, Constructivism. It is truly not difficult to see how little all this had to do with the machine worship which K. Umansky and others mistakenly attributed to him.

He was much more concerned with 'how to liberate man from technological slavery' to get the better of the mechanized world of the modern age – as has been described by one of his first critics, Isakov.[142]

Tatlin's deeply ingrained romantic outlook manifested itself differently, but just as overwhelmingly, in everything he did after his main creation, the Tower.

The Tower was his triumph, but there were tragic undertones mingled with this triumph: the main creation of 'the greatest artist' (as Maiakovskii called him) was never fully understood. And this tragic situation was not merely the consequence of an 'unfortunate coincidence of circumstances' but was to a certain extent an inner necessity. In principle, the effects of such a work of creation should have been long, complex and gradual. On the other hand, of course, it soon became quite obvious that it could not fit in with the traditional course of events.

After the **Monument to the Third International**, Tatlin busied himself for a long time 234–292 with designing utilitarian things while teaching industrial design. This might seem to be in contradiction to his endeavour to solve increasingly greater problems in each and every stage of his artistic career. He stated that 'he proceeded from material constructions of the simplest forms to more complicated ones'.[143] History on the other hand proved that the everyday reality of rebuilding the country after the war (which started in 1921) turned out to be much more demanding than the period of war communism.

Tatlin did not compromise his art by taking on meagre tasks, but he felt he wanted to work on what the historical circumstances determined as priority tasks. He accepted this as an ethical commitment and regarded it as the highest responsibility towards himself and society. He never was a slave of objects, and was indifferent to comfortable living all his life. It seems a paradox that such a person should spend his energy for a long time on 'constructing objects'.

Here his ethical integrity proved itself again. The basic characteristic of the objects Tatlin designed was that they were meant for people for whom ideas were more important than the objective world. These objects lacked pompousness and exhibitionism. One could definitely not become the slave to such objects. Tatlin humanized this work in the same way as he attempted to humanize technology through art.

313–353 After the projects for a 'new way of life'[144] Tatlin, between 1929 and 1932, built (as mentioned above) the one-man flying-construction, **Letatlin**. **Letatlin** too is an object; it is a particularly telling attempt at humanizing technology. There can be no doubt that compared with the earlier artistic phase, this task was immeasurably more complex. The plan for **Letatlin** was conceived in Tatlin's mind long before the start of the actual construction process: it is not unlikely that the basic idea of a flying apparatus was conceived towards the beginning of his career. This is why the time which he chose for the realization of this project is so significant.

340 The period of rebuilding the economy had now been completed. A period of industrialization began with the building of less developed or totally neglected areas of modern industry. A slogan was issued: 'Technology will solve all our problems'. Inventors seeking rationalization in technology were widely supported.

One has to take into account also the changes which were taking place in the artistic world: by this time, there were definite signs of consolidation. The fight between antagonistic artistic groups became even sharper but moved increasingly onto a level of theoretical debate. The 'leftist' art of the revolutionary years now seemed dated even to its once most active followers because conditions had changed fundamentally. The most significant representatives of left-wing art (Maiakovskii, Meierkhol'd, Eisenstein, Dovzhenko, Malevich, the Vesnin brothers, Mel'nikov, Leonidov, Nikol'skii and others) all worked on large-scale works of a programmatic character throughout the whole spectrum of artistic genres, trying to find answers to the new questions. At the same time the position of the traditionalists became increasingly strong in every artistic genre.

It was at such a time that **Letatlin** was created. Tatlin regarded himself as an inventor[145] and therefore he tried to penetrate one of the advanced fields of technology. His romanticism was now not simply programmatic but had a very strong demonstrative character.

Once again he chose one of those classic themes which have intrigued the human mind for centuries, and which are to be found in the most ancient sources of mythology. After the latter-day 'Tower of Babel' he attempted to realize the dream of Icarus, a dream which stemmed from an even more ancient Assyrian myth.

Would Tatlin's apparatus fly or not? He had to believe that it would. But did he not know of the failure of numerous previous attempts? It is perfectly obvious that he consciously took the enormous risk. It is also likely, however, that in his opinion this piece of work was not to be judged first and foremost by its practical usefulness. When he started work on this project, utilitarian in its way, Tatlin held the opinion that art is not utilitarian. He stressed that the artist had the right to indulge in romantic utopias, to advocate beautiful things which might never be realized.

And indeed, let us imagine **Letatlin** taking off into the air. What would have been the result? The already numerous great technological inventions would have been enriched by yet another one which would have been taken for granted soon after by a blasé public – and anyhow, it is not impossible that such a machine is yet to be invented. A work of art, on the other hand, will always preserve its uniqueness.

Letatlin, like the **Monument to the Third International**, was not just a material form but one of Tatlin's manifestos.

It is remarkable that he used not only the experiences of his contemporary, Lilienthal, but also those of Leonardo and even of the anonymous peasant who, according to ancient Russian chronicles, jumped off a tall bell-tower in order to try out his home-made wings.

For the building of **Letatlin** the artist set up a workshop in the tall bell-tower of the old Moscow Novodevichii Convent and it can hardly be a coincidence that both he and his two companions, the young artists Sotnikov and Pavil'onov, tried to look and dress like Russian craftsmen of old.

Letatlin did not take off in the end. For various reasons practice attempts had to be broken off. The well-wishers and the critics postponed passing final judgment until such time as attempts should provide a clear result. At the same time they came to the conclusion that Tatlin 'departed from art into technology'.[146]

For Tatlin, however, 'art going into the service of technology' did not mean that he 'was departing from art into technology'. After the publication of the article which made this suggestion, he publicly declared at the first opportunity that 'he was to return to painting' and 'also wants to take up architectural constructions', and he admitted to 'an inveterate attraction to the theatre from very early on'.[147] Tatlin did not admit to having distanced himself from art, even if this was meant to be appreciative. He simply reminded people that he was almost a universal artist and could carry on working in a number of artistic genres. He remained a believer in the idea of production art and **Letatlin** was the final fulfilment of this idea. But when a production artist is deprived of the realistic basis for his activity he 'has to return' to one of the traditional genres of art, one which was not branded as 'formalistic'. From the available possibilities Tatlin chose painting, architecture and the theatre. And indeed, between 1930 and 1950 he was mostly busy painting and doing graphics but almost entirely 'for himself'.

During these years, however, he followed two different artistic directions in his painting and in his graphics. Compared to his early paintings he chose a new style, which showed familiarity with the experiments of the so-called Paris School. Similar traits are to be found in the paintings of Tatlin's contemporaries, like Lebedev, Tyrsa, Al'tman and others, although there were individual differences. In this context one also must mention Tatlin's artistic 'reconciliation' with Petrov-Vodkin.[148]

In graphics the process was somewhat different. Tatlin continued, as earlier, to experiment with the achievements of genres outside the officially recognized art. In his later graphics he employed anti-aestheticism, one of the major aspects of the artistic avant-garde after the turn of the century, as a means to more complete expression.

Among the architectural tasks of the 1930s there was no place for Tatlin, although he sometimes 'fiddled around' on its 'periphery': he did take part in festive decorations of towns and did some industrial design work.[149] Towards the end of his life he worked as an expert on colour-dynamics in the studio of the architect Rudnev.

From the 1930s until the end of his life the main area of Tatlin's artistic activities was the theatre.[150] Here he could maintain his principles, although sometimes he simply had to leave material form alone and compromise in favour of a misinterpreted 'realism'.

In spite of this, it was the theatre that best suited the ageing Tatlin's taste, character, and creative practice because only the theatre could create a real synthesis of the arts, uniting in itself a visual art in time and space, making a connection between simple handwork and art and other outside factors – which were here held together in an orderly principle to create a spiritual culture.

322–324

313, 318
319
314, 315
317
341–343

410–420

Notes

1 The idea of considering creative artistic activity as pursuing a programme can be found in numerous writings (co-) authored by Tatlin. *See* 'My Answer', p. 185; 'The Work', p. 239; 'The Artist', p. 266; 'Art into', p. 310.

2 *See* 'List', p. 240.

3 А.Ф. Пахомов, *Про свою работу*, Ленинград, 1971, p. 20.

4 From 1913–14, Tatlin's principle in selecting works for exhibition was to regard them mainly as illustrations of chronological and typological stages in the evolution of his artistic method. Therefore, some works, which he saw as vehicles of a certain package of information, appeared at several exhibitions.

5 *See* p. 336.

6 Ф. Татлин, *Пчелы как любопытный предмет естествознания и пчеловодство*, Москва, Грамотей, 1873, p. 338.

7 Е.Н. Татлин, *Сменные бригады на паровозах американских железных дорог*, Харьков,1896, p. 122.

8 Ibid., p. 54. Occasionally Tatlin described artistic creation as invention.

9 Autobiographical themes dominated until 1913: *Sailor (Self-Portrait)* (Ill. 19), *Beginning of the Shipping Season, End of the Shipping Season, Vendor of Sailor Uniforms* (Ill. 25), *At the Harbour, Market at the Harbour, Fishmonger* (Ill. 28), *Composition with Fishermen, Fisherman* (Ill. 29), etc.

10 Of some thirty works for the theatre for which Tatlin designed the setting, at least eight were related to the sea. *See* Syrkina, p. 155; Works for the Theatre, p. 503.

11 Sergel', *On the Sailing-Ship*, was among the few books Tatlin illustrated. *See* Zhadova, p. 130.

12 *See* Syrkina, p. 173.

13 'Slogans', p. 244. The word 'order' has nothing to do with bureaucracy. It is part of a collection of slogans that sum up Tatlin's artistic creed. (Cf., Maiakovskii's poems 'Order to the Army of Arts', 'Order No. Two to the Army of Arts'.)

14 *See also* relevant commentary, p. 263.

15 *See* relevant commentary, p. 393.

16 Cf. Isakov, p. 333; Н. Радлов, 'О футуризме и "Мире искусства"', Аполлон, no. 1, 1917.

17 'The Work', p. 239.

18 Isakov, p. 333.

19 He lived simply but was eager to have a phone, a novelty of the time, installed in his studio.

20 'The Work', p. 239.

21 'Letter to Novitskii', p. 260.

22 'Art into', p. 310.

23 'Initiative Individual', p. 237.

24 'Curriculum Vitae', p. 321; Khodasevich, 1957–70, in Selected Bibliography (Bibliog.).

25 'Curriculum Vitae', p. 322.

26 *See* Bibliog.: Punin, 1923, 'Review'.

27 *See also* Syrkina, p. 155. Tatlin's attraction to Russian historical and folk plays is clear from the fact that he never designed sets for other than Russian historical or costume pieces.

28 The bandore is an old Ukrainian stringed instrument. It was Tatlin's favourite instrument and he himself made several. One of these is kept at the Glinka Museum of Music in Moscow. An accomplished folk-singer, Tatlin could accompany as a performer a group of musicians and singers who took part in the Russian exhibition of folk art in Berlin in 1914. *See* 'Letter about a Trip', p. 181.

29 The picture *The Month of May* has recently become known under the title *Composition. See Tendenzen der Zwanziger Jahre*, West Berlin, 1977, Cat. no. 1/25. It is unlikely that Tatlin gave this neutral title. The former title

seems to be more authentic as the words 'month of May' (*Mai mesiats*) appear on the picture just as in the case of *Staro-Basman* (*Staraia-Basmannaia*). On the latter, *see* n33.

30 'On "Zangezi"', p. 248.

31 Tatlin's works and ideas were probably reflected in Khlebnikov's prophetic design for the architecture of the future and in some of his poems, e.g., 'The City of the Future'. *See* 'Tatlin', p. 336 ff.

32 Arvatov, for example, praised Meierkhol'd's art by comparing him to Khlebnikov and Tatlin. Б. Арватов, *В.Э. Мейерхольд. Сборник к 20-летию режиссерской и 25-летию актерской деятельности*, Тверь, 1923, p. 11.

33 Воспоминания художницы Дымшиц-Толстой. Archive of the State Russian Museum, fond 100, unit 249, pp. 10, 46. At that time Tatlin's studio was at 33 Old Basman Street (today Karl Marx Road).

34 'Questionnaire', p. 262.

35 Н.Ф. Лапшин, Автобиографические записки, Archive of the State Russian Museum, fond 144, unit 452, p. 39.

36 *See* pp. 263–4.

37 Tatlin always referred to 1909 as the year of his first exhibition (Golden Fleece *Salon*). Larionov's *Portrait of Vladimir Tatlin* in a seaman's blouse dates back to 1908 (Ill. 32).

38 Tatlin took part in four exhibitions of the Union of Youth in 1911–14. In 1912 he participated in an exhibition organized jointly by the Union of Youth and the Donkey's Tail, a group of Moscow artists. *See* Tatlin at Exhibitions, p. 489. He did not take part in the exhibitions of other groups of the same circle – Target, The Four, etc. – probably because of his travels abroad and his conflict with Larionov.

39 Larionov painted Tatlin's portrait again in 1910 (Ill. 33). However, he wrote the word blockhead (*balda*) on it. *See also* p. 61 n2.

40 *See also* n62 and 105; Tatlin's and Mansurov's 'Declaration' and commentaries, pp. 257–8.

41 *See* Sarab'ianov, p. 44; Kostin, p. 67.

42 'My Answer', p. 185.

43 *Tatlin (Against Cubism)*, p. 347; *see also* commentary, p. 393.

44 'List', p. 241.

45 *See* Tatlin at Exhibitions, p. 490.

46 The memoirs which retell the story are probably based on Tatlin's account.

47 'The Work', p. 239.

48 *See also* pp. 26 and 34; the commentary 'Constructivism', p. 312.

49 Tatlin's soul-mates and other contemporaries had an exact idea of the meaning of the term counter-relief. The counter-reliefs made, for example, by Alexandra Exter and the Stenberg brothers for the pavilions of the 1923 Agricultural Exhibition coincided with Tatlin's interpretation of the term. Nowadays, however, the term counter-relief is generally used to mean high relief. Thus the high relief made by Lebedeva for Pasternak's gravestone, for example, is called counter-relief in literature. *See* С.Д. Лебедева, *Посмертная выставка произведений. 1892–1967*, Москва, 1969, p. 42.

50 The following examples may be mentioned: Severianin: coined *bezdar'* (talentless person); Khlebnikov: *ladomir* (world of harmony), *trudomir* (world of action), *liudostan* (man's stature); Maiakovskii: *iazykotvorets* (innovator of language), *liudogus'* (goose-man); Mariengof: *guchelet* (he walks on clouds). Tatlin therefore followed the contemporary practice of coining words.

51 *See* p. 334.

52 А.К., 'У В.И. [!] Татлина', *Утро России*, no. 111, 1914.

53 Isakov, 'On Tatlin's Counter-Reliefs', p. 334.

54 As early as 1913 his costume designs for *Ivan Susanin* had the character of technical drawings (Ill. 137–55). Naturally, this style was the most conspicuous in his technical drawings for the *Monument to the Third International* (Ill. 164–206) and for *Letatlin* (Ill. 313–53). The same applies to his later stage designs, some of which he finished with the painting techniques. Cf. *The Flying Dutchman* (Ill. 156–63), Sukhovo-Kobylin, *The Affair* (Ill. 369–83).

55 *See* Bibliog.: Maiakovskii, 1957–64, vol. XIII, p. 188.

56 В. Шкловский, 'Искусство как прием', *Поэтика*, Петроград, 1919, p. 105.

57 The article 'Problems of Artistic Education' differentiates between the training of artists and artistic education. The article was either written by or based on the ideas of Tatlin.Проблемы художественного образования. *Справочник Отдела ИЗО Наркомпроса*, Москва, 1920, pp. 42–3.

58 А.В. Луначарский, *Об изобразительном искусстве*, Москва, 1967, p. 475.

59 Н. Радлов, op. cit., p. 13.

60 He took part in the organization of key avant-garde exhibitions: Tramway V (1915), The Last Futurist Exhibition 0—10 (1915–16), etc., and himself organized The Store (1916). *See* Tatlin at Exhibitions, p. 489..

61 Воспоминания художницы Дымшиц-Толстой, ibid., p. 42.

62 It is not the subject of this paper to compare the characters of Tatlin and Malevich. Suffice it to say that the circumstances of their co-operation and subsequent conflict are indicated by numerous documents, some still unknown. *See also* n40 and 105.

63 'My Answer', p. 185. Highly telling is what the painter Chekrygin wrote of Tatlin in 1921: 'I respected Vladimir Evgrafovich as a sincere artist; however, I did not and do not consider him a clearly thinking theorist'. Ю.А. Молок, В.И. Костин, 'Об одной идее "будущего синтеза живых искусств"', *Советское искусствознание-76*, Москва, 1977, p. 323.

64 Tatlin was under surveillance in 1909–11. A secret report of 1 February 1909 by the commander of the Penza Provincial Police says of the situation at the Penza College of Art: 'In 1905–6 the revolutionary agitation reached, among other schools, the Penza College of Art. Partisan rivalry and hostility developed among the students. First of all, Dean A.F. Afanas'ev and certain faculty members were involved in the political struggle. Some students – who were already members of the revolutionary organization – took advantage of the disorder and uncertainty and carried out effective revolutionary propaganda, that is, enlisting public support to the Revolution and the Party.' The revolutionary organization mentioned was the board of monitors. A police report of 13 May 1909 states that the members of the board were Kriukov, Subbotin, Tatlin, Taran, Minkel'dei and Moskvichev, 'persons with revolutionary views'. (TsGAOR).

65 Cf. 'The Work', p. 239.

66 Radlov, for example, was convinced that the mere recognition of Futurism as an artistic tendency would mean for art a revolution unprecedented since the Stone Age (op. cit. [n16], pp. 16–17).

67 On 12 April 1917 a plenary meeting of the left wing of the Union of Art Workers unanimously passed the following decision: 'We are electing the painter Tatlin as our delegate and sending him to Moscow to contact left-wing artists and their organization there. In case there is no left-wing block there, we commission him to organize one.' (TsGIAL, fond 794, inventory 1, unit 25, p. 46.)

68 The Union of Art Workers was formed after the February Revolution and it existed until summer 1918. It was a mass organization of Petrograd artists, architects, writers, musicians and actors only in name but actually it was a bourgeois organization.

69 The letter of commission is kept at TsGALI.

70 'Curriculum Vitae', p. 323.

71 The Moscow Artistic Collegium of IZO Narkompros included the following officials: Tatlin (chairman), Zholtovskii and Korolev (members of the board), Dymshits-Tolstaia (secretary), Kuznetsov, Mashkov, Morgunov, Malevich, Shevchenko, Konenkov, Udal'tsova, Fal'k, Kandinsky, Ivanov, Franketti, Rodchenko, Strizhiminskii, Fidler, (*Искусство*, 15 Jan. and 1 Feb. 1919). Tatlin headed the Collegium April 1918 to June 1919, while its personnel somewhat changed.

72 *See* 'Memorandum', p. 185; 'Letter', p. 187; Bibliog.: Strigalev, 1975.

73 'Report', p. 237.

74 Ibid.

75 An International Bureau was set up within IZO Narkompros. It was run by the following committee: Dymshits-Tolstaia (head of the Bureau), Lunacharskii, Shterenberg, Punin, Tatlin and Kandinsky. 'The aim of the world-wide activity of the International Bureau is to rally the exponents of new art to evolve a new universal artistic culture.' (*Искусство*, 15 Jan. 1919). The Bureau prepared for publication the first issue of the journal *Internatsional Iskusstv* (the project failed), and it sent appeals to artists in Germany and Great Britain. Tatlin was on the editorial board and wrote theses for an article intended for publication in the journal. *See* 'Initiative', p. 237.

76 Six tendencies were represented in the Studios: Realist–Naturalist, Impressionist, neo-Impressionist, post-Impressionist–Cubist, Suprematist, Futurist. (TsGALI, fond 680, inventory 1, unit 1018, verso of p. 106, 108.)

77 In traditional schools of art professional training in the strict sense consisted of drawing from nature and of solving concrete tasks of composition (picture composition, architectural design, ornaments, etc.). After the Revolution schools were reformed and the study of the general principles of artistic form was introduced. Some of the new subjects were: Materials, Volume and Construction; Volume; Mass; Colour, etc. The blanket term for these subjects was formal disciplines (*formal'nye distsipliny*). Tatlin called them technical disciplines (*formal'no-tekhnicheskie distsipliny*). *See* 'Letter to Novitskii', p. 260; 'Pedagogical Work' in 'Curriculum Vitae' and commentaries, pp. 323, 327-8.

78 The term 'painterly culture' gained wide currency among left-wing artists, especially after the organization of the Museums of Painterly Culture in 1919. However, the term was found narrow as it did not cover sculpture and graphic art. Therefore, these museums were renamed Museums of Artistic Culture. Later they were transformed into Institutes of Artistic Culture: INKhUK, Moscow, 1920; GINKhUK, Petrograd, 1923. The Petrograd Museum of Artistic Culture considered artistic culture as a synthesis of painterly culture and material culture. (LGALI, fond 4340, inventory 1, unit 6, p. 15. At GINKhUK Tatlin headed the Section for Material Culture.)

79 In spring 1919 the Sovnarkom decreed to set up the Russian Academy of the History of Material Culture on the basis of the Russian Archaeological Committee. This is how the name was coined: 'Pokrovskii did not like the name "Academy of Archaeology and Art History", therefore he passed a decree renaming it "Academy of Material Culture". Lenin added the word "History"'. (И.Э. Грабарь, *Письма 1917–1941*, Москва, 1977, p. 29.) Mikhail Nikolaevich Pokrovskii: historian, statesman, deputy commissar for education.

80 'Letter to Novitskii', p. 260.

81 *Справочник Отдела ИЗО Наркомпроса*, Москва,1920. The bulletin contains documents originating from January

1918 to June 1920. The draft educational programmes are not dated but they are apparently based on experiences of the Free State Artistic Studios. In all probability, the programmes were drafted between early 1919 and June 1920 since the bulletin includes the proceedings of the first Russian conference of instructors and students of the colleges of art, 1–10 June 1920. (These, however, are not directly related to the documents to be analysed below.)

82 'Схема учебного плана ГСХМ', pp. 27–32; 'Проблемы художественного образования', pp. 37–45; Искусство и внешкольное воспитание', pp. 50-52;'Программа по изучению искусства в единой трудовой школе', pp. 59–73. The documents, except for the last one, were unsigned as they expressed the views of the whole department. Page 73 carries the signature of V.L. Khrakovskii; however, this was deleted on every copy. It can only be seen when the leaf is turned toward the light. Apparently the organizers decided to publish his contribution without naming the author.

Vladimir L'vovich Khrakovskii (b.1893): artist and industrial designer from Tatlin's circle.

83 The documents are believed to have been written by several hands, but they were published without signature as they expressed the views of the Fine Arts Department. Tatlin, head of the Moscow Fine Arts Department and a senior lecturer, is thought to have collaborated with all the authors. The last two pieces rely on Tatlin's conception, but are not based on it. (As mentioned above, the latter of the two was written by Khrakovskii.)

84 The chapters on painting, sculpture and architecture in the 'Outline' can only represent 'ideal' versions of the programmes of the Studios under Tatlin. The 'Outline' is strikingly similar to the programmes of the period Tatlin spent at GINKhUK (1923–4). The conception of the closing chapter, 'Institute of Artistic Sciences', is reminiscent of the article 'Problems of Art Education', especially of its conclusion. As regards this latter article, Tatlin's (co-)authorship seems almost certain. The content, idiom, structure, argumentation and style are all similar to Tatlin's other early writings, or those written at the time or much later, even in the 1940s.

85 *Справочник Отдела ИЗО*, pp. 38, 40.

86 Ibid, p. 42.

87 It is of no relevance who exactly wrote the two articles. If they were not written by Tatlin, that is an even more eloquent proof of the popularity and high esteem of his views.

88 В.М. Жирмунский, *Теория литературы. Поэтика. Стилистика*, Ленинград, 1977, p. 18.

89 В. Шкловский, *Сюжет как понятие стиля*, Петроград, 1921, p. 4. It is conceivable that Shklovskii interpreted Tatlin's creative practice as convincing proof of his theoretical conception. Shklovskii was a good acquaintance of Tatlin's and he wrote press reviews of his works. Shklovskii, 'On *Faktura*', p. 341; 'The Monument', p. 342.

90 The term 'material form' appears first in connection with the *Monument to the Third International* in 'Curriculum Vitae', manuscript, (1929) (*see* p. 265). Later Tatlin used the term to describe some of his other works, e.g., the models of the setting for *A Comic Actor of the 17th Century* (Ill. 355).

91 *See* В.М. Жирмунский, op. cit. p. 313.

92 К. Малевич, *Супрематизм. 34 рисунка*, Витебск, 1920, p. 3.

93 *See* Bibliog.: Strigalev, 'On Tatlin's Project', 1973. That writing contains a more detailed analysis of the *Monument* than this paper. I intend, however, to correct some of its inaccuracies below. *See* n119 and Bibliog.: Tatlin, 1977.

94 *See* Bibliog.: Punin, 9 March 1919 and *Жизнь искус-*

ства, 24–5 October 1919. Political events of the time prompted him to dedicate it to a broader theme: world revolution and the idea of the International. The allegation that there were two separate designs, and that the first one originated primarily from Punin, is without foundation. *See* Bibliog.: Shapiro, 1976, p. 44.

95 *Справочник Отдела ИЗО*, pp. 40–1.

96 *Жизнь искусства*, 1919, pp. 24–5.

97 The highest technical structure of the time was the Eiffel Tower (300 m), and the tallest block was the Woolworth skyscraper (231 m) built in New York in 1913. Russia's highest structures were the belfry of the Peter-Paul Cathedral (122 m) and the St Isaac's Cathedral (102 m) in Petrograd. The first building higher than 400 m was raised in New York in 1972 (410 m). The Moscow Television Broadcasting Tower (1967) is 533 m.

98 Owing to Punin's unaccountable error, the view gained wide currency that the project comprises only three glass halls (a cube, a pyramid and a cylinder), whereas photos of the model and the sketches clearly show four. *See* 'The Monument', p. 344.

99 *See* Bibliog.: Radlov, 1923, p. 48.

100 *See* Луначарский, op. cit., pp. 61–3 [n58].

101 *See* Bibliog.: *Tatlin*, 1968, pp. 7–8.

102 In the 1910s reproductions of these frescoes appeared also in such popular publications as И. Грабарь, *История русского искусства*, vol. VI, Москва, 1914, pp. 516–17; Ю. Шамурин, *Ярославль. Романов-Борисоглебск. Углич*, Москва, 1912.

103 'The Work', p. 239.

104 *See* Bibliog.: Punin, 9 March 1919.

105 The project got ample and systematic press coverage. Obviously, the artists learned of its progress also through other channels of information. Tatlin was probably interested in publicizing his project even though he was, as a rule, secretive. Secretiveness was one of his favourite 'games'. He was extremely suspicious of colleagues in case they should steal his ideas. This suspicion was most strongly displayed towards Malevich and his students. Once Tatlin destroyed a number of his own works so that Malevich could not see them. (*See* n40 and 62 and n7 to Sarab'ianov's study.) Tatlin was secretive even before his own students – a fact mentioned by all his one-time students.

106 *Жизнь искусства*, 1919, pp. 24–5.

107 Ibid., 11 Dec. 1919.

108 'The Monument', p. 344.

109 Punin's above mentioned work has been the only Soviet publication to carry the two sketches. Photos of the sketches are in Tatlin's archive (Ill. 170-1). The photo of the inclined façade does not show the letters Punin used for the analysis of the sketches.

110 'The Monument', p. 344. Punin confused the initials of Vinogradov's first names: he wrote M. P. instead of P.M.

111 Tatlin selected his associates from those students of the Moscow Free State Artistic Studios who first worked in the studio of sculpture 'without a leader' and then joined his studio. Probably the criterion was their practical aptitude. Shapiro, for example, says he helped Chagall to decorate Vitebsk on public holidays; assisted the sculptor Konenkov in erecting a monument to Stenka Razin; he accepted commissions from fellow students, e. g. Mukhina, to produce wooden models of their sculptures, etc. Meerzon met Shapiro at Vitebsk. Tatlin, Meerzon and Shapiro moved to Petrograd and, as Shapiro recalls, Vinogradov joined them in Moscow at the time of erecting the model for the second time. He also signed 'The Work Ahead of Us' (*see* p. 239) on 31 December 1920. Dymshits-Tolstaia might be wrong in writing that Vinogradov took part in the project in Leningrad as well (cf. n33). Tatlin's most important associates, therefore, were Shapiro and Meerzon. Recent research has established that several artists and students – Pchel'nikova, Terlitskii, Dormidontov, Stakanov, Khapaev and Dymshits-Tolstaia – also helped. М.Ю. Евсевьев, *Художественная жизнь Петрограда в первые послеоктябрьские годы (1917–1921 гг.)* (Thesis for the first academic degree), Ленинград, 1978, p. 13.

112 Пахомов, op. cit., p. 20. In 1921, soon after the completion of the model of the Tower, Meerzon and Shapiro enrolled in the faculty of architecture of the Academy of Arts, and they graduated in 1927.

113 *Жизнь искусства*, 3 Mar. 1920.

114 *Жизнь искусства*, 30–1 Oct. 1920.

115 *Красная газета*, 12 Dec. 1920.

116 The lists of Tatlin's works and the press reports on the project spoke of steel and glass: materials not for the model but for the planned structure.

117 *Жизнь искусства*, 12 Nov. 1920.

118 This view is substantiated by a recently disclosed photo, which is in Troels Andersen's possession. Repr.: *Art et poésie russes 1900-1930: Textes choisis*, Paris, 1979, p. 133.

119 Shapiro puts its height at between 6 and 7 m. See Bibliog.: *Tatlin*, 1968, p. 13. In a conversation with the author of this paper in 1969, Shapiro spoke of the same height (6.57–7 m). Accepting the eyewitness's report as authentic, I entitled a chapter of my paper (Bibliog.: Strigalev, 1973) 'The Seven-Metre Model of 1920'. Ultimately, however, the model was found to have been about 5 m.

120 Its fate can be traced down to 1943 as it was kept in the State Tret'iakov Gallery. It is believed to have been lost when a part of the collection was evacuated. The model of 1925 was a separate work. Therefore, Shapiro's view is mistaken that, except for some component parts, the original model was sent to the Paris exhibition, to be assembled in a rough-and-ready way. *See* Bibliog.: Shapiro, 1976, p. 45. Actually, Tatlin got another commission to produce a model (LGALI, fond 4340, inventory 1, unit 56, p. 98; TsGIAL, fond 941, inventory 15, unit 11, verso of p. 26) and he and his colleagues at GINKhUK made it. The fate of that model is obscure. The last we hear about it is that it was on show at the War and Art exhibition in the State Russian Museum. *See* 'Tatlin at Exhibitions,' p. 496.

121 Tugendkhol'd 'On the Discussion', p. 250.

122 Art Nouveau's attempt to renew architecture brought only a short-lived result.

123 'The Work', p. 239; Iaroslavl' station: commentary on p. 240.

124 'Programme for', p. 242.

125 Tugendkhol'd, op. cit., p. 250.

126 'Art into', p. 310.

127 Ibid., p. 310.

128 'Programme for', p. 243.

129 'Slogans', p. 244.

130 Punin, *Tatlin*, p. 347; С.О. Хан-Магомедов, 'Молодое и старшее поколение художников-производственников на этапе "от изображения к конструкции". Конструктивисты из Обмоху и Татлин (ИНХУК, 1921-2 гг.)'. Труды ВНИИТЭ, *Техническая эстетика*, 1979, no. 21.

131 Taran, INKhUK's director, appointed Lapshin and Dymshits-Tolstaia to help Tatlin to fulfil the mission and rely on the local Museum of Artistic Culture. The staff of the Petrograd Museum embraced the idea of turning the museum into an institute yet insisted on organizational independence from the Moscow INKhUK. (LGALI, fond 4340, inventory 1, unit 6, verso of p. 2). The newspaper article (*Русское искусство*, 1923, no. 2-3, p. 87) reporting on work done by the Petrograd section under Tatlin of the Moscow INKhUK was, consequently, not quite accurate.

132 С.О. Хан-Магомедов, 'Первая творческая организация пионеров советского дизайна – группа конструктивистов ИНХУКа 1921 г'. in: *Художественные проблемы предметно-пространственной среды*, Москва, 1978, pp. 2–3.

133 *See* n48.

134 'Art into', p. 310; 'Constructivism', commentary, p. 312.

135 K. Umansky, 'Die neue Monumentalskulptur in Russland', *Der Ararat*, no. 5/6, 1920, p. 32. The same year, before the completion of the first model, Umansky once again wrote of Tatlin, Bibliog.: Umansky, 1920.
The year 1922 saw growth in the popularity of Tatlin's art in Germany and elsewhere. His works were shown at the first Russian exhibition of fine arts in Berlin and several articles discussed his art. Short reviews by Punin and El Lissitzky appeared in *Veshch'-Objet-Gegenstand* (Berlin) on his Tower (no. 1–2, 1922). Ehrenburg discussed it in a journal article and a chapter of his book. *See* Bibliog.: both of Ehrenburg's works. Both of his writings are illustrated by slightly modified copies of photos of the model of the Monument. These drawings were republished in several books on the era and the Tower was reproduced usually in that form. *See* Bibliog.: Punin, *Veshch'*, 1922.

136 George Grosz, *Ein kleines Ja und ein grosses Nein*, Hamburg, 1955, pp. 171–3.

137 Cf. El Lissitzky's well-known self-portrait in photomontage (1924), which shows the artist's face, an open palm and compasses. El Lissitzky, *Maler, Architekt, Typograf*, Dresden, 1967 (Ill. 114).

138 'Art into', p. 311.

139 For more information *see* Zhadova, pp. 151–4.

140 'Art into', p. 310.

141 *See* Khlebnikov, 'Tatlin', p. 336; on *Letatlin*'s creation *see* Zhadova, pp. 147–51.

142 Isakov, p. 333.

143 'Art into', p. 311.

144 For more information *see* Zhadova, p. 134.

145 When industrialization was on the agenda, Tatlin joined the movement of technical innovation. *See* *Комсомольская правда*. 5 Dec. 1933.

146 *See* Bibliog.: Kronman, 1932, p. 22. Efros put it in sharper terms, saying that Tatlin left art for the sake of things that did not exist. (А. Эфрос, 'Вчера, сегодня, завтра', *Искусство*, 1933, no. 6, pp. 40–1.)

147 Kut, 'An Evening', p. 312.

148 'Speech', p. 313.

149 In 1940 Tatlin helped Shapiro to draw the design of a monument to commemorate a battle with white Finns. (*Архитектура Ленинграда*, 1940, and an unpublished interview with Shapiro in 1978).

150 *See also* Syrkina, pp. 155–79.

Dmitrii Vladimirovich Sarab'ianov
TATLIN'S PAINTING

164–206 If one were obliged to describe Tatlin's craft in only one word, one could scarcely say 'Tatlin, the painter'. His name is enshrined in the annals of the history of art primarily by his **Monument to the Third International**, his counter-reliefs and his early experimental creations in the field of design; his paintings are of only secondary importance. Nevertheless, Tatlin's creative career began with painting. Along with many of his European colleagues he started his work within the traditional framework of easel painting, only to break out of this framework later and to create transitional forms to other branches of art: architecture and the aesthetic shaping of the environment. This same road was followed by Malevich and Mondrian, Rodchenko and Popova, Marcel Duchamp and Le Corbusier, Kandinsky and El Lissitzky, Moholy-Nagy and Schwitters. Much later Tatlin did return to painting and withdrew, so to speak, into his own private world.

However, this period was characterized once again by differentiation according to the traditional branches of art, rather than the all-embracing syntheticism of the 1910s and 1920s, and Tatlin's painting lost its earlier experimental character.

For this reason we will concentrate chiefly on Tatlin's early painting, on his explorations which led to the counter-reliefs. At the same time, these pictures are highly important not only in that they point to the future, but also in that they are significant in the renewal of the language of painting itself, asserting a structural approach within the one-dimensional limits of easel painting.

The beginnings of Tatlin's career as a painter are shrouded in mist. We can only make inferences about his earliest known works, those which came into being before the end of the first decade of the twentieth century, since they are unfortunately unavailable to us.

The Penza College of Art, where Tatlin began his studies, was only the first step on his way to maturity as an artist. Later in his life Tatlin was to remember this period in the following way: 'I was thoroughly fed up with drawing models, who stand on tiptoe, with pieces of candy in their outstretched hands. The professor demanded that we draw this piece of sugar in such a way as to render a perfect illusion of reality. The drawing was successful but somehow it seemed a shameless stupidity to spend time doing such things.'[1]

When Tatlin came to the Penza College its director was the elderly 'Wanderer' artist, Savitskii, who was later to gain the recognition of a few young Russian painters. Pavel Filonov, among others, held him to be a true model of authentic realism. He had, however, scarcely any influence on the young Tatlin, whose teachers were Afanas'ev, a painter with inclinations towards the grotesque satirical, and Goriushkin-Sorokopudov, a Wanderer who was a successful 'parlour painter'. Without doubt, the first of these masters was the more important, and his influence on Tatlin's art is more probable. Afanas'ev was mostly involved in making illustrations to fairy-tales, in which he made use of various elements of folklore. These, however, were nothing more than illustrations and stylizations of the genuine creations of folk art. Nevertheless, Afanas'ev's role is undeniable in paving Tatlin's way towards primitivism, although Tatlin arrived there finally only after his acquaintance with Larionov. The relationship with the latter began at the end of the first decade of this century and broke
84 off after the Donkey's Tail exhibition which opened in 1912, and in which over fifty of Tatlin's works were shown.[2]

At the end of the first decade of this century Larionov exercised considerable influence on him. Tatlin, however, remained practically free of Goncharova's influence during these years, although at this time it was held by many that Goncharova was the initiator of the new ways. Her expressive style became a model for imitation so that even Malevich and Chagall were unable to escape it. In Tatlin's case, however, even Larionov's influence is felt only during the first part of his career: on the landscapes and still-lifes, and on the portraits he produced in the last years of the first decade of the 1900s.

Larionov was only four years older than Tatlin, but by this time he already had a significant artistic past and was familiar with modern artistic tendencies in foreign countries. The two artists met exactly at the time when Larionov's artistic revolt was beginning to have an influence on his fellow students and to disturb the peace of the teachers at the Moscow College of Art; it was later to result in the scandalous Jack of Diamonds and Donkey's Tail exhibitions. It seems that Larionov's rebellious spirit had a great influence on the youthful Tatlin.

85, 84

Tatlin enrolled in the Moscow College of Painting, Sculpture and Architecture probably around 1910, though some sources disagree about this date. At this time Serov was no longer teaching at the College, but Kostin, the researcher of the artist's graphic works, asserts that traces of the Serov tradition are to be found in Tatlin's drawings executed at the beginning of the 1910s.[3] However, it appears more probable that Tatlin, independently of any direct influence, was familiar with the widely popular stylistic elements of Russian drawing of the early twentieth century. Naturally, the time spent at the Moscow College was not without results, on the one hand because the College, which held to the painterly legacies of Korovin and Serov, made all young painters acquainted with the newest problems of Russian painting, and on the other because the transition from the 1900s to the 1910s was a period of ferment when new trails were being blazed, away from the old traditions. To mention only some, Mashkov and Fal'k, Kuznetsov and Larionov, Goncharova and Petrov-Vodkin, Sar'ian and Ul'ianov were just a few of the many who started off from the same point to go and conquer new territories of painting. Tatlin was younger than most of these. However, he did not merely build on their achievements. He also returned to the common source from which all the youth of Moscow was drinking and to which not only the older 'rebels' leaving the College in 1910 were returning, but also the younger students at that time like Chekrygin, Romanovich, Zhegin, Maiakovskii and many others.

Afanas'ev, Larionov and the whole milieu of the Moscow College helped Tatlin's artistic development and influenced him into joining the drift towards what was then called 'Neo-Primitivism',[4] even though Tatlin's own interpretation of this was completely original and individualistic. ·

When one examines the development of Tatlin's artistic career, it becomes evident that its various manifestations are ordered in a unified and well-defined pattern which points in a specific direction.

In order to render a proper sketch of this first period, we must take into account one more factor. At the beginning of the twentieth century the main effort of Russian painters was to leave behind the representational way of looking at things and, accordingly, to create new methods of painting. They reshaped what they saw in nature to suit the inherent laws of painting and finally were able to achieve a reality which neither demands nor tolerates comparison with everyday reality, and which is animated by its own inner impulses.

The most important example to follow was West European, especially French, painting, even for those who had not made the trip to Paris. Shchukin's and Morozov's collections made it possible for those artists who lived in Moscow to become acquainted with the latest output of the Paris school. Cézanne's was the greatest influence. 'When Tatlin just started creating', wrote Punin, the famous critic, who, until now, is the only one to have written a monograph about Tatlin, 'Cézanne was reigning supreme, thus the young artist's task was to approach Cézanne as closely as possible.'[5]

The remark just quoted is excessively categorical. One cannot see even a trace of the supposed imitation of Cézanne in one of Tatlin's first authenticated paintings, the still-life **Carnation**, which was both signed and dated (1908) by the artist. The theme itself, a bunch

13

of carnations in front of a window through which the outdoors can be seen, is impressionistic in character, a purposely accidental selection of a segment of reality. The left side of the foreshortened window-ledge and the base of the flowerpot holding the carnations are cut off by the frame. Only one wing of the window, through which a green garden is seen, has found its way into the 'accidental' cutting off of the picture. The artist has not opened up a large perspective with the sketching in of the landscape. The compositional solution, however, is none the less oriented towards space. Tatlin was here mostly excited by how the interior of the room melted directly into the landscape, that is, by the unity of the interior and the landscape. It is not by accident that he built up the composition in such a way that he lifted a section of the room, however small, into its visual field, thereby enabling the viewer to imagine the place from which the scene opens up to the painter's eye. The still-life has lost all the specific properties of the genre. There is nothing of the still-life in **Carnation**. The objects lose all their solidity and dissolve into the atmosphere. The viewer almost feels as though they are flashing past his eye, since he too is carried off by the movement of the landscape and his attention is not seized solidly by the individual objects. We may call this kind of still-life one of the landscape-type.

The conception of still-life as landscape was quite popular in Russian painting during the first few years of this century. In essence, it was the Russian Impressionists who brought this into fashion. Around the middle of the first decade of this century Grabar' painted a series of still-lifes in which he placed the objects on a table located in a garden outdoors under trees, and this in itself already presaged the union of the two genres. True, Grabar''s style still made it possible for the attention to linger on the objects. Korovin, the most important figure of Russian Impressionism, and later one of Tatlin's teachers at the Moscow College of Painting, Sculpture and Architecture, was also working in the still-life genre at the end of the 1910s, and by placing a bunch of roses before a window joined the interior to the landscape.

It is, however, scarcely tenable to say that Tatlin took this solution from his immediate predecessors or older contemporaries. His pictures have different sources. It is probable that Tatlin spent the summers during the end of the 1910s at the Larionov house in Tiraspol'. As we know, at this time Tatlin and Larionov shared a close friendship and Tatlin fell under Larionov's influence. They would paint their still-lifes and landscapes together, drawing on

12   the work not only of the Impressionists but of Van Gogh as well. Larionov had already painted some still-lifes in which Impressionism had intertwined with the striving for new roads in painting. He himself said several times that he had tried to make use of Van Gogh's and Cézanne's achievements in his own paintings of the period.

This was characteristic of the circle of painters which had formed around Larionov. They were in an advantageous position during the first years of this century, since they could pick and choose from the experiences of Western artists who had advanced in their development and so gained the opportunity to mix and combine the various tendencies. A particular characteristic of Russian impressionistic painting was that, right from the beginning, it absorbed the stylistic qualities of Post-Impressionist painting. This applies also to those painters who remained Impressionists to the end, as well as those in whose careers Impressionism was nothing more than a transitional stage. A good example of the first group is Korovin (whose Impressionism was enriched by decorative elements), and of the second, Larionov.

13   **Carnation** is linked to Impressionism first and foremost by its colour scheme. At the same time, Tatlin tended to use spots of colour more than the 'classical' Impressionists and would cover fairly large areas with thick brown paint. The light blue flashes of light on the glass and window frame became large spots. Tatlin leaves the brown, green, light blue paint unchanged on the canvas over fairly large areas. The way in which the paint is applied begins to play an important role. This is already a foretaste of the future 'body painting' (*korpusnaia okraska*) in which Punin saw a survival of the legacy of the old Russian painterly craft.[6] The

painter used strong contouring on purpose. He used thick, dark-coloured lines to outline the objects. The influence of Van Gogh's method of painting is obvious in the energetic brush-work and in the decisive, energetic strokes which create parallel straight lines.

It would probably be unjustified to spend so much time on this still-life if it did not contain the significant elements of Tatlin's further development. Besides, few of his early pictures which he himself dated have survived. We can compare this work with a lot of pictures, using analogies and a comparison with Larionov, and mentioning the titles of Tatlin's works listed in exhibition catalogues of the early 1910s. According to the latter, the majority of landscapes date probably from 1909–10. Among these may be included **In the Garden**, **The Garden**, **In Turkestan**, **Southern Street**, **In Alexandria**, **The Bazaar**, **Shop**, etc.[7]

In the landscape now known as **Twilight**, which, in its painterly style and colour scheme, stands close to **Carnation** and may be identical to **In the Garden**, or **The Garden**, the solid green colours occur along with various shades of brown and yellow. Vivid light green spots of colour stand out of the depths of the background through a thick web of tree-trunks drawn by brush on top of a pre-worked surface. The contrasts of dark and light colours and dynamic brushwork remind one of Larionov's vision.

The landscape entitled **Summer** also evokes the spirit of the master of Tiraspol', with the minor difference that here the previous colour contrast is complemented by a strident blue.

The picture **Landscape with Well**, painted on the reverse of **Twilight**, was, in our opinion, also painted near the end of the first decade of this century. This work is also reminiscent of Larionov in its theme. A house with an outbuilding, a well, a fence and a few trees: here we have a traditional collection of objects for the picture's composition. The elaboration of its surface and its range of colours are more restrained than in the previous landscape. Grey tones dominate. The landscape style of the Wanderers may easily be seen here in the simple choice of theme and the meagre use of colour.

It is evident that this style of painting shows the effects of Tatlin's studies in Penza, even though the achievements of the Moscow painters who represented the new tendencies in art are also visible. Tatlin's early works, no matter what genre they represent, are all closely tied to the representational tenets. This characterizes also **Man's Portrait** (1909?)[8], one of the early pieces in this genre, which Tatlin rarely attempted at this time. The background is a sketchy landscape painted with broad brush lines. The dark blue contours outlining yellow, green and orange spots of colour conjure up Larionov's large portraits of Khlebnikov and Burliuk. In Tatlin, however, the surface of the painting is more detailed, the drawing is less decisive and the delineation is not as homogeneous as in Larionov. But were this kind of comparison applied to other pictures painted at the end of the first decade of the century it would not be to Tatlin's advantage, since during this period his philosophy as an artist was still in its formative stage and he had not yet found his own independent style.

One could say the same thing about his still-lifes, of which the one with carnations is probably the most successful. **Marigolds** or **Leaves in a Jug** (from the end of the first decade of this century)[9] still have all the signs of a representational outlook, and are still rather far from the Constructivism which was soon to become the individualizing trait of Tatlin's paintings and drawings.

Still-Life with Melon (end of the first decade of this century)[10] is reminiscent of Larionov in the same way – particularly of the still-life with yellow flowers he painted in 1907. The foreshortenings, the shadows cast by the objects, the grey planes of the tables and the floor, and the fruit lying on them are all common to both Tatlin's and Larionov's work. Tatlin's variant, however, seems coarser and more straightforward and ties in more closely with the naturalistic view. It lacks those distinctly painterly elements which always characterized Larionov's work. Tatlin still had a long way to go before he got from his still-lifes to the bouquets of the early 1910s, from the **Man's Portrait** to the **Portrait of the Painter**, or the **Sailor**. In the end, however, it took him only a very short time to arrive at the end of this road: the transition from the first to the second decade of the century.

His sequence of watercolours, which may be located in this period, played an important role in this process. Once again we encounter the problem of chronology since most of Tatlin's watercolours are untitled in the catalogues. But two dated works make it possible for us more or less to locate other works of similar style in this period. These two works are
18, 25   **Sitting Male Figure** (1909)[11] and **Vendor of Sailor Uniforms** (1910).[12]
18   **Sitting Male Figure**, strictly speaking, forms a transition between the works of the first decade and those of the second decade of this century. The 'accidental' breaking of the composition into fragments remains from the previous period, while the new characteristic is that Tatlin was now striving for more solid picture construction within each fragment than before. Because of this, he cut the figure at the waist and positioned it to the left of centre, turning it slightly to the right. This turning away of the figure is balanced by the long table positioned along the diagonal leading to the upper right corner. At this time Tatlin was still keeping entirely to natural forms and was making no effort to reshape them in a radical way. For the time being it is a question only of a few correspondences of form. Tatlin used cylindrical shapes to depict the flowerpots placed one behind the other on the table and the watering-can above the man's head. In the foreground of the picture he built a tower-shaped structure of upside-down pots fitting into one another. He placed these plastic shapes directly opposite the volume of the human form. This system of correspondences did not yet mean that Tatlin had already turned away from naturalistic portrayal, but it did announce the transition to his system of plastic deformation as a means of interpretation of reality.
25   In the watercolour **Vendor of Sailor Uniforms** this change did indeed take place. It is enough to compare the colour schemes of the two pictures to feel immediately the significant difference between them. In the first picture Tatlin achieved unity through the great variety
18   of colours: blue, green, yellow, orange and scarlet are united by the brown base colour. He
25   reduced **Vendor of Sailor Uniforms** to two colours, orange and dark blue, thereby transforming a real variety of colours into a system of dominant ones. He eliminated the element of chance by the placement of the two figures. It is as though the sailor and the vendor are standing on a pedestal designed especially for them. They are equidistant from the edges of the picture, so that the vertical axis of the composition falls precisely between them. The true perspective dissolves and the objects do not move into the picture but slide perpendicularly across its surface, and this is clearly reinforced by the parallel upward-leading boards of the platform on which the figures stand. By means of these devices the artist has created some particularly advantageous conditions for the introduction of the two figures: he has depicted them not as parts of reality in their accidental positions but has fixed them into place in a world created by himself.
      It is not only in the composition and choice of colours that he disregarded reality, but also in the representation of the figures, first of all in their linear characteristics. Here Tatlin worked
34   in his own idiom, which he was later to use in such masterpieces as the **Sailor** and the
77–79 **Nudes** of 1913. In these pictures the contours have become more simple and more tense. Tatlin was searching for a method of sketching in which the line would be conceived as a section of a larger circle or ellipse, sometimes subordinating the natural appearance of the figures to the geometrical configuration. These curved lines filled with tension became characteristic of Tatlin's painterly style. This is precisely what Kostin pointed out about the drawings in his essay 'Tatlin's Drawings of 1912–1914,'[13] in which he remarked that this would become characteristic of the paintings as well, basing his comments, however, only on the naturalistic drawing done at the Ostozhenka Studio. One may nevertheless suppose that Tatlin's new method of depiction had already taken shape earlier, in the watercolours and probably in the numerous drawings included in contemporary exhibitions from 1910 onwards. As in the case of the watercolours, the catalogues did not list the titles of the drawings. So we are able to rely only on the date (1910) found in Punin's book cited above, found under the reproduction of the India ink drawing **Man Picking Up Matches**. Many drawings of this type have survived. It is these which, together with the watercolours we

have already discussed, mark the turning-point in the artist's creativity. We will not dwell on the drawings since they are the subject of another paper.[14]

We must, however, return to the watercolours because these also provide an important basis for a sketch of Tatlin's experimentation in painting. A small unfinished watercolour[15] may have been one of the first formulations of the painting **Fishmonger**. One can sense in 31 it a certain dispersion, a variety of both objects and colour. Although it is already possible to find almost all the shades of colour of the later painting in this watercolour, they do not yet create a harmonious whole. The contours have not yet acquired a real tension. All of this allows us to conjecture that this picture was painted around 1910. Very different characteristics mark the watercolour **Sailor Uniforms**, on the reverse of which may be seen another 26 one, **Fishmonger's Trade**. It may be assumed that these were painted at the same time as, 27 or somewhat later than, the picture **Vendor of Sailor Uniforms** which we have already 25 met. These watercolours, painted on grey paper, have a monumental effect; they are in every respect the equals of oil and tempera pictures.

In the picture **Sailor Uniforms** the vigorous rhythm which permeates the surface draws 26 the objects and the figure into a circular shape. This circular movement spreads from the sketchy object shapes of the background directly into the figure, bending through the lines of the shoulder, curving onwards in the contour of the back and then in the yellow patch of the trouser-legs (practically disregarding the real shape of the leg), continues as a grey line on its predetermined course and finally realizes itself in the contours of various objects. The idea of the curving shape develops further in the lower part of the composition; the broken lines on the pale red surface of the ground (or floor) continue on further, once again curving to the left, in the grey contours of the objects at the left edge of the composition. The painter worked out the interior rhythms within this circular line according to the systems of correspondences which we have already elaborated when we analysed **Sitting Male Figure**.

It is interesting to note that the composition built on a circular motif became a favourite technique in Tatlin's painting. In the picture called **Sailor** the circular movement is around 34 a true centre, the head of the main figure, while in **Sailor Uniforms** the figure is built right 26 into the circle. This watercolour assumes a transitional position in the progression leading to **Sailor** and the **Nude** of 1913, not only in regard to its composition but in the shaping 34, 79 of the figure as well. Tatlin showed a particular interest in the movements of the body. He often turned the head sharply towards the side in direct opposition to the movement of the trunk. He consolidated these body movements by tightening the contours and by giving elastic tension to the figure as a whole.

He uses this same procedure to establish turning or bending movements in his many India ink drawings of the early 1910s which depict the human form in active movement (for example, **Man Picking Up Matches**). The landscape setting has disappeared from the drawings and watercolours, and the human form now occupies the centre of the picture. It was the human body which engaged Tatlin's attention most of all. He positioned his model in **Nude** (1913) in the same way as in the watercolours and drawings: the head and the 79 lower part of the trunk turn in opposite directions. The drawing of the foot has two components – the contour line and the 'construction line'. Thus the watercolours and drawings of the years around 1910 already contain numerous traits which foreshadow the future.

While Tatlin was painting his landscapes and still-lifes under Larionov's influence at Tiraspol', his conception of reality, like Larionov's, was primarily landscape-centred and definitely representational. It was this outlook that he had to overcome. Larionov also passed beyond this stage. He had already painted, during the same period as his landscapes and still-lifes (1907–8), his first scenes of country life, the **Barber-shops**, his first so-called 'signboard' picture, with which he created a new school of Russian art: Primitivism.

At this point, however, Larionov and Tatlin parted company, since Tatlin in no way regarded Primitivism as his chief artistic goal. For him Primitivism was important primarily because it opened the way towards the deformation and reinterpretation of the real world and opened up the possibility of a system of constructing pictures with its own inherent rules, that is, the construction of forms. Tatlin's ultimate goal lay in this constructive task. For him it was the 'construction' in an old icon, a Renaissance picture or a print from the market which was important.

The popular themes and characters most typical of this school also appear in Tatlin's works at the same time. All the artists who were more or less attached to the movement had developed for themselves a limited set of these popular themes. Larionov painted barbers and their clients, country dandies and dames, soldiers' girls and prostitutes. Goncharova was interested in peasants working on the land. Malevich painted peasant women at work. Fonvizin liked circus themes. Tatlin chose fishermen, fishmongers and sailors as themes for his works. The choice was a natural one since he himself had worked as a sailor. Moreover, fishermen and fishmongers were a necessary part of the nautical life with which Tatlin had been so closely linked in his youth.

For the Primitivist painters not only the limited number of themes and characters was important. For their heroes they took people with their own traditions, customs and life-styles. Tatlin's particular world was that of sea-coast towns like Odessa, where he had been several times. The theme of his compositions is unchanging: his sailors are busy with their uniforms at the beginning and end of the sailing season; his fishermen and fishmongers, with huge baskets of fish on their arms, walk up and down through the market among the long tables on which sprawl giant, gutted fish carcases.

27 **Fishmonger's Trade** is an excellent demonstration of how Tatlin worked within a consistent iconography. This watercolour shows the outlines of a man holding a basket with huge red fish-tails hanging out of it – a figure typical for the painter. Its stylistic characteristics relate it to the pictures discussed above, but it is distinguished by painterly freedom and a brighter colour scheme (resulting from the use of spots and lines of black, red and green, colours rather far from each other on the colour scale).

An important place in Tatlin's painting is occupied by the still-lifes done at the beginning of the second decade of this century, which treat objects and space in a completely different
74, 75 way from the ones of the preceding period. We are thinking primarily of two still-lifes with flowers. These resemble each other so strongly that they were without doubt made nearly at the same time.[16] In them there is absolutely no trace of Primitivism. The painter was here occupied above all with the construction of the picture. At the same time the influence of Cézanne and early Cubism is quite apparent.

These still-lifes are no longer as life-like as the ones of Tatlin's 'Larionov period'. There is nothing in them of the accidental or incidental. The fact that both are built up according to the same principle supports this assertion. The flower vase is positioned in the exact centre of the canvas, behind it the vertically slanted table-top, and behind that, the plane of the wall. The two planes merge easily into each other, but we cannot say that the painter is a devotee of surface decorativism; he has not done away with space, he has only deformed it. There is no 'accidental cutting off' or elements of a frame in any of these pictures. Only in the
75 variation called **Still-Life (Flowers)** is the left corner of the table indicated: its foreshortening corresponds to the perspective view of the pipe seen on the right side. This compositional technique makes the overall impression somewhat complicated, though without upsetting the proportions of the picture. The simplification which Tatlin had used in the probably earlier
74 version, the **Bouquet**, is lacking. The spatial expanse of the two pictures is closed and does not extend into the depth of the picture. The painter was striving to resolve the 'inner' rhythm of the composition, by varying one single motif only. The focal point of the **Bouquet** is situated a little high up; the foreshortening of the vase gains emphasis and all the rhythmic lines are directed upward, although they do diverge in the upper corners of the picture.
75 However, in **Still-Life (Flowers)** all the forms 'hang down' as though drawn to the centre
34 point of the composition. A circular movement reminiscent of the 1911 picture **Sailor** and

of the 1913 **Nude** is created. The shape of the canvas in the case of the first still-life is   79
somewhat elongated, while the second is a strict square. Any observable differences between
the two variants are not ones of principle, but point undoubtedly to certain aims of the artist.
For us, however, much more important than these differences are the common, new characteristics which demonstrate the distance of the two flower still-lifes from the earlier still-lifes   13, 14, 15
of the 'Larionov period'.

To these we must add new traits apparent in the painting technique itself. The spontaneous application of paint characteristic of the paintings of the end of the second decade
of the century becomes more and more constructive and rational in execution. The open,
expressive strength now begins to focus itself on the inner concentration of the layers of
paint, the brushwork and the colour. The colour scale has also aligned itself to this striving
for concentration. In the **Bouquet** the colours congregate around the yellow and the white   74
(the bare canvas), but in **Still-Life (Flowers)** around the brown, the dark blue and the   75
green. Tatlin willingly used colour contrasts, but these lean towards the base tone which
unites the whole colour scale.

If we tried to find just one word to describe all the new characteristics in Tatlin's still-lifes, we
would have to introduce the concept of picture-character, which appeared for the first time in   34, 76–79
precisely these two still-lifes, and later in the **Sailor**, the **Nudes** and the counter-reliefs.   113–121

As we can see, Tatlin's development as an artist was very rapid and, although he was
heading in several different directions, all these directions did gradually converge on one
single point: the constructive creation of pictures. The still-lifes of 1911–12 were approaching this with their new interpretation of painterly structure, not entirely free of the influence
of Cézanne and the French Cubists, whom Tatlin knew well from exhibitions and Moscow
picture collections. The watercolours and drawings of the early 1910s followed a road which
led through Primitivism and, by reinterpreting and deforming nature, to the possibility of
constructive composition. The two trends were scarcely different; each striving for union
with the other. The proof of this tendency is found in the men's portraits, the sailor and
fishmonger portrayals, and finally in the series of **Nudes**.

We should like to put on record once again that we are reconstructing the general
tendencies of Tatlin's development as an artist only on the basis of the works to which we
have access. It is probable that a lot of things which we have had no access to will, in the
future, complete or modify the line of development we have sketched. On present information, we know only one of the early portraits that has come down to us from the period in
which we have been tracing the course of Tatlin's watercolour painting. This is **Man's**   16
Portrait, which, according to all evidence, the artist painted at the very beginning of the
1910s.[17] This portrait scarcely goes beyond that early period which reflects the spirit of
Larionov. Certain features, primarily the realistic representation of space, still suggest the old
style. The man's shape has been somewhat shifted towards the left side of the picture, and
it is cut in such a way by the picture frame that its position in space gives the impression
of being rather accidental. This spontaneity is in harmony with the open, unchecked expressivity which is here not yet regulated by any structural severity, as would later be the case
with **Sailor** and other subsequent works.   34

Many elements, nevertheless, bear witness to the transition to Tatlin's mature style. The
painter was striving for standardization of the figure through simplification and tautening of
the outlines. The colour no longer relates to natural experience; the dark blues and reds of
the background are not linked to objects but exist only for themselves, being evoked entirely
by the artist's expressive efforts. The same may be said of the way he uses the brush. The
brush strokes run parallel to each other, fill out large surfaces and create patches of colour
one beside the other on the surface of the picture. Unlike in the later paintings, however,
these do not yet appear as sharply differentiated areas of colour. At the same time, we must
pay attention to the fact that the energetic brushwork used by the artist in this picture also
lived on in the best works of the 1910s, those which belong to the mature period.

35, 34   **Portrait of the Painter** and **Sailor** already signal a new stage; one may suppose that
             they came into being in the early 1910s. Both are documents of Tatlin's mature period, as
31, 77–79   are the **Fishmonger** and the three **Nudes**. **Portrait of the Painter**[18] depicts the upper part
35   of the body of a man wearing a hat, and working on a picture with brush in hand. So far as
             its characteristics of form are concerned, it reminds us of the preceding portrait: the figure
             here occupies the same place on the surface of the canvas as in the other, and its relationship
             to space and the sides of the picture is the same. However, the essential differences between
             the portraits are obvious. The world of **Portrait of the Painter** is somewhat stylized: all
             natural features have disappeared from it. It is not the actual model which dominates. Tatlin
             has created the picture 'from memory'. The impressions created by the objects are subor-
             dinated to the structure of the picture. The model's head is positioned almost exactly at the
             centre of the canvas and the figure fits exactly between the picture frames. Tatlin actively
             uses the motif of the two lines which come together to form an incomplete triangle. A similar
             angle is formed by the bent arm, the chin, the triangle between the nose and the mouth, the
             freely handled lines of the background as well as several other small details. Tatlin made free
             use of this rhythmical motif, independently of perceived reality. His handling of colour is
             restrained. The tone of the suit and hat is grey-blue, of the face greyish brown with a
             yellowish tinge; the background is dull red. In this picture Tatlin has already started to 'smear'
             the paint. He has covered broad surfaces with just one colour, using that particular technique
             of body painting in which Punin, as we have already remarked, saw the continuation of the
             traditions of icon painting.[19]

             All these characteristics of form do not, however, as yet spring from themselves. Tatlin's
             goal here was the creation of character. The taut, energetic movement of the hand which
             finishes up in the tip of the brush, the squinting gaze fixed on the easel, the slightly awkward
             carriage of the angular figure: all render the model's character most effectively in a way which
             is marked by Primitivism. Tatlin had some predecessors in this area. Konchalovskii had
             painted in 1910 a portrait of the artist Iakulov with sabres hanging on the wall in the
             background, accentuating the oriental extravagance and the excessively confident provincial
             features of his model. At the end of the 1900s Larionov portrayed Vladimir Burliuk with a
             dumb-bell in his hand. Mashkov participated in the first exhibition of the Jack of Diamonds
             with a double portrait depicting Konchalovskii and himself wearing shorts and surrounded
             by dumb-bells, holding a violin and music score. These portraits were already in sharp
             opposition to the traditional type of representation of the artist-inventor, inspired performer
             and tribune of the people – of which type Serov, for example, was a representative during
             the same period. Tatlin, however, did not accept the new ideas completely. His artist is
             painting a picture instead of showing himself in the amazing role of weight-lifter or collector
             of sabres. At the same time Tatlin stripped 'creative artistic work' of its halo and depicted it
             as hard physical labour. He made a static photograph, as it were, of the painter's movement,
             thereby giving it a more permanent quality. From this point it was a mandatory step to the
34   self-portrait of the **Sailor**, one of Tatlin's key pieces.[20]
76–79   In this picture, as in the **Nudes**, his painterly strivings of the preceding five or six years
34   gained independent form. In the **Sailor** Tatlin's efforts to typify his figures appear in mature
             form. The model's half-length portrait is completed in the objects visible in the background:
             the silhouette of a ship's cannon and two sailor figures which could also easily be replica-
             tions of the main character. In this way the artist created a situation which is in harmony with
             the strained facial expression of the sailor, a fictitious member of the crew of the cruiser. The
             painter makes this situation felt principally by the taut, wire-like line which delineates not
             only the silhouette of the figure but the framework of the body and all its movements as well.
             With this he fixes the pose and stops the movement of time.

             The transitory moment is made lasting in that Tatlin stretches movement to its utmost,
             finding in any given phase its culminating point: freeing the model from the constraints of
35   time. In this he took a step beyond **Portrait of the Painter**, in which the stabilized

momentum is tied to a concrete chain of actions – the painting of the picture. Here, on the other hand, the reality of the action is negated by the abstract connection of the model and the background and the fictitious interrelationship of the figure and the perspective. It is this which makes it possible to feel in **Sailor** a state of inner concentration, in spite of the activity 34 of movement.

Tatlin turned against the art of the past but remained faithful to it in many respects, maintaining links to it in the most varied ways. The most important of these points of contact was, as we have already mentioned, Russian icon painting. At the same time, we may discover in **Sailor** an analogy, deliberately asserted, with formal classical portraits. This is shown by the assertiveness of the portrayal, the impressiveness of the model, as well as the permanence suggested by the presentation; and yet Tatlin's techniques are quite different from those of the formal portraitists of the eighteenth century.

It is worth mentioning that it was in the same year, 1912, that Mashkov's self-portrait, depicting him with a steamship and sailing ship in the background as though he were at least a sailor or someone associated with the sea, was shown at the Jack of Diamonds exhibition. In this, as in many other portraits of the 1910s, the element of play, disguise and theatricality[21] is emphasized, leading to a certain parody of the formal classical portrait. The Jack of Diamonds and Donkey's Tail masters liked to parody canonical artistic forms. In Tatlin this desire to parody was either lacking or was present only to a faint degree. In his still-lifes with flowers, for example, the irony which characterized Mashkov's still-lifes is lacking, so too is that gibing at the viewer which Lentulov permitted himself in his 1915 self-portrait – which did not get the title **Le grand peintre** by accident – or the shocking provocation of Mashkov's **Female Nudes** or Larionov's **Venuses**.

In the **Sailor**, compositional stability was achieved by entirely different means from those of traditional formal portraits. Even the choice of a square format impelled Tatlin to look for independent means of expression. He was able to find examples for this in icon painting. The signs of hagiographic composition simply leap to the eye in **Sailor** and we may easily imagine that the principal figure and the two small figures in the background are the same. Nor can we avoid mentioning the principle behind the joining of the square and the circle. The striving for geometrical harmony of forms recalls the traditional iconographic types of **Strength of the Redeemer** or **Christ in Majesty**. Naturally, we must not take this to mean that Tatlin mechanically transferred the devices of icon painting – or of Rublev's **Trinity**, say, with its circle inside a triangle – to his own compositions. Rather, we might recognize in the composition the general characteristics of Russian artistic thought. Tatlin, moreover, did not ally himself to the popular variant of Russian icon painting, as did Goncharova and Larionov, but to the classical one. The basis of this classical tradition is the principle of joining circle to square. Tatlin realized this principle through the rhythmical movement of curved lines over a plane, not only in his paintings but in his watercolours and drawings as well.[22] We must particularly emphasize that this movement of the curved line is realized on the surface and does not deepen the perspective at all. Let us observe how the model's head barely covers the two figures in the background, whose small size as compared to the head is not at all the result of foreshortening of the perspective. Neither did Tatlin use the effects of colour to create a new dimension. The colouring of the two small figures and of the cruiser's cannon is in harmony with the sometimes grey, sometimes pinkish, tones surrounding the yellow centre. This is not a real background at all, but upper and lower edges around a centre.

While in **Sailor** the purpose of the portrait itself made the path towards a constructive 34 purity of the painterly composition easier, it was not as easy to achieve this in other works of the same period. We are thinking of the picture **Fishmonger**, which could not have 31 preceded the **Sailor** by very much.[23] The theme of the **Fishmonger** had occupied the painter for some time. We have already mentioned a similar but unfinished watercolour of the same subject, and also **Fishmonger's Trade**, yet another watercolour. Tatlin was 27 evidently striving to reduce overcrowding of superfluous objects, but in such a way as to retain the model and the typical details he had worked out earlier. At the same time, he asserted the compositional principle whereby the large-scale half-size portrait of the main figure should interlock with the small figure of the vendor carrying his basket of fish. He united all these with a moving circular line but, because the centre of the circle is displaced

34
31
to the right, the composition is not as perfectly enclosed as in the **Sailor**,[24] and some accidental elements also slip in. But in spite of its unresolved elements the **Fishmonger** belongs among Tatlin's best paintings. He had opened up nearly every possibility offered by the genre to create a Tatlinesque picture: he brought the composition as close as possible to the constructive notion of movement while giving an immediate feeling of the actual scene.

The fishmonger as it were leans into the picture on the right side. This compositional solution carries the danger that the arrangement of the objects might become incidental – and the relationship of the bodies out of proportion. Tatlin resolved this by vertically tilting the table-top on which the fish carcases sprawl and running it right out of the picture – thus preventing a perspective which might lead into deepening space – and by building up the linear rhythms around the figure of the vendor. It is as though the contours of the objects and figures were layering themselves one on top of the other, a variation on the same melody and, finally, were creating a circle which cannot be contained within the frame of the picture. The painter overcomes the crowding of objects and the variety of lines not so much by leaving anything out as by pulling the two faces into a unity of rhythm and colour. The grey, brown and yellow tones blend into red to create a unified colour effect.

The **Fishmonger** is the best illustration of Tatlin's relationship to Primitivism. The picture in total creates a 'signboard' effect, and Tatlin was able to create the portrait by using the tools of Primitivism, diverging from both the formal portrait and icon painting. At the same time, the construction of the picture is very deliberate, very professional. This is demonstrated by the decisive sketching, the organization of the picture surface and a total elimination of all accidental, superfluous details and devices. Russian Primitivism served to conquer the norms which had reigned earlier in art. Tatlin made use at the beginning of his career of the possibilities this offered, but he did not in any way accept all its consequences.

76–79
The 'classical' tendency in Tatlin's painting reached its height in the **Nudes** which he most probably painted between 1911 and 1913. In the artist's legacy of drawings it is the female nude which dominates. The process of studying nature, assimilating it and reinterpreting it went on at the beginning of the 1910s, in essence, within the framework of this theme. In the Ostozhenka studio drawing was done from live models. Among Tatlin's drawings are some which are true to nature and depict the model's real shape quite accurately, but there are other works which are abstract, generalizing, and which concentrate on revealing the construction of the human body, as though showing its skeleton. In any event, the work of drawing female nudes was closely linked to the perfecting of the artist's constructive intent. It goes without saying that these efforts had to come to fruition not only in his drawings but in his paintings as well.

76
We are acquainted with four of Tatlin's **Nudes**, even if one of them is only from an old photograph.[25] The nudes may also be regarded as a phase in the development of the painter's thought. For this reason we may suppose that they were made one after the other.[26]

It is interesting to compare Tatlin's four **Nudes** either with each other or with pictures of similar subjects by other artists who were working with him from the same model, primarily

80, 81
77, 78
Popova and Vesnin. Although the body positions of two of Vesnin's nudes and two of Tatlin's are obviously similar, the paintings are substantially different. Vesnin finished the face and dramatized the theme by setting the poses within particular situations. Tatlin, on the other hand, made a picture of a state of being. He merely indicated the face with a general area outlined by a sharp contour, and in the figure emphasized primarily the basic elements of the 'mechanics' of the body. Popova's **Nudes** painted at the same time were too closely

linked to the concrete object as she had not yet arrived at its reinterpretation. Compared with his studio colleagues, Tatlin was the most prepared, both in his thinking and in the means at his disposal, to bring into being painting without objects which was 'oriented towards architecture'; but a few years later Vesnin and Popova were also able to realize this objective.

If we compare Tatlin's **Nudes** with each other we may observe, in addition to the common characteristics we have already mentioned, differences which, so to speak, mark the stages in the elaboration of his theme. In the painting which we know only from the photograph we can feel especially the artist's attachment to nature. The position of the nude's body appears accidental. The depiction of the face and body is portrait-like and the model in this picture strongly recalls Vesnin's and Popova's. At this time Tatlin was still not abstracting, but indicating all the details of the face: the straight line of the nose, the strong contrast between the pupil and eyeball, and so on.

The model of the earliest **Nude**, in a semi-reclining position with her hand supported on the divan, fills up most of the canvas from the lower left corner to the top right corner. In the next nude picture the model is seated, not in a chair or armchair, but rather on some kind of pedestal, on which she is leaning with both hands. One gets the impression that she has just risen from a reclining position. Although the shape of the canvas is somewhat elongated in a horizontal direction, it comes close to a square. In the final variation the model is sitting on a special pedestal and the shape of the picture is stretched upwards as though emphasizing the monumental and shapely character of the figure.

In the pictures set up in sequence the background changes by degrees. In the first variation it is a multicoloured yellow and dark-blue patterned cloth arranged in a place which is almost true to life. The hanging drapery forms a right angle with the surface on which the model is lying. In the later variations the concrete nature of the background tends to disappear more and more. The red drapery which forms the background for the second **Nude** is slashed with black stripes. These resemble pleats so little that the drapery itself also loses its texture. The drapery of the final **Nude** is even more abstract: the geometrical forms created by the background are variations of the plastic motifs of the figure.

The plastic treatment of the nude and the interpretation of its position have changed progressively. There is something accidental, 'disorderly', temporary about the body position of the reclining woman. The position and diagonal posture of the figure leaning insecurely on its left elbow breaks up the balance of the picture. In the subsequent pictures Tatlin was trying to reestablish stability. In the variation with red background he created a situation of balance which points beyond the single moment of time, reinforcing it with a psychological motivation by presenting the model in an attitude suggesting deep concentration. He achieved this by nothing more than the inclination of the head, the contour lines and the linear rhythm, since he did not sketch in any of the features of the face at all. It seems as though the model has become entirely motionless, excluded from the turbulence of life, as though having stepped into a different 'state of being'. In the final variation Tatlin returned to an active body movement suggestive of performing an action. But unlike what we have seen in the reclining **Nude**, he brought this action to its logical conclusion, reinforcing it in its final phase. Here Tatlin was using the method of harmonizing movements in various directions which he had worked out progressively in his drawings. He turned the model's head to the left, but her trunk and particularly her legs in the opposite direction. The way in which the figure leans to the side is counterbalanced by the turn of the head, and this makes the balance dynamic. The last two **Nudes** are distinguished by Tatlin's highest mastery. The red of the background of the former links it to old Russian icon painting. The white spots formed by the portions of canvas left bare form harmonious contrasts with the coat of red paint. The surface of the painting is slightly dull, slightly 'rough'. The simplicity of the brushwork creates a decorative impression. In this picture Tatlin has brought together the legacies of body painting[27] and the new tendencies.

76

77

78

79

77

78

79

77

78

79

78, 79
78

79   In contrast to the meditativeness of this **Nude** the final one emphasizes energy, even though this is somewhat restrained: arrested, so to speak, by the limits of the picture. The contrasts create a harmonious whole, a tight unity. It is no accident that we have made the analogy between this picture and icon painting.[28] It is a matter not only of the compositional relationship, the orientation of the picture construction towards the plane, and the rhythms of the lines which create the geometrical shapes, but the characteristic impersonality of the

78   form is also icon-like. While in the earlier **Nude** the meditative appearance of the head
79   position still contained a certain psychological element, in this variation the only important element is the expression of the form. Instead of the positioning and concreteness of the body movements it is the interior movement of the picture which has gained prominence, bringing a concentrated tautness into existence within the confines of the canvas.

79   The impersonality of the final **Nude** opened up new possibilities for Tatlin to depict the human body and the human organism constructed according to predetermined laws. His goal was to discover these but in so doing he diverged from the methods of old Russian icon painting: he did not attempt to depict a figure which would embody ideal values or, even less, one which would embody these ideal values in a physical shell. At the same time, he was reconsidering what was the traditional nude theme, which included, no matter to how small a degree, the element of delight in the female body. This element is lacking in Tatlin's **Nude**. The abstraction is made possible by analysing the constructive basis of an actual

103   phenomenon. It was no accident that he exhibited **Composition-Analysis** in 1913–14 following the **Nude-Composition**. These, in fact, bring to a close the line of development of Tatlin's pre-Revolution painting.[29]

Although we have no accurate facts with which to back up our proposition, we may still safely hazard the assumption that the latter creation is identical with the picture of which Khodasevich writes, quoting Tatlin's own words:

It is unimportant to a true artist whether to portray a Madonna or a strumpet because he solves his own artistic problems through their creation. So the outside of the model may be almost anything. In their time people who placed the commissions wanted Madonnas... Just look, Valechka, 'Madonna and Child'! I, however, see Cranach's idea before me: he was obliged to create a composition out of triangles, and he was able to solve the problem brilliantly. And to make this even clearer (although it is possible that this was to order!) he drew the young lady and child into a triangle – touchingly enough to produce tears! I, on the other hand, understand this and am explaining it to you so that you may see what a wonderful thing springs out of this.[30]

One may find in a private collection in Moscow a watercolour and gouache by Tatlin which is evidently a sketch inspired by a Cranach **Madonna**.[31] It has not been possible to identify this composition with any of Cranach's works,[32] and it reminds us rather of the Italian Madonnas of the end of the sixteenth and beginning of the seventeenth centuries. It seems that the mention of Cranach's name is no accident. In one of the lists of Popova's works[33] is found a nude dated 1913, on the back of which was 'copy of Cranach's **Madonna**.' Until now it has not been possible to find the picture mentioned on the list. However, if we consider the fact that Popova was working with Tatlin in Morgunov's studio and in the Ostozhenka studio in the summer of 1913, we can make the assertion that the same original picture was in front of both Tatlin and Popova. Tatlin, however, did not make a copy, but an analysis, and thence the differences arise.

Tatlin's primary aim is to discover in the real scene those interconnected geometrical shapes which, in their entirety, create a strict and clear composition. The triangles and ellipses fit organically into the rectangle of the paper. Many elements point to the development of his thought on counter-reliefs. Several details remind one of rivets and it seems that the planes are arranged in such a way as to realize themselves eventually in some concrete materials. With this, figurative painting as such has finally exhausted its possibilities and passed on the sum total of its experiences to the construction of objects.

Judging from the exhibition catalogues, from 1914 onwards Tatlin did not concern himself with painting in the earlier meaning of the word. He concentrated on counter-reliefs and theatrical work. There are only a few works related to painting. In the two independent easel painting-like set designs, done for the opera **Ivan Susanin**, he still used the concentric tension of the **Nude** pictures.[34]

138, 139
76–79

Another independent 'picture' was connected to the set designs for **The Flying Dutchman**, on which he worked from 1915 to 1918. This painting was already based on his Constructivist strivings in creating objects; there is considerable rhythmical expressiveness in it. It proved that the artistic achievements of the counter-reliefs[35] could also be used successfully in solving problems related to painting.

157

In a subsequent work, **Board No. 1. Staro-Basman** (Old Basmannaia Street), done in 1917, Tatlin again uses his experience of counter-reliefs, but not to construct objects; rather he places them on a board and projects them onto a plane. The balance of black, red, yellow and golden colours and of geometrical forms characterizes this composition, which shows at the same time that Tatlin was occupied to a certain extent with Malevich's Suprematist ideas and Popova's architectonic compositions.

104

Naturally, the so-called painterly and counter-reliefs also demand colour solutions. In these, however, the function of 'painting' has changed completely. Here Tatlin was trying to preserve the original *faktura* of the paint layers. It was the paint itself which most held his attention, and the colour itself was secondary.

It is possible that in the future new works of Tatlin will be found which will illustrate more accurately the transition in the mid-1910s from painting to the counter-reliefs and the influence of one genre on the other. But even those pictures which we know prove convincingly that Tatlin's constructive approach developed by degrees within the framework of the various painterly genres: show how he expanded these genres, taking a stride out into space with the counter-relief, and how he arrived at the use of concrete material. Constructivism, however, was still only an ideal, an aesthetic mark, even in the counter-reliefs, and not yet a utilitarian goal. It was during the 1920s that Tatlin, reacting to new demands, emerged into the area of the construction of materials, with the organization of everyday life and the aesthetic shaping of the environment. The great mass of experience he had accumulated earlier on was to play a determining role in his plans in these areas.

If we want to clarify the importance of Tatlin's career and creative ideals during the years leading up to the Revolution, we must make reference to his relations with other representatives of the Russian avant-garde. By the middle of the 1910s several new tendencies had developed within the Russian avant-garde movement. One of these was the group of Primitivists, with Larionov at its head. Another tendency was allied to Kandinsky's activities, although he did not return to Russia until 1914. Along with the avant-garde movement and the St Petersburg Union of Youth, a particular position was occupied by Filonov, who stood outside the contemporary art groupings. An independent tendency was created by Malevich, and finally Tatlin became the founder of a still newer one.

Naturally, there also existed numerous other trends in Russian painting, but these were either allied to movements which had flowered in an earlier period or, although forward-looking, had at this time still not reached maturity. To the first type belonged Kuznetsov and Sar'ian from the Blue Rose group, who were working with renewed energy in the 1910s but had retained the symbolic elements drawn from the Art Nouveau sphere of thought characteristic of the first period of the Blue Rose. Iakulov's role was similar. By the second half of the first decade of this century the traits of his particular Orientalizing symbolism had already developed. Later on he did enrich these, in part from the lessons of French art, but the essential elements of his own art remained the same. The Jack of Diamonds group had also come on the scene during the 1910s. They made use of Cézanne's painterly style but, having simplified and rusticized it, they subordinated it to markedly Russian themes – coming to a halt right there.

Later, the artists forming the core of the Jack of Diamonds group and those who were systematically developing painterly language came up against each other. The enemies were Larionov and Goncharova, with their movement, Primitivism, which was linked in theme and its essential formal characteristics to the legacy of Russian popular art and was creating a new artistic idiom based on this. As we have seen, Tatlin was also influenced for a time by this movement. Kandinsky's concepts, however, were foreign to Tatlin. Even less of a link tied him to Filonov's art. The Symbolist and Expressionist interpretation of artistic creativity was also far removed from Tatlin's strivings. His search was directed towards the world of materials; it was this world which he was to shape and to a certain extent spiritualize. His mentality and mode of operation linked him to the Cubo-Futurists but, at the same time, placed him in opposition to them. Malevich and Tatlin became the two main rivals.

An important element in this competition was the desire for artistic discovery. Tatlin and Malevich were exceptionally jealous of each other, keeping track of each other's every move and every new work. Malevich broke with Cubo-Futurism in the middle of the 1910s and created his own abstract Suprematism, bringing into being a tendency of great importance.[36] Malevich was joined by Puni, Kliun, Men'kov, Rozanova, Udal'tsova, Exter and Popova. During these years Tatlin was not so popular and thus could not gather students around himself, but it is also true that some of Malevich's students – for example, Popova and Puni – came under Tatlin's influence. Tatlin's genre, *skul'ptozhivopis'*, a synthesis of sculpture and painting, indisputably found followers among his contemporaries and became absorbed into the idiom of the avant-garde. Malevich was nonetheless able to create in the period before the Revolution an artistic society called Supremus, into which he gathered a large number of followers sympathetic to the art of Tatlin, his arch rival. (The meaning of the Latin word is the chiefest, the most significant, the absolute. Malevich's choice of word signifies that he had created a tendency of the highest order, that is, a reign of an absolute form of painting without objects. His associates were Udal'tsova, Puni, Rozanova, Pestel', Kruchenykh, Kliun, Archipenko and others.) Tatlin's 'defeat', however, was temporary. Taking into account the larger perspective, we must conclude that Tatlin's experiments of the 1910s laid the foundations of the highly significant Constructivist movement, which exercised an international influence from as early as 1920 on, and was, moreover, the source and basis of several other tendencies and groupings.[37]

Tatlin was one of the first to assert the notion that artistic and engineering thinking influenced each other, and that the embodiment of this notion was the artist, who is a builder and organizer of life.

Having created in counter-reliefs a Constructivism which was as yet not utilitarian, Tatlin gave up easel painting,[38] and probably did not return to it until 1929–30.[39] First the counter-reliefs, then the **Monument to the Third International**, then **Letatlin**, and from time to time work on material culture and theatrical work – all this forced into the background his work in traditional painting, which was to become meaningful for him only when the tasks he had set for himself as an artist-constructor had exhausted themselves.

It was the tragic break-up of his career which once more caused his attention to turn to this genre, making it possible for him to express personal feelings.

Tatlin's later painting is traditional. The portrait, the still-life, the landscape now diverge sharply. They do not approach each other in any way nor do they influence each other as before. On the contrary, the painter is now trying for a consistent expression of the specifics of each separate genre. The still-life is never embedded in a landscape; in the portrait attention is focused on the characterization of the face and form; in the landscape on the natural scene. Within the different genres the objects and the motifs themselves have a decidedly traditional character. In the still-lifes there are usually a vase with wild flowers, a book and a skull; in the landscapes a road or trees, with the dark blue vault of the sky in the background. Female nudes appear as bathers, with a bath-towel or sheet in their hands. The portraits often depict a reading figure, and the model is usually sitting in a chair or armchair.

Tatlin's later works recall the paintings of the old masters. The artist often paints on wooden panels and, for the most part, it is these works which are the most successful. By this time he was not using tempera any longer, like some of the artists of the 1910s, and was working only with oil. He was working up the surface of the painting very thoroughly. The colours melt into each other in these pictures and the *faktura* is homogeneous. There are no longer any focal spots of colour on the canvas, the various grades of colour become mixed, creating complicated ensembles and amalgams. Tatlin's ideal has become Dutch painting of the seventeenth century, but he does not suggest or conventionalize any particular style in his pictures. His relationship to nature has changed fundamentally: he was no longer deforming natural shapes. He regarded the study of nature as his chief task, but this was a different attitude from that of the French Impressionists. For this reason it is easy to distinguish Tatlin's early works, in which Impressionism was still one of the components of his style, from the later works, since these are decidedly representational even if he is not satisfied with merely recording superficial incidents.

If we were to try to place Tatlin's later paintings into certain periods we might draw a borderline somewhere around 1940. This, however, does not represent a sharp separating line; the painterly problems of the 1930s often repeat themselves later on. Nonetheless, we may conclude that there are more classical motifs in his painting of the 1930s, when he leans more on the legacies of old paintings, while in the 1940s the strength of his overwhelming desire for self-expression often predominates.

Tatlin's later works offer no complicated analogies of meaning or intellectual adventures to the viewer. In the landscapes there is always a simple motif which can produce an intimate lyrical feeling by itself. Tatlin painted his landscapes in 'traditional Russian' places, in the Volga region and in the countryside around Moscow. In the countryside his favourite themes were a road among trees leading deep into a forest, a lane or a path, the sandy gravel beside a lake, a row of trees or a solitary tree.

In these pictures Tatlin found an opportunity to withdraw and find a refuge for himself. We will comment only on a few significant ones from among his numerous later works.

One of the best creations of this period is the 1933 **Woman's Portrait** painted on wood. 415 Even the body position of the model signals the difference between the early and later painterly concepts. He was not interested in the abstract phases of movement in the fine expression of the female form. The gentle movements of the hand and trunk appear incidental or accidental. The self-absorbed spiritual state of the model is made apparent by the lyrical use of colour. Tatlin achieved a complicated colour effect by combining green, dark blue, yellow and light blue. He laid on the paint in layers and finally applied lines and patches by brush to the top layer of paint, finishing by rhythmically moulding the surface of the picture. The yellow and light blue create two contrasting poles, to one or other of which the other colours placed in the picture's field relate. The model is meditative, her movements are restrained, but at the same time the artist took for granted her existence in space and time. Tatlin laid hold of the course of time, slowed down its movement, but without quite stopping it or fixing it at a predetermined point as he had in the **Sailor** or the last **Nude**. Space appears 34, 79 in its own unique specificity, surrounds the figure and becomes the true stage for its existence. The many layers of paint also help to make the scene concrete, not only by creating an illusion of being in space, but also by the effect of the paint layers on each other. Some of the layers appear to shine through the layers above, others emerge suddenly from the depths to the surface or, on the contrary, are sucked up in to the interior of the picture field.

One of the best still-lifes of the later period is **Flowers**,[40] which Tatlin painted in 1940 on a wooden board. The work is a typical example of the still-lifes of the 1930s and 1940s. The main object, the flowerpot, is positioned exactly in the centre of the not too deep field. Tatlin definitely emphasized the three-dimensional volume of the container. Unity is also achieved here by the merging of the colours; and olive-yellow shades with traces of light blue dominate once again in the colour scheme. Thick white tendrils of flowers coil into the enamel-like *faktura*, this being a typical example of Tatlin's drawing on the flat surface of the picture with his brush.

Occasionally unpainted surfaces are left on the canvas as, for example, in **Bouquet with a Red Ribbon**. Now the canvas seems to become an organic component of the picture's whole colour scheme. The technique, however, is no more than reminiscent of the early paintings.

418 One of the masterpieces of Tatlin's later painting is the still-life **Bouquet** of 1940. This small picture, which the painter himself dated and provided with his own initials, is perhaps the most artistic among the creations of this later period; it exemplifies his brushwork at the time of Tatlin's highest artistic development. The theme itself – a bouquet of flowers on a table, its cut stems tied up with a ribbon – is often found among the later pictures. The construction of this still-life is decidedly symmetrical. The flowers leaning against the table show gracefully against the wall. At first glance the placement of the light and dark spots might seem impulsive, but the careful viewer will discover in them a desire for harmony and balance. An instinctive impetus tamed to harmonious order permeates the rhythm of the brush-strokes used by the painter to characterize the fragile branches, leaves and petals, and at the same time, to form the surface of the painting.

Flowers, branches and leaves become a favoured motif of Tatlin's still-lifes of the 1930s and 1940s. Bunches of flowers placed in jugs, vases, glasses, or simply lying on a table – as if stuck into the surface of the table – offered the artist an opportunity to show his pure inner lyricism hidden within the pictures on nature, and to express a resigned, modest hope in the blossoming of new life and growth.

419 Of the last still-lifes the one known as **Meat** from 1947 deserves special mention. It is an exceptionally strong, solid and dramatic creation. Its material and artistic concentration attests to the fact that the artist himself considered this picture to be significant: to be, so to say, his final *ars poetica*. The brutality of the theme – raw meat and a huge knife – is very striking as compared with the flower still-lifes or the portraits. The painterly treatment also suggests brutality. The piece of meat forces itself nauseatingly on our attention, as in a Dutch kitchen still-life of the seventeenth century. The knife is laid on the table in such a way that its tip is pointed directly at the main object.

Compared to every one of his previous pictures the application of the paint is poignantly, dramatically, tumultuous; the reds and the blacks, the light and dark patches gain even more tragic strength.

The following fact is significant in itself: Tatlin did not exhibit his later works. He considered his painting as a private matter, a part of his personal life. He was consistent in his behaviour and in the views he expressed about painting, its objectives and forms. Naturally, this conception of painting was not the same as he had held in his youth. The older Tatlin's painting and behaviour were obviously strongly influenced by his separation from the prominent tendencies of Soviet art of the thirties and forties, in which there was scarcely any room for personal expression.

Tatlin's later works do not belong to the main line of development of twentieth-century art and, at the same time, are obviously far removed from Soviet art of the thirties and forties. It is worth noting that more than one of Tatlin's contemporaries, artists of the Russian avant-garde of the same period, followed the same road as he and then returned to traditional methods and genres. For Tatlin, just as for Rodchenko or Malevich, the only option was a withdrawal into his own personal sphere.

Notes

1 Quoted by a close associate, Khodasevich. *See* Bibliog.: Khodasevich, 1957–70, p. 71.

2 Evidence of their break is Tatlin's staying away from Larionov's next exhibition, the Target, and that the word *Balda* (blockhead) appears on Larionov's portrait of Tatlin (Ill. 33). The figure 28 in the upper left corner presumably refers to Tatlin's age. If this hypothesis is correct, the portrait was made not in 1911, as is widely believed, but in 1913. *See also* n39 for Strigalev, p. 40.

3 *See* Bibliog.: *Tatlin*, 1977, pp. 34–40.

4 The term was used first by Shevchenko and then gained currency in literature. (А.В. Шевченко, *Нео-примитивизм, его теория, его возможности, его достижения*, Москва, 1913.) Such a tendency can be considered as parallel to German Expressionism and French Fauvism. The Primitivist artist used the idiom of peasant arts and crafts, folk woodcuts (*lubok*), icons of the popular type, and urban folklore, the signboards.

5 Punin, *Tatlin*, p. 389.

6 *See* c 'Body painting', p. 393.

7 It is possible that some of these works are identical with some of the paintings kept in TsGALI and given a later date by the catalogue of Tatlin's Moscow exhibition of 1977. As the pictures' sizes, dates of creation and the techniques applied to them are rarely if ever indicated in catalogues of the time – for example, the catalogue for the Donkey's Tail exhibition (*see* Tatlin at Exhibitions, p. 490) – it is impossible to identify all extant paintings. Several works of Tatlin are thought to have been lost. The painter Khodasevich writes in her above-mentioned memoirs that, presumably in the early 1920s, she saw Tatlin burn some of his works. (*See* Khodasevich, 1957–70, p. 152.)

8 The dating is based on an analysis of the painterly style, which is reminiscent of the above works, and a vague inscription on the upper right margin: *Lantsi*. 1909. The word *Lantsi* presumably refers to the locality where the portrait was made. It sounds just like other place-names in the Tiraspol' district. The painting can be identified, with some reservations, with *Boy*, shown in 1913 at the Jack of Diamonds exhibition. *See* Tatlin at Exhibitions, p. 490.

9 Both can be found in TsGALI.

10 Kept in TsGALI.

11 Tatlin's signature can be found on the left side of the passe-partout around the watercolour, while on the right side there is the inscription: *1909. Penza*. Even if Tatlin signed it only at the time of framing, the style of the work appears to substantiate the dating. The catalogue of Tatlin's Moscow 1977 exhibition refers to it as *Man's Portrait*. *See* Bibliog.: Tatlin, 1977.

12 Reproduced in Punin, *Tatlin (Against Cubism)* 1921, where it is dated 1910. Tatlin certainly checked the manuscript and probably had a vivid memory of events ten years before. Yet I have reservations about the dating as Tatlin was imprecise in dating numerous documents, e.g. the curricula vitae of his last years. Cf. 'Curriculum Vitae', p. 320. The watercolour has been registered in the Saratov Museum under the title *The Sailor and a Chinaman*.

13 *See* Bibliog.: Tatlin, 1977, pp. 34–5.

14 *See* Kostin, pp. 67–72.

15 17 × 15 cm, private collection, Moscow.

16 The *Still-Life* (State Russian Museum, Leningrad) was dated 1912 by Tatlin himself. Both the signature and the date are old and are therefore to be regarded as authentic. The *Bouquet* in the Moscow Tret'iakov Gallery is usually dated 1911. The catalogue of Tatlin's 1977 Moscow exhibition says 1911?. (*See* Bibliog.: Tatlin, 1977, p. 28.) In his *Tatlin* Punin dates it 1912. At the 1913 exhibition of the

Jack of Diamonds (*see* Tatlin at Exhibitions, p. 490) three paintings were entitled *Flowers*. One was dated 1911 in the catalogue and two were undated. Vesnin was mentioned as the painter of one of them. Two out of the three might be identical with Tatlin's above two still-lifes. They can be dated 1911–12 with a measure of certainty. The two works might have been made from the same arrangement: the backdrop cloth has the same pattern and the vase seems to be identical in both.

17 In the catalogue of Tatlin's 1977 Moscow exhibition it is erroneously dated in the 1930s and entitled *The Painter Shchipitsyn's Portrait. See* Bibliog.: Tatlin, 1977, p. 32. Both the style of the painting and the hard-sign at the end of Tatlin's signature on it prove that it is an early work. (Until a reform of orthography in 1918 a hard-sign was put at the end of all words ending in a hard consonant. Translator's note.) Some consider the sculptor and organizer of exhibitions Izdebskii to be the model for the portrait. G. Izdebski Prichard, a resident of New York, the daughter of the sculptor, lends credence to this theory. A comparison with I. Shima's *Portrait of Zdanevich and Izdebskii* 1922, confirms this opinion. Cf. catalogue of Il'ia Zdanevich's exhibition: held in Centre Georges Pompidou, Musée National d'Art Moderne, 10 May–25 June 1978, p. 53. Note the same elongated face and long nose on both pictures.

In 1911 Tatlin exhibited a work entitled *Portrait* in the Union of Youth, while in 1913 at the Jack of Diamonds exhibition he showed *Portrait of the Painter. See* Tatlin at Exhibitions, pp. 489, 490. What is believed to be Izdebskii's portrait is likely to be identical with the first one as its style evokes other works made between 1908 and 1912. In 1910–11 Tatlin exhibited at a show of Izdebskii's in Odessa, where they probably met several times, which made it possible for Tatlin to have painted his portrait.

18 In exhibitions of the early 1910s Tatlin put on show the *Self-Portrait*, the *Sailor* (Donkey's Tail, 1912, *see* Tatlin at Exhibitions, p. 490) and the *Portrait of the Painter* (Jack of Diamonds, 1913, *see* Tatlin at Exhibitions, p. 490). The portrait concerned can be identified either with the *Portrait of the Painter* or the *Self-Portrait*. Although some features of the *Portrait of the Painter* have certain similarities with the *Sailor*, that is ascribable chiefly to Tatlin's painterly style. Moreover, the portrait concerned depicts an older person than does the *Sailor*. That Tatlin exhibited it in 1913 does not contradict the thesis that it could have been painted in the early 1910s.

19 *See* n6.

20 Punin dates it 1912 in his *Tatlin*, but on the back of the canvas there is an inscription: 1911.

21 *See* Г.О. Поспелов, 'Портрет в искусстве раннего "Бубнового валета"', in: *Материалы научной конференции (1972). Проблемы портрета*, Москва, 1973.

22 On the lithographic version of the *Sailor* (Ill. 19), which was reproduced in a postcard form in Kruchenykh's printing office in 1912, Tatlin adjusted the picture to the rectangular format and did not follow the composition of his earlier painting of the same title. The minor figures are placed behind and not on the two sides of the principal figure on the lithograph. As well as being shifted to the background, they have also been cut off, which adds to the importance of the principal figure. This procedure gives more internal space to the lithograph. The contour of the sailor's blouse does not form part of a circle as in the other picture, so the unity of the composition is destroyed. The lithograph *Painter* (1912), which was made on the basis of an illustration for *The Service-Book of the Three* (Ill. 70) was issued in a postcard format, to which it was much better suited.

23 There is the following inscription on the back of the canvas: 'Tatlin, *Fishmonger*, 1911'. A painting with a similar title was on show in the 1911–12 exhibition of the Union of Youth. *See* Tatlin at Exhibitions, p. 489. In the 1912 exhibition of the Donkey's Tail and the Union of Youth (*see* Tatlin at Exhibitions, pp. 489, 490) there were two paintings under a similar title. The whereabouts of the second one is unknown.

24 The *Fisher Lad*, India ink (Ill. 30), which Tatlin later offered as decoration for chinaware, was made at the same time. By enclosing the lad in an oval, Tatlin introduced geometrical composition in genre-painting.

25 The authenticity of a *Nude* (1910), Paris, private collection, reproduced in John E. Bowlt, 'The Blue Rose: Russian Symbolism in Art', *The Burlington Magazine*, August 1976, p. 567, is highly doubtful even if it bears the signature of Tatlin. It lacks Tatlin's Constructivist logic, sketchy representation of space and vividness of colours that are so characteristic of his works in the early 1910s. Although the painterly technique is somewhat similar to Tatlin's pictures of the 1930s, the similarity is so slight that we cannot accept it as Tatlin's.

26 Only the *Nude Composition* (Jack of Diamonds, 1913, *see* Tatlin at Exhibitions, p. 490) among the works on show can be identified with one of the three extant *Nudes*. The one best suited for identification is in the Tret'iakov Gallery (Ill. 79). In his *Tatlin (Against Cubism)*, Punin (*see* p. 347)

also dates it 1913. The other two are also thought to have been painted at that time.

27 *See* n6.

28 Camilla Gray compares Tatlin's *Nude* with the icon in *The Russian Experiment in Art, 1863–1922*, London, 1971, p. 169.

29 The *Composition-Analysis*, oil, was on show in a 1913–14 Union of Youth exhibition. *See* Tatlin at Exhibitions, p. 491.

30 *See* Bibliog.: Khodasevich, 1957–70; p. 88.

31 The *Composition-Analysis*, watercolour and gouache, is presumably related to the above-mentioned oil and is identical with the *Explanatory Drawing* on show at the Second Modern Painting exhibition. *See* Tatlin at Exhibitions, p. 491.

32 Zhadova thinks otherwise: *see* her study on pp. 63–6.

33 А. Веснин, В. Шемшин, И. Аксенов, П. Попов, 'Опись работ Л. Поповой'. (no. 47) Collection Sarab'ianov, Moscow.

34 *See also* Kostin, pp. 67–72, Syrkina, pp. 155–79.

35 *See* Strigalev, pp. 13–43.

36 *See* c 'Suprematist painting', p. 342.

37 *See also* Strigalev, pp. 19, 26, 34; c 'Constructivism', p. 312.

38 It is highly telling that he did not exhibit his paintings in the post-Revolution years.

39 In 1933 he said he would return to painting. *See* Kut, 'Notes', p. 312. He had probably made the return by then.

40 State Russian Museum, Leningrad.

Larissa Alekseevna Zhadova
'COMPOSITION-ANALYSIS', OR A NEW SYNTHESIS?

We are acquainted with the history of the genesis of the 1913 painting **Composition-Analysis** from the memoirs of the artist V. M. Khodasevich.[1] According to her notes the study of Cranach's **Madonna** took an extraordinarily long time. During this time Tatlin prepared not only an oil painting but a sketch as well.[2] Both works can be found in the catalogues of contemporary exhibitions.[3]

103

Tatlin's ideas were obviously foreign to the representatives of both the new and traditional tendencies in art, and his contemporaries paid little regard to the sketch or the oil painting.

Researchers are right to emphasize Tatlin's connections with old Russian artistic traditions. It was in 1913 that he prepared his stage designs for Glinka's opera **Ivan Susanin (A Life for the Tsar)**,[4] in which the influence of Russian icon painting is already evident. This influence can be discerned also in his female nudes of 1913.[5]

137–155

76–79

Composition-Analysis at the same time connects Tatlin's art with the tradition of the European classical Renaissance. According to Sarab'ianov's view it is not of primary importance that one should seek among Cranach's **Madonnas** for the prototype of Tatlin's analysis.[6] He does, however, emphasize that **Composition-Analysis** is a turning-point in Tatlin's art. 'With this, figurative painting as such has finally exhausted its possibilities.'[7] The composition demonstrates a direct relationship with the construction of one of Tatlin's best known **Selections of Materials**.

103

109

Composition-Analysis is, therefore, one of the turning-points in Tatlin's career. It is for this reason that we are dedicating a separate essay to it.

There are several hypotheses concerning the prototype. According to the Cranach specialists:

1 Tatlin has drawn the analysis of an unknown Cranach work,

2 Tatlin combined the motifs of several pictures in his sketch, for example, those of Cranach's Innsbruck picture and [da Vinci's] **Benois Madonna**.'[8]

100, 102

Along with these two hypotheses a third has been proposed by the Soviet art historian and West European Renaissance specialist Grashchenkov: an hypothesis which, until very recently, was shared by Sarab'ianov as well.[9] Grashchenkov and Sarab'ianov were of the opinion that both Khodasevich and Tatlin were wrong, and that the prototype for the analysis was not a work by Cranach but some Italian Madonna with Child from the end of the fifteenth or beginning of the sixteenth century – either a painting or a relief. Its creator might have been either Desiderio da Settignano or some member of the della Robbia family, since the Madonna with her face pressed against that of her Child is quite common in the work of these artists.

If we are to accept the first hypothesis, we must also be ready to hope for the discovery of some new Cranach masterpiece.

Let us suppose that the second hypothesis is the valid one: in Tatlin's drawing the line composition of the upper part of the picture is very close to Cranach's famous **Innsbruck Madonna** because of the diagonal lines of the veil and hair. However, in this picture the manner in which the Child is holding his foot, and the shape of the heads of the two figures, are different from Tatlin's composition. The decidedly plastic modelling recalls rather the **Benois Madonna**. In the **Innsbruck Madonna** the heads are more circular in shape, whereas with Tatlin they are decidedly oval. With Cranach the eyes of Madonna and Child are not exactly in line, whereas Tatlin emphasizes this particular feature. Depicting the eyes of Madonna and Child in this way is quite common in Italian works, in the Madonnas of the della Robbia family and Desiderio da Settignano.

102

100

In favour of the second and third hypotheses is the fact that Khodasevich's mistake is
103   completely possible. She was wrong, for example, in placing the creation of **Composition-
Analysis** in 1915 instead of 1913, and this date is of the utmost importance.[10] It may be
presumed that the watercolour and gouache sketch and the oil painting were done after
Tatlin's trip to Paris. It was during this period that he switched from painting, first to painterly
and counter-reliefs and then to selections of materials.

We must also mention in connection with the third hypothesis that Sarab'ianov has very
recently revised his position and now considers it more probable that Tatlin did in fact make
an analysis of one of Cranach's **Madonnas** rather than of an Italian work. Sarab'ianov came
across a document which attests that Popova also made a 'copy' of one of Cranach's
Madonnas.[11]

After giving due consideration to all the foregoing, the author of this essay is proposing
a new, fourth hypothesis, namely that the prototype of Tatlin's work might have been
99   Cranach's **Virgin-tondo** – the more so since this Madonna was included in Schuchardt's
monograph on Cranach, which was the only summary catalogue available around 1913, and
which was probably available in Exter's library.[12] It is common knowledge that she and her
husband collected books on the history of art.

If we transfer the main structural lines of Cranach's Madonna onto tracing-paper and then
compare them with Tatlin's, we find that in essence they coincide with its linear composition
and may serve as an illustration of the compositional logic of Cranach's picture. This logic
conforms perfectly to the convictions of Leonardo da Vinci, twenty years Cranach's senior.
Leonardo states: 'The whole of philosophy is written in that excellent book which lies forever
open before our eyes – the book of the universe. However, before we are able to understand
it, we must first of all study its language and its symbols. This book was written in the
language of mathematics and the symbols it uses are triangles, circles and other geometrical
shapes. Without being thoroughly acquainted with these we are not able to decipher one
single word and we keep wandering about in a dark labyrinth.'[13] These two things, the
painting itself and the, for Tatlin, encouraging text from Leonardo, together explain the basis
of the analysis. Tatlin had brought the structural construction of classical composition back
to the basic geometrical forms.

103   **Composition-Analysis** is, however, also a synthesis: an independent Tatlin work and, at
the same time, a new interpretation of the Renaissance Madonna and Child theme. The
99   composition of Cranach's **Madonna** is made up of a system of triangles within a circle. Tatlin

has retained the balance of the composition and the central extended triangle which creates the harmony, but has transposed the circular composition into a rectangular plane. He has shaded in the curving contours with colour, thereby changing them into an oval, and has further changed the tranquil circular shapes of Cranach's composition into taut, stretched, oval forms.

If we place a sketch of the chief contours of the analysis over Cranach's **Madonna** it becomes obvious that Tatlin has disrupted the closed order of the Renaissance composition not only by stretching the forms but also by the objectless method of his brushwork. Tatlin, aware of the tenets of Cubism, has brought into his own composition the 'open' rhythm of spatial tension, creating a new unity based on the principle of dynamic balance. The triangle placed at the centre point of the picture obviously forms the relationship between the two compositions. Yet, the different architectonic order of each picture is evident.

Tatlin laid bare the classical method of creating a picture, at the same time reinterpreting it and giving it new constructive essence. On the one hand, he has stripped the composition of the instruments of classical sensitivity and, on the other, has clothed the naked framework with new material values. Just as he does in his painterly reliefs, he makes one feel depth, weight and material values by layering the geometrical shapes one on top of the other. The form reminiscent of the Child really seems to sit with palpable weight on the horizontal baseline of the triangle. The relationships of weight and proportion, the way in which the triangle and the curved forms flow into each other, and the sensitive brushwork leading into uncertainty: all lend the composition a great dramatic strength which was not at all evident in the original. This also demonstrates the struggle which Tatlin waged to achieve a break-through in the traditional repertory of painting.

The vitality and sensitivity of the fabrics were of great importance to Tatlin. As an example let us take a tiny piece of the Madonna's dress which can be seen at the meeting point of two partly overlapping triangles.

As though through a magnifying glass, Tatlin reproduces the *faktura* of the pleated blue dress of Cranach's **Madonna**. (This detail gives additional strength to the fourth hypothesis, since Cranach's other **Madonnas** of this type do not have pleated dresses.)

It is his sensitivity to the material of the geometric forms that differentiates Tatlin from the French Cubists. From the very moment that he recognized and grasped the possibility of viewing and shaping reality in this way, he made use of it for the resolution of his own problems.

Composition-Analysis is an important turning-point and key work in Tatlin's oeuvre.   103
The stability hidden within the classical works appears here in the more naked exposure of the construction and, moreover, in their reinterpretation; in the emphasis on material drawn from, yet distinctly different from the traditional painterly sensitivity; and in a more down-to-earth sensitivity drawn from a much more immediate environment. Tatlin has brought about his innovations through observance of the characteristics of icon painting, which crystallized a Russian tradition which cannot even be approached by European thinking. He was not alone among his Russian contemporaries in reinterpreting this school of painting, which had been reduced to a series of symbols. Malevich's strength also derived from this allegedly 'frozen source'.

In Tatlin's picture the curved lines which frame the closely pressed-together oval shapes of the faces of Mother and Child suggest a spiritual atmosphere which calls to mind the old-Russian icon painter's art. Tatlin observed Cranach's **Madonna** and analysed it, but his hand was guided by the centuries-old conditioning of the icon painter. It was certainly not by accident that he selected this type of Madonna (*Umilenie*, i.e. tenderness), so frequent in Byzantine and old Russian art, in which the faces of the Madonna and Child are pressed together so tenderly, and which is characterized by profound emotional and intellectual portrayal.

It was particularly the tenderness-type of Madonna portrayals of the fourteenth and fifteenth centuries, the classical period of old Russian art, which stood close to Tatlin's heart.

97,98   At that time icon painting was at its zenith and had achieved balance of feeling and form. The similarity of Tatlin's work to the late fourteenth-century **The Virgin from the Don**, attributed to Theophanes the Greek, is clearly evident. At that time this particular icon used to decorate the iconostasis of the Blagoveshchenskii Cathedral in the Moscow Kremlin. In this picture closed ovals define the shape of the heads of Mother and Child. On old Russian icons the heads of female portrayals grow out of characteristically curved and unnaturally long necks. Tatlin made use of this solution in his designs for the women's costumes for

142–151   Glinka's opera, while in **Composition-Analysis**, even though this is not emphasized by the line drawing, the bending of the Madonna's head involuntarily leads us to think of this.

103   We must emphasize that Tatlin was working on **Composition-Analysis** during the period when artists were turning towards old Russian art with great curiosity. In 1913 Larionov organized an Exhibition of Original Icons and Popular Engravings, and two big official exhibitions of old Russian art also opened in the same year.

From the foregoing it is obvious that Tatlin's outlook was greatly influenced by old Russian culture, but also that according to the evidence of **Composition-Analysis** the traditions of the classical Renaissance too had an effect on it. The symbiosis of the refined rhythmics of icon painting and the stereoscopic effect of mathematically exact Renaissance compositional techniques created in Tatlin's art certain 'genes' from which it was possible later for 'material culture', Tatlin's organic constructivism, to evolve. Once he overcame the two-dimensional system of expression of icon painting, Tatlin was able to arrive at a realization in space of material constructions built from complicated geometrical shapes.

Notes

1 *See* Bibliog.: Khodasevich, 1957–70; Sarab'ianov, p. 56.
2 The whereabouts of the oil painting is unknown. Tatlin presented the sketch (1913) to Khodasevich the same year as it was made. After her death Kapitsa received Khodasevich's archive, including the sketch. It is still there, in Moscow.
3 *See* Tatlin at Exhibitions, p. 491; n31 for Sarab'ianov's study.
4 *See* Syrkina, p. 156; Sarab'ianov, p. 57.
5 *See* Sarab'ianov, p. 55.
6 *See* p. 56.
7 Ibid.
8 This is the hypothesis of Dr Werner Schade (Berlin, German Democratic Republic), and it is based on information from Dieter Koepplin (Basel, Switzerland). Schade's letter to Zhadova (21 November 1978) is in her archive, and was not available when these notes were written. Schade's argument is expounded below: 'Cranach painted few pictures in which the Child presses his face to the Madonna. The *Virgin and Child*, Innsbruck, is the best-known exception. (*See* Max Friedländer – Jakob Rosenberg, *Die Gemälde von L. Cranach*, Berlin, 1932, Ill. 317; Ill. 135 is similar.) Only if we accept the hypothesis that Tatlin deviated from the Innsbruck model concerning the position of the Child's legs and followed another example (cf., Ill. 76 in the above collection) can we

agree that the prototype of the *Composition-Analysis* was the *Virgin and Child* of Innsbruck. The Child's posture, however, is highly reminiscent of that of Leonardo's *Benois Madonna*, that is, its mirror image. Furthermore, J. Białostocki, *Europäische Malerei in polnischen Sammlungen*, Warsaw, 1956, reproduces another painting of Cranach's (Ill. 133), which should also be considered since it is reproduced in a book published in Poland in 1912. It can be assumed therefore ...' – the quotation is continued in the text.
9 *See* p. 56.
10 *See* Bibliog.: Khodasevich, 1957–70.
11 *See* p. 56; n33 for Sarab'ianov.
12 Christian Schuchardt, *Sammlung photographischer Nachbildungen Chranachscher Originalgemälde und Zeichnungen*, Weimar, vol. I-II: 1867, vol. II–III: 1871. No. 353.

Alexandra Exter probably had in her library the catalogue published in Poland in 1888 and 1912, which contains a reproduction of Cranach's *Virgin and Child*, Czestochowa. (Katalog Galerii Obrazów w Museum im. Mielczyńskich. Tow. Przyjaciół Nauk w Poznaniu, Poznań, 1888 i 1912. *See also* J. Białostocki, *Europäische Malerei in polnischen Sammlungen*, Warsaw, 1956, Ill. 113.) However, the composition of this Madonna shows no similarity whatever with Tatlin's *Analysis*.
13 Д. Дживелегов, *Леонардо да Винчи*, Москва, 1969, p. 141.

Vladimir Ivanovich Kostin
TATLIN'S DRAWINGS

Drawing was extremely important throughout Vladimir Tatlin's creative life. In one of his autobiographies[1] he wrote that he began drawing at seven years of age and that he drew while on service in schooners and merchant vessels sailing to Egypt, Africa, Turkey and Greece. Very few of these drawings have been preserved and we are more familiar with his academic drawings done in the Penza College of Art (1905–10). In his drawings of male models, Tatlin followed the usual academic demands (that is: presenting the figure firmly, 42 maintaining the correct correlation of parts, conveying volume through chiaroscuro and revealing the muscular system), while at the same time paying particular attention to the architectonics of the male figure. He treated the large form of the torso broadly and gave it a definite weight supported by the two legs. This architectonic treatment of the figures becomes dominant in the academic drawings preserved from Tatlin's last year of study at the Penza College. Although they do not differ outwardly from the characteristic drawings of any academic school, they do reveal the author's wish to bring out separately the clear articulation of the way the individual parts of the body are joined, the lower part of the torso ending in strong columnar legs balanced on the upper part by the arms. It was not the detailed treatment of the muscular system, but the plastic structure of the torso with the hard abdomen and broad chest – these two large and less mobile parts of the body – which turned out to be most important for the still young artist. It is the emphatically constructive nature of the outwardly completely academic drawings that characterizes the personal element that Tatlin brought to his studio works.

At the same time, Tatlin was doing drawings both at home and on his travels in the summers during his years of study at Penza. It is true that we can only judge these works for the most part indirectly since hardly anything from this period has been preserved. But the tasks Tatlin set himself outside class and the works themselves must inevitably be connected with the new artistic ideas which were widespread in those years in the artistic world generally and particularly among the leading young members of the avant-garde. It is well known that Tatlin in his study period became the organizer of the Penza 'left' part of the youth, thereby arousing the suspicion of the gendarmerie that he was involved in illegal 7–10 activity and consequently bringing about a surveillance of him in Moscow, which continued for some time.[2] Beginning in 1908 he became very friendly with the rebelliously-minded Burliuk brothers and Larionov, aligned himself with the artistic interests of the searching youth and began to participate in exhibitions of new art. All this, plus a wide acquaintance through exhibitions, personal collections of contemporary art and journals with the new trends in art of Western Europe, determined his artistic interests.

However, while he joined the ranks of avant-garde artists who threw out the old artistic traditions and maintained their position and slogans in speeches, in his own practice Tatlin combined such innovation with the study of traditions and of ancient Russian icons and frescoes. Together with his teacher Afanas'ev at the Penza College he copied the frescoes in 11 old Novgorod churches and studied their technique and the technology of icon painting, beginning with the preparation of boards, the primer (*levkas*[3]) and the egg-yolk tempera painting. This deep, thoughtful study of the technique and painterly design of old Russian art showed up very strongly and fruitfully not only in his pictorial works but in his drawings as well.

Besides the influence of these national traditions on his creative idiom he was influenced also by the art of a whole number of contemporaries, especially by the works of the great drawing master Serov. In addition, a brief spell of work in a St Petersburg private studio (which Bernshtein directed jointly with the sculptor Shervud) had a certain significance in Tatlin's mastery of plastically accurate drawing. This is what one of Bernshtein's pupils, the artist Lapshin, said about the studio in his unpublished autobiographical notes: 'After the "romantic" studio of Tsionglinskii, where they "created", Bernshtein's studio appeared somewhat strange. Instead of painting from nature they modelled forms using colour as a point of departure ... In drawing they started from anatomy, the skeleton stood beside the model and they hung up anatomical tables all over the studio. As a model for drawing they hung mounted reproductions of Michelangelo's **The Creation of the World**.'[4] Referring to the evidence of Le Dantiu, Lapshin reports that Tatlin and Rozhdestvenskii came to work with Le Dantiu in this studio. The 'elegant Lebedev and Kozlinskii in "culotte" trousers also came here to paint from life.' Le Dantiu considered that 'only the artist Bernshtein can teach drawing'. Tatlin too owed a lot to Bernshtein's method.

After finishing at the Penza College in the spring of 1910, Tatlin went to Moscow, where he became friendly with the young artists A.A. Vesnin, Udal'tsova, Popova, Khodasevich and Fal'k. In the autumn of 1911 he rented an apartment for his own studio at 37 Ostozhenka, and invited them and some other young artists to join forces with him.

68, 69

One of the members of this studio, Khodasevich, a friend of Tatlin's of many years standing who in the 1910s was to help him to carry out some of his plans and works, wrote in her only partly published work **Bylo** ('This Is the Way it Was')[5] that the studio was in an old wing of the house, while there was an icon studio in the garden of the main building, where now and then Tatlin worked on icons modelled after copies or old ones in poor condition.

The studio had no overhead light but was quite large in size. There was a second room with a divan and a gas stove. Tatlin himself stoked the stove, washed the floor, kept things in order and invited the models. All the expenses were shared by the members of the studio. The models came at eleven and were drawn by the artists for four hours until three in the afternoon. Tatlin got up early, and so some came earlier to paint still-life. All were keen on the work and each one strove in his drawings to convey his special conception of nature, but Tatlin's individuality was most apparent. Khodasevich wrote that 'he turned out not just sketches of the female models but completely finished, precisely designed works – monumental, captivating and beautiful in form and colour'.[6] Khodasevich also valued Tatlin's drawings highly: 'What exactitude of hand, bringing a line to a hair's breadth or a thickness of two centimetres, how actually he makes the fine line very thin or broad by pressing the pencil with differing force. Moreover, he is a considerate host. To arrive at such mastery he demanded a great deal of himself.'[7]

The significance of the studio on Ostozhenka in the creative life of Tatlin and his friends is enormous. Here his first great mature artistic works were done; as well as several hundreds of his drawings. These opened up persuasively the basic line of Tatlin's search and that of his friends. Their analysis offers the evident conclusion first of all that this group of young people entered into the solving of the plastic-spatial problems which were common to all searching artists of that time. Their artistic principles also meant a new conception of the world. They not only wanted to break the old aesthetics, stereotyped, antiquated conceptions of beauty and art, they also protested against the social system, which was expressed in the scandalous appearances and exhibitions of the Futurists 'pour épater les bourgeois'. It was not by chance that it was exactly these young Russian avant-garde artists who started with great energy and enthusiasm to build a new culture and art from the very first days of the October Revolution and took pains to realize their ideas concerning the new role of art on a large scale.

Turning back, however, to the studio on Ostozhenka: in 1911–15 the Tatlin studio was, for the time being, busy finding out how, in drawing from nature, the principles of plastic structures of spatial forms, and first of all of the human body, could directly be elucidated on a plain surface. It was necessary to overcome and give up the chiaroscuro and perspective treatment of volume and space which led to an illusory representation often breaking up the unified form of an object and inevitably distorting it. The task of revealing the basic structural characteristics of the figure fascinated them, that is, revealing basic geometric forms to which the torso, head, arms, legs and the manner in which they join one another correspond.

Cézanne's method of reducing all forms of objects existing in nature to basic geometric figures found its true followers in the studio. Thus in Tatlin's drawings, as in the works of his comrades, the Cézannesque Cubist treatment became one of the most important but not exclusive principles in their drawings from nature.

Most of Tatlin's drawings belong to the albums of 1911–14, but drawings on separate and different sheets of paper have been preserved too.[8] With rare exceptions the drawings are not dated or signed. Drawings by other artists, for example by Tatlin's friend Sagaidachnyi, are found in these albums. There are sometimes drawings on both sides of a sheet. All this makes it extremely difficult to establish precisely the sequence of the drawings. Nevertheless, it can be stated that the development of Tatlin's conception of art – which can be assessed from various aspects – was determined by several intricately intersecting tendencies.   43–58 62–67

First of all one must take into account here that before the opening of the studio, Tatlin had just finished his studies at Penza and, according to his own evidence, he had studied for some time further in the Moscow College of Painting, Sculpture and Architecture, which left its mark on him. Particularly noticeable was the influence of Serov's art, especially that of his drawings.

And in fact, many of Tatlin's drawings of 1911–14 were founded on the harmonious movement of the flowing curve of the line which lightly and gracefully surrounds the forms of the female body (which was characteristic of the Serov school also). It is this fine line that determines the structure of the drawings representing a female nude with her arms raised. There are some elements also of Cubist modelling on this sheet – for example, in the treatment of the breast and lower parts of the abdomen – but as the whole effect is based on the curving line, it is essentially not Cubist; it impresses the viewer with its realistic manner and artistically fulfilled, harmonious and elevated style.   49

We see this same method, but still closer to transmitting the natural, living plasticity of the female body, even more closely in another drawing of Tatlin's. Here the lines, sometimes becoming thicker, sometimes almost absent, clearly reveal both the silhouette of the figure and the three-dimensional form of the body.   43

Sometimes, in addition to the basic, clear, firm lines surrounding the whole figure, Tatlin brings in slender elastic lines corresponding not to the form of the figure but going outside it, only in the same direction and as if girdling the whole figure into one whole. With this device the artist connects the drawing of the figure with a part of the space surrounding it, and at the same time emphasizes the primary and basic dynamics of the position.   50

The technique and means in Tatlin's drawings are rich and varied. On many of the sheets in the album the artist draws in one clean line but of varying thickness, without shading or hatching. In some works the line is hard and unbroken and in others it is soft, graceful and intermittent. In some cases the line almost disappears, then is sharply and energetically thickened and widened. Sometimes the drawing in general is formed from thick dark strokes and spots, with only thin lines connecting the separate parts of the figure.   51, 44, 45

In the drawings which we have examined Tatlin analysed the structure of the human body, searching to find its laws of composition. In addition, he relied on the experience of the master close to him and, first of all, as already indicated above, on the traditions of the Serov school and also on the high culture of French graphic art and, in particular, on the works of that magnificent master of drawing, Degas. However, an elastic bow-shape is organically imposed on the soft curvilinearity of these drawings. This originated in Tatlin's work as a result of his very intense and inspired study of the plastic language of icons, which influenced his art greatly, especially his construction of form and rhythm. All that has been said relates to only part of the drawings of his early period, to the drawings which are basically formed by the harmonious curvilinear form.

Tatlin worked on completely different problems in drawings where the human figure is treated as a complex mechanism with the emphasis on the dynamic characteristics of the body. At first it may seem that drawings of this type are carried out completely in the spirit of Cubist demands. In fact, Tatlin usually reduces the proportions of the figure to simple geometric forms and uses the Cubist cut-off, in the form of sharp straight lines which intersect the figure at certain points and move it to the side in space. In this period Tatlin made numerous drawings of this Cubist type. The artist could not and did not want to pass by this plastic approach which influenced the development of all contemporary art: in fact, he studied it.

But given all this, his drawings cannot be classified as Cubist. They rather recall a constructive system of blocks joined together in a peculiar way. Thus, in the drawing of the
54   sitting nude woman the cylindrical legs are put into the big spherical form of the lower part of the torso, and the neck, also in the shape of a cylinder, is put into its upper part. As a whole the drawing reveals the striving of the artist to understand the mechanics of the joining and interaction of the parts of the body, and to understand their dynamic architectonic foundation. Confirmation that he attached special significance to this is provided in a whole series of almost diagrammatical drawings of separate parts of the figure, in places where they join each other.

Thus, one can state that although Tatlin's drawings of this kind do have some features of Cubism, essentially they are intended to move in the opposite direction. The artist's purpose was neither the Cubist breaking down of forms, nor the reconstruction of abstract structures from these dismembered forms, but knowledge of the structural essence of objects, in this case, the human body – the revelation of its living dynamics, the discovery of the mechanical-physical laws of the body's structure.

It should be noted that in these drawings the curvilinear modelling peculiar to his other drawings is not completely absent. It appears more in some works and less in others, as a line combining separate parts, adding a definite lifelikeness to the constructive portrayal of the human figure. It is precisely in Tatlin's works of this kind that the synthetic character of his drawing evolved, where the economical Cubist method is integrated with a living organic curvilinear plasticity and with the constructive inspirations of the most innovative thinking of the artist.

Working in the studio, directing the small group of talented young artists and thus becoming the leader, Tatlin noticeably influenced the whole group. Many drawings preserv-
80, 81   ed by two members of the studio – his closest friend and associate Aleksandr Vesnin and the
60, 61   artist Udal'tsova – confirm this. Both have Cubist elements in their works – cut-offs, geometric forms and displacements. However, in many of Vesnin's drawings the flowing line, which gracefully conveys the pose, a slight turning of the figure and the instantaneous movement are preserved. Udal'tsova draws more decisively, emphasizing the geometry of forms, and often comes to an integral Cubist composition using the entire sheet. Aleksandr Vesnin, although he sometimes follows in this direction, more often conveys the pose with greater attention, trying to conserve lifelikeness in the portrayal of the figure. But these individual differences are still less significant than what generally links their work with Tatlin's: i.e., the revelation of the constructive essence of nature and all its elements, which subsequently led Tatlin to his peculiar constructive use of the organic world and which made Vesnin into an outstanding initiator in modern Constructivist architecture.

After the end of his studies and his intimacy with the left part of the artistic and poetic youth, Tatlin – in addition to his studio work – began to take part in Futurist publications.
71–73   From 1912 his drawings were used to illustrate individual poems by Khlebnikov and Maiakovskii. It is interesting that all the illustrations and many individual drawings differed essentially from the nude studies made in the studio, first of all in content, and also in style and manner of execution. The drawings done either in India ink or with brush or pen attract by their rhythmically refined playfulness of lines and hatching. This applies especially to several

drawings of fishermen with rods in 1912, in which the almost dancing movement of the figure with the floundering fishes flying around him on their lines, and the folds in the clothes in the form of rounded rhythmically recurrent lines, bring these light and graceful works close to the stylized yet lively Japanese graphic art.[9]

Later Tatlin was to apply the idiom he had worked out in his studio studies and drawings made without a model in the most diversified genres: easel painting, works for the theatre, illustrations and design projects. So, for example, in his well-known painterly works of the 1910s, **Fishmonger**, 1911, **Still-Life (Flowers)**, 1912, **Nude**, 1912, **Sailor**, 1911, the pictorial structure of the canvas is supported by a clear-cut, linear drawing or, at any rate, it is organically united with the manner of the drawing.[10]

Tatlin's skill as a graphic artist also appeared in numerous decorations and costumes for theatrical productions. In his coloured drawings for his first theatrical work, **Tsar Maximilian and his Disobedient Son, Adolf**, he drew on the popular woodcut (*lubok*), and to emphasize the grotesque elements inherent in the subject he also employed the means of expression of Primitivism.[11]

His next work for the theatre, in 1913–14, was designing the stage setting and costumes for Glinka's opera **Ivan Susanin (A Life for the Tsar)**.[12] The production was not realized. The form demanded by the subject – the curvilinear forms of medieval architecture which Tatlin projected into the scenes of nature too as psychologically adequate – was essentially identical with the compositional theory he had elaborated in his nude studies and paintings.

Other elements from the drawings made in Ostozhenka Street – Cubistic visions accentuating segments and their interrelationship – also appear in the stage designs for Glinka's opera.

Some time later, in the staging of Khlebnikov's poem **Zangezi** in 1923, Tatlin, completely carried away in two sketches by the creation of new material forms, sets the stage in the spirit of corner counter-reliefs, thus speaking out against the principle of creating the illusion of, and stylizing, reality in stage design and affirming the principle of Constructivism being developed by him and by his comrades at the beginning of the 1910s in the studio drawings in the workshop in Ostozhenka Street.[13]

His brilliant mastery of drawing manifested itself in the costume sketches for the staging of Ostrovskii's **A Comic Actor of the 17th Century**.[14] The curvilinear plasticity characteristic of many of Tatlin's drawings of the 1910s was dominant in them. The graceful silhouettes of the girls in *sarafan* [sleeveless Russian peasant costume] defined by a beautiful melodious line, a strict construction of the figures: all this, found also in the drawings of the Ostozhenka studio, began to resound once again in a new quality in the sketches for Ostrovskii's play.

However, in the course of time Tatlin's drawing changed a great deal.[15] The principle of Socialist Realism announced in the early 1930s and, above all, the official criterion of authentically representing reality, interpreted the relation of art and reality in a way entirely different from that proposed by the various trends of the avant-garde and by Tatlin personally. Many artists set out to comply with the new requirements. The so-called 'leftist' movements, and Tatlin among them, were to face this task. That period brought many changes to Tatlin's activities in different genres. His activity as a graphic artist – mainly due to his commissions by theatres which made his living – was relatively unbroken.

The last pieces of his constructive drawings as described above were his industrial designs for his **Letatlin** prior to 1932.[16] In his other drawings he tried to achieve a more lifelike representation by chiaroscuro and plasticity. He now strove to find authentic plastic ways of expressing the most complicated, psychologically and socially most important, intrinsic features of the person to be represented. His costume designs for Sukhovo-Kobylin's **The Affair** in 1940 were more of social and psychological portrayal. Each sketch is both an appropriate portrait of a character in the play and a dramatic expression of universal human features: rude strength, bureaucracy, wounded dignity and suffering.

29, 30

31, 75, 77
34

38–41
36

137–155
138
139

217–220

354–368

360–368

320, 321

369–383

410–413
420

In Tatlin's last creative period, from the late 1930s, his individual drawings not meant for the stage were, of course, less dynamic, seeking less to symbolize totality and concentrating more on personal life. Consequently, they were more painterly, softer, more attentive to details, subtle transitions and nuances and more determined by the concrete situation and environment.

411

From the end of the 1930s Tatlin again drew many nudes, usually in company with several artists in studios where the models were paid from the resources of the Artistic Fund, as is the custom in the Union of Soviet Artists. In these numerous drawings of models, and in portrait sketches of friends and female acquaintances, great attention is devoted to conveying an environment of light and air, which seems to cover the faces, figures and objects, in contrast to the sharp outlining of the figure on the white expanse of paper in the drawings of the 1910s. The artist makes less use of a well-defined, clear, manly line, more often, on the contrary, turning to a varied type of shading, a washed-out spot and an indistinct contour. A somewhat distorted form, an uncertain volume, mistakes in the portrayal of the figure, quite often appear in the drawings.

The path followed by Tatlin in the art of drawing is divided into three periods.

At the beginning of the 1910s he found in his drawings, which determined the future logic of his development, the way to a dynamic, curvilinear expression of the forms of objects and space: which united traditional Russian visual conceptions with the new ideas of three-dimensional relations. This elaborate form became an essential structural element of his works, from the drawings in the Ostozhenka studio to the taut curved lines in the longeron

313–353

of **Letatlin**.

In the works of material form, the summit of which was the **Tower**, a symbolic monument to the dynamic-constructive essence of man's relation to the world, it was the experiments done in his earlier works that had come to full bloom.

In his third creative period Tatlin withdrew into the shelter of personal life but, as he had always done before, he looked upon man and nature as spiritually and biologically united entities – in his last works he was still striving to find the secret of life.

Tatlin had been drawing all his life, drawings forming the basis of his work in every field of activity. It was always in drawings that he judged the potentialities of his new ideas.

Notes

1 'Autobiography', p. 264.
2 *See also* Strigalev, p. 22; n64.
3 Gum paint, the traditional priming substance of icons. It consists of glue, gauze, chalk and gypsum.
4 *See* notes to Strigalev's study, p. 40 n35.
5 *See* Bibliog.: Khodasevich, 1957–70; Khodasevich, 1980.
6 Ibid.
7 Ibid., p. 75.
8 The albums are kept at TsGALI. Some individual pages are in state and private collections in the Soviet Union.
9 *See also* Sarab'ianov, pp. 49, 54; Zhadova, p. 129.
10 *See* Sarab'ianov, p. 50.
11 *See* Syrkina, pp. 155, 156.
12 Ibid.; and Sarab'ianov, p. 57.
13 *See also* Strigalev, p. 18; Syrkina, p. 161.
14 *See* Syrkina, p. 161.
15 For Tatlin's late paintings, *see* Sarab'ianov, p. 58.
16 *See* Zhadova, p. 147.

М. Овчинниковъ Харьковъ

Е. Овчаренко въ Москвѣ

An asterisk (∗) preceding the caption denotes that in the original Hungarian edition of this book it was published for the first time.

∗ **1** Evgraf Nikiforovich Tatlin, the artist's father.
Photograph owned by S.S. Tatlin, the artist's nephew
∗ **2** Nadezhda Nikolaevna Tatlina, the artist's mother.
Photograph owned by S.S. Tatlin
∗ **3** Evgraf Nikiforovich Tatlin with his children: Sylvia,
Vladimir, in the centre, and Viktor, 1880s.
Photograph owned by S.S. Tatlin

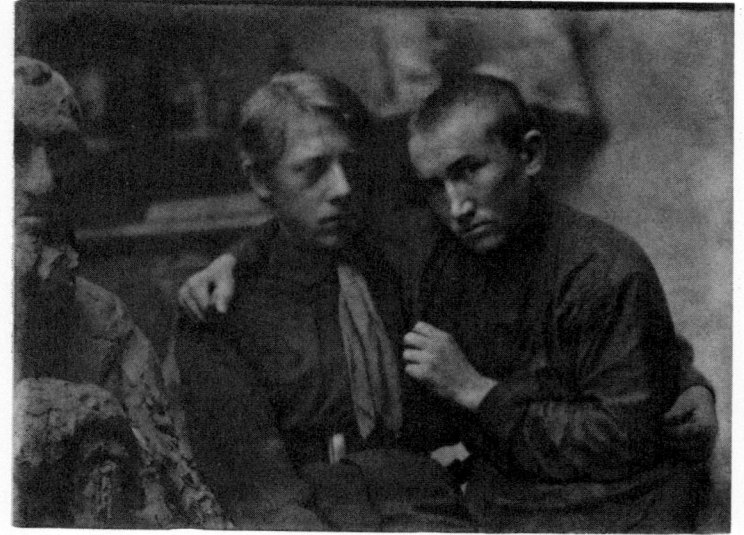

* **4** Tatlin as a grammar school student, with a classmate.
  Photograph: TsGALI, Moscow
* **5** Tatlin and friends in the early 1900s.
  Photograph: TsGALI, Moscow
* **6** Graduation certificate from the Penza College of Art.
  Dated 30 June 1910, Cat. XII/2
* **7–10** Documents from the dossier of the Penza Provincial Police, 1909–11, Cat. XII/1

№ **49** части **5**

ДѢЛО

ДЕПАРТАМЕНТА

ПОЛИЦІИ.

4 ДѢЛОПРОИЗВОДСТВО.

По Пензенской губерніи

Движеніе въ учебныхъ заведеніяхъ

Пензенское художественное училище имени К. Д. Селиверстова.

Начато 190**9** года.

Кончено 190 года.

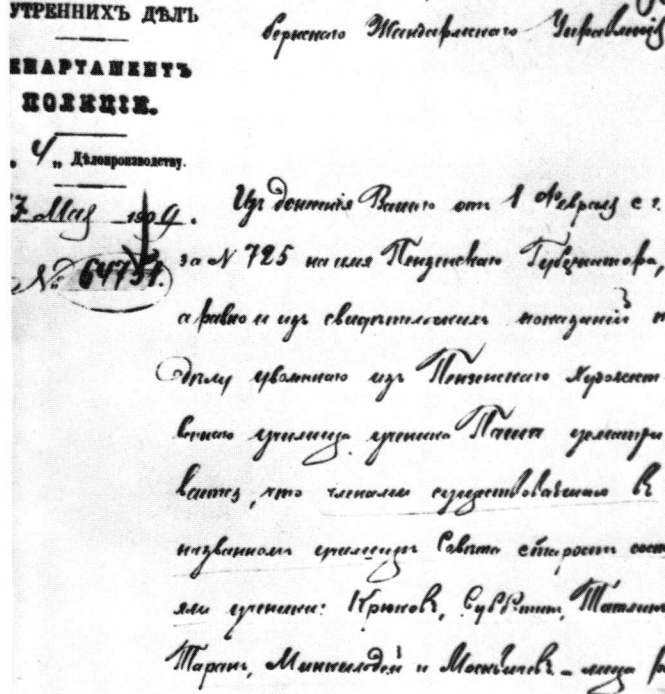

МИНИСТЕРСТВО
ВНУТРЕННИХЪ ДѢЛЪ.

ДЕПАРТАМЕНТЪ
ПОЛИЦІИ.

„ „ Дѣлопроизводству.

Мая 190

№

Начальнику Пензенскаго
Губернскаго Жандармскаго Управленія

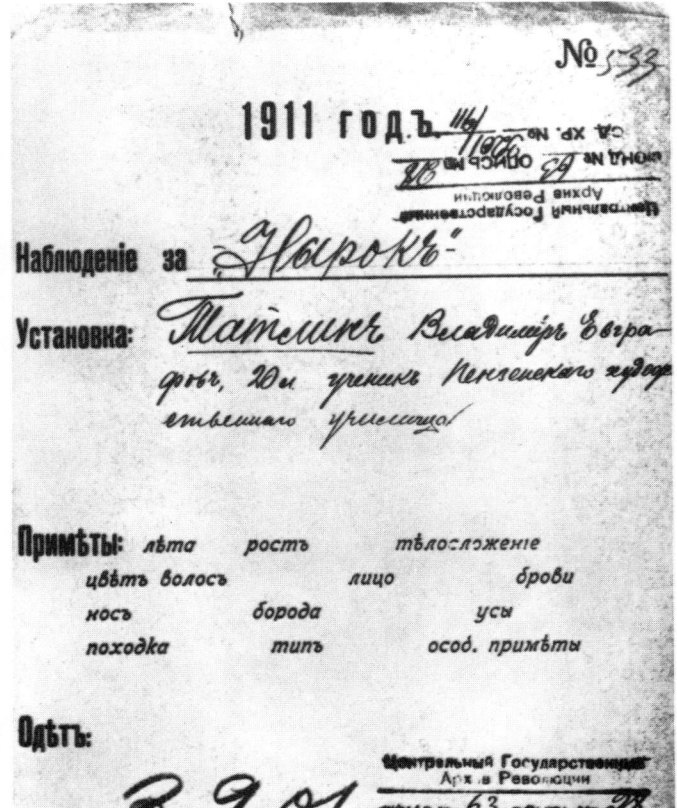

№ 533

1911 годъ.

Наблюденіе за „Шарокъ"

Установка: Татинъ Владиміръ Евграфовъ, 20 л. ученикъ Пензенскаго художественнаго училища

Примѣты: лѣта   ростъ   тѣлосложеніе

цвѣтъ волосъ   лицо   брови

носъ   борода   усы

походка   типъ   особ. примѣты

Одѣтъ:

32 01

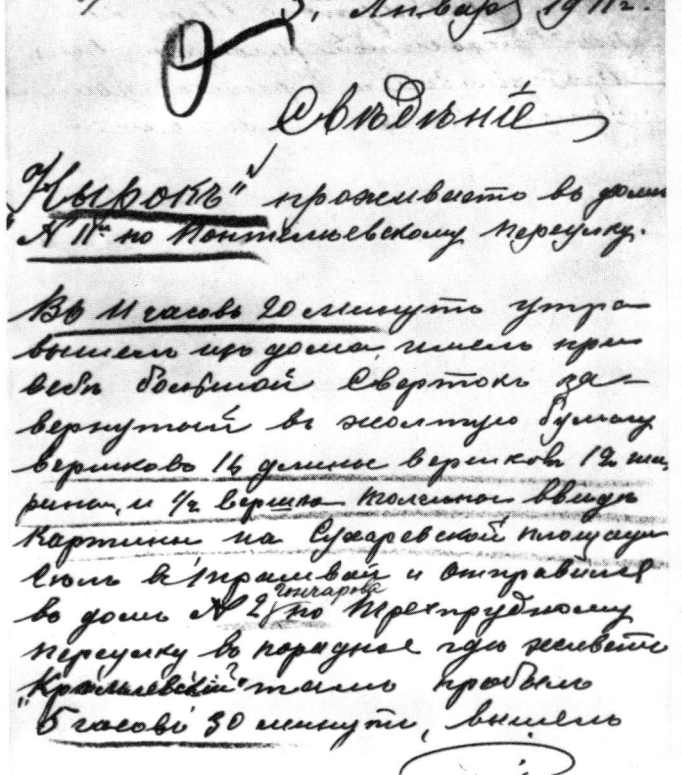

3го Января 1912.

Свѣдѣніе

„Шарокъ" проживаетъ въ домѣ № 11 по Потапьевскому переулку.

* **11** Tatlin, *Apostle on the Cupola of the Church of
St George,* Staraia Ladoga, copy, 1905–10, Cat. I/1

12 Larionov, *Still-Life with Bouquet,* 1909.
State Tret'iakov Gallery, Moscow

13 *Carnation,* 1908, Cat. I/2

* **14** *Twilight*, late 1900s, Cat. I/3
* **15** *Summer*, late 1900s, Cat. I/4
* **16** *Man's Portrait*, 1909(?), Cat. I/6
  17 Larionov, *Portrait of Vladimir Burliuk*, 1910.
  New York, Museum of Modern Art

* **18** *Sitting Male Figure*, 1909, Cat. I/5

* **19** *Sailor (Self-Portrait)*, 1912, Cat. I/16

*   **20** Tatlin, during the sailing years, 1900s.
    Photograph: TsGALI, Moscow
    21–4 The sailing ship on which Tatlin served.
    Photograph: TsGALI, Moscow

25 *Vendor of Sailor Uniforms*, 1910, Cat. I/7

* **26** *Sailor Uniforms*, beginning of 1910s, Cat. I/8

* **27** *Fishmonger's Trade*, beginning of
1910s, Cat. I/9
* **28** *Fishmonger*, 1912, Cat. I/17

29 *Fisherman*, early 1910s, Cat. II/8
30 *Fisher Lad*, *c.* 1912, Cat. I/15
31 *Fishmonger*, 1911, Cat. I/11

32 Larionov, *Portrait of Tatlin*, 1908.
From a private collection in Paris
33 Larionov, *Portrait of Tatlin*, 1911.
From a private collection in Paris

34 *Sailor*, 1911, Cat. I/14

* **35** *Portrait of the Painter,* beginning of 1910s, Cat. I/10

36 Russian popular woodcut (*lubok*). *Feast of the true believers and the apostates*
Reproduction: B.A. Rarinskii, *Russkie narodnye kartinki* [*Russian Miniatures from the Market-Place*], St Petersburg, 1900
37 Goncharova, Décor for Act III of Rimskii-Korsakov's opera *The Golden Cockerel*, TsGTM

38–41 *Tsar Maximilian and his Disobedient Son, Adolf.*
Stage and costume designs, 1911
38 *Panel Sketch*, Cat. VIII/1
39 *Tsar Maximilian*, Cat. VIII/4
40 *Pagan Venus*, Cat. VIII/3

ВЕНЕРИН ЗАДИРЩИК

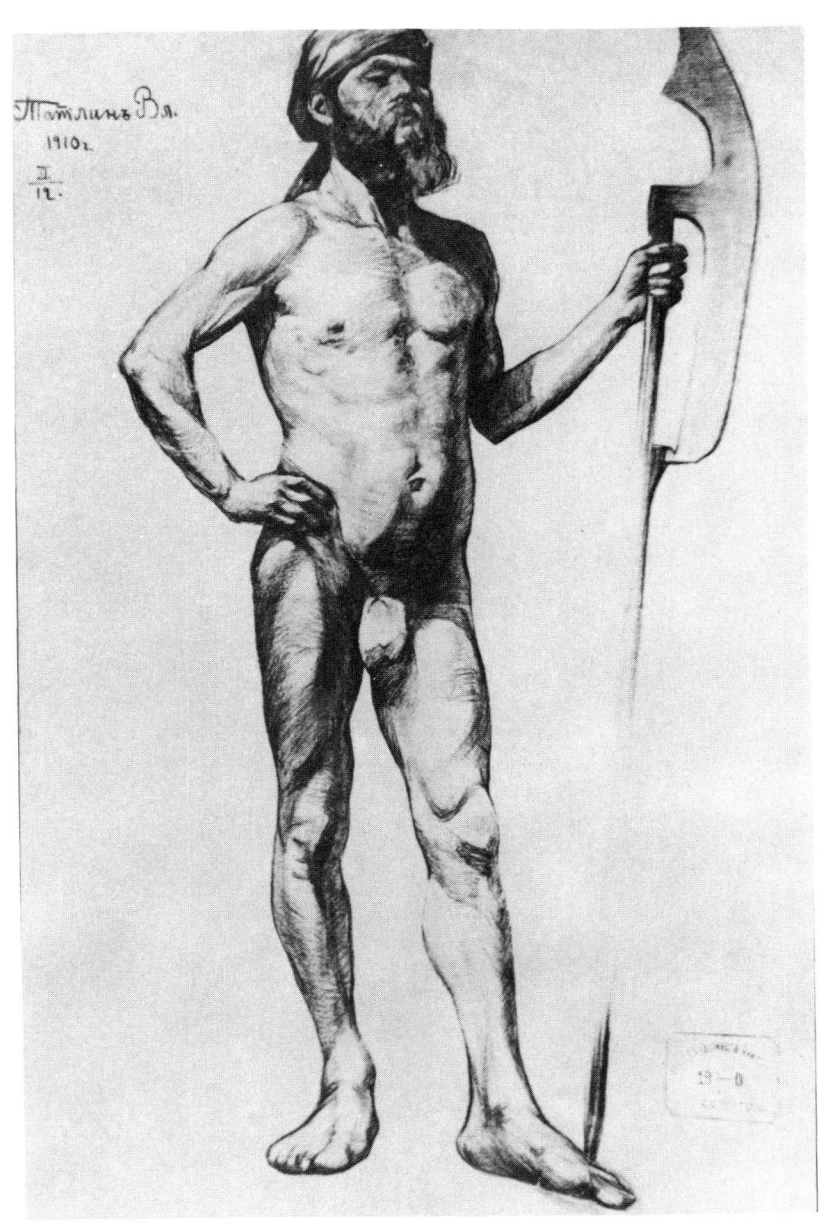

41 *Rowdy Son of Venus*, Cat. VIII/2
* **42** *Male Nude*, 1910, Cat. II/1

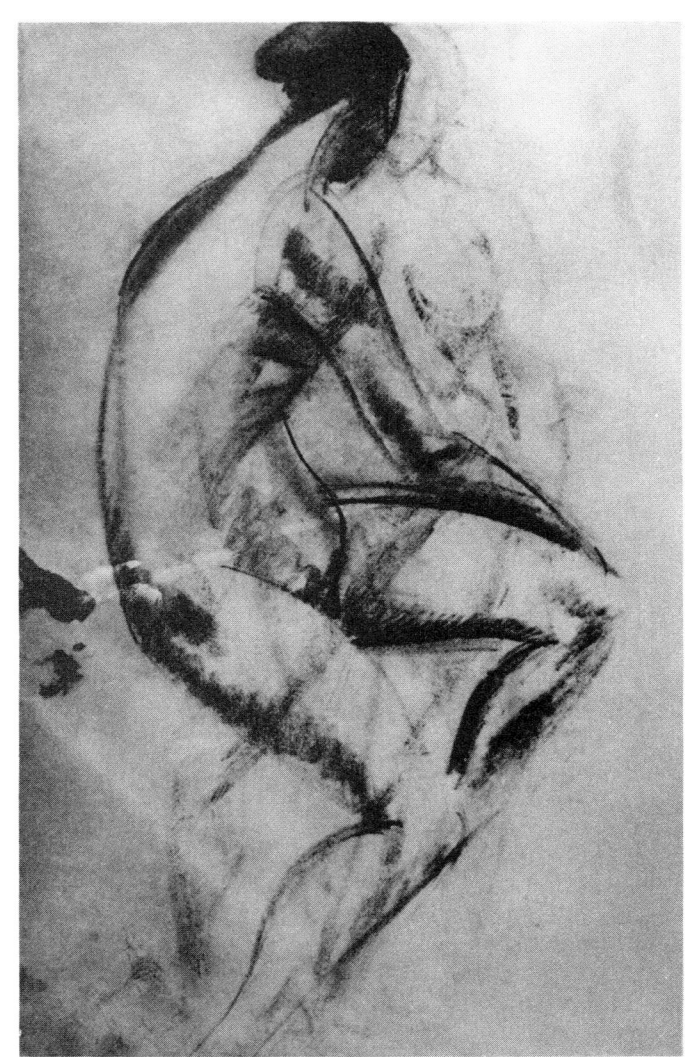

* **43** *Seated Female Nude in Profile*, 1911–14, Cat. II/2b
* **44** *Nude with Arms Crossed*, 1911–14, Cat. II/2e

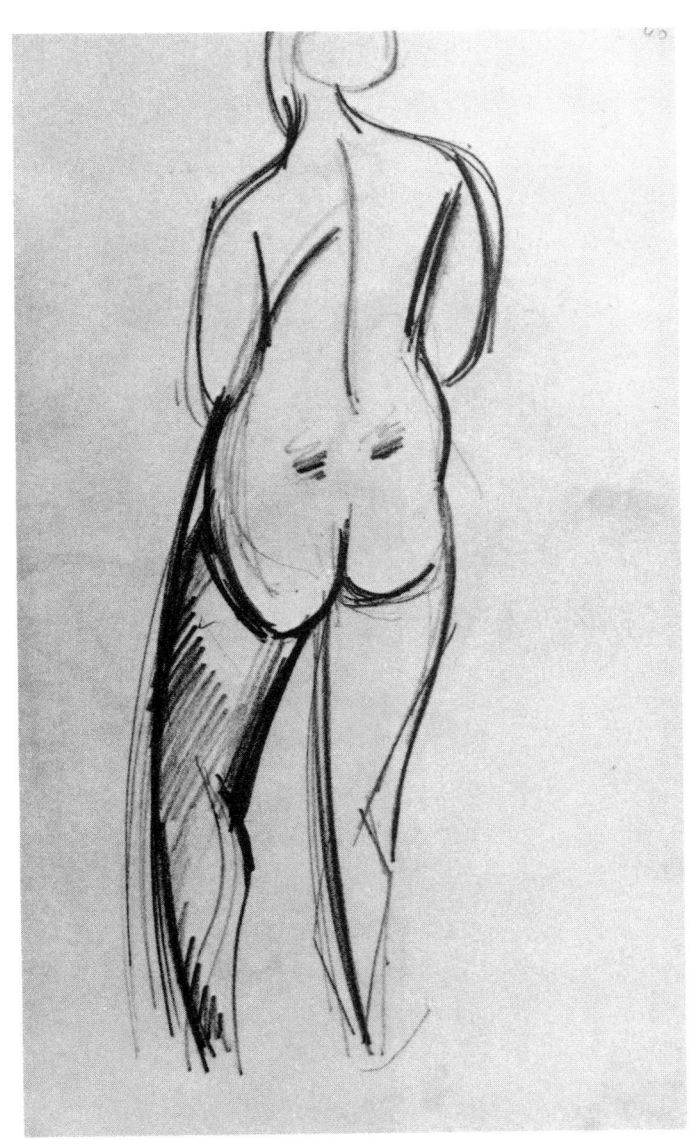

* **45** *Standing Woman*, 1911–14, Cat. II/2f
* **46** *Woman, Rear View*, 1911–14, Cat. II/2i

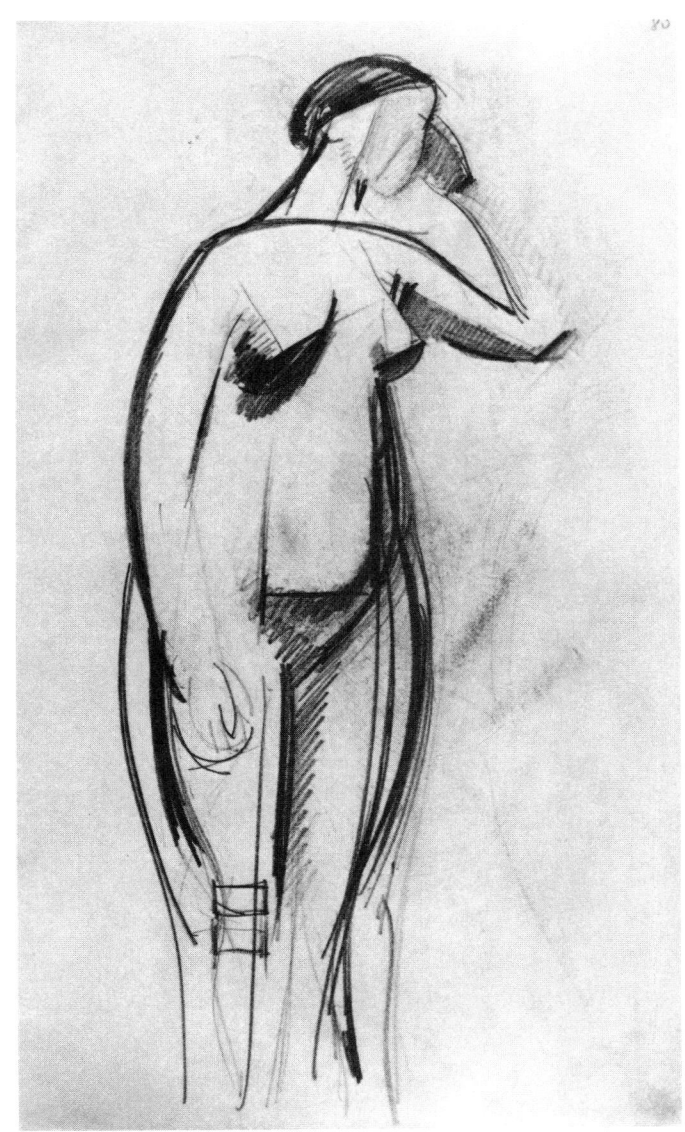

* **47** *Female Nude, Three-Quarter View*, 1911–14,
Cat. II/2h
48 *Female Nude, Rear View*, 1911–14, Cat. II/2g
* **49** *Female Nude with Slightly Raised Arm*, 1911–14,
Cat. II/2a
50 *Oval Shaped Nude*, 1911–14, Cat. II/2c

 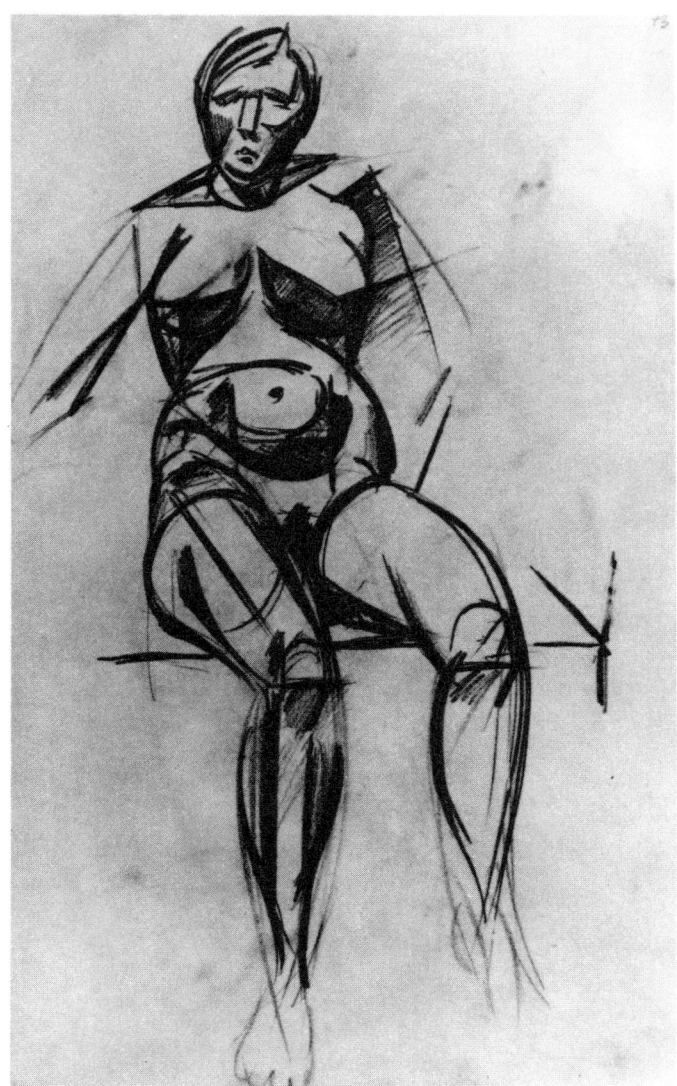

51 *Standing Nude, Front View*, 1911–14, Cat. II/2d
* **52** *Female Nude, Rear View, with Raised Arm*, Cat. II/2j
* **53** *Female Nude*, 1911–14, Cat. II/2m
* **54** *Seated Woman, Front View*, 1911–14, Cat. II/2n

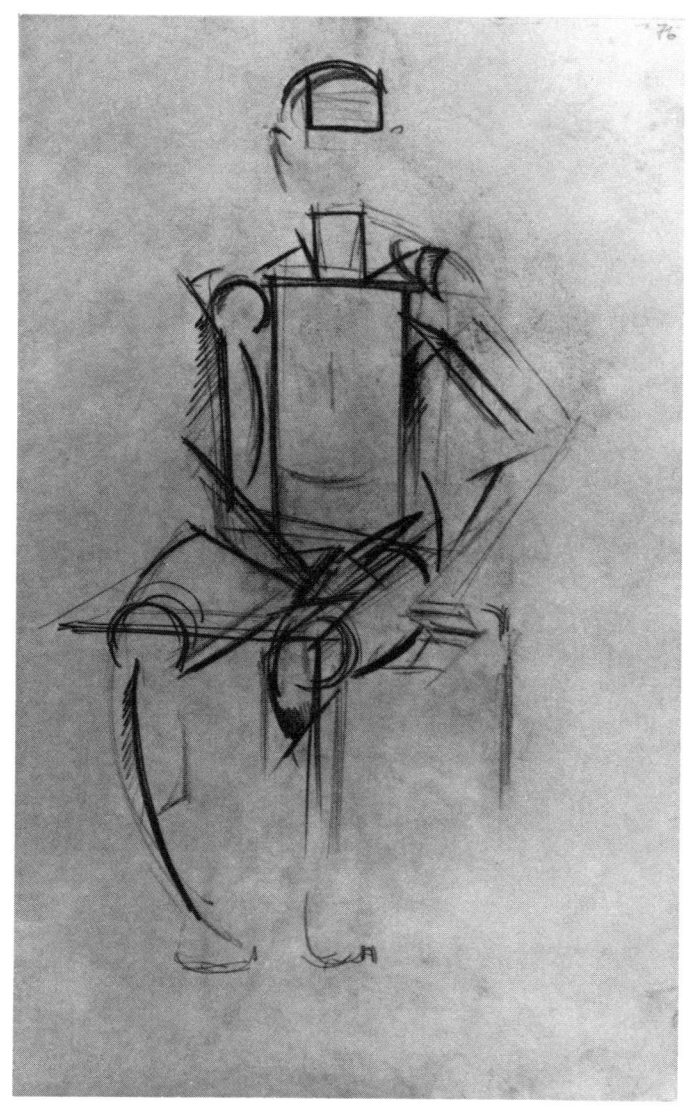

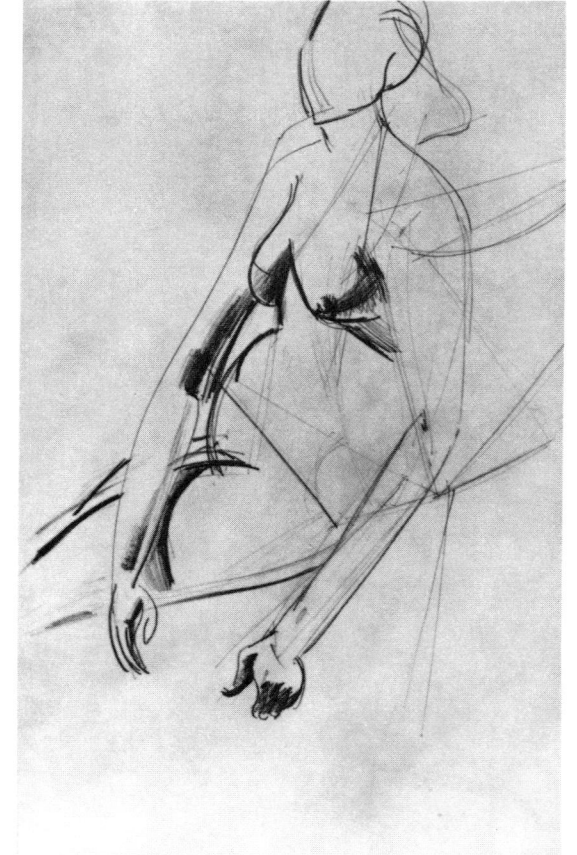

* **55** *Structure of the Front View of a Seated Figure,*
1911–14, Cat. II/2o
56 *Sketch of a Seated Figure,* 1911–14, Cat. II/2l
* **57** *Female Nude, Turning About,* 1911–14, Cat. II/2k

* **58** *Seated Male Nude*, 1911–14, Cat. II/2q
* **59** Popova, *Nude*, 1913. Collection D.V. Sarab'ianov, Moscow

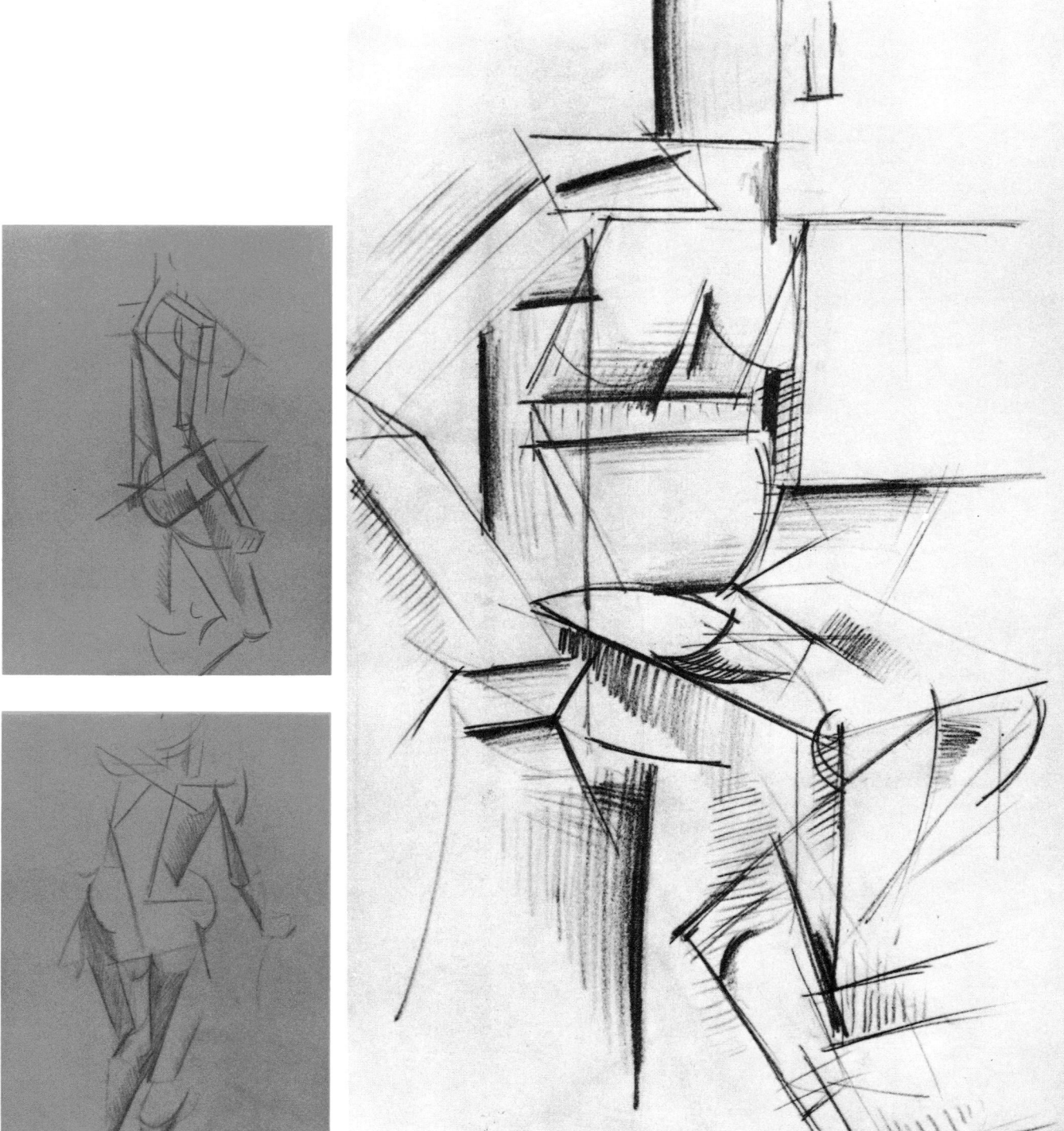

* **60** Udal'tsova, *Female Nude*, 1912–13 (Drawing made in Tatlin's studio) Collection A.A. Drevin, Moscow
* **61** Udal'tsova, *Female Nude*, 1912 (Drawing made in Tatlin's studio) Collection A.A. Drevin, Moscow
* **62** *Three-Quarter View of the Structure of a Seated Figure*, 1911–14, Cat. II/2p

* **63** *Seated Female Nude,* 1913,
Cat. II/4

* **64** *Female Nude with Elbow on Knee*, 1912–14, Cat. II/3
* **65** *Male Nude, Rear View*, 1913, Cat. II/5

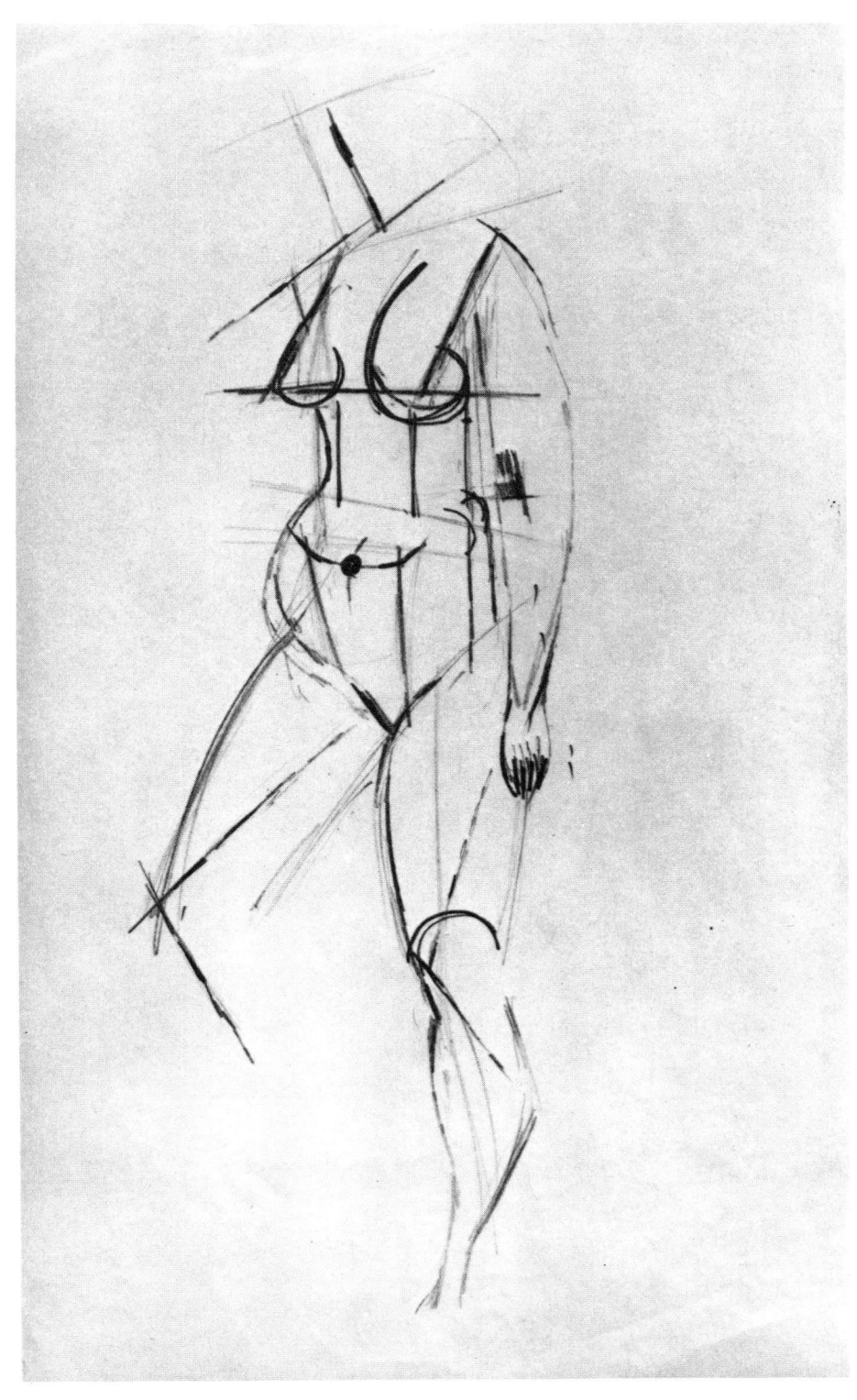

* **66** *Seated Female Nude, Front View*, 1913, Cat. II/6
* **67** *Sketch of Standing Figure*, 1913, Cat. II/7

68 The door of Tatlin's studio
69 No. 37 Ostozhenka Street, where
Tatlin's studio was located from 1910
to 1915. (Today, it is No. 37 Metrostroevskaia Street. Recent photograph)

70 Illustration for Vladimir Burliuk's poem
'Twilight: the Painter with his Wide Brush...', 1913,
Cat. III/4
71 Illustration for Maiakovskii's poem 'Signboards', 1913,
Cat. III/2

72 *Portrait of Vladimir Burliuk*, 1913, Cat. III/3
73 Illustration for Khlebnikov's poem 'Let us be as
Merciless as Ostranitsa', 1912, Cat. III/1

74 *Bouquet*, 1911–12, Cat. I/12

75 *Still Life (Flowers)*, 1912, Cat. I/13

* **76** *Nude*, 1911–12, Cat. I/18
  77 *Nude*, 1912–13, Cat. I/19
  78 *Nude*, 1913, Cat. I/20

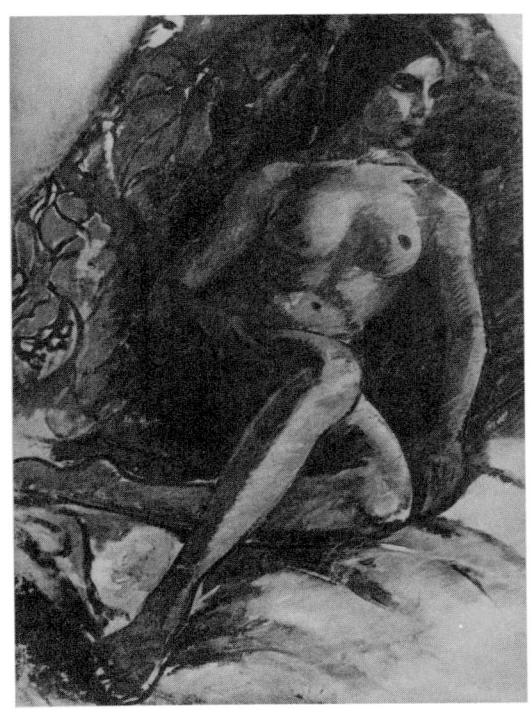 

79 *Nude*, 1913, Cat. I/21
* **80** Aleksandr Vesnin, *Nude*, 1911–14
* **81** Aleksandr Vesnin, *Nude*, 1911–14

82 Survey of New Tendencies in Art, an exhibition – GINKhUK, Section for Material Culture (Tatlin's works on display) 1927. Photograph: State Russian Museum, Leningrad

83 In Lakhernskaia, holiday resort near Moscow, summer 1915.
Left to right: Tatlin, Udal'tsova, unknown, Prutkovskaia, Pestel' (?).
Photograph: Collection A.A. Drevin, Moscow
84 Ticket to the opening of the Donkey's Tail exhibition, 1912, Cat. XII/3

1916 г.

Футуристическая

выставка

„МАГАЗИНЪ".

Брунн Левъ Александровичъ
    Импер. Акад. Худ. Петроградъ. В. О.

1. Трехпланный рельефъ.
2.

Vassilieff Marie
    Paris 21 av. du Maine.

3. Pierette (salon d'automne).
4. Paysage en Espagne (salon d'automne).
5. Portrait d'un jeune homme.
6. Recherche (salon independant).
7. Noture vivante.
8. Tête.
9. Paysage a Paris.
10. Portrait d'un anglais.
11. Fabrique en Espagne (salon d'automne.
12. Portrait de m. K.
13. Perisiene.

Клюнъ И. В.
    Сокольники, 4-й Полевой, 10.

14. Граммофонъ.
15. Озонаторъ.
16. Ариометръ.
17. Футуристическій пейзажъ.
18. Голова пильщика.
19. Пробѣгающій пейзажъ.
20. Автопортретъ.

Малевичъ Казимиръ
    3-й Ямской пер., д. 5, кв. 3.

21. Корова и скрипка.
22. Шахматистъ.
23. Англичанинъ въ Москвѣ.
24. Авіаторъ.
25. Кубическое построеніе
26. Дачникъ
27. Военный портной   1914 г.
28. Дама
29. Шахъ и матъ
30. Лакей съ самоваромъ (Собраніе А. М. Константинова).

Моргуновъ Алексѣй Алексѣевичъ.

31. *
32. „
33. „
34. „
35. „
36. „
37. „
38. „
39. „

Пестель Вѣра Ефремовна
    Москва, Грибоѣдовскій 4, кв. 3 (Плющиха).

40. Чайная (1915 г.).
41. Битоны (1915 г.).
42. Игроки въ карты (1915 г.).

Удальцова Надежда Андреевна
    Смоленскій бульваръ, № 65, кв. 82.

73. Ресторанъ.
74. Этюдъ къ ресторану (соб. А. У.).
75. Музыкальные инструменты.
76. Молотокъ и кружка.
77. Синій кувшинъ.
78. Бутылка и рюмка (соб. К. Е. Татлина).
79. Игроки.
80. Музыка.
81. Мотивъ витрины.

Экстеръ Александра Александровна
    Боярскій дворъ, комната 136.

82. *
83. „
84. „
85. „
86. „
87. „
88. „

Юстицкій Валентинъ Михаиловичъ
    Лопухинскій, домъ 15, кв. 8.

89. Портретъ художника Крастина.

Толстая Софья Исааковна
    Большая Дмитровка, домъ 9, кв. 41.

90, 91, 92, 93, 94, 95 стеклянные рельефы.

Организаторъ

В. Е. Татлинъ.

Тел. 1-88-42.

43. Мертвая натура (1916 г.).
44. Дама съ самоваромъ (1915 г.).
45. Сундукъ и чайникъ (живописный рельефъ. 1916 г.).
46. Художникъ Татлинъ и бандура (1916 г.).

Попова Любовь Сергѣевна
    Новинскій бульваръ, 117.

47. Дама съ гитарой (1915 г.).
48. Скрипка (1914 г.).
49. Портретъ (1915 г.).
50. Рисунокъ къ портрету (1915 г.).
51. Путешественница (1915 г.).
52. Бутылка и стаканъ (1915 г.).
53. Ваза и фрукты (1915 г.).
54. Кувшинъ на столѣ (пластическая живопись 1915 г.).
55. Игра въ карты (живописно пластическое равновѣсіе 1915 г.).

Родченко Александръ Михаиловичъ
    Каретно-Садовая, д. 4, кв. 1.

56. Двѣ фигуры.
57. Рисунокъ къ картинѣ „Двѣ фигуры".
58. Танцовщица.
59.
60.
61. } графика.
62.
63.
64.
65. Натюръ мортъ (обои).

Татлинъ Владиміръ Евграфовичъ
    Москва (Плющ.), Грибоѣд. 4, кв. 3, т. 1-88-42.

66.
67. } угловые контръ-рельефы 1914—1915 г.
68.
69.
70. } рельефы 1913—1914 г.
71.
72. рельефъ 1915 г.

„Домъ Науки и Искусствъ“

Въ среду, 25 мая 1916 г.

состоится

ЛЕКЦІЯ
ФУТУРИСТОВЪ

„Чугунныя
крылья“

ЛЕКЦІЯ БУДЕТЪ ПРОЧТЕНА ПОЭТОМЪ

Димитріемъ ПЕТРОВСКИМЪ

при участіи художника

Владимира ТАТЛИНА

Программа лекціи:

1) Дни Икара.
2) Чугунныя крылья.
3) Современность, какъ плавильный горнъ.
4) Путь отъ пространства ко времени.
5) Существуютъ-ли чистые законы времени.
6) Достиги **ХЛѢБНИКОВА**: „Время, мѣра-міра.
7) Футуризмъ перископъ будущаго.
8) Въ пользу словотворчества.
9) Законы языка (законы языка Русскихъ, опыты.)
10) На смѣну живописи: Законы формъ, закон. вѣса у Татлина и Бруни. О ТАТЛИНѢ.
11) Обзоръ нашего прошлаго въ поэзіи.
12) Чтеніе образцовъ поэзіи (прочтетъ Петровскій).
13) Хлѣбниковъ и Татлинъ О ПЕТРОВСКОМЪ.
14) Футуристы, какъ послы будущаго.
15) Будущее футуризма, какъ миѳъ Тезея и Минотавра.

Начало въ 8½ час. веч.

Цѣны мѣстамъ отъ 25 к. до 3 р.

Лекторъ и ответственный распорядитель
Димитрій Петровскій.

Печатать разрѣшено Начальствомъ
„Акц. О-во Царской Типо-Литографіи и Писчебумажной Торговли въ Царицынѣ о./В.“

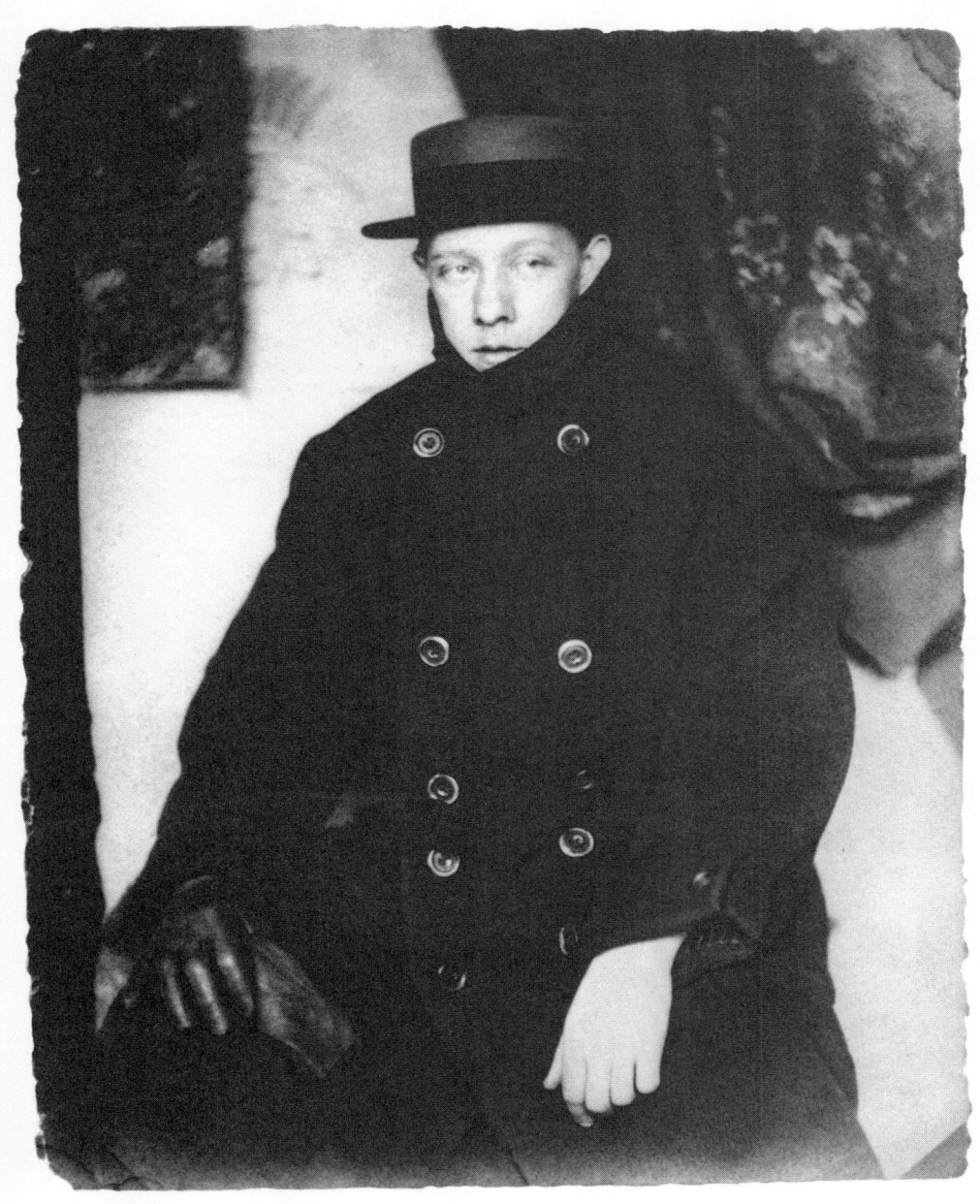

* **89** Poster of the 'Cast-Iron Wings' Futurist lecture, 1916,
Cat. XII/13
90 Tatlin in Paris, March–April 1913. Photograph: TsGALI, Moscow

91–2 Tatlin at the Russian Exhibition of Folk Art, Berlin, posing as a 'blind bandore player', February–March 1913. Photograph: TsGALI, Moscow

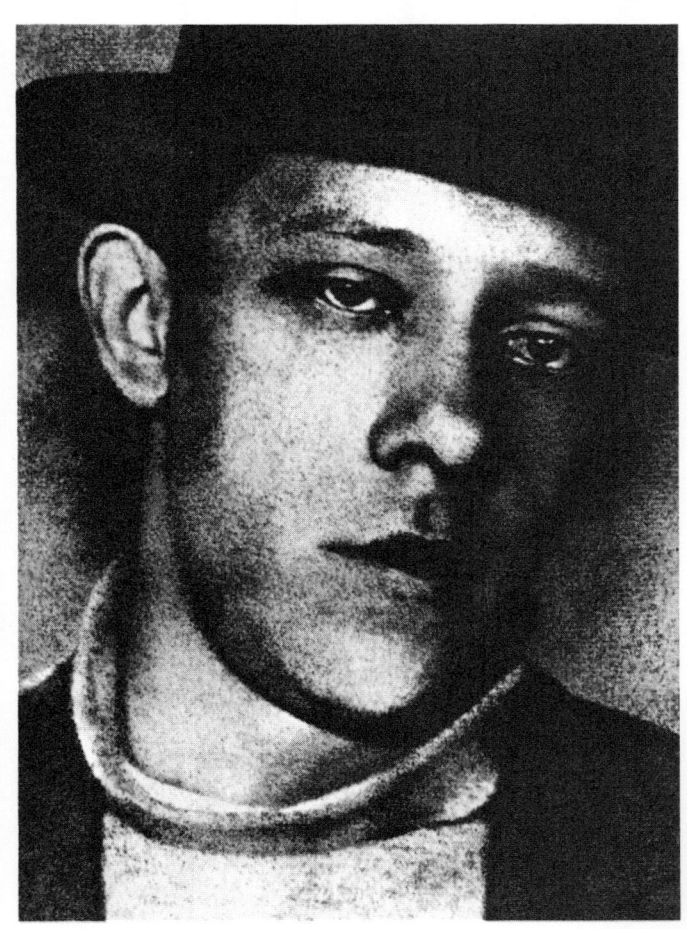

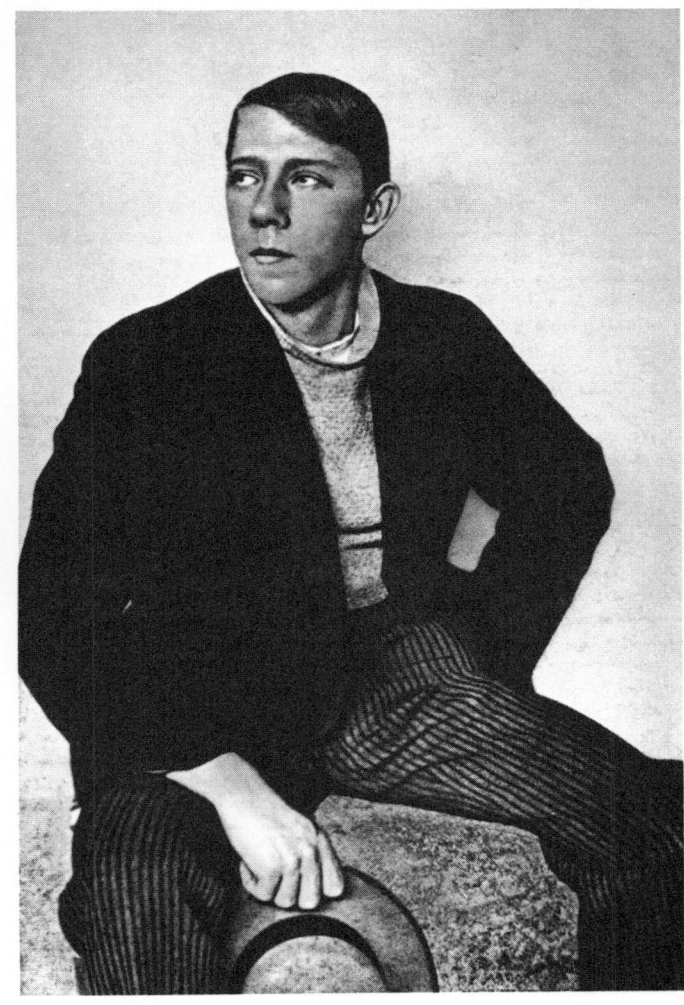

93 Tatlin, 1916. Photograph, TsGALI, Moscow
94 Tatlin, 1916. Photograph, TsGALI, Moscow

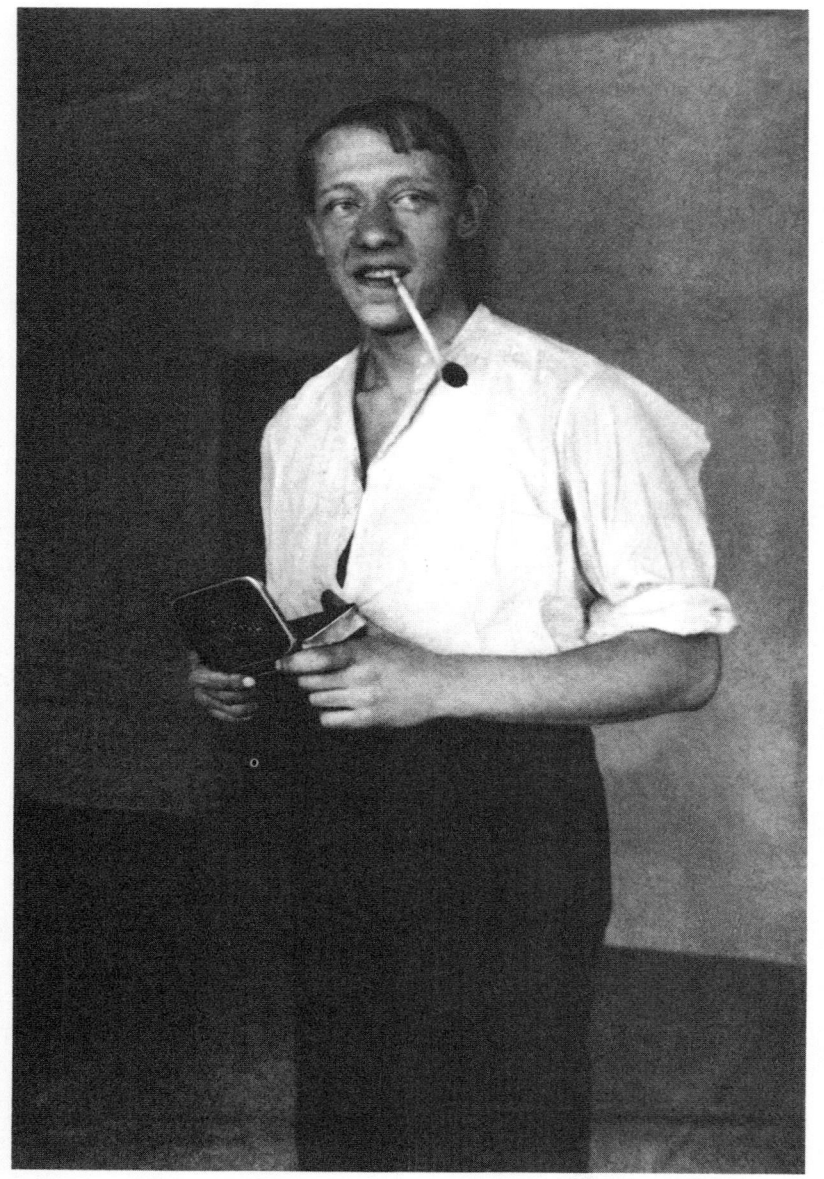

95 Tatlin, *c.* 1917, taken by Rodchenko.
Photograph: Collection V.A. Rodchenko,
Moscow
96 Tatlin (seated in centre), Kliun (behind
Tatlin), and Malevich with his second wife
(on the right)

Larissa Alekseevna Zhadova
TATLIN, THE ILLUSTRATOR AND DESIGNER OF BOOKS

Only a relatively small number of Tatlin's works in the area of book design have survived in comparison with the number of his paintings and designs. Not even the art historians have shown particular interest in these works and, for the most part, have ignored them.[1]

There is no doubt that these were not among the most important of Tatlin's works, yet one cannot deny that in his case even the peripheral works are interesting. His book illustrations, for example, were never made to order but were always the result of some immediate, personal interest. Often they were inspired by some event in his own life, the result of some human or artistic relationship or affection.

Tatlin's first book illustration was a lithograph he prepared for Khlebnikov's four-line poem beginning 'Let Us Be as Merciless as Ostranitsa,'[2] which appeared in 1912 in the collection entitled **Worldbackwards**. This lithograph signals the first contact of these two artistic destinies. Tatlin's final work in the area of book design was the graphic planning of Khlebnikov's **Unpublished Works** in 1940. The first work was the manifestation of their creative collaboration and budding friendship, while the second, in the words of the artist himself, was a salute 'to the memory of the most brilliant poet of the present era'.   73   232, 233

The illustrations for Maiakovskii's poem 'Signboards', which appeared in 1913 in the collection **The Service-Book of the Three**, bears witness to his personal acquaintance with the other great Russian poet of the twentieth century. In 1912 both Tatlin and Maiakovskii had taken part in the exhibition of young artists at the Moscow College of Painting, Sculpture and Architecture. It is probable that they met here for the first time. At that time Maiakovskii was a student at the College. 'The first stage of Maiakovskii's and Tatlin's relationship is signalled by their partnership in the collection of poems and drawings entitled **The Service-Book of the Three**, which was published in Moscow in March 1913. Maiakovskii's poem in the volume, "Signboards", is illustrated with two lithographs – two still-lifes "prepared in the manner of signboards". One of them is the work of the poet, the other is Tatlin's. In consequence, we must regard Tatlin as Maiakovskii's first illustrator (the second being Chekrygin).' So wrote Khardzhiev, a specialist in twentieth-century poetry and painting.[3] The first five years of Soviet culture following the Revolution were embarked upon by Maiakovskii and Tatlin as companions in arms and comrades.[4]   71

In his first attempts at book design Tatlin was already primarily interpreting the intellectual content of the work. His drawings for Khlebnikov's and Maiakovskii's poems were thematic and tied to the motif. He illustrated 'Signboards' with a 'still-life with fish'; in the still-life one sees on a platter the same smoked whitefish which had seized Maiakovskii's poetic imagination as he was 'reading' the 'book of sheet iron pages' of the city – the 'signboards'. In addition to the fish there is also the 'Maggi' bouillon cube whose neon sign whirls through Maiakovskii's poem 'like constellations'. When Tatlin was illustrating Vladimir Burliuk's poem beginning 'Twilight: the painter with his wide brush ...,' he depicted a house painter with bucket and brush in hand. Thus he objectivized the poetic metaphors. In his drawings, purposely simplified, perfunctory forms showing the influence of Primitivism[5] were coupled with precisely executed details. The artistic execution of the publication **Vladimir Evgrafovich Tatlin**[6] (1915) and of Punin's brochure **The Monument to the Third International** (1920) was held by Tatlin to be important because it constituted, to use modern terminology, the 'communicative unity' of material culture and the concept of Constructivism.[7] In this work the unity of his lifelong devotion to an artistic ideal and the purposefulness of an industrial design conception came into being.   70   122–126   182, 183

The booklet **Vladimir Evgrafovich Tatlin** (1915) contains reproductions of some counter-reliefs made up into montages with short texts. Its format was dictated by considerations of content. Perhaps this visual and verbal manifesto of early Constructivism was the first montage of photographic documents in the history of book publishing. Tatlin's principles of book design – strictness, asceticism and the rejection of decorativism – are already evident here. Punin's work **The Monument to the Third International**[8] belongs among the first Constructivist publications. In it the sketchy drawings – which Tatlin called technical drawings – form a visual unity with the text. Tatlin's strictly planned typography in this publication of the first years of the Revolution embraced also the ideals of agitational mass art: flags and slogans, all in a harsh black, red and white colour scheme.

182, 183

The covers of the book **Meeting at the Crossroads**, produced in 1927 while Tatlin was working at the Kiev College of Art, were created in homage to his Ukrainian poet friends Semenko, Shkurupii and Bazhan.[9] Tatlin illustrated Sergel's 1929 book **On the Sailing-Ship** under the pseudonym of LOT.[10]

293
294–297

It is quite likely that the children's book by Kharms, **Firstly and Secondly**, evoked in him personal memories since in the illustrations he endowed the chief character with his own features. We will now look at the preparation of these two books and of Khlebnikov's **Unpublished Works**.

298–312
232, 233

On the Sailing-Ship

This book, whose illustrator went under the name of LOT, was found in Tatlin's personal archive. Even the dust-jacket strengthens the supposition that it is Tatlin who hides behind the pseudonym. Among Tatlin's effects are four photographs of the sailing-ship on which he had served as a sailor in his youth, and the drawing on the dust-jacket very closely resembles one of these photographs. The sails, which appear dark on the photograph, stretch whitely against the wind in the drawing. Thus, Tatlin must have used the negative for a model.[11]

294
21–24

A number of traits exhibited in the illustrations further support Tatlin's authorship. In the drawings the dynamic tension, the way in which the shape of the sailing-ship is resolved – from above, from the viewpoint of the look-out atop the mast – both call to mind the stage design for the **The Flying Dutchman** (1916).[12]

156–163

Other drawings strongly recall the illustrations for **Firstly and Secondly** with their close-up depiction of the human form, and the transverse foreshortening of their hatched, draughtsman-like pencil sketching. The titles on the dust-jackets of both books, executed in sans serif type, are similar. Tatlin also made use of the same kind of typeface on the jacket of the book produced in Kiev.

The 'annotations', which consist of detailed graphic drawings and diagrams of the major types of sailing-ship accompanied by explanatory text, call to mind in their graphic construction the design and written description of the scenic construction of **The Moon on Stage**.[13]

401

On the other hand, the fact that the illustrations seem unconnected with the book's overall design, and instead appear to be individual drawings, does not seem to strengthen the case for Tatlin's authorship.

A decisive argument was, however, put forward by the art historian Khvoinik in a professional opinion, which was found in the archive, about Tatlin's original lost drawings.[14] During the preparation of the reproductions 'eleven of the originals which had been prepared for Sergel's book **On the Sailing-Ship** by the art[ist] Tatlin (pseud. LOT) were lost' ... 'Tatlin is not a productive illustrator. Thus, this circumstance serves to increase the value of his drawings', asserted Khvoinik.[15]

Another telling argument is provided by the discovery of two of the originals of the illustrations. At the same time, it appears that Tatlin served not only as the illustrator of the

296, 297

book but as its 'co-author' as well. According to the testimony of his friends he was a fascinating raconteur. We may well suppose that Sergel' had heard Tatlin's stories of his youth on the high seas and he drew upon them for his own writing.

These drawings are the work of a man who had, himself, spent a long time at sea. They not only bear witness to a deep acquaintance with the various types of sailing-ship but they also faithfully mirror the atmosphere of the sailor's 'peaceful' daily routine and of his mighty struggles with the stormy seas.

The professional opinion mentioned above was written in July 1929, following the publication of **On the Sailing-Ship**. It is probable, therefore, that the illustrations were prepared at the end of 1928 or the beginning of 1929. We may thus put forward the proposition that this work of Tatlin's was 'spadework' for the illustrations of **Firstly and Secondly**, the popular children's book published in 1929.

Firstly and Secondly

With **On the Sailing-Ship**, Tatlin was, first and foremost, the illustrator. In preparing the children's book he was at one and the same time both illustrator and book-designer. This 298–312 made it possible for him to create a harmony between the book itself and its text. We must, however, add that the structural composition of Kharms's[16] modern 'morality story' was helpful to Tatlin's work in many ways.[17]

Tatlin placed each unit of the text and each illustration on a separate page. Since neither the first story nor the concluding text is illustrated, and since only the long story beginning 'For the Fourth Time ...' occupies two pages, thus having two illustrations to itself, the book contains a total of eleven text sections and, including the dust jacket, ten illustrations.[18] The text and the illustration belonging to it do not always fall on facing pages, so that the pacing of the story varies, at times slowing down, at others speeding up.

As the story proves, the very small and the very large stood much closer to both Kharms and Tatlin than did life of normal dimensions.

According to the story, two boys meet the smallest man in the world and a man so tall that when he lies down the boys cannot see the tips of his toes. Tatlin drew himself in the 305, 306 picture of the giant man. The group sets off on its travels and uses many different types of 301–303 transport: a donkey, modern vehicles, and sometimes both together; but all four of them do not seem at all able to travel comfortably at the same time. It is not until the very end of the story that the companions find the mode of transport best suited to each of them. This happens to be in the world of animals: the tallest man rides on an elephant's back, the shortest on a small dog's, and the two boys on a donkey. The title-page depicts the various 299 means of transport, both natural and technological, showing them as coexisting but at the same time mutually obstructive.

The illustrations were prepared in 1929, during the period when Tatlin was researching the relationship between nature and science and was looking for a way to humanize technology, when, after much trial and error, he was beginning to realize his long-cherished plan for a flying machine which was to work on the principle of bird flight: **Letatlin**.[19] Strictly 313–353 speaking, the illustrations in the book contain within themselves a layer of meaning which bears a relationship to the role of the figures, especially to those which 'personify' Tatlin as the 'tallest man'.

In this context it is worth noting that the writer Danin particularly emphasized Tatlin's 'heroic physique' in the same way that he did those of his friends, the poets Khlebnikov and Maiakovskii: '... one could easily miss noticing this scarcely marked motif, though it is of such great importance. It becomes even more dramatic since these valiant knights were defenceless in the world and all alone in the world of art.'[20]

In the illustrations most of the unpleasant events of the trip happen to the character with Tatlin's face, and he is the loneliest and the most defenceless among the travellers. In the last illustration, 'For the Ninth Time', he does finally find the 'mode of transport' which suits him – he rides on an elephant – but his face is screwed into a sour, grotesque grimace.

During the preparation of the book the personal relationships behind the illustrations became more and more important. This is well shown by the difference between the sketch done for the ninth story and the illustration which finally appeared in the book. In the final variant the electric lines which created the dynamics of the composition have disappeared. In the drawing the tall man is sitting on the elephant facing the direction of travel, but with his head turned backwards, towards his companions. In the printed version he is sitting facing the rear, in the manner in which sinners were made to sit on an ass during the Middle Ages. The illustrations were done by a Tatlin who had already suffered many disappointments.

The many possible philosophical interpretations of Tatlin's illustrations for Kharms's text in **Firstly and Secondly** are interesting for children and adults alike. Moreover, the artist who portrayed himself in this story and in this shape has already begun to change the language of his artistry. He is no longer drawing the lines of a self-confident, decisive engineer but is now speaking in the lyrical voice of softer tones.

Khlebnikov's Unpublished Works

232, 233 Tatlin's last work in the field of book art is the portrait of Khlebnikov facing the title-page of the poet's **Unpublished Works** (1940). In contemporary book design pencil portraits of the authors were quite common and artists were happy to furnish these with classical allusions. In Tatlin's drawing, behind the poet's figure, the silhouette of Pushkin's statue in Moscow is sketched in to provide a symbol of the classical tradition. On the hard, raspberry-coloured cover can be seen the silhouette of the poet's profile and, under it, his signature.

Tatlin used the same design for all five volumes of Khlebnikov's **Collected Works**, changing only the colour for each new book and thus creating a uniform series for the first scholarly edition of the poet's works.

The collected edition of Khlebnikov's hitherto unknown works was an important event both as regards the destiny of Khlebnikov's poetic legacy and Tatlin's own artistic career and personal fate. It was in this volume that his friend's poem about him, written in the spring of 1916, appeared for the first time in its entirety.[21]

For Tatlin the fact that Khlebnikov's poem about him appeared before the public in 1940 was exceptionally important. Khlebnikov's verse bears witness to the close relationship between the spiritual and artistic endeavours of the poet and those of the painter; they are 'a team of sun snarers' and 'visionaries'. Khlebnikov was able to anticipate Tatlin's road in 164–206 his poetic programme. The 'visionary of the blades and stern bard of the propeller' created 313–353 the plan for the **Monument to the Third International** and the aerial bicycle, **Letatlin**.

So it is easy to imagine with what devotion Tatlin lent himself to the preparation of the poet's portrait. It is well known that he made several sketches and variations. The writer Danin who, as a student, had become a friend of Tatlin's in 1936, saw these drawings while they were being made as well as later on. He says Tatlin made six or eight portraits of Khlebnikov showing the poet full face and in profile, and in a coat with its collar turned up.[22]

Khlebnikov was the personification of pure intellect in these drawings – a man of gentle temper with an open face. There lurked in him some silent melancholy and reserve. Even for those who had never seen 'the President of the Globe' (that is, Khlebnikov) and had only read his works, Khlebnikov was exactly 'himself' in Tatlin's portrait ... We can see him in the same way in the wonderful drawing which was to become the frontispiece of the 1940, pre-war edition of Velemir Khlebnikov's **Unpublished Works**.

– so writes Danin in his recently published memoirs.[23] According to Danin the original of Khlebnikov's portrait in the book was far superior to the other sketches.[24] It is probable that this sublime and at the same time humanly warm drawing best represented the artist's original conception.

It is different in conception from earlier Khlebnikov portraits by other artists. In 1916 Grigor'ev had tried to capture the characteristics of the poet in profile, but the face reminds one rather of a bird with a hooked beak. Tatlin was well acquainted with Miturich's contemporary tragic works and valued them highly. Miturich had drawn Khlebnikov on his deathbed with documentary exactitude, 'from nature'.[25] This documentary approach was foreign to Tatlin. It is probable that he worked from memory, drawing forth from his own inner world the outlines of his genial friend and spiritual companion, and was, in this manner, able to make the viewer feel much more than he would have from a precise depiction.

As we have already mentioned, book illustrations are relatively rare in Tatlin's work. In his curriculum vitae which appeared shortly before his death he did not even mention his book design work.[26] How can this be explained? It is obvious that Tatlin held the literary text of a book to be the more important and, perhaps, also did not wish, in his capacity as illustrator, to play a secondary role to the author.

Notes

1 *See* Bibliog.: Khardzhiev, 1975, for the only exception.
2 В. Хлебников, *Собрание произведений*, Москва-Ленинград, 1928, vol. I.
3 *See* Bibliog.: Khardzhiev, 1975.
4 *See* 'Maiakovskii on Tatlin', p. 393; and 'Khlebnikov, Tatlin', p. 336.
5 *See* Sarab'ianov, pp. 45, 49; n4.
6 *See* p. 331.
7 *See* Zhadova, p. 134; Strigalev, p. 40, n48.
8 *See* p. 344.
9 Mikhail Vasil'evich Semenko (1892–1937): Ukrainian-Soviet poet, an organizer and theorist of the Ukrainian 'Left Front'. Initiator of the artistic group New Generation (*Novaia Generatsiia*) to which G. Shkurupii and the now widely known Soviet poet Mikola (Nikolai Platonovich) Bazhan also belonged. According to the intentions of the poets, the volume *Meeting at the Crossroads* signalled the beginning of the breaking up of the group.
10 LOT means 'sounding lead'.
11 TsGALI, Moscow.
12 *See* Syrkina, p. 160.
13 *See* 'The Moon', p. 316.
14 И. Хвойник, Заключение эксперта по вопросу о ценности рисунков художника Татлина. TsGALI. The report, in which that professional opinion was expounded, dated Moscow, 3 July 1929, was submitted to the people's tribunal, for Tatlin had appealed to that forum over the lost drawings.
15 Ibid.
16 Daniil Ivanovich Kharms (Iuvachev), 30 December 1905 (17 January 1906) St Petersburg–1942: Soviet writer. Started literary career in the mid-1920s. Member of Oberiu, Leningrad, 1927-30. The children's magazines

Chizh and *Ezh* carried his writings as from 1928. Was on the staff of the Leningrad *Detgiz* children's publishing house. It is a noteworthy fact that Tatlin had contacts with Oberiu. *See* А.А. Александров, 'Материалы Д.И. Хармса в Рукописном отделе Пушкинского дома', in: *Ежегодник РО Пушкинского дома*, 1978, Ленинград, 1980, pp. 64-79. It is usually stressed that Oberiu held kindred views on art with Malevich and Filonov.
17 The tale consists of eleven stories: ten episodes and a conclusion. The opening words, 'Firstly, Secondly', etc., give cohesion to the string of episodes and help sustain the children's attention. Only the conclusion, which promises continuation and is 'unfinished', opens with words other than these ordinal numbers.
18 Five of the original drawings have been recovered. (Ill. 303–6, 311)
19 *See* Zhadova, p. 147.
20 Bibliog.: Danin, 1979, p. 225.
21 *See* 'Khlebnikov, Tatlin', p. 336.
22 Danin's verbal information. The whereabouts of the drawings is unknown. Danin speaks of an as yet undiscovered copy of a portrait which shows Khlebnikov dressed in military uniform.
23 *See* Bibliog.: Danin, 1979.
24 Danin's verbal information.
25 The drawings were exhibited first in summer 1923 on the first anniversary of Khlebnikov's death in the Petrograd Museum of Artistic Culture and then in its Moscow counterpart. Tatlin helped to organize the one in Petrograd. Published first in *Русское искусство* 1923, no. 2–3, p. 98.
26 'Curriculum Vitae', p. 320.

Larissa Alekseevna Zhadova
TATLIN, THE ORGANIZER OF MATERIAL INTO OBJECTS

164–206   The world-wide significance of the architectural design of the **Monument to the Third International** clearly demonstrates why Tatlin until now has been held in esteem primarily as an architect who worked in industrial design. From this point of view, the designing of articles for personal use is certainly of secondary importance. The time is indeed appropriate, however, to examine Tatlin's work as a designer of pieces of furniture, dresses and dishes.[1] Such works, although few in quantity, are nevertheless quite remarkable in their conceptualization.

Researchers have pointed out the important fact that for Tatlin 'material culture' (*material'-naia kul'tura*), 'the culture of material' (*kul'tura materiala, kul'tura materialov*), 'the organization of material into objects' (*organizatsia materiala v veshch'*), 'the construction of material' (*konstruktsia materialov*) and 'the construction of objects' (*konstruirovanie veshchi*) were all synonymous expressions that stood very close to the modern concept of 'design'.[2] Many facts and some newly discovered documents corroborate this.

243   On a Sunday, 27 May 1923, Tatlin gave a lecture in the Museum of Artistic Culture of Petrograd entitled 'Material Culture. Down with Tatlinism.'[3] According to the printed memoirs of a member of the audience he discussed the creation of a new material environment and 'the task of the artist-constructor in the factory'.[4] This lecture was held in the weeks following the opening of the Exhibition of Petrograd Artists of All Tendencies on 15 May
170, 171   1923. Besides presenting for the first time drawings of the **Monument to the Third International**, he exhibited as unseen before a few dress designs, and stage designs and costumes for producing Khlebnikov's supernarrative **Zangezi** in the theatre.[5]

For Tatlin the introduction of the term 'material culture' was a question of principle. One may suppose that it emerged on analogy with the term 'artistic culture' which was widespread among the artists grouped around Tatlin in the first years of the Revolution, and denoted the special aspect with which Tatlin principally concerned himself – designing.[6] His principal preoccupation was that this term surpassed the traditional concept of art, i.e. it broadened the sphere of artistic activity into other domains, such as technology. One then could easily see how the idea of material culture began to take root in his painting and graphic works; so much so that the concept became a distinct natural, organic growth of his development that had very little in common with the idea of material culture as used in archaeology, anthropology and ethnography. Later, probably in order to avoid misunderstandings, Tatlin decided to use the term the culture of material(s). On a contemporary poster advertising the lecture 'Material Culture' the sub-title reads 'Down with Tatlinism'. The juxtaposition of title and sub-title was programmatic for Tatlin. The slogan meant that he protested against the canonization of his artistic methods, and rejected the 'isms' replacing each other in the new art. 'I cast aside as unnecessary a number of "isms" – the chronic sicknesses of contemporary art', he wrote in 1918.[7] Tatlin interpreted material culture as a phenomenon which, independent of changes of styles and fashions, produced artistic formations of lasting value.

At the same time he considered material culture right from the start as a new sphere of professional activity. At the Exhibition of Petrograd Artists of All Tendencies there hung on the wall the 'Order No. 1 for the Group of Material Culture' signed by Tatlin, in which the following appeal was issued: 'Remove from our environment people who have displayed empty slogans not confirmed by their craft.'[8] The group established themselves in 1919–21 in Petrograd under the aegis of the Free Artistic Studios, which had been called initially the

Studio of Volume, Construction and Colours. While the adherents of the Studio were still in the process of being organized (December 1919), Tatlin had already virtually completed his design for the **Monument to the Third International** and had made the necessary preparations for the construction of the model.[9] The evocative name of the studio showed that Tatlin's new type of creative activity began from his formative years as a painter but it did not express accurately the substance of Tatlin's constructive method, because he had given priority to work on material since 1915.[10]

170, 171

This became increasingly obvious in the period between spring and autumn 1920 when Tatlin worked on the construction of the model. This was the time when the studio's name was changed to the Studio of Material, Volume and Construction;[11] hereafter it became widely known under this name. Tatlin was also the organizer of a group in 1922 which soon became the Section for Material Culture within the Museum of Artistic Culture in Petrograd. The latter institution was soon reorganized, and functioned as the State Institute of Artistic Culture (GINKhUK) from 1922 to 1925.[12] Tatlin headed the Section for Material Culture until the summer of 1925. Then, between 1925 and 1927 he was put in charge of the Department of Drama, Film and Photography of the Kiev College of Art, and he gave lectures entitled 'Material Culture' which became a basis for the training of artists. He continued to hold lectures again under the same title in the years between 1927 and 1930 when he was a teacher at VKhUTEIN in Moscow, where he tried the practical implementation of his method during experiments conducted with the students of the faculty of pottery, woodwork and metalwork. The work for **Letatlin** was carried out by Tatlin and his collaborators in the Scientific Experimental Laboratory for the Research of Material Culture of the People's Commissariat of Education (1929–32).

179

244

313–353

Tatlin's view of material culture was expressed clearly in the records of the meeting of the Standing Commission of the Museum of Artistic Culture on 3 September 1923, when the artist read his production report.[13]

Tatlin reports about the work of the Section for Material Culture:
Exhibition of the samples of material culture:
a) the elements of material culture (samples: wood, glass, cloth, paint, etc.)
b) the combination of different materials (relief, counter-relief, etc.)
c) material constructions: objects, partly extant, partly made in the studio – the model of the Monument, stove, dishes, dresses.
The objects produced in the spirit of material culture must be compared to objects produced by principles contradicting ours to illustrate the differences between them.[14]

The major point of Tatlin's report was that he extended the concept of material culture to architecture and to every object having specific spatial relations, that is also to say, design. Hence the concept of material culture became the multiple concept of design-architecture, architectural design, i.e. the shaping of a material environment as a homogeneous entity.

Tatlin went even further: in the pursuit of his goal and endeavours to establish a theoretical basis for the concept of material culture he rendered the concept universal. In his report on the research work being done by the Section for Material Culture in 1924, Tatlin regarded material as 'an unlimited element which alone shapes culture'.[15]

When the concept of material is extended in this way, it is not limited to the material objects associated with architecture or design: colours in painting, words in literature and sounds in music are also included as part of the concrete material world of things. The synthesis of the wide spectrum that the concept entails had inspired Tatlin's stage version of Khlebnikov's supernarrative **Zangezi** in 1923. The theatrical production of this unique work was another example of how the universal interpretation of the material culture began to penetrate other artistic fields. Tatlin extended his concept of material culture to other fields of art, to the theatre, to the film and to photography. His work at the Kiev College of Art is ample enough proof of this. He believed that objects designed in the spirit of material culture must become the objects of a world created by man but inseparable from nature.[16]

216–222

With this conception Tatlin was far ahead of his time; he reached down to the deepest layers of culture. The emphasis on the primacy of material in the process of form-shaping, the effort to achieve organic unity linked Tatlin's conception to the development of popular handicraft in ancient Russia and with its origins in Byzantine and Antique culture. In this context the characteristically Tatlinian 'material slogans' he painted on panels with the technique of icon painting have a symbolic value. It is quite easy to imagine the impression of topicality and eternal validity of Lenin's slogan 'Better fewer but better' being evoked by the colour scheme and brushwork of old panel pictures. Tatlin adopted this principle whole-heartedly. According to his pupil Sotnikov this material slogan, apparently a favourite with Tatlin, was visible to all who entered his apartment.[17] It was a construction consisting of two wooden panels.[18]

316
164–206
313–353

The up-to-date official inscription 'Scientific Experimental Laboratory for the Research of Material Culture', also painted by Tatlin on panel, had multiple meanings.[19]

The peak of the first period of Tatlin's designing work was the project of the **Monument to the Third International**;[20] and it closed with **Letatlin**, the motorless flying apparatus in 1932,[21] but the latter's conception had been worked out much earlier. During this time Tatlin was not painting pictures. In this sense one may regard it as symbolic that on the basis of a sketch made by Tatlin in 1919 – itself the adaptation of a costume-design made in 1911

263, 264 – Chekhonin painted the **Tsarevitch** ornamental plate in the Petrograd (now Leningrad) Porcelain Factory in 1922.[22] This was the last painting of Tatlin's early period but it was made on an object.

It should be mentioned that Tatlin used the term material culture to designate the new sphere of his activity, and also his method of construction. The term material form (*materialo-forma*) appeared only at the end of his work as a designer in 1929. By then he did not need to coin a new term to define a new form of activity but rather one which emphasized the character and quality of his work in any branch of art.[23]

216–222 Contemporaries could not fail to notice the similarities of approach in Tatlin's and Khlebnikov's work.[24] Tatlin, the director, costume and scenery designer of **Zangezi**, one of Khlebnikov's last works, wrote of its production: 'Parallel to the word structure I decided to introduce a material construction. By this means the work of two people with different areas of specialization can be fused into one whole ...'.[25]

Tatlin's production report in September 1923 at the Section for Material Culture reflected the methodological experiences obtained during the production of Khlebnikov's work a few months earlier. The wording of the above-mentioned note made clear that it interpreted material culture as Tatlin's method of design, which was being presented in the exhibition.[26]

'The narrative is built from words as buildings are from building material', declared Khlebnikov in the introduction to **Zangezi**.[27]

'The word is the building unit, the material of linguistic structure, the material is the unit of organized space.' Tatlin's definition went one step further when he delineated the underlying principles of the production of **Zangezi**.[28]

Both Khlebnikov and Tatlin worked for an essential renewal of the language, forms and means of art. The common characteristic of their method was that they penetrated into the deepest layers of the idiom of their own branch of art, and reached down to the elementary expressive force of material in its untouched purity. The basis of Khlebnikov's poetry was its dynamic language-creating internal action. He fashioned the word and the elements of words as plastic material, by which he experimented in connecting and breaking up words. He created new words, gave meanings to phonemes and utilized words of different languages. He borrowed also from ancient forms of literature, from the language of tales, myths, folk poetry. He experimented with 'languages' which had previously had no place in literature: the language of mathematics, of small children, and the 'language of birds.'

The materials of Tatlin's art were wood, metal, glass, plaster, tar, cement, porcelain, cardboard, cloth ... and all materials used by popular handicraftsmen since ancient times.

Tatlin himself did joiner's work all his life: he made wooden benches, billiard-tables, ma-   253
quettes for the theatre and for exhibitions. He also used iron and cement which have only recently
been accepted in art. Experiencing the tactile properties of materials, studying their particularities as the 'prerequisites of form', comparing and combining different forms, materials,
colours and textures in material collections and counter-reliefs, he arrived at the construction
of 'organized space' and thus to the design of the **Monument to the Third International**.   164–206

Tynianov's expression 'conservatives and innovators' applies also to the work of Khlebnikov and Tatlin.[29] Tatlin set forth the basic principles of his method as a general theory and
he applied them in all his later activity and in his lecture series on 'Material Culture'. He
developed this curriculum in its most complete and systematic form in the course of his work
at VKhUTEIN's faculty of woodworking (second, third and fourth courses) and the Ceramics
Faculty. His method improved further in the course of practical work and experiments, and
was realized in the finished products made during the special lessons for designing articles
for personal use.[30] A year later, in 1928, at the Wood- and Metalworking Faculty, Tatlin's
lectures on material culture were turned into a comprehensive school subject of form-design
after integrating in themselves the colour and space disciplines of the basic course. Both the
lectures and the practical lessons became so popular among students that the idea of creating
a special department at the Woodworking Faculty began to take form. It was meant to be
called The Culture of Materials and the Organization of Objects.[31] Finally it did not come off,
probably owing to differences of opinion which in the meantime had emerged between Tatlin
and the teaching staff at the faculty.[32]

So far as Tatlin's relations to his students are concerned, in the working groups he headed   244
he was most likely to be always the soul of the group. His students participated in the work
as technicians making models of his samples or as independent designers, depending upon
their skills and abilities, but in the latter case they continued to work under his direction.
Almost all Tatlin's designs were made with his colleagues and students; many of them are
not even signed; they bear only the stamp 'Tatlin's Studio'. This corresponded fully with his
interpretation of his role as creator and inventor working for the community.

'Invention is always the working out of impulses and desires of the collective and not of
the individual', he wrote in 1919.[33]

Not one of Tatlin's projects has ever been carried out! Building technology has not to this
day dared to construct Tatlin's bold tower. The 'aerial bicycle' **Letatlin** never flew off. The
artist himself had been unable to find the appropriate technical solution. And from his
designs for furniture, dresses and dishes intended for mass production only samples were
produced in the best of cases, and those were mostly handmade.

Late in 1921 Tatlin tried to establish an artistic designing studio at the New Lessner
Mechanical Engineers' Trust. But in the design office nobody understood his ideas and he
was advised to go over to the draughtsmen and 'teach them to draw beautifully'.[34]

In a lecture delivered in 1923, Tatlin 'expressed his dissatisfaction with the authorities who
did not really support his endeavours to work in industrial concerns'.[35]

Despite all odds Tatlin persevered in his struggle to overcome the resistance of managers
and engineers. In the spring of 1929, he established working relations with the Leningrad
Clothing Manufacturers' Trust and planned to contact the Low-Voltage Electrical Factories'
Trust. He wanted to convince those who worked in production that the artist's work was
indispensable for generating better quality industrial products which could contribute to
develop the new way of life.[36] In the spring and summer of 1924, Tatlin delivered at least
six lectures on 'Material Culture and its Role in the Life and Industry of the Soviet Union',
illustrated with sample objects and drawings.[37]

It is easy to imagine the insurmountable resistance and lack of understanding this project
had to face within the turbulence of growing ideological clashes. Tatlin experimented with
creating the Soviet school of industrial design in the mid-twenties during the post-revolutionary period so full of dramatic events. Unlike the fathers of classical Utopias, the creators

of Utopian plans in the first three decades of the twentieth century believed that their plans were necessary and realizable in the near future. Tatlin shared the fate of so many other innovative geniuses of Soviet science, technology and art. Their bold ideas could not be carried out because of the low level of technology and the lack of the necessary material means; the growing resistance of the intellectual environment was also an impediment. These conditions, however, could not diminish the importance of Tatlin in developing a twentieth-century attitude to design.

One would like to believe that these designs may yet become part of some future environment.

Interior Decoration and Furniture Design

164–206   Tatlin's first ideas for interior decoration concerned the furnishing of the rooms in the interior of the **Monument to the Third International**. Punin's article in the March 1919 issue of the journal **Iskusstvo kommuny** gives a fairly good idea of Tatlin's plans:

The simplest form (the cube) will accommodate lecture-halls, gymnasiums, agitation halls and other premises used for different purposes according to requirements. But these rooms cannot be used as museums, libraries or similar offices because they should be able to change their function at any time. The Monument would accommodate an Agitation Centre from where different appeals, proclamations and publications would be sent out on standardized motorcycles and automobiles bearing the emblem of the Monument; this fleet of vehicles would operate as the government's mobile stand-by agitative apparatus. Hence the Monument would contain also garages ... Furthermore, a huge film-screen should be mounted on one of the largest façades of the Monument where, in the evening hours, a newsreel, visible from a great distance, would show the newest political and cultural events. For the sake of direct information there should be a wireless station in the Monument capable of receiving news from all over the world; there should also be a good size telephone exchange and telegraph office together with other means for obtaining information. The Monument would utilize also a recent invention: a projection apparatus would project coloured letters onto the clouds from one wing of the building (the northern one would be particularly suitable). From these letters one could put together slogans related to the day's events. The Monument could also accommodate a series of other, smaller rooms with an artistic function including a hall for exhibiting new works, a printing office, a canteen, etc. The different rooms would be connected with each other by electric lifts and other mechanized vehicles of conveyance. One must emphasize as a basic principle that, firstly, all modern technical equipment promoting agitation and propaganda should be used in the Monument and, secondly, that it should become the centre of the most intense activity ...
Tatlin's plan is based on the synthesis of contemporary engineering discoveries, hence it enables us to richly apply new artistic forms in technology. The radio, the film-screen and the cables are elements of the Monument and at the same time also formal elements. Therefore one must take special care that the Monument should not consist of isolated premises and buildings that are only externally related. It should be completely monolithic and the artist's foremost task is to find that unified form which is at the same time architectural, sculptural and painterly and renders possible the synthesis of the individual forms of different technical apparatuses. It goes without saying that engineers and technical experts of various fields must also be involved in the realization of this Monument.[38]

Tatlin conceived his romantic plan of transformable interior spaces, dynamic installations changeable according to different purposes, a complex system of visual communication and modern transport vehicles which 'would bear the emblem of the Monument' and thus would come to symbolize a superior way of life, the integration of technology and art at a time when the country's economy was at its lowest level and even the minimal technical conditions for realizing his plan were absent.

The idea of projecting images onto the clouds with coloured reflectors was well ahead of its time, as was the synthesis of town planning and colour light painting.

In his first architectural designs Tatlin applied the basic ideas of the programme of material culture: the shaping of environment oriented towards the development of a new way of life and its attendant new social and cultural functions – the Monument was intended to be also a cultural centre. A further aim was to produce new artistic forms and relate them to the newest technical achievements, producing a complex in which every element of the project should be related to every other as parts of a greater whole; and all this was to be realized with the collective participation of engineers and technicians.

Such ideas showed up the 'monolithic' nature of form-shaping including as its means architecture, sculpture and painting, all of which would have been made functional by technology. The dynamic force of mechanics and art would have constituted a coherent unity in the tense balance of material and form.

When later Tatlin had to give up his plans for that monolithic symbolic building and switched over to designing objects for everyday use, for mass production, he altered his programme accordingly. The new programme was aimed at designing objects for everyday use which would serve man in every possible way and advance his cultural and intellectual development. This was essentially a social programme for producing objects which liberated man from the slavery of the consumer attitude and object-fetishism. On the one hand, Tatlin proclaimed the postulate of organic forms in consideration of the human anatomy and individual psychological particularities; on the other hand, of standardized samples. He also said that the artist 'must be able to find for the object the necessary material which can be applied to our climatic and economic conditions'.[39]

The principles of the further development of material culture were expressed in their definitive form in Tatlin's two later articles: 'The Artist as an Organizer of Everyday Life' which appeared in 1929, and 'The Problem of the Relationship between Man and the Object' in 1930. The latter was subtitled 'Let Us Declare War on Chests of Drawers and Sideboards'.[40]

In 1923 Tatlin started to design objects for everyday use with the slogans: 'Not the old, not the new, but the necessary.' 'Not to the left, not to the right, but to the necessary.' He designed stoves and heating equipment, constructed new types of beds, made models of clothes and dishes. The overwhelming majority of artists considered this activity as the degradation of the sublime tasks of art to the level of artisanship. Tatlin, however, persisted in the implementation of his creative programme 'Art into Life'. The moral and aesthetic unity which had always been his fundamental artistic creed gained special significance in those years of crisis in Soviet society and art when a strong resistance had to be overcome to make acceptable an activity and branch of art widely recognized today under the name design. 234

A photo of one of Tatlin's five economic 'standard' stoves has been preserved. These stoves had to give out maximum heat using a minimum amount of fuel: owing to the fuel shortage of the period this was a major requirement. Under the well-known photo there is a technical description of the stove: 'Of the five samples already made of common stoves we shall discuss the one shown in Figure 3: this stove has an economical furnace producing a considerable heating effect with a small expenditure of wood (six logs). The stove is supplied with an oven and a large hermetically sealed chamber capable of keeping water and food hot for 28–30 hours; at the same time with only one furnace it can heat a room of $8 \times 6 \times 6$ arshins* for 48 hours, maintaining a temperature of 14–16 degrees Réaumur.'[41] 245, 246

246

Tatlin's nephew, S.S. Tatlin, who in the early twenties lived with his mother at his uncle's place, still remembers two stoves handmade by the artist. He said that there was a big stove in Tatlin's room, and another one in the room in which he and his mother lived.[42] From this period of his childhood he still remembers that the miraculous stove radiated wonderful heat, and that the application of a special chimney stack was also his uncle's invention. A description of the stove was found recently in the manuscript of a hitherto unknown article of Punin (1924): 239

* 1 arshin = *c.* 30 inches

From the outside it presents a parallelepiped made of tiles without any decorations and of strictly prescribed proportions ... Tatlin's stove consists of a furnace with complicated and adjustable passages which make it possible to heat all of it or only its central part – the air chamber. The latter is so designed that it also serves as a range or, to put it more simply, it is a range covered with an air box; there is a small glass window in one of the sides to peer into the chamber; the chimneys have hooks inside for smoking food ... Tatlin produced neither an electric stove nor even a gas one – in a word, none of those Americanized stoves – but an ordinary wood stove to be used by anybody and all.[43]

When Tatlin designed objects for everyday use he first and foremost followed the traditions of the given cultural environment. The design of the wood stove demonstrates the particularities of the Russian way of life and the people's ingenuity. But Tatlin's stoves were not only technically better and more useful than the iron stoves in widespread use in the difficult years, which were smokey and whose flames readily died fast. Tatlin's stove-designs already contained a tendency of design which later became universal: that in modern apartments technical appliances had to be designed as part of the furnishings. The thick-set forms of Tatlin's stoves evoke the Russian village hut but at the same time they resemble a cube, i.e. he wanted to create modern forms from the popular originals.[44]

In the Section for Material Culture in the Museum of Artistic Culture (later GINKhUK – State Institute of Artistic Culture) Tatlin worked between 1923 and 1925 on design standards for the objects and furnishing of communal rooms and apartments which should be economical, durable and variable according to the 'new way of life'.[45]

There were two studios in Tatlin's section: in the first they made drawings and designs or, according to the term then in vogue, they mounted prototypes; in the second they studied material, especially the properties of 'colour as material', and worked out colour norms.[46]

Discussing Tatlin's painting Punin wrote that he studied colour (colours) more and more as a material. He wrote also that Tatlin liked to cover his canvases with one colour with the traditional technique, the so-called body painting, which characterized the icon- and signboard-painting workshops.[47] It is very probable that Tatlin used these experiences when he worked out his colour norms. Forty such norms were worked out and they were exhibited at GINKhUK and probably presented in lectures.[48] Relying on available pigments – many were missing – Tatlin and his colleagues 'tried to invent new colours and combinations of them'.[49] Unfortunately, until now the missing documents of Tatlin's colour norms have not been found.[50]

255   His next work in the design of everyday objects was the model of the cantilevered chair executed by the college student Rogozhin under Tatlin's direction at the Woodworking Faculty of VKhUTEIN in 1927.[51] Its whereabouts is unknown, but it was reconstructed later

256–258   on[52] from Rodchenko's contemporary photo.[53]

Tatlin commented on the design:

A contemporary furniture factory takes no account of the requirements of the human body in constructing any kind of pattern for furniture. It is interested only in external effect. But a human is an organic being, consisting of a skeleton, nerves and muscles. Because of this a chair should have elasticity. The so-called American chairs give this elasticity, and soft clubhouse chairs give it. But this furniture is exceedingly expensive and cumbersome. The cheap thing is made of bars, it cannot give any elasticity. The chair constructed by us [...] gives a sufficient degree of elasticity. The material is one-inch (in diameter) maple, with strips curved on the principle of bentwood furniture. The construction is in the form of a bridge-girder, and furthermore four one-inch strips completely assure the strength and so to speak the safety of sitting on such a chair. With mass production it will cost even less than a

260   Viennese bentwood chair and will be more comfortable.[54]

259   The Finnish architect Alvar Aalto, who also designed sets of sitting furniture including cantilevered chairs, after much hard work developed a special technology in the twenties and thirties in the course of which he cut multilayered pressed birch plywood and then treated

it with heat. Tatlin's cantilevered chair is based entirely on the traditional Viennese technology. The Thonet firm had started the industrial production of its chairs in Austria in 1841; these were the first classic prototypes of design.[55] The springy curvature of the legs, back and seating surface of the Viennese chairs produced a special plastic form. Despite its originality, this construction left unchanged the stereotyped structure of chairs: the verticals of the four leg supports continue in the vertical line of the back and hold the seat's horizontal plane.

Tatlin's new idea was to abandon the traditional erect framework and the vertical supports. He bent the thin, cylindrical wood into a profile of $\int$ whose curves constituted the three levels necessary for sitting: the curved leg part, the cantilever support of the seat and the form uniting the back and the elbow-rests. The plasticity of form and the construction's technical function reinforce each other. So the doubling of the wooden arches on those very points of the curved legs which bear the greatest tension does not disrupt the form's uniformity but enriches it with a complementary dynamic of rhythms.

The construction's centre of support, which also fixes the transition of the lower curve's vertical to the horizontal of the supporting cantilever, is at the same time also a composition-centre which arranges the tense, dynamic, arched forms into a visual balance. The chair's system of curves is lucid because it fits essentially into the simple stereotype form of a cone intersected by planes: one formed by the seat and two others by the floor-support and the back plus the elbow-rests, respectively.

The Viennese chairs are static. Although Tatlin's chair has no springs, it is not rigid: when one sits down on it the wooden arches are flexible enough to bend a little. From the formal viewpoint this property is expressed in the spatial layout of the graceful construction. The spaces outlined by the softly curving lines appear as the chair's transparent, weightless components. The sculptured form of the seat contrasts with them, and appears as their materialization in space. The seat is covered with leather and shaped with special stitches. The elasticity of the construction allows one to shift the weight of the body from one leg to another if one sits on the chair for a long time.[56]

Since the mid-twenties new standard designs of chairs and armchairs have started to appear in the West. The technical novelty of the varied and original plastic form inventions of Marcel Breuer, Mies van der Rohe, Mart Stam and Le Corbusier was related in the first 262, 261 place to their material, the bent steel tube, and its industrial technology. Tatlin was aware of the most progressive contemporary trends in furniture design; similar experiments were also made in VKhUTEIN.

Tatlin renounced metal and designed chairs from wood because there was a shortage of steel tubes in the Soviet Union at the time. The shortage of funds and material determined his attitude as a born designer, which he formulated in the following way: 'We need to widen the range of our thinking in the area of materials and their interrelationships.'[57] Bearing in mind the existing practical possibilities, Tatlin and his students at VKhUTEIN experimented with available materials to produce no less expressive forms for objects being produced in the Western countries from metal tubes.

So Tatlin tried the technology of Viennese beech furniture on the characteristically 'Russian' maple, and he did not limit its application to furniture design. Two variants of a 254 sleigh are known to have been evolved at VKhUTEIN. Under Tatlin's direction the maple-wood framework was bent to the form of double eights. 'The advantages for us are evident. The material is at our disposal: whole forests, the working of it is not complicated or expensive, and the sleigh is far cheaper. Besides, it is many times lighter than a metal one (it is easy to carry on the shoulder) and in winter it is not unpleasant to the touch since, unlike a metal one, it does not freeze. It is extremely durable.'[58]

It should be pointed out that the novel chair form which Tatlin constructed of wood 255 practically in competition with designers working with metal has stood the test of time doubly. The masterful exploitation of the flexibility and solidity of wood was also a triumph over material because this elastic form developed from arched wood could be applied also

256–258   to metal. The metal reconstructions of the chair made in the Soviet Union and abroad were evident proof. Indeed, in the 1930s Soviet experts were convinced that Tatlin himself had made his chair originally of metal.[59]

Tatlin was not adverse to the creation of metal furniture, unlike Aalto who, it is true, eventually came around to the idea that wood was a more suitable material than the metal
261, 262   chairs and armchairs of the Bauhaus.[60] At the same time Tatlin's approach to material culture and his designing of objects for everyday use had much in common with Aalto's conception. Their views both approached anti-functionalism: both tried to follow 'the phenomena of living nature' in their creative forms. They made generous use of wood as an organic material, because of its natural qualities, they felt it adjusted well to man's psychical and physiological qualities.

If we compare Tatlin's chair with the types of cantilevered chairs made of metal designed
261   in the West in the same period – for instance, Mart Stam's design made in 1926, Mies van
262   der Rohe's in 1927 – Tatlin's chair seems technically primitive. The bundles of the bent construction were tied by hand, and the whole construction and its elements lack the purity and perfection of technical finish. On the other hand, the formal ingenuity of Tatlin's chair is spectacular: to quote Khlebnikov, 'it seems to invite one' since its appearance evokes the association of a man comfortably seated. In Tatlin's album made between 1911 and 1914 there is an analytical drawing of a seated model. The dotted straight and perpendicular lines record the different movements of the hands, shoulders, trunk and legs but the figure's contours constitute a well-balanced arched form. Tatlin's analytical drawing foreshadows the idea of the chair evoking the 'organic construction' of the comfortably sitting human figure; the rounded lines evoke the shape of the future chair.

This anthropomorphism of form-shaping did not mean an excessive stress on anatomy. Tatlin never imitated the form of the human body mechanically: he achieved it through mediation. The specific chair form is the result of well-considered functional aspects: it is an organic structure vibrant in the permanent dynamism of arches – which accounts for its visual expressivity – whereas the composition of cantilevered chairs made in other countries does not suggest the same support of the human body.

Clothes Designs

Tatlin considered clothes designing an important subject in the curriculum of GINKhUK.[61]
His design for a sports coat made from vulcanized material is well known: Tatlin presented
245, 246   it himself in the foreground of the picture of the 'economical stove'. It was reproduced in No. 23 1924 of the periodical **Krasnaia Panorama**, together with a detailed description.

The coat reproduced in the picture has the following typical features. Its shape, wide in the shoulders and narrowing down towards the bottom, results in the following characteristics: heat is not lost out of the bottom, the fabric does not cling to the body but retains a layer of air which, on the one hand better preserves the heat (the principle of the double-glazed window) and on the other, creates more hygienic conditions.
The coat is made in such a way as not to restrict movement and to enable the person wearing it to retain a natural posture: the pockets, for instance, are placed at arm's length… Moreover, the coat has two removable linings – a flannelette one (for autumn) and a sheepskin one (for winter), which can be fastened to the soft waterproof outer part with a special fastening.
Since the coat consists of three separate parts put together when necessary, each of them can be replaced by a new one when the original part is worn out.[62]

247, 250   The principle of the sports coat was probably first worked out as a design for a spring coat for men, of which a large-sized drawing, made in 1923, has survived.[63]
Tatlin's last clothing design, made in the studio of the Institute of Applied Arts in 1925,
248, 249   was a suit and sports coat combination most probably made up in linen cloth which brings

to mind similar contemporary outfits. By then the new type of suit had been fully worked out in its finalized form.

An experimental and transitory form is the so-called lounge suit without trimmings and with a combined collar.

A single design of a woman's dress has been preserved: it has a round, almost sculpted, collar.

251

Tatlin's programme emphasized the new social-cultural function of dress. A montage had been produced in the Section for Material Culture – probably for the Exhibition Room – which illustrated the contrast between the 'old and new'. The photo of Tatlin himself in his sports suit stands upright; it is glued to two other photos in a horizontal position which represent men's suits from the past: one of the figures is in an old-fashioned lounge-suit with bow-tie, walking-stick and hat, and the other is wearing a long double-breasted overcoat, doublet and tie. The position of Tatlin's photo seems to eclipse them, to blur out their presence. Beside the new-fashioned suit there is an inscription written by Tatlin: 'This attire is warm, does not restrict movement, satisfies hygienic requirements, and lasts long.'[64] The old-fashioned suits are accompanied by the following commentary: 'This attire restricts movement, it is also unhygienic, and they wear it only because they think it is beautiful.' The meaning of 'beautiful' in this context is trendy.

246

Materials for the montage were selected from the periodical **Krasnaia Panorama**. Today this confrontation between old and new may seem too direct and a little naïve. But in the period of the NEP (New Economic Policy), when the worst traditions of the past were revived and standards of taste were low, that controversy was very topical.[65] One should only remember Lebedev's satirical drawings made in 1924 with the ironical title **New Way of Life** or his series **NEP** from 1927; he drew puppets in clumsy, flashy attires. In this historical context Tatlin's creations had a clearly social influence. He proclaimed a conception of dressing which had nothing to do with the wearer's social status, did not confer prestige, and liberated people from artificial rules of etiquette and gave them a feeling of freedom. He designed economical and functional models for everyday wear and for every occasion which were beautiful in the modern sense of the word. In his designs he was inspired by sportswear and work clothing. This is evident if one compares his designs of jackets to sailors' working clothes with costume designs he made for the opera and especially to the windbreaker of the helmsman in **The Flying Dutchman**. The coat is waterproof, with a button-in lining, a broad upper section, separately cut shoulder-parts and arms, and stitched-down borders which cover the buttoning.

158

Studies of the history of dress design show that the paraphernalia of soldiers' and sailors' clothes have had a striking influence on dress design.[66] Tatlin's designs evidence this: it was a natural consequence of his career.

He was a descendant of Dutch shipbuilders, the Van Tatlings. His ancestors had been brought to Russia by Tsar Peter I. He knew and loved life at sea and had served several times in the merchant fleet. As a sailor he wore a windbreaker and an angler's cap, so he knew from experience that these clothes were comfortable and practical and even had a beauty about them in their own right. Tatlin's views about dress design differed from those of the Constructivist artists who worked in the Institute of Artistic Culture of Moscow (INKhUK). Rodchenko, Stepanova, Popova and Aleksandr Vesnin thought the primary task was to make working clothes as flexible as possible, but Tatlin designed everyday outfits in which he reconciled the forms of working clothes and formal dress.

20–24

The expressive beauty of clothing may originate in the conception of a human body as a volume or a silhouette. Tatlin's point of departure in dress design was the plasticity of the human body. The laconic forms and sweeping lines of his clothes give them the character of rustic sculptures, and yet they are extremely elegant. The designer emphasized the basic structure of his clothes and worked out all their details down to the last stitch – as, for example, broad, rounded-off shoulders, straight, downwards narrowing cuts, big arm-holes,

248, 249
tight necklines closed with buttons, oval patches on the elbow of his coats, etc. Tatlin knew about contemporary fashion trends, and so Cubist forms and the cut of folk costume shirts influenced his work. He assembled his suits from geometric forms, especially from the many-sided variable rectangle. His sports jackets and suits were created from few elements but he made very good use of geometric planes. By applying them in a relatively complex manner, he obtained the maximum effect. From rectangular patterns he constructed trapezoids and placed curvilinear forms at their base and at the separately-cut shoulder parts and sleeves.

In the contemporary work of most Russian dress designers the expressivity of their patterns was based mainly on their geometrical outline, and the form of the human body was of secondary importance to rhythm – as in the models of Rodchenko and Stepanova. Tatlin, however, did not put much emphasis on the cut for he wished to achieve a specific total expressivity by the dynamic unhindered unity of the dress and the human figure.

252
Tatlin was not by training a professional clothing designer: his activity in this field was only an offshoot of his major artistic production but his principles were nevertheless shared even by Lamanova, the internationally recognized artist, master and theorist of the Soviet dress designing school, who wrote in 1924: 'The correct interpretation of the conception of dressing is opposed to the old idea of following tradition and fashion.'[67] Lamanova explained her theory as follows: 'Fashion has a tendency to level off and does not take into consideration the characteristic build and real and potential imperfections of people's bodies (you need only think of the crinoline or the tight swaddled skirt). Every person is entitled to a harmonious, pleasant appearance however irregularly shaped their bodies may be, either due to the rigours of their way of life or from congenital defects. The more recent ideas on dressing make a conscious effort to improve the proportions of the human body with the help of creative dress design.'[68] This is a possible explanation of Tatlin's method of bringing the human figure into harmony with the form and volume of the dress. He did not trace the body's forms and lines in his sketches of dresses and theatre costumes as is generally done.

Tatlin's and Lamanova's artistic conceptions had much in common. Lamanova emphasized the importance of the material in the form-shaping effect of a dress. Indeed, Lamanova's surviving drawings and articles from her creative programme, which evolved independently of Tatlin's, show that her ideas were identical with those of the representatives of the concept of material culture.

Not only had Tatlin no interest at all in designing one-off garments, he was interested only in setting standard patterns for serial production from the most widely obtainable and cheapest materials. He also worked out a constructive, economical, logically simplified cutting method which, although uncomplicated, was far from schematic.

It is important to note that Tatlin designed his models for his own measurements. He not only controlled the production of his designs for jackets, coats and suits personally in the workshop of the Leningrad Clothing Manufacturers' Trust (so called since 1924), but publicly modelled them himself. He designed his standard models for '150,000,000 people'[69] with the same care and attention as if he had designed them only for himself. Tatlin's values were truly and fundamentally democratic.

'Every era has its own type of *arbiter elegantiarum*; in the era of industrial Cubism this term is applicable to Tatlin. He is a man of style and of beautiful forms; he is carved of one block,'[70] wrote Punin about Tatlin. If a designer designs for himself, his personality becomes decisive. In Tatlin's case the designer was a creative genius whose ideals were shared by the best minds of the Soviet Union at the time. The new dresses were first shown in 1923 at an exhibition in Petrograd.[71] They impressed all press correspondents.

Tatlin's ideas, together with his many suggestions for renewing material culture, were highly appreciated but they could not break through the spiritual and technical obstacles of the period. Several decades later his ideas were accepted as general tendencies all over the world, setting the trend in fashion from the 1960s on.[72]

Household Ceramics

In the 1923 report mentioned above about the work of the Section for Material Culture, Tatlin was one of the first to mention dishes among the objects designed and constructed in the Section. Sketches bearing the stamp 'Tatlin's Studio' from 1923 have been found in 1977.[73] The design for a porcelain **Tea-Set** includes sketches of cup, saucer, teapot, milk-jug, sugar-bowl, and separately the spout of the milk-jug. The drawings prove the designer's superior professional skill. The forms are represented in orthogonal projection which is the standard drawing representation for sketches of crockery. The trapezoid-shaped tea-set is simple and practical. These designs and many others were the organic creative production of Tatlin's programme at the time, all summed up under his motto: 'Not the old, not the new, but the necessary.' With his ingenuity he managed to standardize porcelain dishes in the early twenties when in the Soviet Union technical conditions were still largely manufactural.

He was among the first to start designing metal kitchen dishes, most likely around 1923.[74] His **Multipurpose Dish** remained only at the experimental stage: it was a combination of a pot and a tea-kettle whose cover served also as a frying-pan. The plan remained impracticable probably because he could not solve the problem of placing the frying-pan's handle. It broke the monolithic form of the dish, whereas the pot's handle made it unstable.

In this design Tatlin also tried to find a new, unconventional form which, in his intention, would have fulfilled several functions. According to his interpretation of the new social requirements developed by the Revolution, the dish took on the form and character of a mess tin: this suggests that he followed the well-tested military practice of having separate independent elements which could easily fit into each other as a singular mass form. From this viewpoint his work is strikingly similar to a mess tin which can be put together into a single form and consists of tin, tea kettle, frying-pan, plate, drinking-cup, knife, fork and spoon. This was designed in the same year, 1923, by Bykov, a student of the Metalworking Faculty of VKhUTEMAS, under the direction of Rodchenko.

The novelty in Tatlin's design is the monolithic effect of the body created with energetic and firm curves, the plastic cast handles and the broad, soft-lined profile of the spouts forming an organic unit with the dish's body. The sculpted character of Tatlin's dishes is suggested in the sketches; this distinguishes his work from all other Russian and Western designs.

The other known designs were made by Tatlin's pupils under his direction at the Ceramics Faculty of VKhUTEIN.[75] In the lessons on 'designing everyday objects' Sotnikov, a third-year student, designed in 1930 a **Set of Child's Nursing Vessels** and an ingenious **Teapot** without handles. Sotnikov is today a well-known Soviet porcelain sculptor. He was Tatlin's favourite pupil,[76] and later became his assistant in constructing the flying apparatus. 'I was happy because they admitted me to the Ceramics Faculty. Among my teachers P. Kuznetsov, D. Shterenberg, A. Bruni and O. Pavlenko left imperishable memories, but Tatlin played the most important role in my professional training, being also the closest to me. He taught the designing and constructing of new articles for everyday use. His lectures in this field opened wide vistas and were built on consistent principles. Compromise solutions did not exist for him. "If your work is not good, begin it once again" – Tatlin would say,' Sotnikov declared.[77] Tatlin involved him very soon in his work, and this, according to the students of VKhUTEIN, was a rare privilege.[78]

Two variants have been preserved of the **Child's Nursing Vessel**. The first, despite its formal novelty, looks like a medical vessel, static and clumsy. But, on the other hand, this was the customary form of the earthen vessels made in the studio of VKhUTEIN from organically appropriate material: their tonality and *faktura* had the beautiful smooth effect of ivory. Later Sotnikov began to work with porcelain which was more widely used in Russian industry. In the porcelain factory of Dulevo he changed the form of the **Child's Nursing Vessel**[79] into what was to become its definite form.

265–271
266–269

234

265

275–288
278–281
275–277

278, 279

280, 281   In shaping his **Nursing Vessel** Sotnikov's source of inspiration was the female breast but in his interpretation the classical form became a sculptural design. His drinking vessel – a sculpture – was intended to be a 'living thing', a simple toy, and at the same time a form evoking rich emotional and cognitive associations. Like Tatlin's Tower, the small vessel is oblique, organized around an axle parallel to the axle of the globe.

Despite its small size the principle of its design was its organic integration into the system of the universe. At the same time its oval, streamlined form and its stability in asymmetrical proportions relates it to Tatlin's chair construction.

Today the possibility of this unified conception of objects so different in quality seems highly unusual but the novelty of Tatlin's intellectual and artistic system was this monolithic organization. For him the universe, society, the individual, cosmic and everyday objects, natural organisms and the technical tools produced by man, their supreme manifestation, were of identical value.

280, 281   Coming back to the **Child's Nursing Vessel**, its complicated curvature can be traced
278, 279   back to a simple basic form, a square with sides of 8 cm. The slanting axle is the square's diagonal. The proportions of the vessel are harmonious, its volume being 24 cm³, i.e. a number divisible by eight. (In the first version these proportions had not yet been clear: with a height of 7.5 cm, and a volume of 27 cm³ the form seemed too elongated.) The functional aspects have been considered thoroughly in the design. The vessel is easy to hold, if it falls down it rolls on the earth but does not break. The nickel-plated cover does not allow the milk to spill if the bowl is overturned; its spring-actuated, removable structure makes cleaning easy. In short, it is hygienic.

The nursing vessel was designed for day nurseries, and in its aesthetic and functional planning the designer thought not only of the children but also of their nurses. Ten vessels
282, 283   can be placed in a **Wicker Tray** with compartments, which can be carried easily. Sotnikov himself made the wickerwork from golden yellow Indian cane. The colour and the texture of the materials constitute a harmonious contrast.

This careful designing of a dish-set for nurseries in 1930 was stimulated by social conditions in which the collective care of infants was imperative.

Another of Sotnikov's designs has been preserved: a **Teapot** without a handle – oval and
275–277   streamlined like the **Child's Nursing Vessel**. According to Khlebnikov, both forms are pleasant to hold in the hand. The grooved surfaces which replace the handles have very little heat conductivity: they rise from the curved form as reliefs, and conform to the movement of the human hand holding the teapot so that they constitute an asymmetrical holding surface for the thumb and the other four fingers. This produces a lively rhythm and a connection between the teapot's form and man's everyday activity. Sotnikov produced his porcelain objects in the spirit of material culture under Tatlin's direction. Weight, plasticity, materiality – qualities which are not appreciated in porcelain objects but very important in peasant pottery – had gained major aesthetic value in Sotnikov's works. He extended the range of the properties of porcelain as the traditional material of chinaware, and proved that
284   it was possible to model it as a sculpture. Characteristically, he did not join the two halves of the child's nursing vessel's mould vertically as usual but diagonally: i.e. he shaped the form containing the spout and the neck as one unit, and cut out the apertures later by hand. The white colour of porcelain acquired a special density and purity on the streamlined surfaces. By exploring the new, 'prosaic' possibilities of the material they invented the grooved holding surface cast together with the dish as a special 'porcelain construction'.[80]

Tatlin's experiments included working out porcelain forms which did not conduct heat. His methods differed from those used in Western experiments which, in the late 1930s, tried to achieve the same end by changing the chemical composition of the porcelain mass.

Kozhin was Tatlin's other pupil at the Ceramics Faculty.[81] Since 1938 he had also been
288   working in the porcelain factory of Dulevo. His so-called 'constructive' **Teapot** (also known as **Egg**, 1930) was made under Tatlin's direction and has been the subject of praise by

experts ever since. Kozhin's diploma work belongs to the line of Tatlin's dynamic, statuesque, streamlined dishes whose painting emphasizes and enhances the plasticity of their forms.

There were other bright students at the Ceramics Faculty who attended Tatlin's lectures at different periods, including Ginstling, Vasil'eva, Traskunov, Borkin and Derunov.[82] Some of them became sculptors,[83] others artists in the field of applied arts or ceramics. Of their works Borkin's **Shaving Kit** has been preserved: it is a two-part dish, one for hot water, the other for lather. Borkin's **Pepper Shaker**, dated 1930, has also been preserved: it demonstrates Tatlin's conception that an everyday object should be functional, statuesque in its form and represent some spontaneous idea. Already as far back as 1923 Tatlin emphasized in his lecture, 'Material Culture', that an object 'should be comfortable, durable, suitable to its purpose and also pleasing to the eye'.[84] By teaching this principle and implementing it in practice Tatlin had established in the 1920s a specific design that naturally embodied sculptural values. The objects produced under his direction are functional and satisfy demanding plastic-sculptural requirements: while reconciling the two these objects manifest countless individual ideas and playful associations. Naturally, artists always had to consider technological possibilities. Representation was not a requirement, but the forms had to be expressive in the sense of Tatlin's organic form-shaping principle.

286
287

Letatlin

Letatlin was Tatlin's last work as a designer. It has a special significance inasmuch as it is the quintessence and highest incarnation of his personality in a plastic work.

313–353

Letatlin was the design of an idea, a Utopian one at that, despite all the practical justifications, and one which, according to the practical outlook of contemporary Europe, would have been a senseless undertaking.

Letatlin was a bird-winged apparatus of the engineless glider type, an ornithopter (*ornis*: bird, *pteron*: wing). According to Tatlin's conception, man can fly with the help of his muscles, the flexibility of his body and the oscillating movement of the wings of his apparatus. Flying with it would have been like swimming in the air and would have to be learned in childhood just like swimming in water. The society using **Letatlin** would thus have to consist of strong, physically well-developed individuals.

Tatlin considered the construction of **Letatlin** a part of his programme for material culture like his designs for furniture, dresses or dishes. He thought it would be an 'everyday object' of the future communist way of life. This seemed quite natural in an age when Maiakovskii wrote his poem 'Flying Proletarian', a dream of the future new way of life. Tatlin amazed the writer Gladkov when he spoke of Khlebnikov's Utopian, futuristic fantasies as of the most natural everyday things. 'It seemed as if he were absolutely not interested whether the camp of Khlebnikov's followers grew or not... He considered Khlebnikov's every action and work as the most natural everyday events, and everything opposed to them seemed to him strange and eccentric.'[85]

Together with many of his Russian contemporaries, Tatlin lived the future in the present and tried to convert everybody to his ideas of the future.

In the early thirties when he was working on **Letatlin** many people believed that the distance between the present and the future could be overcome in one generation. There were people in every walk of life who were convinced that the speedy realization of the new air transport vehicle was a social and cultural need. These were Tatlin's followers who countered the arguments of the doubting Thomases. Tatlin's supporters were: Máté Zalka, a Hungarian, at the time leader of the Defence Section of the Writer's Union of the USSR; Vsevolod Vishnevskii, member of the Section; engineer Iurtsev, President of the All-Union Society of Inventors; Smirnov, who worked in the Moscow Metropolitan Council; the pilot Artseulov,[86] an enthusiastic advocate of gliding in the early thirties, and the leader of the section of 'flapping-wing flying' in the club of OSOAVIAKhIM.[87] Test pilots Khapov and

Nefedov and many others supported Tatlin's plan.[88] In 1932 and 1933 the model of **Letatlin** was shown not only at the exhibition of the State Museum of Fine Arts but also in several clubs including the Writer's Union and OSOAVIAKhIM. In the summer of 1933, at the Meeting of Glider Pilots of Moscow and the Moscow District, the model of **Letatlin**, covered with white silk, was taken to the airfield at the Pervomaiskaia (Skhodnia) station near Moscow. It was exhibited in 1934 in the section of inventions of the Polytechnical Museum of Moscow.

Tatlin intended to make his 'aerial bicycle' a consumer article: 'I chose the flying machine as an object for artistic construction because it is the most complicated dynamic material form which can enter into the daily lives of the Soviet masses as an object of widespread use.'[89]

Letatlin was intended as a prototype. According to Sotnikov, who had taken part in the work, the moulds needed for making the flexible wooden elements came from industry. Tatlin and his assistants[90] made three copies of the apparatus, foreseeing eventual mishaps during experiments; the total weight of the construction was 32 kg, the wing surface 12 m², with 8 kg load factor per one square metre. Naturally, manual processing and montage caused a few insignificant differences. In the 1932 exhibition of the State Museum of Fine Arts all three models were on show, two shrouded in white silk covers, the third without, and separately the wickerwork fuselage.

The flapping-wing construction was based on reproducing as accurately as possible the dynamic mechanics of the flight of birds. The proportion of the total weight of the apparatus and the weight of the wings was one to six; this ratio characterizes most birds. The principles of steering and functioning were described by the pilot Artseulov.[91]

As opposed to the rigid construction of engine-driven airplanes, **Letatlin** was built on the principle of elasticity. For the sake of the greatest possible elasticity, Tatlin shaped the main support of the wings from bentwood in the form of a figure eight with complicated curves, and glued whalebone to it for greater firmness. The figure eight, shaped as a double loop, which Tatlin had first used on his wooden sleigh, had an even greater application in this construction. In the period of the first achievements and successes of engine-powered airplanes, when records in height, distance and load-bearing followed one upon another, Tatlin thought that his elastic construction, quite alien to the spirit of the age, was indeed 'the most complicated form which meets the needs of the moment for man's mastery of space'.[92]

Tatlin studied birds for a long time and not for the sole purpose of reproducing the mechanism of their flying. The source of his flying apparatus was a detailed analysis of the wings of living birds which can change their form flexibly during flight, and of their chest and wishbones which function as brakes during their fall. In the mechanical structure of **Letatlin** he reproduced the form of birds' wings with artistic perfection as 'an organic natural phenomenon'. In reality the 'aerial bicycle' is an ethereal kinetic sculpture of wood permeated by space which triumphs over its own weight.

Tatlin had indeed created a homogeneous form which resembled natural forms. He followed his own principle proclaimed as early as 1919: the synthesis of the different branches of art. His assistants had been selected from the students of VKhUTEIN on the basis of this conception. So the collaborators on **Letatlin** included the monumentalist painter Pavil'onov, the sculptors Shchipitsyn and Zelenskii, and only one constructivist artist: Sotnikov.

Letatlin summed up Tatlin's experiences gathered during his experiments into the nature of materials, their functions and technical workability. The bending of wood, started in VKhUTEIN with the chair and the sleigh, reached professional perfection and sophistication in the work on **Letatlin**. He used a multitude of materials: ash, lime, vine, cork, silk cord, Duralumin, steel cable, whalebone, hide rope; their selection and combination were based on their inherent properties and adaptable functions within the construction.

The technical execution of such a grandiose construction never saw the light of day; it never got off the ground. In the professional literature the design for **Letatlin** has often been

332, 333
334
341–343

314, 315

335, 332

333

334

254

317
314
315

255, 254

considered a 'groundless Utopia'. Some argue that in the career of Tatlin, the 'father of Constructivism', and 'the most consistently logical designer of the twentieth century', **Letatlin** marked a decline and total failure. A narrowly technical interpretation of Tatlin's Constructivism in the 1920s contributed to this opinion, but inasmuch as it seeks to belittle the designer it is unacceptable. It is inadmissible also because facts prove that the idea of **Letatlin** was born much earlier than generally believed. Tatlin himself said that his consultants had been the surgeon Geintse and the pilot trainer Losev.[93] Maria Andreevna Geintse, Tatlin's wife and mother of his son Volodia, could only have helped to stuff birds and study their anatomy in the first half of the 1920s, in the years when the artist was principally concerned with interior decoration, dress design and dishes.[94] Late in 1924, or in 1925, Tatlin and Geintse divorced, moved apart and never met again.[95] The chronology of these events is confirmed by Tatlin's joking statement as quoted by Khodasevich in her memoirs. When Volodia, born in 1922, was still a baby, according to Khodasevich, 'Tatlin started to speak of the construction of the model of a flying structure which would be called **Letatlin** and tried out by his son Volodia as long as he was small enough and not too heavy.'[96] According to the writer Begicheva, between 1925 and 1927 theoretical and experimental work preparing the construction of the flying structure progressed at full speed at Tatlin's home in Kiev. Tatlin watched birds – he kept a stork – studied the laws of aerodynamics and the history of gliding. Without doubt this was the period when he became interested in Leonardo da Vinci who had also tried to construct a flying apparatus at the turn of the fifteenth and sixteenth centuries on the basis of the principle of birds' flight. On the wall of Tatlin's room in Kiev there was a death mask of Leonardo da Vinci and a plaster copy of the head of one of his angels.[97]

322–324

In Kiev Tatlin prepared the construction frame, the 'protomodel' of **Letatlin**; the then young Bazhan saw it in his home.[98] But the idea had been born much earlier.

'Tat[lin] took off in his flyer', wrote Khlebnikov as early as 1912 in his collection of new word coinages, where he suggested new Russian terms for the concepts connected with the upswing of the 'flying trade'.[99] In his 'Short Cathechism of Linguistic Neologisms' one must look for the etymological origin of the word 'letatlin' in models like 'flyer' (*letatel*), 'to fly' (*letat*), 'flying contraption' (*letalishche*). According to Khlebnikov's thesis on language, sounds and words are constructed from the 'alphabet of conceptual meanings'. Hence the word **Letatlin** is not the result of a combination but of an integration of two words: 'let' is the root of the verb to fly which is integrated with 'Tatlin' where the last 't' of 'let' merges into the first 't' of Tatlin and creates a radically new concept: **Letatlin**, the flying Tatlin. The new concept means victory over the force of gravity through rising, flying, i.e. it stands for the concept of self-powered movement.[100]

Tatlin and Khlebnikov probably met in the early 1910s; the first proof of their joint work stems from 1912 when Tatlin illustrated Khlebnikov's poem **Let Us Be as Merciless as Ostranitsa**. The poet and the painter were similarly attracted to each other. Khlebnikov was attracted by everything in Tatlin: his personality, his name, his paintings. He saw Tatlin's pictures at the exhibitions of the Union of Youth in 1911 and 1912, in Petrograd and Moscow respectively. Very probably Tatlin's pictures, together with other avant-garde works, inspired the famous sentence in the poet's early manifesto against Symbolism: 'We want words to follow painting boldly.'[101] The poet must also have been attracted by Tatlin's personality, his sailor's past, his skill in crafts, his musical talent and bandore playing. He sensed in him the active man who not only conceived ideas and talked of them but who materially created them in the three-dimensional world of objects. On the other hand, Khlebnikov's language-creating experiments, the spirit of his poetry, his futuristic ideas and fascinating forecasts about mankind's future became a source of inspiration for Tatlin's ideas.[102]

73

Tatlin put into practice Khlebnikov's thesis about 'astral language', the universal language of conceptual meanings whose alphabet should be constituted by plastic signs created by

216–222   art and understood by everybody. When he produced **Zangezi** he tried to ultimately har-
monize colour and plastic equivalents to the 'Astral Alphabet' in which the hero of the poem
expressed his thoughts. Indeed, Khlebnikov's idea that 'the language of stars was nothing
other than the names of the different types of space', 'a little dictionary of the spatial world',[103]
inspired Tatlin's entire work as a designer from the **Monument to the Third International**
to objects of everyday life.

225   Tatlin and Khlebnikov were linked by many inner structural ties and impulses travelling
in both directions. In 1915 Khlebnikov wrote his prose work **Houses and Us**, a vision of
tomorrow's architecture: flower houses, poplar houses, cup houses towering over meadows
and forests in a wholly preserved natural environment. The pure air is not polluted by petrol
vapour because the houses are peopled by 'winged inhabitants'. 'The city viewed from
above: it first reminds one of a curry-comb brush. Will the city of winged inhabitants also
be like this? Swarms of bird-people fluctuate in the streets which show off their roofs below,
instead of their walls. The roofs melt into the infinite blue, far removed from the filth of
dust-clouds... Having forgotten how to walk and never hearing the patter of the hooves of
fellow inhabitants the crowd has learned to flit above town!'[104]

In May 1916 Tatlin and Khlebnikov organized a joint evening programme in the House
of Science and Culture in Tsaritsyn. Khlebnikov's discourse, 'Cast-Iron Wings', was recited.
'The Days of Icarus, Cast-Iron Wings, Our Era, a Melting Furnace... Painting replaced by
Tatlin's and Bruni's laws of form and weight' – these were some major topics of the lecture
89   as they appeared on the poster.[105] In March 1916 Khlebnikov saw Tatlin's reliefs and
86–88   counter-reliefs at the Moscow exhibition The Store, and in December 1915 in Petrograd at
The Last Futurist Exhibition.[106] And it was in Tsaritsyn that Khlebnikov wrote a poem on
Tatlin; it was a poetic vision of Tatlin's bold plans.[107] The poem is a document of Khlebnikov's
faith in the realization of Tatlin's ideas since flying, as has already been mentioned, had been
a common interest since 1912.

Their relationship was closest between 1917 and 1919.[108] At the time of preparing the
227   journal **Internatsional Iskusstv**, Khlebnikov wrote his article 'The Artists of the World'[109]
to encourage Tatlin. It was, in fact, a call to create the universal 'astral language' by means
of fine art.

Tatlin surely knew Khlebnikov's Utopian ideas which called for the preservation of the
actual ecological balance of nature's flora and fauna and for the construction of buildings,
transport vehicles and objects of everyday use with the means of modern technology,
ensuring maximum comfort to man, and at the same time preserving the harmony of their
forms with the natural and human environment.

The idea of the winged 'aerial bicycle' had been maturing in Tatlin for almost two decades,
especially in that period when he designed 'practical' objects of everyday use.

Letatlin proved that Tatlin's idea of material culture was nothing less than the dream of
the unity of 'living objects', 'living technology' and 'living material' compatible with the
harmonious world of that 'second nature' outlined in Khlebnikov's Futurist Utopia.

Tatlin explained that he attributed great importance to creating organic forms because they
could serve as a starting-point for the new relationship between man and his everyday
objects.[110] **Letatlin** was the materialized symbol of this idea, of the unrelenting faith in the
future, in the humanization of technology.

Tatlin's design contradicted contemporary trends in the genre: his works were opposed
to that engineer-like purposefulness analogous with modernity and identified by public
opinion as Constructivism. The basic principle of his modernity was the organic: his furniture,
dress and dish designs, and his flying apparatus diverge from the machine-worshipping
principles of his age. Naturally, his work also contains elements conforming to some of the
common principles of contemporary international Constructivism, but mere practicality was
never Tatlin's first concern: his objects of everyday use had to serve the ideal of human
achievement, and at the same time be practical. Tatlin criticized that 'Constructivism' in

inverted commas which, owing to 'mechanically applying technology', had become a tendency of style throughout Europe in the 1920s.[111] Constructivism is not a style but a method, and as such, has played an important part in Russian art since the 1910s when its problems led from painting to the construction of objects. In the early 1920s Tatlin considered this meaning of Constructivism synonymous with material culture. Although he accepted the label Constructivist attributed to him in the international world of art because he considered himself the founder of that tendency, he himself preferred the term material culture to describe the essence of his work. 'Against the old artistic thinking it is necessary to set the new form: material culture', he wrote in 1930.[112]

'Art into Life' was Tatlin's programmatic slogan, which defined the concept of Constructivism as the social organizing principle of the life of man.

Notes

1 For help in writing this work and finding material and information hitherto unknown or little known, the author thanks the artist A.N. Korsakova, the sculptors A.G. Sotnikov, E.M. Ginstling and V.I. Derunov; V.E. Tatlin's nephew, S.S. Tatlin; the art historian I.N. Punina; M.V. Petrova, head of the Fine Art Archive of the Bakhrushin Museum; the research officer of TsGALI Z.P. Mellit, and the literary critic A.E. Parnis.

2 *See*, e.g., Bibliog.: Strigalev, 'On a Conception,' 1978, p. 30.

3 The exact dating of the report – 1923 – was established on the basis of the number of Sundays by a special periodic table. Contemporary reflections confirm this dating. *See* next note.

4 *See* Bibliog.: Miklashevskii, 1924, p. 60. Written on 28 August 1923. Reference to Tatlin's paper, 'Down with Tatlinism'.

5 *See* 'Tatlin at Exhibitions', p. 494; c 'Supernarrative', p. 397.

6 Here one can trace certain connections with the programmatical document of IZO Narkompros, one of whose leaders was Tatlin: namely, 'The Position of the Department of Fine Arts and Applied Arts on the Question of Artistic Culture'. ('Положение отдела изобразительного искусства и художественной промышленности по вопросу о художественной культуре', *Искусство коммуны*, 16 Febr. 1919.) The ideas of this document became one of the theoretical foundations for the establishment of GINKhUK. In this document, among the elements of artistic culture, material was the first to be named as a means of creating forms.

7 'My Answer', p. 185; 'Tatlin' and commentaries, pp. 331–3.

8 'Slogans', p. 244.

9 'A New Art Teaching', p. 339.

10 *See* the commentaries 'The draft', 'Compared', p. 332.

11 *See* the text on the poster about 'The Exhibition of a Model of the Projected Monument' in the 'SVOMAS Building (former Academy of Arts) in the Studio of Material, Volume and Construction of Professor Tatlin', open from 8 Nov. to 1 Dec. 1920.

12 *See also* 'Report', p. 250; commentaries on 'To the Museums', p. 242.

13 The meeting took place under the chairmanship of Lapshin, with Tyrsa and Tatlin present. Malevich was introduced as a new director.

14 We quote the record in full. LGALI, fond 4340, inventory 1, unit 18, p. 13. This account in many respects served as the basis of the plan for research of the Section for Material Culture in 1924–5. *See* 'Research', p. 254.

15 'Report ... for 1924', p. 256.

16 *See* Shklovskii, 'On *Faktura*', p. 341.

17 The flat looked on to the yard of the VKhUTEMAS-VKhUTEIN building in Miasnitskaia Street, today Kirov Street.

18 One of the panels was fixed to the wall, the other was suspended. As the words were on two planes, the slogan could be read both as isolated words and as a statement. The brownish red letters were in sharp contrast to the richly shaded light red background. The sumptuous colours were achieved by the use of *levkas* (gum paint), an old primer of icons. The letters seemed to be burnt into the texture of the boards.

19 The greyish blue letters were on an ivory white background. The panel was fixed by a special bracing wire over the entrance to the staircase of the belfry of the Novodevichii Convent, leading to Tatlin's 12 m high studio. The icon technique of the panel symbolized the synthesis of handicraft and industrial design.

20 *See* Strigalev, p. 26.

21 It was not Tatlin's last designing work, though the period was marked by his 'return to painting' (*see* Kut, p. 312) and an intensive involvement in the theatre. He drew up standard designs for shops (III. 289) and for the pavilion of animal husbandry at the Exhibition of Economic Achievement (VDNKh), 1930. There is evidence that in 1941 the artist worked on the camouflage of Moscow. After the war he offered his design for a motorcar workshop to the Artistic Fund. The painter Labas, a friend of Tatlin's, who lived next door to him after the war, remembers having seen a drawing-book full of sketches and designs for the workshop. (Information Labas)

22 The sketch referred to was the tsarevich's costume for the production of the Russian folk drama *Tsar Maximilian and his Disobedient Son, Adolf*.

See also Syrkina, p. 155. Taking as model an India ink drawing, *Fisher Lad* (*c.* 1912, III. 30), Tatlin started to make but did not finish another sketch for the plate in 1919.

23 *See* c 'Material form', p. 266; Strigalev, p. 24.

24 Н. Пунин, 'Коммунизм и футуризм', *Искусство коммуны*, 30 March 1919, p. 3; 'On "Zangezi"', p. 395; Б. Арватов, 'Футуризм как социальное явление', in: *Об агитационном и продуктивном искусстве*, Москва, 1930, p. 47.

25 'On "Zangezi"', p. 248.

26 Apparently, this refers to the permanent exhibition in the show-room of the Section for Material Culture, in which individual exhibits were occasionally changed.

27 В. Хлебников, 'Зангези'. 'Введение'. In: *Собрание произведений*, Ленинград, 1931, p. 317.
The supernarrative was finally arranged from pieces on 16 January 1922. *See* Syrkina, p. 160; 'About "Zangezi"', p. 395; c 'Supernarrative', p. 397; 'On "Zangezi"', and commentaries, p. 248.

28 'On "Zangezi"', p. 248. Tatlin put in inverted commas Khlebnikov's thesis as paraphrased and developed by him.

29 Ю. Тынянов, 'Архаисты и новаторы', in: *Сборник статей о поэзии Ю. Тынянова*, 1929.

30 On Tatlin's course in the Metal Department of the Faculty of Woodworking and Metalworking, *see* Bibliog.: Khan-Magomedov, 1977, pp. 35–7.

31 TsGALI, fond 681, inventory 3, unit 114, p. 119.

32 *See* the minutes of the discussion of Tatlin's course, 'Material culture', at a meeting of the art subjects commission of the Faculty in Oct.-Nov. 1928.Протоколы обсуждения курса В.Е. Татлина 'Материальная культура' на заседании Художественно-предметной комиссии Дерметфака ВХУТЕИНа в октябре-ноябре 1928 г.TsGALI, fond 681, inventory 3, unit 231, pp. 237-8. In this period the disciplines of colour (Klutsis) and volume (Lamtsov) were taken from the third course.

33 'The Initiative Individual', p. 238.

34 '…at the meeting dedicated to B. Kushner's report on the engineer's place in production, B. Arvatov took part in the discussion and reported: … the painter and master of the corner and central counter-relief Tatlin appealed in Petrograd to the engineers of the Mechanical Engineers' Trust for permission to enter the factories to teach young people and workers in the factory schools the subject of material design. The engineers did not understand the proposal and in turn proposed to Tatlin that he go to the technical bureau where the draughtsmen work, so that Tatlin, the artist, could teach them to draw beautifully.' 'В ИНХУКе', Художники и производство, *Вестник искусств*, 1922, no. 5, p. 26.
Tatlin's attempt reflected the Constructivist painter's endeavour to help develop industry. The programme was proclaimed by INKhUK in late 1921 or early 1922. (Tatlin was a corresponding member of the Moscow INKhUK.) (*See* n78 on p. 41.) Arvatov, a theorist of production art, promoted Tatlin to first place among the artists of this group. Tatlin, considering himself the leader in the movement, accepted the term Constructivism created by his young followers in INKhUK. *See* 'Autobiography', p. 264; 'Art into', and its commentaries, pp. 310–12.
He accepted the role which the theorists of production art ascribed to him. For this period one can assume not only the closeness of the concepts material culture and Constructivism but also material culture and production art.

35 *See* Bibliog.: Mikhlashevskii, 1924, p. 66.

36 Invitations to Tatlin's lecture, 'Material Culture and its Role in the Life and Industry of the Soviet Union', were distributed along with agitative leaflets, which were signed by members of the Group for Material Culture, May–June 1924. TsGAOR, fond 2555, inventory 1, unit 647, p. 160.

37 В Ленинградский Отдел Главнауки, June 1924, TsGAOR, fond 2555, inventory 1, unit 647, p. 177; *see also* 'To the Leningrad', p. 252.

38 Bibliog.: Punin, 9 March. 1919.

39 'The Artist', p. 266.

40 *See* pp. 266, 267.

41 'The New Way', p. 407.

42 Information from S.S. Tatlin. He lived with his uncle in an apartment located in a back wing of the Academy of Arts in Petrograd in 1920–1. Khodasevich tells in her memoirs how once, dropping in on Tatlin in the apartment in the GINKhUK-Museum of Artistic Culture building (1 Poch-tamtskaia, now Soiuz sviazi Street), she found him building a stove. (*See* Bibliog.: Khodasevich, 1957–70, p. 12.) Tatlin moved to this apartment in 1922 or 1923 and lived there until the autumn of 1925. The known documents indicate that Tatlin worked on stoves in 1923–4. (*See* 'Report', p. 250; 'The New Way', p. 407.) If S.S. Tatlin is not mistaken, this work began earlier, but originally the artist did not attach any professional significance to it.

43 'Routine', p. 403.

44 Malevich emphasized the artistic character of the form of Tatlin's domestic stove and considered this work as 'an exceptionally important fact' from the point of view of involving the artist-painter in the organization of the everyday environment. 'Конструктивная живопись русских художников и конструктивизм', *Новая генерация*, 1929, no. 8, p. 51. Ill. 13 of the journal shows the same stove as the journal *Krasnaia panorama* (because of the carelessness of the editors, printed upside down); and it is dated 1924 according to the date of publication.

45 'Research Plan', p. 254.

46 'Report', p. 250.

47 Punin, Tatlin, p. 347; c 'Body painting', p. 393.

48 'Report', p. 250.

49 'The Artist', p. 266.

50 One can in hindsight see a connection between this 'daubing' work and those colour experiments which Tatlin carried out for the performance of *Zangezi*. 'The experiments he carries out in his studio by "daubing" boards ("The Astral Alphabet" in the performance of *Zangezi*) were actually outstanding works on paint as a material. At first glance this work is simple, but anyone who has worked on paint, and has an educated eye for material, knows that it is difficult: the transformation of raw "tube" paint into a processed, long-acting lively colour without losing the essence of the paint itself…' *See* Bibliog.: Punin, 29 May 1923.

51 Rogozhin, a student of Tatlin, in the autumn of 1927 when Tatlin began to work at VKhUTEIN, was apparently in his first year, since by 1930 he was in his third. TsGALI, fond 681, inventory 3, unit 231, p. 125.

52 A photograph of the chair was exhibited in 1968 in the Museum of Decorative Art in Paris. (In the catalogue, *Les Assises du siège contemporain*, Paris, 1968, no. 278.) A model of Tatlin's chair was first displayed in London in 1971 at the exhibition Art in Revolution. (*See* Tatlin at Exhibitions, p. 500.) The reconstruction is now on show in a permanent exhibition on the history of design in Centre Georges Pompidou in Paris. The artist Solopov and the mechanic Pavlov also made a reconstruction of the chair for Tatlin's 1977 Moscow exhibition. They used Rodchenko's photograph.

53 The photograph first published in: *Архитектура и строительство Москвы*, 1929, no. 10, 1929, p. 10.

54 'The Artist', p. 266. Lobov erroneously named beech as the material of Tatlin's cantilevered chair. М.П. Лобов, 'Мебель факультета по обработке дерева и металлов ВХУТЕИНа', *Архитектура и строительство Москвы*, no. 10, 1929, p. 10.

55 Models of the Viennese chairs were exhibited at the First International Industrial Exhibition in 1851 at the Crystal Palace in London and were awarded a medal of honour. In the twentieth century production was renewed by the Thonet brothers at their factory in Frankenberg. Here, along with traditional bentwood chairs, they turned out the first examples of chairs made from bent metal tubes which became part of contemporary classical design.

56 This feature is not considered in the reconstruction of the chair.

57 'The Artist', p. 266.

58 Ibid., p. 267.
59 *See* Даркин, 'О мебели', *Бригада художников*, no. 1, 1932, p. 22.

A reconstruction of Tatlin's chair in the authentic material, maple wood, does not exist at the present time.
60 Alvar Aalto visited the Bauhaus in Dessau and the exhibition of contemporary dwellings in Stuttgart at the beginning of 1928. While criticizing the standard metal furniture of the Bauhaus masters from the point of view of the material, the Finnish architect-designer highly appreciated its practicality in a technical and constructive sense.
61 In 1925 Tatlin became a member of the council on standard clothing in the Leningrad Institute of Applied Arts. LGALI, fond 3035, inventory 1, unit 27, p. 18.
62 'The New Way', p. 407.

One can suppose that this coat was approved for the development of the new form of normal clothing by the commission of experts of the Leningrad Clothing Manufacturers' Trust. An extract from the minutes of a meeting of this commission, held on 12 April 1924, has been preserved (Korsakova's Collection, Moscow). No data on the manufacture of this model have been discovered.
63 The same model of the coat has been copied and enlarged on tracing-paper as a pattern, apparently by some of Tatlin's students (*en face* and from the back). In this transfer drawing some details are omitted and there is a mistake: the figure on the left is depicted from the back and the legs are copied from the sketch *en face*.
64 The inscription continues: 'Pattern and model produced in the Institute of Applied Arts.'
65 Let us also recall that the comparison of the finished model with the preceding one became one of the productive principles of the contemporary designing methods. It was interpreted by Tatlin as such in the work programmes of the Section for Material Culture (1923–5). (*See* 'Summary', p. 249; 'Research Plan', p. 254).
66 N. Lindinger, 'Designgeschichte', *Form*, no. 26–7–8, 1964; no. 30. 1965.
67 Н.П. Ламанова, 'О современном костюме', *Красная нива*, no. 27, 1924, p. 662.

Nadezhda Petrovna Lamanova (1861–1941): obtained professional training in Suvorova's cutting and sewing course in Moscow. Was organizer and manager of the workshop of contemporary suits in IZO Narkompros and IZO Glavnauka, 1919–20. From 1901 to the end of her life she worked in the costume workshop of MKhAT on theatrical costumes. *See* Т.А. Стриженова, '*Из истории советского костюма*', Москва, 1972.
68 Ламанова, op. cit.
69 This refers to Maiakovskii's poem '150,000,000', which was written by him in the name of 150,000,000 (then the population of Russia) and not signed.
70 Н.Н. Пунин, Искусство и революция, manuscript, p. 78. (Archive Punin family, Leningrad).
71 *See* Bibliog.: Isakov, 1923, p. 2; Punin, 29 May 1923.
72 In 1971 at the Museum of Decorative Art in Paris an exhibition, 'Work Clothing', took place, which was appraised by critics as a revolution in fashion. 'Work clothing has come into fashion, fashion has taken possession of work clothing.' (Dominique Dupré and Gilles de Bur, 'Le vêtement fonctionnel', *Cree*, no. 2, 1971, 5 pp. 50–3.) The authors note that high-quality reforms in clothing occur when they touch on men's suits. It is noteworthy that Tatlin was the only Soviet artist engaged in designing clothes in the first half of the 1920s to give preference to men's suits.
73 Besides Tatlin, the head, the following people worked in the Section for Material Culture: Khapaev, Nekrasov, Kholodov, Kobelev, Zheltikov, Sakovich and Korotkov. It is

difficult to establish which of them carried out the sketches for dishes.
74 The drawing is not dated by the author. However, reference to the china in documents of the Section for Material Culture relates to 1923.
75 Tatlin's work with students continued for some time in the Institute of Silicates (1920–3), where the Faculty of Ceramics was moved after the break-up of VKhUTEIN.
76 Aleksei Georgievich Sotnikov, named first by Tatlin in the list of his students (*see* 'Curriculum Vitae', p. 325), is a Soviet sculptor-potter and Honoured Art Worker of the RSFSR. Born in 1904 in the Kuban in a peasant family; 1925–8: studied at the Krasnodar Art Technical College; 1928–30: Ceramics Faculty of VKhUTEIN; 1930–2: worked with Tatlin on *Letatlin* at the Scientific Experimental Laboratory. From 1934 to the present: sculptor of the Dulevo Porcelain Factory, with a spell in the Army in the war years. Sotnikov's works of animal sculpture, especially birds, are widely known. Worthy of attention is his design of a 40 m steel sculpture of a bird, recently interpreted as a design for a monument on the theme 'Preservation of Nature', 1940, whose erection was planned on a highway in the open steppe. Sotnikov's sculpture is regularly exhibited at Soviet and international exhibitions. (А.Г. Сотников, Catalogue, Москва, 1976.) *See also* 'Сотников', in: В.А. Тиханова, *Скульпторы-анималисты Москвы*, Москва, 1969.
77 *Художники об искусстве керамики*, Москва, 1971, p. 241.
78 The students' difficulties in communicating with Tatlin gave rise among them to a kind of legend. The sculptor Derunov told the author about one incident connected with the task of making a china device for shaving. Tatlin supposedly instructed the students to make a vessel for drinking and for shaving at the same time. Baffled, a student asked: 'Why? There is a glass suitable for both.' Tatlin replied: 'And so Khlebnikov said: I can! am able, shall, (*ia mogu! mogei, ia mogeiu*), that is, he pronounced Zangezi's monologue on man's omnipotence.' Then the students, confused, got down to work.
79 The Ceramics Faculty had daily relations with that factory as the students learned practical skills there.
80 According to Sotnikov's testimony, about one hundred nursing vessels were cast at Dulevo and two holders were made. (Only two old nursing vessels have come to light.) About ten teapots were moulded and fired in a muffle oven in the ceramic workshop of VKhUTEIN. (Not preserved.)

In 1978 Sotnikov reconstructed the authorized version of the teapot and straw holder with ten nursing vessels. They were displayed at the Group Exhibition of the Works of Moscow Artists in 1979 in Moscow. The complexity of reconstructing models of dishes created almost half a century ago is indicated by the dissimilarity of the new teapot model to the original, known from an old photograph. The reconstructed one is larger in size, more static and bears the stamp of Sotnikov's reconciliation with old Russian ceramics in 1930–40.
81 Pavel Mikhailovich Kozhin (1904–75): sculptor-porcelain specialist. Graduated from the Faculty of Ceramics of VKhUTEIN (1926–31); belonged to that last course of the Faculty of Ceramics who graduated in 1931 after the break-up of VKhUTEIN; managed the ceramics laboratory of the Institute of Handicraft Industry in 1932–3, then worked in the porcelain factory at Verbilki; from 1938 he worked in the Dulevo porcelain factory. Named by Tatlin in the list of students. 'Curriculum Vitae', p. 325; about Kozhin *see* Л.А. Крамаренко, *Павел Михайлович Кожин*, Москва, 1958; 'Кожин' in: В.А. Тиханова, op. cit. [n76] pp. 204–312.
82 Esfir' Mikhailovna Ginstling (born 1904): master craftswoman of ceramics, Honoured Art Worker of the RSFSR; Zoia Vasil'evna Vasil'eva; Aron Borisovich Traskunov

(1908–77): sculptor; Vasilii Vasil'evich Borkin: sculptor; Vladimir Ivanovich Derunov (1908–79): sculptor. At the beginning of February 1930 Derunov was accepted into VKhUTEIN on the special recommendation of the Iaroslavl' Artistic Technical College, where he began his education. Under Tatlin's supervision he studied for one semester and went on to practise at the Dulevo Porcelain Factory. Then he studied at the Faculty of Sculpture of the Academy of Arts (end of 1930–36).

83 *See* n76, 78.

84 *See* Bibliog.: Miklashevskii, 1924, p. 60.

85 Е. Гладков, 'О.В. Татлине', in: Книга воспоминаний (manuscript), private collection, Moscow.

86 *See also* Artseulov, 'About *Letatlin*', commentaries, pp. 408–9.

87 OSOAVIAKhIM: Society for the Promotion of Defence and Aero-Chemical Development. Its stern name notwithstanding, it was a benevolent civilian society for aviation and navigation. The society was popular in the 1930s.

88 Artseulov, Khapov and Nefedov came out with their memoirs about the creation and tests of the flying machine at the discussion of the exhibition of Tatlin in the Fadeev Writers' Hall, on 25 February 1977.

89 'Art into', p. 311.

90 Tatlin himself, besides Sotnikov, named Pavil'onov among his assistants working on *Letatlin*. *See* 'Art into', p. 311.

Georgii Sergeevich Pavil'onov (1907–37): between 1926 and 1930 studied at the Department of Monumental Painting at the Faculty of Painting of VKhUTEIN; 1930–2: worked with Tatlin on the flying machine; from 1934 worked in the team of young 'artist-monumentalists', directed by Favorskii.

91 *See* p. 408.

92 'Art into', p. 311.

93 Ibid.

94 'Report', p. 254.

95 Tatlin's wife, who worked as a doctor in a small town near Arzamas, died in 1927 saving a baby from diphtheria.

96 *See* Bibliog.: Khodasevich, 1957–70, p. 14.

97 А. Бегічева, 'Комісар Наркомпроса', *Вітчізна*, no. 2, 1969, pp. 159–170.

98 Here is how Bazhan, a renowned Ukrainian poet, tells about this in a letter to the author on 26 June 1980: 'Semenko told me about Tatlin and about his *Letatlin*, and invited us to visit, to get acquainted and talk about joint work. We arrived. The large room was cluttered with printing machines, sketching tables, bamboo canes bound and supplied with tennis balls where they were fastened. This strange construction exactly like the skeleton of some pterodactyl was indeed the famous *Letatlin*.'

The joint work referred to was as follows: Н. Семенко, Г. Шкурупий, М. Бажан, Зустріч на перехрест, Кіев, 1927.Tatlin designed the book. (Ill. 293) *See* Zhadova, p. 130.

99 The short line in quotations, 'Tat(lin) took off in his *letocha*', (an anapaest) represents a line of an unwritten poem. (В. Хлебников,'Образчик словоновшеств в языке', in: *Пощечина общественному вкусу*, Москва, 1912; В. Хлебников, *Собрание произведений*, Ленинград, 1933, vol. V, p. 255.)

100 The sound 'L' with which the word Letatlin begins was very often discussed and used poetically by Khlebnikov, and moreover in all cases it corresponds to the image or concept of bright, honest, liberating, positively acting forces such as the image of *libertas* and love. The sound 'T' in Khlebnikov's interpretation conflicts with 'L' and bears the sense of weight, gravity, immobility and passivity. 'Художники мира', in: Хлебников, *Собрание произведений*, 1933, vol. V, pp. 218–9; 'Изберем два слова', *see* Bibliog.: Khlebnikov, 1940, pp. 325–9.'

101 'Мы хотим девы слова...' in: Bibliog.: Khlebnikov, 1940, p. 334.

102 *See also* 'Tatlin' and commentaries, pp. 336–8; с 'The meeting of Tatlin and Khlebnikov', p. 396; for *budetlianism* see Strigalev, p. 15.

103 В. Хлебников, 'Художники мира', in: В. Хлебников, *Собрание произведений*, Ленинград,1933, vol. V, p. 219.

The 'Astral Language' is set forth in many articles and interpreted in the poet's artistic works beginning from 1912 right up to 1922. For example, to the sound 'L' corresponds the colour white and a geometrically dynamic 'flying' structure, a 'formation of a two-dimensional body from a three-dimensional one'. (Ibid,. vol. V, p. 218.) The sound 'T' spatially and geometrically denotes 'the negative path of movement induced by the shadow of an invisible point', ('Словарь звездного языка', 'Царапина на небе', vol. III, pp. 376–7; 'Мы и дома, мы и улице-творцы', pp. 276–7.)

104 This work is dated 1915 by Khardzhiev, *see* Bibliog.: Khlebnikov, 1940, p. 412.

105 By courtesy of Parnis.

106 *See* 'Tatlin at Exhibitions', p. 492.

107 'Tatlin', p. 336; *see also* Bibliog.: Petrovskii, 1923.

108 Strigalev, pp. 15, 16; Syrkina, p. 160.

109 В. Хлебников, 'Художники мира', in: *Собрание произведений*, Ленинград,1933, vol. V, pp. 216–9.

110 'The Problem', p. 267.

111 *See* 'Art into', p. 310; n48 for Strigalev, p. 40.

112 'The Problem', p. 268.

Flora Iakovlevna Syrkina
TATLIN'S THEATRE

At one point in his turbulent youth, Tatlin worked as an assistant in the décor workshop of the Moscow Solodovnikov Opera. Ever since that time he felt drawn to the magical world of the theatre.[1] The reason for this was not only that in the first decade of the century Russian theatre attracted the most talented composers, poets and visual artists and thus became the product of their creative co-operation. Tatlin also discovered that because of its synthetic nature it was the theatre, more than any other art form, which was capable of achieving a true unity between life and art: between aesthetic values and social and political issues.

Tatlin became a set and costume designer in 1911. This was the golden age of the World of Art circle, whose members enjoyed their greatest successes in the productions of Diaghilev's company, which brought world-wide recognition for Russian stage-design. It was around this time that painters belonging to the World of Art circle started working for the Moscow Art Academic Theatre and also for the Theatre of Antiquity,[2] where certain forms of acting, stemming from the Middle Ages, were used in order to reintroduce forgotten stage techniques. This was one of the reasons, presumably, why the Moscow Literary and Artistic Circle decided to stage the Russian popular play from the eighteenth century, **Tsar Maximilian and his Disobedient Son, Adolf**. The production was directed by Bonch-Tomashevskii, who was, though an amateur artist, a well-known personality of the Russian theatrical scene after the turn of the century. He himself adapted the popular play for this production and organized the theatrical company 'Tragical Popular Farce'. Tatlin was invited to design the scenery and the costumes. The première took place in October 1911.[3]

38–41

The eighteenth-century play **Tsar Maximilian and his Disobedient Son, Adolf** must have been one of the favourites of Russian popular theatre. This is suggested by the fact that at the beginning of the twentieth century there were no fewer than nineteen versions of the play in manuscript form, all about the fatal conflict between Peter I and his son, the Tsarevich Aleksei. In the Russian popular play, the historical subject-matter was turned into a fairy-tale: apart from Tsar Maximilian and his son Adolf, there were the Goddess Venus, King Mamai, a hangman called Brambeus and numerous other characters from other artistic genres, including Death as an old woman. Both the farcical and tragic twists take on fantastic and exhilarating dimensions in this Russian popular *commedia dell'arte* which pokes fun at the Tsar and makes him pay for his cruel ways.

In Bonch-Tomashevskii's adaptation the historical thread was almost entirely lost. The principal aim of the play became mere fooling around in a coarse, market-place style; in this the principal characters, the pagan Venus, the son of Venus, the grave-diggers and the fools all made a great deal of noise. One can get an idea of the set and the costumes only from a few sketches which have survived.[4] It has been said that Tatlin's set consisted exclusively of painted screens, but one need only look at one of the sketches to see that this is wrong. The sketch shows the throne-room of the royal court. Three steps lead to a platform on top of which sits Maximilian, with his courtiers standing on the second and bottom steps. It is obvious, therefore, that there were not only painted but constructed elements of scenery on stage. The platform could not possibly have been a painted one; it must have been made out of real timber, surrounded by tall screens with tiny windows in them, fairly high up.[5] The steps leading to the platform were covered by two mats (either painted or real) each showing a tree with a dense crown. (Had the steps been painted, the outlines of the trees could not have been broken by the angles of the steps.) The painted backdrop shows the low, broad tower of a palace, decorated with colourful flowers. From both sides of the stage, from high

40

38

up, two huge, bewhiskered wild cats stand 'as if ready to jump', as though to complete this symmetrical, heraldic composition. The painted central arch must have been cut through in order to create a hump-backed platform with stairs leading to it, on top of which was the throne where Maximilian sat between two guards.

36   In Tatlin's design-sketches, reminiscent of miniatures sold in market-places, every motif derives from popular farce: the clumsily carpentered platform, the position of the steps leading to the throne, the painting of the sets, in a word the whole simplistic approach. We have no information about whether all this was in fact realized on stage or not. According to a review of the production, a platform was in fact erected on stage.[6] The article also indicates that the production, so far as the direction was concerned, was quite weak. Another article points out that: 'There was a lot of bustle, noise and colour; it was an expensive, very meticulous, externally good production ... But all its superficial "thoroughness", all its colourful details brought together piece by piece, could not cover over the poverty and insubstantiality of the action itself.'[7]

Tatlin, while making the sets and the costumes for **Tsar Maximilian**, used much of the style both of the design and the text of Russian miniatures on sale in the market-place. These pictures were characterized by an unrepeatable synthesis of impudence, vulgarity of expression

39   and moral purity. One of the costume sketches shows Tsar Maximilian as a Russian peasant with a ginger beard being shorn 'under an earthenware pot': clad in a Russian peasant shirt, with underpants made of a printed material and a pair of white felt boots. He is a typical popular comic figure, a parody of the Tsar, with the suggestion that he puts his royal garments simply on top of his everyday peasant clothes. On his head he wears a 'home-made' crown of horns, on his shoulders a stiff, orange-coloured cloak (orange meant to imitate gold) out of which bundles of black cotton stick out instead of ermine tails. Round his belly there is a wide, bluish-black belt with a huge star indicating some order, and his felt boots too are decorated. The costume is clearly of an improvised character. All the costumes were designed in this spirit.

This was Tatlin's first job as a set and costume designer in which, independently from the World of Art artists (the dictators of stage design at that time), he discovered the parodic nature of the sets and costumes used in popular acting; he even underlined their clumsiness. Tatlin's début took place in the same year that Benois arrived at the summit of his career as a stage designer, completing the setting for Stravinsky's **Petrushka**,[8] in which he evoked the world of popular carnival entertainment with a fine sense of aestheticism. And yet it was not from Benois that Goncharova took her inspiration when in 1914 she was given the task, at his recommendation, of designing the sets and costumes for Rimskii-Korsakov's **The**

37   **Golden Cockerel** for the Diaghilev company. One might also assume that it was Tatlin's opposition to the World of Art's tendency towards stylization that led Goncharova to set free

36   her own true temperament as a painter and to transfer the originality and irony of Russian popular woodcuts to her stage designs for the professional theatre.[9]

Tatlin's first experiment in the theatre was well received, yet he himself was disappointed. We assume that he was happy with the sets, carried out by his painter friends, but he was certainly very unhappy with the badly executed costumes, which hardly resembled his designs. In the end he broke off all contact with Bonch-Tomashevskii's Tragical Popular Farce company. He wrote about this in the press, too, following an article about the production which had been illustrated with his costume designs.[10]

His love for the theatre, however, remained unscathed. At the same time as he was experimenting with counter-reliefs he was working on a stage version of Glinka's historical

137–155   opera **Ivan Susanin (A Life for the Tsar)**.

We do not know whether Tatlin had a contract to work on the design for the opera. Probably not. At any rate, no such document has been found so far. He probably chose Glinka's opera himself (staged at that time according to the official, pro-monarchy ideology) but in 1913–14 he discovered in it the same Russian popular theme. Tatlin acted both as scenic artist and director while designing Glinka's opera. Not all the set and costume designs have survived, but the ones that are known manage to present a clear picture of Tatlin's concept as designer-director. He interpreted the opera as a popular tragedy with Ivan Susanin, the folk hero, as its central figure, in exactly the same spirit as the opera has been played since the Revolution in Soviet theatres under the title **Ivan Susanin**. This is quite obvious from Tatlin's actual design sketches: the inhabitants of the village of Domnino, the folk heroes and the crowd in the finale were given much greater emphasis, whereas the boyars, the Tsar's bodyguard and the *strel'tsy* were portrayed ironically.[11] The setting, too, was presented in an entirely new, visually unorthodox way. The first act is set in the village of Domnino, where the protagonist of the opera lives with his family and which is invaded by Polish soldiers. In the theatre of the nineteenth and the beginning of the twentieth century scenes of this kind were realized with cloth-screens, with varying degrees of verisimilitude depending on the talent of the painter. Tatlin interpreted them very differently. In accordance with the spirit of his counter-reliefs, he elaborated the flat surface of the sketch as a three-dimensional composition. Instead of painted screens, two simple wooden huts resting on ochre-coloured wooden platforms framed the stage. Stage left was Susanin's free-standing hut; stage right, taking up a somewhat smaller space, part of a two-storeyed wooden house could be seen. The porch roof was extended, so that it could be used as another level of action. All along the back of the stage there was a building in light colours, behind which, framed by the blue-black sky, stretched triangles and parallelograms of greenish-yellow roofs above the walls of hardly distinguishable buildings. Despite the heavily symbolic visual presentation, the place of action was accurately determined by the carved window frames and the porch roof. At the same time the roofs and the tense rhythm of the strongly geometric architecture (all in colours ranging between ochre brown, blue, green and black) evoked a tragic atmosphere for the two figures clad in peasant clothes in front of Susanin's house.

141–153

137

This sketch is, in all probability, one of the first Cubo-Futurist stage designs,[12] which later became a tendency on the stage of the Moscow Kamernyi Theatre with Alexandra Exter's collaboration.

Somewhat different in approach, not so close to Cubism and yet still following the system of forms Tatlin devised, was the design for the impenetrable forest of Kostroma, to which Susanin led the troops of the enemy, sacrificing his own life. This set evokes both Tatlin's earlier works and future ones. The way the tree-trunks bend down forming an oval shape is reminiscent of the nude compositions and of the principles of icon painting involved in them.[13] At the same time there is a motif that points forwards to **Zangezi**: the tree-trunk with thorny branches. This, one might say, is the forerunner of the pine-tree in **Zangezi**, the mast in **The Flying Dutchman**, and the bare tree in **A Comic Actor of the 17th Century**. An even more striking similarity can be discovered between the arched, Gothic forms of King Sigismund's throne-room and the compositional principle of Tatlin's **Nudes**. The challenge to explore space even further impelled Tatlin to find new solutions. The throne-room is an obvious transition between the intellectual and practical inquiry into the **Nudes** and the painterly and counter-reliefs.[14]

139

76–79

216–222
163
354–355
138
76–79

One can assume that the setting for the second act, the throne-room in King Sigismund's old Polish castle, venue for the ball, was to have had free-standing sets. This is indicated by the sketch, which shows tall columns by the footlights instead of screens and the outlines of a three-dimensional Gothic interior in the background. The soft ochre tone suggests that this set must also have been made of wood.

138

Tatlin resolved the set for Act IV again in his own way. According to the libretto the first scene of Act IV takes place 'By the gate leading to the Red Square', with the finale 'On the Red Square.' Tatlin wrote on the back of the sketch for this act: 'At the Spassky Gate', or 'To the Spassky Gate', 'To the Entrance'. Yet on the actual sketch there is neither the well-known picture of the Red Square, nor the Kremlin walls, nor the Spassky Tower. Instead, the festivities take place in a composite image of Russian architecture, which includes interior and façade at the same time. Tatlin took the white stone walls, columns,

140

stairs and gateways, now blackened with soot, and united them with the ochre of the arches, which were decorated like the Granovitaia Palace with crimson, brown, black, sky-blue, vermilion and umber-coloured foliated scrolls, leaves and flowers. In front of this solemn and strict background the masses of people clad in white, and the bodyguards dressed in black, white and red, must have stood out with particular beauty. The dominant lines again reveal the strong compositional principle of the **Nudes**, while also reminding one of the principles of Russian icon painting. This work, however, also made it possible for Tatlin to 'step out' – at least potentially – into concrete space and to think in terms of different materials: bringing his stage design close to his counter-reliefs.

The composition is characterized by a specific perception of matter and space which does not, however, merely define a real location. It is composed in the language of plastic values without illustrative references. Thus decorative motifs taken from folklore do not limit the range of associations: they rather help to expand it.

By concentrating so strongly on the expressive power inherent in architectonic proportions, on the language of the materials he used and on the effects of different *fakturas*, Tatlin rethought the possibilities for staging classical operas. He turned the characters into prototypes. Looking at the design sketches, one can see that Tatlin divided the players into two groups: on the one side were the people and on the other those in power. The shapes and forms of the people's costumes do not vary significantly throughout the scenes, although certain changes, marking one occasion or another, do gain some impact. The costumes worn at home in the village were simpler, those worn in Moscow more festive. The basic material for those playing the people was white linen.

In 1885 Vasnetsov designed the famous sets and costumes for Rimskii-Korsakov's **The Snow Maiden**, produced by Mamontov's company. He was the first designer to dress the peasant choir in white, handwoven linen decorated with real embroidery, appliqué[15] and printed patterns. Tatlin used the same linen and embroidery on his costumes in a different way. His costumes were more generalized, more monumental. They reminded one of stone buildings and were decorated in such a way as to have a kind of constructed 'ornamental layer'. A choir of such figures was to sound forth in triumphant celebration at the Spassky Gate. In the shining whiteness of this victorious festival Tatlin had only Antonida, in mourning for her heroic father, dressed in black.

Tatlin obviously consulted icon paintings before designing his costumes: local colours, flat surfaces, the emphasizing of silhouettes, the treatment of folds in the garments – all point in that direction. Without stylization, he fell back on the traditions of Russian painting in order to express more exactly the characteristic silhouettes, gestures and rhythms of the figures in their costumes. Thus, he was able to stress Antonida's timid, sad gesture, Vania's adolescent clumsiness, the majestic bearing of the marching bodyguards, the haughtiness of the aggressive *strel'tsy*, the cautious steps of the stealthy boyar.

In Tatlin's designs the basic shape and cut of each costume are precisely shown. The talent of the future dress designer is already apparent here. And yet, in the years of their creation and first appearance at exhibitions and in the papers, Tatlin's designs were met – as were the designs for **Tsar Maximilian** too – with a total lack of understanding by theatre-historians, critics and other theatrical experts. Drizen, who, it seems, had a particularly refined theatrical taste, wrote about Tatlin's designs for **Tsar Maximilian**: 'I can picture the face of the dressmaker who receives Mr Tatlin's costume designs for **Tsar Maximilian**. What can be done with them? How does one turn these little lines into something tangible without any guidelines whatever on the final execution of the costumes? Or does the artist's task stop at sketchily drawn ideas and all the rest, all the details, are up to the wardrobe-department to rack their brains about?'[16] The costumes for **Ivan Susanin** were received with similar lack of understanding. This time it was such an expert in theatrical design as Efros himself who spoke out against Tatlin. He was of the opinion that Tatlin's costume designs could not be realized on stage and the paradoxical expression he invented for them was 'untheatrical

142, 143
145–148
150, 151

140
145, 154

146, 154
141, 149

theatricality'.[17] Efros failed to recognize the white linen costumes of the peasant choir in the apparently 'bodiless' whiteness of the paper and the drawing. A few years later, however, he would understand and praise Alexandra Exter's designs for the Kamernyi Theatre, which were inspired by Tatlin's. These costume designs prove not only Tatlin's gift as a theatrical artist but also that he was a true director as well, inasmuch as he could interpret a play independently and give the characters an emphasis that deviated from the conventional view, building scenery to support his interpretation.

Tatlin's second venture into the theatre did, however, also earn some positive notices.

The author of one of the reviews, for instance – unlike Efros, a militant defender of the young designer Tatlin – pointed out the novelty in the set and costume designs:

Tatlin interprets the theatre in a very daring and individual way ... the set and costume sketches for **A Life for the Tsar** are among the most interesting designs in the theatre for the last few years. It is astounding that there is no theatre which would actually want to use these designs or which would commission the young and talented artist to design some new production. ... At the risk of challenging the authority of certain dictators of scenic design I would even venture to suggest that in Tatlin's sketches ... there is ultimately more subtlety in the use of colours, sensitivity to popular decorative art, more resourcefulness in the application of architectural forms, than in any one of Korovin's works.[18]

No more of Tatlin's stage-designs were realized before the Revolution. True, in 1911 Meierkhol'd, having seen potential in Tatlin's work, invited him to design the sets and costumes for his film based on Sologub's **Spectral Charms**, a gloomy, mystical novel. 'That thing, gloomy and mystical through and through, was deeply foreign to me even then', wrote Tatlin years later.[19] This comment suggests that the Russian 'modern style' fashionable just after the turn of the century (a specifically Russian version of the European Art Nouveau, to which Meierkhol'd also subscribed) was decisively rejected by Tatlin. Remembering his meeting with Meierkhol'd Tatlin notes, not without irony, that instead of the mystical 'strange tree' he was supposed to design, 'I built a huge ship's mast with all the proper nautical attachments – rigging and observation towers. Clamber up the mast, up the tree, that is, play to your heart's content. But when Meierkhol'd saw my tree-mast he was horrified.'[20] This then marked the end of their collaboration. What Tatlin tried to prove when offering Meierkhol'd a mast instead of a tree is obvious. This was his way of radically rejecting Sologub's script: the expression of his protest against the purely illustrative films made at that time. It was this that he countered with the perfection he so much admired in the strict, rational forms of a ship's rigging. We must however add that the Soviet writer Danin[21] gives a slightly different account of this incident in his memoirs about Tatlin. As a student during the second half of the 1930s, Danin was an enthusiastic admirer of the artist, and they often met. The story Tatlin must have told his young friend probably took place in the earliest stage of the above-mentioned unhappy collaboration. Meierkhol'd – according to Tatlin – 'asked me to draw for him a grove ... Sologub's young heroes ... were supposed to hang out there, telling each other whatever they had to tell each other. I on the other hand drew a tree ... In a grove there is no harmony ... Vsevolod [Meierkhol'd] said he wasn't happy with this solution. I replied that I could not oblige with a grove. He then replied that he would not accept my tree ... I then said that my tree was a hundred times better than any grove could ever be. He then started to scream and shout about my messing up his conception! Why, you think a painter has no concept?! – said I.' It is very likely that the always stubborn Meierkhol'd then demanded that the stubborn painter come up with a different tree 'more mysterious and mystical', more suitable for Sologub's decadent play. And this is, presumably, when the shocking mast-tree was conceived. A few versions of the sketches have been found.[22] There is one with a huge, crownless and barkless tree with straining, muscular branches, and another which is geometric, resembling a mast. 'Presumably', writes Danin, comparing Tatlin's own words with the interview given to **Sovetskoe Iskusstvo**, 'the grove-version was already a simplified one, like the mast-version, only from a different point of view. The grove was the start, the mast the finish.' Besides other valuable information in Danin's memoirs, it is of particular interest that Tatlin says he does not perceive the same harmony in a grove he does in one single tree. This is a good example of Tatlin's determined search for plasticity of form and volumetric harmony, whether in painting, counter-relief or stage design.

156–163 In 1915–18 Tatlin worked, without a commission, on the costume and set designs for **The Flying Dutchman**, from an artist's and director's point of view. His imagination was stirred by this opera by the young Wagner (conceived while he was still under the influence of Beethoven), especially since Tatlin as a young man had travelled the sea for several years and knew the power of the elements and the heroism of the humans subjected to it. During 163 the search for documentation on this subject, large sheets of tracing-paper were discovered on which Tatlin had tried out variations of drawings of masts, rigging, observation towers, different decks, sails: sloping slightly, sometimes in harsh lighting, sometimes in soft. Some of the drawings depict the different planes of the decks and huge fragments of the sides of the ship. The sloping and shifting vertical lines cannot be contained within the limits of the paper, giving an idea of their great height; similarly, one can almost feel the motion of the waves by looking at the angle at which the masses of the deck meet the horizon. These motifs are also recognizable in the final version of the set design, which Tatlin painted on a 156, 157 horizontal canvas taking into account the proportions of the stage. The Cubo-Futurist set was built out of yellowish-grey timbers which gave the impression that the deck had gone through a violent shipwreck disaster; above it were sloping, silvery masts, yellowish-black hanging sails, and huge masses of blue-black sea and sky. The tempest was created by a rhythmical whirlpool of waves which constantly unbalanced the ship and which the sloping, almost horizontal masts could no longer keep in control. The sharp contrast of a leaden-blue with yellowish and greyish-black shadows suggests a tempest at sea with its thunder and lightning. It is therefore the material concreteness that lifts the vision of a ship in distress out of the local sphere to a level where the individual drama – the tragedy – gains momentum 158–162 as part of an abstract controlling principle. The costumes are designed as rhythmically as the sets. The huge figure of the helmsman wears a massive dark robe, long boots and hat. His 159 body and the steering-wheel build one single complex. Here the structure of the costumes for both the seamen and the nuns is different from the conception Tatlin employed when working on **Ivan Susanin**. This time, Tatlin stressed first and foremost the weight and volume of the forms. The black, white, light-blue and ochre colours of the costumes stand out sharply and the characters fit well into the massive, gloomy colour scheme of the sets.

The materials for **The Flying Dutchman** set were to be concrete materials: Tatlin had particular plans for the colour and *faktura* of the wood, the ropes and the wires he meant to use. Unfortunately, he was unable to turn this project into reality.

During the years preceding the Revolution, only one of his three designs completed during seven years of theatrical work was used on stage.

A greater part of his work for the theatre was yet to come.

Shortly after the Revolution it was his collaboration with Khlebnikov that, after his earlier experiments, provided the impetus for theatrical work and brought him the project for 216–222 **Zangezi**. Their friendship had taken root presumably as early as 1916. According to a 207 manuscript found during research for this article, dated 2 November 1917 (old style: a few days after the Revolution, that is), Khlebnikov and Tatlin together prepared a production. Author and director was Khlebnikov, set and costume designer was Tatlin.

The 'artistic collective' apparently consisted of thirteen actors and actresses, none of them professionals but rather amateurs and students. Khlebnikov gave the production the title **Selection of Objects**, and it was to consist of three pieces by himself: **Death's Error**, **Madame Lenin** and **Thirteen in the Air**.[23] According to Khardzhiev, the project was cancelled.[24] Apart from the above-mentioned document, no other references or set designs have been found. And yet these facts, however slight, are significant inasmuch as they establish Tatlin's and Khlebnikov's theatrical collaboration in 1917. Whatever the fate of this production, the preparations for it probably gave Tatlin the first impulse to search for a clear idiom of form that would correspond with Khlebnikov's poetic language.

When in 1923, a year after Khlebnikov's death, Tatlin decided to stage **Zangezi** posthumously, it had already been sufficiently prepared for a scenic realization.

216–222

Zangezi is Khlebnikov's last work. His dream about the future of mankind takes shape above all in daring word-creations. The poet uses the words of the philosopher and prophet Zangezi to open up, for the benefit of ignorant people, the secrets of the universe, nature and society, with the help of a 'universal language' comprehensible to everyone. The scene of the action is accurately described by the author, so accurately that it may very well have been an actual place. There are 'mountains', there are 'slopes dense with conifers', a tall 'pine tree that covers part of the rock' and 'black stones'. But the language of the description is packed with unusual images. 'A rough, steep rock, resembling a needle under a magnifying glass. The rock stands among steeply sloping stones which have been grown over by forests, like a shepherd's crook resting against a wall. It is connected to the main stone by a bridge formed by a landslide falling upon it like a straw-hat. The area on the bridge is Zangezi's favourite place. From among the roots the main stone appears in black layers. A tall pine tree, blazing with the violent blue waves of its foliage … The roots twist in knots where the angles of stone books stick through … the road of the weeping night. Living black stones stand between the stumps like threatening bodies of giants going off to war.'[25]

The description is very suggestive, characterized by images of material constructivism; the rough, steep, lonely rock; the needle and shepherd's crook; the square formed by the bridge; the straw hat on the needle; the waves of foliage; the black layers of stone; the angles of stone books: this was sufficient for the artist to determine a strictly metaphoric language for the design. And then there is the dramatic poem itself, which the author called a supernarrative (*sverkhpovest'*)[26] meaning 'architecture made of stories' while a story is 'architecture made of words'. The architectonic strictness of the work's structure, the visual architectural character of the word-creations, the perfection of *faktura*, helped the artist to create a form of correspondences among the objects. 'Parallel to the word structure', Tatlin declared, 'I decided to introduce a material construction.'[27]

The set for the production did not gain its final shape for some time. In one of the first sketches – discovered while researching archives for the present paper – Tatlin partly returned to the composition principle of **The Flying Dutchman**: on top of a huge, sloping mast he placed the needle-sharp points of branches. Zangezi was to stand behind this on a platform formed by the capital of a solid column. This was designed to stand stage left. The wide, bow-like span of a bridge was to take up the centre and right of the stage, supported by another column on that side. The ropes hanging from the bridge were presumably meant to symbolize roots. Evidently Tatlin was eager to integrate his construction organically into the interior of the house where the production was to take place.

219

Another pencil sketch shows an almost symmetrical construction. Tatlin erected three tree-trunk masts, one on each side of the wings and one in front of the backdrop, which as we saw, consisted of differently levelled steps. Corresponding to the one which is placed stage left in the foreground, there is a stretched parallelepiped on the right. On the most sloping 'mast' further back to the right (two figures, presumably from the cast, sit under it) is a pointed branch ending in a thin, living pine-twig. An arrow shows the direction in which it is moving. In the background is part of a 'mast' which is bent down like a fallen tree. Above it there comes unexpectedly into a composition which has so far consisted of volumes and flat surfaces, a real window frame and, in the foreground, another real object: a little cage. But this sketch was not carried out either, although some details were used by the scenographer. The model that was eventually made shows significant changes in the concept: Tatlin used more simple, flat surfaces instead of three-dimensional forms. He put up three

220

216

screens in the wings, three on each side of the stage. Instead of a backdrop three surfaces of different sizes were constructed. The two most important constructed elements of the set were placed centre-stage front.

213
215   A photograph of the production, as well as Lapshin's print **The Production of Zangezi** and a drawing in a newspaper which accompanied Tufanov's article,[28] show that the set eventually used was much better than any of the previous sketches. As it happened, the play
209, 210   was not produced in the theatre but in the assembly room of the Museum of Painterly Culture, in a realistic space that is, so that its architectural components – marble columns and buttresses – became part of the set.

The high, arched ceiling of the room made it possible to utilize its height more than anything else. Compared with the earlier sketches the stage was now more centred, had more a vertical character which in turn emphasized the central part of the set. A parallelepiped, cylinder and blocks led up tier upon tier to Zangezi's platform, as in the construction of the
213, 214   **Monument to the Third International**. This is clearly visible both in the print and in the photograph. From the inclining top of the rock a number of ropes dangled down, and there were surfaces with texts written on them.

Regrettably, it is very hard for us today to define the nature of materials and textures Tatlin used for the set. The same applies to the stage machinery used to set the stage in motion. The poster for the production, which the author discovered during the preparations for the
211   1977 Tatlin exhibition in Moscow, reads:

The Museum of Artistic Culture
No 9 Isaakievskaia Square
presents the production on
Wednesday   30th May of
KHLEBNIKOV'S
POEM
ZANGEZI
directed by the constructor TATLIN
participants are:
MACHINES, PEOPLE, A PROJECTOR
Tickets are available from No 9 Isaakievskaia Square between 12 noon and 4 p.m.

We have no information about the nature of the above-mentioned machines. As to one of the materials used for the preparation of the set, the artist's nephew, S.S. Tatlin, supplied a valuable piece of information that part of the set was covered in tree bark. This is not at
220   all unlikely and is confirmed by the sketch with the window frame and the birdcage. The side verticals of the foreground and background, and part of an apparently fallen pine-tree, which lay under the window frame, were not completely sketched in in the corners. On the left-hand side of the sheet one can read in the artist's handwriting an abbreviated form of the words 'tree bark'. As we know, Tatlin interpreted Zangezi's speech as 'a slowly moving ray, as it were, from the thinker to the uncomprehending crowd',[29] as a ray of light in the realm of darkness in the strictest sense of the word. The photograph, the print and the drawing
214, 213   illustrating Tufanov's article all show Tatlin in the role of Zangezi, sitting on the top of the
215   construction; people turn towards him from down below.

The projector, too, had an important role to play as a means of enhancing and concentrating the plot; the constantly moving shadows it threw made the action more dynamic. The
213   same spotlight served, presumably, to enliven the texture of the materials. On the print one can see the sources of this theatrical light positioned off stage: at about the level of the floorboards and a little higher.

The production of **Zangezi**, for which Tatlin was director, set and costume designer, and principal actor, was put on by the Experimental Amateur Theatre of the Museum of Artistic

Culture, in the Isaakievskaia Square in Petrograd. The players were painters and students of the Academy of Arts, the University and the Practical Technological Institute, as in the first but unrealized version directed by Khlebnikov himself. 'This is intentional', said Tatlin, justifying his choice; 'professional actors have been brought up in the traditions both of the old and of the contemporary theatre. **Zangezi** is something too new to be subjected to existing traditions, whatever they are.'[30]

The majority of the actors wore daytime clothes, with the exception of those playing the characters of 'Repentance' and 'Laughter'. The existing costume-designs[31] are, in line with the spirit of the sets, symbolic and Constructivist in their execution. The actors' faces were covered by masks. 'Repentance's' mask was a triangle pointing downwards without either nose or mouth, the eyes were holes densely lined with black circles: resembling a tragic gasmask. The front of the costume was a wooden board covering the whole body except for the bare legs. Tatlin reinterpreted 'Repentance's' words from Khlebnikov's poem 'There is sorrow in every piece of wood'. He wrote this on the sheet with the costume design and even underlined it. The bare legs of the figure symbolized the poverty of a beggar, the board a coffin-lid and the gasmask the symbol of war.

221, 222

'Laughter's' mask was a cylinder rounded at both ends, the openings for the eyes were two straight lines, the 'stubby' nose formed a perfect triangle and its laughing mouth a wide semicircle. The design corresponded only partly with Khlebnikov's description and characterization:

> I am a jolly glutton, stout and round,
> a sponge and drain for anger – I'm Laughter...[32]

Tatlin's 'Laughter' wore a white shirt, black trousers, a belt and bast shoes like a peasant. The figure is drawn as a construction depicting the 'hammer and sickle', with the head-mask forming a part of this emblem. 'Laughter' was the opposite of 'Repentance', thus symbolizing 'Happiness', which had become associated with the concept of Soviet rule.

Tatlin, in embodying 'Laughter' in the form of an anthropomorphic emblem, was following the spirit in which the poems of Khlebnikov's final creative period were conceived. Perhaps the poem entitled 'Hammer' also influenced Tatlin in his use of the hammer and sickle emblem for 'Laughter's' costume, especially since in the poet's mind dead metal can turn into a living body and soul:

> ... the effort of ores,
> re-incarnated iron sheets
> with iron beams
> becoming gentle and bold boys,
> bad egg or blockhead
> slowly, one rebellious piece of iron hair after the other
> an iron bulge on his dark paunch ...[33]

'Laughter' corresponded with a shield hung up high in the room on which was written 'CCCP' (USSR). According to one critic and eyewitness, Tufanov, 'On the stage there are machines, a stage-light and a tower for the hero of the poem **Zangezi**. In the middle of the stage there is a board inscribed "people", while at the far end of the hall above the audience similar boards say "birds" and "gods".' Just before the final curtain 'a canvas unfolds above the stage with the inscription: 28 June 1922; the date of Velemir Khlebnikov's death'.[34] This suggests that to a certain extent at least the production could be regarded as an animated, theatrical poster. The performance '... opens with a choral song of the birds... and a song of the gods'. Later Punin interrupted the action: standing on a platform, he commented on Khlebnikov's poetic word-creation. After that the thread of the plot was taken up again with the 'astral songs', Zangezi's anthem, followed by folk scenes, turbulent and wild expressions of joy on hearing the 'astral language'. The participation of a choir, the interpretation of the poem's text and the music which accompanied the performance (written especially for **Zangezi** by the young composer Druskin): all this partly connects the production to the forms of popular plays.

216–222 **Zangezi** was performed three times: on 11, 13 and 30 May 1923. Opinions varied: Punin praised it, Iutkevich poked fun at it, while Tufanov, a guardian of purity of style, objected to the fact that 'Repentance' and 'Laughter' were portrayed by living people and criticized Tatlin for borrowing the 'ecstatic character'[35] from 'ancient acting techniques'.

One thing is certain though: no other contemporary work of art ever achieved such a perfect harmony of literary and visual Constructivism. In **Zangezi** sight and text fully corresponded.

Zangezi was Tatlin's last Constructivist piece for the theatre.

We know little about Tatlin's other designs for the theatre in the 1920s, immediately after **Zangezi**. There is a brief newspaper notice from 1925 saying that Tatlin was working on the sets for Jules Romains's **Cromedeyre-le-Vieil** at the Gor'kii Dramatic Theatre in Leningrad.[36] But there is no trace of this play in the repertoire of that theatre, which means that it was not put on after all. There is another small notice in a newspaper in 1926, mentioning that Gzhitskii's play **At Dawn (In the Footsteps of the Stars)** was staged at the Kiev State Children's Theatre with sets and costumes designed by Tatlin.[37] Tatlin also designed the sets for **Bum and Iula**, based on Hans Andersen's fairy-tale, for the same theatre.[38] The production was directed by the talented Kozhich.

Not one of the sketches for these plays has turned up to this date. Presumably the artist himself did not attach much importance to them since he did not include them in any of the lists he compiled of his works for the theatre.[39]

After the 1923 **Zangezi** production, the next entry in his list is **A Comic Actor of the 17th Century**, staged twelve years later in 1935. Even if we count the set designs he did between 1925 and 1926, there is still a great gap in Tatlin's theatrical work.

The years between 1926 and 1935 saw great changes in the Soviet theatre. In stage design, Constructivism was replaced by easel painting, whose representatives were organized in the Society for Easel Painting (OST).[40] These artists set out to achieve the effects of painting on stage. Such naturalistic tendencies in set design were inevitably counter-productive for the development of the theatre as a whole.

354–368 In 1935 Tatlin was invited to design the sets and costumes for Ostrovskii's comedy **A Comic Actor of the 17th Century**. The play is about the birth of the Russian professional theatre, where the first actors worked in an atmosphere of ignorance, prejudice and general hostility. The author set the theme within the framework of a love story and used a great deal of illustrative detail from everyday life; neither the theatre itself, nor actors working in it, were shown.

The artistic directors of the Second Moscow Art Academic Theatre, under Bersenev's leadership, were concerned first and foremost to portray the birth of Russian acting at the time of the first Romanovs,[41] a period in history 'when the true genius of the people struggled with the grey mediocrity of the official world'.[42] The directors, Gurov and Ermilov, tried to neutralize the genre-type character of the play in order to emphasize the satirical character of the plot. The theatre commissioned Vasilii Kamenskii to write a prologue, an interlude and an epilogue to the play. These were to help the audience identify with the atmosphere of first rehearsals and first nights, of the training and acting of the inexperienced young lads who were collected by the Tsar's command for Gregori's troupe.[43]

So another stage action was incorporated into the actual plot, a primitive passion-play from the seventeenth century. It was the dramatization of the biblical story of Adam and Eve, performed by the first Russian professional theatre company. The characters in the play were: God, the Serpent, Angels, Adam and Eve, plus a Highwayman and a Hangman.

When the question arose who should be commissioned to design the sets the choice, according to Bersenev, 'fell on the painter Tatlin because he is on principle an enemy of all genre-types and Naturalism'.[44]

Tatlin, as set and costume designer, always saw many different layers of interpretation in a play. He first read it through to try to understand the author's basic conception. He was happy to work on a play by Ostrovskii. 'The play itself captivated me', he wrote. 'In designing it I made up my mind to emphasize the bigotry and niggardliness – those distinguishing features so vividly depicted by the great dramatist.'[45] He interpreted his set and costume designs symbolically, avoiding Naturalism and letting the humour and satire prevail. In his theatrical work Tatlin was eager to find the materials best suited to evoke the required image. In the case of **A Comic Actor** he thought the most appropriate was wicker, as used in the complicated structure of garden fences, frames, baskets and mats. According to Müller, who had only recently been appointed chief of the production department, a cartful of wicker arrived at the theatre's storehouse on Tatlin's orders. When Tatlin found out, however, that some of the wicker had been used in the production[46] before **A Comic Actor** for some bridge railings, he refused categorically to use this material, saying: 'The wicker has already been used, I need something else.'[47] He was eager to achieve an unusual visual effect, something that would stir the imagination of the spectators. At the same time he insisted on using natural products. This meant that it had to be wood once again, and Tatlin perhaps recalled the wooden structures he had worked out for earlier unusual designs, such as those for the village of Domnino in **Ivan Susanin**. 'At that time', said Tatlin, 'Moscow was almost entirely wooden, only the churches perhaps were of stone, and that not always. So wood is the main material element in the production's design.'[48]

This was neither the first nor the last time in Tatlin's theatrical practice that he fell back on one of his earlier experiments. Despite the originality of his constructive solution for **A Comic Actor**, it was organically related to the set of the village of Domnino, as it was to **Zangezi** and **The Flying Dutchman**. The model, and later the set, for **A Comic Actor of the 17th Century** was made of plywood. While working on the model Müller recalls,

216–222
354–359

Tatlin fell in love not only with the form but also with the material. I remember once… Tatlin complaining that he could not fit one component of the plywood set into the basic construction… at that time I was not familiar with Tatlin's constructive devices… so I advised him to do it with a piece of string. 'How can you say such a thing', Tatlin exclaimed. 'Why, a piece of string is an alien form!' It was then that I realized that analysing and connecting different objects into a perfect whole was for Tatlin a science, not being studied by any institute or laboratory at that time. Then I suddenly recalled the exhibitions organized by Dobychina's Artistic Bureau[49] on the Field of Mars, where Tatlin demonstrated his constructions…[50]

These recollections by one of the senior personalities of the Soviet theatre deserve our attention. Tatlin's abstract, self-standing paintings and counter-reliefs gained a definite, utilitarian character in his scenic concepts. We only need to remember those exercises he introduced to his students at the Faculty of Drama, Cinema and Photography of the Kiev College of Art in 1928: he suggested they try compositions based on a circle, organizing shapes in space in such a way that each component would be interdependent on the adjacent one and, when set in motion, would 'flow' organically into the other. In 1935 Tatlin built a set on a circle. It was rather fantastic and symbolical, but it was a homogeneous and concrete architectural construction. He fastened plywood planks onto a frame around a 12-metre-diameter stage platform, creating a many-faceted stereoscopic construction which revealed the interior of a hut, a hillock in front of the hut in the form of a ramp descending to the edge of the revolving stage, a room with another stage for the mystery play, and a courtyard with a high, covered porch. At the bottom of the ramp, next to a fence, there stood a bare tree with only one branch and a little box for starlings. Had it not been for these two

129, 130

354
356–359

small details, one could have taken the tree for a mast. But most of all, the tree resembled the drawing of the pine-tree in one of the early sketches for **Zangezi**. In this tree there was also a hidden mechanical device which Tatlin saved for the final scene.

It is characteristic that in almost every one of his theatrical projects Tatlin completed and solidified his scenic composition with a tall, vertical element: sometimes a mast, sometimes a tree or a tower of some sort. This feature determined the basic rhythm of his stage constructions.

Tatlin was very particular about the development of the stage action in time and space, designing the spatial environment in close harmony with the above. The accelerated rhythm of the script for **A Comic Actor**, for instance, gave Tatlin the idea of putting on stage a homogeneous composition built on a revolving platform which made instant scene-shifting possible: every turn gave the audience a different setting. This sort of set design meant that Tatlin intruded on the actual directing – by moving the circle he was able either to bring the action close to the footlights or to remove it to the back of the stage. The actors no longer needed to sit and wait inside a defined space but could be shown walking to the required position. This in turn led to a new type of behaviour by actors on stage, with some unexpected effects on their 'body language'.

Tatlin consciously worked on introducing cinematographic effects to the stage. In his own words, '…the artist… tries to make a static theatre setting, even one like a pavilion, as dynamic and mobile as possible, to create action on stage on many planes, to make the scenery have something of the mobility and "flow" of a cinema film.'[51] Tatlin therefore attempted to transfer to the stage the possibilities already inherent in the cinema, which offered more scope for variety. He attempted to turn the stage into a space which could incorporate the dynamic changes the cinema offered with its close-ups and medium-shots. His sets built in the form of a circle did not follow the traditional pavilion shape but were built on the principle of the motion picture frame. They were similar to motion pictures in that Tatlin, in fixing the place of action on one point of a circle, considered that it could be seen equally from every angle in the auditorium as in the cinema. At the same time the

356   intentionally traditional character of the stage remained intact. In the final scene the young comedians were seated one behind the other on the sloping ramp as though it were a boat. With long sticks they gave a parody of rowing, as if performing the traditional popular farce **The Boat** – while the construction was set in motion and they were 'carried' upstage. The simple, mechanized branch of the tree waved them cordially good-bye.

In **A Comic Actor** there was no painted scenery. Tatlin had this to say on the subject: 'True to my principles of working with material, I naturally avoid backdrops and other painted scenery. Construction is the basic principle of design, in close relationship, however, with other design elements, lighting in particular.'[52] Thus outside the round construction the stage was draped with cloth curtains. Instead of wings there were parts of houses made of plywood. At the back, stage right, a fraction above the main scenery, stood a model of Ivan the Great's Bell-tower, a reminder of where the action took place.

The fact that Tatlin had chosen the material most appropriate for the play did not mean he had already made a final decision on the textures and colours for the production. In the

354   case of **A Comic Actor** he found it necessary to work further on the surface texture of the plywood. For the roofs and fences he used sheets of it, inside the hut he mounted the wood in horizontal strips reminiscent of beams. These variations of rhythm were also emphasized by variations of colour. He stained the roofs, the house and living-room walls, and the porch to make them look old, as if stained by time. The new rehearsal area for the comedians retained its light colour, a visual contrast between the young Russian theatre and the old city of Moscow. A further variation on the texture of the plywood was provided by rustic pieces of furniture, carved out of pine and treated with a blowpipe to bring out even more strongly the pattern in the wood. The props consisted of wooden pots and pans, icons, towels and a sheepskin coat turned inside out, placed on the bed. According to Müller, 'Tatlin was so successful in evoking the atmosphere of a peasant hut that there seemed to be a smell of rye

bread in the auditorium.'[53] In the rehearsal scene of the comedians, the picture of the seventeenth-century stage was just as evocative of the improvisatory character of the popular theatre. To accompany the scene which showed the Garden of Eden at the moment of Eve's temptation, Tatlin designed a Tree of Knowledge. Its trunk consisted of barrels of different sizes piled on top of one another; its foliage was represented by six ordinary brooms sticking out of the top one. An appropriate addition to this ironic treatment was a Serpent-Devil, wearing boots on his hands and feet, dragging a whip-like tail behind him. Eve was dressed in man's trousers and a Russian shirt, on top of which artificial breasts were fastened.

368

In designing the costumes Tatlin used his old method once again. First he created the images for the characters by determining their personalities, outer appearances, their place in the action and in the setting. At the same time, he was also interested in individual, personal characteristics, an interest he also showed towards his models in his later period of painting and drawing. He drew sketches of every actor, fixing their gestures, facial expressions, the movements of their eyes. He also drew whole scenes with groups of actors. He often developed personal contacts with them.[54]

360–368

Apart from their actual purpose, these sketches may be seen as works of art in their own right. The brilliantly depicted characters helped the actors not only to see themselves in make-up and costume, but also to find how to behave on stage. Bersenev had a very high regard for Tatlin's role in the production in which, after all, both the director and the actors were very young: '... the artist succeeded in creating a remarkable unity of scenic architecture, presenting a unified artistic image of the seventeenth-century, wooden Russia ... he staged a production in which the right combination of theatricality and realistic acting dominated.'[55]

The same year, 1935, Tatlin designed the sets and costumes for another play. Still vivid in everyone's memory was the alarming news of the shipwrecked *Cheliuskin*, trapped and crushed in the ice of the North Pole: of the heroic survival attempt by members of the expedition, of the camp they improvised on top of an iceblock, and the airplanes which eventually came to their rescue. It was now that Tairov put on the play **Let us not Surrender**. The story was written by Semenov, one of the members of the *Cheliuskin* expedition. During these years the Moscow Kamernyi Theatre was particularly preoccupied with the creation of the genre of 'heroic theatre'. Vishnevskii's **An Optimistic Tragedy** had just opened there for the first time with Constructivist designs by Ryndin. Tairov invited Tatlin to design the new play presumably because he saw in his work an emphasis on three-dimensional solutions making good use of space, which was close to the theatre's own ideas. Tatlin accepted the invitation. He was drawn by the prospect of returning to the sea, even if only to a theatrical version of it. He was looking forward to constructing the sinking ship and the ice floe. He was still very much a seaman and a constructor. On the basis of the available sketches we can guess at the main principles behind the 1935 production.[56] The audience could see only part of the ship's dark silhouette against the background of the polar twilight. This made the ship appear enormous. At first the action takes place on the deck and in the cabins (Tatlin built a number of small interiors in the ship's side, which were illuminated as necessary), then on top of a single, slightly sloping block of ice. Tatlin designed this so that it would wobble, by using a counter-balance. He was eager to show the audience the real danger these heroes were subjected to, the uncertainty of their fate on top of the drifting, fragile ice floe. This of course called for a new approach from the actors too. As it happened, members of the expedition, some of whom acted as advisors during the preparation for the production, did not agree with this solution, saying that the ice was in fact quite stable. 'To be true to life', said Tatlin not without bitterness, 'we had to renounce such an artistic image.'[57] Still, with the help of the excellent lighting equipment, the pride of the Kamernyi Theatre, Tatlin was able to evoke on stage a cold chiaroscuro, the gloomy, stern horizon, and the bare colours of the northern night. The play was taken off quite soon, partly because of weaknesses in its dramatic structure, partly because of its superfluous documentary character, which weakened its artistic authenticity on stage.

Tatlin returned to the subject of the sea four years later during his work for the Moscow
Theatre of the Lensovet (Leningrad Municipal Soviet). Shtein's **Kronshtadt (Spring of '21)**, an historical drama about the Revolution, was directed in 1939 by Plotnikov.

Its subject is the suppression of the white guards' revolt in Kronshtadt. The stage equipment was less than adequate to cope with the number of scene changes: from the battleship *Sevastopol'* to the fragile surface of the spring ice, the flat of the Baroness Wilcken, the Nikolaevskii station, the room of the communist sailor and the headquarters of the revolutionary command, etc. There was no revolving stage. How could one change the scenes quickly? Tatlin had no choice but to use the actual stage curtains. He projected onto the curtain the scenes on the ship, in the form of an upper deck with two muzzles and the flag of the tsarist army. The greyish-white curtain was drawn to the left so as not to obscure the 'screen'. Some episodes were played in front of the curtain during scene changes. The side and back curtains acted as a diaphragm varying in size to define the playing area by narrowing or broadening it. Judging by the black-and-white sketches found, the scenery was made of wood and metal, or of imitations of these materials. Apart from a greyish-black and a silvery-white no other colours were used. There is no longer any trace of the chaotic, whirling forms used in **The Flying Dutchman**. The scenery is concrete and to the point: the lower deck in the hold with the bunks along the side; the window of the prison cell tightly enclosed by a drawn, dark curtain; the once richly and comfortably furnished dining-room with a *burzhuika* [iron] stove (typical of interiors during the Civil War), the badly furnished, bare room.

It is quite obvious, however, that Tatlin was particularly concerned with those scenes which would not at first appear to require much scenery: those taking place on the thin spring ice of the Gulf of Finland.[58] At the beginning of the play, it is on this surface that Baron Wilcken returns secretly to Kronshtadt after crossing the border to lead the revolt against the communists. And the epilogue as well as the final battle in which the revolutionary troops storm Kronshtadt are also played on this ice-field. There was only one way the set designer could contribute to the action and to the work of the actors: by turning the wooden stage boarding into part of the set. Tatlin was keen to solve this problem not only because of the subject-matter of the play, but also because of the very challenge to him in the construction of the scenery.

The sketches suggest very deft solutions. Onto the structure of the boarding he built a remarkable construction consisting of movable pieces of timber of different sizes. These could be pulled in and out like the lids of old school pencil-boxes and thus spaces were created at various points in the flooring. These could be lit from beneath by a blue projector light, suggesting threateningly glittering water surfaces which would alternately rise and subside from among the blocks of ice. Tatlin himself also built out of wood a kind of see-saw, which seemed to make the ice-blocks wobble. On the margins of one of his sketches Tatlin has written: 'Water surface between ice-blocks', 'Ice – wood to be pulled out', 'Light from down below', 'State of balance'. Tatlin achieved the required stage effect without using realistic stage-props but simply with the help of appropriate lighting cues.

In this way the set designer placed the actors into a very visual multi-dimensional environment, which challenged them to unusually active stage behaviour.

Tatlin's idea of wobbling ice-blocks, which could not be used in **Let us not Surrender**, was realized in **Kronshtadt**. 'The sets for the production were designed by Tatlin. They are monumental and laconic at the same time. There is not one piece of unnecessary naturalistic detail and yet they convey great power of expression,' wrote an unknown reviewer.[59]

Tatlin often gave his characters autobiographical features. He identified with one of the figures when he did the illustrations to Kharms's book,[60] for instance. Here, among the costume-designs, the sailor Kudrin carries Tatlin's self-portrait from the thirties. Kudrin, according to the plot, is a devoted follower of the Revolution and his lines include the statement: 'I believe in Lenin.'

384–391

385

386, 387

156–163

298–312
391

In 1940 the Central Theatre of the Red Army produced with Tatlin's participation a play called **The Affair**, the second part of Sukhovo-Kobylin's classic trilogy.[61] It is a tragedy and also a manifesto against the bureaucracy of the Russian autocracy: it is a law case, or rather a never-ending legal dispute, concerning the theft of a solitaire diamond from the daughter of a landowner, Muromskii. This 'affair' reflects as in a drop of water the autocratic handling of matters in the courts, the money-grubbing of the civil servants and the unavoidable fate of the victims in the Russia of Tsar Nicolai I. The play is made up of caricatures. The protagonists can be divided, depending on their social role in the bureaucratic system, into two groups and classified on the one hand as 'Bosses', 'Employers', 'Civil Servants', or on the other as 'Nobodies, that is Private Persons', or generally as 'Non-entities'. This classification is directly related to the positions of the play's participants either within the official hierarchy or without. In this way the author mastered the forms of the satirical drama from the very beginning, continuing in his own way the Russian literary tradition of Gogol' and Saltykov-Shchedrin.

369–383

The task for Popov, as artistic director of the theatre and director of the play, and for Tatlin as designer was to find an appropriate form for this in the production. Tatlin paid great attention to the author's script, which combines broad social criticism with detailed psychological characterization. He built as it were a citadel of bureaucracy on stage, an alien and hostile world for honest 'Private Persons'. As material for the model (and later for the actual sets) he chose toughened plaster and the 'velvety surface of lime-wood': a contrast between the dull, rough, cold walls and the light texture of varnished wood. Tatlin did not use any paint on the sets: he let the natural colours prevail. 'Here, the colours of natural materials mean exactly the same as the colours of the palette for the painter,'[62] he said at a discussion in 1940 in Moscow. The combination of the grey, coarse texture with the brilliant yellow created the threatening atmosphere for the action. Through endless open doors one could glimpse other rooms, all similar, suggesting the same endless labyrinth as the 'affairs' which no one could ever sort out. There was not one superfluous detail, only the most necessary ones visually related to the action itself. Tatlin even took the table in the Chancery from a drawing by Agin,[63] not as a naturalistic illustration but simply as a typical piece of furniture characteristic of the era. The curtains were decorated with coats of arms and crowns. In the courtroom, which had the same curtains, the table appeared enormously long. This effect was achieved partly by its positioning (diagonally across the stage from front to back) and partly by using several specially constructed tables with a foreshortened perspective. According to Danin, who watched Tatlin work on the model for this scene, 'The long table in the courtroom had the shape of an elongated trapezoid, slightly sloping towards the auditorium, its furthest edges reaching as far as the statue of the blindfolded Themis. It looked like a long, narrow, raised axe. In actual fact, Tatlin merely stressed the law of perspectives: a right angle at the back of the stage does, inevitably, create the effect of a trapezoid. Tatlin shaped wooden armchairs too in the form of trapezoids framing the table on both sides....'[64] Thus the axe-shaped table and the small axe-like armchairs gave the impression of a terrifying parade of executioners. This setting was crowned by a chandelier hanging above the table: an iron spider, extending its greedy feelers above the whole of the stage. The statue of Themis in its niche was a sharp contrast to its gloomy surroundings. This was not the classically cold statue of the Goddess of Justice as usually seen in official buildings, but a charming, playful, flirtatious society lady. In Tatlin's words, 'She is not just a Goddess, but such a woman as to attract the Duke for some reason... holding the scales as one would a fan.'[65] The stone walls and the rigid, motionless creases in the wooden curtains suggested the unshakeability and unchangeability of this glittering, cold environment. This is where the victims of the play are brought, people who are incapable of shaking this soulless world. Even the Muromskii family's flat is only '... a little more comfortable, and everything else is a wasteland'.[66]

369, 370

Tatlin assigned a specially important role to the *faktura* of varnished wood which, following the dramatic situations in the play, could react quite differently to light. It was, for example, brightly lit for the scenes which take place during business hours at the Chancery, so as to show the overwhelming mass of shining, yellow filing cabinets; but in the scene when Muromskii appears at night, the cabinets are hardly distinguishable in a weak light from below, just sparkling threateningly into the darkness. Tatlin designed the lighting to serve the play's dramaturgic structure.

The objective world of the scenery for **The Affair**, with its expressive textures, shapes and lighting, is inherently related to Tatlin's early counter-reliefs, in which he first explored the dimensional characteristics of various materials and their mutual effects. This was noted by one of the most gifted stage designers of the 1920s-1940s, Dmitriev: '... this is one of the best theatrical works for many years. Every detail expresses exactly the same as does the play, and the artist has succeeded in avoiding mere everyday naturalism. Tatlin did not need to compromise. I have the feeling that these sets could not have happened without his counter-reliefs. One ought to introduce the teaching of counter-reliefs ... here we have questions of space, sculpture, volume... perhaps the work Tatlin did in his counter-reliefs is in fact a construction in space of paintings, a construction which is neither architecture nor sculpture, but a specific positioning of materials in space ... a most perfect utilization of stage-space.'[67]

371–383   Working on the characters of **The Affair**, Tatlin analysed with unusual accuracy their psycho-physiognomical features: with a very sharp pencil, drawing on sheets first coated with a soft watercolour, he defined them in the minutest detail. In accordance with the author's directions Tatlin classified them according to their rank, without preconceptions, disregarding all earlier standard interpretations.

377–379   While Lidochka's role was normally considered to be of secondary importance, Tatlin, taking into account the previous part of the trilogy, **Krechinskii's Marriage**, saw her in a process of development; he built her previous life story into her present character: the spoilt girl that she once was has turned into a victim. Tatlin took great pleasure in picturing himself and his close friends in books he illustrated or in parts of plays he worked on. Lidochka in particular shows a certain similarity to the artist's mother, an extraordinary woman of her time, a student of the Bestuzhev courses[68] and a poet. This unorthodox interpretation of Lidochka was also noted by the critics: 'Tatlin is perhaps the first artist to understand fully the spirit of Sukhovo-Kobylin and who deeply identifies with the tragic tone of his work. Lidochka is usually interpreted as a colourless little ornament. But from Tatlin's sketches Lidochka looks at us with the eyes of Dostoevskii's heroines; Tatlin has uncovered her inner world.'[69]

383
376   The circle of characters called generally 'Non-entities', or Private Persons, to which Lidochka also belongs, was by no means a uniform group. Lidochka and her father were victims who accepted their sufferings. Razuvaev, the manager of Muromskii's estates, although a peasant, was a very dignified figure of a man. Muromskii's sister, Atueva, in earlier portrayals a well-meaning but not very intelligent woman, was for Tatlin one of the causes of the tragedy. In the first part of the trilogy she is the one who desperately wants the naïve Lidochka to be introduced to the lady-killer and card-player Krechinskii. In the sketches Atueva is not an innocent person: her face, her narrow lips expressing a forced smile, her frown, all suggest arrogance. Her tiny eyes are penetrating and angry. She has a straight posture, while the tall collar of her dark dress supports her sagging cheeks. She wears a feather shawl over her shoulders as importantly as if it were made of expensive fur. And to finish off her costume there is a seductive bright little ribbon across her forehead, which is, of course, totally out of place. Tatlin saw her as a parasite living off her rich brother; as a woman who, unhappy with her lot, tries to preserve an air of independence and importance.

The other characters, from the highest 'Bosses' to the lowest 'Civil Servants', are rather homogeneous. They represent the entire body of civil servants in the courts, who live according to their egoistic interests on the same intellectual, psychological and moral level: the only thing that differentiates them is their position in the service. Rank leaves its mark on their posture, facial expressions and every gesture. But despite their common, negative characteristics, they all have their own, emphatically individualized features as well. The conceited Duke is a well-groomed man with sensual lips, whose cheerless face with its bushy moustache has an expression of proud ignorance. He wears with solemn dignity his braided uniform and the gilded breastplate that is supposed to preserve him from misfortune. Varravin's coarse and angular face is that of a tyrant. He is ugly and yet vain: despite his indented nose and narrow forehead he walks with importance and thrusts out his chest with all his decorations at every opportunity. On the other hand the lowly civil servant is the embodiment of a slave mentality. In Tatlin's drawings of such functionaries it is always the eyes which are the most remarkable. Tatlin observes very carefully this naturalistically physiognomic area: the Duke's eyes are tired and indifferent, Varravin's are like a wolf's, Tarelkin's like those of a criminal, Schmerz's like a fox's, while the lowly civil servant stares cross-eyed in his effort to please. These carefully naturalistic descriptions are in fact subtly worked-out masks of vindictiveness, hypocrisy, greed, careerism and servility, incorporating, of course, Tatlin's own experiences. He concentrated so strongly on the psychological expressions of each face that he presented the civil servants, with the exception of the Duke, as almost fleshless. The costumes, painted lightly in watercolour, are made strangely transparent with a few light patches. The feet are barely suggested in pencil. Tarelkin does not seem to have any legs at all under his empty cloak. Through this unusual combination of mask-like faces and costumes which express the transience of the characters, Tatlin wanted to create the visual features of that fantastic bureaucratic machinery which is the central theme of the trilogy from **The Affair** to **Tarelkin's Death**, and which motivates the whole of the action.

374, 375

371

373
382

Tatlin's interpretation was not shared by many. Popov, the director, had quite different ideas about **The Affair**, having discovered in Sukhovo-Kobylin's play dramaturgical similarities to Ostrovskii's works. So he approached the production and the acting from a genre-like interpretation. This inevitably meant a change in the designer's concept. The Muromskii family's flat, for instance, which was empty and bleak in Tatlin's design, was found by the director to be much too shabby, so to make it more comfortable and opulent he gave it a picture, a tea-table and other such objects, which had no immediate connection with the action. There was no parquet floor on stage. Instead of wooden curtains very solemn brocade drapery was used in the production. The actors wore very accurately tailored, brand new costumes, and the director categorically prohibited treating them in any way which would make them look more shabby and worn. On top of all this, the statue of the fastidious Themis, created by the sculptor Zelenskii, was made by a badly qualified prop-maker. Tatlin rushed around the theatre, furious at how his ideas had been distorted. And he was not angry on his own behalf: 'This is not a matter of Tatlin but of Sukhovo-Kobylin and of the theatre itself.' On the first night, when all involved with the production appeared for the final curtain, Tatlin left the theatre in protest. 'In the fifty-sixth year of my life, not once was I given the satisfaction of completing a job in the theatre without interference,' he exclaimed bitterly.[70]

The truth is, however, that even the badly carried-out final version of the sets and costumes compared favourably with the production itself. The critics, who had seen Tatlin's models and sketches in advance, gave them enthusiastic notices. They were cold towards the actual production, accusing the director and the actors of misunderstanding Sukhovo-Kobylin's play.

'Tatlin's talent', wrote one theatre historian, 'has not lost its originality. It has become... even richer... It is a long time since we have seen scenery of such psychological impact, such deep understanding of the characters in this drama. Each of his sketches is not only a costume-design but an accurate formula for a human character. It is a great pity that the Central Theatre of the Red Army was unable to keep in their production what Tatlin discovered in Sukhovo-Kobylin's work.'[71]

The writer Leonid Grossman, who made a special scholarly study of the dramatic work of Sukhovo-Kobylin, also analysed the production by the Central Theatre of the Red Army. He praised, first and foremost, the exceptional virtues of Tatlin's set and costume designs, then spoke in very ironic terms of the work of the director and criticized the acting: 'V.E. Tatlin splendidly created the atmosphere of the Chancery and other offices with their masses of yellow filing cabinets stuffed to the brim with affairs... the director failed to grasp the "grotesque" elements in the play... The actors did not always give a proper interpretation of Sukhovo-Kobylin's heroes.'[72]

Today, Tatlin's set and costume designs are included among the classic works of Soviet stage design.

In the list of the set and costume designs he compiled (which is not exhaustive), Tatlin mentions plays in which his participation was previously unknown. There is for instance the play **Pushkin** by Globa at the Sverdlovsk State Dramatic Theatre. This is mentioned at around the time of the controversy surrounding his designs for **The Affair**. One of Tatlin's defenders, Kozlov, himself a designer, praised it as being a living confirmation of Tatlin's regard for principle and his anti-Naturalist approach. 'I was overwhelmed by Tatlin's conception for the characters and the scenery ... there were no painted backdrops ... he used grey silk, the forms of which were changed during the various acts according to the requirements of the action. In one act one could see the Statue of Peter the Great and the Peter-Paul Fortress... this was one scene. For the duel, he used the same silk to create a totally different scene and time (he put up two or three trees as well)... if he had done it differently, there would have been no real changes of scene at all.'[73]

The principle of combining differently coloured textiles according to the tone of the production with a selection of the most characteristic real objects which could be associated with the action (monuments, architectural detail, etc.) was also used by other anti-Naturalist designers of the Soviet stage in the thirties. Dmitriev in particular used this method in his stage adaptation of Lev Tolstoi's novel **Anna Karenina**. Stanislavskii, too, when staging Gogol's **Dead Souls**, demanded of the set designers (to no avail in the end) that they come up with mobile backdrops which could serve as the framework for each episode. Tatlin was always opposed to the requirements of illustrative realism and the influence of Naturalism on stage.

In August 1940, when at Tatlin's request a meeting was called to discuss the models and sketches for **The Affair**, Gremislavskii, the then head of the production department of the Moscow Art Theatre, spoke out in Tatlin's defence. A highly-educated man, he was immediately interested in the daring theatrical ideas and energetically defended Tatlin against those sceptics who insisted that the models were impracticable because of the enormous weight of the wooden curtains and the plaster. Gremislavskii also said he would suggest Tatlin as designer to the directorate of the Art Theatre.

392–396   There is an entry in the diary of rehearsals[74] for Kron's play **Deep Reconnaissance** about two meetings after the rehearsals on 21 and 23 May to decide on the choice of designer. As well as the director, Gremislavskii was present at both meetings, and it is more than likely that Tatlin was commissioned on his recommendation. The critics, of course, were right to complain about the slackness of composition, the didactic and often one-dimensional approach, 'the mannered stereotypes forced upon the human characters in the play'.[75] But Tatlin obviously found some challenge in the play or he would not have taken it on. Described by the critics as 'a production drama through and through', the play still intrigued him, with its heroes searching for oil in an arid desert called 'Death Valley': dedicated geologists living in this bleak land under the severest conditions.

In June 1941 part of the company of the Moscow Art Theatre left to go on tour just when the Great Patriotic War broke out. The rest kept working busily on **Deep Reconnaissance** in Moscow under Kedrov. Tatlin was also involved in the work, which did not come to an end because of the war. Kron even added to the play scenes dealing with wartime as well as pre-war events – making the production topical.

The diary of rehearsals pedantically notes the regular course of rehearsals; the instructions given the actors on the interpretation of their characters; the meetings discussing the sets and costumes, and so on. During this time there often came upsetting news from the front and air-raid warnings interrupted work. The other part of the company managed to return safely from burning Minsk, but all the sets and costumes taken on tour were destroyed, among them P.V. Vil'iams's splendid designs for **Tartuffe**. To make things even worse, Tatlin was struck by a personal tragedy. His only son, at the front, had been wounded several times and was finally killed on the battlefield. Meanwhile, in threatened Moscow the theatres played every night to packed houses. Plays like **Ivan Susanin**, **Joan of Arc**, **William Tell** and **Cyrano de Bergerac** were filled with true, patriotic sentiments. But laughter was also needed to break the tensions: the fairy-world of the operetta and the grotesque humour of the circus.

From the diary of rehearsals for **Deep Reconnaissance** one is able to reconstruct Tatlin's daily routine. On 17 June he had meetings with Kedrov and Gremislavskii, on 27 with Kedrov and Kron, while regularly attending rehearsals. On 12 July, only two weeks later, Tatlin's temporary sets were used for rehearsals held on the ground floor foyer of the theatre.[76] This means that he knew already at that time quite clearly what sort of scenery he was going to design. He presented the models for the first and second acts on 26 August. Kedrov accepted them after minor changes. On 27 August the sets for the second act were mounted on the stage itself according to Tatlin's model. On 26 September Tatlin received the cast list and started work on the costumes. The rehearsals went on until the end of October and were not interrupted in 1942 when the company was evacuated to Saratov: without Tatlin, but using his designs. The collaboration with the author was continued the same year when the company moved on to Sverdlovsk. Rehearsals took place, with the temporary sets, in the club of the People's Commissariat for Internal Affairs. On 3 October 1942 the models for the second and third acts were presented and discussed, and the go-ahead for the fourth act given. According to this factual account of the production there were some changes made in the sets for the second act. Tatlin, like the rest of the theatre collective, worked day and night. Finally on 4 February 1943 the sets were transferred to the stage on his instructions, with him establishing details such as props and lighting. This time his suggestions were accurately followed. This is clear, for instance, from the entry: 'Put several objects in the hall according to Tatlin's instructions.'[77] On 10 March the sets for the fourth act were ready, and finally, on 8 June the first preview was held in the chamber theatre of the Art Theatre. (The production was given the State Prize of the Soviet Union.) Tatlin's role in the creation of this production was remarkable.

394–396

Tatlin did not take long to find the form and texture for the scenery. He used wood and stone as basic materials. He built the interior and the façade of both barracks and working rooms out of wood, plus the tower of a mine where the rock-samples were extracted. There it was again, Tatlin's favourite, vertical construction, a kind of tower, which – even if a comparison with the **Monument to the Third International** would be too bold – has much in common with the stage construction of **Zangezi**. His Constructivist way of thinking could be favourably applied even to the then prevailing naturalistic requirements, especially with a subject like this. This explains the use of rocks and stones on which the camp was set up – the hard, bare layers of ground-rock of an empty wasteland – all fixed on stage onto a wooden frame. Real rock-samples were used and placed on wooden shelves of the living-room and laboratory. The texture of the timber was well matched by the sack-cloth (there were sacks of rock-samples) and metal equipment such as shovels, pick-axes and a few simple props necessary in the course of the action: all of which the artist turned into a single, structural collage. Tatlin's clever use of lighting gave a specific colouring, a major departure from the merely illustrative effects which were traditional in the practice of the Art Theatre.

216–222

In addition to the wooden stage-construction for **Deep Reconnaissance** Tatlin designed a 'constructed' moon. He rejected, and rightly so, the traditional, transparent way the moon had so far been realized on stage, usually serving as no more than part of the

401

background, saying that such methods fail to suggest 'any feeling of the air and space surrounding the moon as we see it in real life'[78] – again, a far-reaching reference to the time when Tatlin imagined his constructions would gain cosmic proportions.

He tried out several versions of the moon – one out of papier-mâché, one out of wood. The object that served as moon in the actual production was a flat, metal disc, the edges of which were turned back at an angle. The disc, hung into the stage area from above, approximately two to three metres away from the backdrop, was lit by a projector.

It must be said, however, that this sort of stage moon was not invented by Tatlin. Rabinovich used a similar one as early as 1930 for Markish's play **Earth**, a production of the Moscow Jewish Theatre. And Aleksandr Tyshler, who worked in the Gypsy 'Romen' Theatre (the first of its kind in the world, established in the thirties), used a copper plate for his version. Tatlin's experiments with the construction of a stage moon were published as well: in this he was helped by Gremislavskii, who at that time was administrator and director of the Stage Experimental Laboratory of the Art Theatre. This small, original, experimental studio made exciting experiments not always in line with the prevailing trends of the time, and was able to publish the results. These publications were distributed among a number of theatres and amateur companies in the country. One of the first brochures of this kind was the one by Tatlin.[79]

In those years the work of designers was either not mentioned in the reviews at all or only briefly dealt with in one or two stereotyped generalizations of praise or criticism. This was the case with Tatlin's role in **Deep Reconnaissance**, which is why an article written in 1943 by the renowned Soviet theatre historian and critic Morozov is of particular importance, even if he could not assess the significance of the designer's work in the context of the whole of the production: 'It would seem that the setting for the play could have offered splendid possibilities for showy, exotic "landscapes". The production could easily have turned into a show of pretty pictures. Fortunately this was not the case. The scenery (the work of V.E. Tatlin) fulfilled its true functions....'[80] It was not without good reason that the author of this review expressed his misgivings about 'exotic' sets, for at that time there was already a danger of glamorous, ostentatious scenic design.

As well as **Deep Reconnaissance** Tatlin designed another four productions for Moscow theatres during the war. These were all plays by Soviet authors and all dealt with the war.

During the last decade of his life Tatlin worked regularly and a great deal for Moscow theatres.[81] Between 1944 and 1952 he designed one, sometimes two plays a year. Apart from Ostrovskii's play, these were all by Soviet dramatists. The plays varied in their subject-matter: life at sea, the war, history, or fairy-tales. We have almost no information on most of these productions except for their titles on old posters and in Tatlin's list. What remains of his designs is far from complete. It is very likely that for many productions the artist made his models straightaway and that, during work on the production, these were taken to pieces to be sent to the various workshops and were never reassembled. Another reason why it is so hard to reproduce some of Tatlin's designs is the fact that, in part, he too started using painted backdrops, painted scenery that is.

What, one might ask, made Tatlin accept the use of painted scenery? It probably became increasingly difficult for the ageing artist to fight the prevailing trend in Soviet stage design. Also, during and following the war, there was a shortage of expensive drapery and other basic materials for set-construction. Even if he did make certain compromises, Tatlin never ceased to oppose in principle the ostentatious decorativism that overtook the Soviet stage towards the end of the forties and the beginning of the fifties. Some documents show that whenever possible Tatlin preferred to use constructed sets. There is for instance a drawing in cross-section for the interior of a half-demolished house which, judging from a note in Tatlin's handwriting, he designed for Shtok's **Fog Over the Bay**, in 1945.[82] It shows a building where a bomb has fallen on the roof, fallen walls and a corner of a room where one can glimpse traces of the lives of those who once lived there. A propeller on the wall of course belonged to a pilot. The windows hang crookedly, the doors have been ripped out. In the corner is a temporary iron stove, and a couch stands by the window. A fine pencil drawing was to suggest the landscape beyond the walls of the house.

Life at sea is depicted in the design made for the 1946 première of **Captain Kostrov**. This shows the captain's cabin on a freighter. The composition has three levels: part of the bridge is shown in cross-section; underneath is the captain's cabin, cramped but friendly, with a lamp hanging from the ceiling, a small bookcase, a desk and an armchair; and underneath there is the engine-room with a sign saying: 'Signaller Krenkel'.

399

The vertically elongated composition is framed by curtains on both sides. Tatlin thus divided the stage into architectural proportions.

The designs for Lavrenev's **For Those at Sea**, staged by Bersenev in 1947 at the Moscow Theatre of the Lenin Komsomol, can be reconstructed only with the help of some small sketches, a few watercolours and Sokolova's eye-witness account of the production.[83] These sources indicate that Tatlin managed once again, as far as circumstances allowed, to realize a Constructivist idea. The article describes the work as follows:

Characteristic for the stage designer artist Tatlin is a passion for a heroic, romantic approach, firmly chosen colours, 'natural materials' like wood, plywood and metal. He is fond of the contrast between black and white, and seldom chooses bright colours, preferring the contrast of light and shadow. These characteristic aspects of his art are again clearly recognizable in the production of **For Those at Sea**. The first act... evokes a premonition in the spectator of the approaching tragedy. In the darkness the sea sparkles with light, but this is ultimately swallowed by the dark colour that is the basic tone for the whole production. The evening closes with the same grim picture, a winter night on the pier... The artist does not express in his sets the play's optimistic conclusion... In this closing scene, heroic colours too should burst forth... Tatlin is much stronger in his execution of interiors, the sailors' cabins for instance. He combines wood, glass and metal with great professionalism and taste....[84]

While giving Tatlin his due, the critic at the same time criticized the set's bleakness and asceticism, the lack of colour and the joyless tone. Tatlin's sketches are indeed bleak: only a small part of the deserted pier on its supports appears, sometimes in bluish-black darkness of the night sea, sometimes in a greyish fog. It was useless to expect from him the monumentality, the vivid colours of panoramic, magnificent landscapes, which were characteristic of the stage at that time.

During these years Tatlin worked on stage and costume designs for several children's plays: two for the Central Children's Theatre, one for the Club for Young Talents and one for the Moscow State Youth Variety Theatre. The available sketches indicate that Tatlin treated children as if they were adults.

The stage adaptation of Iroshnikova's short story **Somewhere in Siberia** was directed by the young Tovstonogov in 1949. It is the story of young Komsomol boys and girls, hardly out of school, who replaced their fathers and older brothers in a Siberian factory during the cruel winter of the Battle of Stalingrad. The strict, laconic language of Tatlin's stage architecture (the workshops, the factory gate, etc.) conveyed the terrible conditions there as well. 'V. Tatlin with a few expressive elements helped the director to create the atmosphere of the factory during the war years',[85] states one review. Another critic, as if to complete the previous line of thought, wrote: 'Tatlin's sets are very successful. His love for the *faktura* of wood is especially justified in scenes like the factory gate and the offices of the party organization.[86] But behind the words of praise one can detect a hint of criticism of the artist's use of his favourite material, wood. In those years Tatlin must have been the only artist to use wood for his designs, and, what is more, in its natural form.

This is all the more interesting as Tatlin had not constructed an abstract, symbolic composition on stage since 1930. All his stage designs more or less complied with the requirements of realism. But the stage aesthetics of the time nurtured such stubborn preconceptions against natural materials and all 'constructions' made out of them, however realistically they were treated, that the mere fact of using wood seemed to be a threat to realism.

Tatlin, as so often in the past, used his own experiences in the characterization of the heroes in the play. Here, in this piece about young heroes, there is a little lad called Vania Kochenev, who dreams of running away to the front – like the young Tatlin when he ran away to sign on a sailing ship. This character wore clothes (a pullover and a long scarf) just like Tatlin's.

During the forties and the beginning of the fifties Tatlin mostly painted backdrops with constructed scenery in the foreground. One of these was a design for Shvarts's **A Far Country** about children evacuated during the war.[87]

There is an interesting sketch for an unknown production which is painted with unusual expressiveness. Almost in the middle of the composition, between the dense green foliage of the trees, are drawn the fine outlines of a bare, tall pine-tree with a slightly bent trunk: reminiscent of the proud mast in **The Flying Dutchman**, or of one of the versions of the tree in **Zangezi** and the happy, waving tree in **A Comic Actor of the 17th Century**. This sketch shows the last in his family of trees, resurrected in the glowing colours of his late painting period, a fitting conclusion to his favourite triple theme of sea, nature and height. Its tone is similar to the painting **Meat** conceived in 1947; these are eruptive, dramatic confessions about himself and the world with little apparent relevance to the subject-matter.

In this period of his life Tatlin hardly painted any landscapes. But he did paint a great number of stage pictures of nature for minor plays which were soon taken off and forgotten, like the production of **Cup of Joy**.[88]

We know that Tatlin collaborated in no fewer than thirty-one stage productions. It is more than likely, however, that this is not the full extent of his work for the theatre. There are still a lot of materials for research: on his work in the Ukraine, in his Kiev period, for example, or during his wartime evacuation to Siberia.

His work in the theatre, which went through considerable transformation in forty years, included revolutionary innovations but most of all, despite the pressure of circumstances, he tried to emphasize the importance of the transcendental unity of perceived and actual reality, a concept which he formed around 1920 about the mission of art. This is why he later came into conflict with directors and with the production departments of theatres.

It is possible to work in the theatre only in a case where the artist is dealing with a director who is organically close to him in his creative method, which means for some to work with an experimentalist director, a bold, talented man who is not afraid of going astray in the search for new paths. Work in the theatre is very attractive. But it will lose all value if you have to convince yourself that more concessions are required from the artist than from the director.[89]

Tatlin was able to put his ideas into practice mainly during the period between **Tsar Maximilian** and **Zangezi**. But he also managed to get on with Bersenev and Plotnikov, Kedrov, Gremislavskii and the young Tovstonogov, especially when the approach of designer and director was the same or at least similar. But often in the theatre he suffered from failing to realize his aims.

During the first period of his working life, in the seven years before the Revolution, Tatlin was one of the pioneers of stage design. His designs for **Tsar Maximilian**, created in opposition to attempts at stylization, preceded Goncharova's world-famous designs for **The Golden Cockerel**. In the second and shortest period of his theatre work he turned to scenic Constructivism, his unique achievement, even if this resulted in only one actual production, **Zangezi**.

In his third period, which started around the middle of the thirties and lasted until 1943, he fought a great and often successful battle against Naturalism on stage. The set designs for **A Comic Actor of the 17th Century** and **The Affair** were created during this time. Finally, his fourth and last artistic period (1944–52) was taken up with an almost catastroph-

397

400

354

419

38–41

37

216–222

354–368
369–383

ic, often humiliating fight against the illustrative or decorative approach to stage design of that time. Giving in to the pressure that weighed down the whole of Russian culture and especially artists of his generation in those years, Tatlin made an attempt to combine constructed sets with painted, illustrative ones. For the first time in his life he made concessions, but even so he worked against the ruling trend.

Tatlin's work in the theatre could, from one point of view, also be seen as belonging to the Russian visual arts, painting in particular. At the beginning of this century the blossoming Russian stage culture drew painting into its magical world, so that set and costume designs stood out as independent works of art – as specific and fruitful products of the encounter between Russian artistic traditions and the European *style nouveau*. Stage designs became not merely an applied genre, but were seen as pictures. Having said this, there can hardly be any question why Tatlin, with his multitude of activities and his conscious alternation between various genres, remained loyal to the theatre until the end of his life.

It is obvious that in the circumstances of the time he hoped to realize the ultimate potentialities of a life devoted to art – consciously chosen at the beginning of his career – in the theatre. It is also obvious that among those of his contemporaries who were aware of the logic and the demands of current events, Tatlin's personality, thanks to a fortunate combination of history and genius, carried the signs of his being among 'the chosen few'. By triumphing over the deepest depths he set out to reach the greatest heights. The fact that in the meantime one of the technical revolutions of the age had taken place did not mean much to him, except in so far as it was useful for him to be able to conquer the universe and give some warmth to people in need until he reached his aim. During the thirties he had to face the reality that the utopia of a role for the artist in shaping reality had collapsed. It was the theatre, one among many of the areas he worked in, that helped Tatlin survive. It would be daring and unfounded to compare Tatlin's and Bulgakov's work. And yet, they can be brought close to one another by the uniquely complex medium of the theatre.

Despite its naturalistic-didactic tendencies since the thirties, the theatre has been the only artistic form in the Soviet Union to allow, through the multitude of its means and methods, references to broader perspectives, even if these are disguised in metaphors.

And although opportunities there too became more and more restricted, it was in the theatre that Tatlin could eternalize the principles of his life and art: man's physical and spiritual ascent, and his ultimate freedom.

Notes

1 For help in granting me access to little known archives, precious works of art, printed and typewritten documents, and for allowing me to use their communications on Tatlin's theatrical designs, the author thanks Tatlin's companion, the painter and graphic artist A.N. Korsakova; the set and costume designer G.V. Medvedeva; M.V. Petrova, head of the Fine Art Archive of the Bakhrushin Museum; the art historian L.A. Zhadova; the painter and teacher V.N. Müller, a former senior director of MKhAT-2; and the literary historian A.E. Parnis.

2 Organized by the theatrical expert Drizen in St Petersburg in 1907, its directors were Evreinov and Sanin; stage designers Rerikh, Dobuzhinskii and Bilibin. It worked for only two seasons: 1907 and 1911.

3 The play was staged ten months earlier by the Union of Youth in St Petersburg, where the sets and costumes were designed by the painters Le Dantiu, Sagaidachnyi and Spandikov. Some erroneously associated the set and costume designs of the Petersburg performance with Tatlin: *see* Bibliog.: *Tatlin*, 1968; М.В. Давыдова, *Очерки истории русского театрально-декорационного искусства XVIII— начала XX вв.*, Москва, 1974, p. 176.

4 Some are kept in museums, others were reproduced in journals of the time; but no detailed description has yet been found, either in contemporary press reviews or in archives.

5 Consequently, it was a mistake to call the drawing kept in the Leningrad State Theatre History Museum *Panel Sketch*.

6 Н. Лопатин, 'Рождение театра,' *Студия*, 29 Oct. 1911, p. 7. No names or titles are mentioned, yet the date and description appear to refer to the performance discussed. (The review says: in preparation for the performance wood was planed, scaffolding was built and some scenery was painted: a curtain displaying three figures of nymphs or goddesses.)

7 Макс-Ли, 'Трагический балаган,' *Студия*, 5 Nov. 1911, p. 7.

8 Diaghilev staged it in 1911.

9 *See* Давыдова, op. cit. pp. 176–7.

This book is the first to mention Tatlin's name in the history of costume and set design. However, the author describes his characters as 'extravagant, provocative and grotesque', in the exaggerated and unrestrained manner of caricatures. The rigorous reviewers of the time did not raise such objections, as at that time lifeless stage design was considered as mere routine which hindered progress. The author confronts Tatlin with Goncharova. As she put it: 'Tatlin's openly primitive characters and set designs do not reflect what we can see in Goncharova's décors: the organic integration of Russian popular woodcuts.' We cannot accept her view as she compares the set design of two works of entirely different genre, dramaturgic structure and idiom. Is it at all possible to stage in a similar way a Russian folk play and Rimskii-Korsakov's opera, based on Pushkin's tale and presented as an opera ballet?

10 'Letter to the Editor', p. 181.

11 In the sixteenth and seventeenth centuries bodyguards formed the guard of honour of grand dukes and the tsar. During receptions at the court and military parades they wore silvery white caftans and carried halberds. The guards' school was disbanded by Tsar Peter I in 1698. The *strel'tsy* were a military corps of musketeers. The corps was formed by Tsar Ivan IV in 1550 and abolished by Peter I in 1699.

12 'The first Futurist theatrical performance in the world' was held in the Lune Park in St Petersburg on 2, 3, 4 and 5 Dec. 1913. It consisted of two pieces: Maiakovskii's tragedy *Vladimir Maiakovskii*, and Matiushin's opera, *Victory over the Sun* (libretto by Kruchenykh and prologue by Khlebnikov). Filonov and Rozanova designed the sets for the first and second acts and Shkol'nik for the prologue and epilogue of the tragedy. Malevich designed the sets for the opera. These Futurist sets were painted panels backstage, which did not penetrate the actors' area of play. On the other hand, Tatlin's set designs evoke the feeling of space and of the *faktura* of built sets.

13 *See also* Sarab'ianov, p. 54; n4 for Zhadova, 'Composition-Analysis', p. 66.

14 *See also* Strigalev, p. 18.

15 Appliqué is an ornamental work that was widely used in Russian folk costumes until the late nineteenth century. It is either rectangular or round and is made of a variety of materials.

16 The clipping of the newspaper article was preserved in Korsakova's archive. The name of the newspaper and the date of publication are unknown.

17 *See* Bibliog.: Efros, 1914, p. 43.

18 А.К., *Утро России*, Москва, 15 May 1914.

19 'Artist or', p. 314.

20 Ibid.

21 *See* Bibliog.: Danin, 1979.

22 Bakhrushin Central State Museum of Theatre History, Moscow.

23 Tatlin drew the invitation in black ink, which has by now faded. The text is as follows: 2 November '17

Selection of Objects. 1) 'Death's Error' 1/2 h[our]
                        2) 'Madame Lenin'
                        3) 'Thirteen in the Air'
Author: V. Khlebnikov
Director: V. Khlebnikov
Costume, setting: Vl. Evgr. Tatlin
Performed by 13 members of the artistic collective.

The copyright of these plays belongs to
Vikt. Vl. Khlebnikov,
Vlad. Evgraf. Tatlin
and Artur Serg. Lur'e
Violation of this right incurs 300,000 roubles
in fine. Proceeding shall be conducted by
Vlad. Efgraf. Tatlin.

                              Velemir Khlebnikov
               Vladimir Tatlin, Artur Lur'e

On Khlebnikov, the relation of Khlebnikov and Tatlin, *see* Khlebnikov, 'Tatlin', p. 336 and commentaries; 'The Initia-tive' ... 'Khlebnikov', p. 238; 'Punin, *Zangezi*' c 'The meeting of Tatlin and Khlebnikov', p. 396.

Artur Sergeevich Lur'e: composer, experimental artist; had lively links with Futurist painters and poets. Headed the Section for Music of Narkompros after the Revolution.

24 *See* Bibliog.: Khlebnikov, 1940, p. 413.

25 *Собрание произведений В. Хлебникова*, Ленинград, 1933, vol. III, p. 318.

26 *See* Punin, 'About "Zangezi"', c 'Supernarrative', p. 397.

27 'On "Zangezi"', p. 248.

28 'On the Stage Production', p. 400.

29 'On "Zangezi"', p. 248.

30 Ibid.

31 The designs, which had been published earlier and were thought to have been lost, came to light during preparations for Tatlin's 1977 Moscow exhibition.

32 *Собрание произведений В. Хлебникова*, Ленинград, 1933, vol. III, p. 360.

33 Ibid. p. 92

34 Tufanov, 'On the Stage Production', p. 401.

35 'About "Zangezi",' p. 395; *see* Bibliog.: Iutkevich, 1923; 'On the Stage Production', p. 400.

36 'Художник В.Е. Татлин оформляет пьесу "Кромдейр-Старый" в ленинградском БДТ' *Вечерняя Красная газета*, Ленинград, 6 Jan. 1925.

37 'Хроника', *Киевский пролетарий*, 23 Feb. 1926.

38 Information from literary historian Parnis, who was told this by an old Ukrainian actor.

39 *See* 'Works for the Theatre', p. 503.

40 The OST consisted of relatively young artists, with differing talents. They considered easel painting as the most important genre. Tatlin and his avant-garde colleagues, who advocated various artistic techniques, rejected easel painting because of their world outlook. The OST artists included among their subject-matter motifs that referred to life in their own time in order better to express the social transformation under way in the Soviet system. In the early 1930s several OST members replaced Constructivists in the theatre. Some of them, e.g. Vil'iams, Volkov, Shifrin, Tyshler and Pimenov, undoubtedly made numerous new and noteworthy contributions. The OST existed between 1924 and 1932, when it merged with the Union of Soviet Artists, which united all the artists of the Soviet Union. *See* В. Костин, *ОСТ (Общество станковистов)*, Ленинград, 1976.

41 The Romanovs, Russia's last dynasty of tsars, reigned between 21 Feb. 1613 and 2 Mar. 1917 (old style). Here reference is made to the reign of Tsar Aleksei Mikhailovich, Peter I's father, when the first court theatre was formed.

42 Комик XVII столетия. МХАТ-II, Москва, 1935, p. 5.

43 Johann Gottfried Gregori (?–1675): German pastor, resident of Moscow's German section. Strove to organize Russia's first professional drama company. Relied both on German scholastic acting and the so-called Anglo-Saxon theatre. Was commissioned in mid-1673 to recruit children of burghers and clerks for a troupe of 26 and set up an actors' school.

44 *See* n42, p. 7.

45 'Artist or', p. 314.

46 Stage adaptation of Chekhov's short story 'In the Ravine' (*V ovrage*), 1935.

47 В.Н. Мюллер, Воспоминания о В.Е. Татлине (manuscript).

48 'Artist or', p. 314.

49 Dobychina organized numerous exhibitions, including The Last Futurist Exhibition, in her St Petersburg gallery in the early years of the century and then in the early years of the Soviet power. In the early 1930s she was deputy director of the State Russian Museum, Leningrad.

50 В.Н. Мюллер, op. cit.

51 'Tatlin in the Theatre', p. 316.

52 'Artist or', p. 314.

53 В.Н. Мюллер, op. cit.

54 The author of this study went to see Tatlin in his scantily furnished flat in Maslovka Street in the winter of 1944. Tatlin showed her some of his works, including sketches for the *Comic Actor*. He spoke happily, with childlike naivety and with some embarrassment of the characters: the boyar Matveev, Gottfried, Kochetkov, Kliushin, Vania, the young comedian boy in Eve's costume, the Serpent, the Robber, God the Lord and the Archangel. He was telling about young comedians of the seventeenth century as if he had had a personal contact with them all, as if they had sat for him as models. Showing sketches one by one, he said these youngsters were taken into the company by force, they found it very difficult to learn their parts, and were often beaten up. He also spoke of their subsequent careers. In the sketches the characters of the comedy and of the mystery play were represented sometimes ironically and sometimes with sympathy.

55 *See* n44, p. 8.

56 No model or photo of the décor has been preserved. The photos available show only the actors. The sketches and photos are kept in the Bakhrushin Museum of Theatre History.

57 'Tatlin in the Theatre', p. 316.

58 The anti-Soviet revolt in Kronstadt took place 2–17 March 1921. The situation became extremely complicated as mild weather started to melt the ice on the Gulf. The plan of staging an attack on Kronstadt from Petrograd across the ice was in danger, and it was feared that Kronstadt could be isolated from Petrograd.

59 *Театральная неделя*, 9 Sept. 1940, p. 28.

60 *See* Zhadova, p. 131.

61 Aleksandr Vasil'evich Sukhovo-Kobylin (1817–1903): author of the comedy *Krechinskii's Marriage* (1855), the drama *The Affair* (1861), and the comedy *Tarelkin's Death* (1868). The three form a trilogy and were published by the author under the title *Pictures from the Past*. The last two reflect the author's experiences of a lawsuit in 1850–5. The trilogy speaks of man's defencelessness against the civil service and the police. Comic and tragic situations are placed in satirical and grotesque perspective.

62 Стенограмма обсуждения оформления 'Дела' Сухово-Кобылина в Центральном театре Красной Армии, происходившего во Всероссийском театральном обществе в Москве в 1940 году. (Manuscript in private collection.)

63 Aleksandr Alekseevich Agin (1817–75): Russian graphic artist, an early exponent of realist book illustration. He portrayed stock figures and scenes from life in Petrograd. Illustrated Gogol's *Dead Souls*.

64 *See* Bibliog.: Danin, 1979, p. 232.

65 *See* n62.

66 Ibid.

67 Ibid., the painter Dmitriev's contribution.

68 'Curriculum', с 'Bestuzhev courses', p. 326.

69 *See* Bibliog.: Shneiderman, 1940.

70 *See* n62.

71 *See* n69.

72 *See* Bibliog.: Grossman, 1940.

73 *See* n62, the painter Kozlov's contribution.

74 А. Крон, Глубокая разведка (rehearsal diary), 1940–1, p. 33. Archive MKhAT.

75 Ю. Калашников, 'Глубокая разведка, пьеса А. Крона в Московском художественном театре', *Литература и искусство* [Москва], 4 Sept. 1943.

76 *See* n74.

77 Ibid., p. 77.

78 'The Moon on Stage', p. 316.

79 Ibid.

80 М. Морозов, 'Глубокая разведка. Новая постановка Московского художественного театра', *Труд*, Москва, 30 June 1943.

81 From 1944 on, the painter Korsakova, Tatlin's faithful companion in his last years, made costume designs for nearly all these plays.

82 We have no documents on this performance, but the sketch, which is in the Bakhrushin Museum and was identified during the preparation for Tatlin's 1977 Moscow exhibition, corresponds to Shtok's description of this scene.

83 Н. Соколова, 'Опыт оформления спектакля', *Советское искусство*, 14 Mar. 1947.

84 Ibid.

85 В. Любимова, 'Воспитание комсомолом', *Литературная газета*, 23 Mar. 1949.

86 Ц. Богомазов, '"Где-то в Сибири." Спектакль Центрального детского театра', *Вечерняя Москва*, 2 March 1949.

87 Central Children's Theatre, 1944.

88 Written by Vinnikov, it was performed in the Theatre of the Moscow Soviet in 1950. The play centres on the construction of a reservoir that will supply water for the dry lands of the collective farms. Tatlin created numerous paintings for the performance. They show the raw earth of ploughed land, the new dam decorated with a red flag, a white stone house and young trees in blossom.

89 'Tatlin in the Theatre', p. 315.

PART TWO: DOCUMENTS
1 Tatlin's Writings

Events that occurred in Russia before 1 February 1918 are referred to according to the Julian Calendar (old style). The Julian Calendar was behind the Gregorian Calendar by twelve days in the nineteenth century and by thirteen in the twentieth century.

St Petersburg became Petrograd in August 1914, and was renamed Leningrad in January 1924.

Words deleted by the author (Tatlin) in handwritten manuscripts, explanations of abbreviations, remarks and corrections of the editor and translator, and explanatory titles of untitled pieces are in square brackets. The titles in square brackets have been added by the editor to documents without titles.

Emphasis in the original is indicated here by italics.

The dates at the end of the documents are in parentheses for dated pieces and in square brackets for those dated by the editor.

Letter to the Editor [Studiia]

D[ear] Mr Editor,
In 'Studiia' no. 5 of this year you print drawings of 'Tsar Maxem'ian' and 'The Goddess   39, 40
Venus' for the performance in the Literary and Artistic Circle.

These drawings of mine as well as a number of others were made by me for the production of 'Tsar Maxem'ian' by Mr. Bonch-Tomashevskii. But when I saw how far the realization of the costumes was from my sketches, that it was, to be frank, a distortion of them, I found it necessary to withdraw from this 'tragedy'.

Thus I have nothing to do with the production of 'Tsar Maxem'ian.' And I am extremely surprised that the directors of the 'Popular Farce' used the drawings of mine they still *happened* to have by giving them to 'Studiia' to illustrate something I had no part in.

Vladimir Tatlin, artist
(1911)

'Письмо в редакцию,' Студия, no. 7, 12 November 1911, p. 20.

In no. 5 of the journal (pp. 5, 6) are printed not two but three costume sketches by Tatlin: *Rowdy Son of Venus* (Ill. 41), *Pagan Venus* (Ill. 40) and *Tsar Maximilian* (Ill. 39). In no. 6 (p. 8) is a drawing by the artist El'skii showing an actor in the costume of *Death* from the actual production. Judging from this drawing, the costumes in some measure lost the sharpness of Tatlin's sketches. (*See* Syrkina, p. 155)

Tsar Maxem'ian and his Disobedient Son, Adolf (or in the modernized version *Tsar Maximilian and his Disobedient Son, Adolf*, which gave rise to various readings in the literature on it and in Tatlin's own references: Tsar Maxem'ian and Tsar Maximilian and others too) was a Russian folk drama from the beginning of the eighteenth century, which parodied the story of Peter the Great's relations with his son Aleksei. In its 'vulgar' farcical form the drama poses deep ethical problems which lead to a tragic outcome.

Bonch-Tomashevskii, Mikhail Mikhailovich (1884–*c.* 1920) an amateur producer enthusiastic about the revival of the old folk theatre. Organized the Tragical Popular Farce theatre putting on *Tsar Maxem'ian* in St Petersburg (January 1911) and Moscow (October of the same year) in the Literary and Artistic Circle. In Moscow there was one performance, which was not a success. True, the surviving review (Макс-Ли, 'Трагический балаган,' *Студия*, no. 6, 5 November 1911, p. 7) is by an author who was against turning to old Russian artistic traditions on principle, a view totally opposed to the position of Tatlin and those like him amongst the innovative young Russian writers and artists of that time. Of the staging of the play it was said: 'There was a lot of bustle, noise, and colour; it was an expensive, very meticulous, externally good production ... But all its superficial "thoroughness", all its colourful details brought together piece by piece, could not cover over the poverty and insubstantiality of the acting itself.' The designers for the St Petersburg production of *Tsar Maxem'ian* were Le Dantiu, Sagaidachnyi and Spandikov (*see Опись выставленных ... памятников русского театра из собрания Л.И. Жевержеева, Петроград*, 1915, pp. 72–5) – all of whom were close friends of Tatlin in those years.

[Letter about a Trip Abroad]

D[ear] S[ir],
I hereby inform you that I am willing to accept your invitation on the following conditions:

To perform not 5 hours a day, according to your letter of 24 January this year, but 3 hours, from one o'clock as indicated in my letter to Chekhonin. If you wish me to perform more than 3 hours and apart from the evenings, in the mornings too (from 11 a.m. to 1 p.m.), then the honorarium will be not 400 but 800 marks (plus apartment and depr[ecation] ...)

In either case travel there and back (3rd-class ticket) at your expense.

I agree to perform in folk costume.

Conditions of payment:

an advance of 150 marks before my departure from Moscow, 125 marks on 20 February, the rest on 7 March (n[ew] style).

With greatest respect,
Tatlin.
[1914]

TsGALI, fond 2089, inventory 1, unit 2, p. 15, back.

Draft letter to an undetermined person written in an album of Tatlin's drawings, dated by its contents as after 24 January 1914. The letter states the conditions on which Tatlin agreed to accompany the Russian Exhibition of Folk Art to Berlin. (*See also* Strigalev, p. 20, n28)

Chekhonin, Sergei Vasil'evich (1878–1936), a Russian artist working in many areas of decorative art, joined the administration of IZO Narkompros at the same time as Tatlin. He was then the main artist of the State (now Lomonosov) Porcelain Factory and artist of numerous pieces of so-called 'agitational porcelain'. In 1922 he decorated a plate on the basis of Tatlin's sketch *Tsarevich* (a variant on the theatrical costume theme – III. 263). From 1928 on lived in France.

[Letter to Shkol'nik]

Most respected Iosif Solomonovich,
From 26 April on I will be out of Moscow, and in case of letters or a postal order please send them care of Aleksandr Aleksandrovich Vesnin, Trubnikovskii Lane, no. 19, apartment 31 (Moscow).

With sin[cere] resp[ects]
Tatlin.

Don't forget the slide for the lecture, if not of the nude then of the boy with fish.
[Sent] from Eropkino, 30(IV)13.   (1913)

State Russian Museum, manuscripts section, fond 121, unit 67.

Postcard, sent to St Petersburg from the village of Eropkino near Moscow (location not determined).

The text shows that Tatlin returned from abroad before 26 April 1913 (*see* 'Letter about a Trip', p. 181). Thus he spent less than three months in Berlin and Paris (where he went after Berlin), and not just over a year as Tatlin wrote in later biographical materials (see 'Questionnaire' p. 262; 'Autobiography', p. 264).

The slides mentioned displayed two of Tatlin's works shown at the Jack of Diamonds exhibition in St Petersburg in April 1913 under the names *Nude Composition,* later known as *Nude* 1913 (III. 79), and *Boy* (perhaps the *Fishmonger* of 1912). (*See* Tatlin at Exhibitions, p. 490)

Shkol'nik, Iosif Solomonovich (1883–1926), an artist and active participant in the Union of Youth, was a friend of Tatlin.

Vesnin, Aleksandr Aleksandrovich (1883–1959), an architect, theatre artist, painter and graphic artist, was in the 1920s the leading figure of architectural Constructivism, and carried out most of his architectural works in collaboration with his brothers Leonid and Viktor Vesnin. In the 1910s a close friend and sympathizer of Tatlin.

[Letter to Benois]

Most respected Aleksandr Nikolaevich,
During our conversation in St Petersburg at the World of A[rt] exhibition, you expressed the desire to come and see my studio, look at my work, [and talk]. Since you'll be in Moscow for a while, I'd suggest you come a little later, about the end of December or beginning of January. I'm at present preparing for exhibitions, so my works are not in the state I'd like you to see them in.

Returning to our conversation, I wanted to tell you that, if my paintings as well as my drawings should be accepted for the World of Art, I'd like to join the World of Art societies, on the usual conditions, i.e. I should not take part in other exhibitions. I should like to show my paintings in the exhibition as well, but last year in Moscow my paintings were not accepted for the W[orld of] A[rt], although it was suggested that I show my drawings, which I did this year. If it should be proposed to me to take part as an exhibitor I'd accept with pleasure, but for my part I would ask that my drawings be accepted without a jury.

Respectfully,
TI

37 Ostozhenka, tel. 29-20   [1913]

TsGALI, fond 2089, inventory 1, unit 2, p. 36.

Draft of a letter in an album of Tatlin's drawings and sketches relating to 1912–14. Since Tatlin participated in the World of Art exhibitions only in 1913 the letter must be dated after 3 November 1913, the opening of the relevant World of Art exhibition, and apparently before mid-December. The same works were on show in Moscow in December. 'Tl' is a frequently found signature of Tatlin's in the 1910s. '37 Ostozhenka' is the address of Tatlin's Moscow studio at that time.

The draft of another letter is in a second album of Tatlin's drawings of the same period (TsGALI, fond 2089, inventory 1, unit 2, p. 93a). It is addressed to one Rabinovich who was involved in the organization of the World of Art exhibition, and refers to Tatlin's participation in it:

V[asil'evskii] O[strov] Fifth line, 44, [St Petersburg]. Rabinovich (…) Information for the catalogue. Sketches of sets and costumes for the opera *[A Life for the Tsar]:* **27** items.

Tatlin

37 Ost[ozhenka]

Tatlin sent the letter before November 1913. Its contents are typical of Tatlin's manner of exhibiting, in that he never gave clearly differentiated characteristics of his works such as dates, materials, dimensions or frequently even titles; sometimes he referred to whole series of works under the same title. (All this creates additional difficulties in studying Tatlin's artistic legacy.)

Both letters show Tatlin's attempt to win acceptance to the World of Art even at the cost of shunning exhibitions of other societies. He had no links with Larionov's group any more as his participation in the 1913 exhibition of the Jack of Diamonds brought no close co-operation. The Union of Youth, whose exhibitions had included Tatlin's works since 1911, was in a state of decline. Aware that his latest works, selections of materials and painterly reliefs (*see* Strigalev, p. 13) were unacceptable to Benois and his circle, Tatlin, cunningly, 'flirted' with the World of Art (and exhibited with it in November–December 1913), while at the show of the Union of Youth (November 1913 to January 1914) he showed works unacceptable to the World of Art. A double review – a favourable appraisal and a critical one – was given in the journal *Apollon* (no. 9, 1913, p. 66), whose views were similar to those of one of its leading art contributors, Benois.

In 1914 Tatlin was invited by the World of Art to participate in the exhibition entitled Moscow Artists in Aid of the Victims of the War. Taking advantage of the fact that there was no jury, Tatlin exhibited in addition to his sketches for *A Life for the Tsar* his painterly reliefs, which caused a scandal and led to his final break with the World of Art (*see Утро России*, no. 304, 7 December 1914).

Benois, Aleksandr Nikolaevich (1870–1960), a Russian artist, art critic and art historian, organizer and leader of the artistic society World of Art, supported during the first stage of his activity any kind of renewal of Russian art, but in the period immediately following sharply diverged from the representatives of the new innovative trends, which had gone significantly further in artistic reform than he had proposed. From 1926 Benois lived in France.

Rabinovich (better known as Roslavlev), Miron Il'ich (1888–1948), an architect and ardent neo-Classicist, he directed the logistics of World of Art exhibitions before the Revolution.

World of Art, an artistic society active intermittently between 1900 and 1924 and organized by Benois and Diaghilev, sought a *rapprochement* with certain avant-garde tendencies at that time in Western art, the renewal of the language of all the arts and their synthesis, but combined with this a refined type of retrospectivism and stylization. The World of Art prepared the ground for the future development of the avant-garde in Russian art of the beginning of the twentieth century, and many of its leading masters were either direct or indirect teachers of the future representatives of new artistic trends, including Tatlin. Tatlin was an independent exhibitor at the exhibitions of the World of Art in 1913, showing sketches for the production of the opera *A Life for the Tsar:* in Moscow 29 items and in St Petersburg 24 items, whose exact titles did not always figure in catalogues. (*See* Tatlin at Exhibitions, p. 491)

A Life for the Tsar (Ivan Susanin), an opera by Glinka (1836), the first Russian historical opera of monumental-epic character, is still performed today. There is no information on any theatre commissioning Tatlin to undertake the designing of this opera. One may suppose that it was commissioned by L.I. Zheverzheev, the president of the Union of Youth society, a patron of the arts, publisher and collector: he acquired all Tatlin's sketches for *Tsar Maximilian,* and in the album in which the above letter appears there is yet another draft letter (p. 63, reverse, indistinct and almost illegible) from Tatlin to Zheverzheev at the Union of Youth asking for a grant to travel to St Petersburg to become acquainted with the production of *A Life for the Tsar.* According to the reminiscences of the artist Vera Pestel' (State Lenin Library, manuscripts section), these sketches were regarded by Tatlin as work 'for money'. The designs for Glinka's *A Life for the Tsar* in 1912–13 and Wagner's *The Flying Dutchman* in 1915–16 (Ill. 137–163) are probably the only examples of theatrical works which he 'designed on his own initiative and exhibited sketches' for them.

[Letter to Anna Darmolatova]

January 1914

Dear Anna Dmitrievna,
Thank you for your note. I'm living in Moscow, and am none the less painting pictures which, I'm sorry to say, you won't like, and there's no hope a time will come when you might say that what I'm doing is any good.

Sarra Dmitrievna said decisively, once and for all, that my pictures are an abomination, and that during the exhibition she did crossword puzzles so as not to see them, but you were kind and didn't say anything.

(1914)

TsGALI, fond 2089, inventory 1, unit 2, p. 63 back. Handwritten in India ink.

Unfinished letter in an album of sketches, dated January 1914. Addressed to one of the three Darmolatova sisters, who were friends of Tatlin at that time. The letter refers to a Petrograd exhibition of the Union of Youth (10 November 1913 to 10 January 1914), where Tatlin exhibited four new works, the most important being *Composition-Analysis* (III. 103). (*See* Zhadova, pp. 63–66; Sarab'ianov, p. 56) The letter illustrates the difficulties the 'new art' encountered even among close friends and those of similar artistic views; it also illustrates Tatlin's deep emotional and psychological vulnerability, which was most characteristic of him although usually hidden behind an external abruptness and roughness of manner.

Darmolatova (married name: Radlova), **Anna** Dmitrievna (1891–1949), a poet and translator, she started publishing in 1916. Her husband was a stage director. (*See* 'Radlov', p. 243)

Darmolatova (married name: Lebedeva), **Sarra** Dmitrievna (1892–1967), was a well-known Soviet sculptress and the wife of a friend of Tatlin's, the painter and graphic artist Lebedev. She later became one of Tatlin's closest friends, and 'understood' and appreciated his work more fully than anyone. After Tatlin's death she kept a large collection of his works and documents, which she gave to TsGALI in the 1960s (fond 2089, personal collection of V.E. Tatlin, consisting of 38 units).

On the Organization of an 'Artistic Society' on New Principles

It has been my constant aspiration, my dream, to find a way out of the present most unhappy artistic reality and into new conditions of artistic life by uniting artists of all directions into a harmonious family, bound together by mutual respect on the basis of its service to art.

When you realize that over 40 percent are not accepted for exhibitions and thrown overboard, it becomes clear why such resentment and impatience reign amongst artists.

This is something abnormal, and one must aspire with all one's strength to eradicate such abnormality.

We must present the artistic guild with a vigorous call to unite, and I believe that precisely those who have been rejected, who are blamed above all for partisanship and irreconcilability, will be the first to stretch out their hands in reconciliation.

(1914)

'К организации "художественного общества" на новых началах', Новь, по. 152, 23 December 1914, p. 10.

Tatlin's answer to a question on this theme raised by the newspaper's editors. At the same time as Tatlin, various other artists responded to the same topic: Dudin (who was against the organization of a society uniting all trends and putting on exhibitions without a jury), Lentulov (who was for it but did not believe it would be possible to create it) and Leblanc (whose reply was similar to Tatlin's).

The thoughts expressed in this note were basic to Tatlin; after the Revolution he tried to put them into practice, in his administrative work as head of the Moscow Department of IZO Narkompros, and in his social activity. (*See* 'Memorandum', p. 185, 'Programme', p. 242)

My Answer to 'Letter to the Futurists'*

Having been interested since my childhood in art which is perceived through the eye, I have some reservations about my writing, which I have never really perfected.

I agree with you that the Futurists are too busy with cafés and embroidery of various quality for emperors and ladies.

I explain this by a 3/5 loss of focus in their artistic vision.

Since 1912 I have been appealing to the members of my profession to improve their eyesight.

Having constructed corner and centre reliefs of a superior type, I cast aside as unnecessary a number of 'isms' – the chronic sickness of contemporary art.

I am waiting for well-equipped artistic 'depots' where an artist's psychic machine might be repaired as necessary.

I appeal to all those in my guild to pass through the suggested gateway and throw off the old to admit a breath of anarchy.

Tatlin

*Anarkhiia, no. 27 [Tatlin's note.]

(1918)

Татлин, 'Отвечаю на " Письмо к футуристам",' Анархия, по 30, 29 March 1918.

Tatlin's reply to an article by Baian Plamen' (pseudonym). (Баян Пламень, 'Письмо к тов. футуристам', Анархия, no. 27, 25 March 1918). In the 'Letter' the author appealed to the Futurist artists to serve the Revolution, and distinguished Revolutionary Futurism (giving a number of names, singling out Maiakovskii in particular) from Futurism which was socially passive, serving the bourgeois way of life by designing café interiors and artifacts (by which was meant the Moscow Café Pittoresque, designed at the end of 1917 and beginning of 1918 by the painter and stage designer Iakulov heading a large team of Tatlin, Rodchenko, Bromirskii, Udal'tsova, Drevin and others – III. 132–3). The question of the proper orientation of the arts in the conditions created by the victory of the Socialist Revolution was extremely topical in those days. Very shortly afterwards (in the first half of April 1918) the principles of Soviet governmental policy on the arts were formulated, both in a creative sense (the plan for 'monumental propaganda' and a number of simultaneous measures) and in an organizational one (strengthening the position of IZO Narkompros). Tatlin played an active part in this work.

Memorandum of the Moscow Artistic Collegium of the People's Commissariat of Education to the Council of People's Commissars, on the Erection in Moscow of 50 Monuments to Outstanding Figures in the Area of Revolutionary and Social Activity, in Philosophy, Literature, Sciences and the Arts

On the initiative of the President of the Council of People's Commissars comrade Lenin, the People's Commissar of Education comrade Lunarcharskii proposed to the Artistic Collegium at its meeting of 27 May that monuments should be erected to outstanding figures in the area of revolutionary and social activity, in philosophy, literature, sciences and the arts.

The monuments should be erected in boulevards, public gardens and the like in all districts of Moscow, with quotations or maxims engraved on the pedestals or surroundings, so that these monuments should appear like street rostra from which living words should fly to the mass of the people, stimulating minds and consciousness of thought.

The whole difficulty of putting this idea into practice is to ensure that its speed should not be at the expense of the artistic side, since the state as it now is cannot and must not be the initiator of poor taste.

This is why the Collegium has laid down entirely new principles for the organization of this work, principles which until now have perhaps never been applied or tested in our country or indeed in the whole world.

The principle for the plan as laid down by the Collegium is, on the one hand, to enlist the forces of as many young sculptors as possible and, on the other, to involve the broad masses of the people in artistic creativity.

In earlier times, under a bureaucratic regime, conditions for competitions were such that those who worked for them or on assignment were either notorious star-artists or artists who were materially provided for and could take part in them regardless of loss of time. The results of such competitions are well known: works erected by these artists are now being removed from their sites. Young artists still huddled in their garrets and dark rooms, weary and forgotten, without any civil rights. In art everything that was new and fresh was pursued and persecuted by all possible means. There are any number of examples.

Such was the position of the artist in our country, particularly of the innovative artist.

There is only one solution to this: to enlist the young and fresh forces of artists of the aforesaid profession, precisely those elements who were barred by all manner of means from social work, and give them the opportunity to express themselves freely today in the Free Republic.

Rejecting therefore the giving of prizes, the Artistic Collegium considers it appropriate to give a sculptor the opportunity to express himself freely, merely providing for him materially for the time of his work. The Collegium also considers it necessary to eliminate the usual jury for competitions and rely instead on a public showing, and judging of the projects on the sites for which they are intended.

No more than three months should pass from the date the competition is announced to the completion of it, and during this time sculptors should prepare their projects, in the form of a bust, statue or relief, from some light material such as plaster, cement or wood, and put them up in the place they are meant for. After this the public at large will judge which projects should be completed in hard material such as bronze, marble or granite, and then a commission will be given to the sculptor who designed the work. Thus each work should be completed by about the end of September of the current year.

The Moscow Artistic Collegium believes that only by organizing the whole matter in such a way can it carry out the ideas of comrade Lenin as soon and as artistically as possible. Believing also that this will both revive our dead artistic reality and throw a spark into the artistic consciousness of the people, the Moscow Artistic Collegium is sure that in the Council of People's Commissars the proposal will also meet with lively sympathy and will not be deferred for an indefinite time.

TATLIN
Director of the Department of Fine Arts,
Secretary, DYMSHITS-TOLSTAIA
(1918)

Докладная записка Московской художественной коллегии при Народном Комиссариате по вопросам просвещения в Совет Народных Комиссаров о постановке в Москве 50 памятников великим людям в области революционной и общественной деятельности, в области философии, литературы, наук и искусств, Известия ВЦИК, no. 155, 24 July 1918; Искусство, *no. 2(6), August 1918, p. 15.*

The exact dating of the text, to 18 June 1918, appears in a later publication of the 'Memorandum'.
(Б.Н. Терновец, '15 лет советской скульптуры', *Искусство,* no. 3, 1933, pp. 152–3.)

This is an official document prepared by the Moscow Artistic Collegium and signed by its leaders. There was also an addendum to it, a second document which defined more concretely the memorandum's general ideas, with the title: 'Moscow Trade Union of Sculptors Competition Rules and Conditions for the Erection of 50 Statues of Great People of the Revolution, Public Figures, Philosophers, Writers, Artists, Musicians, Performing Artists, Scientists.'

Both documents were drawn up by the Collegium together with the leadership of the Moscow Trade Union of Sculptors: TsGALI has earlier memoranda by the sculptors Korolev and Konenkov (fond 2701, inventory 1, unit 137,

p. 1 and reverse; unit 136, pp. 1–2), parts of which are both in content and wording close to the 'Memorandum' and the 'Competition Conditions'. Both documents were discussed at the Sovnarkom meeting of 17 July 1918, as a result of which the 'Competition Conditions' were officially confirmed and then printed together with the corresponding Sovnarkom resolution, the 'Memorandum' and the preliminary list of suggested figures to whom monuments would be erected (Известия ВЦИК).

The text of the 'Memorandum' as presented to Sovnarkom originally ended with the paragraph: 'Furthermore, the Collegium requests that the Council of People's Commissars present a list of figures to whom monuments should be erected.' This paragraph was deleted for the document's official publication since by that time the task of compiling a list of monuments had also been given to IZO Narkompros.

The text of the 'Memorandum' was printed more than once in the Soviet press, but with an incorrect month in the date: 18 July instead of 18 June 1918 (*see Искусство*, no. 1, 1939, p. 152 and subsequent publications). The 'Memorandum' is one of the basic documents which define the tasks and manner of organization of the 'plan for monumental propaganda' put forward by Lenin in the spring of 1918. In the Soviet Republic the leadership of all areas of cultural life was entrusted to the People's Commissariat of Education (Narkompros). Within Narkompros worked a separate Fine Arts Department (IZO), which was headed by two artistic collegia, for Moscow and Petrograd (with the central leadership remaining in Petrograd until 1919). The construction of 'monumental art' was entrusted to Narkompros, IZO and also the local soviets of Moscow, Petrograd and other towns.

Dymshits-Tolstaia, Sof'ia Isaakovna (1888–1963), a painter who participated in the avant-garde movement of the 1910s and 1920s, was executive secretary of the Moscow Artistic Collegium of IZO. She worked with Tatlin and in 1919 moved with him from Moscow to Petrograd. (Her memoirs are in the manuscripts section of the State Russian Museum: fond 100, unit 249.)

[Letter to Lunacharskii]

Most respected Anatolii Vasil'evich,
During your visit to Moscow you gave particular attention to the question of putting up monuments and expressed the desire that some of these should be finished, if possible, for the October celebrations.

The Fine Arts Department, as well as the Trade Union of Sculptors, undertook all measures to carry out fully the given task. The work was speeded up as much as possible without affecting the high quality and care of execution, and at the present time we can inform you *that about 30 monuments will be completed by November.*

Together with representatives of the Trade Union of Sculptors I visited all those who are working to create monuments and I can say with a feeling of deep satisfaction that these works are not only the monuments of outstanding individuals but at the same time are monuments to the Russian Revolution, monuments of an attitude of the state towards art unknown before the present time, monuments of free creativity in a socialist state.

The work on monuments is being carried out by artists with great enthusiasm and effort; their awareness of the sympathy of the working masses, in the persons of their representatives the People's Commissars, for their creations serves as moral support in this difficult work. Regrettably, this awareness has recently been overshadowed by unfortunate occurrences. We have learnt that comrade Vinogradov (assistant to c[omrade] Malinovskii) sees the direction and result of the work to create monuments in a tendentious way, is bringing his totally unfounded opinion to the attention of c[omrade] V.I. Lenin and in this way is attempting to cast a shadow on the activity of the Fine Arts Department.

We hope that you will not refuse to meet our wishes and will take on the task of dispersing the rumours spread by our department's ill-wishers, and will acquaint c[omrade] V.I. Lenin with the true state of affairs.

With the greatest respect,
Tatlin
[1918]

Литературное наследство, vol. LXXX, *В.И. Ленин и А.В. Луначарский, Переписка, доклады, документы, Москва, 1971, p. 78. The original is in the Central Party Archive of the Marxism-Leninism Institute of the CPSU Central Committee, fond 5, inventory 1, unit 2174.*

On the original is the handwritten notation: 'Send to comrade Chairman of the Council of People's Commissars V.I. Ul'ianov (Lenin). A. Lunacharskii', which was done. The letter was sent from Moscow to Petrograd and forwarded from there to Lenin in Moscow sometime between 18 September and 10 October 1918. (On its publication in *Literaturnoe Nasledstvo* it was incorrectly dated 'by its content' to the end of August 1918. For the justification of the above dating and the significance of the letter, *see* Bibliog.: Strigalev, 1975.)

The letter concerns the conflict between Narkompros and the Moscow Soviet in the matter of the organization of 'monumental propaganda', and is only one of a number of documents on that theme (*see*, for example, op. cit., vol. LXXX, pp. 74–5, 76, 82–3, 84, 89). On 10 July 1918 Lunacharskii had sent a letter to Lenin asking him to help eliminate this conflict and 'entrust the matter of monuments either wholly to the Moscow Soviet or wholly to Narkompros' (op. cit., vol. LXXX, pp. 74–5). This letter was signed not only by Lunacharskii but also by the chiefs of the Moscow Museums and Fine Arts Departments (the first signature is illegible, the second is Tatlin's). Tatlin, as chief of the Moscow Department of IZO, was the main representative of Narkompros in carrying out 'monumental propaganda' in Moscow.

Lunacharskii, who in 1918 was directing the activity of the Moscow Department of IZO from Petrograd, came to Moscow four times before the circumstances described, and on each occasion dealt with questions of monumental art. In the first half of April his conversation with Lenin on the whole idea of monumental propaganda took place; the decree 'On Monuments of the Republic' was prepared and adopted; and the Moscow Artistic Collegium, which included Tatlin on its staff, was formed. At the end of May, when he came again, the order was given to the Moscow Collegium to prepare the memorandum on the organization of monumental propaganda (Tatlin at this time was chairman of the Collegium). At the beginning of July Lunacharskii participated in the discussion by Sovnarkom of questions concerning the unsatisfactory progress of monumental propaganda and of a number of organizational measures to improve it. (The conflict between Narkompros and the Moscow Soviet emerged at that time.) Finally he came at the end of August, after the distribution of commissions for monument projects (the contract for which was drawn up on 15 August). It is this last of Lunacharskii's visits which is referred to at the beginning of Tatlin's letter.

Sovnarkom had discussed the question of the unsatisfactory progress of monumental propaganda on 8 July 1918, and directed the three organizations in Moscow responsible for the matter (Narkompros, the Commissariat of Artistic-Historical Properties of the Republic, and the Moscow Soviet) to select a person satisfactory to all who would be entrusted with personal responsibility for carrying out monumental propaganda in Moscow (*see* Ленин, *Полное собрание сочинений*, Москва, 1965, vol. L, p. 182). On 9 July the Moscow Soviet entrusted these duties to an architect in its employ, N.D. Vinogradov. Tatlin's letter was in reply to an enquiry from Lunacharskii after he had received Lenin's telegram of 18 September 1918 (Lenin, op. cit., vol. L, p. 191). Lenin, who had received from Vinogradov the Moscow Soviet's complaint about Narkompros's inactivity in the matter of monumental propaganda, demanded an explanation and the names of those personally responsible. However, that part of Vinogradov's information was not objective, as was then brought to Lenin's attention by Lunacharskii, by his deputy in Moscow M.N. Pokrovskii (*see Искусство*, no. 4, 1967, pp. 52, 54) and by Tatlin's letter, which was forwarded to him. Consequently, when on 7 October 1918 the Moscow Soviet again tried to complain of Narkompros's inactivity, Lenin did not believe the new complaint and categorically demanded from the Presidium of the Moscow Soviet a more responsible attitude towards its duties in the matter of monumental propaganda (Lenin, Collected Works, vol. XLII, Moscow, 1969, pp. 104–5). Thus Tatlin's letter is of considerable additional interest in the context of Lenin's documents on monumental propaganda. When IZO learned of the contents of the Moscow Soviet's complaint of 7 October, it sent a further explanation of the letter's lack of objectivity to Lenin on 19 October (*Литературное наследство*, vol. LXXX, p. 63).

That 'about 30 monuments' would be ready in time for the October anniversary, as Tatlin maintained, was quite true. This figure appears more than once at the time: in the periodic press of those days there is published a series of postcards for the anniversary with pictures of the sketches for 30 monuments, and Tatlin headed a joint commission of representatives both of IZO Narkompros (Konenkov, Korolev, Dymshits-Tolstaia) and of the Moscow Soviet (Vinogradov, Zaporozhets) for the erection of the '30 monuments' now ready. (*Известия ВЦИК*, 22 September 1918, no. 230.) In fact, only 17 of the several dozen portrait statues ready in Moscow in 1918–19 were erected.

Vinogradov, Nikolai Dmitrievich (1885–1980), an architect who in the first years of the Revolution was deeply involved in the implementation of the plan for monumental propaganda, later worked mainly as an architectural restorer.

Malinovskii, Pavel Petrovich (1869–1943), an architect, Soviet statesman and member of the Bolshevik Party from 1904, in 1918 headed the People's Commissariat of Artistic-Historical Properties of the Republic, which in an organizational sense was a part of the People's Commissariat for Education. It was abolished by the summer of 1918.

97–8 Theophanes the Greek, *The Virgin from the Don*, late 14th century,
State Tret'iakov Gallery, Moscow

99 Cranach, *Virgin-tondo*, 1525. Whereabouts unknown
100 Leonardo da Vinci, *Benois Madonna*, 1478, Hermitage, Leningrad
101 Cranach, *Virgin and Child*, Episcopal Palace, Częstochowa
102 Cranach, *Virgin and Child*, Parish Church, Innsbruck
* 103 *Composition-Analysis*, sketch, 1913, Cat. I/22

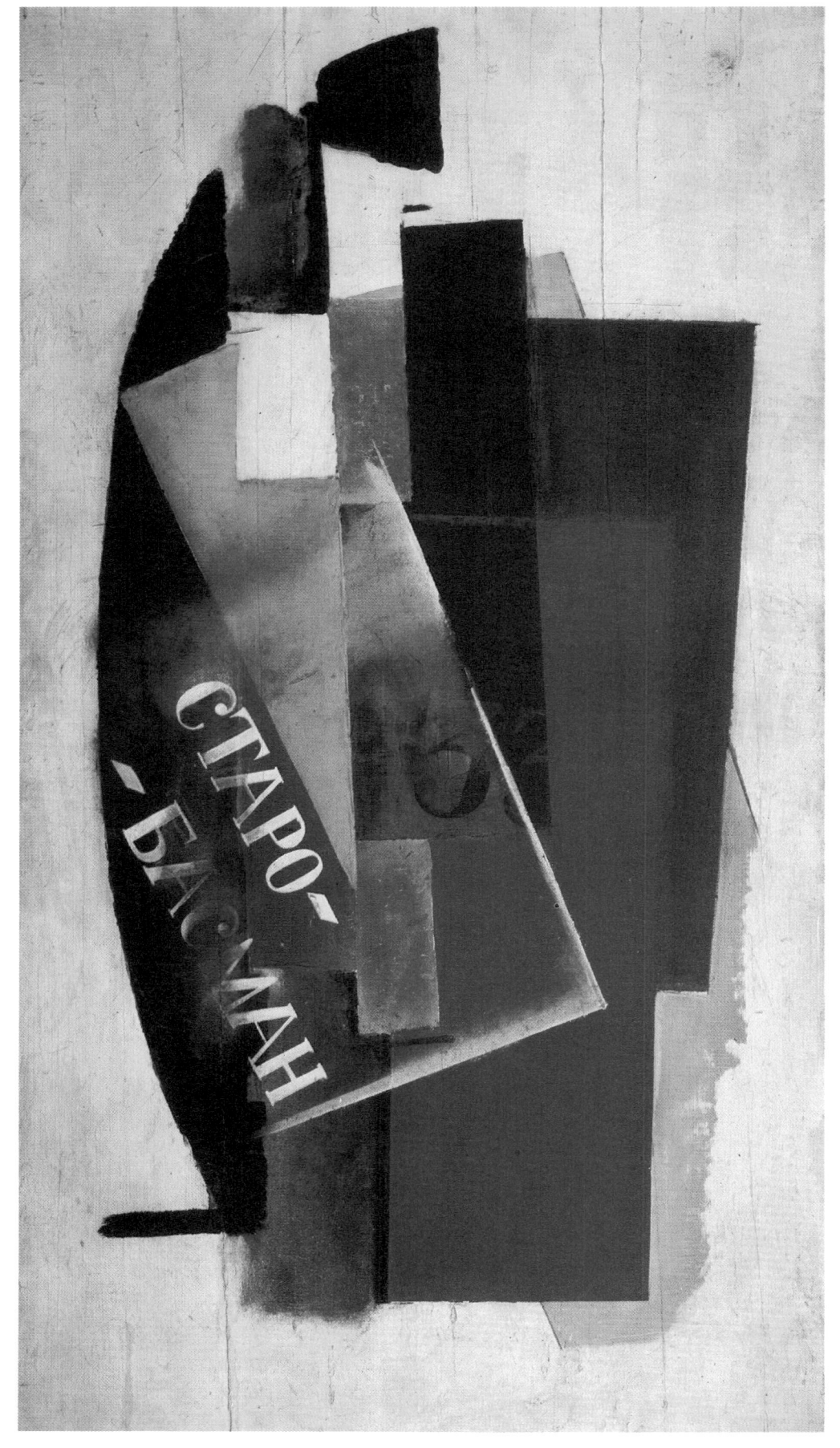

104 *Board No. 1 Staro-Basman*, 1917, Cat. IV/8
105 *Composition (The Month of May)*, 1916, Cat. IV/7

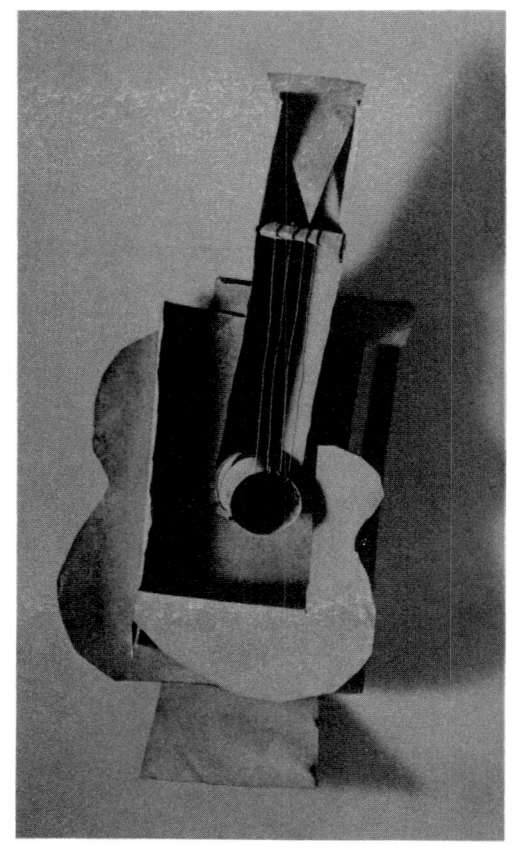

106 Picasso, *Violin*, 1912, State Pushkin Museum, Moscow
107 Picasso, *Guitar*, 1912, Nasjongalleriet, Oslo

108 *Painterly Relief*, 1913–14, Cat. IV/2

109 *Selection of Materials,* 1917, Cat. IV/10

110 *Selection of Materials,* 1917, Cat. IV/9

111 *Bottle* (Painterly relief), 1913, Cat. IV/1

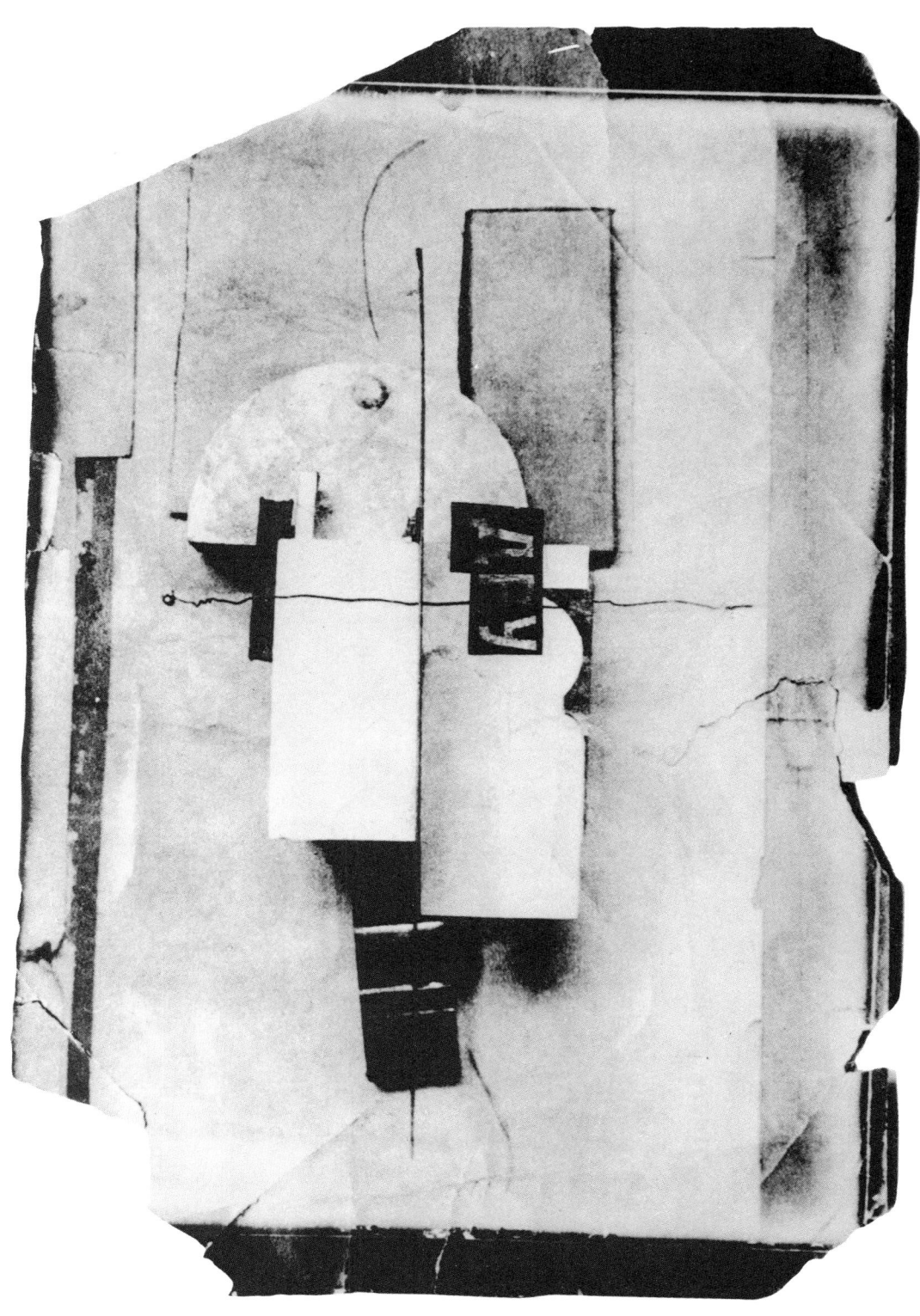

112 *Painterly Relief,* 1917, Cat. IV/11

113 *Counter-Relief,* late 1910s, Cat. IV/16
114 *Counter-Relief,* late 1910s, Cat. IV/14

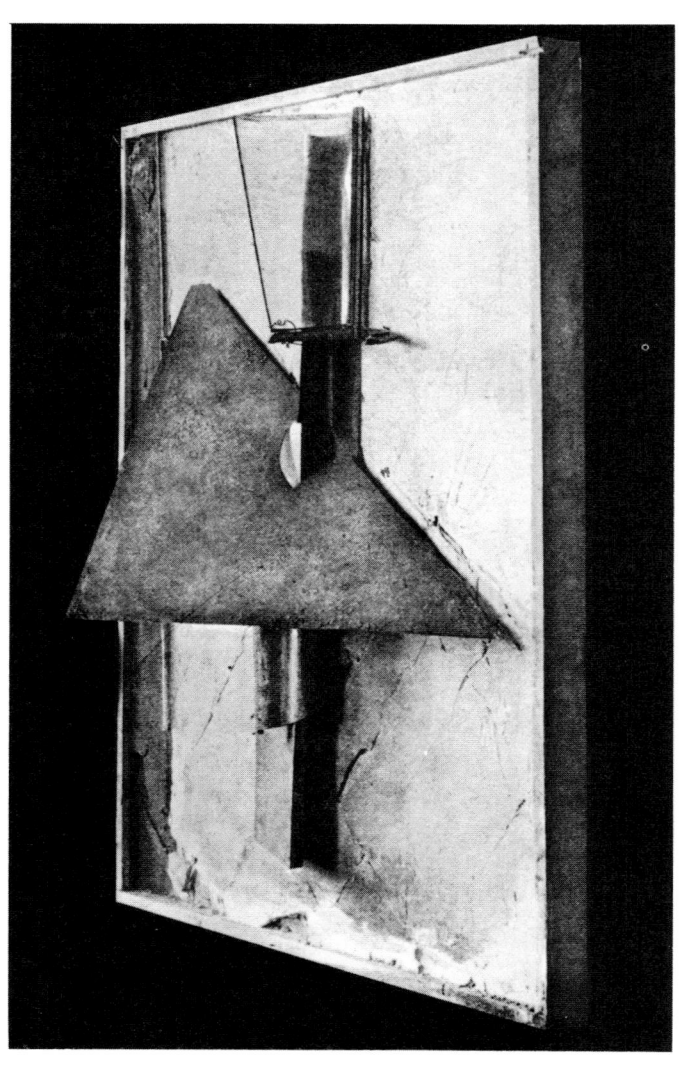

115–6 *Selection of Materials*, 1914, Cat. IV/5a,b

117 *Counter-Relief*, late 1910s, Cat. IV/15

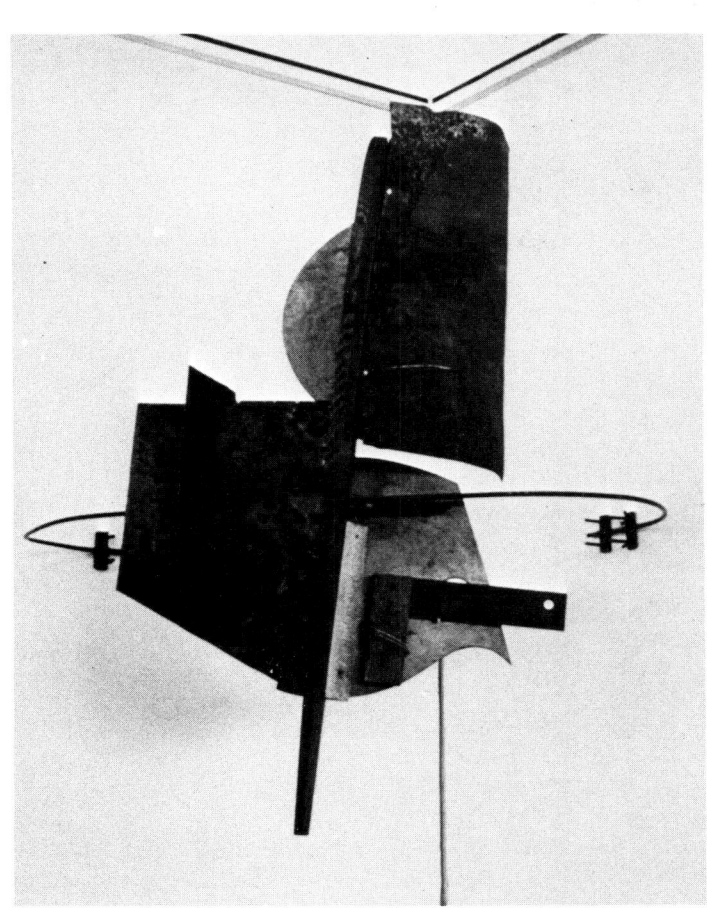

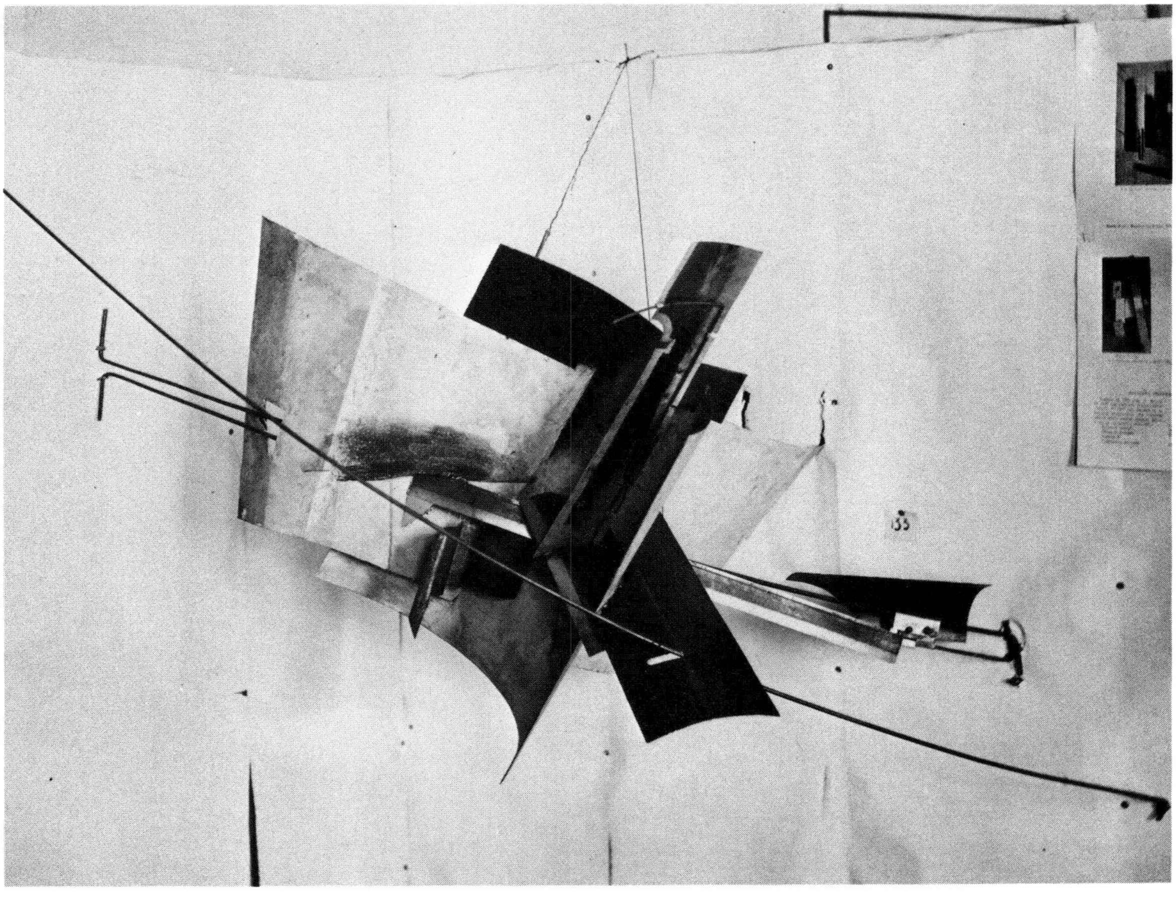

* **122–3** Manuscript of the booklet *Vladimir Evgrafovich Tatlin*, October 1915, Cat. XII/5
124 Cover of the booklet *Vladimir Evgrafovich Tatlin*, Cat. XII/6; III/5; IV/6b
125 An inner page of the booklet, Cat. XII/6; IV/3; IV/4; IV/13b▷

Владиміръ Евграфовичъ ТАТЛИНЪ.

(19$\frac{17}{xii}$15 г.)

В. Е. Татлинъ. „Угловой контръ-рельефъ“ (деталь). 1914—1915 г.

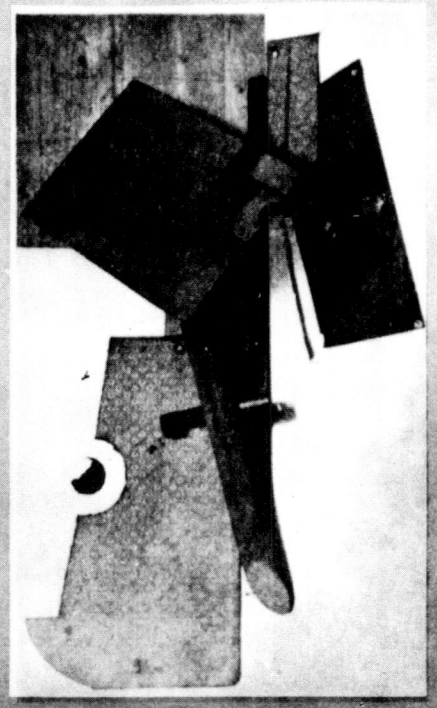

В. Е. Татлинъ. „Живописные рельефы". („Первая выставка рельефовъ" 1913—1914 г.).

ВЛАДИМІРЪ ЕВГРАФОВИЧЪ ТАТЛИНЪ.

Родился въ 1885 году въ Москвѣ. Въ 1910 году окончилъ художественное училище. Съ 1909 года выставлялъ, въ качествѣ экспонента, свои станковыя работы (масло, темпера, акварель, фреска и пр.) на слѣдующихъ выставкахъ:

„Бубновый валетъ",

„Общество женщинъ",

„Трамвай В",

„Современная живопись",

„Ослиный хвостъ",

„Міръ Искусства",

„Союзъ молодежи",

Салонъ „Золотого Руна",

„Выставка живописи 1915 года"

и на рядѣ сборныхъ, какъ футуристическихъ, такъ и внѣпартійныхъ выставокъ Петрограда и Москвы.

Ни къ татлинизму, ни къ лучизму, ни къ футуризму, ни къ передвижничеству,

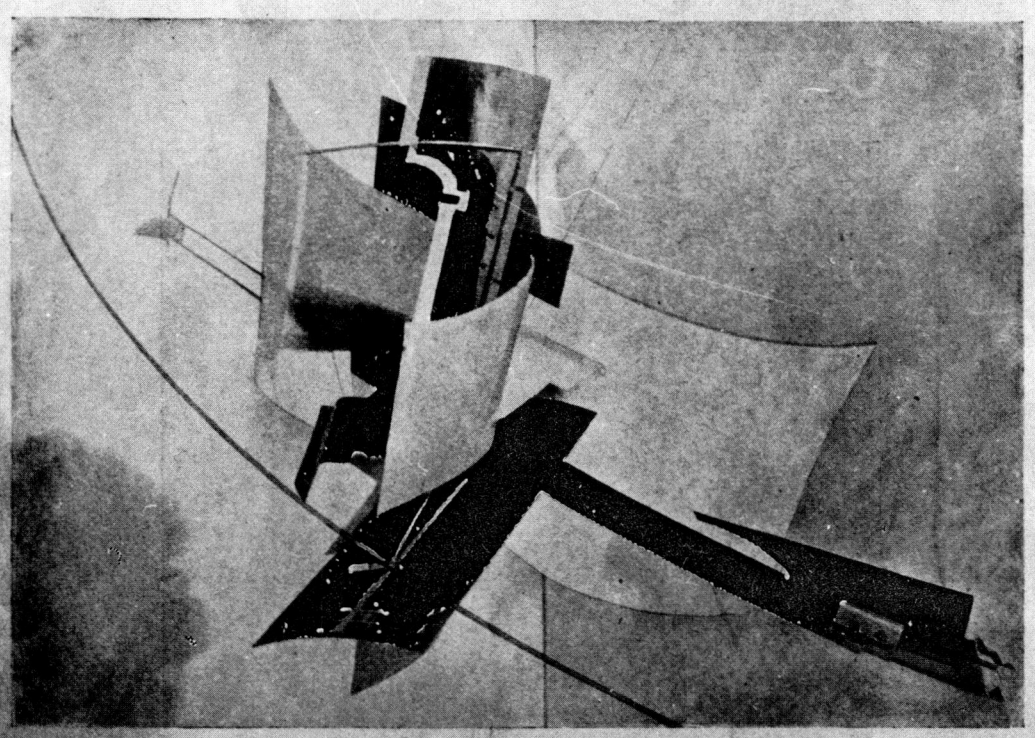

В. Е. Татлинъ. „Угловой контръ-рельефъ". (1914—1915 г.).

ни къ прочимъ группамъ не принадле-
жалъ и не принадлежитъ.

Въ выставочномъ сезонѣ 1913—14 г.
устраивалъ самостоятельную выставку
своихъ работъ подъ названіемъ „Первая выставка живописныхъ рельефовъ" (Москва, Остоженка, 37).

Въ работы эти входили матеріалы:
дерево, металлы, стекло, штукатурка,
картонъ, левкасъ, гудронъ и пр.; поверх-
ности этихъ матерьяловъ обрабатывались
шпаклевкой, реполиномъ, вапами, припо-
рашиваніемъ пылью и другими спосо-
бами.

Въ 1915 году въ мастерской Татлина
построены были „Угловые контръ-
рельефы", которые въ текущемъ сезонѣ
выставляются на „Сборной" выставкѣ
въ Москвѣ и на „Послѣдней футуристической выставкѣ" въ Петроградѣ.

В. Е. Татлинъ. „Угловой контръ-рельефъ". (1914—1915 г.).

Изданіе «Новаго Журнала для Всѣхъ». Петроградъ, Эртелевъ, 3. Тел. 107—88.

ТИП. Т-ФА „НАШЪ ВѢКЪ", ПЕТРОГРАДЪ, МАЛ. ПОДЬЯЧЕСКАЯ, С. :., № 12.

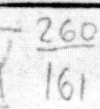

новый
ЖУРНАЛ
для всѣхъ.

260
161

Народная картинка: „Аника воинъ и смерть".

ПЕТРОГРАДЪ.   **№ 12.**   **ДЕКАБРЬ 1915.**

126 Back cover of the booklet, Cat. XII/6; IV/6a
127 Cover of *Novyi zhurnal dlia vsekh*, 1915, Cat. XII/7

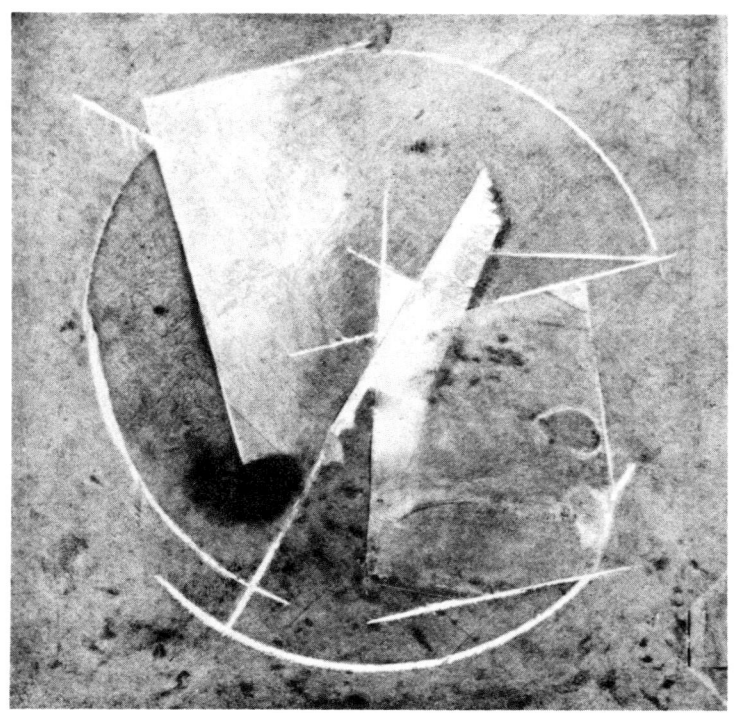

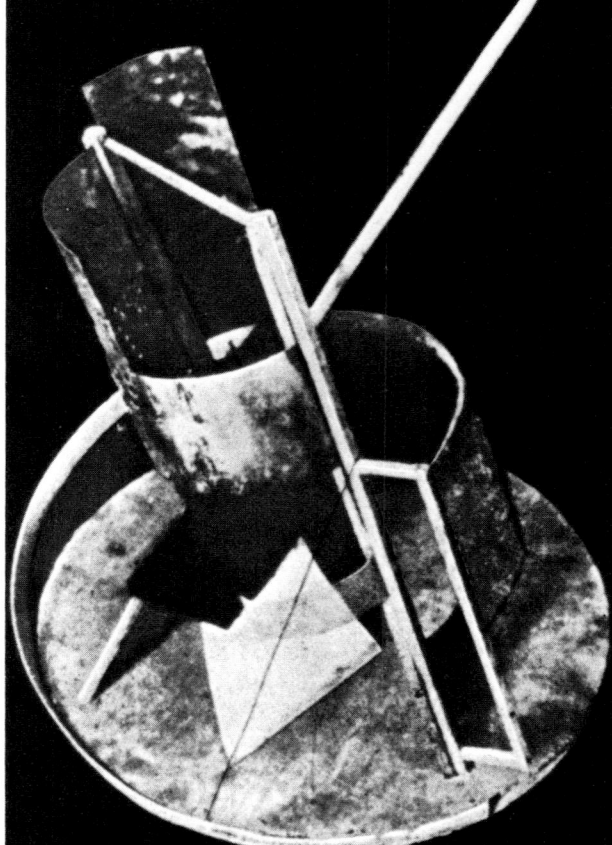

128–31 Works of Tatlin's students prepared under his direction

128 *Painterly Relief*, 1921, Cat. XI/1

129 *Composition* on the theme 'The Selection of Materials', 1926–7, Cat. XI/2

130 *Composition* on the theme 'The Selection of Materials', 1926–7, Cat. XI/3

131 A.I. Damskii, *Composition* on the theme 'The Selection of Materials', end of 1920s, Cat. XI/4

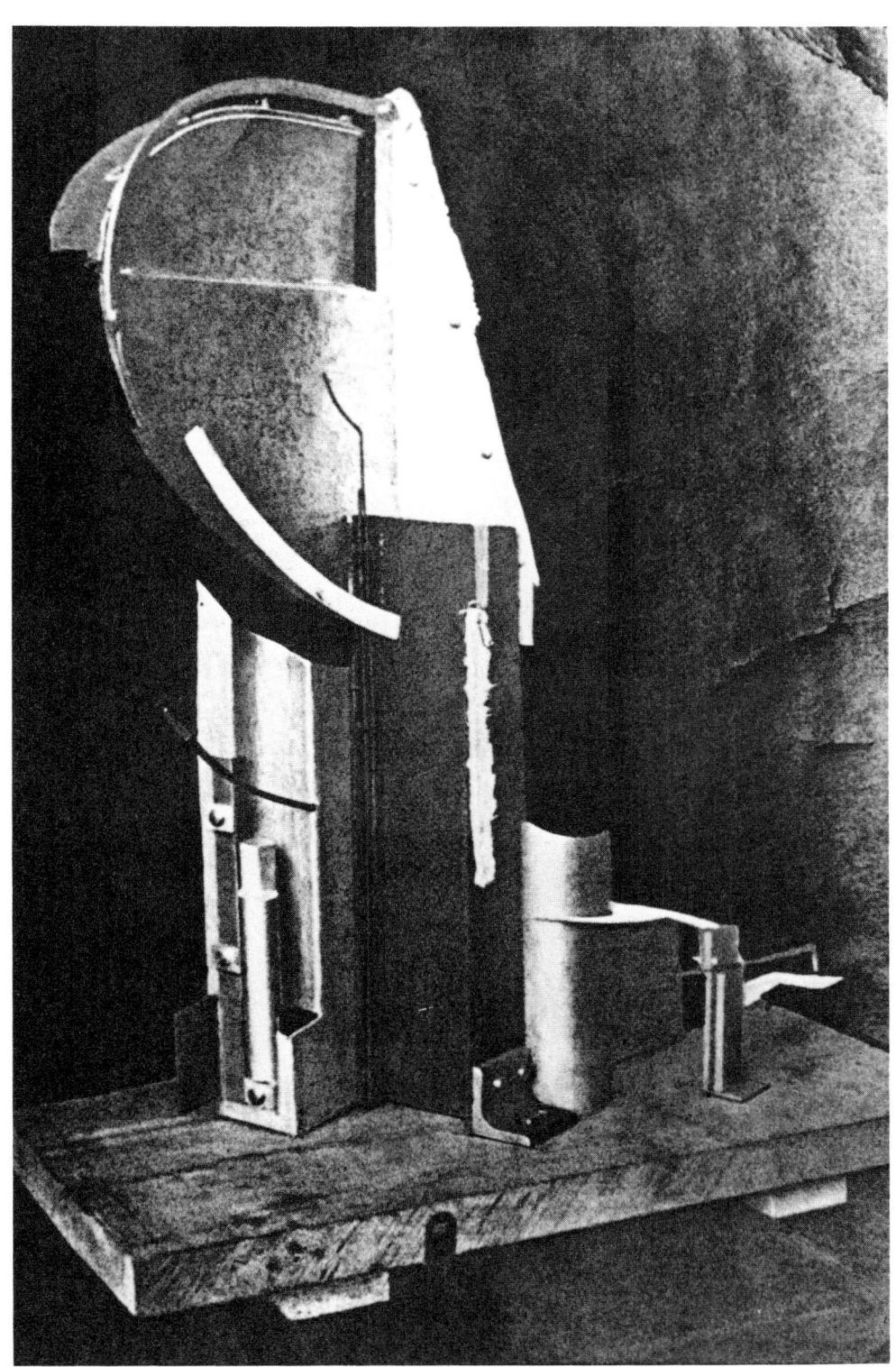

132–3 Interior of the Café Pittoresque, Moscow (details), 1917–18, Cat. IX/1

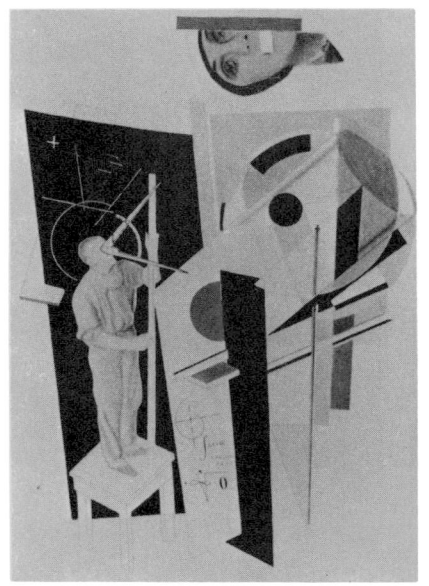

134 El Lissitzky, *Tatlin at Work*. Illustration for Il'ia Ehrenburg's short story 'Vitrion', *c.* 1922
135 Raoul Hausmann, *Tatlin at Home*, 1920, Moderna Museet, Stockholm
136 George Grosz and John Heartfield with the poster 'Art is dead. Long live Tatlin's Machine Art' at the Berlin Dadaist Exhibition, summer 1920. Photograph: Gertrud Heartfield

137–55 Glinka, *Ivan Susanin* (*A Life for the Tsar*), stage and costume designs, 1913–14
* **137** *Domnino Village*, Cat. VIII/5

138 *King Sigismund's Throne Room,* Cat. VIII/6

139 *The Forest,* Cat. VIII/7

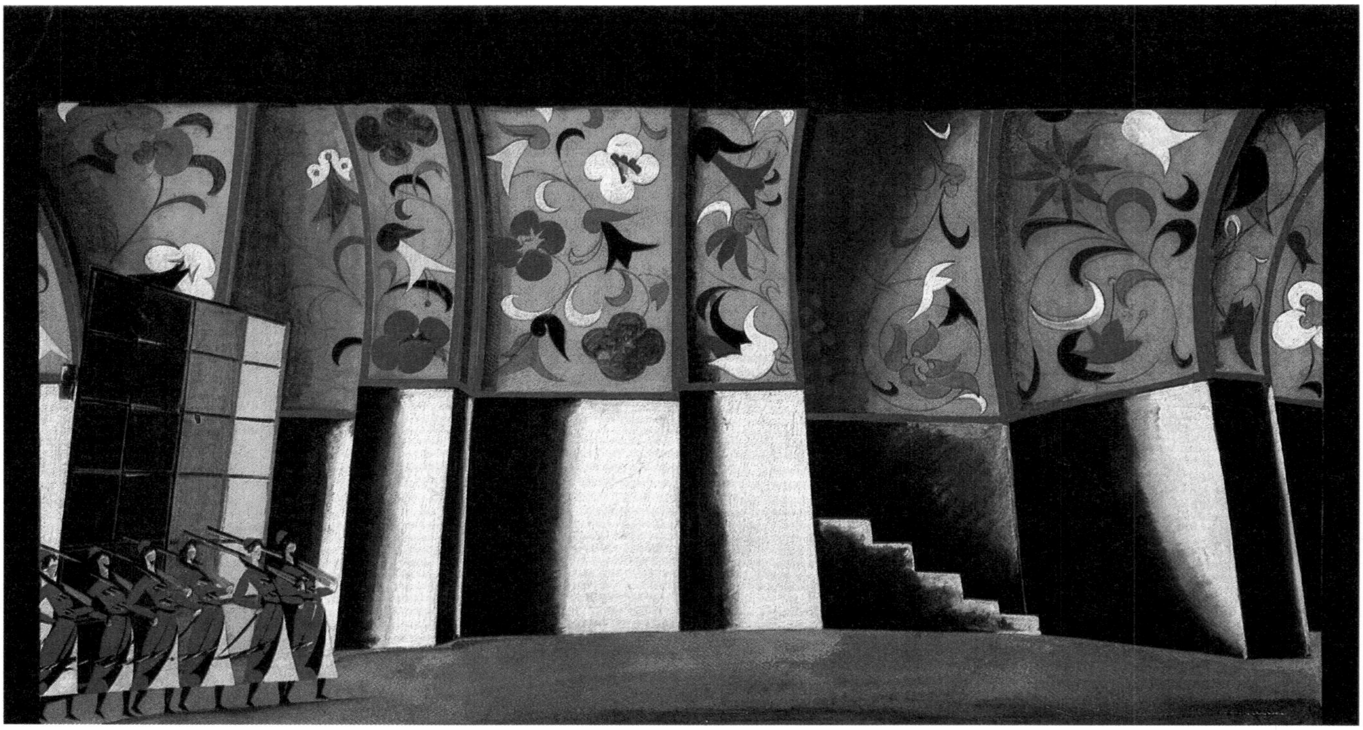

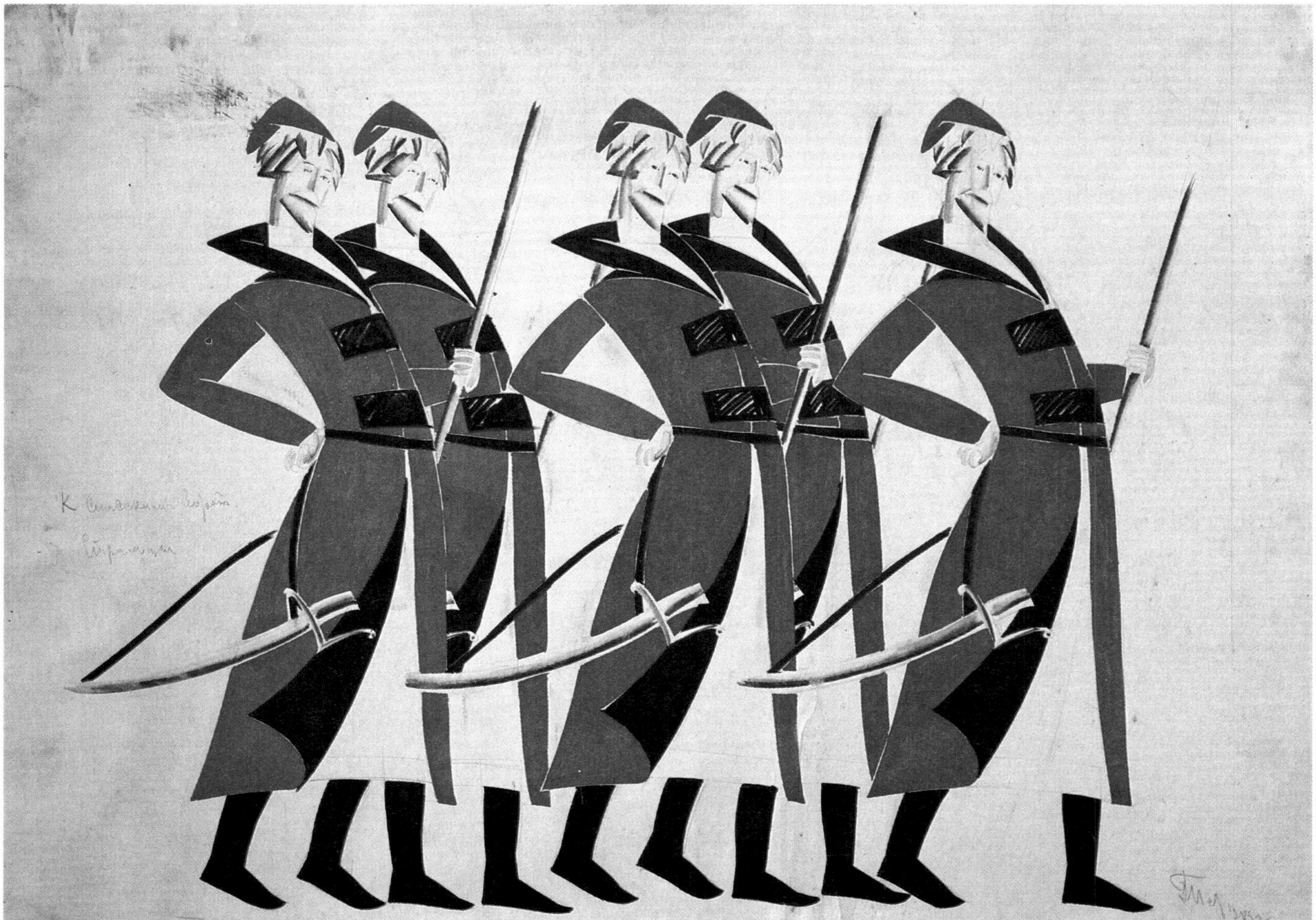

140 *At the Spassky Gate,* Cat. VIII/8
141 *Strel'tsy,* Cat. VIII/22
* **142** *Russian Woman's National Costume,* Cat. VIII/13
143 *Russian Woman's National Costume,* Cat. VIII/15

* **144** *Boyar Girl*, Cat. VIII/17
* **145** *Antonida*, Cat. VIII/16
* **146** *Vania*, Cat. VIII/9

* **147** *Russian Woman's National Costume*, Cat. VIII/11
* **148** *Russian Woman's National Costume*, Cat. VIII/12
* **149** *Boyar*, Cat. VIII/18

150 *Russian Woman's National Costume*, Cat. VIII/10

"Иван Сусанин"
Къ Спасскимъ воротъ

* **151** *Russian Woman's National Costume*, Cat. VIII/14

* **152** *Imperial Guardsman*, Cat. VIII/21

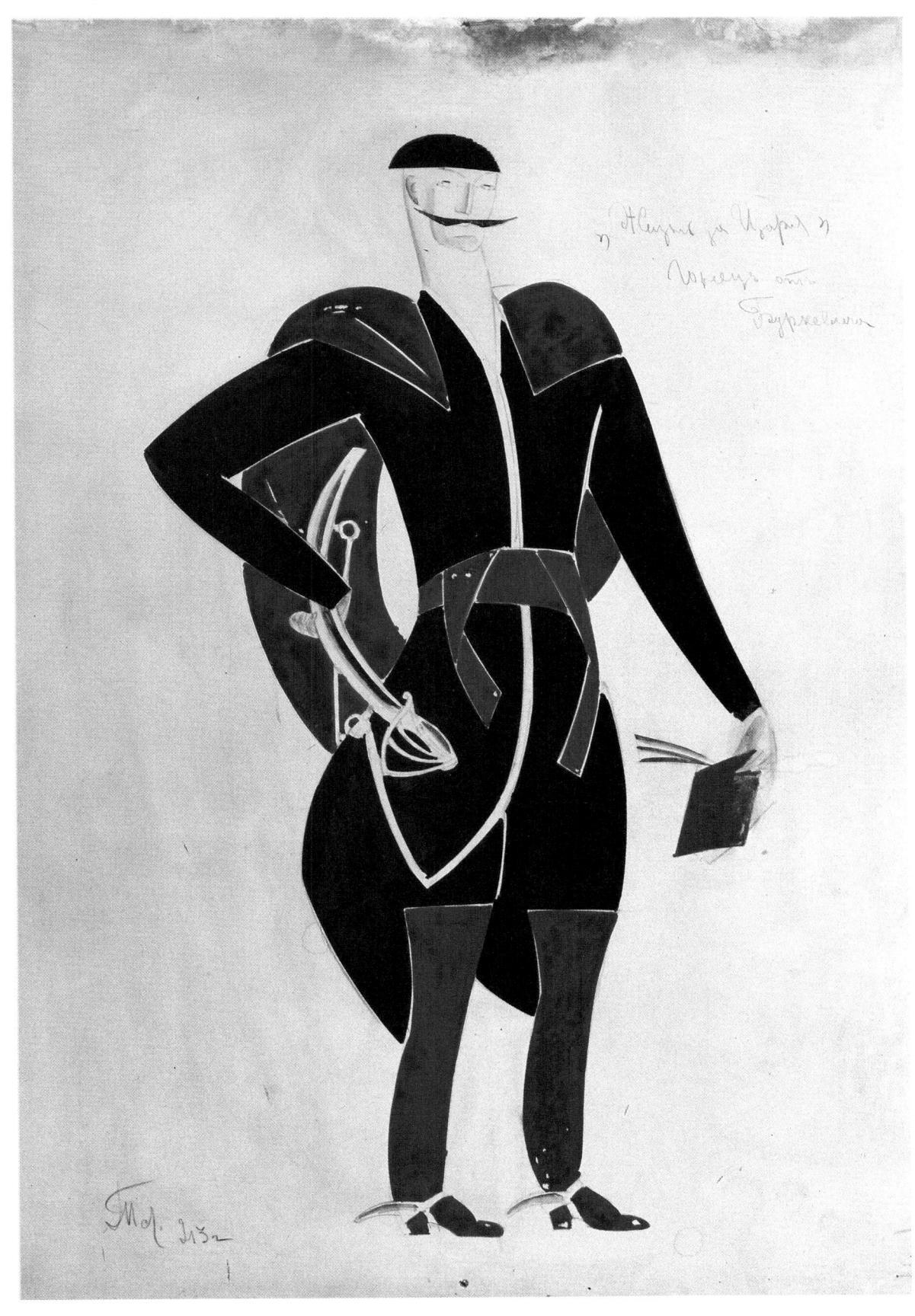

* **153** *Burkevich's Runner*, Cat. VIII/20

Милой Сарре Дмитриевне!

т, и

154 *Antonida and Vania*, Cat. VIII/23
∗ **155** *Embellishment to the Scenery*, Cat. VIII/19
156–63 Wagner, *The Flying Dutchman*, stage and costume designs, 1915–18
∗ **156** *Ship's Deck*, Cat. VIII/25

* **157** *Ship's Deck,* Cat. VIII/24

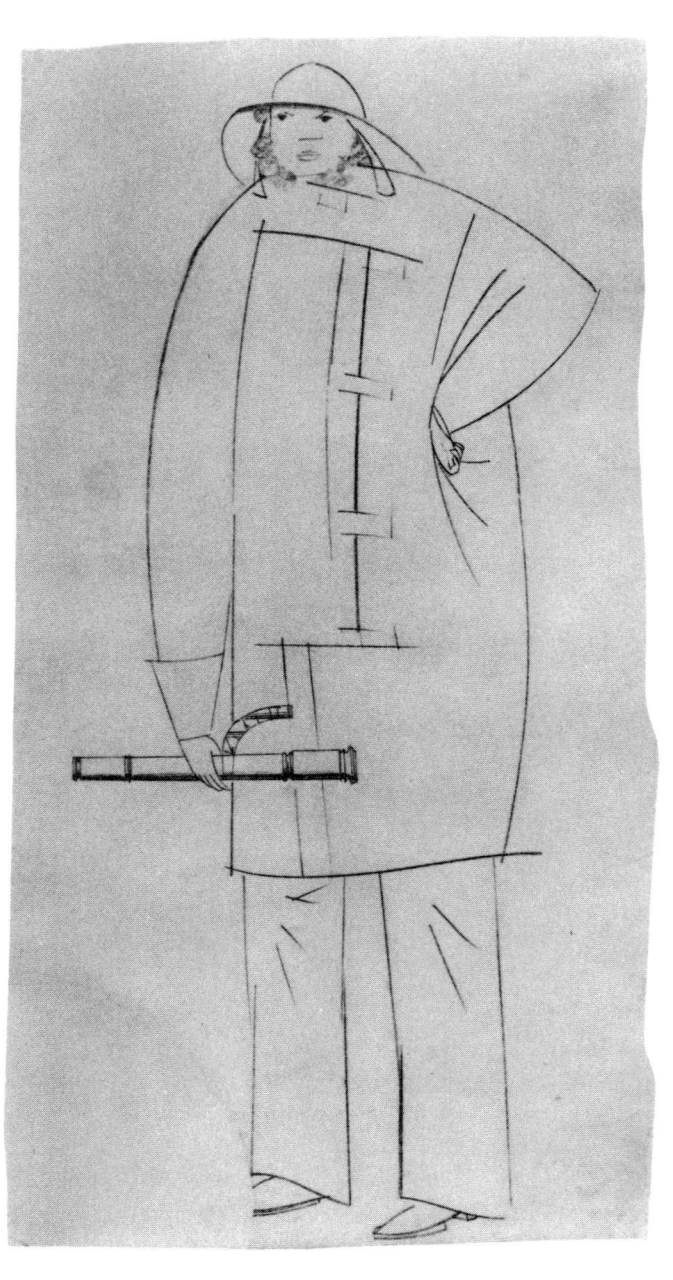

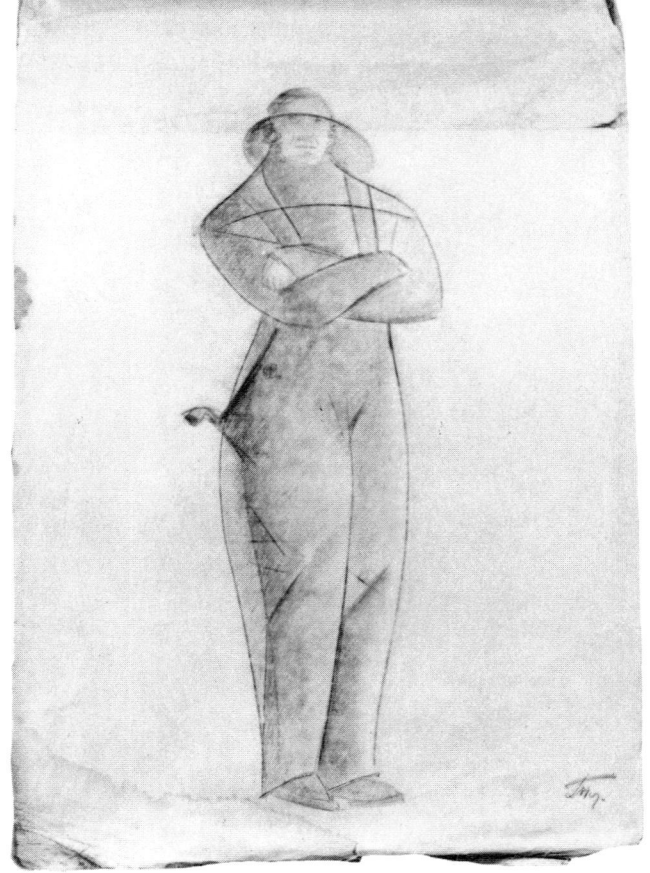

* **158** *Helmsman*, Cat. VIII/28
* **159** *Nun*, Cat. VIII/30
  160 *Sailor*, Cat. VIII/29
* **161** *Helmsman*, Cat. VIII/27
* **162** *Woman's Costume*, Cat. VIII/31

* **163** *Mast,* Cat. VIII/26

[Report on a Museum of Contemporary Art]

From the life of the past we have inherited both museums and private houses containing valuable works of art which have been selected on the basis of individual taste: thus these cannot become institutions for the artistic education of the wide masses of the people. So into these museums should go works of art which in principle fully represent the best examples of masters put forward by the people.

The Artistic Collegium should undertake the creation of a new museum, and the Museums Collegium the reorganization of old museums according to principles suitable to the New Russia.

The Artistic Collegium, fully recognizing its authority to create a museum from works of living art, considers it timely and urgent to adopt the following principles:

1) An immediate concern for the organization of a Museum of Contemporary Art of the city of Moscow, into which should be placed all the best works of living art.

2) The acquisition of works for the Museum of Contemporary Art, and the Museum itself, to fall within the exclusive competence of the Artistic Collegium.

3) The procedure for acquiring works of art to be organized by the Collegium as a whole.

4) The Collegium to draw up a list of artists whose best works should be placed in the Museum of Contemporary Art. The choice of works for the Museum to be left to the artist himself.

5) All private galleries and collections (which have valuables for the Museum of Contemporary Art), as well as that part of the Tret'iakov Gallery which corresponds to the functions of the Museum, to be brought together and classified in it with the participation of the Museums Collegium, the transfer and security of the collection's works being left to the full competence of the collectors.

All works from private collections should be provided with a plate with the name of the collector.

Tatlin
Dymshits-Tolstaia
[1918]

TsGALI, fond 665, inventory 1, unit 31, p. 1. Typed copy.

Museum of Contemporary Art: suggestions to create such an institution were made by circles close to Tatlin even before the Revolution. (И. Школьник, 'Музей современной живописи', *Союз Молодежи*, Санкт-Петербург, no. 2, 1912).

The report was prepared in the summer of 1918. The art historian A.M. Raikhenshtein told us that at a meeting of the Narkompros Artistic Collegium on 28 July 1918 the report was mentioned as having been already adopted by the Moscow Artistic Collegium. The report represents the first document including the programme for establishing a museum of contemporary art and has as its aim the formation of a new type of museum. (Tatlin was a member of the Museums Collegium of Narkompros from its foundation in May 1918 at the latest.) The practical activity of organizing such museums (known as 'museums of artistic culture', or 'painterly culture') got under way from the end of 1918 with the active participation of Tatlin. Between 1921 and 1923 he was not a staff member. Between 1923 and 1925, after the Petrograd Museum of Artistic Culture was reorganized as GINKhUK, he was a staff member. In May 1923, at the regular museum conference, Punin and Tatlin gave a joint report, 'On Museums of Artistic Culture' (whereabouts unknown).

Dymshits-Tolstaia, *see* 'Memorandum' p. 187; commentary.

The Initiative Individual in the Creativity of the Collective

Theses

1) The initiative individual is the collector of the *energy* of the collective, directed towards knowledge and invention.

2) The initiative individual serves as a contact between the invention and the creativity of the collective.

3) The viability of the collective is confirmed by the number of initiative units distinguished by it.

4) The initiative individual is the refraction point of the collective's creativity and brings realization to the idea.

5) Art, always being connected with life at the moment of change in the political system (change of the Collective-consumer), and being cut off from the collective in the person of the artist, goes through an acute revolution. A revolution strengthens the impulse of invention. That is why there is a flourishing of art following a revolution, when the inter-relationship between the initiative individual and the collective is clearly defined.

6) Invention is always the working out of impulses and desires of the collective and not of the individual.

7) The world of numbers, as the nearest to the architectonics of art, gives us: 1) confirmation of the existence of the inventor; 2) a complete organic connection of the individual with the collective numeral. There is no error in Khlebnikov's example. 1) 'In a series of natural numbers, prime numbers, indivisible and non-recurring, are scattered. Each of these numbers carries with it its new numerical world. From this it follows that among numbers too there are inventors.' 2) 'If we take the principle of addition, and add one more to a thousand individuals, the arrival and departure of this individual will be unnoticed. If we take the principle of multiplication, then a positive singular multiplied by a thousand makes the entire thousand positive. A negative singular multiplied by a thousand makes the whole thousand negative. From this it follows that there exists a complete organic connection between the individual and the collective numeral.'

[1919]

TsGALI, fond 665, inventory 1, unit 32, p. 11. Typewritten copy.

Theses for an article for the *Internatsional Iskusstv,* as well as article theses prepared by Lunacharskii, D. Shterenberg, Khlebnikov, Malevich, Kuznetsov and Dymshits-Tolstaia (located in the same fond).

Dated by the time of preparation for the proposed, although unrealized, issue no. 1 of the journal.

By collective Tatlin means a society which first and foremost is new and building socialism. Tatlin regards the artist as an example of the 'initiative individual'. Thus the main theme of the article is the role of the artist in the new society as Tatlin conceived it. In a narrower sense the views set out here were extended by Tatlin to include the activity of creative collectives of artists, as particular cases of a general situation. These views should be taken into account when considering Tatlin's social and creative activity at the head of various 'collectives' he organized: in these cases the role of the 'initiative individual' always belonged entirely to Tatlin. [The Russian word title reads *Initsiativnaia edinitsa*, where *edinitsa* means unit, individual, singular, etc.]

In the concluding part are quoted the theses of Khlebnikov (from a text unknown from other sources), who was fascinated by mathematical research and sought mathematical laws of historical and social development.

Khlebnikov, Velemir (Viktor) Vladimirovich (1885–1922), a Russian and Soviet poet, was from 1910 a leading figure in the literary-artistic movement of Russian Futurists (or *budetliane,* in Khlebnikov's terminology). (*See* Strigalev, p. 15) On Khlebnikov and Tatlin, who were close friends and linked too by their creative endeavours, *see* 'On "Zangezi"', p. 248; Khlebnikov, 'Tatlin', p. 336; N. Punin, 'Zangezi', p. 395; Syrkina, p. 160; Zhadova, p. 135.

[Letter to Neradovskii]

Most respected Petr Ivanovich,
I have been entrusted from Moscow with Levitan's picture. Regarding this period of Levitan very valuable too I am submitting it to you for your consideration.
6. XII. 1919

Tatlin
(1919)

State Tret'iakov Gallery, manuscripts section, 31/1550.

This letter concerns an episode connected with the centralization, replenishment and redistribution of museum collections in the post-revolutionary years. It illustrates Tatlin's close co-operation with the Museums Department of Narkompros and his frequent travels between Moscow and Petrograd in those years.

On **Levitan** *see* the commentaries to 'Curriculum Vitae', section 'My teachers', p. 322. Which of Levitan's pictures and which period of his creativity is meant by Tatlin in his note is unknown.

Neradovskii, Petr Ivanovich (1875–1962), artist and art historian, was curator of the Artistic Department of the State Russian Museum (1909–32) and a member of the board of directors of the State Tret'iakov Gallery (1925–28). He was also one of the 'task-force of three' (with Dobychina and Punin as chairman) which in 1932 prepared the exhibition 'Fifteen Years' Work by Artists of the RSFSR' in the State Russian Museum. (*See* Tatlin at Exhibitions)

The Work Ahead of Us

The principles on which our fine art – our craft – stood were discredited, and any connection between painting, sculpture and architecture was lost, as a result of which individualism appeared, i.e. the expression of merely personal habits and tastes, and artists in their treatment of material reduced it to the level of being distorted in relation to one of the branches of fine art. So, at best, the artist decorated the walls of private dwellings (individual nests) and left us a series of 'Iaroslavl' stations' and a mass of forms which are comical now.

What happened in '17 in a social sense had been carried out in our fine craft in 1914, when 'material, volume and construction' were established as a principle.

Distrusting the eye, we place it under the control of touch.

In 1916 in Moscow there was an exhibition of laboratory models made of real materials (exhibition of reliefs and counter-reliefs).

An exhibition in 1917 gave a number of examples of materials selected on the basis of more complex research into the material itself as well as its resultant movement, tension and the interrelationship between the two.

This research into material, volume and construction allowed us in 1918 to begin creating an artistic form of a selection of materials like iron and glass, as materials belonging to modern classicism, equal to marble in the past in their austerity.

In such a way it becomes possible to combine purely artistic forms with utilitarian goals. For example: the project of a Monument to the Third Communist International (Exhibited   181 at the Eighth Congress).

The fruits of this are models which give rise to discoveries serving the creation of a new world and which call upon producers to control the forms of the new life around us.

V.E. Tatlin
T. Shapiro
I. Meerzon
P. Vinogradov

Moscow, 31 December 1920

В. Татлин, 'Наша предстоящая работа', VIII Съезд Советов (Ежедневный бюллетень съезда), по. 13, 1 January 1921, p. 11.

The article in the New Year's literary issue is signed 'V. Tatlin' in the table of contents, but under the article itself are also the signatures of his assistants in constructing the model of the Monument to the Third International. In its contents the article characterizes the stages of Tatlin's personal creative path and only its penultimate paragraph relates to the work in which all those who signed it participated. The article occupies an important place in Tatlin's legacy. It shows how he tried to use each of his not numerous printed statements to characterize his own creative path as a series of consecutive stages logically developing out of one another and always intended for further development in the future. Moreover, the exposition is extremely laconic; concrete details are omitted or 'straightened out' for the sake of the overall picture. In this respect the article relates closely to a number of Tatlin's other published and unpublished autobiographical materials. (*See* 'V.E. Tatlin', p. 331; 'My Answer', p. 185; 'List', p. 240; 'Autobiography', p. 264, 'Curriculum Vitae', p. 320)

For an understanding of Tatlin's world view, and that of many other cultural figures of those years, it is important to pay attention to the author's testimony about having a kind of premonition of social upheavals, of the coming revolution in the professional consciousness of artists, and about his works being perceived by them as steps on the path to such a premonition.

The article was written and published in connection with the display of the model of the Monument to the Third International at the exhibition for the Eighth All-Russian Congress of Soviets (Ill. 181). Both the Congress and the exhibition took place in Moscow, in the building of the Great Noble Assembly, given over after the Revolution to the trade unions as the House of Unions (Ill. 166). Which of his exhibitions in 1917 Tatlin means is unclear. In actual fact the article relates to a number of exhibitions in which he participated in 1914–16. The words about the possibility of 'creating an artistic form of a selection of materials like iron and glass' in 1918 suggest that the projected Monument to the Third International may have been conceived as early as that year.

The Iaroslavl' Station in Moscow (erected in 1902, architect Shekhtel') is one of the outstanding examples of the 'Modern style' (Russian Art Nouveau).

Shapiro, Tevel' Markovich (b. 1898), an architect, studied in 1918–19 in the sculpture division of the Free Artistic Studios (SVOMAS: the future VKhUTEMAS) in Moscow. In 1919 he moved to Petrograd, and joined the 'creative collective' which 'drew up the detailed project and built the model' for the *Monument to the Third International*. In 1921–27 he studied in the architectural faculty of the Academy of Arts, where his diploma project was a building conceived as a monument to the heroes of the Revolution. (Академия художеств. Архитектурный факультет. *Сборник композиционных работ студентов*, Ленинград, 1929, pp. 66–7.) He subsequently designed projects and built in Leningrad. He co-operated with Tatlin a second time in 1940 in a casual work: the competition project for an obelisk on one of the sites of a battle against the white Finns (*see Архитектура Ленинграда*, no. 4, 1940, p. 8). Shapiro was a consultant to Swedish specialists in 1967 who reconstructed Tatlin's model (Ill. 202, *see* Bibliog.: *Tatlin*, 1968). Since that time his interest in the work he once helped to create has been renewed. In 1976 and 1977 Shapiro himself reconstructed two such models – the first of cardboard, a metre high (Ill. 205), the second of wood, metal and plexiglass, about five metres high, and in the permanent exhibition of the Shchusev Museum of Architecture in Moscow –, and made designs and many drawings for such a model; in 1976 he published an article 'A Manifesto of Revolutionary Romanticism. On the Possibilities of Recreating a Model of V.E. Tatlin's Tower.' (*See* Bibliog.: Shapiro, 1976, pp. 43–5).

Meerzon, Iosif Aizikovich (1900–41) was a Soviet architect. The first biographical details which are of interest to us, including his graduation from the Academy of Arts in 1927, correspond to Shapiro's (his diploma project on the same theme is printed in the same collection, pp. 66–7). Subsequently he taught in the architectural faculty of the Academy of Arts, and died at the front.

Vinogradov, Pavel Mikhailovich (dates unknown) was the third of Tatlin's assistants on the model. Vinogradov joined the 'creative collective' at the time of its organization in Moscow, but only went up to Petrograd for a short time. He helped in the mounting of the model for the exhibition in the House of Unions.

On the other participants in the work on the model *see* Strigalev, p. 30 and n111.

List of Works

I List of works from 1910 to 1913

74   'Bouquet' (oil). Tret'iak[ov] Gallery (Moscow).
31   'Fishmonger' (gum paint). Museum of Paint[erly] Culture (Moscow).
      'Picking up Matches' (India ink).
      'Nude' (oil).
      'At the End of the Sailing Season' (watercolour).
34   'Sailor' (tempera). Mus[eum] of Paint[erly] Cult[ure] (Petrograd).
      'Window' (oil). Mus[eum] of Paint[erly] Cult[ure] (Petrograd).
      'Fishermen.' Mus[eum] of Paint[erly] Cult[ure] (Petrograd).
137–163   Theatr[ical] Draw[ings] to [operas of] Glinka and Wagner.

II (Construction of material) 1913–1919

Selections:
109–121   Relief: Wood – nickel.
      Relief: Wood, cardboard.
      Relief: Wood, iron.

Relief: Stucco, iron, glass, asphalt.
Selections of a more advanced type (counter-reliefs):
Corner relief: iron, primer, aluminium.
Centre relief: cable, celluloid, whitewash.
Corner relief: netting, parquet, [fabric] cotton.

III 1920–1921. Constr[uctions] of materials

Development of the design for the Monument to the Third International   164–187
1) Drawings (sketches)
2) Constructional drawings
3) Model of the Monument to the Third International

Slogans 1913
1) Let us place the eye under the control of touch
1920
2) Through the discovery of material to [the creation of] a new object.

[1921]

Список работ. Handwritten original in the possession of A.N. Korsakova, Moscow.

The List. Judging by the contents and manner of exposition, this is a draft note composed by Tatlin for N. Punin's book *Tatlin (Against Cubism)*. (*See* p. 347)

The text gives the impression of having been written in haste: it is written in pencil on both sides of a large sheet of paper; many words are unfinished, some crossed out (both indicated here by square brackets), there is almost no punctuation (here the most necessary punctuation marks have been inserted), and no unified format of exposition for such information has been observed. At the same time the option that Tatlin copied the list from the text of the printed book, is excluded. From the manuscript it is clearly evident that while it was written down, it was continuously corrected: many words are written above the original ones. For example, the material of *Fishmonger* was first indicated as 'oil', and 'gum paint' was written above; instead of the name *Fishermen* was originally written *Return*; in the list of materials for one of the reliefs 'fabric' was crossed through and replaced by 'cotton'. Other words in the original 'version' could not be deciphered. In Punin's book this text is used in its entirety, but is regularized by the editor and provided with a note to the effect that 'the present list does not exhaust Tatlin's works but indicates the main ones'.

In the list printed in the book (besides Punin's editorial revisions) there are two additions: in the section of works from 1913 to 1919 are added '*Board No. 1*, egg, oil, primer, Museum of Artistic Culture, Moscow' and '*Relief*, zinc, palisander wood, fir'. Both these works are reproduced in the book and this was probably one of the reasons for adding them to the list.
    The list drawn up by the artist, not that by the book's author, became the basis for establishing and studying Tatlin's artistic legacy, and he himself used it too (cf. 'Autobiography', p. 264; 'Curriculum Vitae', p. 320); in practice Tatlin never expanded this list which referred to the period before 1920. He used a similar method for information on the works of subsequent years: he considered his works from the point of view of principal stages in his whole creative path and showed them, at exhibitions too, as illustrations of such stages. Hence the considerable reduction in their numbers as compared with the actual number known to the public, the repeated showing of the same works at exhibitions of different years, his lack of care in describing them (dating, etc.), the showing and exhibiting them in series, the lack of concrete information in order to 'straighten out' the general course of his development, etc. This was one of the reasons why, already in his own lifetime, he was seen as a not very prolific artist, 'hardly taking a brush in his hands for decades', etc. (All this, as has been said, makes the elucidation and study of Tatlin's artistic legacy most complex.)

To the Museums Department of the Petrograd Directorate of the Institutions of the Academic Centre

The association of artists Union of New Tendencies in Art, learning that in the Russian Museum a significant number of the works of the so-called left artists which have been acquired at various times over eight years are not exhibited in the public rooms but are kept in closed areas as things in storage – and some of the works previously shown have been removed – has charged its representatives, with the permission of the appropriate institutions, to enquire into the actual state of affairs, and as a result, after hearing its representatives' report, brings the following to the attention of the Museums Department:

A comprehensive knowledge of the state of contemporary Russian art for visitors to the Russian Museum is possible only if space is given in the Russian Museum *equally* to all tendencies worthy of it on the basis of their record and importance in art.

The tendencies in Russian painting have up to now been served in the best possible way by the administration of the Russian Museum, which was concerned with the overall representation of views, but this cannot be said of the new tendencies. Such a state of affairs is explained by the fact that representatives of these particular tendencies have not had representation on the administration of the Russian Museum.

Taking this into consideration, the Union of New Tendencies thinks it necessary to include in the composition of the Russian Museum's directorate representatives of the Collegium of the Museum of Artistic Culture, while correspondingly allowing the Russian Museum through its representatives to take part in the work of the Museum of Artistic Culture.

President of the Union of New Tendencies in Art,

Tatlin
(1922)

В Музейный отдел Петроградского управления учреждениями академического центра. LGALI, fond 4340, inventory 1, unit 7, p. 107. Typescript, certified copy dated 23 March 1922.

The letter published here probably had some influence on the appointment shortly afterwards of Punin, one of the active organizers and collaborators of the Museum of Artistic Culture, to the directorate of the Russian Museum, and on 9 December 1922 a division of new art was opened in it.

Union of New Tendencies in Art: At the beginning of the 1920s Tatlin organized the 'Left' artists of Petrograd into the 'Union'. The activity of the Union was not clearly defined in an organizational sense but it was of an active and varied character. (*See* 'Programme', p. 242 and commentaries.)

State Russian Museum, founded in 1895, was the main depository of materials on the Russian fine arts of all periods and genres in St Petersburg/Leningrad. After the Revolution the Museum began to acquire works of contemporary Russian art, which in this official Museum (named in pre-revolutionary times after Aleksandr III) had previously been absent.

Museums of Artistic Culture (or Museums of Painterly Culture) were museums of a new type founded in Petrograd, Moscow, Vitebsk, Kostroma, Nizhnii Novgorod and projected for other towns too. Their aim was to collect, exhibit and study works (mainly, but not exclusively, contemporary) which characterized as fully as possible the professional side of the development of the fine arts (*see* 'Report', p. 237).

The Petrograd Museum of Artistic Culture was organized in 1919, opened to the public in April 1921, and had the task of 'popularizing the ideas of artistic culture and the new art'. The Museum's sections were devoted to research from 1923 on; in October 1924 it was transformed into the State Institute of Artistic Culture (GINKhUK). On this *see* Л.А. Жадова, Государственный институт художественной культуры (ГИНХУК) в Ленинграде in: *Проблемы истории советской архитектуры*, no. 4, Moscow, 1978, pp. 25–8. Directors of the Museum (and GINKhUK) were successively Al'tman, Taran, Lapshin, Punin (the latter two for only a short time) and Malevich (from 15 August 1923). Tatlin, beginning in 1921, was a member of the Permanent Commission (and all its specialized commissions), taking an active part in its leadership but not occupying any paid position; from 1 November 1923 (and in practice even earlier) he was on the staff of the Museum–GINKhUK as chief of the Section for Material Culture. He left as of 1 October 1925.

Programme for the Exhibition 'A Survey of New Tendencies in Art'

The exhibition 'A Survey of New Tendencies in Art' has as its aim to mobilize all the artistic forces of Petrograd working in the area of the new art, in painting, theatre, music, sculpture and building. The exhibition has no jury.

Works of artists not participating in other organizations are exhibited.

By exchanging views with those who visit the exhibition, with excursion groups and representatives of artistic and professional organizations, and by arranging lectures, discussions, shows and demonstrations, the exhibition's organizers acquaint the broad mass of visitors with the main tasks of the new art and with its individual branches as elaborated by various artistic groups. On Mondays, N.N. Punin lectures on 'Formal Elements of the New Art', on Thursdays and Sundays comrade B.V. Ender gives explanations of works from the studio of M. Matiushin, and V. Tatlin gives explanations of those from his own studio. On Sundays too S.E. Radlov's theatrical studio and the Moscow studio of comrade Foregger show their works. The exhibition will continue until the end of July.

The Main Slogans of Tatlin's Studio:
1) Painting + engineering – architecture = construction of materials (a + v–o = k);
2) Organized material is a utilitarian form;
3) Let us place the eye under the control of touch;
4) Through the discovery of material to [the creation of] a new object.
   [...]

                                                                                  (1922)

LGALI, fond 4340, inventory 1, unit 6, p. 43.

Original manuscript, most probably written in Tatlin's hand. On page 42 is a typed copy of the same text with a few minor variations (in punctuation, etc.), giving however certain nuances of meaning to the text, which was evidently intended to serve as an announcement about the coming exhibition. After the slogans of Tatlin's studio it has two further sections (written in the same hand): 'The Main Slogans of S. Radlov's Studio' and 'The Main Slogans of Constructive Music'.

The exhibition 'A Survey of New Tendencies in Art' opened on 15 June 1922 in the halls of the Petrograd Museum of Artistic Culture in an eighteenth-century building, which was formerly the home of the Miatlev family, which before the Revolution housed Count Zubor's Institute of Art History. The address was no. 9, Isaakievskaia Square, and Tatlin in those years lived in apartment 1 of the same house, but with his entrance through the courtyard from no. 2, Soiuz sviazi Street (formerly Pochtamtskaia Street). The exhibition was one of the main events organized by Tatlin in the Museum of Artistic Culture. On learning of Khlebnikov's death on 28 June 1922, he added to the exhibition works devoted to the poet's memory. (*See* 'Letter to Miturich', p. 245)

Tatlin exhibited old and new works but no list has come down to us. His *Nude* (1913), and several experimental works concerned with the study of colour and material, including *Pink Board*, were certainly there. *See* articles by Lapshin and Punin: Жизнь искусства, 1922, no. 25, 27, 29 (11 and 25 July); Bibliog.: Radlov, 1923.

The programme of the exhibition broadly characterizes Tatlin's creative and organizational activity at that time. The text and particularly the slogans are of fundamental importance for the understanding of Tatlin's creative method. (*See* Bibliog.: Strigalev, 1978).

Punin, Nikolai Nikolaevich (1888–1953), an art historian, was a member of the Collegium of IZO Narkompros and fully participated in its activity. (*See* 'The Monument', p. 344 and commentaries; 'Punin, Tatlin', p. 347 and commentaries.)

Matiushin, Mikhail Vasil'evich (1861–1934), painter, sculptor, musician and art theoretician, was an active participant in the avant-garde movement in Russian art. In the Museum of Artistic Culture–GINKhUK he headed the workshop (section) for Organic Culture, which was concerned with research into psycho-physiological aspects of the perception of art.

Ender, Boris Vladimirovich (1893–1960), an artist and one of the pupils and closest collaborators of Matiushin.

Radlov, Sergei Ernestovich (1892–1959), a theatre director who worked in Petrograd and Moscow and was an active participant in the Petrograd mass productions of the 1920s, in 1920–2 headed the Theatre of Popular Comedy which he had organized. He was the brother of the artist N.E. Radlov, who had shown a bitter intolerance of the new tendencies and criticized Tatlin personally. (*See* Bibliog.: Radlov, 1923).

Foregger von Greifenturn, Nikolai Mikhailovich (1892–1939), theatre director and participant in the Theatrical October movement, ran the so-called Foregger's Studio (Mastfor) in Moscow. At the exhibition, the Petrograd Studio of Ritual Theatre under M.D. Tuberovskii replaced Foregger's Studio.

[Tatlin's Slogans]

177–178 [1] Engineers and bridge-builders, make calculations for an invented new form.
181   [2] ... Prepare parts of the Monument to the Third International.

[1920]

243   [3] Material culture. Down with Tatlinism.

[1922]

[4] Not to the left, not to the right, but to the necessary.
234   [5] Not the old, not the new, but the necessary.
[6] Remove from our environment people who have displayed empty slogans not confirmed by their craft.

[1923]

A selection of slogans from various sources.

The tendency to draw up a creative concept in the form of a slogan or several slogans was widely practised in the art of the revolutionary years and was characteristic of Tatlin in particular.

He displayed slogans along with his works (*see* 'Programme', p. 242) and included them in his 'List of Works' (p. 240) which was then incorporated in Punin's monograph on his creative activity (p. 347). We have here six slogans known to the compiler (apart from those listed in the above documents or included in the text or titles of other documents), although in fact there were many more.

[1] From a photograph (Ill. 177, 178) of the model of the Monument to the Third International exhibited in Petrograd in November–December 1920 and recently discovered. The model was exhibited in the former mosaics workshop of the Academy of Arts. Over the model hung the slogan 'Long Live the Third International', and on the walls are no fewer than four slogans reflecting Tatlin's creative conception. The slogan quoted above was the second from the top on the left if we face the windows. Three other slogans can be seen only in part on the existing photographs. On the left wall, above the one quoted, is: '[Effect]uating a form of large volume, [let us van]quish the form by...' On the right wall at the top is '[Through the dis]covery of mate[rial] to model[s...]' (cf. 'List', p. 240; 'Programme', p. 242); in this variant we already note Tatlin's appeal to create 'models' (i.e. standards or 'norms', as was generally said then, by Tatlin too) for mass production ('Summary', p. 249; 'Research Plan', p. 254; 'Letter to Novitskii', p. 260). Under this slogan is the most undecipherable one: '[... metal]-workers [...]s, build [...] [...]ical.'

The above slogan has semantic parallels in the slogan 'painting + engineering – architecture = construction of materials' (*see* 'Programme', p. 242: 'Tugendkhol'd's article', p. 250; 'Art into', p. 310). All these texts express Tatlin's particular position regarding architectural creativity.

[2] From a photograph of the same model in Moscow (from the end of December 1920 to 1922) in the foyer of the House of Unions (Ill. 181). First printed in the book *Заблудившийся Трамвай. Arts et poésies russes, 1900–1930*, Paris, 1979, p. 133. The slogan is on one side of the model's round pedestal and is a fragment of the complete text. Like the previous slogan [1], it expresses Tatlin's attempt to realize in practice his conception of the relationship between the 'initiative individual' and the 'collective' (*see* 'Initiative Individual', p. 237). Such an effort to stimulate new forms of epic creation was by no means unique at that time: for example, V. Maiakovskii published his poem '150,000,000', also in 1920, anonymously, suggesting 'that anyone complete and improve' his work (В. Маяковский, *Полное собрание сочинений*, vol. I, Moscow, 1955, p. 26).

[3] From a poster announcing a lecture by Tatlin in the Museum of Artistic Culture (Ill. 243).

The term Tatlinism is mentioned at the end of 1915 in the booklet *Vladimir Evgrafovich Tatlin* (*see* p. 331), where it was said that he 'has never belonged and does not belong to Tatlinism, Rayonism, Futurism, the Wanderers, or any other group'. Similarly, his 1922 lecture 'Material Culture. Down with Tatlinism' was not the only address he gave of this type, but was part of his overall programme.

Such a proposition can be explained by two mutually related considerations. First, Tatlin was in principle opposed to viewing the development of art as a succession of 'isms', and considered his own merit to lie in introducing a new creative method and new type of works which, in his opinion, should be more enduring than individual, transitory 'isms' (*see* 'My Answer', p. 185). Hence Tatlin's difficulty in working out his own terminology, his understanding of the term Constructivism only as designating a creative method, and his difference from others in his treatment of it (*see* 'Art into', p. 310). Second, Tatlin thoroughly disliked any attempt to canonize what had already been achieved, as well as the imitations which followed such new canons. Cf. a similar position in a later polemical article by Meierkhol'd: 'Meierkhol'd against Meierkhol'dism' (1936).

[4] Quoted from Isakov's article 'Artists and the Revolution'. (С. Исаков, 'Художники и революция,' *Жизнь искусства,* no. 22, 1923, p. 2.)

[5] Quoted from Punin's article 'State Exhibition'. (*See* Bibliog.: Punin, 29 May 1923.)

Both slogans are mentioned in connection with Tatlin's participation in the Exhibition of Pictures of Petrograd Artists of All Tendencies: probably a selection of Tatlin's slogans was shown at this exhibition (Ill. 234). Both slogans provide important features of the same thought which bore fruit creatively at precisely that time, during the initial stages of the reconstruction and development of the country's national economy after the Civil War.

[6] Quoted from Miklashevskii's book *Hypertrophy in Art* (*See* Bibliog.: Miklashevskii, 1924). It was reprinted in Kronman's article 'Departing into Technology'. (*See* Bibliog.: Kronman, 1932.) There it is cited as para. 2 of 'Order no. 1 for the Group of Material Culture'. The full text of this 'Order' is unknown, but presumably the whole 'Order' was a list of a number of Tatlin's creative propositions. The thought expressed in this slogan reflects Tatlin's principle that proclaimed tasks should necessarily correspond to artistic practice, i.e. they should be empirical. Such a thought was particularly topical at a time when numerous manifestos and declarations were proclaimed, often with no foundation in practice. (Cf. Tatlin's later article against 'Constructivism' in inverted commas, *see* 'Art into', p. 310).

[Letter to Miturich]

Miturich!

Listen, when we learnt of Khlebnikov's death, we marked the occasion *as soon* as we possibly could, since it was the main thing that had happened to us in all this time. In the exhibition we constructed planes which extended out into space and which overpowered all the exhibition pieces in their intensity and size.

They were of various dimensions. Planes painted black, 16 arshins by 2, 6 by 3, 8 by 2, and so on. There were up to 10 posters and on them was written: 'Khlebnikov has died – date.' People told me that this produced a deep impression. There were discussions of how to arrange a speech in his honour, but in Petrograd no one can say anything about him (Khlebnikov). I'd ask you to send me his 'Boards of Destiny', addressed to Tatlin, Petrograd, 2 Pochtamtskaia, apartment 1. Regards to the Isakov family. I shake your hand.

Tatlin
[1922]

TsGALI, fond 527, inventory 1, unit 338, p. 1.

Original letter evidently written shortly after the closing of the exhibition A Survey of New Tendencies in Art (*see* 'Programme', p. 242), i.e. no earlier than August 1922.

The news of Khlebnikov's death (28 June 1922) came during the exhibition, which had opened on 15 June, and the newly-made planes were included among the exhibits already on display. In metres their dimensions were: 11.36×1.42; 4.26×2.13; 5.68×1.42.

This letter probably gave Miturich as well as Tatlin himself the idea of arranging a special exhibition in memory of Khlebnikov. This opened in the White Hall of the Museum of Artistic Culture on the anniversary of Khlebnikov's death, 28 June 1923; editions of his publications, documents and also artistic works devoted to Khlebnikov were shown. Tatlin organized the exhibition, which consisted of 494 items, 441 of which Miturich brought from Moscow.

On **Khlebnikov** *see* 'Punin, Zangezi', p. 397; Khlebnikov, 'Tatlin', and commentaries, p. 336; 'Initiative Individual', p. 237.

Miturich, Petr Vasil'evich (1887–1956), an artist (mainly a graphic artist), took part in the avant-garde movement in Russian and Soviet art of the beginning of the twentieth century. He was a close friend of Khlebnikov, keeper and publicizer of his artistic legacy; later he married Khlebnikov's sister, the artist V.V. Khlebnikova. Tatlin and Miturich were friends for many years.

The Isakov family were Moscow friends of Miturich and Khlebnikov. (*See* 'Isakov, On Tatlin's Counter-Reliefs', p. 333; c 'Isakov', p. 335)

Boards of Destiny were those works by Khlebnikov in which the poet gave an overall account of his research into mathematical laws of history. Miturich helped to prepare them for printing (they are published in part).

[Letter to Maiakovskii]

Maiakovskii!
I have learnt that in the House of Unions they're exhibiting a samovar instead of my model of the International under the same title. I'd ask you to take the necessary measures at once

and announce it loudly at a meeting or lecture, you know yourself how to go about it. It's necessary to raise a scandal so as to keep the thing. I shake your hand.

Tatlin
(1922)

V.A. Rodchenko Archive in Moscow.

Original letter dated by the author 19 August 1922. The letter was probably sent to Moscow from Petrograd, where Tatlin lived at the beginning of the 1920s.
On the House of Unions, *see* 'The Work', p. 239, and its commentaries.

Maiakovskii, Vladimir Vladimirovich (1893–1930), one of the leaders of avant-garde Soviet art. He and his closest comrades regarded Tatlin as a leader of Constructivism. On the relations of Tatlin and Maiakovskii *see* 'Maiakovskii on Tatlin', p. 393.

The first model of the Monument to the Third International. Its further fate can be followed only with difficulty. In 1929 (*see* 'Autobiography', p. 264) the model was in the State Russian Museum and shortly afterwards Tatlin suggested the Museum should buy it (as attested by Tatlin's letter to Punin of 1930, in a private archive in Leningrad). Probably up to that time the model was in the Museum only for safekeeping. In 1933 it was acquired by the State Tret'iakov Gallery, where it was restored by A. Sotnikov under the supervision of Tatlin. In 1943, during the evacuation of part of the collection, what remained of it was probably written off.

To the Head of the Petrograd Directorate of Scientific and Artistic Institutions, Kristi

The Union of New Tendencies in Art, after hearing at its meeting of 18 December reports by its members, comrades Tatlin, Punin and Lapshin, on the hanging of works by new artists in the Russian Museum, has resolved to bring the following to the attention both of the Council of the Artistic Department of the Russian Museum and to the corresponding organ of the directorate: while noting with satisfaction the hanging of works of the new art in rooms of the Museum which are open for viewing, the Union nevertheless considers that the hanging of works of new artists as carried out by the Russian Museum, in the opinion of the entire Union, does not give a complete representation of the development of painting in recent decades and excessively complicates any overall understanding of precisely those works which by all objective indications may be considered as leading the formal development in new painting.

Believing also that artists might be useful in advising the Museum on the hanging of works which have come out of their circle, the Union requests the Council of the Russian Museum:
1) In the very near future to reorganize the rooms in question.
2) For assistance in the hanging, to invite member-artists of the Union who, while remaining within the limits of the material and space already provided, could present their plan for the placing of pictures.

The Union hopes that the Russian Museum will not fail to inform the Department of its decision in the near future.

President, Tatlin.
Secretary, A. Taran.

3/I/1923
Address of the Union: 2 Pochtamtskaia Street.

TsGAOR Leningrad, fond 2555, inventory 1, file 375, p. 81.

The typewritten document continues and develops the action of the Union in the area of museums. It was written in connection with the opening on 9 December 1922 of a Department of Contemporary Art in the Russian Museum. Punin played a large part in the organization of this, representing the Museum of Artistic Culture in the

Council of the Russian Museum's Artistic Department, not without the influence of Tatlin's Union (*see* 'The Museums Department', p. 241).

Tatlin, in suggesting the personal participation of artists in the showing of contemporary art, was in essence raising the question of introducing principles he had been working on for a new type of museum into a Department of Contemporary Art even of such a traditional art repository as the Russian Museum. Written diagonally across the top in Kristi's handwriting is the directive 'Take the present circumstance into account'.

Pochtamtskaia Street (now Soiuz sviazi Street), 2, the address of Tatlin's apartment, is given as the address of the Union of New Tendencies in Art.

Taran, Andrei Ivanovich, a painter appearing here as secretary to the Union of New Tendencies in Art (*see* p. 242), was assistant to Tatlin as president of the Union. At the same time Taran was from 1921 to 1923 director of the Museum of Artistic Culture, in which Tatlin participated in his turn as member of the Museum Council and organizer of the Museum's Material Culture group.

Punin: *see* 'The Monument', p. 344; 'Tatlin', p. 347; 'About "Zangezi"', p. 395; 'Routine and Tatlin', p. 403 and commentaries.

Lapshin, Nikolai Fedorovich, was deputy director and for some months acting director of the Museum of Artistic Culture from 1921 to 1923.

[Letter to Matiushin]

Mikhail Vasil'evich,

The question of licences is the same for everyone. None of us received one, there's no money. Nevertheless this question is urgent for all of us. I'll raise it at the first meeting and we'll excel in not paying, since no one has any profit from our business. We shall send our resolution to the Trade Union with a representative. On the other hand, if the Museum arranges an exhibition it can, I think, manage without a licence. As for income tax, you won't be asked for it without a licence. For tax matters and exemption from any kind of monetary deduction you should ask for a certificate from the Academy. I have done so myself all this time. The Academy counts you as a professor and cannot refuse you.

Yours, Tatlin

$\frac{7}{II}$[19]23

IRLI (Pushkin House), fond 565 (legacy of Matiushin).

New Economic Policy (NEP): with the development of reconstruction and the NEP in 1923 a monetary reform was carried out, replacing the devalued millions and billions of the previous years with a stable currency (*chervonets*, worth 10 gold roubles). The change to the new rate took place gradually and required a change in state job schedules, wage tariffs and the introduction of differential taxation. For employment in any enterprise outside of government institutions (a trade, commerce, 'free professions' and others) a licence was issued, taxable according to professional income. It was particularly difficult to determine how and how much to tax artists, writers, etc. and this caused a great deal of confusion. (*See* for example К.И. Чуковский, '*Чукоккала*', Москва, 1979; also Maiakovskii's well-known poem written three years after the document quoted above, 'Conversation with a Tax Inspector about Poetry', and related documents in: В. Маяковский, *Полное собрание сочинений*, Москва, vol. VII, pp. 119–26 and vol. XIII, pp. 90–5.)

The letter: at the time the above letter was written Tatlin was a member of the Permanent Commission of the Museum of Artistic Culture (LGALI, fond 4340, inventory 1, unit 13, p. 12), where he was active in various ways but did not have any regular paid position (the staffs of all Soviet institutions were reduced as much as possible in the most difficult year of 1921). Only at the end of 1923 was the Museum's staff increased somewhat and Tatlin 'is employed by the Museum of Artistic Culture as a member of the Museum and receives a basic rate in category 16 (in a 17-category scale) of 41 roubles 40 kopeks in the new currency'. From 1 November that year staff position of Director of the Section for Material Culture was created for him (LGALI fond 4340; inventory 2, unit 5, p. 2; unit 2, pp. 9 reverse –10).

The institutions mentioned: The Union mentioned in the letter is the Trade Union of Art Workers (Rabis); the Museum is the Petrograd Museum of Artistic Culture (later GINKhUK); and the Academy is the Academy of Arts, which had again received this name in 1921.

Although in fact they hardly participated in the work of the Academy at this time, Tatlin and Matiushin were still considered to be professors there (until 1924 and 1926, respectively). At the time of the reform of the Academy in 1921 they had suggested that a faculty of new tendencies in art should be organized there as well as the academic faculty, but their suggestion was not accepted.

On **Matiushin** *see* 'Programme for the Exhibition'; commentary, p. 242.

On 'Zangezi'

On 9 May this year in the Museum of Painterly Culture (9 Isaakievskaia Square) a performance + lecture + exhibition of material constructions is taking place.

216–222 The theme is taken from V. Khlebnikov's last work before his death, 'Zangezi'. This piece is the height of Khlebnikov's creative achievement. In it, his work on language and the study of laws of time are fused in the form of a supernarrative.

N. Punin will give a lecture on Khlebnikov's laws of time. The phonetician Iakubinskii will talk about Khlebnikov's word-creation.

The performance of 'Zangezi' is based on the principle: 'The word is the building unit, the material is the unit of organized space.' According to Khlebnikov's own definition, the supernarrative is 'architecture from stories' and a story is 'architecture from words'. He looks at the word as plastic material. The properties of this material make it possible to manipulate it for the building of the 'government of language'.

This view of Khlebnikov's gave me opportunities for working on the production. Parallel to the word structure I decided to introduce a material construction. By this means the work of two people with different areas of specialization can be fused into one whole, in order to make Khlebnikov's creative work accessible to the masses.

Khlebnikov takes a sound as an element. Within it is the impulse to give birth to words. The sound 'CH', for example, evokes the words *chashka, cherep, chulok, chan* [meaning cup, skull, stocking, vat]. All these words give the idea of an outer shell, one body in the shell of another. The sound 'L' talks of a reduction of energy as the surrounding area at the point of application grows: *lodka, lezhanka, ladon', list, lit'* and so on [meaning boat, stove-couch, palm, leaf, to pour]. In one of the 'packs of planes' of which 'Zangezi' is made up there is a series of such 'thing-like sounds', as in the 'Song of the Astral Language':

Where a swarm of green KHAs for two,
And the EL of clothes during a run,
A GO of clouds over people's games,
A VE of crowds around an unseen fire,
And LA of work, and PE of game and song...

and so on.

To reveal the natures of these sounds I have taken surfaces which are diverse in their material and treatment.

The 'Song of the Astral Language' and in general everything 'Zangezi' says is a slowly moving ray, as it were, from the thinker to the uncomprehending crowd.

This contact is established by means of a specially designed apparatus. In 'Zangezi' there are places where the energy of word-creation is at its most tense.

It was necessary to introduce machines which by their motion again provide a parallel to the action and at the same time fuse with it.

'Zangezi' is something so structurally diverse and difficult to perform that the scenes on stage, being restricted in space, are unable to contain the action. In order to direct the 213, 214 spectator's attention, the projector's eye slides from one place to another, bringing in order and sequence. The projector is also necessary to reveal the properties of the material.

212

The actors are young people: artists, students of the Academy of Arts, of the Mining Institute and the University. This is intentional; professional actors have been brought up in the traditions both of the old and of the contemporary theatre. 'Zangezi' is something too new to be subjected to existing traditions, whatever they are. For this reason it is better to mobilize young people untouched by the theatre, so as to reveal Khlebnikov's work as a revolutionary event.

V. Tatlin
(1923)

В. Татлин, 'О"Зангези"', Жизнь искусства, no. 18, 8 May 1923, p. 15.

The printed text includes a number of printer's errors: Khlebnikov's 'supernarrative' (*sverkhpovest'*) was printed in the first paragraph as 'supernovelty' (*sverkhnovost'*) and there is an omission in the quoted poem. The misprints are corrected here not just by the sense but according to Tatlin's own corrections on the cutting he kept from the journal. In two places punctuation marks had to be corrected, although from the sense there should have been more corrections – the printing of the journal at that time was very careless.

Zangezi is a dramatic 'supernarrative' by Khlebnikov (*see* 'About "Zangezi"', p. 395). For its performance Tatlin took on the functions of producer–director and designer, as well as the actor who played the title role. It was performed three times, on 11, 13 and 30 May (there is documentary confirmation of the first two of these performances). Tatlin displayed the sets and costumes for *Zangezi* (Ill. 216–22) at a number of exhibitions starting in 1923. (*See* Tatlin at Exhibitions, p. 489) On Tatlin's work on *Zangezi, see* 'Kut's Notes', p. 312; 'Artist or', p. 314; 'Tatlin in the Theatre', p. 315 'Curriculum Vitae', p. 320.

Iakubinskii, Lev Petrovich (1892–1945): a Russian linguist and literary specialist, joined the Society for the Study of Poetic Language (OPOIaZ) in the 1920s and was published in *LEF*. (*See also* 'About "Zangezi"', commentaries and notes, pp. 395–400)

Summary of the Programme of the Section for Research on the Construction of the Object (Material Culture)

The main task of the Section is material culture. The work of the Section is purely practical and is the continuation of the work on material culture carried out by V.E. Tatlin since 1913.

I

Research into methods and types of utilization of materials in the construction of objects of everyday life – in the past:

1) Kinds and processing of materials.
2) Techniques for processing materials.
3) Construction of the object.

II

The determination of new methods and types of utilization of materials in the construction of objects of everyday life:

1) New kinds of processing of materials.
2) New kinds of techniques for processing materials
3) New kinds of construction of the object and its standardization.

As the work shows its results, the Section will organize periodic demonstrations of them with explanatory talks.

Tatlin
(1923)

LGALI, fond 4340, inventory 1, unit 21, p. 79. Typescript with Tatlin's signature.

The document is registered as having been presented to the administration of the Museum of Artistic Culture on 6 December 1923.

The Section for Material Culture (the original name of which, as the above letter shows, was the Section for Research on the Construction of the Object) was directed by Tatlin from its creation until the autumn of 1925. In

October 1923 research sections were created in the Museum of Artistic Culture. During this time those who worked in the Department included Khapaev, Nekrasov, Kholodov, Zheltikov, Kobelev, Sakovich, Korotkov (not more than two or three at a time).

[Extracts from Tugendkhol'd's article 'On the Discussion of a Memorial to C[omrade] Lenin']

[...] The artist Tatlin (creator of the famous project for a Monument to the International) is even against the participation of architects in the building, allowing for only constructivist-artists and engineering technicians.

[...] In Tatlin's opinion, for this monument which will be a triumph of the technical side of engineering, we should bring in everything that characterizes our late leader as an innovator and revolutionary *in all areas* of knowledge and human thought in general. It must have an enormous capacity and include a large number of elements of a dynamic and utilitarian character. 200–300 telephones for the use of visitors. A huge auditorium. An information office to let the world know of events in the Soviet republic. A powerful radio and so on [...]

(1924)

'Известия ВЦИК', no. 46, 24 February 1924, in: 'О памятнике Ленину', Ленинград, 1924, p. 111.

In the article Tugendkhol'd summarized the results of a questionnaire he had sent out to leading architects, artists and literary figures in connection with a nationwide discussion of measures to perpetuate the memory of Lenin. He made it a point to reproduce the original wording (that is why it is republished in this section: editor's note). As well as Tatlin's opinions are given also those of Exter, Ivan Fomin, Moisei Ginzburg, Lev Il'in, Norbert, Nivinskii, Roslavlev, Rostislavov, Shchuko, Shchusev, Aleksandr Vesnin and Zelinskii.

Tugendkhol'd, Iakov Aleksandrovich (1882–1928), was a Russian and Soviet art historian specializing in twentieth-century art.

Report of the Section for Material Culture under the Museum of Artistic Culture to the Leningrad Division of the Main Directorate of Scientific Institutions

In 1922 the Section had two divisions:
1) A workshop (Paint as material), the tasks of which were to reveal the property of materials, both in the sense of what has been accomplished in the past and is now being accomplished, and to set the goal for the future.
2) A division for the organization of heterogeneous materials:
   a) an assembly workshop and
   b) a drafting room.

The first task of these two workshops was to discover the properties of materials by analysing them and to provide a number of patterns: a new norm – which would be a pattern for production in the USSR.

In 1923 rooms were allotted in the Museum of Artistic Culture so we could carry out a number of projects, and a number of new forms were suggested in sketches: for a clothing norm and other projects which were shown at exhibitions of the Museum of Artistic Culture and of the Union of Art Workers (Sorabis) and others.

The work of 1922–23 began with a small number of employees and, apart from comrade Tatlin, the first to join their number and work constantly with them was comrade Kholopov, a former student of the Academy of Arts working in its Workshop for Material Culture from 1920 under the direction of his professor, comrade Tatlin, in the Academy of Arts.

All these employees formed a group working on the analysis of properties of heterogeneous materials and their artistic application to our new way of life in the USSR.

What has been done and can now be shown?

1) There are forty norms for standard colours.
2) There are three samples for standard stoves.
3) There is one set (consisting of four separate parts) of new clothing-norms for workers.

What besides this has not been done?

1) Developing and intensifying work [in the creation of colour-charts] on colour-norm[s].
2) Work on the organization of colour-norm material.
3) Intensifying and broadening our tasks in the analysis of heterogeneous materials.

A permanent record is being kept of all the work and this in due course will serve for printed material to explain long-standing questions about how these tasks fit into our new construction. The work is being carried out in the closest contact with those corrective measures provided by life itself, in that our employees have been working since January of this year in factories of the Leningrad Clothing Manufacturers and Low-voltage Electrical Factories Trusts, and are arranging contacts and joint work projects with the other trusts in Leningrad.

An account of the work is provided by the cycle of lectures and showing of designs from 1922 to 1924 inclusive in the Section for Material Culture of the Museum of Artistic Culture, for

1 The People's Commissar of Education, A.V. Lunacharskii, and the Academic Centre as one of his departments,
2 For all scientific and scholarly institutions,
3 For institutes of higher technical education in Leningrad, and their professional faculties,
4 For military and sports organizations and their clubs.

On behalf of the Group for Material Culture,   the Director, Tatlin

Leningrad, 27 May 1924

TsGAOR, fond 2555, inventory 1, file 647, p. 155. Typescript.

The report: Tatlin signs this (as he also does 'To the Leningrad Division', p. 252) with the words 'on behalf of the Group for Material Culture', in accordance with his own view on the role of the 'initiative individual in the collective' (*see* 'Initiative Individual', p. 237).

This Report (or more exactly its theses) is chronologically the first document on the history, structure, results and employees of the Section for Material Culture of the State Institute of Artistic Culture (GINKhUK), which was usually called the Museum of Artistic Culture.

Tatlin, the founder of the Section, attributes the beginning of its work to the year 1922.

The account by the Museum's acting director, Lapshin, of its activity for the first half of 1923 is dated 27 June 1923 (TsGAOR, fond 2555, inventory 1, file 475, p. 66), and the 'Report of the Section for Material Culture' by its director Tatlin is dated 3 September of that year (*see* Zhadova, p. 135). These testify to the 'active work' of Tatlin's workshop in the first half of 1923 'on the object as a product of artistic material culture'. This also confirms the first showing of the results of this work at the exhibitions A Survey of New Tendencies in Art in the summer of 1922 and Exhibition of Petrograd Artists of all Tendencies and In Memoriam Khlebnikov in spring and summer 1923, indicated in the text as exhibitions of the Museum of Artistic Culture and of Sorabis (*see* Tatlin at Exhibitions, pp. 493, 494).

Tatlin was the first artist to create a research workshop as early as being on the staff of the Museum of Artistic Culture. It served as one of the reasons for the reorganization of the Museum into a scientific research institute in October 1923. Tatlin personally viewed the Group for Material Culture, and subsequently the Section for Material Culture in GINKhUK, as a direct continuation of the Studio on Materials, Volume and Construction directed by him from 1919 to 1921 in the Academy of Arts, which in the above text he calls simply the Workshop for Material Culture.

It is interesting to note that work began on colour as material even in the Academy of Arts workshop.

Forty colour-standards for performances, interiors, object constructions, developed by the middle of 1924: this number is first mentioned in the above document. In the language of that time they were called colour-norms.

The information in the report about **samples for stoves** and **clothing designs** is confirmed in press publications (*see* 'The New Way', p. 407).

The **Leningrad Clothing Manufacturers' Trust** was an organization of sewing factories, one of which prepared patterns for clothing models designed by Tatlin. (*See also* 'Research Plan', p. 254).

The **Low-voltage Electrical Factories' Trust** united five factories which prepared communication equipment (telephones, etc.) working with a low-voltage current.

Lectures, demonstrations of models. The publicizing of 'design' as we should say today, in the form of lectures with demonstrations of models is judged in the report to be an extremely important way for the Section for Material Culture to present its account. Judging from an invitation card in the same archive file, Tatlin gave a lecture on 18 May 1924 in the Museum of Artistic Culture on 'Material Culture and its role in the Production and Life of the USSR' (of the same document, p. 159). According to Sotnikov's reminiscences of lectures in the VKhUTEIN, Tatlin was an excellent speaker. (Sotnikov's personal communication.)

To the invitation card is attached an explanatory sheet which says in particular: 'The lecture on material culture and its role in the production and life of the USSR aims thoroughly to shed light on the tasks of production in our country, and also to discover the place of the artist-constructor in production, in relation to improving the quality both of the manufactured product and of the organization of the new way of life in general...' (p. 160).

Khapaev, Nikolai Alekseevich (1896– ?), went over with Tatlin from the Academy of Arts to the Group/Section for Material Culture under the Museum of Artistic Culture–GINKhUK. In a questionnaire in the autumn of 1923 he calls himself an artist-constructor and talks of the beginning of the work on the analysis of materials in 1920–21 (TsGAOR, fond 2555, inventory 1, file 647, p. 30).

To the Leningrad Division of Glavnauka

In reply to your memorandum no. 4195 of 9 June 1924, the Section for Material Culture informs you that it is in no way working in isolation since all the research which takes place in the Section is presented in the form of special reports and lectures which have recently been organized, since 25 May, for six different institutions and enterprises, and will continue until July.

In its turn the group of employees has charged me to inform you that, according to the terms for research work, even those employees who are not directly engaged in the work are not allowed in certain areas of the Section for Material Culture for five or six days until the varnishes and oils have dried, since too much circulation raises dust and ruins the quality of our experiments. Furthermore, investigations and experiments which are being carried out in a laboratory cannot be shown before they have been mounted, and when they have been they must be shown to institutions
1) concerned with production,
2) having a direct connection with production,
3) carrying out ideological and scholarly work for the consolidation of the USSR (i.e. to all party organizations).

In view of what has been said I would ask the Leningrad division of Glavnauka to confirm the work procedures of the Section for Material Culture under the Museum of Artistic Culture so that the administrative–economic apparatus of the Museum should not bring confusion into the quietly progressing work of the Section for Material Culture.

On behalf of the group of employees,
Director of the Section for Material Culture, Tatlin.
Leningrad, Section for Material Culture of the Museum of Artistic Culture

12 June 1924

TsGAOR, fond 2555, inventory 1, file 647, p. 177.

The document is a typescript with Tatlin's signature. It is registered as being presented to the administration of PUNU on 12 June 1924. The well-edited text of an 'official paper' was evidently written by Tatlin with the help of one of his colleagues or friends.

This explanatory and informational paper is an answer to the firm warning of the director of the Petrograd Directorate of Scientific and Artistic Institutions (PUNU) Kristi, 'that the Section for Material Culture should be closed' if Tatlin continued to isolate the Department's work from GINKhUK 'in an administrative–economic and scientific sense'. (PUNU memorandum [Kristi] of 9 June 1924, p. 175 of the same file.) Tatlin, known for his suspiciousness and his morbid fear of plagiarism, allowed neither employees of other sections nor representatives of the administration onto the premises of the Section for Material Culture – including the director himself, Malevich, a long-standing rival and competitor to Tatlin. In the summer and autumn of 1924 he boycotted sessions of the GINKhUK directorate, and wrote reports on his section's activity for 1923–4 and its work plan for 1924–5 only under pressure from higher organizations (*see* p. 254).

Exhibition of the Section for Material Culture: Tatlin officially refused to participate in the Synoptic Exhibition of GINKhUK for 1925 (15 May to 8 June), but nevertheless arranged an exhibition of the work of his department in the so-called showroom of the Section for Material Culture. Apparently models, sketches and drawings were brought together representing the artistic and design activity of Tatlin's Section which had been mentioned in the press but not published (*see* 'The New Way', p. 407). The exhibition of works from Tatlin's workshop in this showroom during the period of GINKhUK's Synoptic Exhibition was essentially an integral part of it. On the night before the exhibition opened, evidently in order to preserve secrecy, Tatlin took the critic Isakov and another acquaintance into the Section's exhibition by breaking the door leading from his apartment to the display room. As a result Malevich, the director of GINKhUK, officially declared that he 'disclaimed all responsibility' for the Section for Material Culture, and was supported by the director of PUNU, Kristi (PUNU's letter of 16 May 1924 in the same file, p. 156). At the time when GINKhUK's Synoptic Exhibition was being prepared, Tatlin and his colleagues engaged in publicizing the section, talking about its work first and foremost to people directly connected with production. Judging by this document, Tatlin gave six lectures during the period from 25 April to 12 June. (On the lecture of 18 May *see* 'Report', p. 250) All these lectures took place in the room of the Section for Material Culture's exhibition, where it was convenient to demonstrate the models.

Tatlin, the artist-constructor: Tatlin who as early as the end of 1923 had defined his area of specialization as that of an artist-constructor (*see* his employment form for the Petrograd Museum of Artistic Culture–GINKhUK of 14 November 1923: TsGAOR, fond 2555, inventory 1, file 647, p. 29), at this period of his activity was evidently closely involved with the movement of productionist artists.

[Letter to Spandikov]

Dear Eduard Karlovich,

I'm in Barnaul. The local travelling conditions are intolerable. As for painting, the conditions for working at it are impossible, you have to limit yourself to sketches, more is impossible. There's a demand for 'art junk', but the clients are fanatic in relation to their 'aesthetic' requirements. If it's bad in Petersburg it's nightmarish here. I have learnt from experience: I eat well and heartily and... that's all.

    I was in Biisk. I didn't manage to find Mikh. Khris. Bader. I inquired in the provincial land office [Gubzemupravlenie] and the department of local ec[onomy].

Sincere regards,
'maestro' V. Tatlin
24/9/24

Unfortunately, for certain reasons I haven't an address until my next letter.

(1924)

State Russian Museum, manuscripts section, fond 134, unit 72, p. 1. Handwritten original.

This letter has so far been the only documentary evidence of Tatlin's trip to western Siberia, although there is a brief mention of it in the reminiscences of the poet Martynov. Talking about a New Year's tree put up by the young artists of Omsk 'as an outrageous denial of an ancient custom' and decorated 'symbolically, expressionistically and cubistically,' Martynov maintains that such a tree 'would be appreciated by Tatlin himself, who came, as I learnt later, to Omsk in those very years as an instructor of the all-Russian council of the as yet undissolved Proletkul't in order to inquire into the activity of workers' theatres. Tatlin, if it was he and not some other Tatlin, I think would have approved of our tree.' (Леонид Мартынов, Воздушные фрегаты, Москва,1974, p. 124) Tatlin was not an employee of the Organization for Proletarian Culture (although possibly he may have carried out some assignments for it); at that time he worked in GINKhUK and was probably on a visit to western Siberia to become acquainted with local artistic life and the work of museums. In particular it was in Barnaul that the most recent Museum of Artistic Culture had been established.

Spandikov, Eduard Karlovich (1875–1929), an artist and lawyer, and an active participant in the Union of Youth, took part in the performance of *Tsar Maximilian* in 1911 in St Petersburg as artist and actor. He was a long-time acquaintance of Tatlin.

Bader, M.Kh: this person has not been identified yet.

Research Plan of the Section for Material Culture under the Museum of Artistic Culture for 1924 and 1925

Division of Coating Materials

Broadening and intensifying work on a paint-norm. Checking and selecting from existing standards in the workshop from 1923 and 1924.
Conclusions based on the above standards of 1923 and 1924.
Selection and establishing of new standards applicable to the new way of life. (For performances, homes, objects etc.)
Research into economic means of painting.

Division on the Organization of Material into the Object

1) Establishing the tasks.
2) Analysis both of old objects and of their parts.
3) Comparison of materials.
4) Construction of the object.
5) Establishing pattern-norms for mass production.
6) Research into production in the USSR.
7) Research into production abroad.

20 October 1924   Director of the Section for Material Culture
                                                                    V. Tatlin
                                                                    (1924)

LGALI, fond 4340, inventory 1, unit 31, p. 74. Typed copy corrected by hand.

The plan continues the direction of work which had become traditional in the Section for Material Culture ('Division on the Organizaton of Material into the Object'), and is supplemented by the previously unknown division of 'Coating Materials.' The latter drew up a plan for the future and also reflected the variety of work already carried out when Tatlin was considering 'colour as material'. Its results were shown at the exhibitions A Survey of New Tendencies in Art (1922) and Exhibition of Petrograd Artists of all Tendencies (1923). (*See* Tatlin at Exhibitions, pp. 493; 494.) The ideas in this plan and similar documents formed Tatlin's working programme in subsequent years, particularly when he was teaching in the Kiev College of Art (1925–7) and in VKhUTEIN (1927–30). (*See* 'The Artist', p. 266; 'The Problem', p. 267)

Report of the Section for Material Culture's Work for 1923–1924

Taking into account the anarchical state of the organization of materials, the principal basis for which is industrial and domestic production, as well as all kinds of experimental tendencies directed towards raising the level of material culture in the sense of using and shaping materials artistically;
Recognizing, besides this, that the present everyday life in the country and the towns is also in an anarchical state in terms of the economy and the artistic shaping of life itself;
In view of this the section for Material Culture sets itself two tasks:
1) The shaping of materials.
2) The shaping of everyday life.
To accomplish these tasks the Section carried out work in the following divisions:
1) Division of Coating Materials.
The task of the division was to broaden the possibilities of use:
a) of colour selection, based on ways of preparation.
b) to find normative ways for preparing individual coating materials in the sense of making them acceptable to the eye and to everyday life.

This division made in 1923–4 forty patterns for colour-norms, and preparations of bases for norms – developing primers and applying coating materials (with whitewash and oil).
2) Division on the Organization of Material into the Object.

The task was to use the accumulated experience on material culture (relief and counter-relief), and apply these experiments to the organization of everyday life, taking mass production into account. The Section undertook a number of experiments:
a) Experiment on developing a pattern for clothing-norms.

The division worked out a plan for a clothing-norm, with preparatory drawings and sketches, contacted factories of Leningrad Clothing Manufacturers' Trust and jointly produced a set of clothing-norms for the working citizens and townspeople of the USSR. The set took the form of three items: 1) A man's overcoat; 2) A jacket; 3) A smock.
b) Experiment on developing household objects: a norm for fireplaces for workers' apartments, three different types.

In 1923 and 1924 the research work concluded with a number of lectures on the theme 'Material Culture and its Role in the Production and Life of the USSR'. The lectures were given to specialist workers, professional faculty and students of institutes of higher education, and evaluations were made by means of a questionnaire. The lectures were accompanied by demonstrations of the above-mentioned designs.

The working staff of the Section in 1923 and 1924 did not exceed 9 persons. The research workers were:

1 Khapaev,
2 Kobelev,
3 Kholodov,
4 Nekrasov,
5 Geintse,
6 Vinogradov.

Of these, active participants were: Kobelev, Khapaev and Nekrasov, and Kholodov.

Geintse was entrusted with work involving microscopic research.

Vinogradov had been sent to complete courses on civil engineering.

The section has an accessory-assembly shop, in which work was carried out on the assembling and preparing of necessary parts. In this shop two Section workers are employed: a fitter, Nikolaev, and a metal-worker, Sokovich.

1 November 1924   Director of the Section for Material Culture, Tatlin
Leningrad

TsGAOR, fond 2555, inventory 1, file 647, pp. 337–38, typescript.

The report: the Director of PUNU, Kristi, has written diagonally across the top left-hand side the instruction 'Request an expanded version of the account. 5. 11. Kristi.'

Tatlin wrote this account of his Section very late and after more than one reminder not only from the GINKhUK directorate but also from Kristi, personally. (The other section directors, Malevich, Matiushin and Punin, had given their accounts by the end of June 1924.)

The distinctive empiricism (material concreteness) of Tatlin's creative thought, his basic inability to give verbal and theoretical expression to his research, his lack of clarity and the extreme brevity of his formulations led, however, to Kristi's negative reaction and demand for more.

This is one of the programmatic documents of Tatlin's activity as Director of the Section for Material Culture of GINKhUK. While repeating with a few slight variations information on the Section's structure, lecture work and results of its activities (three items are indicated rather than four in the set of clothes, evidently a result of the author's habitual carelessness over things that had already been produced. Cf. 'Report', pp. 250, 256), Tatlin in this document tries for the first time to give an historical-sociological foundation to two basic directions of the work which from the beginning had been characteristic of the Section for Material Culture (i.e. the 'Division of Coating Materials' and the 'Division on the Organization of Material into the Object') as a prototype of a design-office in the USSR. (*See also* 'Research Plan', p. 254)

In this report Tatlin made the first attempt to define in words the extremely important socially-forming principle of 'Material Culture' or, as we would say now, his own creative design-conception: the designing of objects as a means of creating new forms for everyday life ('shaping of everyday life').

New information is reported here on the creation of colour patterns for painting, both in the practical sense of the task's complexity (1, creating bases and primers, 2, selecting the colours and components of coating materials) and in the aesthetic one of what are acceptable criteria psychologically (for the eye) and socially (for everyday life).

In this document, which is characteristically programmatic as far as his own development is concerned, Tatlin looks at the experimental work on the relief and counter-relief as the genesis and empirical methodological basis for the designing of objects. It is noteworthy that in the 'employment form' of 14 November 1923 Tatlin answers the question about his academic career thus: 'Work on Material Culture from 1923 on (looking for new ways to shape our everyday life).' TsGAOR, p. 29 of the same archive file.

Khapaev, N.A.: *see* 'Report', commentary, p. 252.

Kobelev, Kholodov: details as yet undetermined.

Nekrasov, Evgenii Nikolaevich (b. 1902), a painter, worked in the Group/Section for Material Culture on research into materials from 1922 on.

Geintse, Mariia Andreevna, Tatlin's wife from 1921 to 1925, was a doctor. Tatlin's mention of surgeon M.A. Geintse's participation as one of the assistant-consultants in the building of **Letatlin** (Ill. 313–53) in his well-known article of 1932 can be illuminated for the first time in this report. The early beginning (1924) of preparatory (microscopic) research, particularly the preparation of birds for studying the flight mechanisms of their wings, here receives documentary confirmation.

Vinogradov, *see* 'The Work', p. 239 and commentary.

Nikolaev, Sokovich, P.I.: no available information.

Report of the Section for Material Culture's Research Work for 1924

Taking into account that the industrial and domestic production inherited from the old world, including painting, as well as our experience in both town and country in all its manifestations, is in a state of anarchy: production is splintered into chance productive units, experience is abnormally individualized and without unity of form. Recognizing also that the shaping principle of culture, production and experience is material, the Section for Material Culture sets itself the task of:

1) Research into material as the shaping principle of culture.
2) Research into everyday life as a certain form of material culture.
3) The synthetic forming of material and, as a result of such formation, the construction of standards for new experience.

To realize these tasks the Section carried out the following work:

I Experimental research into coating materials. The work was carried out in the direction of broadening the use of coating materials, determining new means of preparing surfaces. The Section showed a number of colour selections which, thanks to their particular colour qualities, could find an application in production; moreover, the Section found for certain coating materials normal methods of preparation (colour-norms), thanks to which materials of this kind can be widely used in our everyday life. In connection with the demonstration of new standards two lectures were given by the director of this work:

1) Colour as coating material (against Impressionism and other 'isms'.)
2) Specific colour fields in various cultural epochs.

II Experimental research into the properties of material.

Work was done and developed on the shaping of material in space; to this purpose research was undertaken into the construction of reliefs and counter-reliefs, our experience in analysing a fully material volume was broadened, and finally the significance of material as an unlimited element which uniquely shapes culture was confirmed. At the synoptic exhibition patterns of reliefs and counter-reliefs of classical construction were shown, in connection with which two lectures were given:

a) form as a result of material volume;
b) the development of spatial perceptions from recent tendencies in art to the counter-relief.

The shaping of materials in the conditions of contemporary everyday life. In this division the Section worked out two patterns in several variants of clothing-norms and a fireplace-norm. Patterns of clothing-norms were designed in a number of sketches and drawings, of which 1) A man's overcoat; 2) A jacket; 3) A smock; 4) Trousers, one set for workers and citizens of the USSR (townspeople), were realized by the Department of Material Culture jointly with the factories of Leningrad Clothing Manufacturers' Trust.

The design of a fireplace-norm for workers' apartments was developed in three variants: a model of a complex stove-range with all the means for preparing and preserving food, the model of a simplified stove, and the model of an economical stove. The demonstration of new models was accompanied by lectures.

Material culture, contemporary everyday life and production.

Besides this, a number of conversations were held with specialist workers, workers who were students of institutes of higher education; evaluation forms were collected.

At the synoptic yearly exhibition all the designs were shown and accompanied by necessary explanations.

The Section's staff:

The scientific staff: Khapaev, Kobelev, Kholodov, Nekrasov, Geintse.

Specialist workers: Nikolaev, Sokovich.

The Section has an accessory and assembly shop, in which work was carried out on the assembly and preparing of necessary parts for developing demonstration patterns.

Director of the Section for Material Culture, V. Tatlin
Leningrad, 10 November 1924

TsGAOR, fond 2555, inventory 1, file 647, pp. 348–9. Typescript with Tatlin's signature.

This new version of the Report of the Section for Material Culture is written ten days after the previous one in response to PUNU's request for 'an expanded version of the account' (*see* 'Report', p. 255). In the title the time span of the account, 1923–4, has been shortened to 1924.

In its facts and, in part, in its composition, this document repeats with slight variations the report of 1 November and in many ways the report of 27 May (*see* 'Report', pp. 254, 250).

The new account, which is not longer than the previous one, gives certain new interpretations to the theses of 'Material Culture' as well as individual points of clarification.

Tatlin makes clear, for example, that when he talks of the sociological-historical foundation to the Section's aims he means the contemporary condition of industrial and domestic production in Russia in an aesthetic sense.

This creative concept of Tatlin's 'Material Culture', connected at this period with the slogans he proposed 'Not to the left, not to the right, but to the necessary' and 'Not the old, not the new, but the necessary' ('Slogans', p. 244; III. 234), led him in these years of Russia's economic chaos to such an original 'necessary' design as that of a wood stove. Subsequently in the 1920s this tendency would be developed in his programme by his turning to traditional native materials like wood, rather than metal, in furniture design.

Tatlin formulates the social and cultural functions of Soviet design more accurately by setting himself the task of research into everyday life, that is into a way of life 'as a certain form of material culture' with the aim of 'shaping' or 'forming' it: i.e. of improving and changing it.

In confirming 'material as an unlimited element which uniquely shapes culture' Tatlin tries to give his own creative concept a theoretical foundation. In other words, as well as universalizing the concept of material culture (*see* Zhadova, p. 135), Tatlin attempts to realize what was most distinctive in it as a strictly artistic way of constructing – its creation of forms in volume and space – in a formulating design.

In Tatlin's report of 27 May, and in his two accounts of 1 and 10 November 1924 of his section's work (pp. 250, 254, 256), we have the history of the Group/Section for Material Culture from 1922 to 1924 inclusive as the history of a composite experimental-research design-centre or design-workshop, as we should say today, with its own productive base and its own office for publicizing a new sphere of activity.

To the Leningrad Division of Glavnauka
Declaration by the Director of the Section for Material Culture Tatlin and the Director of the Experimental Section of the Institute of Artistic Culture Mansurov

The past working year of our research institute has shown the complete isolation of this institute from other scientific and artistic institutions, and it has also become clear that the internal work of our departments is proceeding under unfavourable conditions created by the administration in the person of the director, who, having charge of the formal-theoretical section, uses the work of other departments with the aim of publicizing one tendency (Suprematism), legitimizing his scientific method by administrative means. Moreover, the structure of the administrative and scientific organs of the Institute's directorate, in the absence of a constitution, is arbitrary and does not correspond to the desired form and general interests of all five sections.

We request that this be taken into consideration, and also in the interests of a more stable foundation for the whole matter, and for the regulation of both the institute's external and internal life, we request that someone objective be named director of the Institute of Artistic Culture, who commands respect both in scientific-artistic and party circles and who is also well acquainted with questions of contemporary art and general politics.

V. Tatlin
P. Mansurov

4/XII/1924

TsGAOR, fond 2555, inventory 1, file 647, p. 364.

Original manuscript in India ink written by Mansurov, with the signatures of Tatlin as Director of the Section for Material Culture (staff position) and Mansurov himself as Director of the Experimental Section of GINKhUK (a supernumerary position).

Mansurov, Pavel Aleksandrovich (b. 1895), a painter, graduated from the Baron Shtiglits Artistic College and the School of the Society for the Encouragement of the Arts. In autumn 1923 with the agreement of the new Director of the Museum of Artistic Culture, K.S. Malevich, he was confirmed as the supernumerary Director of the Section for painting technique, shortly to be renamed the Experimental Section.

Malevich followed with interest Mansurov's research work on the relationship between the creation of forms in nature and the artistic activity of man (he considered painting technique, building, etc. from this point of view). In June 1924 Malevich, as Director of GINKhUK, applied for a trip abroad for P.A. Mansurov for research purposes (same archive file, p. 173).

By the beginning of December 1924, when the above declaration was written, Mansurov, who had previously been friendly towards Malevich, had become extremely resentful of the Institute's director, who at the same time headed the Section for Theoretical Analysis of Form (Section for Painterly Culture). The paid (staff) position of departmental director which Mansurov was trying to obtain was given to Punin, naturally with Malevich's approval. Indeed it was in autumn 1924 that Punin had actively begun to reform the Section for General Methodology.

The declaration: It may be supposed that it was Mansurov who initiated the idea for such a declaration, easily involving Tatlin in an action directed against Malevich. Tatlin's long-standing jealousy of Malevich in an artistic sense was aggravated by the latter's position as Director of the Institute, as administratively he had gained the upper hand. An idea (dating from the end of 1921) to create a branch of the Moscow INKhUK on the basis of the Petrograd Museum of Artistic Culture, under Tatlin's directorship, came to nothing (*see* Strigalev, n78, p. 41).

Mansurov's subsequent fate is typical. In spring 1925 he was officially removed from the list of GINKhUK's employees by Glavnauka. However, he continued to work there without authorization and made use of GINKhUK's Synoptic Exhibition for 1926 to publicize his own declarations ('Letter from the Countryside to the City') which were unrelated to art, adding to the tense atmosphere surrounding GINKhUK which soon led, in December 1926, to the Institute's being disbanded. Mansurov himself emigrated to France, where he still lives.

Tatlin's and Mansurov's criticisms of Malevich as Director of GINKhUK can hardly be justified. Since 26 October 1923 the 'Regulations of the Institute of Higher Artistic Knowledge' (as it had originally been thought to call GINKhUK, organized on the basis of the Museum of Material Culture) had been in force. (Minutes of the meeting of the Council of the Museum of Artistic Culture of 17 October 1923: TsGAOR, fond 2555, inventory 1, file 647, pp. 7, 9.) These Regulations were discussed at subsequent Councils, elaborated by Malevich and reported by him to PUNU (same archive folio, file 475, pp. 88, 118–19). Judging from numerous documents and testimonies of GINKhUK's members, Malevich allowed section directors complete independence in their activity.

Malevich, Kazimir Severinovich: *see* Sarab'ianov pp. 44, 57, 58.

Filonov, Pavel Nikolaevich (1883–1941), a painter, theorist and educator, he worked out the conception of 'Analytic art', which he realized in his art and teaching activity. He urged a transformation of the Museum of Artistic Culture into a research institute – GINKhUK – and was the first head of the Section for General Methodology (Ideology).

Punin: *see* 'To the Head', commentary, p. 246.

To the Director of the Leningrad Division of Glavnauka, Kristi

From the Director of the Experimental Section of the Institute of Artistic Culture Mansurov and the Director of the Section for Material Culture Tatlin

On our own behalf and further to the declaration we ask you to offer the position of Director of the Institute of Artistic Culture to S.K. Isakov, who is highly competent in matters of art of the past and the new art, is completely loyal to various tendencies in art, a party member, and has wide connections with the art-historical and scientific organizations of Moscow and Leningrad.

                                                                                                  Tatlin
9/XII[19]24   P. Mansurov

TsGAOR, fond 2555, inventory 1, file 647, p. 363.

Original manuscript in India ink written by Mansurov, with the signatures of Tatlin and Mansurov.

The document is an addition to Tatlin's and Mansurov's action against Malevich in their declaration of 4 December 1924 (*see* previous document).
   This document may have been written at Tatlin's suggestion, since its authors propose for the position of GINKhUK's director an old friend of Tatlin's, Isakov, Sergei Konstantinovich (*see* 'Tatlin's Counter-Reliefs', p. 333 and commentaries).

To the Committee for the USSR Section of the International Exhibition in Paris
Declaration of Artist-Constructor Tatlin

At the Committee's suggestion I have made a model in honour of the Comintern for showing   186
at the Paris Exhibition. In view of the model's complex structure and its size (3 metres high)
it has to be sent in dismantled form.
   For the model's assembly and proper mounting at the exhibition I have to be present, and thus I would propose that the Committee organize my trip to Paris.
   In order to receive a grant of 275 roubles for the model's construction I signed a contract which provides for it to become the property of the Committee. I signed this contract so as to begin work as early as possible and complete it by the given deadline. In fact I consider that I have been paid too paltry a sum for the huge expenditure of energy and materials. I would assess my model as being worth three thousand gold roubles. And I cannot transfer ownership rights to the Committee for 275 roubles. If the Committee should not find it necessary to acquire the model for three thousand roubles, then it should be returned to my workshop, and I would ask you to urgently send me your agreement.
   The Commission which accepted the model, in the persons of the chairman D.P. Shterenberg and the secretary, agreed with me about the incorrect evaluation of the exhibit and promised to send me an extract from the minutes of the commission's meeting in Moscow at which this question is to be decided.
   The model and cases to pack it in are ready. I would urgently ask you to send your decision.
                                                                                                  Tatlin
Leningrad, 9/2 Vorovskii Square and Soiuz sviazi Street, apartment 1

                                                                                                  [1925]

TsGALI, fond 941, inventory 15, unit 20, p. 11 and back.

Original manuscript in black ink with Tatlin's signature. Registered by the administration of the Committee for the Exhibition's Soviet Section on 16 February 1925.
   In autumn 1924 the young Soviet republic was given *de jure* recognition by France, the first major capitalist power to do so. The Soviet government accepted the French proposal which followed at the end of October 1924 to participate in the International Exhibition of Modern Decorative and Industrial Arts, which opened in May 1925 in Paris. On 15 November 1924 a Committee on the Organization of the Soviet Section of the Exhibition was

established (TsGALI, fond 941, inventory 15, unit 13, p. 38), and included Lunacharskii (Chairman), Shterenberg (Commissioner of the Soviet Section), Tugendkhol'd, Maiakovskii, Kristi and others.

At a meeting of the Committee for the USSR Section on 16 December 1924 a personal invitation to Tatlin to participate was confirmed (Protocol no. 9 in TsGALI, fond 941, inventory 15, unit 13, p. 38).

Kristi, the Committee's Leningrad representative, sent this to Tatlin on 29 December 1924.

At the Committee's meeting of 6 January 1925 it was recognized as 'desirable to have at the exhibition a model of the Monument to the Third International' and to allow the grant of 275 roubles requested by its author for its preparation (Protocol no. 16, same archive file, p. 62).

Tatlin constructed the second model of the tower with unprecedented speed. By the end of January it was already at an advanced stage and on 10 February 1925 was accepted by the Commission for showing at the Exhibition. (See 'Protocol of the meeting on the question of examining and selecting the Leningrad exhibits for the USSR Section of the International Exhibition of Decorative and Industrial Arts in Paris.' Chairman M.P. Kristi, secretary Ia.M. Gessen; commission members D.P. Shterenberg, D.A. Arkin and invited experts P.I. Neradovskii, S.K. Isakov, N.N. Punin. TsGAOR, fond 2555, inventory 1, file 737, p. 114.)

The Committee on the Organization of the USSR Section at the International Exhibition refused Tatlin a trip to Paris for lack of means. However, at the same time Kristi in his letter to the Committee of 27 January 1925, while indicating that he managed only with great difficulty to convince the artist to transfer ownership rights of the model to the Committee, recognizes the justice of the author's claim in view of the disparity between the model's real worth and the extremely modest grant allowed to Tatlin (TsGAOR, fond 2555, inventory 1, file 737, p. 84).

The same was confirmed by D.P. Shterenberg at the above-mentioned Commission of experts when the model was accepted on 10 February 1925. He further drew the conclusion that if the model were not sold it should be returned to its author and the amount allowed him regarded only as a grant. (See the above-mentioned Protocol.)

The second model of the Monument to the Third International enjoyed a great success at the 1925 International Exhibition in Paris and its author was awarded a gold medal.

In spring 1926 the model was returned to Leningrad (in two boxes) and on 16 March 1926 it was received by GINKhUK. (See 'Detailed list of objects sent from the USSR Section', TsGAOR, fond 2555, inventory 1, file 737, p. 202.)

Tatlin at this time was already working in Kiev. Evidently the model was returned to the author and then bought from him by the State Russian Museum, where it was shown in 1930 at the exhibition 'War and Art' (see Tatlin at Exhibitions, p. 496).

Gessen, Iakov Matveevich, was the deputy director of PUNU in Leningrad.

Shterenberg, David Petrovich (1881–1948): a painter, was People's Commissar for Arts in 1917–18, head of IZO Narkompros in 1918–20, and commissioner of the Soviet Section at the Paris exhibition.

Arkin, David Efimovich, was an art historian.

Neradovskii: see 'Letter to Neradovskii', commentary, p. 239.

Isakov: see 'On Tatlin's Counter-Reliefs', commentary, p. 335.

Punin: see 'Programme of the Exhibition', commentary, p. 243.

[Letter to Novitskii]

Most respected Pavel Ivanovich,

I am writing to you from Kiev. You will remember me, as I do you very well from Leningrad when you came there. I am working in the Kiev College of Art, where I'm directing and managing the Drama-cine-photo Department. The Department is divided into two sub-departments. One graduates artists for theatre and cinema design, and the second sub-department artists for cinema photography. It's something new, is only in its second year of existence and so far has only two courses. The complete course should take four years to complete.

This is something I'm very interested in and I would like to continue with it, but my isolation from the artistic environment obliges me to ask you (as the head and rector of VKhUTEMAS) to find me a place in your institute. Here I have the position of professor of the first category. In the theatre I worked as artistic decorator and designer, but I also know the mechanical side of the stage, and during that time I 'mechanized' several stages. In the Kiev College, as additional work, I was formally in charge of 'technical disciplines (space)'.

As the founder of the idea 'art into life' I worked in the woodworking industry on the development of new models for furniture, and also worked in sewing trusts on the development of a clothing-norm.

Until my move to the Leningrad Academy I was one of the leaders in VKhUTEMAS [at that time it was in fact the Free State Artistic Studios].

My record before the Revolution: I had a studio on Ostozhenka Street (Moscow) from 1912 until the October Revolution and instructed drawing and painting. From [19]18 I was in charge of IZO Narkompros and, as a professor of VKhUTEMAS [Free State Artistic Studios], instructed for one and a half years. In 1921 I moved to Leningrad [in 1919, to Petrograd], where I was a professor-instructor in the Academy of Arts [Petrograd SVOMAS]. In 1925 I was invited as professor to the Kiev College of Art, where I am still working now.

I attach to this letter a certificate from Leningrad, which can serve as my record of service and as a partial curriculum vitae.

I would ask you to inform me of your decision at my address Kiev, 7 Dikaia Street, apartment 1, Tatlin.

With my sincere respects,   V. E. Tatlin
1/IV/27
P.S. If you need any further papers or information, let me know.

(1927)

TsGALI, fond 681, inventory 3, unit 26, p. 272. Original manuscript.

To the letter is attached an official certificate of Tatlin's employment activity in Soviet and educational institutions (same archive file, p. 273). On the letter is Novitskii's instruction: 'To the Dean of the Wood- and Metalworking Faculty. I recommend to your attention an application from Tatlin, an outstanding inventor and constructor of objects. 17. IV. P. Novitskii.'

VKhUTEMAS (Higher Artistic and Technical Studios) was an institute of higher artistic education in Moscow formed at the end of 1920 from the Free State Artistic Studios, which had replaced in 1918 and 1919 the Stroganov Artistic-Industrial College and the Moscow College of Painting, Sculpture and Architecture. When Tatlin's letter was sent (1927), VKhUTEMAS was reorganized into VKhUTEIN. Dermet is the Russian acronym for VKhUTEIN's Woodworking Faculty, of which Tatlin became associate professor, then professor after 1927.

Kiev College of Art was created in 1917 on the basis of the Ukrainian Academy of Arts (from 1922 the Institute of Plastic Arts). Tatlin worked in the Kiev College of Art from 1925 to 1927.

Novitskii, Pavel Ivanovich (1888–1971), an art critic and art historian, was the rector of VKhUTEMAS–VKhUTEIN from 1926 to 1930.

[Letter to Neradovskii]

Most respected Petr Ivanovich,
I am leaving you five drawings for 'The Flying Dutchman', which I brought to your apartment, and I would ask you to submit them to the (Moscow) Purchasing Commission for consideration.

156–163

Five of these things I can sell without breaking a set, since they were made for one theatrical production. For my part I would ask you to explain to the commission that my work is of long-term significance and for this reason I cannot sell them for a cheap price.

$\frac{14}{V}$ 27   With my sincere respects,
                                                                                          Tatlin

Kiev, 7 Dikaia Street, apartment 1 or c/o 2/9 Isaak[ievskaia] Sq[uare] and Poch[tamtskaia Street]: Mariia Andr[eevna] Geintse

(1927)

State Tret'iakov Gallery, manuscripts section, 31/1551.

The drawings were made by Tatlin in 1915–18. (*See* 'Theatrical Work', p. 324; commentaries, p. 328)

The letter: Since Neradovskii worked at the same time in the State Russian Museum and the State Tret'iakov Gallery, Tatlin specifies that he is offering his drawings to the latter (Moscow Purchasing Commission). All the five drawings were purchased and the next year four of them were shown at the Exhibition of Acquisitions for 1927–1928 by the State Purchasing Commission for Acquiring Works of Fine Art. (*See* Tatlin at Exhibitions, p. 496)
    At the end of the letter Tatlin, who just at that time had made arrangements to leave for Moscow (*see* 'Letter', p. 260), gives his Kiev address and the Leningrad address of his old apartment in the GINKhUK, where at that time his wife M.A. Geintse (*see* 'Art into', p. 310; c'Geintse', p. 256) and four-year-old son Vladimir (1923–43) were living.

Neradovskii: *see* 'Letter to Neradovskii', p. 238 and commentaries.

Questionnaire

1 *Surname, name, patronymic:* Tatlin, Vladimir Evgrafovich.
2 *Year and place of birth:* 12 December (old style) 1885 in Moscow.
3 *General education:* practical school up to the 4th class in Khar'kov.
4 *Special education (where, with whom, special educational establishments completed):* At the College of Painting, Sculpture and Architecture (1902–1904) [1902–1903] under K. Korovin and Serov.
   Penza College of Art (1904–1909) [1905–1910] under A.F. Afanas'ev.
   VUZhVZ [Higher Institute of Painting, Sculpture and Architecture] (1909–1910).
5 *Can you indicate which artists or individual works of theirs had a [direct] influence on your works?:* A.F. Afanas'ev, M. Larionov, Picasso.
6 *Have you been abroad and where?:* In Paris at Le Fauconnier, Metzinger and Picasso (1913–1914) [1913]. I have been in Germany, Egypt, Syria, Turkey, Greece and Italian colonies in Africa.
7 *Under whom and where did you work abroad?:*
8 *What types of art from those shown below did you or do you work on?:*
   a) *monumental compositions:*
   b) *easel compositions:* yes
   c) *landscape:* yes
   d) *portraits:* yes
   e) *illustration:* no
   f) *theatrical design:* yes
9 *Of what artistic societies are you a member?:*
   Golden Fleece, Union of Youth, World of Art – as external exhibitor, Donkey's Tail, Jack of Diamonds.

(1928)

TsGALI, fond 1938, inventory 1, unit 59, p. 1.

Typed form filled in by hand in ink; there are notes in pencil, including 'Biography' opposite question 5. It is possible that the questionnaires were accompanied by biographical descriptions (cf. 'Autobiography', p. 264)

The Moscow College of Painting, Sculpture and Architecture (MUZhVZ) was the leading artistic educational institution of pre-revolutionary Moscow (founded in 1832). It did not, however, have the status of a 'higher' educational institution until 1917, and Tatlin is inaccurate in writing 'VUZhVZ', where the first letter stands for 'higher'.

The Penza College of Art was founded in 1897 by Sileverstov and named after him. V.D. Burliuk, Taran, Sagaidachnyi and others studied there at the same time as Tatlin.
    Tatlin more than once indicated the same two periods of study at MUZhVZ, interrupted by a time at the Penza College. This information is, however, inaccurate: he studied in MUZhVZ from 1902 to 1903, and graduated from Penza not in 1909 but in 1910. Information on his second period in MUZhVZ is not available: his name is not in the lists of those graduating from there in 1910 (*see also* 'Autobiography' and commentaries, pp. 264–66; 'Curriculum Vitae' and commentaries, pp. 320–29).

Korovin, Konstantin Alekseevich (1861–1939), was a Russian artist, painter and theatre designer, a member of the Academy of Arts (from 1905), and a member of the World of Art and Union of Russian Artists. He was one of the most popular teachers among the students at MUZhVZ.

Serov, Valentin Aleksandrovich (1865–1911), was a Russian artist, painter, graphic artist and theatre designer, a member of the Academy of Arts (from 1895), a member of the Society of Itinerant Exhibitions (Wanderers), World of Art and Union of Russian Artists. He significantly renewed the language of Russian decorative art and in retrospect may be seen as a precursor to the innovative experiments of the beginning of the twentieth century. He taught painting in MUZhVZ, usually together with Korovin, and exercised the greatest authority among the students.

Afanas'ev, Aleksei Fedorovich (1850–1920), a Russian genre-artist, was an external student of the Academy of Arts, took part in the exhibitions of the Wanderers, illustrated the tales and poems of Ershov, Pushkin and A.K. Tolstoi, and made drawings for journals. From 1905 to 1908 he was director of the Penza College of Art. He has sometimes been confused with Aleksandr Nikolaevich Afanas'ev (1826–1871), the well-known literary expert and historian (*see* Bibliog.: Abramova, 1966).

Larionov, Mikhail Fedorovich (1881–1964), a Russian artist who studied at MUZhVZ, was an acknowledged leader of the avant-garde movement in Russian painting and had enormous authority among his contemporaries and the younger artists. He promoted Rayonism (*luchism*) as a new trend in painting, and in works close to those of the Italian Futurists he tried to convey the movement and dynamics of light; in other works he drew on popular prints (*lubki*), signboards, children's drawings and also icons, combined with a study and assimilation of the experiments in contemporary French and German painting. He lived in Paris from 1914 onwards. Tatlin was linked to Larionov both by his artistic endeavours and as a friend, but later quarrelled with him. (On Larionov and Tatlin *see also* Sarab'ianov, p. 44; n2.)

Picasso, Pablo (1881–1973). In Russia the work of Picasso became known very early, through his participation in Russian exhibitions and the collections of Shchukin and Morozov etc., and excited the keen interest of the artistic youth with avant-garde tendencies. Picasso's work undoubtedly strongly influenced Tatlin. (*See* Strigalev, p. 18) It became, however, an impetus for Tatlin's own strivings, as Punin correctly wrote in his book on Tatlin, to which he quite deliberately gave the sub-title 'Against Cubism' (*see* p. 347; El'konin, 'What I Remember about Tatlin', p. 438).

In question 5 Tatlin crossed out the word 'direct', wishing to emphasize that the influence he acknowledged of the three listed – and very different – artists in no way indicated a dependence on them in his own work. (On the time Tatlin spent in Germany and France *see* 'Letter about a Trip', p. 181 and commentaries.)

Metzinger, Jean (1883–1957), a French artist, representative and popularizer of Cubism, was, together with A. Gleizes, the author of a book on Cubism which had two Russian translations in 1913. This is the main reason for his being known among Russian artists. (*See also* 'Punin, Tatlin', p. 347)

Golden Fleece was a journal which organized the annual *Salon* of the Golden Fleece, in which Tatlin says he exhibited once, in 1909 (*see* 'Autobiography', p. 264), though documentary confirmation of this has not been found.

Union of Youth (1910–17), an artistic society in St Petersburg/Petrograd, which united representatives of the avant-garde movement in various branches of the arts. Its president and to some extent patron was Zheverzheev. The Union of Youth arranged annual exhibitions of painting and was active in publishing. The members of the society were: Khlebnikov, Rozanova, Shkol'nik, Spandikov, Filonov, V. Markov (Matvei) and others. The Moscow artists who took part in its exhibitions were: V.D. and D.D. Burliuk, Larionov, Goncharova, Malevich, Maiakovskii, Shevchenko, Morgunov and others. Tatlin participated in four exhibitions, in 1911–14 (*see* Tatlin at Exhibitions, pp. 489, 491). He was accepted as a member of the society in January 1913.

World of Art *see* 'Letter to Benois', c, p. 183.

Donkey's Tail, a Moscow union of young avant-garde artists, broke away from the Jack of Diamonds in 1912 and organized a joint exhibition with the Union of Youth, first in St Petersburg and then in Moscow. To counterbalance the westernizing tendencies of the Jack of Diamonds it based itself on the traditions of Russian icon painting, signboards and *lubki,* as well as on Oriental art. Participants in it were Larionov, Goncharova, Malevich, Tatlin, Shevchenko, Le Dantiu, Sagaidachnyi, Zdanevich, V. Markov (Matvei), Fonvizin, Morgunov, Bart and others.

Jack of Diamonds, a society of Moscow artists which was directed towards the development of Post-Impressionist tendencies (so-called Russian Cézannism), formally founded in 1911, after its first exhibition in 1910. Between 1910 and 1916 it organized joint exhibitions of Russian and foreign artists. In 1916 the nucleus of the Jack of Diamonds joined the ranks of the World of Art. Tatlin took part in its 1913 exhibition, where founder members of the union showed their works (Konchalovskii, Kuprin, Lentulov, Mashkov, Rozhdestvenskii, Fal'k, Exter and others) as well as a number of French and German artists (G. Braque, A. Derain, K. Van Dongen, P. Picasso, P. Signac, M. Vlaminck, H. Le Fauconnier, F. Volloton, A. Marquet, A. Kubin and others) and external exhibitors amongst whom were Tatlin, Grishchenko, Dymshits-Tolstaia. In October 1917 Tatlin was accepted as a member of the Jack of Diamonds but left it after several days since he did not agree with the views of its leaders. (*See* Bibliog.: Lapshin, 1977)

Tatlin and the artistic societies: Tatlin was always at the centre of the social and professional activity of artists who had similar views to his own but, apparently, he preferred not to tie himself down by official participation in artistic societies. None the less, in addition to those already listed, he joined the 'left block' of the Union of Art Workers (March-November 1917 in Petrograd), the Moscow Trade Union of Artists and Painters (from summer 1917), and at the beginning of the twenties headed the Petrograd Union of New Tendencies in Art (*see* 'To the Museums Department', p. 241; 'Programme', p. 242). He did not belong to LEF or any other organization of Constructivists, although he considered himself, and was generally acknowledged to be the father of Constructivism (*see* 'Art into', p. 310).

Autobiography

I was born in 1885. My father was a mechanical engineer, my mother a poet and a member of [the] Narodnaia Volia [organization], who published in journals of the 1880s. My mother died when I was two. My father died when I was 13. At the age of 13 I left my stepmother and my home, and began an independent life.

As a boy of fourteen, still in Odessa, I became ship's boy on a sailing ship and went on a voyage abroad for the first time.

From then on a significant period of my young years was spent serving on various ships of the Russian Navigation and Trade Company of the volunteer fleet: Evgeniia Ol'denburg-skaia (steamship), Mariia (sailing ship). In Voronezh – on small sailing ships. I went to Syria, Turkey, Egypt, to the Italian colonies (to Tripoli in Africa).

I drew from my early childhood (from the age of seven). During my sailing period I drew as well, and in the interim periods in the winter I worked in artists' studios (private ones) in Moscow.

In 1902 I entered the College of Painting, Sculpture and Architecture in Moscow, but after two years I was thrown out for lack of ability.

In 1904 I entered the Penza College of Art, from which I graduated in 1909. [1905–1910]

I continued to work in the summer periods in private studios in Moscow. While I was still a student at the College of Art I began to take part in art exhibitions in Moscow (1909, Golden Fleece) and from 1910 my works began to be noticed in newspapers and journals.

After graduating from the College of Art I continued to study and from 1911 had my own studio on Ostozhenka Street, where there were no more than 3–4 young people, with whom I worked on painting and drawing.

68–69
42–67

In 1913 I went to Paris, where I continued perfecting my work in private studios. Two months before the beginning of the war I returned to Moscow and continued working and exhibiting at exhibitions.

86

In 1915 I formed a group of young artists and we arranged an independent exhibition of Futurists, The Store (on Petrovka Street in Moscow). [This exhibition, alternately called The Shop, was actually in 1916.]

Before the Revolution I was active socially, organizing the left artists; I was also president of the artists of the 'Left-Wing Federation', which later became included in the Union of Painters, where I continued this work right up to the split of the Union.

In 1917 I was active socially, participating from the beginning in the organization of the Union of Art Workers, right up to the beginning of my work in Narkompros, and also in the IZO section of the Soviet of Workers', Peasants' and Red-Army Deputies.

In 1918 I organized the IZO Department and Museums Department in Narkompros, and at that difficult time, when it was not easy to collect specialists, I none the less enlisted them and worked with them for a year and a half, while I was Director of IZO and chairman of the collegium.

At the same time as this I was invited as a professor to VKhUTEIN in the metalwork division. [To the Free State Artistic Studios (PGSKhUM or SVOMAS) in the painting division].

In 1920 I was invited to Leningrad by the Academy of Arts [it was then the Petrograd SVOMAS and the correct date is 1919], where I was professor in the department or workshop of the faculty of material culture for two and a half years.

At this period [no later than the beginning of 1919] Narkompros charged me with carrying out a project of material-form in honour of the Comintern.

In 1921 the work was completed and shown in Leningrad in the Academy of Arts and in Moscow the same year in the House of Unions at the Congress of Unions. [The work was finished and exhibited in Petrograd from 8 November to 1 December 1920; in Moscow from the end of December 1920 to 1922.] 176–180 181

Afterwards in 1925 a model of the Comintern was sent to the international exhibition in France (Paris). 186, 187

Through the press and exhibitions this work became widely known, both here in the USSR and abroad, in the West and in America.

Working on the culture of material and developing this from 1914 on, in 1922 [1923–1925] I worked out patterns for new clothes in a factory of the Leningrad Clothing Manufacturers' Trust and also carried out work in the scientific-technical bureau of this trust. 247–251

Carrying out propaganda at the same time for new forms in everyday life (by lectures) I showed at them designs for new clothes among the proletarian youth studying in various Soviet higher educational establishments in Leningrad.

In 1923 I transferred to the Museum and later Institute of Painterly Culture, where I was in charge of the Section for Material Culture.

In 1925 I was invited to the Kiev College of Art, where I stayed two years, and where I had the position of professor and was in charge of the Theatre-cine Department.

In 1927 I was appointed to VKhUTEIN in Moscow to the metal-wood [working] faculty, in charge of the department on the culture of material, where I am working now.

The influence of my art is expressed in the path taken by the Constructivists, of whom I am the founder.

The influence of my art in the West is shown in the statement by the Dadaists in 1921 (their banner with the slogan 'the machine art of Tatlin' – Berlin) [in 1920], and also in the Bauhaus (Weimar and Dessau). 136

Working with materials, I have felt the whole time a considerable lack of means, since this area demands greater material expenditure than paints and canvas.

My works are in all the large people's museums and galleries of Moscow, Leningrad and the provinces.

The best known of them are the following:

1912 'Nude' (oil), Russian Museum, Leningrad — 78

1912 'Still-Life' (oil), Russian Museum, Leningrad — 75

1912 Theatrical drawings (tempera), Tret'iakov Gallery, Moscow. [He is referring to the sketches for 'A Life for the Tsar'] — 137–155

1913 'Sailor' (tempera), Russian Museum, Leningrad [1912] — 34

1913 'Still-Life' (oil), Tret'iakov Gallery, Moscow [1912]

1916 'Board No. 1' (wood and paint), ditto, [1917] — 104

1914 'Counter-Relief' (metal and wood), ditto, [1917, Selection of materials]

1920 'Material-form in honour of the Comintern', Russian Museum, Leningrad — 164–206

Tatlin
1929

Private collection, Moscow, manuscript.

The Autobiography belongs to the very small number of Tatlin materials which contain direct autobiographical information. (*See* 'Questionnaire', p. 262; 'Curriculum Vitae', p. 320) Only in this autobiography does Tatlin speak in relative detail about his service in the fleet (in the original the lines which list the ships and places where Tatlin has been are lightly crossed through by the author) or say that he was thrown out of the Moscow College (which happened in 1903).

Tatlin is inaccurate in calling his mother a 'Narodnaia Volia' member (*narodovolka*), probably meaning to say a 'populist' (*narodnitsa*), i.e. someone who shared views widely held among the democratic intelligentsia, but not a member of the militant revolutionary party 'Narodnaia Volia' (People's Freedom). Tatlin's father was still alive in 1903 (TsGALI, fond 680, inventory 2, unit 1801).

In Tatlin's studio, which was on Moscow's Ostozhenka Street, no. 37, a group of young artists worked on drawing and painting from 1911 to 1915, including Fal'k, Khodasevich, Popova, Udal'tsova, Aleksandr Vesnin. (*See* Kostin, p. 68)

The Store exhibition (1916), alternately translated as 'The Shop', was one of the first undertakings organized by Tatlin; its participants were Bruni, Dymshits-Tolstaia, Exter, Iustitskii, Kliun, Malevich, Morgunov, Pestel', Popova, Rodchenko, Tatlin, Udal'tsova, Vasil'eva. Tatlin showed reliefs and counter-reliefs (totalling 7 items) at the exhibition. (For a review of it *see Аполлон,* no. 3, 1916, p. 61.)

The Left Federation ('young people') was one of three factions forming in the summer of 1917 the Moscow Trade Union of Painters, which on 21 November 1917 delegated Tatlin to the Artistic Section of the Moscow Soviet of Workers' and Soldiers' Deputies, where from autumn 1917 to spring 1918 (before the organization of IZO Narkompros) he worked on the commission for protecting monuments of art and antiquity. (*See also* Strigalev, p. 24)

Union of Art Workers (Soiuz Rabotnikov Iskusstva, or more accurately Soiuz Deiatelei Iskusstva: SDI): *see* n67, 68 to Strigalev, p. 41. Tatlin joined the 'left block' of this and immediately after the October Revolution, together with a significant part of the 'left block', left the organization (*see also* 'Autobiography', p. 264).

On Tatlin's work in the Artistic and Museums Collegia of Narkompros *see* 'Memorandum', p. 185; 'Report', p. 237. At the beginning of the 1918/1919 academic year the Second Free State Artistic Studios (GSKhM, previously MUZhVZ) granted Tatlin a painting studio which he ran until 1920; in 1919 he received in the Petrograd Free State Artistic Teaching Studios (SVOMAS, previously the Academy of Arts) a workshop 'of material, volume and construction', which he ran until 1921.

On the Museum of Artistic Culture *see* 'To the Museums Department', commentary, p. 242.

On the Kiev College of Art *see* 'Letter to Novitskii', commentary, p. 260.

On Constructivism *see* 'Art into', commentary, p. 312.

On the influence of Tatlin's art in Germany *see* Strigalev, pp. 35, 36.

The Bauhaus was a new type of higher artistic educational establishment created in Weimar in 1919 by progressive German architects and artists headed by Walter Gropius. It later moved to Dessau. The Bauhaus sought to end the nineteenth-century schism between the artist and the technically expert craftsman by training students equally in both fields. The leaders of the Bauhaus were intensely interested in the development of Soviet art (particularly in Tatlin's activity) and took account of much of its experience in their own works.

Material-form was a new term by which Tatlin began to designate his Constructivist-spatial works from the end of the twenties. We find it here in written form for the first time. (*See* Strigalev, p. 24; Zhadova, p. 136)

The Artist as an Organizer of Everyday Life

A new everyday life requires new objects. But very little is done in this area. In particular, in regard to furniture the problem remains acute even at the present time.

Everything that we're doing now in the way of constructing new furniture is only an attempt to imitate the West. It's fashionable there just now to reform furniture by constructing it from bicycle tubes. There were attempts here too to go the same route. But then we came up against a shortage of the material: iron tubes. As in the past, to overcome such a problem, we tried to invent new colours and selections of them, we are now studying the phenomena of materials in the most detailed way. We need to widen the range of our thinking in the area of materials and their interrelationships, looking for the prerequisites for form within the material itself. And from different materials we achieve the same objects. Let's take for example [...] a sleigh. A sleigh of bicycle tubes, commonplace in America, is no use for us in the USSR. And here the artist, organizing new forms of everyday life, must be able to find for the object the necessary material which can be applied to our climatic and economic conditions. A sleigh made from bent bicycle tubes is no use in our conditions for a number of reasons: the severe winter makes the material extremely fragile, the sleigh is often heavy, expensive and so on. We replaced the tubes by strips of maple curved according to the principle of Viennese or bentwood furniture. The advantages for us are evident. The material is at our disposal – whole forests – the working of it is not complicated or expensive, and the sleigh is far cheaper. Besides, it is many times lighter than a metal one (it is easy to carry on the shoulder) and in winter it is not unpleasant to the touch since, unlike a metal one, it does not freeze. It is extremely durable.

260, 254

A contemporary furniture factory takes no account of the requirements of the human body in constructing any kind of pattern for furniture. It is interested only in external effect. But a human is an organic being, consisting of a skeleton, nerves and muscles. Because of this a chair should have elasticity. The so-called American chairs give this elasticity, and soft club chairs give it. But this furniture is exceedingly expensive and cumbersome. The cheap thing is made of bars, it cannot give any elasticity. The chair constructed by us [...] gives a sufficient degree of elasticity. The material is one-inch (in diameter) maple, with strips curved on the principle of bentwood furniture. The construction is in the form of a bridge-girder, and furthermore four one-inch strips completely assure the strength and so to speak the safety for sitting on such a chair. With mass production it will cost even less than a Viennese bentwood chair and will be more comfortable.

255

260

All our life, and production too, is overburdened by things, and mainly things which contain other things. We are also striving to eliminate these, to take from them only certain parts and introduce those parts into a building's architecture (shelves into the recess of a wall and so on). What do we use in constructing one object or another? Modern technology is working on those questions first and foremost. But that is not enough. Besides 'what', 'how' is very important, the organic form is important. For this we take and analyse existing objects, we use technical constructions as models for the forms of everyday objects, and finally, we also use as models the phenomena of living nature. Such are our principal tasks in working on the organization of the new object in the new way of life. We are moving towards their solution.

(1929)

'Художник – организатор быта' (Статья профессора ВХУТЕИНа В. Татлина), Рабис, по 48, 25 November 1929, p. 4.

The article is illustrated by photographs of examples of items manufactured under Tatlin's direction: a chair (by the student Rogozhin – Khan-Magomedov convincingly dates this work 1929) and two frames of wooden sleighs. The article clearly shows that the chair, which is usually considered to be of metal (*see*, for example, *Бригада художников*, no. 1, 1932, p. 22) and on another occasion is said to be made of beech (*Строительство Москвы*, no. 10, 1929, p. 10), is made of maple. On the reconstruction of the chair *see* Ill. 256–8; Zhadova, p. 140. In this article Tatlin talks for the first time of the organic methods (i.e. observed as 'phenomena of living nature') of his form-creation. Such a method was characteristic of him even earlier, but by the end of the twenties had become completely crystallized in connection with the work on *Letatlin*. (*See* Zelinskii's interview, p. 309; Rakhtanov's essay, p. 309.)
     The subject of this article is directly continued in the next one.

The Problem of the Relationship between Man and Object

Let us Declare War on Chests of Drawers and Sideboards

We are now waging war for a collective way of life.

Socialist cities, 'green cities', communal residences, palaces of culture are being built. In this construction there arises before us in all its breadth the problem of *man and object*.

The object in our conception must become not a sign of social distinction but that unit which is called on to realize specific functions allotted to it. At moments this object may disintegrate, become only a part of the whole, but continue to fulfil some functions.

Against the old artistic thinking it is necessary to set the new form: material culture.

Working in this area since 1914, first alone and then with a group of students, I became convinced that our industry will be able to produce objects of high quality only when the artist-production worker takes a direct part in the organization of the object.

A way of thinking based on the culture of material makes it possible to take account both of the properties of individual materials and of the most advantageous features of their interrelationships. In such a way the artist, in creating an object, furnishes himself with a palette of different materials which he uses on the basis of their properties. Taken into account here are colour, texture, density, elasticity, weight, strength, etc., etc.

With the task of creating a concrete everyday object with determined functions, the artist of material culture takes account of all properties of suitable materials and their interrelationships, the organic form (man) for which a given object is created, and finally the social side: this man is a worker and will use the object in question in the working life he leads.

Here must be considered the maximum functionality of the object which can be achieved when there is a great understanding of the properties of materials. This factor creates the possibility for an intelligent selection of materials for a functional object, and for the introduction of completely new and hitherto unexplored materials. This in turn gives a completely exceptional result: an object which is original and radically different from objects in the West or in America. This last fact is very important inasmuch as our everyday life is being built on completely new principles.

The demands we make of an object which has to serve us are considerably greater given the conditions of everyday life here than the demands made in capitalist countries.

Our everyday life is built on healthy and natural principles and an object from the West cannot satisfy us. We must search for completely different points of departure for creating our object. It is for this reason that I show such a great interest in organic form as a point of departure for the creation of the new object. I came to the unalterable view that studying organic form will give the richest material for the creation of a new object.

All our life, and production too, is overburdened by objects, and mainly things which contain other objects. We have to strive to eliminate these, to take from them only certain parts and introduce those parts into a building's architecture (shelves into the recess of a wall and so on). What do we use in constructing one object or another? Modern technology is working on those questions first and foremost. But that is not enough. Besides 'what', 'how' is very important, the organic form is important. For this we take and analyse existing objects, we use technical constructions as models for the forms of everyday objects, and finally, we also use as models the phenomena of living nature. Such are our principal tasks in working on the organization of new objects in the new collective way of life.

V. Tatlin
(1930)

'*Проблема соотношения человека и вещи. Объявим войну комодам и буфетам*', Рабис, по. 15, 14 April 1930, p. 9.

The headings over the article – 'Let us live in a new way!', 'The force of habit of millions is the most terrible force', 'Let us blow up the Bastille of stagnation, backwardness, darkness! Let us break up a decayed way of life!' – are not Tatlin's: his article was printed in a regular, recurring section of the journal. As illustrations, under the heading 'Woodmetal [*Dermet*] of VKhUTEIN. Diploma works', three photographs are printed showing the set of furniture made by P. Galaktionov (directed by Rodchenko) and a wooden transformable table.

In its subject and material the article is closely related to the preceding one, and their final paragraphs, except for insignificant variations, are the same.

164 Simplified version of the model of the Monument to the Third International at the May Day parade in Leningrad in 1926, Cat. V/5

165 The Mosaics Studio at the former Academy of Arts in Leningrad, where the first model of the Monument to the Third International was built. Recent photograph
166 House of Unions, Moscow, where the model was displayed during the Exhibition in Honour of the Eighth Congress of Soviets, end of 1920 beginning of 1921. Photograph, taken at the time, legacy L. A. Zhadova
167 Tatlin in 1918. Photograph: TsGALI, Moscow
* **168** Tatlin's certificate of membership of the Museums Committee of the People's Commissariat of Education, issued 30 May 1918, Cat. XII/16
169 Tatlin (on the left end) at the unveiling of the monument to Sofia Perovskaia in front of the Moscow Station building. Petrograd, 20 December 1918.
In the centre are Lunacharskii and Shterenberg.
Photograph: Leningrad Archive of Film, Photo and Sound

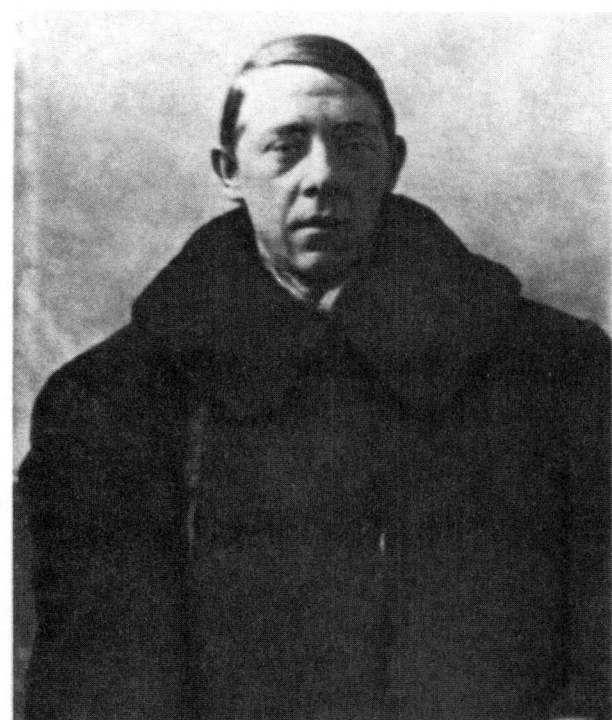

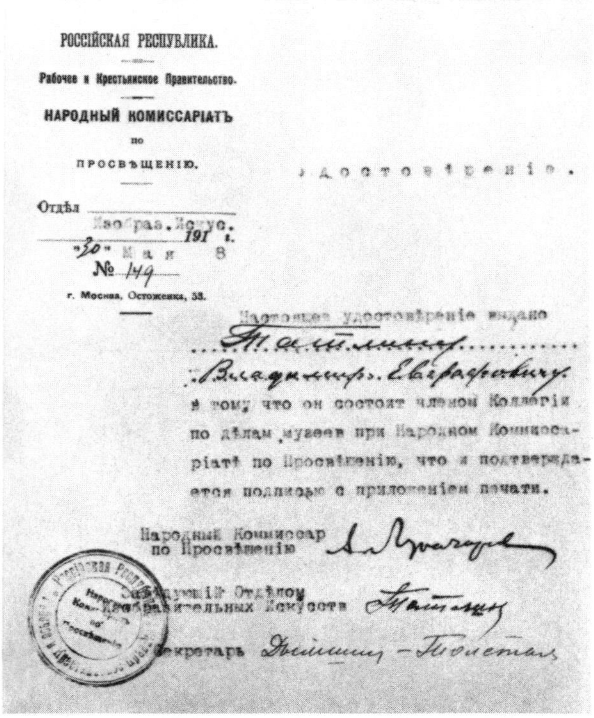

РОССІЙСКАЯ РЕСПУБЛИКА.

Рабочее и Крестьянское Правительство.

НАРОДНЫЙ КОМИССАРІАТЪ
по
ПРОСВѢЩЕНІЮ.

Отдѣл
Изобраз. Искус.
"30" Мая 1918 г.
№ 149
г. Москва, Остоженка, 53.

Удостовѣреніе.

Настоящее удостовѣреніе выдано
Татлину
Владимиру Евграфовичу
в тому что он состоит членом Коллегіи по дѣлам музеев при Народном Комиссаріатѣ по Просвѣщенію, что и подтверждается подписью с приложеніем печати.

Народный Комиссар по Просвѣщенію А. Луначарский

Завѣдующій Отдѣлом Изобразительных Искусств Татлин

Секретарь Дымшиц-Толстая

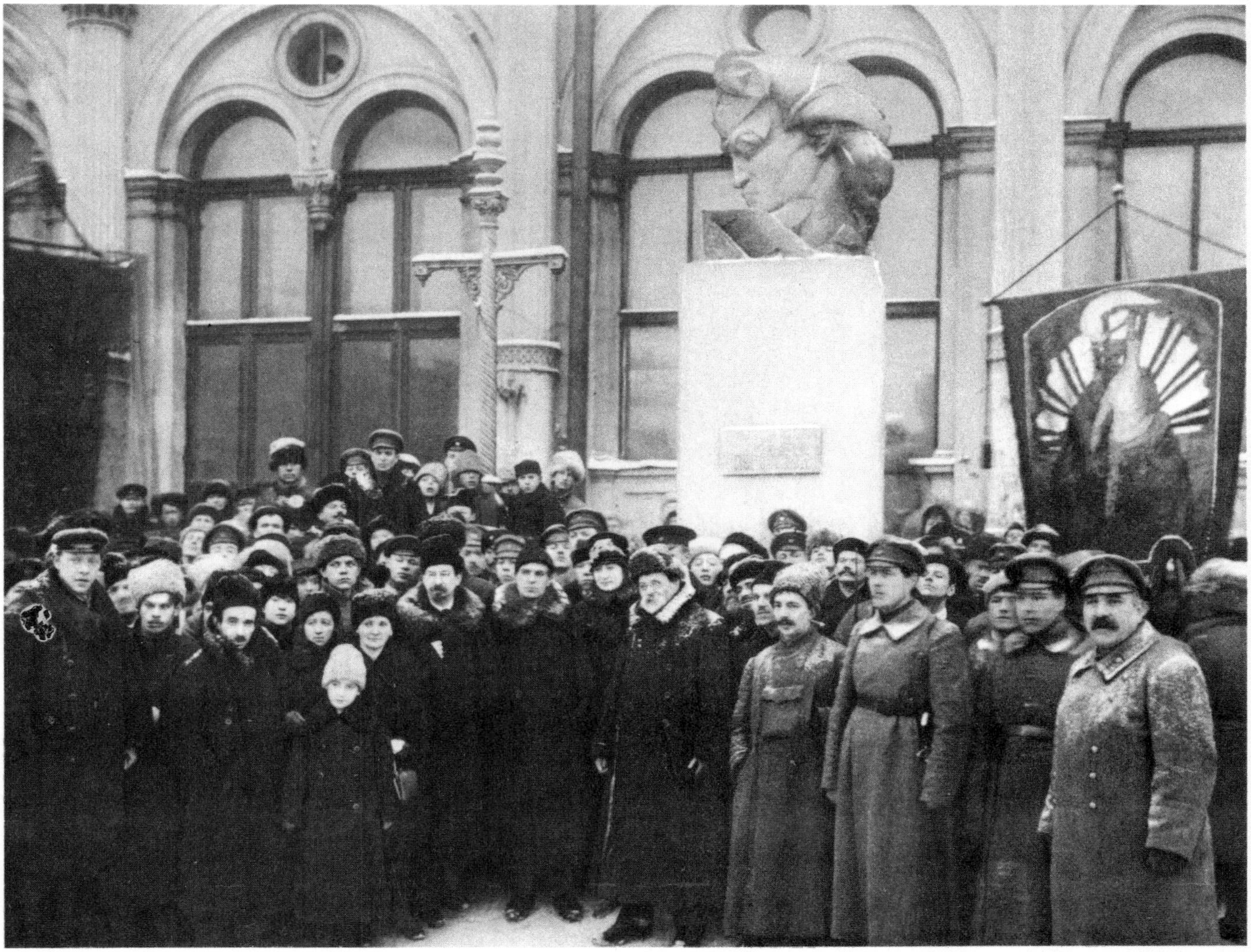

170 The Monument to the Third International, sketch of the inclined
axis, 1919, Cat. V/2
171 Sketch of the vertical view, 1919, Cat. V/1

172–8, 181 The first model of the Monument to the Third
International, 1920. Cat. V/3
172 The construction of the model, 1920. Cat. V/3b
173 The construction of the model, 1920.
From left to right: Dymshits-Tolstaia, Tatlin, Shapiro,
Meerzon, Cat. V/3a

174 The model in the Studio of Materials, Volume and Construction, in the Mosaics Studio of the former Academy of Arts, Petrograd, November 1920, Cat. V/3c
175 The same, from a different perspective, Cat. V/3d
176 The Mosaics Studio of the former Academy of Arts. Recent photograph

177 Model of the Monument seen from above. Same location, Cat. V/3f

178 The Tatlin Studio Collective in front of the model. Tatlin, third, Shapiro, fourth from left, Cat. V/3e

Отдел Изобразительных Искусств Наркомпроса

ВЫСТАВКА

Модель проэкта памятника

III-му КОММУНИСТИЧЕСКОМУ ИНТЕРНАЦИОНАЛУ

художника В. Татлина

В здании Свомаса (бывш. Академия Художеств) в мастерской — об'ема, материала и конструкции — проф. Татлина

Вход с 3-ей линии Васильевского Острова

Об'яснения будут даны строителями памятника

Выставка открыта с 8 ноября по 1 декабря

В день открытия 8-го ноября, с 12 ч. до 16 ч. дня, в мастерской проф. Татлина состоится Художественно-Политический

МИТИНГ

Приглашаются представители профсоюзов, воинских частей и судовых команд.

Отдел Раздан № 114. — 5.000 экз.   17-я Государственная типография, 7-я рота, 26.

179 Poster for the exhibition of the model of the Monument to the Third International, held in the Mosaics Studio of the former Petrograd Academy of Arts, 1920, Cat. XII/18
180 Entrance to the Mosaics Studio of the former Academy of Arts. Recent photograph
181 The model of the Monument in the foreground of the colonnade of the House of Unions, Moscow, end of 1920 – beginning of 1921, Cat. V/3g

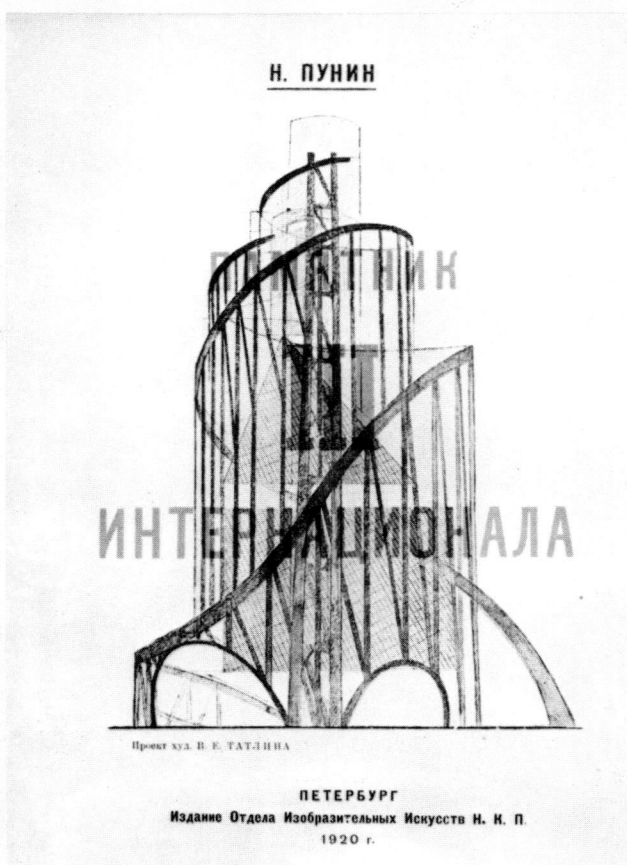

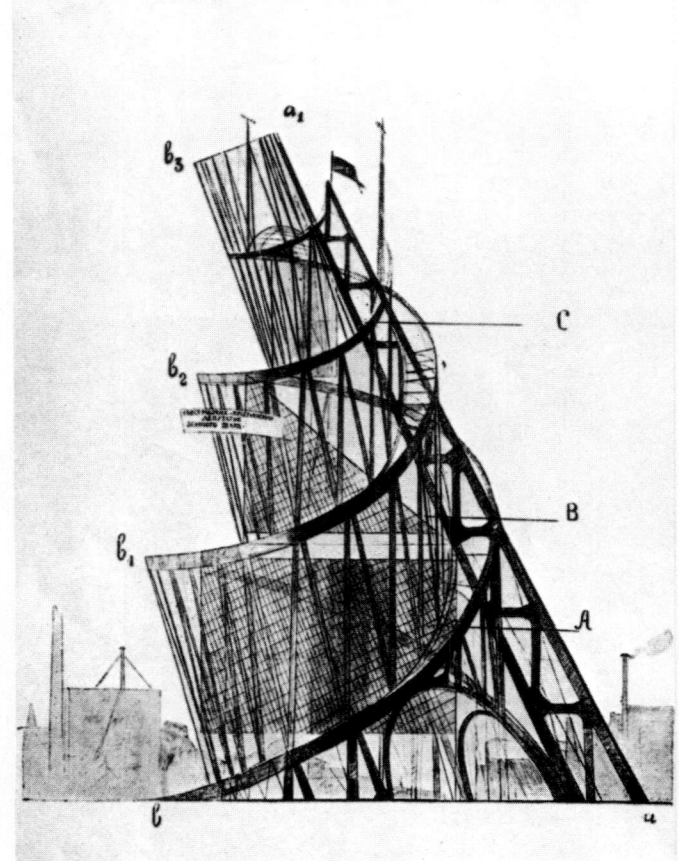

182 Punin, *The Monument to the Third International*, brochure, 1920, cover, Cat. III/6a
183 Punin, Illustration for the brochure *The Monument to the Third International*, 1920, Cat. III/6b

184 N.N. Punin, *Tatlin (Against Cubism)*, cover, 1921,
Cat. XII/19
185 Il'ia Ehrenburg, *A vse-taki ona vertitsia*... [*For all that,
it turns*...], illustration, 1922, Berlin and Moscow

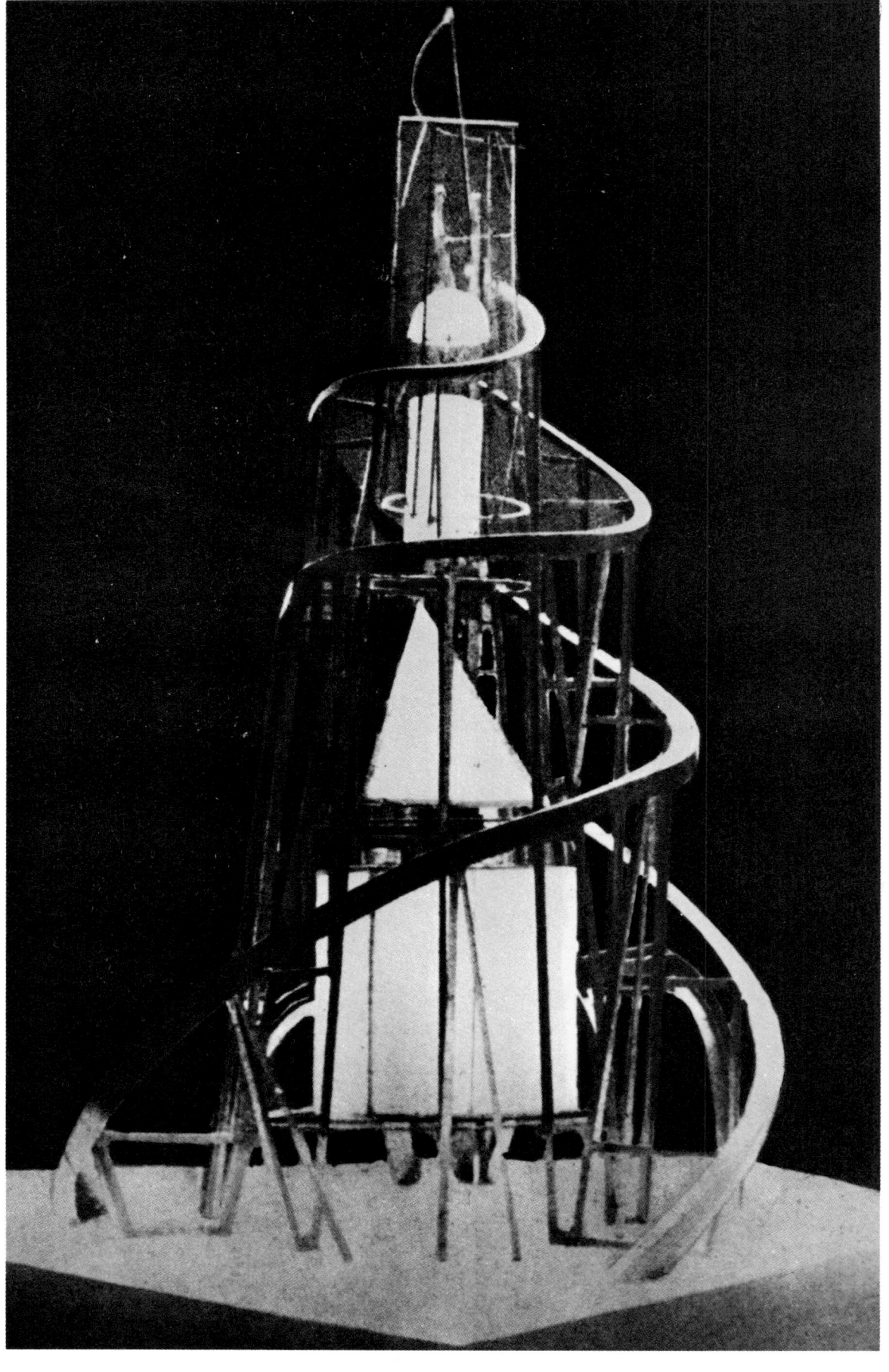

186 The second model of the Monument to the Third International at the Paris International Exhibition of Modern Decorative and Industrial Arts, 1925, Cat. V/4a
187 Detail of the exhibition, Cat. V/4b

188 The Eiffel Tower, Paris, 1889.
Recent photograph
189 Sukhov, Radio Tower, 1918–22, Moscow.
Recent photograph
190 The structure of the Eiffel Tower viewed from below
191 Sukhov, The structure of the Radio Tower viewed from below.
Recent photograph
192 *Cranes in Leningrad Harbour*. Photo graphic by O. Bakharev

193 Pieter Brueghel the Elder, *Tower of Babel*, 1563
Kunsthistorisches Museum, Vienna
194 The minaret of the Great Mosque, Samarra, Iraq, 9th century.
It is probable that European travellers of the Middle Ages considered it a copy of the Tower of Babel. Recent photograph
195 The Leaning Tower of Pisa

196 *The Tower of Babel*. Fresco in the Voskresenskii Cathedral at Tutaev, 17th century
197 School of Pskov: *The Presentation in the Temple*, 16th century. Pskov State Museum of History, Architecture and Art
198 Borromini, *Sant'Ivo della Sapienza*, Rome, 1642–60

199 Robert Delaunay, *The Eiffel Tower*, 1911.
The Solomon R. Guggenheim Museum,
New York
200 Umberto Boccioni, *Bottle* (Projection),
1912.
New York, Museum of Modern Art
201 Hermann Obrist, *Design of a Monument*,
1898.
(Museums Bellerive), Sammlung des
Kunstgewerbemuseums, Zurich

202 Model of the Monument to the Third International (Stockholm reconstruction made there), 1968, Cat. X/2a

203 Model of the Monument to the Third International (Stockholm reconstruction exhibited in Venice), 1970, Cat. X/2b
204 Model of the Monument to the Third International (London reconstruction), 1971, Cat. X/3

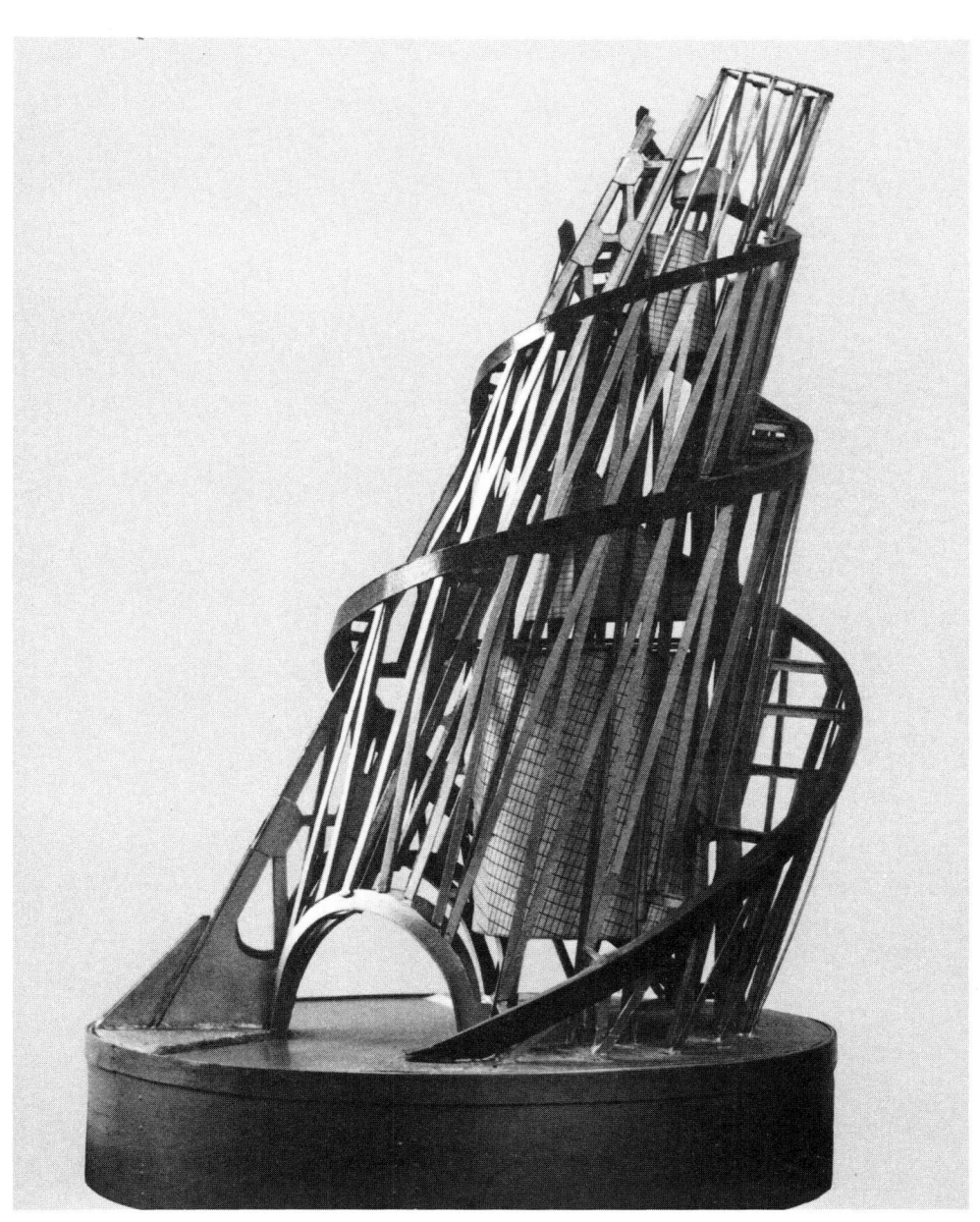

205 Model of the Monument to the Third International (Moscow reconstruction), 1976,
Cat. X/4

206 Model of the Monument to the Third International (reconstruction), 1979, Cat. X/5

* **207** Contract for the staging of Khlebnikov's *Selection of Objects*, 1917, Cat. XII/14
208 Photograph of Velemir Khlebnikov

209 Miatlev House, Leningrad.
Recent photograph
210 The White Hall of Miatlev House in Leningrad, where
Zangezi was performed in 1923.
Recent photograph
211 Poster for the stage production of Khlebnikov's
Zangezi, 1923, Cat. XII/23
212 Tatlin among the performers of *Zangezi* in the White
Hall of Miatlev House, 1923 (Punin seated at left).
Photograph: TsGALI, Moscow

213 N.F. Lapshin, Illustration for Punin, 'About "*Zangezi*"',
Zhizn' iskusstva, no. 20, 1923
214 The production of *Zangezi* in the Museum of Artistic
Culture, Petrograd, 9 May 1923
215 I.N. Popov-Voronezhskii's illustration for Tufanov's
article 'On the Production of Velemir Khlebnikov, *Zangezi*',
Krasnyi student, no. 7–8, 1923

216–22 Velemir Khlebnikov, *Zangezi*, stage and costume
designs, 1923
216 Model of stage setting, Cat. VIII/36

* **217** *Stage Design*, Cat. VIII/33

* **218** *Stage Design*, Cat. VIII/32

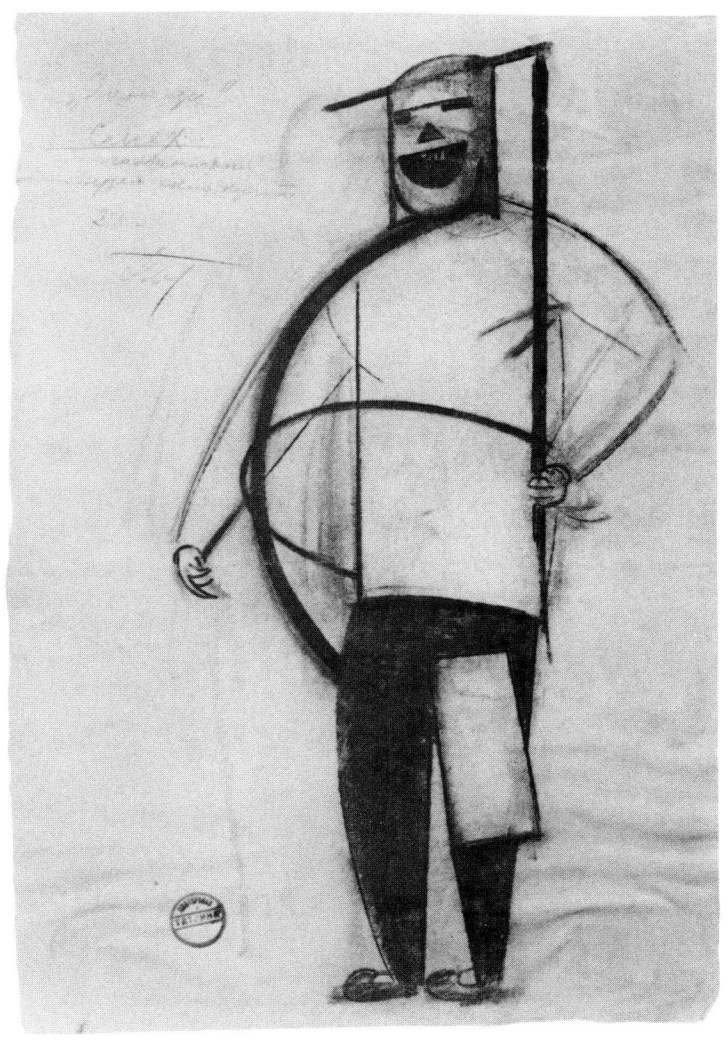

* **219** *Stage Design*, Cat. VIII/34
  220 *Stage Design*, Cat. VIII/35
  221 *Repentance*, Cat. VIII/38
  222 *Laughter*, Cat. VIII/37

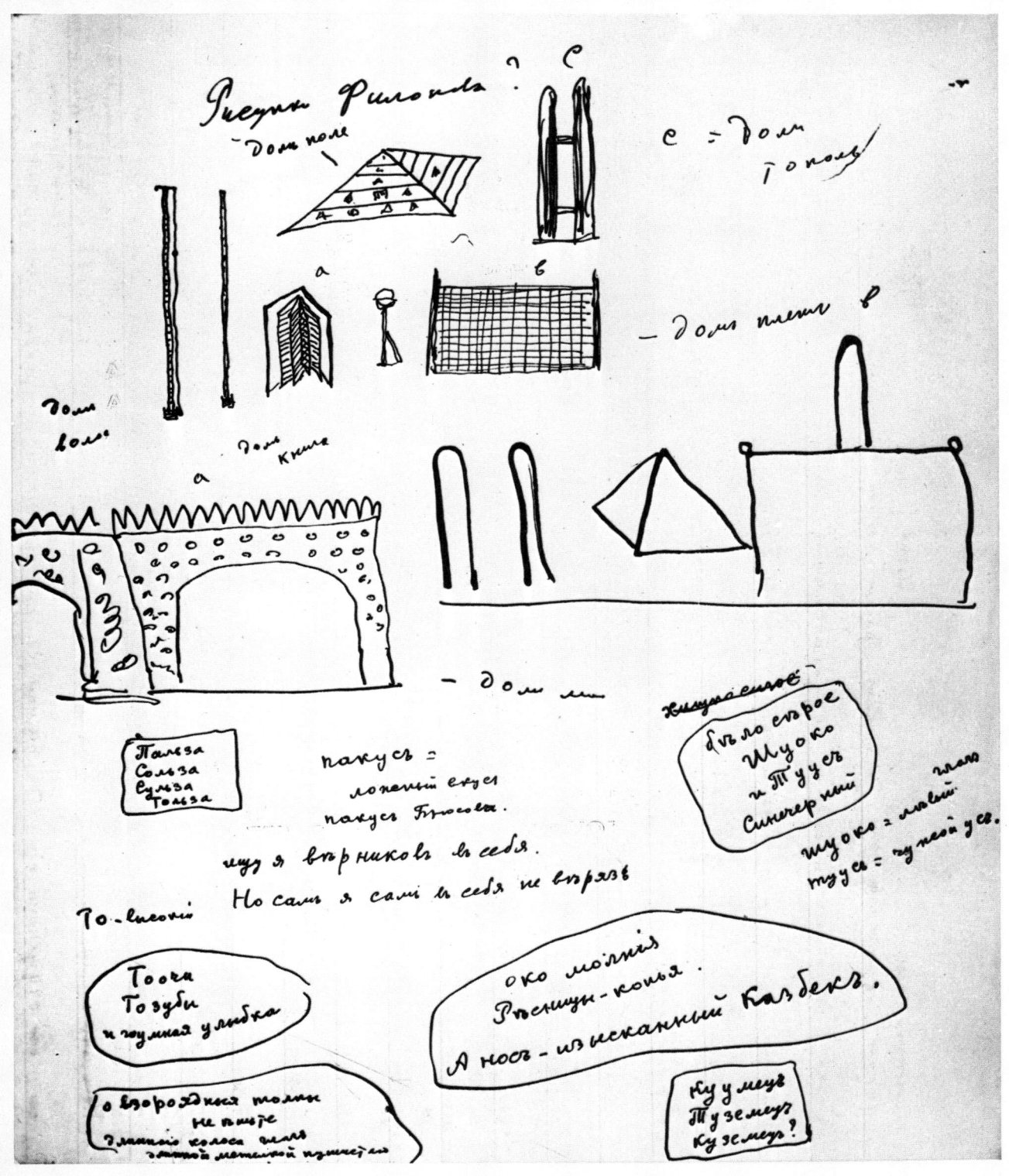

* **223** Khlebnikov, *Portrait of Tatlin*, 1915–6, Cat. XII/10
224 Khlebnikov, 'Architecture of the Future', sketches, 1915–6, Cat. XII/8
* **225** Khlebnikov, 'Architecture of the Future', sketches, 1915–6, Cat. XII/9

226 Tatlin and V.P. Smirnov during the 1930s

* 227 Detail from the manuscript of Khlebnikov, 'Artists of the World', with drawings by the author, Cat. XII/17

* 228–30 Tatlin's inscription in the three-volume set of Khlebnikov, *Collected Works* presented to Smirnov in 1933, Cat. XII/26

* 231 Typewritten copy of Khlebnikov's poem 'Tatlin', 1916, Cat. XII/12

Читай и чугай
Гениального поэта
Велимира
т.к. без подлинного
искусства нам
Социализма не
построить

Другу милому
Васе
от Татлина

33г
Москва
7 июля

В. Хлебников
Т. 1

В знак помощи
и проталкивания
в жизнь моих
замыслов. Ты
Вася и есть
мой настоящий
друг

Татлин

33 г
Москва
7 июля

В. Хлебников
Т. 2

Читай настоящего
поэта Велимира
подлинному
другу

Татлин

Москва
33г 7 июля

Т. 3

ТАТЛИН Татлин

Татлин тайновидец-лопастей
И винта певец суровый,
Из отряда солнцеловов,
Паутинный дол снастей,
Он железною подковой,
Рукой мертвой завязал (в топ).
В тайновидении жизни
Смотрят, что он показал.
Так неслыханно и веще
Жестянные - кистью вещи.

Вел. Хлебников,
г. Царицын, 1916 г.

ВЕЛИМИР ХЛЕБНИКОВ

НЕИЗДАННЫЕ
ПРОИЗВЕДЕНИЯ

ПОЭМЫ И СТИХИ
Редакция и комментарии
Н. Харджиева

ПРОЗА
Редакция и комментарии
Т. Грица

Государственное издательство
«*Художественная литература*»
Москва 1940

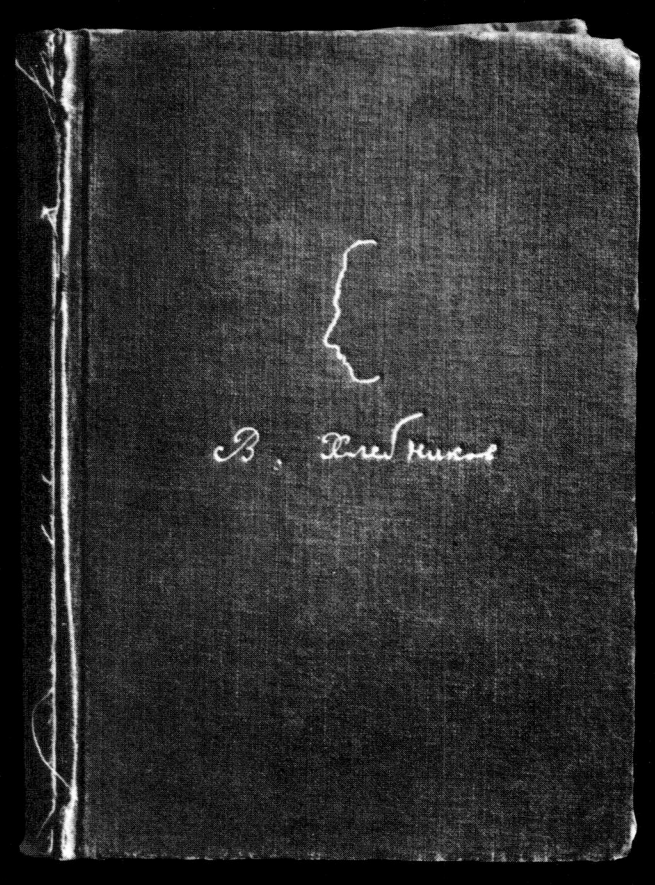

232 *Portrait of Khlebnikov*, 1940,
Cat. III/10b
233 Cover of V. Khlebnikov, *Unpublished
Works*, 1940, Cat. III/10a

[From Zelinskii's Interview 'Letatlin']

[...]

[A] I don't want this object to be approached in a purely utilitarian way. I created it as an artist. Look there at the curve of the wing: I consider it aesthetically perfect. Does not 'Letatlin' give the impression of something aesthetically complete? Like a soaring gull? Is it not true? But a gull can fly behind a ship for weeks, supporting itself only on air. I consider that my apparatus can also support a man in the air. I calculated the mathematical side, the resistance of the material, the surface of the wings. But you have to learn to sail on it in the air as we learn to swim in water, ride a bicycle, etc.   313–353

[Q:] What is the principle of flight for this apparatus?

[A:] The principle of a glider. But my wing has three kinds of movement, as has a bird, except for the tail. Moreover the wings can make small flapping movements. You can 'rock' yourself in the air. A man lies in the middle on his chest, puts his feet and hands into the straps and   325–327
attacks the wind...

[Q:] How did you come to this idea?

[A:] It's several thousand years old, from the time of Icarus in antiquity. I proceeded from an organic form. I observed young cranes, how they learn to fly. I bought cranes and learnt from them. Young cranes are just as helpless before the wind as we people. Why then can we not learn to soar like birds by learning their techniques? Moreover I want to give back to man the sensation of flight. The machine flight of the aeroplane has taken it away from us. We do not know our bodies' sensations of movement in air.

[Q:] What is the practical purpose of your apparatus?

[A:] The same as gliding. Doesn't the proletariat need it? It is early to speak of the future of aerial cycling, when the apparatus itself has not been tested. But in spring we'll take tents and off we'll go to try it on the hills. But besides this I should like to emphasize the aesthetic side of the matter. Here art is going into the service of technology. [...]

(1932)

Вечерняя Москва, no. 80, 6 April 1932.

The article – from which the above are quotations – is the earliest publication about Tatlin's new work, the flying machine *Letatlin* (1929–32). ['Letatlin' is a play on words, made by combining Tatlin's name with the Russian verb *letat'*, meaning 'to fly' – translator.]

Zelinskii, Kornelii Liutsianovich (1896–1970), a literary specialist and critic, at the beginning of the twenties was one of the organizers of the literary group of Constructivists, its leading and most radical theoretician. In 1930 he published an article 'The End of Constructivism' (К. Зелинский, 'Конец конструктивизма', *На литературном посту*, no. 20, 1930), and became a pertinacious opponent of the tendency he had earlier advocated, criticizing it as 'bourgeois' and 'imitating the West'. Zelinskii criticizes Tatlin's activity and his new work from a technological and vulgarly sociological position, finding completely unacceptable the organic or, in today's language, 'bionic' method of form-creation which was at the basis of this work.

[From Rakhtanov's Essay 'Letatlin – An Aerial Bicycle']

[...]

A tall man spoke on stage:

'Calculations? But let the comrade engineers not take offence at me. Have you asked a   339
crow what the calculations for its wings are?...

'Have you asked why it flies?' the tall man continued. 'No? You should have. I was a sailor. Gulls flew behind our stern without getting tired. They flew three days and still didn't get tired. There was a storm, the wind reached an enormous force, but they didn't care, the worthy birds fly and don't get tired. [...]

'Birds are arranged more perfectly than aeroplanes. They're plastic in their construction, while aeroplanes are rigid. Birds have living, soft wings while aeroplanes have dead, rigid ones. [...]

313–353 'In "Letatlin" there won't be a passenger as in a Junkers, i.e. a person who's bored, sitting in a leather chair and suffering from air sickness.

'First of all in "Letatlin" there's no room for a leather chair. A chair weighs a lot and "Letatlin" is a very light bird. To put a chair into "Letatlin" is as absurd as to put a chair on the wings of a flying bird.

'A man in "Letatlin" will lie in the position of a swimmer. And do the flying. He will work with his arms and legs as he already works when he's swimming.

'And that will be aerial swimming. And for this swimming he'll need to expend no more energy than for ordinary swimming. [...]

260 'Birds learn to fly from their infancy, and people should learn it too. When they make as many "Letatlins" as they now make Viennese (bentwood) chairs, then children will have to learn to fly from about the age of eight. This human age roughly corresponds to two weeks for a bird. In all the schools there will be flying lessons, because then it will be as necessary for a person to fly as it is to walk now.' [...]

(1932)

Пионер, по. 9, 1932, p. 12.

The article: For the heading are mounted the silhouettes of two *Letatlins* (without fabric) and the photograph of a crane. The essay is a record of Tatlin's speech in the Moscow Writers' Club on 5 April 1932, at an evening specially devoted to a demonstration of *Letatlin*. Reprinting this essay many years later as 'Спираль художника' (in: И. Рахтанов, *На широтах времени. Рассказы и очерки.* Москва, 1973), the author edited his original text very slightly in a literary sense, and considered it necessary to stress that his essay, written when the speech was still fresh in his memory and then shown to Tatlin, 'came out something like a verbatim report', and conveyed Tatlin's 'manner of speech, his vocabulary and syntax'. (Ibid., p. 334.)

Rakhtanov, Isai Arkad'evich (1907–79), was a Soviet author who wrote a great deal for young people.

Art into Technology

Technology in a period of reconstruction determines everything.
Stalin

Existing forms used in the art of building (in architecture), in technology, and partly in aviation, acquire a certain fixed and schematic character. Usually this is a combination of simple rectilinear forms and forms having the simplest curvature.

In architecture, the use of curvature and forms of complex curvature (resulting from the complex movement of a straight line or curve) is still of a primitive character as far as the forms used in building are concerned, and all of it is limited to the ordinary intersection of the simplest bodies; this leads to monotony in the sense of a constructive-technical resolution and also locks the artist into a narrow range of generally accepted building materials. This is clearly seen in projects for world-wide competitions in modern architecture. As for 'minor forms', in this area artistic creativity has been totally dominated by a narrow range of formal achievements of the past; the elements of non-objectivism, which are in essence extremely primitive forms of artistic thinking, did not develop further and did not lead to the creation of the synthetic object necessary in life itself.

Note: The 'Constructivists' in inverted commas also operated with materials but abstractly, for the sake of formal tasks, mechanically applying technology to their art as well. 'Constructivism' in inverted commas did not take into account the organic connection of materials with its own efforts and work. In essence a form necessary to life itself is born only as a result of the dynamics of such interrelationships. It is not surprising that the 'Constructivists' in inverted commas turned into decorators or took up graphic art.

Work in this area, which includes furniture and everyday objects, is still only beginning, while the birth of new cultural institutions for our everyday life – in which the working masses will live, think and reveal their talents – will demand of artists not only external decoration but above all will demand objects which correspond to the dialectics of the new everyday life.

My attention was drawn to the idea of becoming acquainted with aviation, since the particular conditions of aviation (the mobility of the machine and its interrelationship with its environment) create a greater change in the variety of forms and constructions than is the case with a static type of technology.

Research led me to the conclusion that indeed, qualitatively, there is in aviation more variety in curvature of form, in the use of different materials, than there is in architectural forms. But I think that the use of curved surfaces, and experimental work in this area, is insufficiently developed there too.

Thus:

1) A monotony of forms (essentially not conditioned by technical requirements) leads to a limited range of materials and a monotonous use of them, and to a certain degree creates a stereotyped attitude in the cultural and material designing of objects, which leads in turn to a monotonous resolution of the constructive tasks.

2) The artist who has experience with a range of heterogeneous materials (who, without being an engineer, has studied the question that interests him) involuntarily sets himself the task of solving technical design by means of new material relationships, with the aim of finding new challenges and inventing a complex form on this basis, one that should of course be studied technically in the process of its further development. The artist must confront technology with the fact of the new interrelation in material forms and his work on them. Forms of complicated curvature require other plastic, material and constructive interrelationships – these elements can and must be mastered by the artist, whose method of creation is qualitatively different from that of the engineer.

And so:

1) I chose the flying machine as an object for artistic construction because it is the most complicated dynamic material form which can enter into the daily lives of the Soviet masses as an object of widespread use.

2) I proceeded from material constructions of the simplest forms to more complicated ones: these were clothes, objects of everyday life, up to the architectural construction in honour of the Comintern. The flying machine at the present stage of my work is the most complicated form which meets the needs of the moment for man's mastery of space. 234–292 / 164–206 / 313–353

3) As a result of this work I came to the conclusion that an artist's approach to technology can and must pour new life into outmoded methods which often resist the tasks of a period of reconstruction.

4) My apparatus is built on the principle of using living, organic forms. Observations of these forms led me to the conclusion that the most aesthetic forms are indeed the most economical. Work on the shaping of material in this direction is indeed art.

5) The work was completed according to my plans and consultations in which comrades surgeon M.A. Geintse and flying-instructor A.V. Losev participated.

The building of the apparatus was carried out in the scientific-research laboratory 'on the culture of materials' with my colleagues A.G. Sotnikov and Iu.S. Pavil'onov. 316, 315 / 317, 314

V. Tatlin
(1932)

В. Татлин, 'Искусство в технику!' in: Выставка работ заслуженного деятеля искусств В.Е. Татлина (Catalogue). Государственный Музей изобразительных искусств, Москва-Ленинград,1932, pp. 5–8.

The article was reprinted in *Бригада художников,* no. 6, 1932, pp. 17–8, without the motto and the two concluding paragraphs.

The text is included in a collection of materials 'From the Comintern Tower to *Letatlin*. We discuss artist V. Tatlin's model'. This includes a statement from the editors, an article by Artseulov (*see* p. 408), an article by Kronman and a number of illustrations, among which are two draft-sketches for *Letatlin.*

The title – 'Art into Technology' – can be compared with Tatlin's statement that he was the founder of the idea 'art into life,' (*see* 'Letter to Novitskii', p. 260). On the exhibition whose catalogue carried the article *see* Tatlin at Exhibitions, p. 496. The main exhibits were three *Letatlin* machines and their components. Works of previous years shown in part and only in the form of photographs were the Monument to the Third International and 'works on the shaping of everyday life' and documents. The poster invited to the exhibition 'artists, aviation workers, engineers, anatomists and Soviet society at large'. The catalogue (Ill. 336–8) also contains Artseulov's above mentioned article and a brief list of exhibitions and photo illustrations related to *Letatlin.*

Constructivism: The article 'Art into Technology' is Tatlin's summary conceptual document characterizing his understanding of Constructivism, his concept of uniting the methods of technical and organic form-creation, and his criticism of 'Constructivism in inverted commas' (*see* Strigalev, p. 34).

Constructivism was a term first suggested by artists in Moscow who had views similar to Tatlin's, at the very beginning of 1921 (while the Tower for the Comintern was being exhibited in Moscow), and was later accepted by Tatlin as successfully designating the methodology and creative tendencies close to his. (On Tatlin's terminology, cf. Bibliog.: Strigalev, 'On a Conception of Design', 1978.) In 1923 the literary group of the Constructivists was formed, and in 1925 the Union of Contemporary Architects (OSA) was organized; the ideas of Constructivism were close to those of LEF. But the term soon came to be applied generally to the whole of the avant-garde Soviet art of the 1920s, replacing in this respect the earlier term Futurism, which was characteristic of the years before and shortly after the Revolution.

Tatlin with justice considered himself the 'father of Constructivism' but he very early started to emphasize his differences from those who used this term, as he considered it, inappropriately: e.g. from architects whose 'Constructivist' method was basically functionalist, from stylists and imitators, etc. (*see* slogan 6 in 'Slogans' and commentary, p. 245).

Geintse: *see* 'Report', commentary, p. 256.

Losev, A.V., was a flying instructor who helped Tatlin in his work.

Sotnikov: *see* Zhadova, p. 145 and n76. In 'Curriculum Vitae', p. 325, he is mentioned as Tatlin's student.

Pavil'onov, Georgii (Iurii) Sergeevich (1907–37), artist and painter. (Sotnikov's and Pavil'onov's initials are given incorrectly in the article as A.S. and Iu.V., respectively.)

Besides those named Tatlin was also helped by two VKhUTEIN students: sculptor A.E. Zelenskii and painter A.B. Shchipitsyn.

[From Kut's Notes 'Return to Painting. At an Evening for the Artist Tatlin']

[...]

Tatlin not only acquainted the audience with the outlines of his colourful life, full of creative achievements and failures, but also revealed with great frankness his current intentions and plans.

313–353   After boldly challenging our ideas on engineering with his 'Letatlin', *the artist now wants to return to painting*, with which he began his artistic career.

The artist also wants to take up architectural constructions, continuing that line of his

164–206   creativity which was so gloriously marked by the monument to the Communist International which shook the whole world.

Tatlin admitted that he has an inveterate attraction to the theatre. While still a youth he worked as an apprentice in the scenery studios of the Solodovnikov Opera and primed over fifteen thousand metres of canvas for scenery. After the Revolution Tatlin produced V. Khleb-

216–222   nikov's romantic poem 'Zangezi' in Leningrad and attempted to work with Meierkhol'd. But the construction he made for Meierkhol'd's proposed production of F. Sologub's 'Spectral

Charms' turned out to be in such screaming contrast to Meierkhol'd's intention that it ended in a prolonged friction between them.

[...]

(1933)

Вечерняя Москва, no. 8, 10 January 1933.

These short notes summarize Tatlin's speech of the previous evening in the Moscow House of Artists, at a 'meeting' with art workers. The speech contains a number of autobiographical items which are not known from other Tatlin documents, and reflects Tatlin's reaction to a series of printed and oral statements in 1932 on his exhibition in the State Museum of Fine Arts and on *Letatlin*. In reply to the charge made by such statements that Tatlin was 'departing into technology' (*see* Bibliog.: Kronman, 1932), the artist decisively affirms his 'return to painting' and also his return to work as a theatre artist and architectural designer.

A. Kut (pseudonym of the journalist A.V. Kutuzov), wrote frequently in the periodical press of the thirties on questions of culture and art.

Solodovnikov Opera, a Moscow opera house belonging to the entrepreneur Solodovnikov, which functioned until 1908, in the building which now houses the Central Theatre of Operetta.

Meierkhol'd, Vsevolod Emil'evich (1874–1940), was an avant-garde theatrical director and actor. Meierkhol'd himself and his contemporaries considered that there was a definite correspondence between his creativity and Tatlin's, even if this took place in different branches of art. In 1917 Meierkhol'd proposed making a film based on the novel *Spectral Charms* and invited Tatlin to be the artistic designer (*see also* 'Artist or', p. 314).

Sologub (Teternikov), Fedor Kuzmich (1863–1927), Russian writer and poet, belonged to the older generation of Russian symbolists.

Spectral Charms (*Nav'i chary*), Sologub's novel-trilogy (1907–8), contained motifs of pessimism, mysticism and morbid eroticism typical of that stage of his career. The title of the novel became applied to designate the decadent movement of that time.

On the performance of Zangezi *see* 'On "Zangezi"', p. 248.

[Speech at a 'Creative Evening' for Petrov-Vodkin]

Here a lot has been said and everything is revealed. I just wanted to say a few words about my personal attitude to Petrov-Vodkin from the time when he was starting his work, when I found him in Leningrad, to the end. I think now that there were different relationships among artists then: when there was one artist then it was fine, two and there's already an argument, three and there's almost a fight. Each somehow stood firm and followed his own line. Then we met like hedgehogs without understanding one another's inner condition.

I consider that now such a time has passed. So much has happened both in life and in the progress of art that I personally am changing to a completely different condition. And I must say openly that attitudes towards us and attacks made on us are often deeply unjust in the case of artists who are genuine masters.

I fully recognize the work of Petrov-Vodkin as that of a great master who is both connected with the preceding age and a real force today. The situation is most critical. We must stretch out our hands to one another. A master must feel that there is a genuine power in the man who holds a trade in his hands, who has painting as a weapon. With this weapon he can speak. Anyone who doesn't know this secret isn't worth anything. People who will work in the spirit of Petrov-Vodkin should be told this openly. [...]

Without criticism, without discussion of our works we won't go very far. Without this our work isn't worth anything, it's just soap-bubbles.

I only wish Petrov-Vodkin that he may get better physically and be sure to get abroad for that purpose, so his health may be put back on the right tracks. (Applause.)

(1933)

State Russian Museum, manuscripts section, fond 105, unit 33, p. 13.

Typed transcript of the **shorthand minutes** of a 'creative evening' for Petrov-Vodkin in the Moscow Division of the Union of Soviet Artists (MOSSKh) on 25 May 1933. (For the present publication this text has had a certain minimum of literary editing, since the whole transcript, not just of Tatlin's speech, was made very carelessly – the editor.) At the evening, Kuznetsov, Lentulov, Uitz, Gerasimov, Goncharov and others spoke as well as Petrov-Vodkin himself.

Petrov–Vodkin, Kuzma Sergeevich (1878–1939), Russian painter and member of the 'second generation' of the World of Art group.

[From the Article (Signed 'Sh.') 'Artist or Constructor. Tatlin Designs Ostrovskii']

[...]

'For the first time,' Tatlin relates, 'I made my debut as a theatrical artist in 1913 [in 1911]. Then I designed the production of "Tsar Maximilian", put on in the Literary and Artistic Circle. Then in 1916 [in 1917] I was invited by V.E. Meierkhol'd, who was working at the time in cinematography, to design a production of "Spectral Charms". That thing, gloomy and mystical through and through, was deeply foreign to me even then.

'The results of my attitude to this material were not long in having their effect,' Tatlin recalls. 'Meierkhol'd asked me to make a mystical "strange tree" for the production. He evidently had in mind a huge spreading tree with incredible branches and roots sticking out of the ground. But I treated the "strange tree" in my own way and built a huge ship's mast with all the proper nautical attachments – rigging and observation towers. Clamber up the mast, up the tree, that is, play to your heart's content. But when Meierkhol'd saw my tree-mast he was horrified. This production wasn't destined to take place.

'Then I began work in the theatre as early as 1923 in Leningrad. The Theatre of the Institute of Artistic Culture [Museum of Artistic Culture, Petrograd] put on Velemir Khlebnikov's "Zangezi" and I worked with enthusiasm.

'Now, after a long interval, I have returned to the theatre. True, in this time there have been isolated attempts to draw me into theatre work, but all the time I was busy with other things, and then the dramatic material often didn't satisfy me. So I refused Meierkhol'd's suggestion to design Maiakovskii's "Bathhouse", a play I didn't like.

'The work suggested to me by MKhAT-2 attracted me with the possibility of showing Ostrovskii as a playwright of everyday life by depictive means. In building models for the sets I treat each thing as profoundly belonging to everyday life. Hence too the basic realistic line in this work of mine. So in designing the production I try to introduce into the elements of the design a material environment to characterize the setting and characters of Ostrovskii's play as fully, vividly and richly as possible.

'The play itself captivated me. In designing it I made up my mind to emphasize the bigotry and niggardliness – those distinguishing features so vividly depicted by the great dramatist.

'At that time Moscow was almost entirely wooden, only the churches perhaps were of stone, and that not always. So wood is the main material element in the production's design.

'True to my principles of working with material, I naturally avoid backdrops and other painted scenery. Construction is the basic principle of the design, in close relationship, however, with other design elements, lighting in particular.

'I provide a volumetric and spatial material-form, which can be presented in motion. This form is very diverse and a slight turning of a scenery platform is sufficient to change the set, from a street, say, to a living-room. The whole production is set within drapery wings.

'The construction is built to be seen equally well from the stalls and any part of the upper circles.'

(1934)

Советское искусство, no. 43, 17 September 1934.

In the first part of **the article,** after a general evaluation of Tatlin's creative path, is the statement 'In conversation with our reporter V.E. Tatlin shared his reminiscences... and intentions ...'. In its exposition the article attempts to convey Tatlin's direct words. It is illustrated by a photograph of Tatlin's model for the set of the play *A Comic Actor of the 17th Century* (Ill. 355).

The authorship of this article may perhaps be attributed to I. Shneiderman (only the initial 'Sh' is given) on the grounds that he later published an article written in the same key on Tatlin's work in designing the production of *The Affair* (see Bibliog.: Shneiderman, 1940).

On the production of **Tsar Maximilian** *see* 'Letter to the Editor', commentary, p. 181.

On Meierkhol'd's intention to produce **Spectral Charms** *see* 'From Kut's Notes', commentary, p. 313.

On the **performance of Zangezi** *see* p. 248; 'About "Zangezi"', p. 395.; 'On the Stage Production', p. 400.

The Bathhouse, a satirical comedy (1929) by Maiakovskii, was produced by Meierkhol'd, with the participation of the author, in 1930. It was designed by the architect Vakhtangov and artist Deineka.

Second Moscow Art Academic Theatre (MKhAT-2): functioned from 1924 to 1936.

A Comic Actor of the 17th Century, an historical comedy (1872) by Ostrovskii, is written on the theme of the beginning of the professional theatre in Russia. (*See* Syrkina, p. 164) MKhAT-2 performed it with a prologue, interludes and epilogue specially written by Kamenskii.

   With the designing of this production Tatlin began, after a lengthy interval, a long cycle of theatrical works, and he considered the beginning of this work (which he relates to 1933 or 1934) a kind of turning-point in his career (*see* 'Return', p. 312, 'Curriculum Vitae', p. 324). It is more for tactical considerations that he emphasizes his 'everyday' and 'realistic' approach to the play. More accurate was Bersenev's appraisal (*see* Syrkina, p. 164). There were two variants of Tatlin's design (*see* next article, p. 315). The models of the set have not been preserved (the costume designs: Ill. 360–8).

On the term **material-form** *see* 'Autobiography', commentary, p. 266.

[From the Article 'Tatlin in the Theatre. A Conversation with the Artist']

[...]

Velemir Khlebnikov's 'Zangezi' was Tatlin's first experiment of work in the theatre. That was in 1923 in Leningrad [Petrograd]. This performance, in which Tatlin was actor, producer and designer, took place in the Museum of Artistic Culture on Isaakievskaia Square. Both the performance and its creator had a sensational success, Tatlin received many congratulations from directors, but not one invitation for work. The artist on his own initiative designed and exhibited sketches for theatrical costumes and scenery. They were acquired by picture galleries, they received recognition, but the artist, who so much wanted to work in the theatre, continued to work away from the stage.

   'Why?'

   'Probably because of my bad character,' the artist growls good-naturedly. 'When an artist goes to work in the theatre in his fiftieth year one has to suppose that his character is already completely formed and he'll hardly have the power to change it to please directors. It is possible to work in the theatre only in a case where the artist is dealing with a director who is organically close to him in his creative method, which means for some to work with an experimentalist director, a bold, talented man who isn't afraid of going astray in the search for new paths. Work in the theatre is very attractive. But it will lose all value if you have to convince yourself that more concessions are required from the artist than from the director.

   'The first intention in designing the production of "Let us not Surrender" was changed considerably. The first version of the model was built not so much on the principle of "resemblance" to the actual setting in which the men on the Cheliuskin found themselves as with the idea of creating an artistic image for their camp. It was the artist's aim to convey to the audience the feeling of alarm, constant danger, lack of stability, to force the actors to move over an unstable surface, an oscillating surface. After consultations with specialists – Otto Iul'evich gave us his advice too – it turned out that the model was untrue to life in many ways. The ice-floe the camp was pitched on – several metres thick – simply couldn't oscillate noticeably from the weight of people on it. To be true to life we had to renounce such an artistic image.

'We had to seek the solution to the problem by other means.

'Lighting is extremely important in such scenery. The Kamernyi Theatre, which has excellent imported lighting equipment, will be able here to achieve the necessary results. We just have to be careful that enthusiasm for the pleasant, at times pleasantly softening, lighting which is fine for a production like "Egyptian Nights" shouldn't lead us to mistakes in the Cheliuskin production, which demands more severity, restraint, cold chiaroscuro.

'The work on "The Comic Actor" in MKhAT-2 wasn't without compromises either. What the spectator will see on stage falls short of the original version of the model in the sense of inventiveness and mobility of the constructions. The fault lies with the stage conditions of MKhAT-2. Still, the very limited movements of a stage circle allow the director, if he pays careful attention to the model, to solve the problems the artist has set before him. The main difficulties lie in the fact that the artist too tries to make a static theatre setting, even one like a pavilion, as dynamic and mobile as possible, to create action on stage on many planes, to make the scenery have something of the mobility and "flow" of a cinema film.'

[...]

(1935)

Литературная газета, no. 54, 24 September 1935.

The anonymity of the article emphasizes the attempt to convey as fully as possible the contents and intonation of what Tatlin said. The two concluding paragraphs contain a description of the model for the set of *A Comic Actor of the 17th Century*. The article is illustrated by a sketch for a woman's costume for this production. (There is a misprint in the signature: N. Tatlin.)

On the **production of A Comic**..., *see* 'Artist or', commentary, p. 315.

On **'theatrical works on his own initiative'**, *see* 'Letter to Benois', and commentaries, pp. 182–3.

Shmidt, Otto Iul'evich (1891–1956), a Soviet scientist and explorer of the Arctic, headed the Cheliuskin expedition.

The Kamernyi Theatre Moscow, founded by Tairov, functioned under his direction from 1914 to 1950. It aimed at 'pure theatricality', which it contrasted to both naturalistic and the conventional symbolist theatre.

Egyptian Nights was a production by the Kamernyi Theatre (1934) based on motifs from Pushkin, G.B. Shaw and Shakespeare, and designed by V.F. Ryndin.

The production **Let us not Surrender** was put on by Tairov in 1935. (*See also* Syrkina, p. 167).

The Moon on Stage

The drawback of existing methods of showing the moon on stage – by a transparency cut out in the sky; a lamp with a round, flat, mat glass; a spot painted on a backcloth, etc. – has always been the total lack of any feeling of the air and space surrounding the moon as we see it in real life.

401   In trying to find a way of overcoming this drawback I settled on one technique which certainly gives the right effect. It consists of the following: a disk for the moon of the desired

dimensions is made from papier-mâché, a board, metal, etc. The main requirement is an absolutely smooth surface. In cross-section, the front side of the disk is slightly convex, equally and smoothly receding to the edges, which are curved towards the back, thus giving the fully streamlined form of a flattened globe. The back side is flat or even concave – this has no importance.

If the disk is made of papier-mâché from a preparatory mould of plaster from a clay model, or is planed from one or more boards glued together, then particular attention must be given to its surface. All the uneven parts must be filled in. Then the disk is covered with a base and when it is dry it is carefully rubbed down with pumice and sandpaper. It is essential to get an *absolutely smooth surface.* It is better to make the base the same colour as that intended for the moon – 'moon-coloured', orange, reddish (coppery) and so on – or to paint it using a spray or a soft brush.

Particularly interesting is a disk made of metal – brass, tin, etc. It must be made of a whole piece of metal, not welded; it must be smoothly curved, like the profile shown in figure 1, to give the impression of having been stamped out mechanically. Such a disk is not painted at all since its main value is in the actual metal as material. A disk prepared in such a way is hung on two thin wires, the thinnest possible, and attached to a fly at the appropriate height. The distance between them and the backdrop should be no less than 2–3 metres.

The second problem is how to illuminate this disk. This is done by a projector with a tube attached to the lens to prevent the light from scattering, and with an aperture which will give at the necessary distance a spot of light the same size as the disk. But since in most cases the projector – even when hung as far back and away from the illuminated object, i.e. the disk, as possible – will be at a slight angle to it, the round aperture will give an elliptical spot. To avoid this it is necessary, once the diaphragm has been opened to the required diameter, to replace it with a permanent mask which is not round but is distorted, so that when the light is aimed at the disk at the determined distance and angle it will give a round spot on the disk.

The disk's colour is determined either by its own colour – and then one uses a white light – or by a colour-filter over the projector. Then the same white disk can be used on different occasions.

The effect can be achieved more simply by replacing the convex disk by a completely flat one. In this case the edges should be as thin as possible, and cut at an angle towards the back, giving a profile like this: [There is an isosceles trapezium standing on its acute angle in the original text.] When the spot of light is thrown on this disk the lens should not be placed in sharp focus. The edges should be soft and diffuse, passing into shadow, and so giving a certain feeling of volume and roundness. Such a way of showing the moon was used for the production of the play 'Deep Reconnaissance' at the Moscow Art Theatre.

(1944)

В.Е. Татлин, 'Луна на сцене', Издание Сценической экспериментальной лаборатории при МХАТ СССР им. М. Горького. Москва,1944, (six-page brochure with illustrations).

The brochure: The illustrations consisted of a working diagram for 'the moon' in its basic version and a profile of 'the moon's disk' for the simplified version. Tatlin's brochure was the first in a series published by the Art Theatre which popularized specially developed methods for overcoming problems of theatrical design (*see,* for example, Б.А. Попов, *Автомобиль, мотоцикл, трактор. Шумовое сопровождение спектакля.* Москва, 1947).

In the brochure Tatlin speaks of his own experience of production design but, as in a number of other cases, his intentions for the technical side were not fully carried out by the theatre: the artist publicizes them by means of the brochure and only in its conclusion mentions the simplified version which he himself had to use out of necessity. Tatlin's theatrical works of the 1930s and 1940s were marked by the originality of the constructions, treatment of materials, manner of lighting, etc. In this particular case the principle for the suggested arrangement is that of a hanging construction, a favourite device of Tatlin's since his counter-reliefs. But his daring constructive ideas and the perfection he demanded for their practical realization were none the less aimed at creating the type of scenic illusion which prevailed in the theatre of that time, which was in principle foreign to Tatlin.

Deep Reconnaissance: *see* Syrkina, p. 172; 'Curriculum Vitae', p. 324.

[Speech at a Re-election Meeting of the Section of Theatre Arts of the Moscow Branch of the Union of Soviet Artists]

I did not hear the summary report and hesitate to talk about it. Probably there is much that is good in the work of the executive body, but there are failures too. The failures have been spoken of here and probably the people involved know this and will correct them in good time.

The executive of our Section has certainly been cold and remote at times; sometimes even applications were lost and no one received an answer. I'll say frankly that I was even hurt by this.

Theatre artists, of course, work somewhere on the margin, and how can the Section bring together and engage the interest of artists? Naturally by personal contact.

A man is working entirely in the theatre on the one hand, and then on the other hand there's the Section. How can it attract him? It can attract and interest us by providing each of us with what we want and need.

Perhaps with some improvement in our lives. [...]

I am 63. I don't always have work in the theatre: there are empty bubbles [idle periods], very big ones, sometimes you're left hanging in the air. Of course our new executive should consider all this and, as far as it can, prevent such times. [...]

The place we're meeting in here could be very lively and valuable if the executive took a little more active interest in artists.

But there are difficult times now. A group of my comrades and I have fallen into a very difficult situation: suddenly one morning you read in the paper – they name names – that in the thirty-first year of the Soviet Union's existence there exist people in the USSR occupied with something that sounds today like, say, astrology. That's what happens. But in reality that isn't so.

How could it happen that without the knowledge of the Section's executive an article was printed in which people who have been working in the Soviet theatre for fourteen years suddenly turn out to be some kind of 'Frenchmen', Cubists perhaps, who have been preserved in some inexplicable way? But there just aren't such people here now.

Only if my work were judged, analysed... [...] But in fact nobody analysed anything in this case. You wake up in the morning and suddenly there's this. And there's even 'antisocial' written there!

And where should I be able to count on finding a defence if not in the Section's executive? I hope the Section's executive will help me in this.

(1948)

TsGALI, fond 2422, inventory 1, unit 174, pp. 95–7.

Uncorrected verbatim report of a review and re-election meeting of the executive of the Section of Theatre Arts of the Moscow Branch of the Union of Soviet Artists, 14 April 1948.

At the meeting B.R. Erdman and N.A. Shifrin gave reports on the executive's organizational work for 1943–8; thirteen artists took part in the discussion. The meeting took place shortly after the adoption of certain Party decrees in the area of ideology and art (on the repertory of theatres, on the opera *Great Friendship*, on the journals *Zvezda* and *Leningrad*); at the same time the atmosphere of the meeting also reflected the difficult material situation of the early post-war years.

Tatlin's work was mentioned in both summary reports and in a number of speeches at the meeting, since shortly before it an article had been printed in *Sovetskoe iskusstvo* sharply criticizing the Section of Theatre Arts of the Branch of the Moscow Union of Artists which, it maintained, had become a refuge for formalist artists Tatlin, Tyshler and a number of others.

The meeting did not agree with such criticism. In Erdman's report in particular it was said: 'Take Tatlin, who provides one realistic production after another and works even in those theatres where formalism would be unimaginable: in the Art Theatre, in the Theatre of the Lenin Komsomol' (ibid., p. 16). The same view is expressed in Shifrin's report. For example: 'Tatlin gave very powerful productions this year: *Deep Reconnaissance, Captain Kostrov* and *Fog over the Bay*, and a play which hasn't been performed yet, *The Battle of Grunwald*' (ibid., p. 41).

[Speech at a Discussion of the Artist Shifrin's Works]

I think that such a showing of an artist, whether a theatrical artist or not, should not take place. The most important consideration in fact is how high he carries the banner of an artist.

What I have heard here about Nisson Abramovich's exhibition doesn't raise any objections from me. I agree that this is on a high level, and Shifrin fully deserves the praises I've heard.

I should just like to point out that there should be as much benefit as possible to Shifrin himself from this showing. What is said in discussion and criticism should always bring great benefit both to Shifrin himself and to us, the spectators. If we hear praise the whole time, if all are content, then he too will go home, get into bed and say 'very good', and go to sleep. We have to find some way of preventing him from going to sleep, so that he should adopt a critical attitude towards himself, set himself a number of questions.

I myself am sorry to say I don't have a pin to prick him with, and so I agree with the rest. If I look at these landscapes – it's been said of them perhaps they're a grey colour. I myself have no conception of such gradations in real life. Because colour generally in nature is almost always – or even always – active. And of course, if we grade life according to the seven colours of the palette as we have them, then they are insufficient to express all the emotions in the artist's own perception of nature.

So I see another side. And I see that Nisson Abramovich sees this side too.

When I look at what is outwardly called 'grey': 'He has a grey sky', they say, 'and there it's grey' – it's not so, because the grey here nevertheless can't be called simply grey. It has painterly character, it's active, this colour. That is why it's so interesting and valuable. It causes a certain thrill, and this acts on one's perception too. You look at it and it's effective, it impresses.

[...]

If you see fishes in the water, then they too seem to be grey, but they're actively grey. That's even not grey, but a sparkling silverness. So the grey colour here is a sparkling colour which can compete with whatever you want – with blue or gold.

But if you see some green permanent wave or another colour, then there'll be nothing active in it all the same. Very often one can see an uncultured attitude with paint: sometimes the colour is simply taken from a tube as gaudily as possible. One's told: 'Yes, yes – make it as flowery as possible, it's very good and beautiful.' But in fact it's very bad and ugly, uncultured and generally no good for anything.

But here the paint has been worked, each colour served up to us, and so it's expressive. It has content. Even a separate colour draws the eye to look at it.

Now I'd like to turn to something else, I'd like to say this: here it's said all the time that theatre artists should hold exhibitions of their stage models or sketches over five years. That's quite wrong.

If you go to many people's apartments, they have things piled up and gathering dust, things they love, through which they made some response relative to nature and recorded it. And no one knows what it's for.

I often visit Shifrin and have seen his things. But many of the things exhibited are completely new to me.

I want to say that it's necessary at last for artists to show their faces, particularly theatre artists. Where do they show themselves? On stage. But who sees them? Only the director or theatre people, and the wide public doesn't see them.

I'll criticize myself a little: I consider my work not yet ready, not completed. [...]

(1949)

TsGALI, fond 2422, inventory 1, unit 177, pp. 19, 20, 20 back, 21.

Uncorrected transcript of a meeting of the executive of the Section of Theatre Arts of the Moscow Branch of the Union of Soviet Artists with its membership, 5 October 1949. The text has received minimal literary editing (using in part someone's attempt at some date to edit the beginning of Tatlin's speech). On the agenda for the meeting was a discussion of Shifrin's works exhibited by way of a report on his working visit to Ples in 1947, and a discussion about exhibiting the works of artists of the Theatrical Section. The artists who spoke were: Kozlinskii, Rabinovich, Erdman, Tyshler, Bebutova, Volkov and others.

Shifrin, Nisson Abramovich (1892–1961), was a theatrical artist and painter.
Tatlin spoke as a supporter of a broad showing of the works – i.e. not limited to purely theatrical ones – of theatre artists. (It should be borne in mind that Tatlin did not exhibit his painting for the last twenty years of his life.)

In his conclusion, not here quoted, Tatlin refers to the proposed accounting for his own working trip to Ples, which also took place in 1947.

Curriculum Vitae of Honoured Art Worker Tatlin

Moscow, 6 Petrovsko-Razumovskaia Avenue, apartment 40, tel.: D3-29-66
[...]

Consisting of 17 pages
1) Contents	p. 1
2) Brief Survey	2 and 3
3) Parents and Early Childhood	4
4) Education and Professional Education	5 and 6
5) My Teachers	7
6) Exhibitions and Debates	8
7) The Sailor	9
8) About Myself	10
9) Tatlin as an Art Activist and Organizer	11
10) Pedagogical Work	12
11) Theatrical Work	13 and 14
12) My Students	15
13) Works Acquired by Museums and Galleries	16
14) Prizes, Awards and Titles	17
15) Reviews and References	18

Brief Survey
[...]
My professional career runs from 1909, when I started to exhibit my things at exhibitions and my works were discussed by the public and the press.

1917. To accept or not to accept the October Revolution, that wasn't a question for me. I wholly devoted myself to an active, creative, social and pedagogical life.

I worked as an easel-painting artist. My things were acquired by museums – (State Tret'iakov Gallery, Russian Museum, the Bakhrushin State Museum and others).

128–131
278–281
284–285
129–130

I worked as a professor in higher artistic institutes (Leningrad, Moscow, Kiev). My students are active Soviet artists and many of them have a high rank and have received government awards.

For more than twenty years I have worked as a theatre artist – in the Theatre of the Red Army, in MKhAT, the Theatres of the Moscow Soviet and of the Lenin Komsomol, in the Central Children's Theatre and others. In most there are positive reviews in our periodic publications, and also a number of productions designed by me were awarded a Stalin Prize.

In 1933 I was given the title of honoured art worker by the Soviet of Commissars.

I am now 68 and my health is deteriorating. But despite everything I work as an artist as and when I can. [...]

Parents and Early Childhood

My father Evgraf Nikiforovich Tatlin graduated as a mechanical engineer from the Technological Institute in St Petersburg and joined the Brest railway in Moscow as a railway engineer. As a leading engineer of that time he was sent abroad to study special questions related to railways. When he returned to Moscow he wrote and published a book, 'Crew Shifts on the Railways', published in 1888 [in 1893 and 1896].

My mother was a poet in the '80s and '90s. She graduated from the Bestuzhev courses. Her poems were printed in progressive journals of that time. Her work was close to that of Nekrasov, Polonskii. My father and mother met at Polonskii's funeral, where my mother read her poems for the poet's death. [Polonskii died later.] I was born in 1885 in Moscow on the Prechistenka Street. There were three children in our family and when we were young we lived together.

My mother died in 1887, when I was 2, and my father, after two years as a widower, remarried and the family moved from Moscow to Khar'kov. My father left government service and became chief engineer and director of a factory.

While we were still young we lived well enough, but when I was of school age and put into an elementary school my life started to deteriorate noticeably because of my stepmother's influence on my father.

Education and Professional Education

From my childhood I had a disposition for drawing (from the age of seven). At home and indeed everywhere I constantly scribbled with paper and pencil and loved it. At that age I was not attracted to the sciences. The reason for this (I now think) was the frequent beatings my father gave me because of my poor progress at school.

When I finished elementary school I was sent to a practical school. When I was in the fifth form my father died and I didn't want to stay with my stepmother, so one night I ran away and from Khar'kov I went to Odessa. I was in my fourteenth year and I became ship's boy on a sailing ship, on which I went on my first voyage to Turkey – Sinop – and to Bulgaria – Burgas, Varna. This I repeated more than once, while I was still learning.

Having earned some money as a ship's boy, I went to Moscow, where I succeeded in meeting young artists, with whom I made friends (they were older than me) and started to paint icons with them.

These were my first teachers and comrades, Levenets and Kharchenko. They prepared me for Art College. And so I entered the Penza College of Art in 1898 [1905], from where I graduated in 1903 [1910]. I graduated successfully and was given a recommendation to the Academy of Arts, where I could get in without an examination. And in spite of this I had to leave again on a long voyage to earn money. After which I returned to Moscow and entered the College of Painting, Sculpture and Architecture. While I was studying I had no resources and I often had to interrupt my studies to earn some money. By then I was of age and was hired as a sailor, going away on long voyages.

Once (when I was already a student in the senior classes) I had to make a long break in my studies, which prevented me from graduating from the College. Then I started to work independently, and finally I went abroad to perfect my work, where I studied the art of the past in the Louvre and modern art too at exhibitions. At that time those who graduated from the College of Painting, Sculpture and Architecture were also sent abroad to perfect themselves.

I worked there, and when I returned to Moscow I organized an exhibition with my comrades, in 1913–14.

My contemporaries at that time in the College were: Pavel Ivanovich Ivanov, now an architect; Nikolai Semenovich Zaitsev, a painter; Lysenko, a painter; Rybakov, a painter; Iov Kornilovich Altukhov, a sculptor; we studied together in evening classes (drawing).

I have to say that some of the students in the College of Painting, Sculpture and Architecture were critical of the concepts in art which were being taught by our teachers at that time, and this in part hindered one from thinking of graduating from the College. And that too led to my leaving the College.

My Teachers

In the College of Art my director was the artist Aleksei Fedorovich Afanas'ev, who painted scenes from the life of the people, and he also painted frescoes with the artist Riabushkin. His works are in the Tret'iakov Gallery. Frescoes very much interested me then.

I also studied with Ivan Silych Goriushkin-Sorokopudov. He directed the model class.

At that time the works of the senior classes were sent every year to the synoptic exhibition at the Academy of Arts and my works had success, so when I graduated from the College I was given a recommendation on the strength of which I could enter the Academy without an examination. But at that time I was strongly connected to the young Moscow artists, and I went to Moscow and a year later entered the College of Painting, Sculpture and Architecture, where Korovin, Serov, Levitan, Pasternak, Kasatkin and others were teaching.

All these artists were connected with and belonged to the exhibition organizations Union of Russian Artists and World of Art, and we – a group of young people – didn't share their views on art; and already then new artistic tasks were being promoted in art.

This led to our organizing an exhibition outside the College, where we showed pictures and proclaimed new aims, declarations and manifestos.

Exhibitions and Debates

Before the Revolution there were a number of artistic societies which organized exhibitions in St Petersburg and Moscow. There were the Union of Russian Artists, the Union of Youth, the World of Art, Jack of Diamonds, Golden Fleece and others, which invited us (the young) to participate in their exhibitions although we weren't members of these societies, and we gave them our things for exhibitions. Besides this we organized independent exhibitions (of our *group*) and also exhibitions for individual young artists. This was from 1909 to 1918. These exhibitions went successfully for us and the press always noted them and printed photos of our works in journals.

Besides these appearances we were connected at that time with a group of young poets. Amongst them were: Khlebnikov, Maiakovskii, Kamenskii and others. We often appeared with them and organized joint debates and reports in the lecture rooms of the Polytechnical Museum (Moscow).

These reports and debates, in overcrowded rooms, were very stormy, and served us in our struggle with the philistinism and stagnation of that time. They also served as universities for us. They educated us, if we add to that our meetings and heated round-the-clock arguments about art.

The Sailor

In the intervals between the College of Art and the College of Painting, Sculpture and Architecture I went on long voyages to earn money, and this also gave me the opportunity of seeing ships, the sea, various foreign countries, people, fishes and birds, which I then already observed keenly. And all this suggested various ideas to me, which subsequently I realized in part.

On my voyages I saw more than once Turkey, Syria, Libya, Lebanon and Egypt. I called into the ports of Constantinople, Beirut, Haifa, Jaffa, Smyrna, Port Said, Alexandria, Tripoli, Rhodes, and others.

I want to say that besides giving me a wage this was an education for me as an artist.

84–89

21–24

About Myself

From 1909 on – from my first appearances at exhibitions – my art at that time was abstract, and when the Revolution came we weren't ready to be useful in our art to the broad strata of society. And I personally had to undertake considerable reworking of my art. But as far as I could I tried to be useful for our new life. And I produced things which were shown here in the USSR and were also sent abroad. At that time our country started to put certain new demands on art.

Then the artists had to do a great deal of work on themselves. In particular I too had to reeducate myself as an artist and first of all to determine where to direct my efforts, where they could be most usefully applied. And I decided to go and work in the theatre. I in fact began this work as a realist artist in 1933, [designing – the beginning of the word is illegible] productions on Soviet themes or on the old classical themes.

Tatlin as an Art Activist and Organizer

From 1913 [1917] until 1918 inclusive I was an active member, organizer and president of the Union of Painters, which in 1918 went entirely into Rabis.

From 1917 I was a member of the IZO section of the Soviet of Workers', Peasants' and Red Army Deputies (Moscow, Kremlin).

Tatlin was the first artist who went to work for Soviet power.

In 1918 the People's Commissariat of Education charged me with organizing the Fine Arts Department, of which I was director one and a half years. At that time my superiors were com[rades] Krupskaia and Lunacharskii.

In 1918 I was charged with organizing museum specialists, having created the museums 168 department (organizing a collegium in it as a consultative body), which also looked after the protection and organization of museums and the state's art treasures.

At the same time I was also involved in pedagogical work.

Pedagogical Work

From 1910 to 1913 [1911–15] in Moscow, on 37 Ostozhenka, I had a studio I shared with 68, 69 the artist A.A. Vesnin, in which I taught young people drawing and painting.

From 1913 [1916] to 1920 on 33 Basmannaia Street (Moscow), I had a studio in which I taught a group of young people drawing and painting.

From 1918 in VKhUTEMAS [SVOMAS] I ran a workshop and as professor was in charge 128 of drawing, painting and composition (in Tatlin's workshop) until 1924 [1920] inclusive.

From 1921 [1919] to 1924 I was in the State Free Artistic Studios (Leningrad, former Academy of Arts). I ran my workshop as a profess[or] and was in charge of: drawing, painting, composition.

At the same time as this I worked in the Institute of Painterly Culture – department of drawing, composition and designing objects of everyday life (patterns), from 1922 to 1925 inclusive.

From 1925 in the Kiev College of Art I ran the theatrical section in the Faculty of Painting 129, 130 as a professor and taught basic subjects in theatrical design, drawing and composition until 1927 inclusive.

From 1927 I worked in VKhUTEIN in the Faculty of Ceramics, where as a professor I 275–288 was in charge of drawing, composition and designing [models for ceramic products] to 1931, until the closing of VKhUTEIN.

From 1931 to 1933 the Faculty of Ceramics was transferred to the Silicates Institute, where as a professor I was in charge as an artist of [basic subjects] composition, designing and drawing.

From 1927 I was at the same time involved in pedagogical work in the Faculty of Wood 244 and Metalworking of VKhUTEIN, where as a professor I was in charge of [basic subjects] composition, designing and drawing until the closing of VKhUTEIN in 1931.

Theatrical Work

List of productions designed by me in Moscow and in the country, and also costume drawings and sketches made by me for productions:

38–41 1) 1912 [1911]. I designed the production: 'Maximilian and his Son Adolf'. Put on in Moscow in the Literary and Artistic Circle.

137–155 2) 1914 [1912–13]. I made set and costume sketches for the opera 'Ivan Susanin' (Glinka). St[ate] Tret'iakov Gal[lery].

156–163 3) 1915–1916 [1915–18]. I made set and costume sketches for the opera 'The Flying Dutchman' (Wagner).

216–222 4) Khlebnikov's 'Teacher' [Zangezi]. Production in the Miatlev House, Leningrad, 1922 [Petrograd 1923].

The works indicated were exhibited at the exhibitions of the Union of Russian Artists and the World of Art and acquired by the State Tret'iakov Gallery (Moscow) and Russian Museum (Leningrad) and were noted in the press of that time.

Before the Revolution in general I worked four years for the theatre.

After the Revolution from 1933 to 1952 inclusive I designed productions in the capital's theatres without a break. Some of them:

354–368 4) Ostrovskii (MKhAT-2) 'A Comic Actor of the 17th Century', producer Bersenev.

5) 'Let us not Surrender' ('The Cheliuskin Men'), producer Tairov, Kamernyi Theatre.

384–391 6) 'Kronshtadt'. Theatre of the Lensoviet, producer Plotnikov.

369–383 7) 'The Affair' by Sukhovo-Kobylin, Theatre of the Red Army, producer Popov.

8) 'Pushkin', by Globa, Sverdlovsk State Dramatic Theatre.

9) 'Natasha Moskvina', by Mikhalkov. Stanislavskii Studio.

10) 'A Far Country', by Shvarts, State Central Children's Theatre.

11) 'For Those at Sea', by Lavrenev. Theatre of the Lenin Komsomol.

12) 'For Those at Sea', Theatre of the Cinema Actor.

392–396 13) 'Deep Reconnaissance', by Kron, MKhAT, producer Kedrov.

401, 399 14) 'Captain Kostrov', by Faiko, State Theatre of Drama, producer Okhlopkov.

15) 'Somewhere in Siberia', Central Children's Theatre, producer Tovstonogov.

16) 'Enough Simplicity in Every Wise Man', by Ostrovskii. State Realistic Dramatic Theatre.

17) 'Secretary of the Regional Committee' (by Surov), Theatre of the Moscow Soviet, producer Zavadskii.

18) 'Twelve Months', by Marshak. House of Young Talents.

19) 'The Wonderful Pot' [The Wonderful Treasure], House of Young Talents, producer Lishin.

20) 'The Truth about my Father' [The Truth about his Father] by Berezin. Literary and Dramatic Theatre, producer Bebutov.

21) 'Cup of Joy', Theatre of the Moscow Soviet, producer Zavadskii.

22) 'Emissary of Peace.' Literary and Dramatic Theatre, producer Bebutov

and others. More than once in the press and in speeches at discussions of my theatrical works it was pointed out that Tatlin was one of the leading artists of the Moscow theatre and that productions designed by me were always well received by the public of the capital.

There are also a large number of references from producers of various Moscow theatres, who highly appraised my work in the theatre over the course of two decades.

The overall number of years I have worked in theatres designing productions is: from 1912 to 1916 inclusive four years, and from 1933 to 1952 inclusive 19 years. 4 years + 19 years = 23 years in all.

[...]

My Students

I give the names of my students who have now proven themselves as theatre artists, ceramic-sculptors [and others]; their names are already known to the public, and some of them have been awarded high honours – the Stalin Prize or the title of honoured art worker.

1) Sotnikov, Aleksei Georgievich – sculptor and ceramicist (VKhUTEIN and the Silicates Institute, Moscow).

315, 317
275–284

2) Umanskii – theatre and cinema designer (Kiev College of Art). The main artist of the Kiev P91ema Studio. Winner of the Stalin Prize.

3) Vinogradov, M. – architect (Leningrad).

5) Shtoffer, Ia. – theatre designer.

6) Kaplunovskii – cinema designer, main artist of the Moscow Cinema Studio, honoured art worker and winner of the Stalin Prize (Kiev College of Art).

7) Kozhin – ceramicist and sculptor (VKhUTEIN, Moscow) and others.

288

Works Acquired by State Museums and Galleries

1) 'Sailor' (tempera), 1918 [1912] (Russian Museum, Leningrad).   34

2) 'Still-Life' (oil), 1918 [1912] (Russian Museum, Leningrad).   75

3) Costume sketches and drawings for the play 'Maximilian and his Son Adolf' (Russian Museum), 1916 [1911].   38–41

4) Set and costume sketches for 'The Flying Dutchman' (Wagner), State Tret'iakov Gallery (Moscow).   156–163

5) Set and costume sketches for 'Ivan Susanin', State Tret'iakov Gallery (Moscow).   137–155

6) 'Nude' (oil), State Tret'iakov Gallery, 1927 [1912].   79

7) Monument to the Comintern. Model of wood, metal and glass, State Tret'iakov Gallery (Moscow), 1928 [1920].   164–206

8) Sketches, drawings and model for the play 'A Comic Actor of the 17th Century', Ostrovskii, Bakhrushin State Museum.   354–368

9) Costume sketches and drawings and model for the play 'The Affair' by Sukhovo-Kobylin, acquired by the Bakhrushin State Museum (Moscow).   369–383

Prizes, Awards and Title

On the instructions of Narkompros I completed the Comintern Tower (steel and glass) – [the project] was shown at the 192[0] exhibition in Leningrad and the same year was taken to Moscow, where it was shown at the Eighth Congress of Soviets (in the House of Unions).

177–179
181

In 1925 it was built a second time for the International Exhibition in Paris, where it was awarded a prize.

Of the theatre works, two designed by me, 'Deep Reconnaissance', at MKhAT, and 'Secretary of the Regional Committee', were awarded the Stalin Prize.

392–396
401

In 1933 the Soviet of People's Commissars gave artist professor V.E. Tatlin the title of Honoured Art Worker.

(1953)

Manuscript, 21 pages, TsGALI.

The text was written in 1952–3 in ink and pencil (the pages of the basic text renumbered in Roman numerals from I to XVII). On page II is an insertion outlining Tatlin's career up to and including 1953; he was still in employment that year; on p. III is written 'I am now 68' (*see* p. 320) although Tatlin, who died in May 1953, would have been 68 only in December of that year; on p. XIV Tatlin gives 1952 as when he finished working as a theatre artist (*see* p. 324).

The text was written in at least two stages: pencil insertions are made on the completed manuscript. One of its purposes was an application to receive a higher pension, which is reflected in the lay-out of the first few pages. In its composition the manuscript is divided into sections by theme, each beginning on a new page; the last section, the promised 'Reviews and References', is missing.

This **Curriculum Vitae** is Tatlin's most complete autobiographical document. It provides a considerable amount of information and detail and in this respect is of great significance. Individual factual errors can be explained partly as lapses of memory and partly as the attempt of an old artist to somewhat 'modernize' the account of events in a manner more appropriate, as it seemed to him, to the time when the manuscript was prepared. On the title sheet, besides the heading, is given the address of Tatlin's last home (today house no. 2); his studio was in the same quarter ('quarter of artists') at the following address: 5 Verkhniaia Maslovka Street, studio no. 77 (today's house no. is 1).

On **Brief Survey:**
Tatlin characterizes his position in the days of the October Revolution by repeating a corresponding sentence from Maiakovskii's well-known autobiography 'I Myself' (cf. В. Маяковский, *Полное собрание сочинений*, Москва, vol. I, 1955, p. 25).

According to Resolution no. 74 of the Soviet of People's Commissars of the RSFSR, 17 January 1931, 'Professor of the Moscow Institute of Silicates and Building Materials, comrade V.E. Tatlin' is given the 'title of honoured art worker'.

On **Parents and Early Childhood:**
E.N. Tatlin, the artist's father, was sent in 1892 to the USA on the instructions of the Minister of Communications S. Iu. Vitte, to study the experience there in the deployment of railway staff; in 1893 he published 'An Account of a Trip to Study a System of Shift Crews on American Railways' Locomotives', in: Е.Н. Татлин, 'Отчет о поездке для изучения системы сменных бригад на паровозах американских железных дорог', in: *Журнал Министерства путей сообщения*, no. 5, 1893, then republished as a separate book *Shift Crews on American Railways' Locomotives* (Сменные бригады на паровозах американских железных дорог. Харьков, 1896).

St Petersburg Practical Technological Institute, founded in 1828, was from 1862 to the end of the nineteenth century the only higher educational establishment in Russia which prepared broadly-qualified engineer-technologists.

The Brest Railway, one of the main railways in pre-revolutionary Russia, linked Moscow with the western provinces and West European countries; its administration was in Moscow.

Tatlin's mother: Bart, Nadezhda Nikolaevna.

The Bestuzhev courses represented the first higher educational establishment for women (1878–1914, with an intermission) and had philological-historical and physics-mathematics faculties.

Nekrasov, Nikolai Alekseevich (1821–78), a great Russian poet and democrat.

Polonskii, Iakov Petrovich (1819–98), a Russian lyric poet, was a liberal in his social views. Tatlin's parents could not have met at Polonskii's funeral and probably Tatlin has confused his name with someone else's. No attempt has yet been made to find Bart-Tatlina's poems.

Prechistenka, a street in Moscow, is now Kropotkin Street.
V.E. Tatlin had an older brother and sister. (Compare this section with 'Autobiography', p. 264.)

On **Education and Professional Education:**
Here Tatlin gives most detailed information about his education, with a large number of concrete facts; the picture presented is on the whole a true one, but there are factual inaccuracies in the details and a tendency to characterize this stage somewhat more 'smoothly' than it went in actuality. (On Tatlin's years as a student *see* 'Questionnaire', p. 262; 'Autobiography', p. 264.)

Tatlin began his studies in the Moscow College of Painting, Sculpture and Architecture (MUZhVZ), 1902–3, continued them in the Penza College (1905–10), and then once more, according to his own information, studied in MUZhVZ (1909–10). All the artistic establishments of pre-revolutionary Russia except for the Higher Institute under the Academy of Arts in St Petersburg were considered as secondary education, and successful graduation from one of them gave the right to enter the Academy to complete one's higher education. Documentary evidence of a specific recommendation of this nature for Tatlin has not been found. Tatlin gives two reasons for leaving MUZhVZ before his formal graduation: constant material difficulties and dissatisfaction with the artistic direction of the official education there.

Altukhov, Iov Kornilovich (b. 1884), a sculptor, worked at the end of the 1960s in the village of Khot'kovo in the Moscow district.
On Tatlin's other co-students no information has yet been found.

On **Tatlin's visit to Western Europe** *see* 'Letter about a Trip', p. 181; 'Letter to Shkol'nik', p. 182; 'Questionnaire', p. 262. In Paris Tatlin undoubtedly visited the Louvre, but his main interests were directed towards the most recent artistic phenomena.

Exhibitions in 1913–14: In 1913–14 Tatlin participated in the exhibitions of the Union of Youth (2), Jack of Diamonds, World of Art, Modern Painting (2) and organized in his studio (1914) a personal First Exhibition of Painterly Reliefs. (*See* 'Tatlin at Exhibitions', p. 491)

On **My Teachers:**
On Afanas'ev, Korovin and Serov *see* 'Questionnaire', commentaries, p. 263.

Riabushkin, Andrei Petrovich (1861–1904), the son of an icon painter, was an historical painter and genre artist. Tatlin's direct reference to his interest in frescoes and his being professionally involved in icon painting, is of particular interest.

Goriushkin-Sorokopudov, Ivan Silych (1873–1954), a painter who graduated from the Academy of Arts (1902, a student of Repin), was the author of genre and historical compositions, and taught from 1908 in the Penza College of Art.

Levitan, Isaak Il'ich (1860–1900), a landscape artist and teacher in MUZhVZ.

Pasternak, Leonid Osipovich (1862–1945), a painter, graphic, genre and portrait artist, the father of the poet Boris Pasternak and a teacher in MUZhVZ. He lived in England from 1921.

Kasatkin, Nikolai Alekseevich (1859–1930), a genre painter whose work had a marked social tendency, was a teacher in MUZhVZ and the first artist to receive the title 'people's artist of the RSFSR' (1923).

Union of Russian Artists was a group of Russian painters (1903–23) who earlier had belonged to the Society of Itinerant Exhibitions (The Wanderers) and to the World of Art; in 1910 the St Petersburg artists left the Union after reviving the World of Art. On the World of Art *see* 'Letter to Benois', p. 183. On the exhibiting of slogans, manifestos, etc. as well as artistic works *see* 'List', p. 240; 'Programme', p. 242; 'Slogans', p. 244.

On **Exhibitions and Debates:**
On Union of Youth, Jack of Diamonds, Golden Fleece *see* 'Questionnaire', commentaries, p. 263; On Tatlin's participation in a World of Art exhibition, *see* 'Letter to Benois' and commentaries, pp. 182–3; on Khlebnikov, 'The Initiative Individual', p. 238; on Maiakovskii, 'On Tatlin', and commentaries, pp. 393–5.

Kamenskii, Vasilii Vasil'evich (1884–1961), a poet and playwright, one of the pioneers and organizers of the avant-garde movement in Russia (from 1909), befriended many artists and took part in their exhibitions. On his work with Tatlin on the production of *A Comic Actor of the 17th Century*, *see* 'Artist or', ries p. 314.

The Polytechnical Museum (Moscow), the oldest Russian scientific-technical museum, was founded as an institution in 1872; the debates about the new art in the lecture-rooms of the Polytechnical Museum, beginning with the pre-revolutionary years but mainly in the years following the Revolution, have gone into history as events of great social significance.

On **About Myself:**
Tatlin, like Maiakovskii, Meierkhol'd, Eisenstein and many other artists, saw his own and his colleagues' art as corresponding to the spirit of the Revolution, and close to it. (Cf. 'My Answer', p. 185; 'Memorandum', p. 185; 'Initiative Individual', p. 237; 'The Work', p. 239) Hence Tatlin's feeling that his creative position was one with his social-political position in those years. In the 1930s to 1950s a negative attitude prevailed towards the greater part of the artistic phenomena of the revolutionary years, which were seen as 'formalist' or 'foreign to the people'. In the last years of his life Tatlin, wishing to preserve an attitude of respect towards his social position and activity during the revolutionary years, found it necessary to speak of this separately from the general description of his own creative path (cf. 'About Myself', 'Tatlin as an Art Activist' [pp. 323] and a number of other passages). In evaluating his work Tatlin now emphasizes the significance of this stage, which began, as he maintained more than once, in 1933 and had a qualitatively different (realistic) character. He notes in a restrained but dignified fashion the importance of his works of the early period, without giving their dates – and it is this perhaps that motivates his old man's cunning in 'correcting' the dating of his early works by six, eight and even fourteen years in the section 'Works acquired by Museums and Galleries'.

On **Tatlin as an Art Activist:**
Tatlin's social and professional activity began no later than 1911, but he received formally important social duties for the first time in 1917 (*see* Strigalev, p. 23). Tatlin was not only one of the first artists to work actively with Soviet power but he also influenced others by his example and authority. On his work in the Moscow Section of IZO and the Museums Department of Narkompros *see* 'Memorandum', p. 185.

Rabis, the Trade Union of Art Workers, from 1921 published a journal of the same name, in which Tatlin's articles were published: *see* 'The Artist as', p. 266; 'The Problem', p. 267.

Krupskaia, Nadezhda Konstantinovna (1869–1939), from 1917 to 1920 was Deputy People's Commissar of Education under Lunacharskii; wife of Lenin.

On **Pedagogical Work:**
In his studio on Ostozhenka street (now Metrostroevskaia Street) in 1911–15 Tatlin directed classes in painting and drawing for a group of young artists of roughly the same generation as himself (*see* Kostin, p. 68; 'Autobiography', p. 264). The studio on Staraia Basmannaia Street (1916–20) was Tatlin's individual studio where his colleagues and later students of the Free State Artistic Studios came, but there were no classes in this studio.

Tatlin was director of a studio in the painting division of the Second Free State Artistic Studios (SGKhM, formerly MUZhVZ, the future VKhUTEMAS and VKhUTEIN) in 1918–20. At the same time in 1919 he began directing the studio of materials, volume and construction in the Petrograd Free State Artistic Teaching Studios (SVOMAS, formerly Academy of Arts, which name was adopted again in 1922). On Tatlin's work in the Museum – later Institute – of Artistic Culture *see* 'To the Museums Department', p. 241; 'Report', p. 250; 'Research Plan', p. 254. The Institute of Artistic Culture was only in part concerned with training specialists (through graduate work). On his work in the Kiev College of Art *see* 'Letter to Novitskii', commentary, p. 261. In this College Tatlin was in charge of 'formal-technical disciplines' (TsGALI, fond 681, inventory 2, unit 208, p. 52). (On his work in VKhUTEIN *see* 'Letter to Novitskii', p. 260) Tatlin worked in the Institute of Silicates and Building Materials from 1931 to 1933. The courses led by Tatlin in higher educational establishments were specific in their content and title, but in this text he uses the more usual designations 'drawing, painting' and, when revising it, adds in almost every paragraph 'composition'.

On **Aleksandr Vesnin** *see* 'Letter to Shkol'nik', p. 182.

On **Work in the Theatre:**
Tatlin's list of his theatrical works (23 titles as number four is repeated twice), although not complete, is drawn up on a completely different principle from the 'canonical' list of his work in other genres (cf. 'List', p. 240; 'Autobiography', p. 264; the list of works in the present article in the section 'Works acquired by State Museums and Galleries', p. 325). Even in the last variant of the 'canonical' list Tatlin includes only five productions he designed for the theatre, but in this section he tries to show as fully as possible his basic professional activity of the last twenty years. The actual calculation of the length of his theatrical career begins with a mistake in the year (1912 instead of 1911), and the period from 1917 to 1932 is omitted, although Tatlin did at this time have occasional encounters with the theatre (cf. Bibliog.: *Tatlin*, 1977, pp. 46–7). On the other hand his intensive work from 1933 to 1952 is emphasized in every possible way.
    On the production of *Tsar Maxem'ian see* 'Letter to the Editor', p. 181.
    On *Ivan Susanin* (*A Life for the Tsar*) *see* 'Letter to Benois', p. 182.
    On *Zangezi* (here called *Teacher*, as it was referred to during the course of the play) *see* 'On "Zangezi"' p. 248.
    On the production of *A Comic Actor of the 17th Century see* 'Artist or', p. 314; 'Tatlin in the Theatre', p. 315.
    On *Let us not Surrender see* 'Tatlin in the Theatre', p. 315.
    On Tatlin's participation in the World of Art exhibition *see* 'Letter to Benois', p. 182.
    Tatlin did not participate in any of the eighteen exhibitions of the Union of Russian Artists.
    On *The Affair*, the second play in Sukhovo-Kobylin's trilogy, *see* Syrkina, p. 169.
    On *Deep Reconnaissance see* Syrkina, p. 172; 'List of Works for the Theatre', p. 503.
    The Truth about his Father (not *The Truth about my Father*).
    On the other pieces *see* in the 'List of Works for the Theatre', p. 503.

Tovstonogov, Georgii Aleksandrovich (b. 1915), a producer and actor, worked in Moscow from 1946 to 1949; since 1950 he has worked in Leningrad.

Bersenev (Pavlishchev), Ivan Nikolaevich (1889–1951), producer and actor, worked twice with Tatlin: as a theatre manager (*see* 'Artist or', p. 314) and as producer of *For Those at Sea*.

Tairov, Aleksandr Iakovlevich (1885–1950), producer, actor and (with A. Koonen) the founder and artistic director of the Kamernyi Theatre (1914–50), usually produced all the Theatre's productions himself. (*See* 'Tatlin in the Theatre', p. 315)

Kedrov, Mikhail Nikolaevich (1894–1972), actor, producer and teacher, was artistic director of MKhAT from 1946 to 1955.

On **My Students:**
On **Sotnikov,** *see* Zhadova, p. 145; 'Art into', p. 310. Sotnikov did not work in the Silicates Institute.

Umanskii, Morits Borisovich (1907–48), a theatre and cinema artist, graduated from the Kiev College of Art in 1930 and worked in theatres in the Ukraine.

Vinogradov, M. is perhaps P.M. Vinogradov (who in Punin's brochure *Pamiatnik III Internatsionala* was also given the initials M.P. instead of P.M.), one of Tatlin's assistants in constructing the model in 1920. (*See* 'The Work', p. 239)

Shtoffer, Iakov Zakharovich (1906–51), a theatre artist who graduated from the Kiev College of Art in 1928, worked in theatres in Kirgizia, Moscow and Leningrad.

Kaplunovskii, Vladimir Pavlovich (1906–52), a cinema artist and director, graduated from the Kiev College of Art in 1928.

Kozhin, Pavel Mikhailovich (1904–75): *see* Zhadova, p. 146.

On **Works acquired by State Museums and Galleries:**
The list of Tatlin's works is based on the 'canonical' list of 1921, later repeated in 1929 with a few changes (*see* 'List', p. 240; 'Autobiography', p. 264). This time the changes are more substantial: if in 1921 the list consisted of

18 'items' and in 1929 of 9 'items', in 1953 there are only 6 of the old items and 3 new ones. All the new ones are works for the theatre, including for the first time the designing of the play *Tsar Maxem'ian*, that of *A Comic Actor of the 17th Century* (inaccurately named by Tatlin with the Russian word *vek* instead of *stoletie* for 'century') and *The Affair* – i.e. works belonging to a new stage, those most valued by Tatlin and which received most public acclaim.

The dates of all the works have been brought considerably forward in time: *Sailor* and *Still-Life* are given as 1918 instead of 1911; *Tsar Maxem'ian* as 1916 instead of 1911; *Nude* 1927 instead of 1913, and even *Monument to the Comintern* as 1928 instead of 1919–20. The reasons for these changes are unclear, although apparently they have been made consciously as opposed to Tatlin's frequently encountered carelessness or forgetfulness over dates (cf. 'List', p. 240) That Tatlin deliberately changed these dates can be shown by comparing certain dates within this same 'Curriculum Vitae'.

[Letter about Work on Models]

Mikhail Nikolaevich!
I'm informing you of how matters stand with four models which you gave me to carry out with my team.
1) Model for *Western Siberia* – the last stage of the elaboration of *faktura* is under way. Gustomesov is doing the work. A month is needed to complete it, perhaps even one and a half months.
2) Model for *Volcanoes* (Kamchatka). The *faktura* has been given to G.M. Bespalova, for which she was offered, and she agreed, 2,000 roubles after the model's acceptance by the Artistic Council and yourself. Furthermore I am supervising and directing the work on this.
3) Model for '...' [The word in inverted commas (a geographical term) is illegible.] The reliefs in the model have been carried out (their coating) by the artist A.N. Rudovich. She started the *faktura* two and a half months ago. She made many preliminary versions, but her determined work in this time did not give positive results. Now this model is being given to a different artist.

Model for *The Central-Russian Highlands*. There is a great deal of difficulty with this model because of its extreme complexity, and it is simply not feasible *qualitatively.*

Many artists have looked at it, thought over techniques for carrying it out and as a result all have refused because of the qualitative impossibility of carrying it out. The relief-contours in cardboard are feasible, but further work has been halted for the reasons indicated, as I told you two months ago.

You promised to come on 15 April 53, but unfortunately you couldn't do this.

It's very desirable for you to find a way of coming to see me in my studio in the next few days.

53 $\frac{\text{March}}{26}$ Sincerely, Tatlin

Original manuscript from the archive of A.N. Korsakova, Moscow.

Draft letter (or unsent letter) written by Tatlin within two months, or even less, before his death – the date of 26 March at the bottom of the letter conflicts with the mention in the text of the date 15 April as being already passed; evidently it was a slip of the pen, and should be corrected to 26 April.

The addressee has not been determined.

The letter throws light on yet another aspect of Tatlin's work, the creation of three-dimensional teaching aids for the Geographical Museum which at that time was being prepared for its opening in the skyscraper of the Moscow Lomonosov State University (MGU).

Gustomesov, Leonid Vasil'evich (b. 1910), an artist who, in the last years of Tatlin's life, worked with him and was a close friend.

Rudovich (Korsakova), Aleksandra Nikolaevna (b. 1904), an artist who from 1944 to 1953 was Tatlin's close friend and constant companion, designed costumes for a number of productions for which he was artist; she preserved his most significant archives, the main part of which she made available for the Tatlin exhibition in 1977 and then gave to TsGALI. In the 1970s she made numerous portraits of Tatlin, both paintings and drawings.

2 Writings on Tatlin

Vladimir Evgrafovich Tatlin

17 December 1915

Born in 1885 in Moscow. In 1910 graduated from arts school. Since 1909 has *exhibited* his 122–126 easel paintings (oils, tempera, watercolours, frescoes and others) at the following exhibitions:

Jack of Diamonds,
Society of Women,
Tramway V,
Modern Painting,
The Donkey's Tail,
The World of Art,
The Union of Youth,
The Golden Fleece Salon,
Exhibition of Paintings of the Year 1915

as well as at a number of joint (both Futurist and non-party) exhibitions in Petrograd and Moscow.

Has never belonged and does not belong to Tatlinism, Rayonism, Futurism, the Wanderers or any other group.

During the exhibition season of 1913–14 he arranged his first independent display of works under the title 'The First Exhibition of Painterly Reliefs' (Moscow, 37 Ostozhenka Street).

The following materials were used in making the reliefs: wood, metal, putty, glass, plaster, cardboard, primer, tar, etc.; the surfaces of those materials were treated with putty, gloss paints, dust sprinkling and other means.

In 1915 Tatlin's studio produced 'Corner Counter-Reliefs', which are exhibited in the current season at the collective exhibition in Moscow and at The Last Futurist Exhibition in Petrograd.

Владимир Евграфович Татлин, 17 December 1915, [буклет] *Новый журнал для всех, Петроград, 1915, p. 4.*

The booklet was the first programmatic document related to the artist's work. The booklet (Ill. 122–7) presented three large reproductions of corner counter-reliefs and two reproductions of painterly reliefs. It is worth mentioning the size of the booklet's pages: 37.3 cm × 27 cm. A masterpiece of book-printing in its own right (displayed in the 1977 exhibition Book Covers by Russian Artists from the Beginning of the Twentieth Century – *see* Tatlin at Exhibitions, p. 501), the booklet has preserved for us pictures of two lost counter-reliefs (Ill. 125). The anonymous text probably conceals a joint authorship of Tatlin himself and Udal'tsova.

The date on the cover suggests that it was supposed to appear in print in time for the opening of The Last Futurist Exhibition, 0—10, where Tatlin exhibited his corner counter-reliefs for the first time. However, the absence of the title of the exhibition on the cover as well as of any reference to it in the text itself suggests that the importance attached to the booklet exceeded that of temporary exhibition publications.

Publications for The Last Futurist Exhibition, 0—10: a leaflet with three declarations by Malevich, Kliun and Men'kov; a leaflet with a joint declaration by Puni and Boguslavskaia, as well as Malevich's pamphlet *From Cubism to Suprematism (A New Realism in Painting).* (К.С. Малевич, 'Письма к М.В. Матюшину', публ. Е.Ф. Ковтун in: *Ежегодник РО Пушкинского дома,* 1974, Ленинград, 1976.)

The artistic rivalry between the two groups found its expression in the form of these manifestos. The name Last Futurist Exhibition derived from Malevich, who at that time was busy working out the theory of Suprematism. To preserve the unity of the Futurist movement, he let his friends persuade him to delay publicizing his Suprematism. (*See* Eugen Kowtun, 'Die Entstehung des Suprematismus', in: *Von der Fläche zum Raum, Russland 1916–24,* Katalog der Ausstellung in der Galerie Gmurzynska, Köln, 1974, p. 32.)

The manifesto by Tatlin's group visually declared the creative orientation of the master of the counter-relief. Not being a theoretician, Tatlin attracted and convinced his supporters mainly through the example of his own work. (*See* Strigalev, pp. 13, 22) Its authors tried to imbue the text with an impersonal (anonymous) quality of general significance. This supposition is confirmed by a comparison between the printed text and the surviving draft copy recorded by Udal'tsova from Tatlin's words (Ill. 122–3).

The draft outline for the text of the booklet. This almost illegible document was discovered by Drevina in Udal'tsova's notebook entitled 'Thoughts on Art,' where she used to record her notes, drafts of her articles on art and letters on the same subject. The draft copy of the text was probably recorded by Udal'tsova in early October 1915. (The next entry in her notebook is dated 10 October.) A diary entry of 19 October 1915 also confirms the possibility of her collaboration with Tatlin.

The draft outline was written by Udal'tsova in pencil in a large but dense hand in an all-purpose ruled notebook with the stamp of the famous Moscow department store *Mir i Mereliz* on its cover. A few pages are missing from the notebook after the draft. Udal'tsova is thought to have written on them the final version of the text to be submitted to the publisher in Petrograd. The draft is in the form of notes with numerous abbreviations and omissions of logical links. In the process of recording their thoughts, the authors repeated numerous statements and also crossed out liberally. We reproduce below the main part of the draft without any changes (except for the elimination of dashes and some repetitions):

The artist V.E.T. Born in such-and-such a place.

Graduated from Art School in 1909. Participated in exhibitions since 1909. Don[key]'s Tail, Union of Youth, W[orld] of Art, Tramway V. The year 1915.

Was not a member of any societies or gr[oups], participated in exhibitions only... Afanas'ev, Picasso, Mikhailovskii, Mashkov, Tsionglinskii, Bernshtein, Goriushkin-Sorokopudov, Larionov, Picasso, Mashkov, Picasso.

I started working on another project with various materials.

My stage designs for the production of *A Life for the Tsar* were mentioned in the press. They were shown at the exhibition J[ack of] D[iamonds]. I started working on materials in 1914 and in the spring of this year, on May 2, my creations in painting which I call paint[erly] rel[iefs] were for the first time exhibited in Russia. Since 1913 have been working with materials, their juxtaposition, painterly rel[iefs].

While working in that direction I have reached the stage of my present works which I call counter-reliefs.

Compared to its draft outline, the text of the booklet omits certain facts from Tatlin's biography as an artist, such as the list of his teachers, while some other facts are misrepresented: for instance, the first exhibition of painterly reliefs was shown on 10–14 May 1914 whereas the text gives the date as 1913–14. Tatlin graduated from the Arts School in 1910, instead of 1909, as is correctly stated in the printed text. On the other hand, only the printed text contains Tatlin's programmatic thesis proclaiming his rejection of Tatlinism, Rayonism and Futurism. Here for the first time the term Tatlinism, probably coined by his colleagues and admirers, made its appearance in print.

Tatlinism: the term was used by Khlebnikov in 1918 to describe Tatlin's art: 'Perhaps in the future there will appear next to Benois, the irrepressible negativist Burliuk or the beautiful unhappy Filonov, an obscure bard of city suffering; there will be enough room on the walls for Larionov's Rayonism, for the abstract paintings of Malevich and Tatlin's Tatlinism'. (Published under the pen-name Vekha in *Красный воин*, no. 85, 20 December 1918. This information was provided by Parnis, who discovered a number of previously unknown articles about artists written by Khlebnikov.) Tatlin himself had a very negative attitude to the term Tatlinism as well as to all kinds of isms in general, and in 1922 he advanced the motto 'Against Tatlinism' (*see* 'Slogans', p. 244; Zhadova, p. 134).

The phrase about the corner counter-reliefs does not occur in the draft copy and is probably of later origin. The counter-reliefs were apparently still in the process of creation. The emergence of the term counter-relief is in itself very significant, as is Tatlin's own emphasis on the fact that he himself created terminology for his works. (*See* Strigalev, p. 19.)

The artists mentioned: what makes this document so exceedingly valuable is the fact that here for the first time the artist mentions the names of the masters who influenced him. While basically coinciding with later autobiographical information of this kind (*see* 'Questionnaire', p. 262, 'Autobiography', p. 322), this record provides more detail and accuracy. It confirms indirect evidence provided by Lapshin concerning Tatlin's attendance at Bernshtein's drawing studio that functioned in Petersburg/Petrograd from 1907 to 1916.

Judging from this document, in his earlier years he was familiar with the studio of Tsionglinskii.

In this first autobiographical document Tatlin mentions Mashkov and Mikhailovskii among the teachers and artists who influenced him. Tatlin was probably attending Mashkov's studio during the period when it was jointly supervised by Mashkov and Mikhailovskii (1907 and 1911–12). This was probably after Tatlin's arrival from Penza in the seasons of 1910–11 and 1911–12. In his autobiographical notes Mashkov mentions Tatlin among the artists 'seriously' studying in his studio. (*Илья Машков* [Автор-составитель И.С. Болотина], Москва, 1977, p. 400.) The artist Mikhailovskii is known 'to have introduced' Mashkov to the old masters. (Ibid., p. 402).

For more on the exhibitions, *see* Tatlin at Exhibitions, p. 489; 'Letter to Benois', p. 182, 'Questionnaire', p. 262. The collective exhibition in Moscow is probably The Store, an exhibition organized by Tatlin at that time and shown in March 1916.

Udal'tsova, Nadezhda Andreevna (1886–1961), was an artist. On her return from Paris, where she had studied in 1911–12 under Jean Metzinger, A. Le Fauconnier and D. de Segonzac, she worked in Tatlin's studio in

Ostozhenka Street. After Larionov left for Paris in 1914, she was, during a confrontation between Tatlin and Malevich (*see* Strigalev, p. 22; Sarab'ianov, pp. 57, 58; El'konin, 'What I Remember', p. 438) among the best-trained young avant-garde painters who supported Tatlin. On Udal'tsova's activity after the Revolution in February 1917, *see* Н. Удальцова, 'Из воспоминаний', *Искусство*, no. 3, 1940, p. 34. After October 1917 she was a member of the Moscow Artistic Collegium of IZO Narkompros and taught in the Moscow Free State Artistic Studios, the future VKhUTEMAS. On Udal'tsova *see* 'Удальцова, Надежда Андреевна', in: *Старейшие советские художники о Средней Азии и Кавказе*, Москва, 1963, pp. 220–5.

S.K. Isakov, On Tatlin's Counter-Reliefs

The artistic life of 1915 concludes with The Last Futurist Exhibition, which has recently opened in Petrograd. V.E. Tatlin's exhibits deserve special attention. They are extremely interesting not only in a purely artistic sense but also as the first clear indication of where, and in what, one should seek the way out of the frustrating dead-end of modernity. While leaving a more detailed interpretation of Tatlin's art for one of the winter issues of the journal, we find it necessary to describe at this stage (albeit in most general terms) the main line of approach to Tatlin's creations, to present that particular point of view from which these seemingly eccentric and incomprehensible works of art appear in a completely different light.

A distinctive feature of contemporary art is its 'retrospective nature'. In their effort to comprehend the colossal shift taking place in present-day reality, artists are looking for directions in the past. They look backwards. Alexandre Benois is trying to convince himself and others that 'the classics' have the clue to all the riddles. But how can we believe him?

The chasm separating the material and spiritual life of the antique world from our age, which is ruled by technology, is too great.

We have to discover our own paths.

A Greek would work with marble and discover the secret of the ratio producing the beautiful when using that marvellous material for the purposes of building and sculpting.

Our material is different, it is metal. It should be regarded not only in the static sense but predominantly in a dynamic one.

An artist's creative vision should be oriented towards comprehending the very nature of metal, towards understanding its hidden power and potential, which are expressed through numerical relations other than those discovered by the Greeks.

An artist should look for directions and instructions on how to overcome the tyranny of the machine, how to liberate man from technological slavery, in the same source that gave birth to all modern technology.

For in modern life the machine plays a colossal role, it governs destinies.

Was it not the growth of industry, the hypertrophy of technology, that rejected the greatest commandment of humanity 'Thou shall not kill' and forced the whole of mankind to plunge into streams of fraternal blood?

The phrase 'From Kant to Krupp' sounds smart. But it is short-sighted.

Remove militarism, get rid of the cannon. Then for the transient 'From Kant to Krupp' will be substituted the even more horrifying 'From Christ to the Machine'.

It was proved long ago that a machine turns a robot-like man serving it into its appurtenance, reduces him to the level of a screw or a gear. Precisely in the same way the machine manipulates us all every minute and at every step.

The artists, however, do not seem to see or understand the source of universal slavery. They either sing hymns to their ruler or hide from modernity in museum and libraries; bury themselves in works of art, become antiquarians. Following Ruskin and William Morris they plunge into the depths of the Middle Ages; following Benois they revive the eighteenth century and are ready to resurrect Classicism anew.

The Futurists were the first to call attention to modernity.

But poisoned by Impressionism, they shifted the centre of gravity towards man's inner world, towards psychological perception. They ignored material itself, objects themselves, their unique interaction and hidden energy. They were carried away by the poetry of dynamics. They started singing praises to the machine.

Rodin, however, already associated the development of plastic arts with the development of pure technology. And our own critics, too, were happy to point out sculptors' innovations in treating materials: wood and stone.

Something was prompting the right choice of direction.

And yet, when it was rumoured that instead of painting Picasso had been making some reliefs in which he combined wood with metal, paper and individual objects, that very attempt appeared totally incomprehensible.

I shall not dwell here on the question whether the transition to reliefs of Picasso, who started from Cézanne's painting, was necessary. It will be a topic for a special article. Naturally, when Tatlin's reliefs, which showed him to be an independent, mature artist and not an imitator of Picasso, were displayed at last year's Tramway V exhibition, they caused bewilderment and a torrent of ridicule.

The public had become so used to the eccentricities of the 'Futurists' that without too much concern they included the modest Tatlin, who was totally absorbed by his creative search and was a stranger to any kind of self-promotion. The works he has exhibited this year clearly show to even a superficial spectator that any talk of affectation is definitely out of place. Tatlin's works are so simple in appearance, so obviously constructive and so far removed from any attempt to produce a sensation, that to use such an accusation against them would be absurd and impudent.

It is obvious to anyone that before him are the results of some serious, thought-consuming effort to resolve an extraordinarily difficult problem: *material* and *tension*.

To combine various kinds of materials so that their juxtaposition would be justified by an innate artistic intuition; to shape their surfaces in this particular, and not any other, way; to treat these surfaces with various finishes in order to achieve the desired visual effect and balance its different parts – this is, in a few words, the essence of working with material. It contains the solution of the 'surface tension' problem. There is a tremendous tension, a tremendous amount of potential energy in the way a sheet of iron is bent and a sheet of aluminium is pressing on it at an angle, in the way it is cut through by the metal corner. The impression of tension is further intensified by the wires which pierce the relief like arrows. Whereas in Tatlin's 'painterly reliefs' of last year the centre of gravity was in the material, in this year's 'corner counter-reliefs' it is 'tension' and 'strain' that are in the foreground. That is why the artist called them 'counter-reliefs'. A 'counter-attack' as a response to an ordinary attack must exceed it in its energy. 'Counter-reliefs' are reliefs with a particularly pronounced tension.

The principle of constructiveness is so clearly manifest in Tatlin's new creations that they even remind one of the so-called 'shaped parts' of mechanical equipment. This is their guarantee of inner justification as well as the proof of correct intuitive understanding of the laws of mechanics. Here, however, the similarity between them ends. The divergence steps in: the 'shaped parts' are totally oriented towards practical use, the 'counter-reliefs' towards artistic interpretation.

It goes without saying that Tatlin's works are only the first step in the right direction. An indisputably gifted artist in love with his dream, he will not hesitate to continue on his path. It is also indisputable that there may be other approaches to the problem he poses.

One thing is important, extremely important: the artist contemplates the idol of the present-day reality with wide-open eyes. Through revealing the hidden life of the material that determines the course of our industrial life and generates a sharp discrepancy between our ideology and our reality, through comprehending the laws of energy residing in matter and by transposing them into the plane of the beautiful, he becomes the master of the material world and generates the hope that one day the whole of mankind will find the means and the strength to cast off the humiliating yoke of the machine.

С.К. Исаков, 'К "контррельефам" Татлина', Новый журнал для всех, Петроград, по. 12, 1915, pp. 46–50.

Art criticism of the time: at the time when new art was not understood even in the circles of younger artists and was totally spurned by the general public, critics who understood, and a periodical that would publish their reviews, were a matter of paramount importance for artists. (*See* 'Letter to Darmolatova', p. 184 and commentaries.) Some of them tried to approach the problem by themselves and to find ways to solve it. As early as 1913 the painter Rozanova wrote an article 'The Basic Principles of New Art and Why it is Not Understood' (О.В. Розанова, 'Основы нового творчества и причины его непонимания', *Союз молодежи*, no. 3, 1913, pp. 14–22.) The majority of avant-garde artists tried their hand at art criticism. Incidentally, in the same notebook that contains Udal'tsova's outline of the text of *Vladimir Evgrafovich Tatlin* (*see* p. 332) there is a draft version of what appears to be an article on 'The Attitude of the Critics and the Society towards Contemporary Russian Art'. 'At the moment Tatlin and I are trying to make a reputation for ourselves and to attract serious critics. We have a journal that has already reviewed Tatlin's work,' she wrote in her diary on 19 October 1915 (Drevina's personal archive, Moscow).

The artists dreamed of professional critics who would share their ideas. Maybe that was why Udal'tsova and Tatlin refrained from acknowledging their authorship when composing the text of the booklet. (*See* p. 331.)

Isakov's article, probably hinted at in Udal'tsova's diary quoted above, provided the first true support for Tatlin and other artists from his circle. It was a serious and sagacious attempt to comprehend the inspiration and essence of Tatlin's evolving Constructivism, to identify the problems he was dealing with: aesthetic exploration of technology and humanization of the industrial civilization of the twentieth century. The same journal published the booklet *Vladimir Evgrafovich Tatlin*. Its five illustrations were used in Isakov's article.

Isakov, Sergei Konstantinovich (1875–1953), was an art historian, art critic, teacher and sculptor. He graduated from the Physics and Mathematics Department of the Moscow State University and for a period taught physics in a grammar school. As from 1907 he worked as an assistant curator of the Academy of Arts' Museum; in 1915 he published two catalogues of the museum's holdings. In 1918 he was the head of the Museums Division at the Petrograd Department of Museums and Preservation of Artistic and Historical Monuments; subsequently he worked at the Museum of the Revolution in Petrograd, the State Russian Museum and the State Institute of Art Study. From 1934 until 1953 he was the head of the Academy of Arts' Museum and professor of the history of Russian art.

The date of the article is probably the months of October and November, but in the course of preparations for the opening of the Last Futurist Exhibition 0—10, where the corner counter-reliefs made their appearance, it underwent some alterations and additions, apparently when it was already in galley-proofs. Hence the promise of a more substantial article in the near future – which, however, failed to materialize.

It was during that period that Isakov, the head and senior member of the creative association Apartment No. 5, had become a friend of Tatlin and the first critic who shared his ideas. Isakov discussed Tatlin's art in his later articles of the 1920s.

Apartment No. 5 belonged to the Isakov-Bruni family and was located on the premises of the Academy of Arts (its windows overlooked the Neva Embankment and the Fourth Line of Vasil'evskii Island); in 1914–16 it was one of Petrograd's artistic centres. (Isakov was L.A. Bruni's stepfather.) Among the frequent visitors to the apartment were the composer Lur'e, the poets Mandel'stam and Kliuev, who were often joined by Khlebnikov and Maiakovskii as well as the artists Udal'tsova, Rozanova, Tatlin, Puni, Kliun and Miturich. The nucleus of the creative association Apartment No. 5 was formed by the young artists Bruni, Miturich, Tyrsa, Al'tman, L'vov and their fellow-traveller Punin, a young art critic. In those years Tatlin soon became their leader. 'He was awaited as an event capable of fulfilling one's expectations and moving things forward, as a leader was awaited. And indeed, he brought along new tastes, a new understanding of art, a spontaneous will to create, an irrepressible faith in the future of "Constructivism"... At the same time, his every judgment, every idea on art propelled us, as it were, into a new culture, into the future. We could only listen to him and adjust our personalities to that huge machine emanating energy and blowing up centuries-old strata of painterly culture in order to rearrange them anew', as Punin subsequently recalled (Н.Н. Пунин, Квартира № 5, in: Искусство и революция [fragments of manuscript] pp. 77–8. Punin family archive, Leningrad.)

Benois, Alexandre: *see* 'Letter to Benois', and commentaries, pp. 182–3.

Ruskin, John (1819–1900), **Morris,** William (1834–96), in the age of the Industrial Revolution they initiated the movement of reviving the arts and crafts of old. Isakov gives a polemically one-sided evaluation of their work.

V. Khlebnikov, Tatlin

I

Tatlin, a visionary of the blades	Татлин, тайновидец лопастей
And a stern bard of the propeller,	И винта певец суровый,
From the team of sun-snarers.	Из отряда солнцеловов.
He tied a cobweb dale of rigging	Паутинный дол снастей
Into an iron horseshoe	Он железною подковой
By that deathly grip of his.	Рукою мертвой завязал.
Tongs like the speechless blind	В тайновиденье щипцы
Gaze into the mystery vision	Смотрят, что он показал,
Of what he has shown.	Онемевшие слепцы.
So unheard-of and clairvoyant	Так неслыханны и вещи,
Are the tin things touched by brush.	Жестяные – кистью вещи.

II Tatlin

Tatlin, a visionary of the blades	Татлин, тайновидец лопастей
And a stern bard of the propeller,	И винта певец суровый,
From the team of sun-snarers.	Из отряда солнцеловов,
He tied a cobweb dale of rigging	Паутинный дол снастей
Into an iron horseshoe	Он железною подковой
By that deathly grip of his (into a sailor's knot)	Рукой мертвой завязал (в топ)
In the mystery vision of life	В тайновидении жизни
Gaze at what he has shown.	Смотрят, что он показал,
In such an unheard-of and clairvoyant fashion	Так неслыханно и веще
Are the tin things touched by brush.	Жестяные – кистью вещи.

III

Tatlin, a visionary of the blades	Татлин, тайновидец лопастей
And a stern bard of the propeller	И винта певец суровый
From the team of sun-snarers.	Из отряда солнцеловов.
He tied a cobweb dale of rigging	Паутинный дол снастей
Into an iron horseshoe	Он железною подковой
By that deathly grip of his (into a sailor's knot)	Рукой мертвой завязал (в топ).
In the mystery vision of life	В тайновидении жизни
Gaze at what he has shown	Смотрят, что он показал
(The speechless blind)	(Онемевшие слепцы)
So unheard-of and clairvoyant	Так неслыханны и вещи
Are the tin things touched by brush.	Жестяные кистью вещи.

I. 'Tatlin, a Visionary of the Blades,' published in *Khlebnikov*, 1940, *see* Bibliog.

The first three lines of the poem made their first appearance in the article 'Letatlin' by Zelinskii (К. Зелинский, 'Летатлин', *Вечерняя Москва*, 9 April 1932).

The autographed copy of the poem was given to the publisher by Tatlin. The artist had cherished the manuscript like a treasure, 'religiously or like a conspirator'. (*See* Bibliog.: Danin, 1979) Quite understandably, before giving the manuscript to the publisher, the artist – who had been growing increasingly distrustful over the years – not only sought advice on the matter from his friend Smirnov but also asked him to make a typewritten copy of the poem. His misgiving were justified: '...when Khlebnikov's *Unpublished Works* appeared in print Tatlin, during one of his visits to Smirnov, told him that the text of the poem, the autograph of which he had submitted to the publisher, was published inaccurately, in a garbled form, while the manuscript itself had somehow been lost' (from a tape-recorded interview by K.M. Smirnov with V.P. Smirnov on 29 February 1980; Zhadova's legacy).

II. We were able to discover a new version of Khlebnikov's poem about Tatlin, in which the wording differs from the published version in a single line. In addition, it has the title 'Tatlin' written by hand, possibly by the artist himself.

It is impossible to say at present whether something went wrong when the poem was transcribed from the manuscript in the process of publication or whether Khlebnikov's manuscript itself was interpreted in a different way. (As we know, one of the characteristics of his creative process consisted in continuous reworking of the texts and as a result in his manuscripts words and whole lines are crossed out, some words are written above the lines, some words are added...)

I–II. It is obvious that the poem exists in two different versions. When comparing the two one cannot help concluding that Smirnov, while correctly reading the line 'v tainovidenii zhizni' (in the mystery vision of life), probably omitted another line: 'v tainoviden 'e shchiptsi' (tongs...gaze into the mystery vision).

III. The reconstructed text was tentatively suggested to us by the literary historian A.E. Parnis.

Khlebnikov, Velemir (Viktor) Vladimirovich (1885–1922), a poet. (*See* commentary 'Khlebnikov', p. 238; commentary 'The meeting of Tatlin and Khlebnikov', p. 396)

The poem was written at the end of May 1916 in Tsaritsyn. While on active army service in Tsaritsyn, Khlebnikov was sent to a penal platoon. Tatlin went there to visit his sister Sylvia (then a resident of Tsaritsyn). Tatlin and a friend of Khlebnikov, the poet D. Petrovskii, who was on a visit there, decided to help Khlebnikov by organizing a poetry recital (*see* Zhadova, p. 150). On 25 May, at the Tsaritsyn House of Science and Arts, Petrovskii read a lecture written by Khlebnikov. Khlebnikov himself was not allowed to participate in the recital by the army administration. After the lecture Petrovskii – possibly with Tatlin – recited the poetry of Maiakovskii, Aseev, Burliuk and Khlebnikov, as well as his own poetry.
   The evidence of Tatlin's participation in preparing the lecture for the recital is found in the following comment by Petrovskii: 'We changed the title into "Wings of Cast Iron" and shortened the text a little too. We retained Khlebnikov's numbers and Tatlin's blades called "wings of cast iron".' (*See* Bibliog.: Petrovskii 1923, pp. 151–2.)

Tatlin and Khlebnikov: The spiritual affinity between Khlebnikov and Tatlin is evident from the very appearance of the poem itself as well as from the fact that many images used by Khlebnikov to describe Tatlin can be attributed to the author himself. Both were 'from the team of sun-snarers', both were 'visionaries' each in his own sphere.
   'In a sense the image of Tatlin is associated in my memory with the image of Khlebnikov. Tatlin possessed the same creative spontaneity, freshness of perception and sharpness of imagination in the sphere of plastic forms and lines as Khlebnikov did in the sphere of words' – so writes the composer Lur'e, a friend of both the poet and the artist when they were young. (А. Лурье, Наш Марш, typescript, p. 13, A.E. Parnis' archive). In the reminiscences of the writer Danin we read: 'It is worth mentioning that both Tatlin and Khlebnikov as well as Maiakovskii were tall as Grenadiers. But when mentioned casually, this detail would pass unnoticed. And yet it is indispensable! It dramatizes the vulnerability of those Grenadiers in life and homelessness in art' (*see* Danin, 1979, p. 226). On the profound affinity between their creative potentials, as well as the identical course followed by their human destinies in art, *see* Strigalev, p. 16; Syrkina, p. 160; Zhadova, p. 149. Khardzhiev interprets the poem as 'a kind of a microguide-book for The Last Futurist Exhibition 0—10 and the The Store exhibitions. They displayed Tatlin's painterly reliefs and corner counter-reliefs.' (*See* Bibliog.: Khlebnikov, 1940; Khardzhiev, 1970.)
   It is also possible to conceive of another interpretation of this poem – as the poet's anticipation-projection (and spiritual support) of the artist's plans and projects oriented towards the future (*see* Strigalev, p. 13; Zhadova, p. 150). Khlebnikov's influence on Tatlin was indispensable and multidimensional. The influence, however, was obviously mutual. It is logical to assume that Tatlin's encounter with Khlebnikov in Tsaritsyn in 1916 was accompanied by a mutually productive exchange of ideas, concepts and projects. Tatlin's counter-reliefs – 'the tin things touched by brush' – are perceived by Khlebnikov as 'unheard-of and clairvoyant', that is they predict the world of the future whose material environment will be built on completely different, novel principles. Tatlin's counter-reliefs must have influenced Khlebnikov in 1915–16 and provided a stimulus for the first wave of his prognostic verbal design of the architecture and material-spatial environment of the future. (Лунев (В.В. Хлебников), 'Мы и дома', in: *Собрание произведений В. Хлебникова, Ленинград*, vol. IV, 1930; В.В. Хлебников, 'Лебедия будущего', 1915–16; 'Письма двум японцам', 1916; 'Предложения', 1916, in: *Собрание произведений В. Хлебникова*, Ленинград, 1933, vol. V.).
   It was discovered subsequently that some of those prognoses had been supplied with illustrations made by the poet himself. (*See* Е. Ковтун, А. Павилихина, 'Утес из будущего', *Техническая эстетика*, no. 5–6, 1976, pp. 40–2; Л. Жадова, 'Поиски художественного синтеза на рубеже столетий', *Декоративное искусство*, no. 8, 1976, pp. 38–42). Parnis has recently discovered a few more architectural drawings by Khlebnikov in the manuscript of his prose work 'Houses and Us' (III. 225).
   One of the items in Khlebnikov's lecture printed in the booklet advertising the Tsaritsyn recital (discovered and placed at the disposal of the present authors by Parnis) proclaimed: 'Painting will be substituted by the laws of form, the laws of weight in Tatlin and Bruni.' It demanded a continuation, as it were, which might have subsequently been realized in a poetic form. There are reasons to believe that the poet gave the hand-written text of the poem to the artist as a surprise gift while still in Tsaritsyn.
   A portrait of Tatlin done in pencil by Khlebnikov (*see* III. 223) has survived to this day. Sketched in a bold manner, it is similar to published works by the poet: *Self-Portrait* (1910?); *Portrait of A. Kruchenykh* (1913) and *G. Petnikov's Portrait* (1917), (*see* Bibliog.: Khlebnikov, 1940, p. 381). The date '25 May' in pencil at the bottom of the drawing suggests that it was made on 25 May 1916, the day of the Tsaritsyn recital at the House of Science and Arts. However, the address written on the reverse side of the drawing – 'Arbat, 12 Denezhnyi Lane, apartment 12' – which appears as Tatlin's address in the catalogue of The Last Futurist Exhibition 0—10 – may suggest that the portrait was completed as early as 1915. The catalogue of the next exhibition, The Store (*see* III. 86–8), which took place in 1916, gave a

different address for Tatlin. There are a number of portraits in pencil of the poet apparently made by Tatlin in the 1930s. (*See* Zhadova, p. 132; Ill. 232.)

Petrovskii recalls that in Tsaritsyn Khlebnikov used to call Tatlin 'an architect' (*zodchii*). That view of him continued into later years. Thus on 20 December 1921 he made the following notes:

The thought of Kr(uchenykh) and Khl(ebnikov)	Мысль КР(ученыка) и ХЛ(ебникова)
To entrust	Поручит(ь)
Tatlin	Татлину
With building a tiny chapel	Построит(ь) часовенку
For manuscripts, for storing things for	Для рукописей хранилище вещей
fu[ture] mankind	бу(дущему) человечества
An iron skull	Железный череп
A common cast-iron forehead	Общий чугунный лоб
Preserving our deeds and thoughts	Хранящий наши дела и мысли
So that mice of time	Чтобы мыши времени не сгрызли их.
Will not come and nibble them away.	(Записная книжка Велемира
	Хлебникова. Москва, 1925)

The second wave of Khlebnikov's prognostication occurred in 1919–22 during the social and cultural reforms introduced after the October Revolution. In his collected works (*Собрание произведений В. Хлебникова*, Ленинград, vol. V, 1933) there are a number of poems about the city of the future, about Moscow as well as prose works. (В. Хлебников, 'Утес из будущего', 1921; 'Радио будущего', 1921; in: op. cit, vol. IV, 1930.) Many of the ideas expressed in those Utopian articles have been almost totally realized.

The initial stage of that period was also characterized by the creative interaction between Khlebnikov and Tatlin. The latter suggested that the poet should write an article for the first issue of the journal *Internatsional iskusstv*. The article was called 'Artists of the World'. It also had another title: 'The Written Language of the Terrestrial Globe; the System of Hieroglyphics Common to the Nations of the Planet.' (В. Хлебников, 'Художники мира,' in: op. cit., 1933, vol. V.) The pictorial alphabet of the 'astral language' designed by Khlebnikov himself for the manuscript of his article 'Artists of the World' is still awaiting publication.

The reverence Tatlin felt for Khlebnikov all his life is manifest in the inscriptions he made on the three volumes of Khlebnikov's collected works belonging to his friend, Smirnov. Volume I: 'Read and study Velemir, a poet of genius, for without true art we shall never build socialism. For my friend from Tatlin.' (*See* Ill. 228) Volume II: 'As a token of friendship for your help and assistance in realizing my designs. It is you, Vasia, who is my true friend.' (*See* Ill. 229) Volume III: 'Read the real poet Velemir. To my true friend.' (*See* Ill. 230) All the inscriptions are dated '33 Moscow, 7 July' and signed by the artist on separate sheets of paper, which were enclosed in the books.

Miturich, Petr Vasil'evich (1887–1956), an artist close to Tatlin as a member of the creative association Apartment No. 5 (*see* p. 335), who with Khlebnikov during the last years of the poet's life had been working on 'spatial graphic paintings' somewhat analogous to Khlebnikov's 'astral alphabet' (*see Petr Vasil'evich Miturich*, 1887–1956, Exhibition Catalogue, Moscow: 1978, no. 75 and 76). After the poet's death Tatlin tried to realize Khlebnikov's alphabet in plastic form in his work on *Zangezi* (*see* 'On "Zangezi"', p. 248; 'On Tatlin', p. 393; on the relations of Miturich and Tatlin, *see* El'konin, 'What I Remember about Tatlin', p. 437).

A Studio Headed by Tatlin

The equipment of a new studio which will be directed by Tatlin has been started at the Petrograd Free State Artistic Teaching Studios. It will be equipped with metalworking machine tools and joiners' benches. As is known, Tatlin has been working with iron, wood and bronze rather than with clay or marble. He produces objects which can be immediately utilized, so to say.

'Мастерская руководителя Татлина', Жизнь искусства, no. 37, 14 December 1918, anonymous news item.

The news item appeared during the formative stages of the Petrograd Free State Artistic Teaching Studios (PGSKhUM) immediately after their ceremonial opening on the premises of the former Academy of Arts, which had been abolished by the decree of Sovnarkom of 14 April 1918. (*See* А.В. Луначарский об искусстве. Речь, произнесенная на открытии Петроградских свободных художественно-учебных мастерских, 10 октября 1918 г. Изд. Отдела ИЗО, Петроград, 1919.) (Справочник Отдела ИЗО Наркомпроса, Москва, 1920, pp. 3–4.)

It seemed absolutely imperative that the process of reforming art education should involve both Tatlin – who, in his own words, was 'the first artist who went to work for Soviet power (*see* 'Curriculum Vitae', p. 323) – and his colleagues, the avant-garde artists, in the teaching activities at the Moscow and the Petrograd Art Studios. The fact that in the autumn of 1918 Tatlin lived in Moscow co-ordinating the work of the Artistic Collegium IZO Narkompros did not seem extraordinary in those times of high mobility. It is also known that Tatlin had an intention to leave for Petrograd in the spring of 1918 (*see* Воспоминания художницы Дымшиц-Толстой, 1905–1941. State Russian Museum, manuscripts section, fond 100, unit 249, p. 25 of a typescript).

A week before the publication of the above communication, the newspaper *Iskusstvo kommuny* (Petrograd) published a news item 'On the Teaching Activities at the Reformed Academy of Arts' containing the following information:

'There are studios specializing in 1) architecture: Benois, Kosiakov, Fomin, Munts, Shtal'berg, Il'in, Rudnev and Dubinetskii; 2) painting: Kardovskii, Andreets, Beliaev, Petrov-Vodkin, Popov, Rylov, Savinskii, Shukhaev, Karev, Baranov-Rossine, Al'tman, Puni and a studio without an instructor; 3) sculpture: Matveev, Ginzburg, Shervud, Lishev and Zalaman. Soon the studios of Tatlin, Malevich and Shterenberg will be open.

'Each studio has been asked to present its constitution: a brief description of its artistic goals, the method of work …'

'Об учебной жизни в реформированной Академии художеств', *Искусство коммуны,* 7 December 1918, p. 2).

The author of the communication in *Zhizn' iskusstva* may have taken the desired future for the existing present when he was writing about the set-up of Tatlin's studio in the Petrograd Free State Artistic Teaching Studios. That, however, does not diminish the significance of the project for a new type of studio, devised by Tatlin, which he may himself have described to the reporter.

The plan of the studio: already during his work on the counter-reliefs Tatlin merged creative art and production process into an organic whole called by him 'fine craft' (*see* Strigalev, p. 15; Bibliog.: Punin, 9 February 1919). According to the memoirs of Dymshits-Tolstaia (*see* commentary 'Memorandum', p. 187), Tatlin's private studio in Staro-Basmannaia Street (*see* n29, 33 for Strigalev's study) where he had been working since 1916 'looked more like a joiner's workshop' (State Russian Museum, manuscripts section, fond 100, unit 249, p. 14). In later years the industrial appearance of Tatlin's studios in the Free State Artistic Studios (Moscow) and the Petrograd Free State Artistic Teaching Studios was a constant source of astonishment to his contemporaries.

While contemplating a project for a State Studio under his own supervision, Tatlin advanced in a systematic way the principle of the inseparability of art and labour, the fusion of artistic and industrial activities. He was convinced that only a studio where the distinction between the 'pure' and the applied arts was abolished could reform the academic school of art that provided the basis for PGSKhUM.

In retrospect, this romantic plan for a new kind of studio anticipated the nature of a modern design studio with its own experimental-industrial basis. In the spring of 1919 Tatlin could express his view of his own role as an artist-supervisor of the Studio in the summary of his article ('The Initiative Individual', *see* p. 237).

Art into life. This newspaper communication of late 1918 for the first time presents Tatlin as the originator and practitioner of the idea 'art into life'. In 1927 he would write about it as an historical fact (*see* 'Letter to Novitskii', p. 260)

Tatlin conceived the Studio as a creative collective producing 'objects' that would promote the idea of 'art into life'. In the context of this idea 'the materials of life' – iron, wood, bronze – are contrasted with the traditional 'materials of art' – marble and clay. In 1920 Tatlin would call iron 'the material of modern Classicism' equal to marble (see 'The Work', p. 239).

Veshchism [*veshch'* means object in Russian – translator's note]. Judging from the published text, Tatlin participated in creating the theory of 'objectness'. This theory served as a transitional stage towards the aesthetics of Constructivism and industrial art, Productivism. This controversial theory, important in its time, was expounded and interpreted in 1919–22. (*See* Punin, *Tatlin*, chapter 6; as well as articles by Ehrenburg and Lissitzky in the journal *Veshch'-Objet-Gegenstand*, Berlin, 1922.)

The idea of the project. The above publication on Tatlin's studio might be used as an argument in favour of the possibility that Tatlin conceived the idea of the project of the Monument to the Third International in 1918 and already at that time planned to execute the project on the premises of PGSKhUM. (*See* Strigalev, p. 29; 'The Work', p. 239 and commentaries, pp. 239–40). The following communication printed a year later in *Zhizn' iskusstva* proves this.

A New Art Teaching Studio

The Collegium in charge of Arts and Crafts has approved the project of setting up a new art teaching studio headed by V.E. Tatlin. The new studio will be called the Studio of Volume, Construction and Colours. It will also have affiliated sections of metalwork and paint-processing. The studio will be functioning under Tatlin's general supervision and the students will be taught by four instructors: a joiner, a mechanic, a house painter and a specialist in mosaics. The students will be working as apprentices. It will also be their duty to clean the benches and tools, as well as look after the condition of the materials.

The new studio will be located on the premises of the former Academy of Arts and will carry out Government orders for various works of art.

'Новая художественно-учебная мастерская', Жизнь искусства,*12 December 1919, p. 3, anonymous news item.*

The news item appeared at the time when the author of the project of the Monument to the Third International (which by then had been designed and approved) was contemplating the construction of a model for it in premises already provided, namely the mosaics studio, which was large enough (10 m × 5 m) and high enough (7 m). Interestingly, one of the instructors at Tatlin's studio was a specialist in mosaics. The dimensions of the studio further confirm the height of the first model as 5 m, which follows from comparing its proportions with the size of the studio as it appears on old photographs which have been preserved (III. 176–8, 180). The so-called mosaics wing of the Academy of Arts, Third Line of the Vasil'evskii Island, was built in 1851 as a mosaics studio and has been functioning as such ever since without any reconstruction (III. 165), except during 1920–1 when the art teaching studio under Tatlin was set up on its premises.

The project for the new studio in the 1919 newspaper item is discussed and elaborated in great detail, probably from the author's words. The art teaching studio is conceived as a combination of a school, research centre for creative design and a production workshop, while the teaching process itself is associated with practical work on orders placed by the government. In the structure of this art and design school-workshop one can trace a certain connection with the Bauhaus studios during the initial period of their development, although, according to the previous communication of 1918 (*see* p. 338), Tatlin had conceived the idea of the new production art school before the Bauhaus was even opened (4 April 1919). (*See* Hans Maria Wingler, *Das Bauhaus 1919–33 Weimar, Dessau, Berlin,* 1962; Lothar Lang, *Das Bauhaus 1919–33. Idee und Wirklichkeit,* Berlin, Zentralinstitut für Formgestaltung, Berlin, 1965.)

The studio's name. According to this report, Tatlin's studio was initially called Studio of Volume, Construction and Colours. At the beginning of the work on the model of the Monument in 1920, the studio was renamed Studio of Materials, Volume and Construction.

Work in the studio. Tatlin indeed realized a lot of what he had been hoping for. He and his colleagues were both constructing the Monument to the Third International and learning in the process. In the early autumn of 1920 the works of students from the individual free studios were exhibited at the former Academy of Arts. (It was probably one of those exhibits which was reproduced in Punin's monograph.) (*See* p. 347, III. 128)

On Tatlin's student assistants in the Studio of Materials, Volume and Construction, *see* 'The Work', p. 239 and commentaries.

The VKhUTEMAS. After the foundation of VKhUTEMAS in Moscow (Sovnarkom Decree of 18 December 1920), there followed a reorganization of the higher artistic college in Petrograd in 1921, which for a short period was given back the title of the Academy of Arts. Instead of the former studios a system of departments was introduced – of painting, sculpture, architecture – with a common curriculum. On 6 October 1921 the faculty of painting requested that Tatlin vacate the mosaics studio (Academy of Arts Scientific Library, fond 789, inventory 28, unit 32, p. 29). In October 1921 the Presidium of the Academy of Arts discussed the question 'of the possibility of the future existence of the Academy-based studios headed by Tatlin, Matiushin and Guminer'. (Ibid., p. 30, as well as М. Спасовский, 'Художественная школа', *Аргонавты,* no. 1, 1923, p. 76.)

Tatlin's plan: faculty of new tendencies. In the course of the reorganization of the higher artistic college, Tatlin, as the chairman and founder of the Union of New Tendencies in Art (*see* 'To the Museums', p. 241; 'Programme', p. 242) and on behalf of its members, suggested that alongside the academic departments 'a faculty of new tendencies' should be set up. A special commission for designing the plans and curricula for the new faculty was organized. Among its initial projects there is Tatlin's and Matiushin's joint plan for opening 'a faculty of material and organic culture'. (*See* Б.Н. Капелюш, 'Архивы М.В. Матюшина и Е.Г. Гуро', in: *Ежегодник РО Пушкинского дома за 1974 год,* Ленинград, 1976, p. 10.)

The 'Faculty of New Tendencies' did not open in the autumn of 1921. Tatlin's students were told either to leave the school or to register at one of the general departments. In September Shapiro and Meerzon enrolled in the Department of Architecture in the Academy of Arts. Many ideas for the Faculty of New Tendencies were implemented, but that was later and not with the support of the Academy but of GINKhUK.

Tatlin's plan: special research studio. Between the autumn of 1921 and the spring of 1922 Tatlin had been participating in the process of joining the Academy of Arts and the State Working and Teaching Studios of Decorative Art (the former Shtiglits school), which resulted in the creation of the Petrograd Higher State Artistic and Technical Studios. There Tatlin once more suggested opening 'special research studios' supervised by himself, Matiushin, Malevich, Lebedev, Tyrsa and other artists from the Union of New Tendencies in Art. The 'special research studios' were supposed to become a kind of research institute associated with the school. (Academy of Arts Scientific Library, fond 789, inventory 29, unit 39, pp. 30, 31.)

In his attempts to set up a new faculty – the research studios – Tatlin even nominated himself for the position of Rector of the Academy of Arts. The architect A.E. Belogrud was voted by secret ballot to become Rector, receiving twenty votes as compared with Tatlin's one. (*See* minutes no. 2 of the meeting of the Council of the Academy of Arts 12 February 1921, Academy of Arts Scientific Library, fond 789, inventory 28, unit 32, p. 66.)

V. Shklovskii, On *Faktura* and Counter-Reliefs

One often reads lamentations about the difficulty of expressing one's ideas in art.

Poets used to fill their verses with such complaints. Gornfel'd could not help feeling sorry for the poor poets and wrote an article 'Agony over Words'.

There is a well-known approach to artistic form, i.e. to art itself, as an interpreter translating certain ideas of the artist from the language of his soul into a language comprehensible to the beholder. For the proponents of this view, words in literature and oils in painting are a grievous necessity. These artistic 'means of expression' were required to be first of all transparent and inconspicuous; artists conceded to these demands verbally, but in their studios they continued doing things in their own way.

What makes art delightful?

The external world does not exist. Objects do not exist and are not perceived; words, barely apparent and hardly articulated, do not exist.

The external world is outside art. It is perceived as a series of hints, a series of algebraic signs, as a collection of objects possessing volume, but not a material aspect, a *faktura*.

Faktura is the main distinguishing feature of that specific world of specially constructed objects the totality of which we are used to call art.

There is a profound difference between the word in art and the word in life: its role in life is that of a counter in the abacus, whereas in art it has a *faktura* and a sound, it is fully articulated and perceived in full measure.

In reality we are flying through the world like Jules Verne's characters flying to the moon in a cannon-ball. But *our* cannon-ball has no windows. The whole effort of a poet and a painter is aimed first and foremost at creating a continuous and thoroughly palpable object, an object with a *faktura.*

A poet whose creative material consists of formal structures creates new objects out of the word both as a sound and as a concept. Good and evil in art have a *faktura*. One should not assume that when art undergoes changes it becomes better. The very notion of improvement and ascent is anthropomorphic. Artistic forms change.

Art has its moments not exactly of decline but of dissolution in alien elements. Such are, for example, the works of our Wanderers.

In this case art functions despite the elements which participate in life, in the same way as a bullet in the chest participates in the life of the body.

One cannot claim that Repin is not an artist at all, but one should remember that he is an artist in so far as he was dealing with the creation of a certain type of object – canvases covered with oils.

On the other hand, artists, while thinking that they are solving some purely artistic problems, frequently do not solve but merely demonstrate them, which results in a kind of painterly algebra, i.e. 'an unfinished painting' – essentially a prosaic object.

The *Suprematist* school can be included in such painterly symbolism. Their works are postulated rather than executed. Their structure is not oriented towards continuity of perception. Although in this case 'the question under discussion' is not the harm caused by religion or serfdom but the relation of the red rectangle to the white background, it is essentially an 'art pregnant with ideas'.

Of the Russian artists it is Tatlin and Al'tman who have approached closer than anyone else the problem of creating constructed and continuous objects of art.

Al'tman did it in a number of paintings which revealed his orientation towards *faktura*; their sole meaning consisted in juxtaposing surfaces with various imperfections. Tatlin did it by leaving painting altogether.

At the exhibition of the students of the Academy (the free studios of Vasil'evskii Island) I have seen the works from Tatlin's studio; unfortunately I have not seen his own work: the model of the Monument to the Third International.

This model will be exhibited in November and then it will be possible to discuss it in detail. At this stage one can only say that Tatlin has left the art of painting and the paintings that he was so good at, and has started opposing one object taken as an entity to another.

I have seen a piece produced by one of his students. It is a large quadrangle of parquet different sections of which have a different *faktura* and present several surfaces disappearing one behind another, as it were; one part of the quadrangle is covered by a piece of bronze of irregular shape to which some strips of tracing paper are fastened in front of the main plane of the work.

The ultimate task of Tatlin and Tatlinists is probably a creation of a new world of sensations, a transference of methods for producing works of art to producing 'objects of everyday life'. The ultimate goal must be the creation of a new palpable world.

A counter-relief, a pencil study, bits and pieces of a new paradise where there are no names and no empty spaces, where life does not resemble our current 'flight in a cannon-ball', our existence from one moment to the next as if travelling from one station to another without noticing the road itself.

The new world should be continuous.

I do not know whether Tatlin is right or wrong. I do not know whether the bent tin sheets in his students' compositions can grow into the hammered counter-reliefs of the new world.

I do not believe in miracles, but that is why I am not an artist.

В. Шкловский, 'О фактуре и контррельефах', Жизнь искусства, 20 October 1920.

Shklovskii, Viktor Borisovich (b. 1893), a writer, critic, literary scholar and a member of OPOIaZ (Society for the Study of Poetic Language, 1914–24), together with Eikhenbaum, Tynianov, Iakubinskii, Zhirmunskii and others. He was one of the founders and theorists of the so-called 'formalist school' in literary scholarship (on the 'formalist method' *see* 'About "Zangezi"', and commentaries, pp. 395–400) which regarded works of prose and poetry as independent formations with their own unique devices and means of expression: material (language and word) and laws of construction (device, structure).

Shklovskii's article was the first to express clearly the idea that Tatlin's counter-reliefs contained formative principles and ideas that made it possible for Tatlin and his followers to proceed from painting to the design of the material-spatial environment. That particular orientation of Tatlin's work may have served as an impetus for a subsequent revision by Shklovskii of his own creative-scientific methodology, which had suffered from one-sided-ness and made him aware of the inseparability of content and form in a work of art. (On the exhibition of the students of Tatlin's studio, *see* 'Work in the studio', p. 340.)

Gornfel'd, Arkadii Georgievich (1867–1941), a literary scholar representing the psychological trend in Russian linguistics which the Formalist school opposed. His book, *Agony over Words* (*Muki slova*) of 1906 viewed the art of writing as an eternal struggle with words.

Repin, Il'ia Efimovich (1844–1930), an outstanding member of the Society of Itinerant Exhibitions (Wanderers). Shklovskii's evalution of his work from the standpoint of the Formalist school is one-sided and tendentious. The Wanderers tackled poignant social issues with the boldness of the film-makers of the 1920s and 1930s.

Suprematist painting. Shklovskii analysed the ways of depicting and perceiving space in connection with the practice of Suprematist painting in a separate article, 'Space in Painting and the Suprematists'. (В. Шкловский, 'Пространство живописи и супрематисты', Искусство, no. 843–4, 1919.)

Al'tman, Natan Isaevich (1889–1970), an artist close to Tatlin, in the 1910s a member of the creative society Apartment No. 5. (*See* Isakov, 'On Tatlin's Counter-Reliefs', p. 335) He was the author of the famous decoration of the Uritskii Square (today Palace Square) in Petrograd for the celebration of the first anniversary of the October Revolution, as well as of a series of drawings, *Leniniana* (*see* Б. Арватов, *Натан Альтман*, Берлин, 1924).

V. Shklovskii, The Monument to the Third International

(The Most Recent Work by Tatlin)

164–206   Days chase one another like railway carriages overloaded with various strange-looking vehicles, cannons and crowds of people shouting something. Days are roaring like a steam-hammer – blow after blow until all blows merge together and it is no longer possible to hear them – just as people living close to the sea are no longer aware of the sound of the water. The blows are thundering somewhere in one's chest, beneath consciousness. We live in the silence of thunder.

In this mighty air the iron spiral of the project twice the height of St Isaac's Cathedral has been born. This spiral is falling sideways supported by a sturdy leaning structure.

This is the basic outline of the project of the Monument to the Third International designed by the artist Tatlin.

The bends of the spiral are connected through a network of leaning supports and their transparent nest holds three revolving geometrical bodies. A cylinder below takes a year to make a turn; a pyramid above turns once a month, and a sphere makes a full turn every day. The waves from the radio station situated on the very top of the spiral perpetuate the monument in the air.

170

It is the first time that iron has reared like a horse and is now searching for its creative formula.

In this age of building cranes beautiful as the wisest among the Martians, iron had the right to go berserk and remind people that ever since the time of Ovid our epoch has gratuitously adopted the name of 'iron age' without producing any iron art.

The monument can produce lengthy discussions. The bodies revolving within its own body are lightweight and small compared to its huge 'common' body. Their rotation itself hardly alters its appearance and is perceived as a task rather than a realization. The monument is permeated with a certain utilitarian mood: this spiral – even if it does not wish to be a tenement building – has nevertheless been somehow utilized.

According to the project the lower cylinder should accommodate the World Sovnarkom while the upper sphere should house ROSTA.

The word in poetry is not just a word: it produces dozens and thousands of associations. A literary work is permeated with them as Petersburg's air is permeated with snow in a blizzard.

A painter or a counter-relief artist does not have the freedom to confine the movement on a canvas or between the supports of an iron spiral within this blizzard of associations. These works of art have their own semantics.

It seems to me that Tatlin incorporated the Soviet of People's Commissars into his monument as new artistic material and used it together with ROSTA for the sake of artistic form.

The Monument is made of glass, iron and Revolution.

As for the feasibility of the Monument – i.e. the technical possibility of its execution – it seems at first glance that the artist's intuition produced a technically logical object, although its logic is certainly different from the logic of, say, a water pump.

The Revolution must not be criticized, it has to be supported; and we have to stride forward in order to promote its weight and speed.

В. Шкловский, 'Памятник Третьему Интернационалу', Жизнь искусства, 5, 8, 9 January 1921.

Shklovskii's article came out two and a half months after 'On *Faktura*', as its sequel. (This is why the two are juxtaposed here.)
'Twice the height of St Isaac's Cathedral', i.e. twice as high as the biggest cathedral in Petrograd – an apt visual image conveying the scale of the Monument to the Third International. In reality, according to the project, it was supposed to be four times as high: St Isaac's Cathedral is 101.52 m high; the tower was designed to be 400 m. Shklovskii is mistaken when he writes about three geometrical bodies. There were four. (*See* Strigalev, p. 27.)

ROSTA, the Russian Telegraph Agency, was the central information and propaganda agency of the young Soviet state. Numerous left-wing painters and graphic artists worked for it during the Civil War. They produced hand-made propaganda posters, 'ROSTA windows', so called because they were placed in shop-windows. Maiakovskii worked for ROSTA between October 1919 and January 1921.

N. Punin, The Monument to the Third International

(A Project of the Artist V.E. Tatlin)

In 1919 the Fine Arts Department of the People's Commissariat of Education [IZO Narkom-pros] commissioned the artist V.E. Tatlin to design a project for a monument to the Third International. The artist Tatlin started work immediately and designed the project. Then the artists V.E. Tatlin, I.A. Meerzon, M.P. Vinogradov and T.M. Shapiro came together in an association, a 'creative collective', developed the project in every detail and built the model for it.

164–206

The main concept of the Monument originated from the organic synthesis of architecture, sculpture and painting, which had to produce a new type of monumental art combining a purely artistic form with a utilitarian one. In accordance with this idea, the project of the Monument presents three large glass halls within a complex system of vertical axes and spirals. These halls are located one above the other and their different shapes are in harmony with one another. Special mechanisms ensure their motion at different speeds. The lowest hall (A) in the shape of a cube moves around its axis once a year and is designed for legislative purposes. It can accommodate conferences of the International, sessions of international congresses and other representative legislative meetings. The next room (B) is pyramidal and revolves around its axis once a month; it is designed for executive purposes (the Executive Committee of the International, secretariat and other administrative executive organs). Finally, the upper cylinder (C), revolving at the speed of one turn per day, accom-modates informational centres: an information bureau, a press and publishing centre, a prin-ting press for proclamations, pamphlets, manifestos – in a word, the whole variety of mass media for disseminating information to the world proletariat, including telegraphs, film projectors for the large screen located on the axes of the spherical segment (a_1–b_3) as well as the radio station with its masts rising above the monument. There is no need to point out the various possibilities of equipping and setting up all the rooms: the project does not provide any details, and they can be discussed and elaborated in the course of subsequent work on the Monument. It should be mentioned that, according to Tatlin's design, the glass halls should be equipped with double partitions creating a vacuum (like a thermos), which will facilitate maintenance of the right temperature in the halls. Individual parts of the monument as well as all the rooms will be connected with the ground and one another only by means of complex electric lifts designed to accommodate different rotation speeds of the halls. Such is the technical backbone of the project.

The Artistic Importance of the Project

A social revolution by itself does not change artistic forms but provides the environment which slowly alters forms of art. The idea of propaganda through monumental art has not changed sculpture or sculptors but shifted the very principle of plastic expression reigning in the bourgeois world. The Renaissance tradition in plastic art could appear contemporary until the feudal-bourgeois roots of the capitalist countries had been destroyed. The Renais-sance went up in smoke but only now is Europe clearing away its smouldering ruins.

It is true that communist governments will for some time make use of the classic Graeco-Roman tradition as a means of monumental propaganda, but only because the governments are forced to do so, just as they are forced to turn to professionals of the pre-Revolutionary school. The figurative (Greek and Roman) monuments present a double opposition to our times. They cultivate individual heroism and distort history, torsos and heads of heroes and gods do not correspond to the modern understanding of history. These forms are too personal for the mile-long rows of the proletariat; at best they express the character, feelings and thoughts of the hero, but who will express the mental and emotional tension of the collective thousand? A type? But a type specifies, limits and reduces the mass to one level. This latter is livelier, more complex and more organic.

But even when presenting a type, figurative monuments contradict the spirit of our time even more, owing to the limited nature of their means of expression and static character. The propaganda value of such monuments among the noise and bustle of a vast city is negligible. The contemplators on the granite pedestals may be able to notice much but are not noticed themselves. They are fettered by the form developed in the reign of loggias, mule transport and stone cannon-balls. A war-time telephone wire is more conspicuous than the memorial of a hero; a tramway power pole looks more like an obelisk; city dwellers will recall Ferdinand Lassalle more frequently from book-covers and newspaper titles in libraries than when passing under his proud head. Lassalle stands unseen and unnecessary from the moment the unveiling of the monument was over...

A monument should share the social and public life of the city and the city should live in it. It must be indispensable and dynamic in order to be contemporary. The forms of contemporary propaganda in plastic art lie on the other side of depicting man as a unit. These forms are discovered by an artist who has not been crippled by the feudal-bourgeois Renaissance tradition but also has been working as a labourer on the three units of contemporary plastic consciousness: material, construction and volume. When working with material, construction and volume Tatlin produced a new form in the world of monumental art. Such is the form of the Monument to the Third International.

A year ago the best artist of the Russia of workers and peasants, who has proved his knowledge of the toiling masses by his very life, was commissioned to design a project for the Monument to the Third International. The project is remarkable not only for its total significance as a phenomenon of modern artistic life, but it can also be perceived as a major breakthrough in the vicious circle of the overripe decadent art of our time. The pursuit of art transcends the twentieth century, outlining segments of development for all aspects of art. Regarding myself to a certain extent competent in questions of art, I believe that this project qualifies as an international event in the world of art.

The most complex problem of culture is being resolved before our very eyes: a utilitarian form becomes a pure artistic form. Classicism becomes possible once again, not as a revival but as an invention.

The ideologists of the international workers' movement have long been searching for the classical content of socialist culture. Here it comes. We declare the present project to be the first work of revolutionary art that we can send – and do so – to Europe.

In the project the form rests on two axes (aa_1 and bb_3) engaged in a permanent conflict with each other. The upward movement from a to a_1 is disrupted at its every point by the spiral movement from b, b_1, b_2, b_3 to the line aa_1. A confrontation between these two mutually opposing movements must result in a rupture (so typical of 'Cubism', which is left far behind) and the death of the utilitarian idea, but the spirals coming from the opposite direction take the movement towards aa_1 (and bb_3) and carry them through the movement of the main post (girder aa_1) upwards, producing a dynamic image loaded with the powerful tension of eternally agitated and colliding axes. The whole form is vacillating like a steel snake held together and united into a structure through one common movement of all its parts so as to rise above the ground. The form strives to overcome the material and the force of gravity; the force of resistance is great and massive; by flexing its muscles the form is searching for the way out along the most resilient and dynamic lines the world knows of – the spirals. They are full of movement, aspiration and speed, and they are as tight as a creative will and an arm-muscle strained with holding a hammer.

183

The utilization and organization of the spiral in a contemporary form enriches the composition. Just as a triangle with its balanced parts is the best expression of the Renaissance, a spiral is the best manifestation of our spirit. An interaction between the weight and the support is the purest (classical) form of statics; the classical form of dynamics is a spiral.

Societies with antagonistic classes have been fighting for the possession of the land, the line of their movement is horizontal; the spiral represents the movement of liberated humanity. A spiral is the ideal expression of liberation; with its heel pressed into the soil it escapes the ground and becomes a sign, as it were, of the liberation of all the animal, earthbound and reptile interests.

Bourgeois societies were fond of developing animal life on the land; while cultivating the soil they would set up shops and banks; bourgeois existence was enacted on a public square in front of the audience in order to make a show of it. Creative humanity buries its animal life underground; one cannot see where the co-operatives are working; the square is the place for propaganda, games and festivities; liberated life is rising above the ground and the raw materials of the land. The home – a dwelling as well as a public place – is moved to the layers above the ground as an expression of modernity and the meaning of modern existence. At the same time it is the meaning of a major artistic form.

Any form's content can be adopted and limited by its utilitarian purpose, since the latter is none other than an organization of the content. Forms devoid of practical significance – and those have been in the majority up till now – are simply non-organized forms: and, perhaps, the principle of organization has for the first time been fully realized in art. The Monument relies on the concentration of the legislative (Hall A), executive (Hall B) and informational (Hall C) initiative, all the halls being placed in the upper levels of the space according to the above mentioned principle of modernity. The purity of the initiatives, their ideal quality when freed from the demands of the material, is symbolized by this as well as by the material (glass) too. The art devoid of creative idealism which forms the core of intuition is an art of impure rhythms. Rhythms have so far resisted all attempts at being broken up into the elements of material culture, the latter determining the growth and the conditions of life; but existence itself is rhythms. Intuition flows in harmony with them. Their purity and saturation define the degree of one's talent and I know of no purer and more complete rhythms than those in Tatlin's works. He has the most sensitive eye for the material and defines the borderlines of rhythmical waves precisely through a juxtaposition of materials. We take a wave segment confined between the properties of glass and iron as a basis, as a unit of rhythm. Just as the spatial measure of a sound is a result of multiplying the number of oscillations by the wave length, the measure of a material rhythm is the relation of glass to iron. There is a kind of harsh, red-hot simplicity concealed in a juxtaposition of these two most primitive materials, both of which in the same degree owe their birth to fire. These materials are elements of contemporary art. The form produced by their juxtaposition generates rhythms of such enormous and powerful amplitude that they evoke the birth of an ocean.

To materialize that form means to embody dynamics with the same unsurpassable greatness as a static nature is embodied by a pyramid. We declare: only the might of the multimillion proletarian consciousness could throw into the world the concept of this monument-form; it must be materialized by the muscles of that might, since we have here an ideal, live and classic manifestation of the international union of the workers of the globe in a pure and creative form.

Н. Пунин, Памятник *III Интернационала, издание Отдела ИЗО Наркомпроса, Петроград,* 1920, 8 pp., two illustrations.

Punin, Nikolai Nikolaevich (1888–1953), an art critic, theorist and art historian. (В.Н. Петров, 'Н.Н. Пунин и его искусствоведческие работы', in: Н.Н. Пунин, *Русское и советское искусство,* Москва, 1976, pp. 7–32.) He was a friend of Tatlin, a member of the creative association Apartment No. 5 (*see* Isakov, commentary, p. 335) and the artist's colleague in IZO Narkompros, the Free State Artistic Studios, as well as in the Museum of Artistic Culture and the State Institute of Artistic Culture. He was the first to study Tatlin's art, and devoted to him numerous pages in his articles and reviews.

The brochure. At the time of writing the pamphlet, when the model of the Monument to the Third International had not yet been finished (the text is dated July 1920 while the model was completed in November 1920), Punin perceived the great significance of the project for the contemporary artistic culture. Itself a document of art history of that period, the pamphlet-manifesto remains the main source of information on the author's interpretation of his project, as conveyed in the judgment and personal evaluation of a professional art critic belonging to the artist's intimate circle of friends and colleagues. (Punin is mistaken when writing about the three glass halls inside the tower: there was a fourth, hemispherical one; and Vinogradov's initials are mistakenly reversed.) The brochure of IZO Narkompros is believed to have been published in December 1920 when the model was exhibited at the Eighth Congress of Soviets in Moscow (Ill. 181).

An original piece of art criticism written in a publicist manner, this 'agitational pamphlet' for new art was illustrated by Tatlin in the spirit of the first revolutionary publications (in red, black and white), which makes it especially valuable. It also contains some unique reproductions of the drawings for the project: the vertical façade of the tower on the cover (Ill. 182) and the leaning one (28×22 cm, zincography) (Ill. 183).

The pamphlet was preceded by Punin's exposition of Tatlin's original plans in the article 'On Monuments' (*see* Bibliog.: Punin, 9 March 1919), including the only surviving description of the designs for the interior decoration of the halls of the Monument (*see* Zhadova, p. 138)

The pamphlet provided in many aspects the basis for Punin's monograph *Tatlin (Against Cubism)*, which has hitherto been the only monograph on the artist.

Punin's article 'Tatlin's Tower' *(Veshch'-Objet-Gegenstand)* presents the author's shortened montage of the text of the pamphlet (*see* Bibliog.: Punin, 1922).

Meerzon, Vinogradov and Shapiro: *see* 'The Work', p. 239.

The monument to Lassalle by the sculptor Sinaiskii was on Nevskii Prospect and was unveiled on 7 November 1918.

N. Punin, Tatlin (Against Cubism) [excerpt]

I
Exposition

We have brought up Tatlin's name primarily to define the point of possible convergence of the numerous different forces opposing French Cubism today. By the latter we understand the totality of methods followed by the French school and aimed at an integral realization of painting on the surface – approximately within the limits of the tasks pointed out by Gleizes and Metzinger.[1] We accept the term 'integral realization of painting' as the best possible term for the definition of the kind of synthetic construction of reality which is primarily meant by Cubism. Our task is therefore doubly unrewarding: first, because we declare in advance that we shall be engaged in polemics and, second, because the polemics will involve some truly great masters of painting who also happen to be excellent theoreticians. But the present circumstances of the Russian school are such that its future existence depends to a considerable degree on the intensity of its struggle with Paris; as for Tatlin, there seems to be no better way of showing the importance of this artist than by making him a point of departure in our campaign – inevitable in the final analysis – against France. The time (at least that at my disposal) is not ripe yet for an objective evaluation of Tatlin; we do not feel like prophesying idly; we prefer to fight for a more or less remote yet real future. If it turns into the present in the course of that struggle, then so much the better for us, and the shorter will be our reckoning with certain varieties of Futurism. We know the latter in its two main interpretations – of which the Italian one can no longer be of any interest to us and bears hardly any relation to Tatlin. As for Futurism as the realm of time, we are just on the threshold of an era that will cancel out the past, just as spatial time is cancelled by the time of light. Then many of us will probably find ourselves in the folds of time: we are silent in the face of such

[1] Д. Глез и Ж. Мессенже, *О кубизме.* Пер. С. Низен под ред. Матюшина. Изд. Журавль. [Albert Gleizes–Jean Metzinger, *Du Cubisme,* 1912]

immensity and all the more confident that Tatlin will always ride the wave of any dimension. Within the limits of our polemics, however, the following words will suffice: 'I am gripped by uncontrollable excitement when I visualize the day and the year when artists will comprehend the whole significance of this form and finally realize that there is no other path but this one.' (*Iskusstvo kommuny*, no. 10.)

II
The Eye

Many masters of the Russian school, whose importance in general I am not going to deny, show a hopeless confusion of traditions and methods. Tatlin belongs to those who have followed an unadulterated course of development. In some cases the strength of one's talent lies in none other than the firmness of one's will-power.

In their unselfish wanderings around the world the Russian artists of recent decades most often return to Paris, invariably claiming descent from Manet and Picasso. Perhaps it is Tatlin's very misfortune that he had been born neither Manet nor Picasso? Just because Gleizes and Metzinger had a premonition of the forms of objective beauty, this does not mean that they were foreseeing *culture*. In Picasso's art the study of material was reduced to the interplay of *fakturas*; the basis of this interplay being Verlaine's 'nous voulons les nuances encore'. Picasso cannot be accepted as the dawn of a new era. Contiguous refracted epochs will always have something in common, but 'can logic ever make the wine in a chemist's retort and in a connoisseur's glass identical?' Picasso, however, is on the other side of the divide: the crux of the matter is not even in invention but in artistic culture and tradition. The future belongs to those who are amazingly incapable of the beautiful (*Beaux arts*), for it was precisely the latter that ruined 'la belle France'. The beautiful has irreversibly become French since the time of the Impressionists; that, however, did not make the French European, let alone universally human. Owing to the intensive efforts of the French School art has been identified with the Romantic, the individual and the aesthetic, which prevents it from being classical, real and professional. The thousands of miles separating Paris from Moscow enable us to observe the wave coming from the opposite direction: professional classical realism.

Tatlin cannot be accused of aestheticism (*Beaux arts*)[1]. His eye (taste) is undeniable. Tatlin wrote: 'Since 1912 I have been appealing to the members of my profession to improve their eye.' And they did not listen to him. The capacity and precision of this eye approaches great perfection: it is the most powerful receiver of modernity. Many sincere practitioners of visual art would have given up their craft had they realized the impact of this eye but, since nobody did give up, they could not have realized it; some have been hypocritical. When people wish to get to know an artist they usually study his works; in the case of Tatlin it would be more useful to study his eye, developed in the process of his work.

To see this means to be an artist. The French masters understand their tasks differently; they see the artist's prerogative as looking for the beautiful. Even such serious masters as Gleizes and Metzinger conclude their book with the words, 'and the faith in beauty will give him the necessary strength', overlooking the fact that beauty – even if it is taken seriously – is only one of the possible combinations and the least stable one at that. When it becomes the axis of the creative effort it deprives the artist of his profession. How can a feeling be a profession? Parisian aestheticism, with its copies in Munich, Helsinki or Petersburg, was instrumental in the decline of the professional spirit and in the upsurge of dilettantism. Owing to his innate professionalism, Tatlin has been improving his eye in the name of a mighty and steadfast professionalism.

[1] Once, scrutinizing a truck in Basmannaia Street, I became aware of the purity of Tatlin's taste.

НИ К НОВОМУ, НИ К СТАРОМУ, А К НУЖНОМУ.

* **234** Poster with Tatlin's slogan 'Not the old, not the new, but the necessary', 1923, Cat. XII/21
235 Façade of the Kiev College of Art. Photograph from 1927, legacy L.A. Zhadova

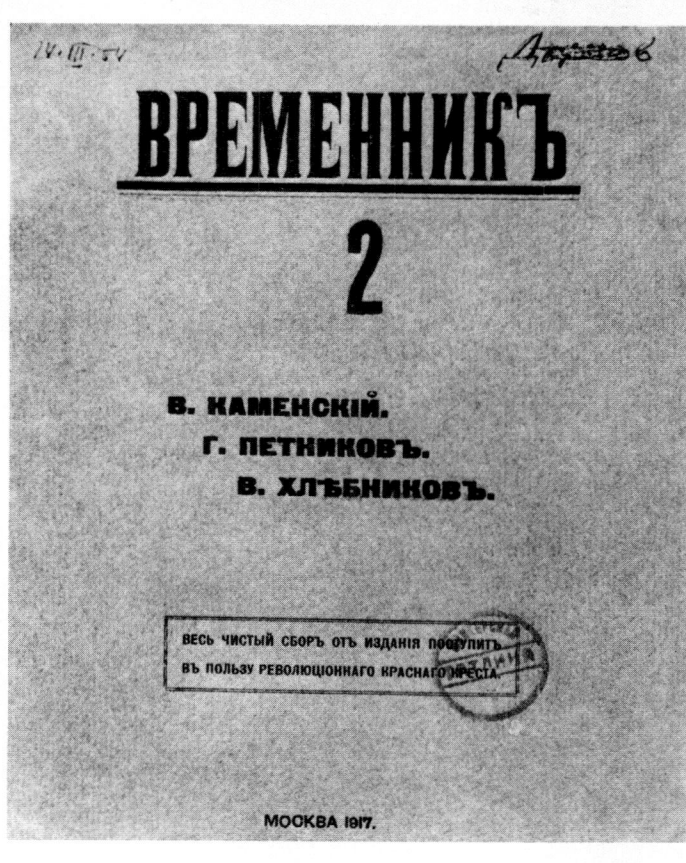

ВРЕМЕННИКЪ

2

В. КАМЕНСКІЙ.
Г. ПЕТНИКОВЪ.
В. ХЛѢБНИКОВЪ.

ВЕСЬ ЧИСТЫЙ СБОРЪ ОТЪ ИЗДАНІЯ ПОСТУПИТЬ
ВЪ ПОЛЬЗУ РЕВОЛЮЦІОННАГО КРАСНАГО КРЕСТА.

МОСКВА 1917.

236 Tatlin with his wife and son, Vladimir, Leningrad, 1924–5.
Photograph: TsGALI, Moscow.
237 Courtyard of Miatlev House in Leningrad giving access to the State Institute of Artistic Culture (GINKhUK). Windows of the former Section for Material Culture and of Tatlin's apartment can be seen in the picture.
Recent photograph
238 Cover of a periodical bearing the stamp of Tatlin's studio, 1917, Cat. XII/15
* **239** Page from the manuscript of Punin, 'Routine and Tatlin', 1924, Cat. XII/22

25
ФЕВРАЛЯ

1921
ГОДА

ВЛАДИМИР ИЛЬИЧ ЛЕНИН
БЫЛ В ЭТОМ ДОМЕ
В КОММУНЕ ВХУТЕМАСА
БЕСЕДОВАЛ СО СТУДЕНТАМИ
ВЫСШИХ ХУДОЖЕСТВЕННЫХ
МАСТЕРСКИХ

ПЕТРОГРАД
МУЗЕЙ ХУД. КУЛЬТУ
ИСАКИЕВ. ПЛ. Д. 9.

В. ВОСКР. 27 МАЯ в 7ч.
В ПЛАНЕ МУЗ. РАБ
В. Е. ТАТЛИН
СДЕЛ. ДОКЛАД. НА ТЕМУ
МАТЕРИАЛЬНАЯ
КУЛЬТУРА
(ДОЛОЙ ТАТЛИНИЗМ
ВХОД

240–2 The VKhUTEMAS–VKhUTEIN building in Moscow.
Recent photographs
243 Poster for Tatlin's lecture 'Material Culture', 1923, Cat. XII/20
244 Tatlin as professor on the Faculty of Wood and Metal Working of VKhUTEIN with his students, late 1920s. Taken by Rodchenko.
Photograph: Collection V.A. Rodchenko.

НОВЫЙ БЫТ

Отдел материальной культуры при музее Художественной культуры (Главнаука), ведя исследовательскую работу в области изыскания новых форм, одной из основных своих задач поставил опыт по реорганизации быта.

В основе этой работы — максимум внимания к простейшим, окружающим нас вещам. Художник должен органически участвовать в создании новой вещи, а не только пользоваться старыми вещами. В связи с этим Отдел выработал задание и уже удалось даже заготовить образцы одежды, отопительных приборов, мебели и пр. На характеристике этих образцов мы остановимся.

Характерные черты данного на рисунке пальто следующие: несколько расширенная в плечах и торсе (корпусе) и суженная книзу форма создает следующие качества: тепло не выдувается снизу, материал не облегает (создается воздушная прослойка), — с одной стороны удерживая этим лучше тепло (принцип двойной рамы), с другой создает более гигиенические условия.

Пальто сделано с таким расчетом, чтобы движения человека в нем не были стеснены, и дает возможность сохранить естественное положение, напр. карманы располагаются соответственно для рук (рис. 1). Кроме того, пальто имеет две сменных пристежных подкладки (фланелевую (осенью) и меховую (барашек) зимой), эти прикрепляются к мягкому непромокаемому верху гнездо специальным шнуром.

Ввиду того, что пальто состоит из трех отдельных, по мере надобности скрепляемых, частей, то каждая из них, по износу может быть заменена новой. Костюм сконструирован по тому же принципу в общих чертах покроя. Рукава куртки и брюки также сужены к низу. Жилет совсем отсутствует. Комбинированный воротник может быть застегнут наглухо. Каркасный приклад целиком отсутствует. Пальто и костюм выполнены совместно с трестом Ленинградодежды.

Из пяти выработанных образцов нормальных печей поясним указанный на рисунке № 3 печь, эта имеет экономическую топку, обеспечивающую при небольшой затрате дров полезный большой тепловой эффект. Печь снабжена духовой и большим герметическим шкафом, который сохраняет воду и пищу горячими в течении 28—30 часов и одновременно при одной топке обогревает помещение, размером 3 куб. ар. при 6-ти ар. высоты до 48 часов сохраняя температуру от 16° до 14° по Реомюру. Помимо того, разрабатываются новые конструкции кроватей и др. предметов.

Работа ведется коллективной группой сотрудников, в число которых входит художник Татлин, возглавляющий одновременно заведывающий указанного отдела Материальной Культуры

1—4) Фасон нового типа пальто: сделан с таким расчетом, чтобы движения человека в нем не стесняли. Пальто служит и летом и зимой с переменной подкладки. 2) Зав. Отд. Матер. Культуры худ. Татлин 3) Новый тип печки, обеспечивающей большое тепло при небольшой затрате дров. В духовом шкафу пища сохраняется горячей в течение 28—30 часов.

245 Novel heater, one of five designs of the economical stove, 1923, Cat. VII/2

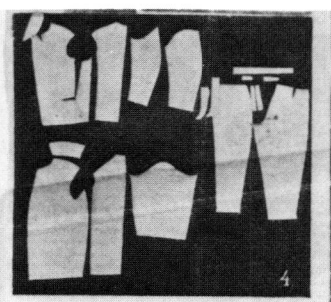

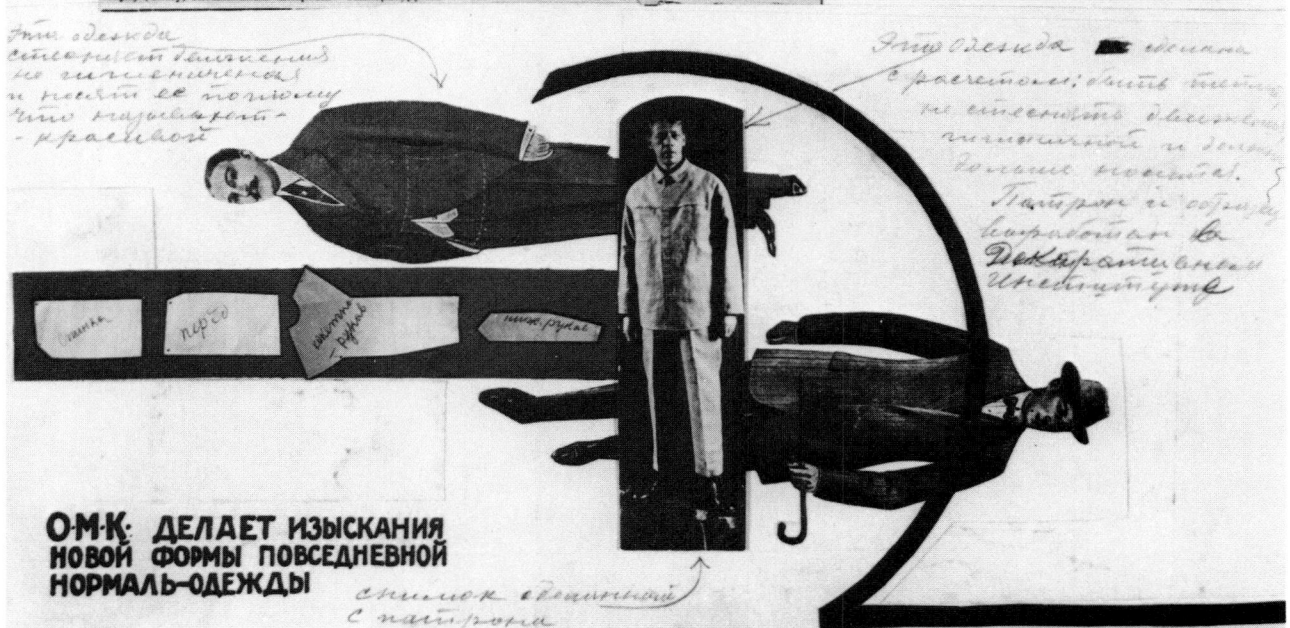

246 *The New Way of Life*, montage illustrating the work of the Section for Material Culture in the design of a new type of clothing, 1923–4, Cat. VII/9

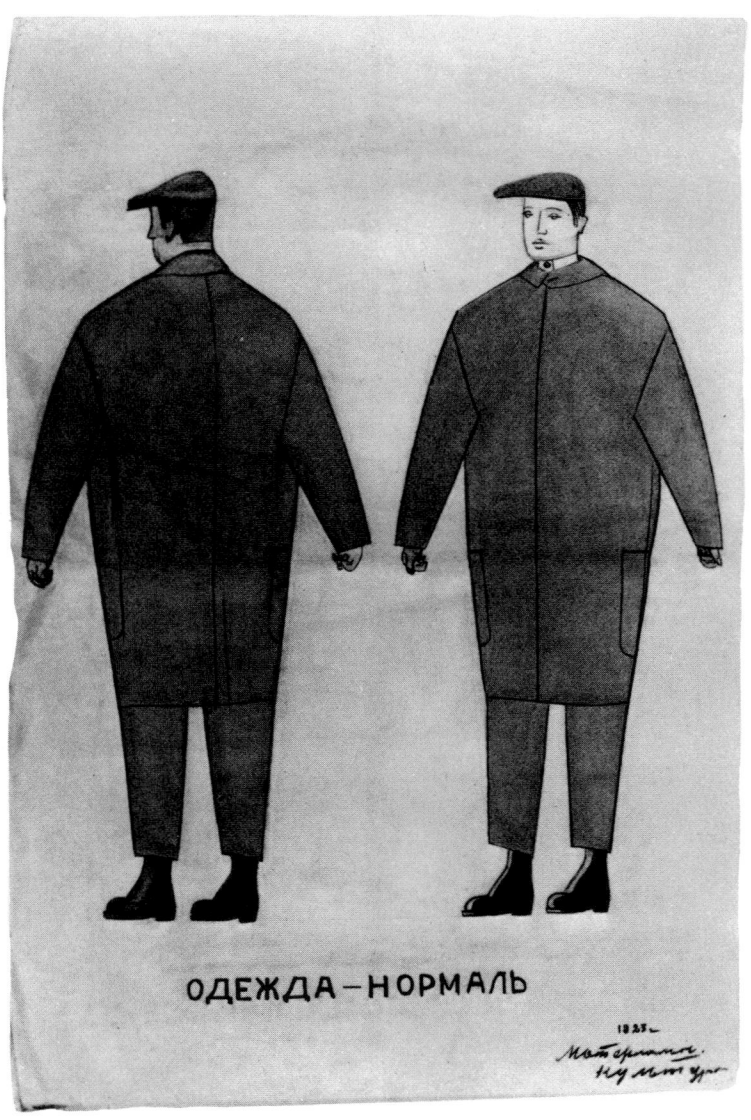

ОДЕЖДА–НОРМАЛЬ

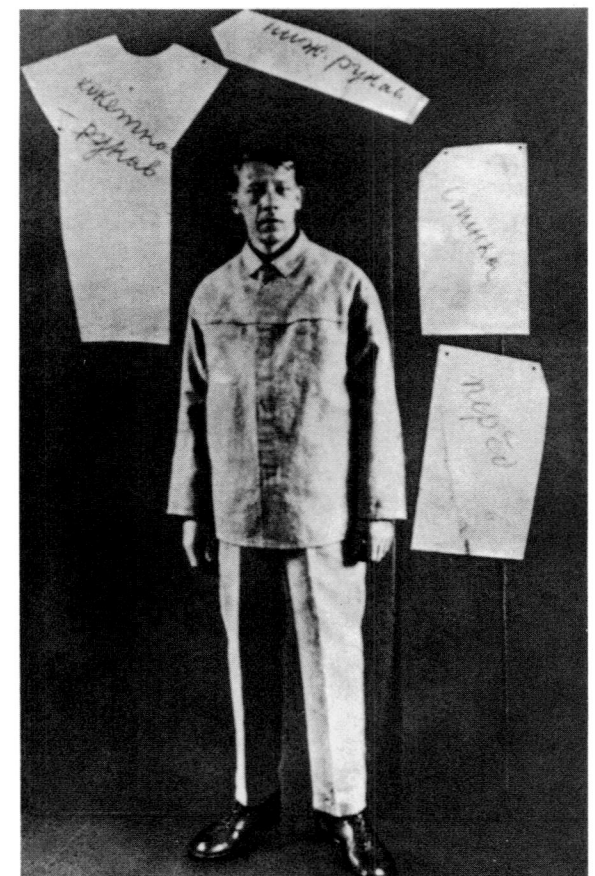

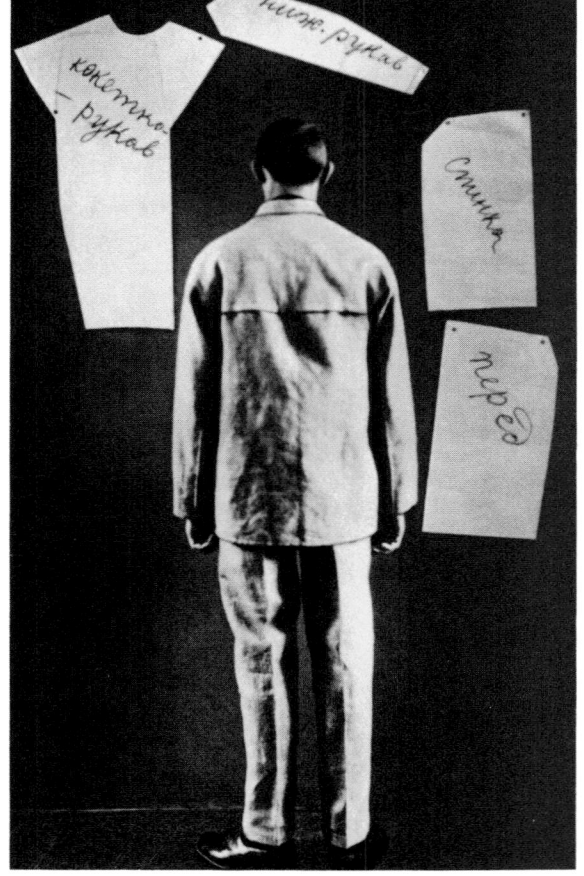

* **247** Design for man's coat ('Utility clothing'), 1923, Cat. VII/6
248–9 Novel street clothing, pattern, 1923–4, front and rear views, Cat. VII/8a,b
250 Design for man's coat, 1923, Cat. VII/5

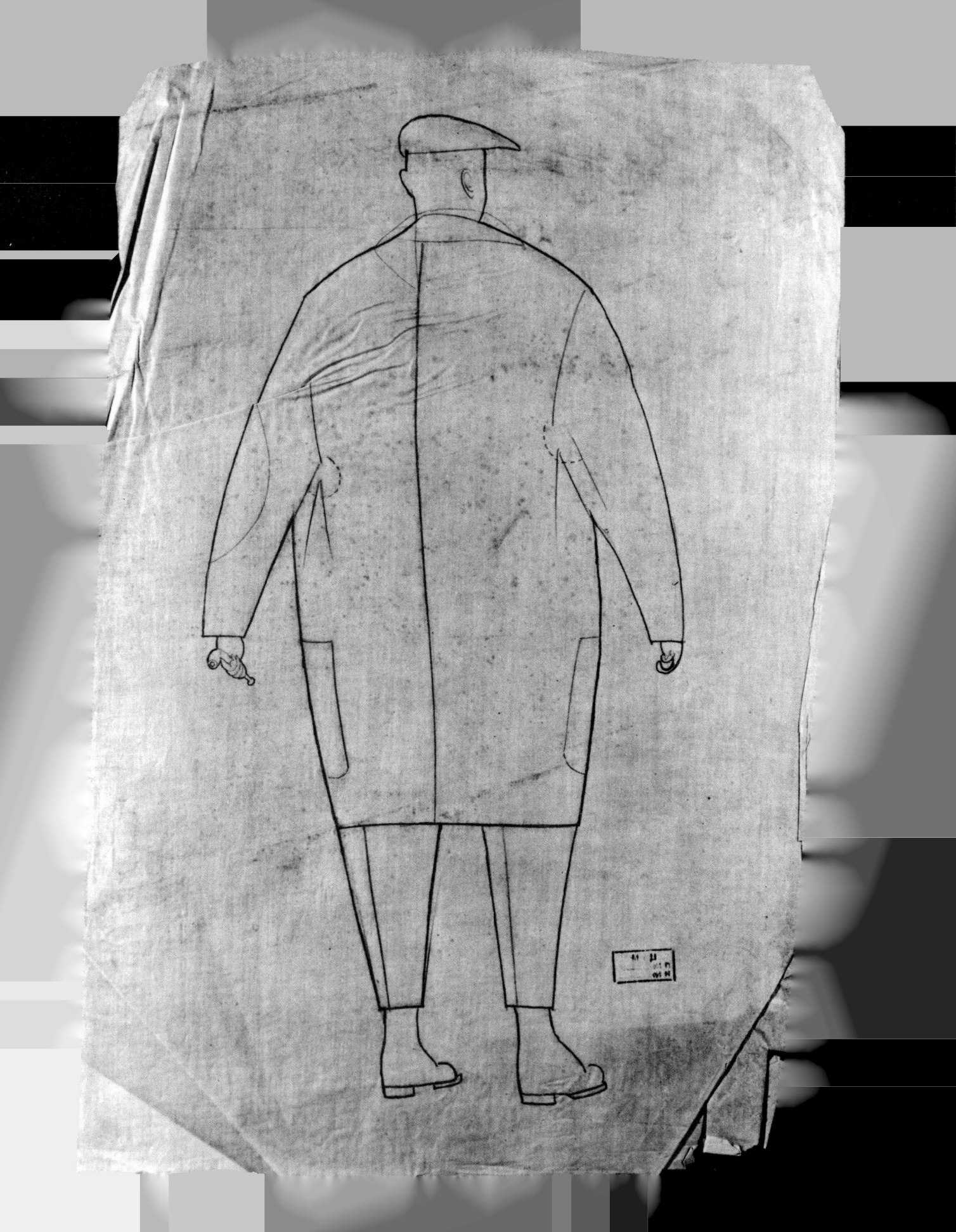

251 Design for woman's clothing, 1923, Cat. VII/7

252 N. Lamanova, Diagrams of clothing models, 1920s

* **253** Bench, designed and constructed by Tatlin, late 1910s, Cat. VII/1

254 Sledge frame, late 1920s, Cat. VII/4

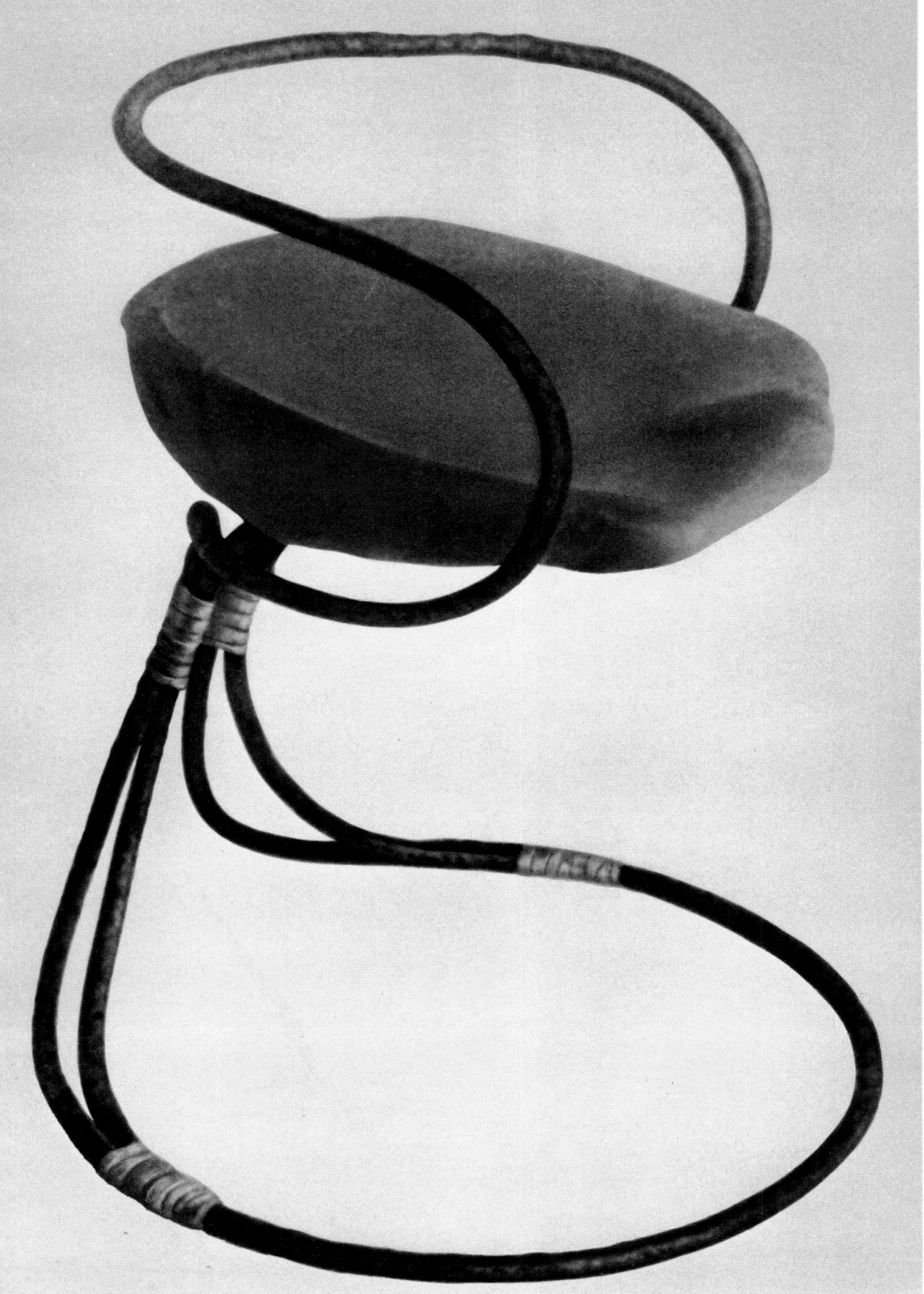

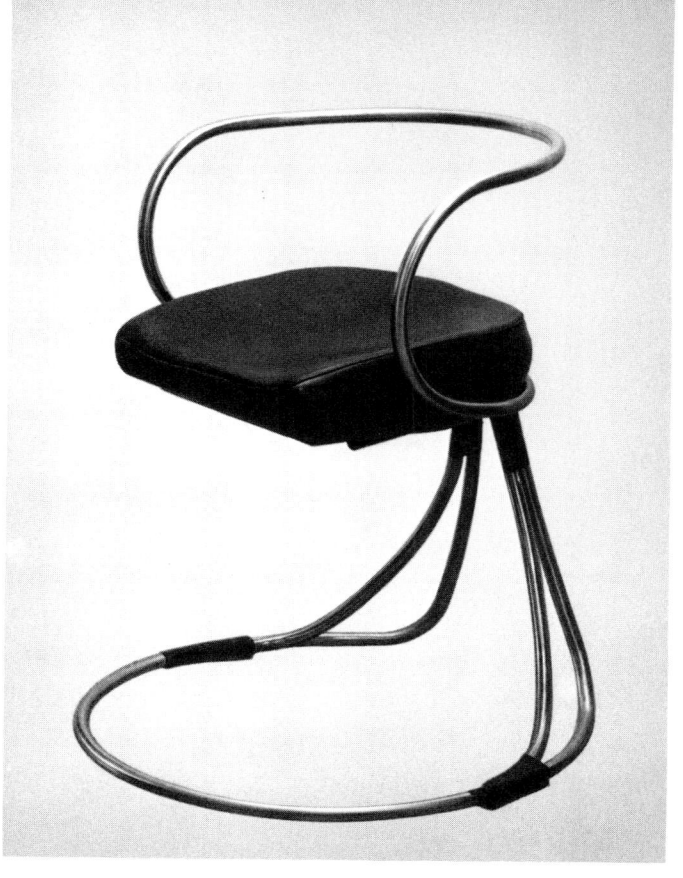

255 Design for model chair, 1927, Cat. VII/3
256–8 Model of the Tatlin–Rogozhin chair (reconstruction), Cat. X/6

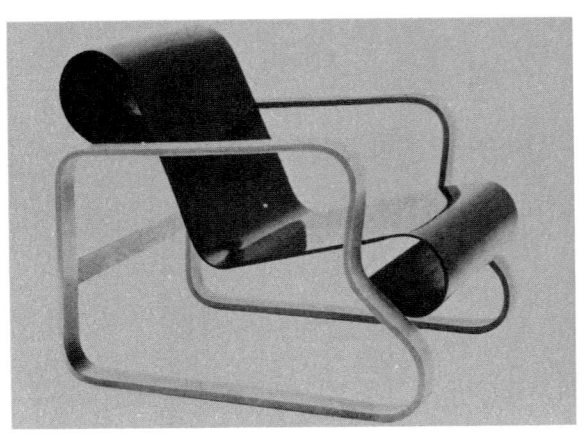

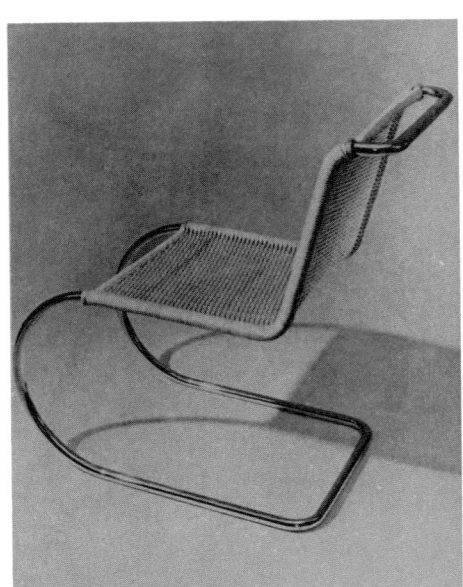

259 Alvar Aalto, Model chair (no. 402) early 1930s
260 Model chair no. 14 of the Thonet Factory, 1859
261 Mart Stam, Model chair (no. 533), 1926 (Bauhaus)
262 Mies van der Rohe, Model chair (no. MR 533), 1927

263 *Tsarevich*, painted plate, 1922, Cat. VII/10a

264 Signature and stamp on the bottom of the plate,
Cat. VII/10b
265 Design for multi-purpose metal dish, 1923, Cat. VII/17

266 Design for teapot, 1923, Cat. VII/13
★ 267 Design for teacup, 1923, Cat. VII/14

268 Design for sugar-bowl, 1923, Cat. VII/16
269 Design for milk-jug, 1923, Cat. VII/11

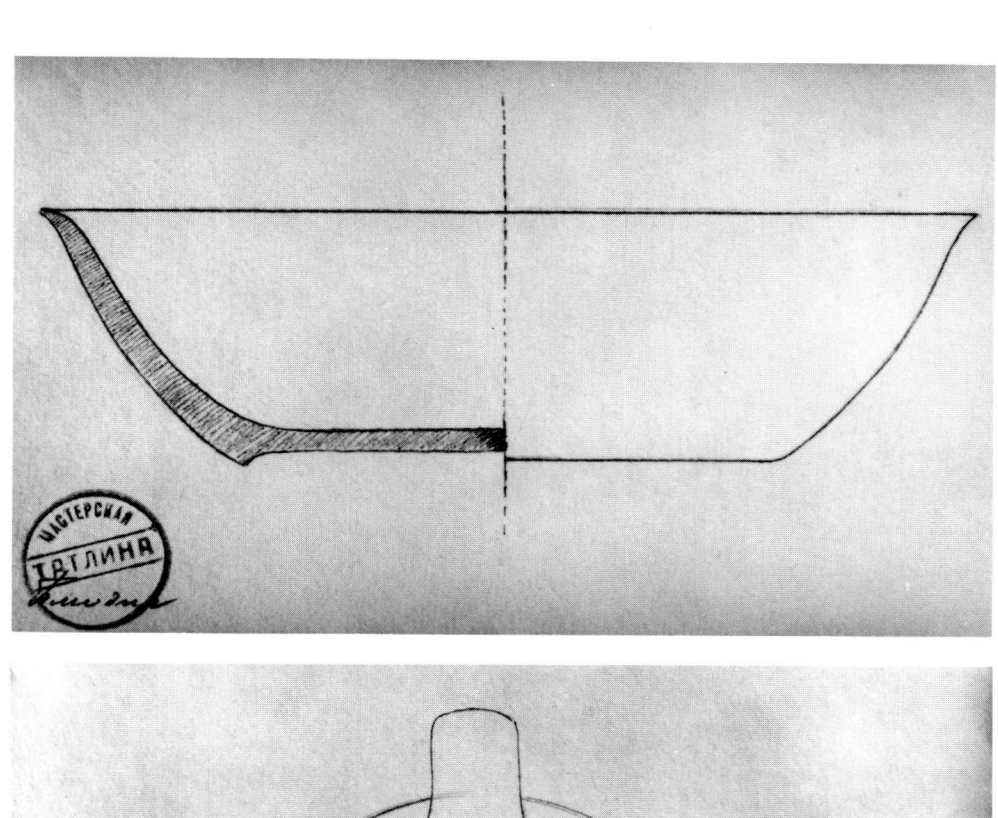

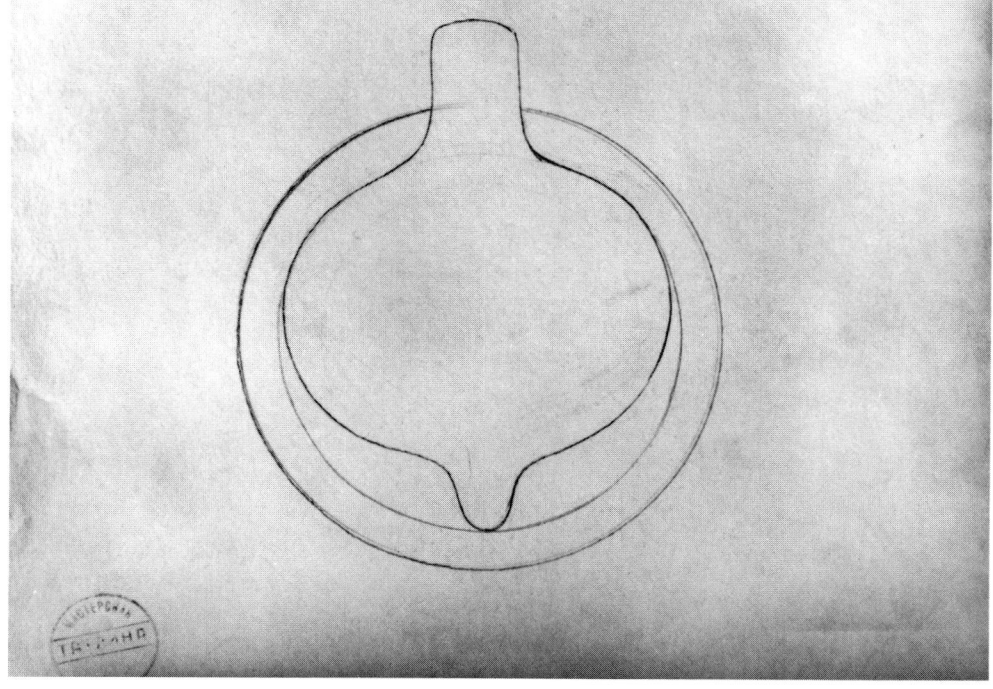

* **270** Design for dish, 1923, Cat. VII/15
271 Milk-jug viewed from above, 1923, Cat. VII/12

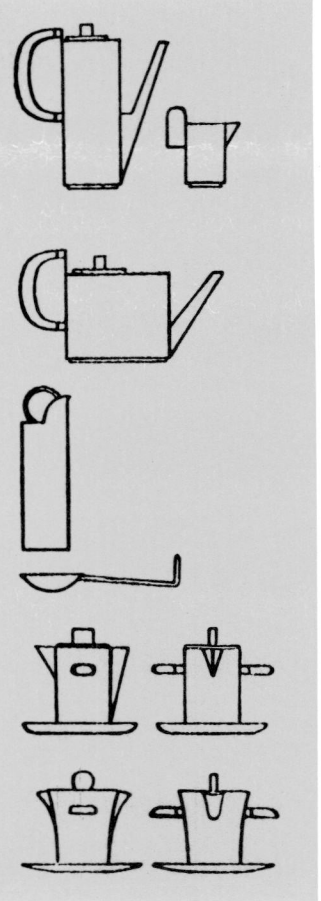

272 Dorofeev, Tea-set, late 1920s (VKhUTEIN)
273 Marianne Brandt, Models of dishes, 1923–4
274 W. Wagenfeld, Dish models – diagrams, 1923–4 (Bauhaus)
275 A.G. Sotnikov, Teapot, 1930, Cat. XI/7

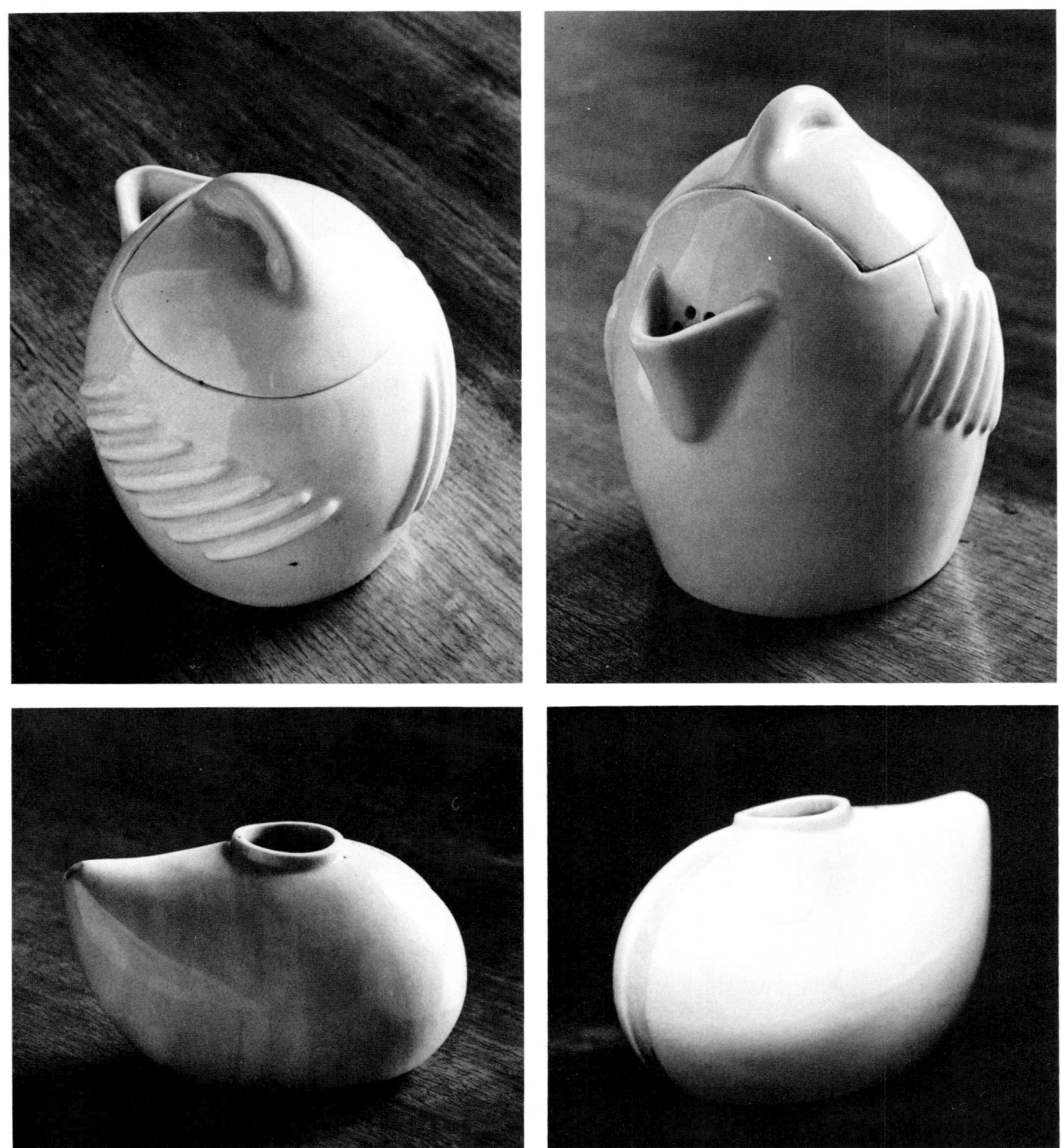

276–7 A.G. Sotnikov, Teapot. Reconstructed by the artist, Cat. XI/12
278–9 A.G. Sotnikov, Child's nursing vessel (First version) 1930, Cat. XI/5a

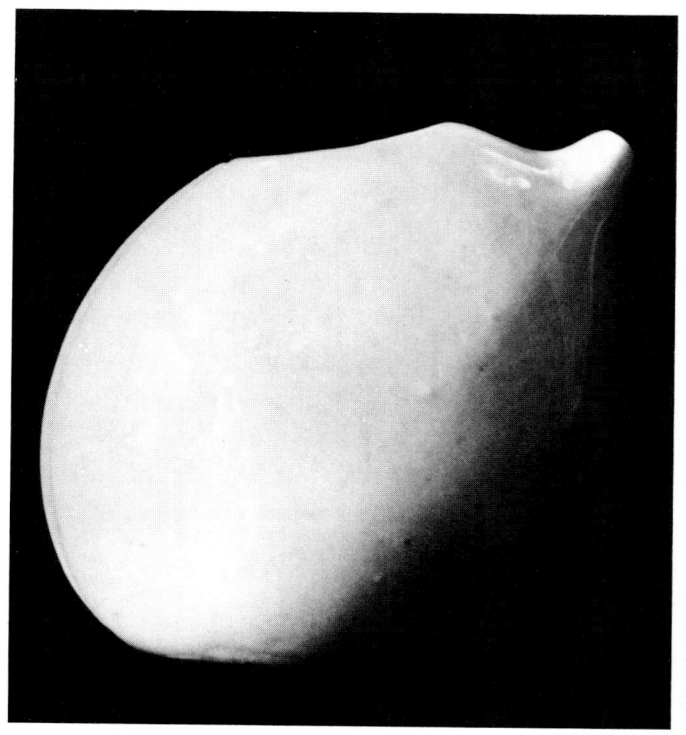
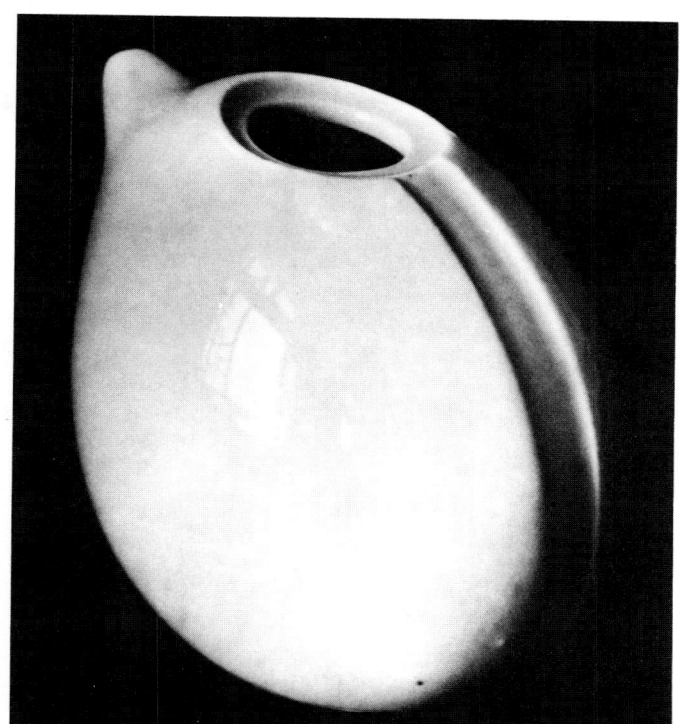
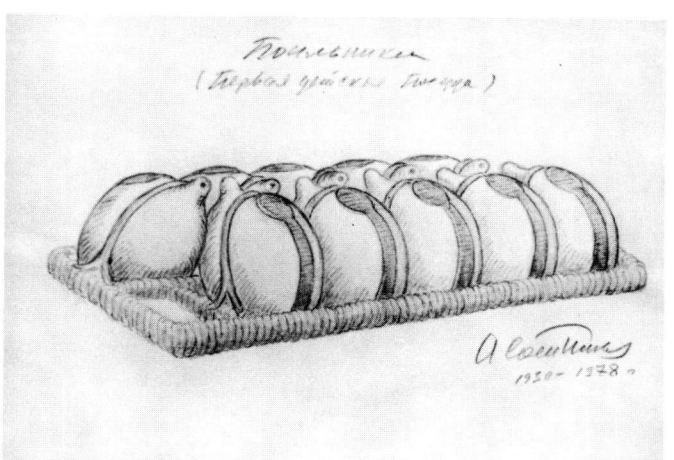

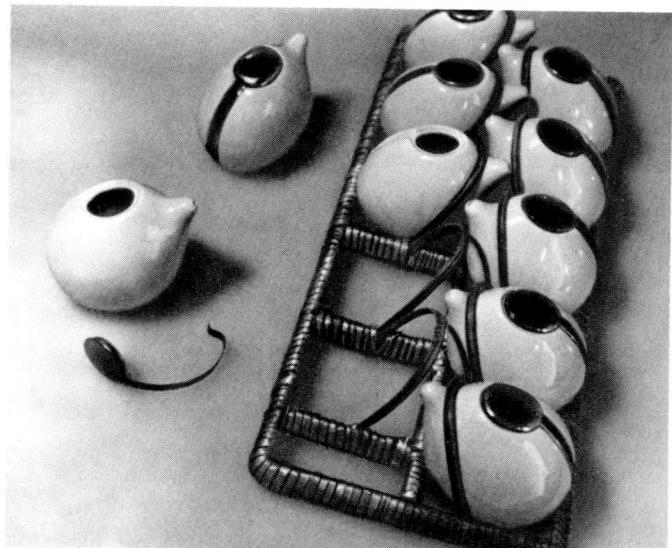

280–1 A.G. Sotnikov, Child's nursing vessel (Final version) 1930, Cat. XI/6
282 A.G. Sotnikov, Wicker tray with compartments for ten children's vessels. Sketch for the reconstruction, Cat. XI/9a
283 A.G. Sotnikov, Wicker tray with compartments for ten children's vessels. Reconstructed by the artist, Cat. XI/9b
284 A.G. Sotnikov, Child's nursing vessel with casting mould, Cat. XI/5b

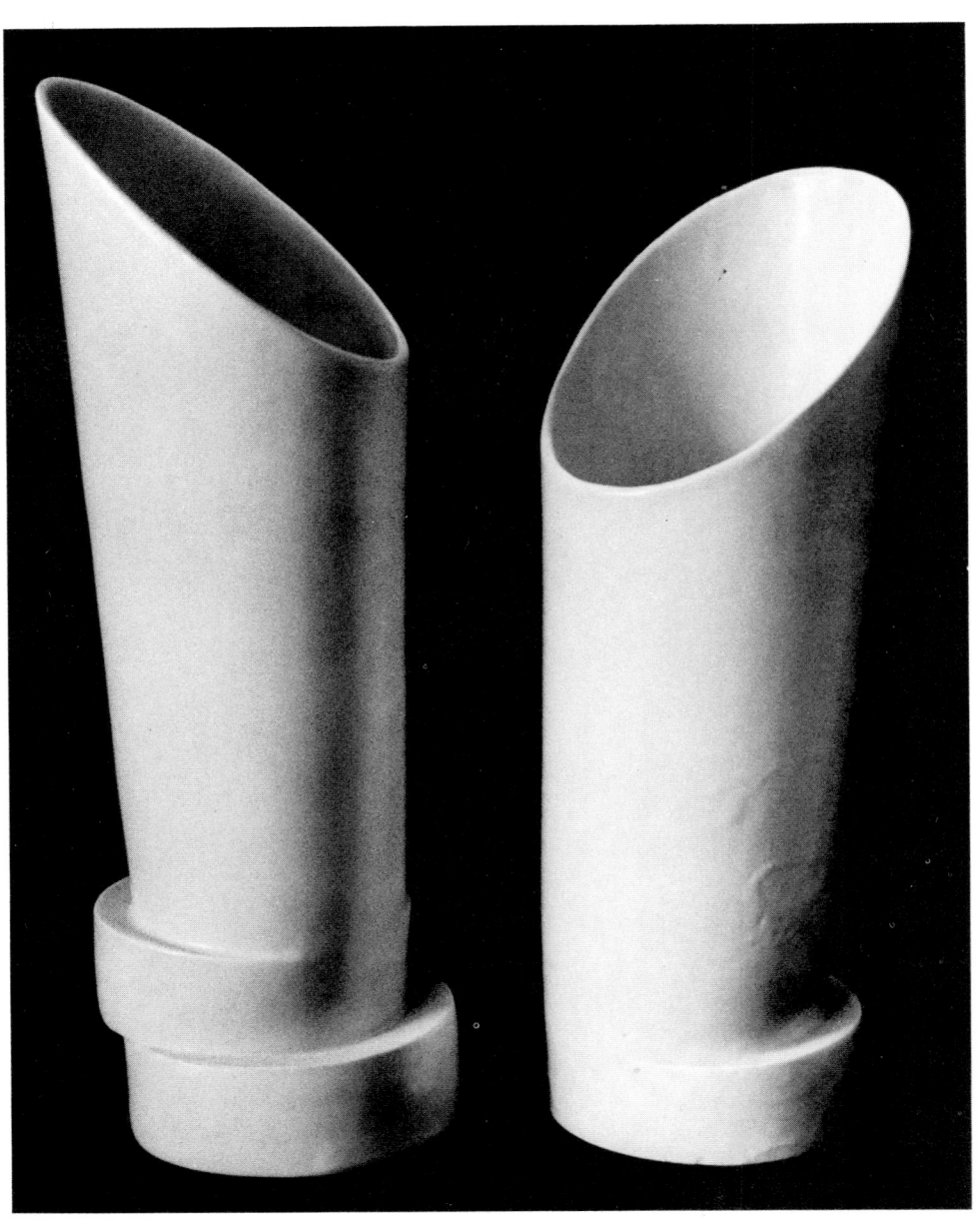

285 E.M. Ginstling, Twin vases ('Flight') 1931, Cat. XI/8
286 V.V. Borkin, Shaving kit, 1930 (reconstruction) Cat. XI/13
287 V.V. Borkin, Pepper shaker, 1930 (reconstruction) Cat. XI/11
288 P.M. Kozhin, Teapot ('Egg') 1930 (reconstruction) Cat. XI/10

290–2 Maiakovskii's catafalque and funeral procession, 1930, Cat. IX/2

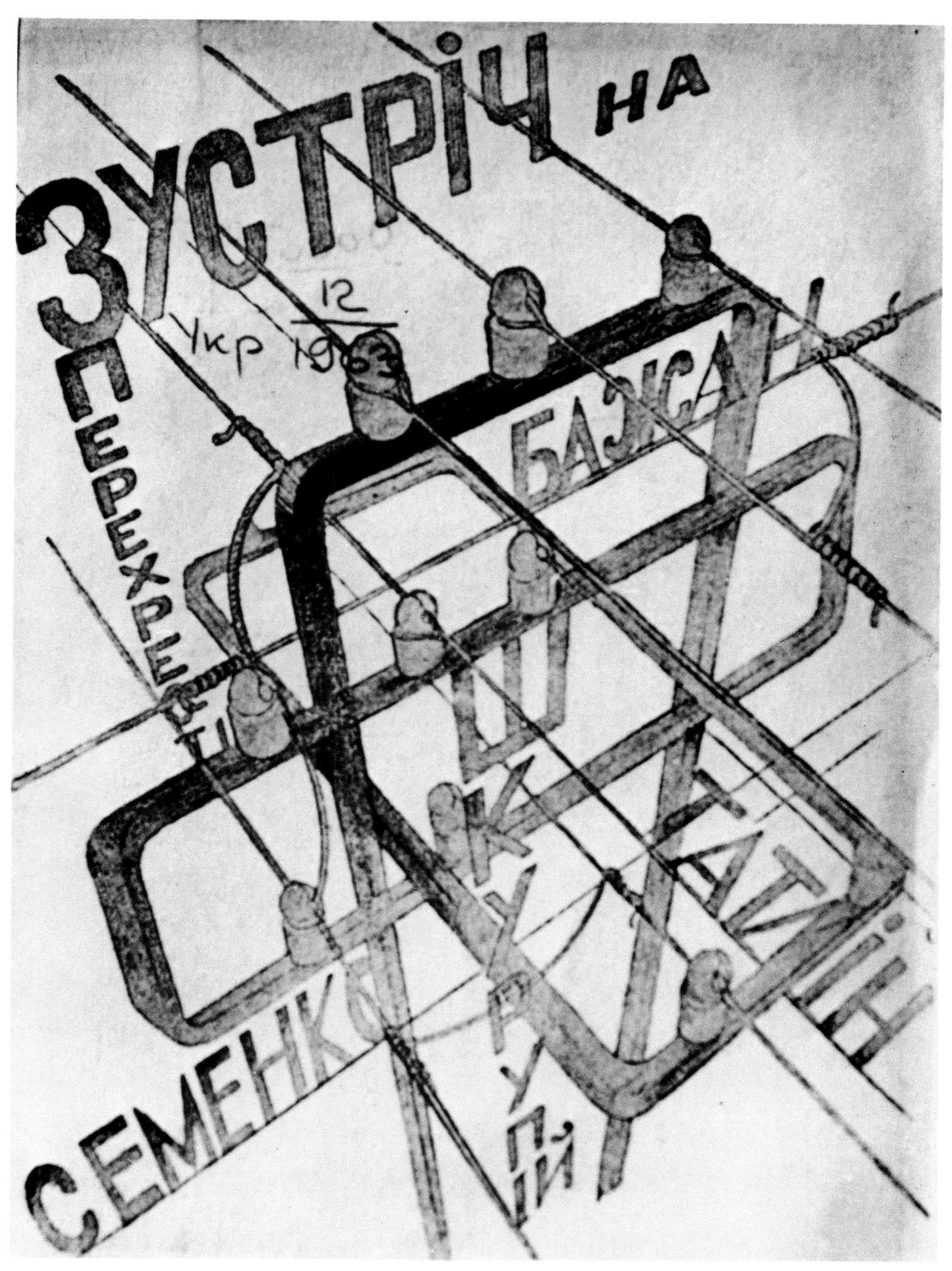

293 Cover of Bazhan, Shkurupii, Semenko and Tatlin, *Meeting at the Crossroads*, 1927,
Cat. III/7

294–7 Illustrations for S. Sergel', *On the Sailing-Ship*, Cat. III/8
294 Cover, 1929, Cat. III/8a
295 *The Sailing-Ship Chernomor*, Cat. III/8b
* **296** *The Crew at Lunch*, sketch, Cat. III/8c
* **297** *Storm*, sketch, Cat. III/8d

Сергель. На парусном судне

Рис 4 стр. 10.

Сергель. На парусном судне

Рис 9 стр. 82.

ДАНИИЛ ХАРМС

ВО-ПЕРВЫХ И
ВО-ВТОРЫХ

ОБЛОЖКА И РИСУНКИ
ХУДОЖНИКА В. ТАТЛИНА

ГОСУДАРСТВЕННОЕ ИЗДАТЕЛЬСТВО
МОСКВА   1929   ЛЕНИНГРАД

298–312 Illustrations for D. Kharms, *Firstly and Secondly*,
1929, Cat. III/9
298 Cover, Cat. III/9a
299 Title-page, Cat. III/9b
300 *For the Fourth Time*, 2nd illus. (p. 11), Cat. III/9g
301 *For the Seventh Time* (p. 17), Cat. III/9k
302 *For the Sixth Time* (p. 15), Cat. III/9j

* **303** *For the Fifth Time*, sketch, Cat. III/9h
* **304** *For the Third Time*, sketch, Cat. III/9c
* **305** *For the Fourth Time*, sketch, Cat. III/9e
* **306** *For the Eighth Time*, sketch, Cat. III/9l
  307 *For the Fifth Time* (p. 13), Cat. III/9i
  308 *For the Third Time* (p. 7), Cat. III/9d
  309 *For the Fourth Time* (p. 9), Cat. III/9f
  310 *For the Eighth Time* (p. 19), Cat. III/9m

* **311** *For the Ninth Time*, sketch, Cat. III/9n
  312 *For the Ninth Time* (p. 21), Cat. III/9o

Identification of beauty with pleasure for ever moulded French art into the forms of individualism. The limitation of reality permitted by the French masters, who saw it only as beauty (taste) and pleasure (personality), put certain limits on them as well: they gradually lost the sense of the real together with a professional approach to painting, and became absorbed in aestheticism, symbolism, mysticism and everything romantic. Although they were proclaiming individual liberty, this does not provide any evidence of their true freedom. The latter acquires strength and meaning only when it has a purpose. 'For bits of freedom gained by Courbet, Manet, Cézanne and the Impressionists, Cubism substitutes infinite freedom.' The infinite is immeasurable. How can it be made into a measure of the superior reality that we call art? And how can this measure be applied when mankind is in fetters, for reality is precisely what we cannot suggest to others.[1]

The eye of the French artists is limited by individual freedom and 'aesthetic' emotions, it is weakened and enslaved. To revive the eye means to revive realism, equally indispensable and mandatory. We regard as the gravest mistake of the dying (French) school its distortion of real relationships. The art developed out of false relationships, hypertrophied emotions and illusion is a great art. An eye devoid of an objective criterion records too many details; gradually even art itself turns into a detail; the incidental is elevated to the level of the mandatory; the individual is preferred to the classical. The Impressionists transformed painting into the art of light; the Cubists decided to resurrect painting; together with painting the wholeness of reality, i.e. life itself, should be resurrected. The generations of artists who will find their strength in art to purify traditional realism will reinforce the gains of the last decades. Then the Monet–Picasso period will be understood as a crisis of European art, after which the classical European realism – more profound, richer and rejuvenated by that crisis – will shine forth even more brightly. The academics accusing Monet and Manet of Expressionism had their own reasons for it, but their misfortune was that they themselves were corpses. The eye that saw as they did in the Salons of the 1870s was neither perverse nor healthy; it was dead, and many years of vacillation had to elapse before the eye could be revived, exercised and only then restored to its proper functioning. Tatlin's efforts in this direction surpass everything that has been accomplished so far; once again there is an opportunity for the objectively truthful and real-world outlook for which art can become real when reality becomes art. Individual relations of accidental form are exorcised with the severity and decisiveness that only great masters are capable of; emotional irritations of the hypertrophied and deformed eye are regarded as sick and are removed. Art is revived, the eye is rehabilitated. The intensive work of the rehabilitation of the eye is an essential, necessary task of the time; at the same time it is the content of the greater part of Tatlin's creative activity.

III
Material and its Volume

Cézanne occupies only one page in the history of the Impressionists: he foresaw the Cubists – hence his boundless influence on art. Methods elevated to principles, i.e. a school, limit inventiveness, especially that of a young art. For that reason an artist passing through Cézanne would be more alive than one passing through Cubism. Cézanne is more talented than any school or trend, which is why he is more likely to excite talents. Indeed, an artist responding to art is happier with Cézanne than with Monet or Gleizes. When Tatlin just started creating, Cézanne was reigning supreme, thus the young artist's task was to approach Cézanne as closely as possible, to emulate him as best he could. The degree of proximity in

[1] Cf. 'For only that is real which we ourselves suggest to others.' Глез и Мессенже, p. 38.

this case is none other than the magnitude of the talent. Schools and disciples, especially those of little ability, more often than not tend to interpret great masters by thinning and weakening them; it is far more profitable to copy them inch by inch. Tatlin's *Bouquet* (in the Jack of Diamonds exhibition, 1910) is an obviously Cézannesque piece, Impressionist on the one hand, and foreshadowing Cubism on the other. Tatlin could not be any closer to Cézanne, nor could he admire him sincerely. Gifted artists, however, even when they submit to the force of an influence are slaves in a lesser degree than those wretched ones who, having formally left the authority of their great teacher (or more often a great school), never stop cringing in a most shameless and miserable way. On the surface of the canvas where he glorifies Cézanne, Tatlin protested – probably unconsciously – against himself and his great master. That protest, unnoticed at the time, today presents a clear evidence that in 1910 we had before us a young talent whose significance it was hard to determine.

According to Bernard, Cézanne used to say: 'There are neither lines nor modelling, but only contrasts; when there is a wealth of colour, there is a completeness of form.' Pigment is for Cézanne no more than colour which he constantly holds in chromatic relationship. Cézanne suffered from that very eye disease that we now call Impressionism. Contrary to his protestations, for him, as for all the followers of that school, the material world drowned and dissolved in light. Although he did make form (volume) more profound, he did so only inasmuch as it could be defined through colour; his volumes are no more than fullness of colour. An eye perceiving reality in a more profound and simple way than Cézanne – a normal eye – felt very soon the necessity to correct Impressionism. It was necessary to find the basis for the corrections. They were to be found in the traditions of Russian art.

Until the reign of Peter the Great, Russian painting had worked with pigment as a painting material, as the result of dye pigment; although it used to gravitate towards one-dimensional (flat) and even decorative colour structure, never – with some rare exceptions – was colour perceived by icon-painters as the relationship within the chromatic scale. Hence the beautiful tradition of a powerful and healthy art was still preserved in the schools of icon-painting and house-painters' workshops. The so-called body painting, conditioned by an old and firm technique, is to a certain extent a national characteristic of Russian painting.

Tatlin unconsciously absorbed both that technique and that understanding of colour, preferring these subsequently to the French manner of painting. In *Bouquet* there is still only a blind instinct, but very soon this instinct would take him to a new path pursued by a centuries-old powerful culture. Such an early and unique choice of direction promised a rich future. It turned out to be even more fulfilling, since the artist managed to apply his creative powers with perfect purity in the direction which, once chosen, he never lost again.

Colour understood as material inevitably led to work on materials in general. A professional consciousness found such material first of all in the surface destined to become the painted surface. One had to forget everything outside that surface and, when it was impossible to forget, one had to abbreviate, to stop taking it into account and recognizing it. A war was waged against naturalist recollections, against chance, the accidental and the individual. That struggle was carried out energetically and decisively. It provided the content for the works that followed: *The Return, Fisherman, Nude*. Tatlin engaged in that struggle at the same time as French Cubism, yet he was against Cubism, fighting on the wide, exposed front, along a line of development that filled a three-year period. 'To illuminate means to disclose, to colour, i.e. to reveal in a particular way,' write Gleizes and Metzinger; Gleizes and Metzinger, however, suffered from an eye disease that we now call Cubism. During the first period of the development of the school they conceived colour as a function of the forms of reality, but since they learned to see from the Impressionists they understood colour as chromatic relationships even during the second period which was more or less liberated from naturalist recollections.

For Tatlin, to colour meant above all to study the dyeing pigment; to colour in a certain way meant to work a surface by means of paints. Colour is given objectively, it is a reality and an element; colour relationships are independent of spatial relationships existing in reality. Red is equally red, whatever the amount of light between it and the eye; ochre on the boards of a fence and ochre at the tip of a brush are not qualitatively different, they can differ only when their chemical composition and the painting technique are different. Working a surface by means of paints is the practical task of the painter. But surface, like paint, is a kind of material: painted, possessing dimensions, volume and texture, it can be fluid or hard, brittle or resinous, elastic, dense and heavy, and like any other material it searches for its form. Material without form is an element one can conceive of (Picasso) but not study and certainly not work on.

Form is an apportionment of the world, a line of its discovery, signs of material laws established by art. Every art is coloured by the origin of the form. We do not claim anything more than the difference in intensity between the Cubists and Tatlin.[1] Besides, as signs of the laws of matter, forms are not elementary; they merely express our attitudes to the elements of the world; they are not given but derived. Yet the laws of the world are normative though approximate, which is why the forms in question are not part of our personality but rather of that 'particular kind of eternity diligently stored away by mathematicians and philosophers', to whom we legitimately, in our opinion, add artists. Art was defined through its attitude to form; we use the latter to establish borderlines, as far as art can be divided. Old painting as concluded with Picasso accepted form as an element presenting us with colour and space. We postulate the primacy of colour (material) and space (volume) whose interaction produces form. The fragmentary information reaching us from Paris, from which we have been isolated for more than six years, consistently repeats the news that in his latest works Picasso has returned to the 'Ingres tradition'. It confirms our view mentioned above. The French school of painting is dying within its own tradition. An art incapable of transcending form and destroying the notion of its elementary nature and primacy, finds itself in an inescapable circle. The laws thereby established by art are objective and sufficient for the eye to obey them willingly. Different materials tend to assume certain forms: it is not expedient to use glass where wood is more suitable. It is precisely the goal of the artist to find the forms to express their materials as completely as possible and to produce lasting unions. In the world of painting such unions are unique.

We do not wish to be accused of superfluous exactitude and a tendency to impose mathematical methods on painting. Our desire to be scientific in art is not identical with the desire of mathematicians. But we would be negating both mathematics and art if they were transformed from the tools of human cognition into closed, self-justifying worlds. We do not know and shall probably never know where geometry ends and painting begins, for the world to which we apply geometric measures along with the measures of art has no knowledge of either the former or the latter. By disturbing the unity of the universe we intend to grasp this unity's quality and above all its reality, for – to repeat it again – reality is precisely that which we ourselves can neither communicate nor suggest to others. Space studied by a geometrician as one of the properties of the universe is equally indispensable for an artist, since for him it is, too, a property of the universe. And when mathematics is enriched by a new knowledge of space it is thereby enriching art as well. We are no longer astonished at Cubism's discarding the refuted notion of space and teaching us a plastic perception of a new one, but we have reasons to reproach the Cubist artists for searching for their plastic dimension of space in their own personalities, thus confining themselves within the same illusions that used to limit the Naturalists. A sense of depth on Picasso's canvases is by no means less illusory than in the paintings of a Russian Wanderer, whereas we want to see more powerful efforts destroying the illusory essence of our notions of space. We believe that only an art that does not

[1] 'Besides, the difference between the Impressionists and ourselves lies only in intensity: we do not claim anything more than that.' (Gleizes and Metzinger)

find its elements on the surface of the ready-made forms of reality as they appear to us but, on the contrary, constructs these forms out of materials and dimensions of live experience – the art of Tatlin – is capable of such an effort. It does it by attributing real spatial relationships to new works of art. Following Tatlin we call these works corner and central counter-reliefs of a higher type.

Since the Impressionist era one can observe a growing orientation towards the real understanding of space, resulting in the creation of a new objectively extended construction. The Impressionists pulverized the world; they made us aware of the depth of the light, but the light excluded all form. Very soon the inborn instinct of the real motivated the masters of painting to restore visible forms in their illusory space on the surface. But even that proved insufficient; the reaction to Impressionism as to one of the gravest diseases of the eye was too strong. It was necessary to search for a more palpable depth that would provide our sense of reality with at least some confidence in the concreteness of the illusory worlds arising on the two-dimensional surface of a painting. The Cubists satisfied that need by destroying banal notions of perspective. They connected the concept of depth with non-Euclidian geometry, introducing time where a three-dimensional space proved inadequate. However, the Cubists' spatial enrichment of painting was no less illusory than all the efforts in that direction by their predecessors. Their activity was grappling with extraordinary difficulties in vain: the surface, resisting all attempts at extracting from it either depth or sequence in time, defied all efforts aimed at its destruction. One had to look for the way out not merely beyond the canvas but beyond the whole tradition of European art. This way out has been found by those artists strong enough to study dimensions in real spatial relationships. This principle underlay Tatlin's first counter-reliefs.[1]

We do not wish to be misunderstood. Our method of investigation applied to a particular sphere of modern painting, and furthermore our conclusions will strike some as being too abstract. However, we ourselves do not permit this in our attitude to art. Certainly not because art is mysterious and beautiful but because the live reality embodying plastic forces of the universe is too concrete. The rhythms we live by are strangled. The struggle carried out by life is precisely the struggle with concreteness saturating the world; we do not have the strength to weaken the pressure exercised by that powerful concreteness; when the rhythms are no longer capable of serving our needs we use our minds, knowing that the mechanical work accomplished with their help is an illusion born out of the relativity of human cognition. If at the same time our own belief is transferred to those whom we address we may regard our efforts as fruitful. That is why we apply crude abstractions even to such complex, live constructions as counter-reliefs. We are also convinced that there was nothing in what we said that might prevent those who have eyes to see and to understand.

[1] We do not wish to determine who was the first to examine live space. Most probably it was done by the first discoverers of the Universe. The question whether Picasso or Tatlin built the first painterly relief is of much more significance to us.

(1921)

Н. Пунин, Татлин (Против кубизма). Издание Отдела ИЗО Наркомпроса, Петроград, 1921, 26 pp., 16 illustrations.

Punin: *see* commentary on p. 346.

The date of the text's completion (February 1921) proves that the book must have been started right after the pamphlet (*see* p. 344) and was written intensively throughout late 1920 and early 1921, i.e. during the exhibition of the model of the *Monument to the Third International* in Petrograd and Moscow or immediately afterwards.

The writing of the monograph in the circumstances attending the appearance of one of the first outstanding works of Soviet art – in the atmosphere of public meetings, controversy and struggle around it – was in itself an 'act' determining the meaning and pathos of the book. With it Punin introduced into Russian art criticism a new type of monograph (without the artist's biography) dealing with current issues in art and written in a romantic and elevated style. On the frontispiece is a dedication 'to the students of the Free State Studios' and the date 'February 1921'. The author, an active member of the Department of Fine Arts, participated in the reform of art education, so his dedication was not accidental. The frontispiece reproduces a 1916 photograph of Tatlin (*see* III. 94); at the end of the book there are eleven black-and-white reproductions of his works from various creative periods, three photographs of the first model for the Monument and a reproduction of a project executed by one of the students at the Studio of Materials, Volume and Construction.

Against Cubism is a manifesto-type subtitle. It clearly indicated the basic idea of Punin's monograph, which proclaimed the innovative character of Tatlin's art and his contribution to the general aim of achieving a leading place for Soviet artistic culture on the world scale. However, Punin's comparative method and arguments are not based on in-depth research. His only source of information on Cubism was the Russian translation of *Du Cubisme*. He had not seen any of Picasso's recent works, and ignored artistic tendencies in France and elsewhere in Western and Central Europe which had evolved from Cubism. Punin profitably developed the point of Tatlin's creative transcendence of Cubism already touched upon by Isakov (*see* p. 334). In his book, Punin – so far from focusing exclusively on Tatlin's art – began a revaluation of the artistic tradition which nurtured the most recent trends in Russian art. He sums up the same ideas in a 1923 article, 'Review of New Tendencies in the Art of Petrograd ' (*see* Bibliog.: Punin, 1923). Here he overcomes his insistence on Tatlin as an unparalleled innovator and places Malevich and Matiushin next to him as the 'initiators' of the search for a new art that would overcome Cubism – a search pursued by a wide circle of young artists: Miturich, Bruni, Tyrsa, Lebedev, Lapshin and others, whose painting and drawing he analyses extensively.

The chapters of the monograph: I. Exposition; II. The Eye; III. Material and its Volume; IV. The Formula of Saturation; V. Rhythm; VI. The Object and a List of Tatlin's Works. (About the latter *see* 'List', p. 240.) The list of works ends with Tatlin's two programmatic mottoes: 1913: 'Let us place the eye under the control of touch'; 1920: 'Through the discovery of material to [the creation of] a new object.'

We have reproduced the first three parts of the monograph, dealing with the basic principles of the author's approach. At the end of the third part we have omitted a paragraph connecting that part with the following ones.

The works referred to: Gleizes and Metzinger, *Du Cubisme,* (*see* 'Questionnaire' and 'Metzinger', pp. 262, 263) was published in Russian in two translations – the one mentioned by Punin (Petersburg, 1913) and another one under the initials M.V. (Moscow, 1913).

At the end of part I Punin quotes his own words from an article (*see* Bibliog.: Punin, 9 February 1919) in which commenting on the achievements of the Suprematists and on Tatlin's temporary silence, he predicted a new upsurge in Tatlin's creative activity that was indeed to follow soon.

'Cézanne according to Bernard' (p. 390) refers to Cézanne's opinions reported by his friend Émile Bernard. Punin must have used the Russian edition of Bernard's book. (Э. Бернар, *Воспоминания о Сезанне,* Москва, 1912, translated by Konchalovskii.)

The paintings referred to: On Tatlin's *Bouquet see* Sarab'ianov, p. 51. *The Return* – the original title for *Fishmonger* (*see* Sarab'ianov, p. 49 f.). *Nude* – probably identical with the one reproduced on III. 79 (*see* Sarab'ianov, p. 54) Subsequently Punin would differentiate it even more sharply from Cubism as being strongly associated with the Russian icon through both its composition (the formal structure) and light. (Н.Н. Пунин, 'Новейшие течения в русском искусстве' (1-я лекция), in: *Традиции новейшего русского искусства.* Издание Государственного Русского музея, 1927, p. 8.)

Body painting (*korpusnaia okraska, korpusnaia zhivopis'*): body paint (*korpusnaia kraska*), which was used in old Russian icon painting, is a non-transparent paint mixed with white body colour. Punin uses the term body painting to describe raw surfaces with homogeneous tonality and without glazing.

Budetlianstvo – 'As for Futurism as the realm of time' – refers to Khlebnikov's '*budetlianstvo*'. (*See* Strigalev, p. 15.)

[Maiakovskii on Tatlin]

[1] ... He mentioned the names: Picasso and Tatlin. Picasso is a Cubist, Tatlin is a counter-reliefist.

[2] ... I am looking at the catalogue of the Russian art exhibition in Berlin that happens to lie on his [Picasso's] table. I ask: 'does it really satisfy you – to take apart a violin for the thousandth time yet again, to produce, as a result, a violin made of tin that no one would even buy, is impossible to play on and designed exclusively for hanging there and delighting the artist's eye?
Here a Russian, Tatlin, is presented in the catalogue. For a long time he has been saying that, instead of mutilating the beautiful tin and iron, now used for tasteless constructions, artists should provide them with form.'

[3] ... Besides our organizational work, we have produced the first art objects of the post-October epoch (Tatlin's Monument to the Third International, Meierkhol'd's Mystery-Bouffe, Kamenskii's Sten'ka Razin).

(1923)

[1] *'Открытое письмо к А.В. Луначарскому', in: Владимир Маяковский, Полное собрание сочинений в 13 томах, Москва, 1952, vol. XII, p. 17* (published first: *Вестник театра*, 30 November 1920).
A polemic piece of writing (excerpt), a response to Lunacharskii's contribution to the discussion of the play *Dawns*, performed in the First Theatre of the RSFSR (22 Nov. 1920).

[2] *Владимир Маяковский, 'Семидневный смотр французской живописи' (Главка 'Пикассо'), in: Владимир Маяковский, op. cit., 1957, vol. IV, p. 246.*
Except from his article 'Seven-day Survey of French Painting'. The text was made into a book, reworked and supplemented in January 1923 from the sketches written during Maiakovskii's trip abroad in the autumn of 1922 and published that same year.

[3] *Владимир Маяковский, 'За что борется Леф?' in: Владимир Маяковский,1959, vol. XII, p. 42.*
The article was first published in March 1923 in the journal *LEF*, no. 1, as one of three editorials printed in the section entitled 'Programme'. It was written by Maiakovskii and signed by all members of the editorial board: N. Aseev, B. Arvatov, O. Brik, B. Kushner, V. Maiakovskii, S. Tret'iakov and N. Chuzhak.

Maiakovskii, Vladimir Vladimirovich (1893–1930), a poet, publicist and painter: a leader of the avant-garde in the Soviet Union. Creative and personal contacts between Maiakovskii and Tatlin had their beginnings in the pre-Revolutionary years. Both participated in the movement of young poets and artists. Tatlin was the first to illustrate Maiakovskii's works (*see* Zhadova, p. 129). There was a project for a joint Maiakovskii–Tatlin stage design for *Mystery-Bouffe* in Petrograd (the production failed to materialize). In late 1920 Maiakovskii and Meierkhol'd asked Tatlin to provide stage designs for the Moscow production of *Mystery-Bouffe*. He was prevented from doing this by his preoccupation with the preparations for exhibiting the model of the Monument to the Third International in Moscow. Nor were they able to work together on the first production of Maiakovskii's *The Bathhouse*. (*See* 'Artist or,' and commentary, pp. 314-15.) Maiakovskii saw the model while it was still in Petrograd and he not only accepted the project but immediately became its vehement defender and popularizer. According to a contemporary, he called it 'the first monument without a beard' at the public meeting in the Cézanne club in VKhUTEMAS, where Tatlin made a report on his project and showed the photographs of the model. (*See* Bibliog.: Khardzhiev, 1975.)

That meeting must have taken place around 10 December 1920 (before the model was taken to Moscow). On 14 December the artist Kliment Red'ko, then a student of VKhUTEMAS, wrote in his diary: 'Tatlin says: My own path leads to the material, i.e. the architectural form. ...In my opinion Tatlin is a practical creator of genius who caused a revaluation of values. His great achievement is in designing the project for the Monument to the Third International.' (*See* Bibliog.: Red'ko, 1974.)

[2] It is quite likely that Maiakovskii mentioned the project for the Monument to the Third International during his encounter with Picasso in Paris in the autumn of 1922, when discussing the first exhibition of Soviet art abroad (Berlin, 1922), where Tatlin presented his works preceding the project. (*See* Tatlin at Exhibitions, p. 493.)

[1] Maiakovskii's highly polemical article, contrasting Tatlin with Cubism and Picasso, echoes Punin's view (*see Tatlin*, p. 347) and testifies to the paramount importance of Tatlin's creative contribution and Constructivism for Maiakovskii's efforts to popularize the new role of Soviet art in the West.

[2] In his Parisian sketch Maiakovskii developed and elaborated his own view of the relationship between Tatlin's art and Picasso's – a view previously expressed in his 1920 'Open Letter to A.V. Lunacharskii'. When Maiakovskii's meeting with Picasso took place in late 1922, the positions of the French and the Russian artist differed even more. In 1922 the poet wrote thus about Constructivism with Tatlin at the head of the movement in plastic arts: 'For the first time it was from Russia and not from France that a new word in art – Constructivism – emerged. One is even astonished to find this word in the French lexicon.' ('Записки Людогуся' [Маяковский], Париж, in: *Владимир Маяковский, Полное собрание сочинений в 13 томах*, Москва, 1957, vol. IV. p. 212. Tatlin appears in Maiakovskii's poetry (*see* 'To the Workers of Kursk Who Extracted the First Ore – a Temporary Monument Executed by Vladimir Maiakovskii.' ['Рабочим Курска, добывшим первую руду, временный памятник работы Владимира Маяковского', *Владимир Маяковский*, op. cit., 1957, vol. III, p. 161]).

It was to Maiakovskii that Tatlin wrote (on 6 August 1922) requesting him to look after the safety of his 'temporary monument', i.e. the model of the Tower of the Third International, at the time when the fate of the model was a source of anxiety to him. (*See* 'Letter to Maiakovskii', p. 245.) In 1925 Maiakovskii, in his capacity as a member of the organizing committee of the Soviet section at the International Exhibition of Modern Decorative and Industrial Art, made every effort to bring about the construction of a second model of the Monument to the Third International, which was displayed at the exhibition (Ill. 186–7) and won its author a gold medal.

[3] It was programmatic that in his editorial in the first issue of *LEF* Maiakovskii should include the Monument to the Third International among 'the first works of art of the October era'. The journal of the Left Front of Arts – *LEF* – was founded and edited by Maiakovskii and was published in 1923–5 (seven issues appeared). In his draft plan for *LEF* in late 1922 in the section '3. The Practice of Art (Samples)' Maiakovskii listed the following poets and artists whose works he intended to popularize: 'Maiakovskii, Aseev, Tret'iakov, Pasternak, Kruchenykh, Neznamov, Kamenskii, Bol'shakov, Tatlin, Rodchenko, Lavinskii, Popova, Stepanova, the Constructivists.' (*See Владимир Маяковский*, op. cit., 1961, vol. XIII, p. 405.)

Tatlin also happened to be the artist who attended Maiakovskii on his last journey. Assisted by the students from VKhUTEIN, Tatlin himself mounted a hearse on a lorry to transport Maiakovskii's corpse across Moscow to the

Novodevichii cemetery. The sides of the vehicle were hung with sheets of white tin, which made it look like a huge metal socle-pedestal carrying the coffin upholstered with red cloth. (III. 290–2)

Mystery-Bouffe produced by Meierkhol'd: a stage production of Maiakovskii's play by Meierkhol'd (*see* 'From Kut's Notes', commentary on p. 313) in collaboration with Maiakovskii on 7 November 1918 in Petrograd and with Bebutov on 1 May 1921 in Moscow.

Sten'ka Razin – 'The People's Heart' – a long poem by V. Kamenskii, published in book form in Moscow in 1918.

N. Punin, About 'Zangezi'

There are some events the meaning of which becomes clear only long after they have taken place. Such an event was Tatlin's production of Khlebnikov's heroic poem 'Zangezi'[1]. The poem was performed twice[2] before a full house, tense with attention, and yet even some well-meaning and sincere people were saying: 'We have not understood a single word.' So difficult it is to comprehend and appreciate the unusual and the unfamiliar. 'Popularization' cannot help here; Tatlin did everything to facilitate the understanding of the production: the actors were students of the College of Mining and the Academy of Arts and not professionals, in order to avoid distracting the audience from the poem itself and obscuring its meaning through actors' mannerisms; commentators explaining the poem were introduced;[3] finally, Tatlin himself provided a simple and clever parallel to the linguistic material of the poem with the paintings produced in his studio.[4] And all that proved insufficient. People failed to understand the most significant part – the one that did not even seem capable of causing any perplexity and should have been self-evident.

The cause of such incomprehension lies, to my mind, in our predisposition for the habitual as well as for a horrible and victorious rationalism in art. Nobody cares to feel – everybody prefers to analyse, a veritable 'formal method'[5] [an omission in the text] – our contemporaries. Typically, one of those who claimed that he 'did not understand a single word', after the talk by Professor Iakubinskii[6] (in which, after the first part of the performance, he briefly interpreted the formal structure of the poem), said: 'Now I am starting to understand something.'

Khlebnikov's poem can be understood only after perceiving its irrationalism.

… I am singing and raving
I am hopping and dancing on the rock[7]

'Zangezi' is not an experiment in plot structure or a laboratory for neologisms, neither is it a rationalistic composition according to the laws of fate; it is one of the most synthetic plotless mysteries of our age,[8] a marvellous stupendous shawl, a cloth hanging over our century; Khlebnikov is a weaver; death, war, revolution, bankruptcy of Western European science, language are the yarns for his loom.[9] One cannot perceive his poetry otherwise, one cannot even ask the question that the audience during those two evenings – wrongly – asked whether his laws of time[10] and the theory of word roots were correct and scientifically grounded. But even if they were, indeed, silly and untrue (which nobody dared to say), even then their poetic significance would remain intact. One is reminded of a comment by Pushkin: poetry should be a little bit silly. Was art not fighting against its sworn enemy, rationalism, already in his time?

Tatlin produced 'Zangezi' according to the principle 'the word is the building unit, the material is the unit of organized space',[11] thereby equating the artist's work and the poet's. But I do not consider that to be the main thing; the novelty lies elsewhere. Tatlin is a sufficiently great master to avoid errors in exhibiting poetic and artistic genres, to find the contact and unite heterogeneous material into a single whole. And who would dare to question Tatlin's sense of the material (his taste) after everything he has done and everything that has been said about him in the past few years? It is far more important and interesting that 'Zangezi' was on the whole Tatlin's production, i.e. he was in this case the creator of the theatre and the action – he was producer, actor and artist at the same time. The task was the more difficult since 'Zangezi' was not a play but a poem which had to be presented on stage, i.e. one had to invent or rather, to find dramatic action in it. At the moment I am not going to describe the devices Tatlin used to solve that problem (he discussed some of them in his article 'O Zangezi' ['On Zangezi'] in *Zhizn' iskusstva*, no. 18)[12] or to discuss his technical ingenuity and wit; I would only like to declare that, to my mind, Tatlin is one of the most sensitive people we have so far as the theatre is concerned.[13]

One may be an expert in stage techniques and acting techniques, one may have a substantial theatrical experience and never commit an error in the realm of the theatre as an art[istic] form – and yet remain alien and dead to the spirit of the theatre. In fact, that is what happens very often. In Tatlin the true living spirit of the theatre lives on. When Gauss in his time read a short paper by Lobachevskii he wrote to Bolyai that an obscure Russian mathematician is the only person in the world thinking in the spirit of geometry.[14] To think and to feel in the spirit of the material (or, in a wider sense, form) one works with, is probably one of the objective signs of what we call genius and is in any case a mark of significant talent.

209, 210 The fact that the hall of the Museum of Artistic Culture where Khlebnikov's poem was staged was permeated with the spirit of the theatre despite the 'domestic' character of the production and the 'crudity' of its technical side,[15] gives us the right to claim that we witnessed an initiative of a powerful theatrical charge.[16] It may even be likely that the limited means of expression (for instance, the absence of professional, i.e. worn out, actors turned into

213–215 robots),[17] as well as elementary lighting techniques (two simple lights wandering across the hall), the absence of costume and make-up for the majority of the performers, contributed towards heightening that spirit: laying bare, as it were, the very essence of theatre, its unique power over time and space. Even so, all the missing elements (the stage, the theatrical machinery, elaborate lighting, etc.) were absent by chance: but it was Tatlin himself who excluded professional costumes, make-up as well as curtain and wings; thus, here we deal with a conscious act, with a will guided by a higher instinct or what we call intuition. It is

209, 210 to the power of intuition that we are indebted for the small hall of the Miatlev House[18] (rather than the academic theatres,[19] innumerable vegetating studios and FEKS[20], filled with the true spirit of the theatre, old like art itself and young at heart no matter what the Alexandrians[21] do and the Eccentrics[22] say).

That is why the production of 'Zangezi' is an event; it is prevented from being understood and impressive by those very same Alexandrians and FEKS; their day is today: Tatlin's and Khlebnikov's day is still somewhere ahead. But when it does come people will recall those two evenings more than once, racking their brains in an effort to reconstruct what happened, and those reconstructing it will be applauded not just by stars alone.

Н.Н. Пунин, 'Зангези', Жизнь искусства, 1923, no. 20, 22 May 1923, pp. 10–12.

The manuscript of the article has not survived; the above text has been reprinted from the journal version. The text in the journal had some bad misprints, distortions and omissions; all those errors have been corrected in the present publication without special mention.

The theatre of Khlebnikov frequently attracted the attention of his contemporaries. Only one of his plays was produced on stage in his lifetime: a production of his play *Death's Error* (in which he participated) in September 1920 in Rostov.

The meeting of Tatlin and Khlebnikov was not accidental. As early as November 1917 Tatlin and Khlebnikov conceived a project for producing a number of his plays – *Death's Error, Thirteen in the Air* (the text of this play has been lost) and *Madame Lenin* (*see* Syrkina, p. 160, Ill. 207) – with Khlebnikov intending to produce the plays on stage himself. (It should be mentioned in parenthesis that Meierkhol'd was in that same year planning to produce *Death's Error* in his studio on Borodinskaia Street, together with the artist Dmitriev.) Interestingly enough, as Punin recalled later, in December 1917 he and the composer Lur'e, who wrote the music for *Death's Error,* went to request Lunacharskii's permission to use the Hermitage theatre for the production of that play by Khlebnikov. (Н.Н. Пунин, 'В дни красного Октября', *Жизнь искусства,* no. 816, 8 November 1921.) That visit to Lunacharskii might have been connected with the above mentioned project of Tatlin to produce Khlebnikov's plays.

Zangezi is a multidimensional programmatic work by Khlebnikov (a 'supernarrative' [*sverkhpovest'*], to use his own term), presenting a montage of his works written between 1920 and 1922, self-contained and different in genre. It was probably the idea of this monumental work that Khlebnikov had in mind when writing to Maiakovskii in February 1921: 'I am contemplating a work that would require the participation of the whole of mankind, all three billions, for whom acting in that play would be mandatory. But ordinary language is not suitable for this work and I have to create a new one, step by step.' (В. Хлебников, *Собрание произведений*, Ленинград, 1933, vol. V, p. 317.) Almost immediately after the publication of *Zangezi* (it appeared in bookshops in the latter half of August 1922), Tatlin decided to produce it on stage. The following item appeared in the magazine *Zhizn' iskusstva*, no. 39, 3 October 1922: 'The Union of New Tendencies in Art is planning to arrange a number of performances of various arts on the premises of the Museum of Artistic Culture (9 Isaakievskaia Square). The following productions are supposed to take place: *Zangezi* by Khlebnikov, directed by Tatlin and Radlov; *Victory over the Sun* by Kruchenykh and Khlebnikov, directed by Matiushin and Malevich [the latter wrote only the prologue to that play-opera – A.P.] and *Death's Error* by Khlebnikov, as well as a number of public lectures and debates: Malevich "Proving through Painting", Matiushin "Spatial Realism", Punin "Astral Language", Lapshin "A Critique of Painting", and S. Radlov "On the New Theatre".'

Radlov. It is not accidental that this programme, almost exclusively devoted to Khlebnikov (or linked with him in some way) and including Punin's lecture, mentions Radlov's name among the circle of Khlebnikov's friends and followers. (Every item in the programme had some relation to Khlebnikov.) Radlov was a well-known left-wing theatre producer, an author of some experimental productions in the Theatre Research Studio, who was genuinely interested in the 'trans-rational' language of Khlebnikov and Kruchenykh (С. Радлов, *Десять лет в театре*, Ленинград, 1929, pp. 114–15, 119, 123). He also highly valued Tatlin's art and regarded him as 'a fine master'. However, the Tatlin–Radlov creative union was evidently soon to break up because of theoretical differences. Tatlin considered *Zangezi* to be 'too innovative a play' whose stage production should reject all 'existing traditions' and, most important, engage in its performance 'people untouched by theatre' ('On "Zangezi"', p. 249). Radlov, who was trying to create his own stage constructivism, could not agree with this basic premise of Tatlin and believed that 'only the talent of the actor will save the theatre' (*Жизнь искусства*, no. 1, 3 January 1923). Radlov's two 1923 articles which mention Tatlin obviously resulted from their arguments. (С. Радлов, 'Непременно ли конструктивизм?' *Театр*, no. 11, 11 December 1923, p. 3; С. Радлов, 'О чистой стихии актерского искусства, in: *Арена*, Петроград, 1924, p. 101.)

The musicologist Druskin, in those days a young composer and creator of the music for that production, recalls Radlov as a potential producer of *Zangezi*: 'The play *Zangezi* by Khlebnikov with my music was performed in the Miatlev House; I cannot recall the name of the producer but I do remember the arrogance with which Sergei Radlov, then already a well-known director, gave his refusal when a shy 18-year-old – the author of the music – approached him with the request to direct the production.' (М.С. Друскин, *Исследования. Воспоминания*, Ленинград, 1977, p. 254.)

Supernarrative. A wide range of issues tackled in that supernarrative, including Khlebnikov's meditations on the path taken by humanity from prehistoric times towards the future, echoed in many ways the cosmic ideas that Tatlin put into his project for the Monument to the Third International. First of all, Tatlin the designer, 'a visionary of the blades and a stern bard of the propeller' according to Khlebnikov's poetic formula, could not help being carried away by the Constructivist poetics of the several planes in *Zangezi* that make up the supernarrative. Tatlin created or, rather, constructed a synthetic production (a 'performance plus a lecture plus an exhibition of material constructions', as he himself defined it) in which he functioned in three guises – as the director, the artist and the leading actor. Tatlin was to a certain extent continuing the tradition of the first Futurist productions of 1913, *Victory Over the Sun* and *Vladimir Maiakovskii*, in which the authors (Maiakovskii and Kruchenykh) also functioned as directors and actors (Maiakovskii also as artist) – as well as the first production of Maiakovskii's *Mystery-Bouffe* directed by Meierkhol'd together with the author. Tatlin's incorporation of the publicist element into the production of *Zangezi* (the interruption of the performance by lectures and exhibits – posters, material constructions – as well as directly addressing the audience), and the deliberate use of non-professional actors, go back to the two Futurist productions of 1913 which, according to Kruchenykh, were 'the first experiments of the publicist theatre'. (А.Е. Крученых, Наш выход [reminiscences], TsGALI, fond 1334.)

We have been able to find out that the performers' recitation of *Zangezi* was co-ordinated by Vysheslavtseva, a reciter and linguist studying recitation (*Красная газета*, 8 May 1923; С.Г. Вышеславцева, 'О моторных импульсах стиха', in: *Поэтика*, Ленинград, 1927, p. 61).

It is worth mentioning that Khlebnikov's description of Tatlin in the poem dedicated to him 'from the team of sun-snarers' ('Tatlin', p. 336) is directly related to the leading idea and the title of Kruchenykh's opera *Victory over the Sun*, which was highly appreciated by Khlebnikov. Tatlin had worked 'with enthusiasm' on the production, and both 'the performance and the author enjoyed a great success'. (*Советское искусство*, no. 43, 7 September 1934; *Литературная газета*, no. 53, 24 September 1935.)

Press reaction. Tatlin's innovative production received positive as well as extremely negative reviews.

The 'trans-rational' poet Tufanov, like Punin, had a very high opinion of the production (*see* p. 400.). On the other hand, negative views were expressed by the literary critic Kazanskii, (Б. Казанский, 'Хлебников в постановке Татлина', *Записки передвижного театра*, no. 58, 5 June 1923); by Iutkevich, a budding director and stage designer (*see* Bibliog.: Iutkevich, 1923), and by the theatre critic Red'ko. (А. Редько, 'Заумный театр', in: А. Редько, *Театр и революция театральных форм*, Москва, 1926, pp. 112–13.)

We should also mention Miklashevskii, a theatre historian and director, who wrote in his book *A Hypertrophy in Art*: 'I have discussed Tatlin extensively since I consider him the most outstanding and gifted representative of

Russian Constructivism who displayed his talent in the sphere of stage production (*Zangezi*) ...' (*See* Bibliog.: Miklashevskii, 1924, p. 66.)

Tatlin returned to the idea of a new production of Zangezi. According to Bruni–Bal'mont's verbal testimony, in 1925 in Bruni's apartment on the premises of VKhUTEMAS Tatlin and Bruni discussed the possibility of staging the supernarrative. That same year at an exhibition in the Tsvetkov Gallery (Moscow) Tatlin displayed two studies for the first production of *Zangezi*. During 1925–7, while teaching at the Kiev College of Art, Tatlin conceived another project for a production of *Zangezi*, recalled by the director Begicheva. (А. Бегічева, 'Комісар Нарком- просу', *Вітчизна*, n. 2, 1968, pp. 159, 160, 163, 167.)

In 1965 M.P. Kholodnaia told the present writer that in Kiev Tatlin approached a well-known Ukrainian director, Kurbas-Les', with a suggestion to produce *Zangezi*: 'Tatlin beautifully recited Khlebnikov's poetry, pronouncing some parts of it as Khlebnikov himself would have done – "swallowing" the endings and whispering – imitating him marvellously. He was obsessed with the idea of staging Khlebnikov in the College of Art; he wanted to make use of his previous production and to introduce a female choir; he was even teaching them to pronounce some words of Khlebnikov – but he did not carry it through, as he left Kiev.'

According to the verbal testimony of Pavlovskii, a student of Tatlin, in 1928 Tatlin tried once again to stage *Zangezi* and, as in 1923, he was going to direct the new production using only non-professional actors – the students of VKhUTEMAS.

The tradition. The 1923 production of *Zangezi* on the amateur stage of the Museum of Artistic Culture started its own tradition and it should be seen not only in the context of the Constructivist theatre of the 1920s, but also in connection with the theatre of the absurd started in the latter half of the 1920s by the Oberiu (a Post-Futurist group from Leningrad), as well as in connection with the innovative tendencies of some productions of the Soviet theatre in the 1960–70s.

Khlebnikov's work in general, and his theatre and the experiment of Tatlin's production of *Zangezi* in particular, doubtlessly influenced the dramaturgy of the Oberiu (*see* p. 402), their provoking performances full of theatricality and, according to one of them, his own practice of stage direction. It is interesting that among the audience at *Zangezi*'s performance was Bakhterev, one of the future Oberiuts, subsequently a poet, playwright and producer of the Oberiuts-style plays *My Mum is Covered in Watches* by Kharms and A. Vvedenskii (1926) and *Elizaveta Bam* by Kharms (1928). In the same White Hall of the Miatlev House where Tatlin produced *Zangezi*, three years later a production of *My Mum is Covered in Watches* was planned in which Bakhterev participated as a stage designer and one of the directors. (On the continuity between the production of *Zangezi* and that first play of the Oberiuts – which was never actually produced – *see* I. Bakhterev's reminiscences (И. Бахтерев, 'Когда мы были молоды- ми', in: *Воспоминания о Заболоцком*, Москва, 1977, p. 77ff). In a letter of 14 January 1967 addressed to the present author Bakhterev communicated some remarkable facts not mentioned by any reviewers of the production of *Zangezi*: 'The performance was to take place not only on stage but also in the foyer during the intermission, for which Tatlin's 'astral boards' were moved from the stage and Tatlin himself, dressed as Zangezi, was to talk about the connections between the word and its visual incarnations in texture... For the Oberiuts' creative work Khleb- nikov's discoveries were of crucial significance. All of us believed that we were continuing his work.' It is worthy of notice that there was a direct contact between Tatlin and Leningrad Post-Futurists, who traced their roots to Khlebnikov and announced in a group manifesto their orientation towards the left painting of Filonov and Malevich. In 1929 Tatlin made illustrations for a book of verse for children by the leading Oberiu poet Daniel Kharms. (*See* p. 133 n16).

Notes

1 Punin's belief proved to be prophetic. Only very recently has there been an attempt by the historiography of Soviet theatre to define the role and significance of Tatlin's production of Khlebnikov's *Zangezi*. (Д. Золотницкий, *Будни и праздники театрального октября*, Ленинград, 1978, pp. 27–9. A.M. Ripellino, *Majakovskij e il teatro d'avanguardia, 1959, p. 48.)*

2 There were three performances of Zangezi: on May 11, 13 and 30, 1923 in the great hall of the Museum of Artistic Culture. (*See* the poster for the production, Ill. 211; Bibliog.: Zhadova, 1980, p. 207.)

3 The author means his own paper as well as those of L.P. Iakubinskii (1892–1945), a linguist and literary scholar, one of the founders of OPOIaZ (*see* 'On "Zangezi"' commentary p. 249). The text of Iakubinskii's paper on Khlebnikov's language–creating art is, unfortunately, unknown; Punin most probably read his paper, previously presented on 11 September 1922 at the meeting of the Free Philosophical Association. (On this paper by Punin *see* Н. Лапшин, 'Поэт времени', *Жизнь искусства*, no. 37, 19 September 1922.) 'Khlebnikov introduces the world to a new stage of development as opposed to the nineteenth century with its spatial consciousness and measures; he lives with the awareness of time – Time, a measure of the world. In all his poems we see this "multitemporality" [*raznovremen'e*] starting with rhythm and ending with imagery. Through "The Trumpet of the Marians" [the title of one of Khlebnikov's declarations – A.P.] he announces a new division of the realm of time into the countries of the old men and of the young ones. Khlebnikov found a measurability of events, their law' – such was Punin's view of Khlebnikov. (*See* also Tufanov, p. 400.)

In introducing his production the 'explanatory' lectures by Iakubinski and Punin, Tatlin followed a tradition founded by Meierkhol'd and Maiakovskii: in 1918 Lunacharskii said an introductory word before the premiere of *Mystery-Bouffe*. (*See* 'Maiakovskii on Tatlin', commentary p. 395.)

4 In his article on the stage version of *Zangezi* Tatlin wrote: 'Parallel to the word structure I decided to introduce a material construction. By this means the work of two people with different areas of specialization can be fused into one whole, in order to make Khlebnikov's creative work accessible to the masses.' (*See* 'On "Zangezi"', p. 248). Some students from Tatlin's Studio of Volume, Construction and Colours collaborated with him on the production of *Zangezi* as artists-designers. One of them, Khapaev, who was involved in the material realization of sound and colour, wrote in his autobiographical sketch of 1923: 'In 1923 I was engaged in some research work for the production of *Zangezi* and made fifty samples of flat surface (material ones).' (TsGAOR, fond 2555, inventory 1, file 647, p. 30, information Zhadova.)

As stage designer and producer who conceived the stage version of *Zangezi* as 'a performance + lecture + exhibition of material constructions', Tatlin doubtless considered the whole production to be a result of the collective effort of 'Tatlin's Studio'. Immediately after the performance of *Zangezi* the drawings for the production (stage designs and costumes) were displayed at the Petrograd Exhibition of Artists of All Tendencies which opened on 15 May 1923; the drawings were listed not as individual works by a single artist but were marked with a round seal inscribed 'Tatlin's Studio'. (*See* Bibliog.: *Tatlin*, 1977, p. 8; 'The Initiative Individual', p. 237.)

5 The 'formal method' theory in literary scholarship analyses a literary text on the formal level denying its content structure. Such a one-sided approach to art was typical of the Russian formalist school in its early period (1914–24); subsequently representatives of this school combined formal analysis with semantic interpretation of the text. Followers of the formalist school, particularly members of OPOIaZ, were closely connected with the theory and practice of Russian Futurism. Iakubinskii was a representative of that school, cf. his early writings on poetic language in: *Поэтика*, Петроград, 1919. For more detail on the formal method *see* V. Erlich, *Russian Formalism. History – Doctrine*. The Hague, 1954; A. Hansen-Löwe, *Der Russische Formalismus*, Vienna, 1978.

6 On Iakubinskii *see* n3 and 5; *Краткая литературная энциклопедия*, Москва, vol. VIII, 1975, columns 1069–70.

7 Fourteenth surface of *Zangezi*: В. Хлебников, *Собрание произведений*, Ленинград, vol. III, 1931, p. 343.

8 It is interesting to note that Punin was one of the first to review Meierkhol'd's production of *Mystery-Bouffe*. (Н. Пунин, 'О "Мистерии-буфф" Вл. Маяковского', *Искусство коммуны*, no. 2, 15 December 1918.)

9 These themes and ideological strata of the supernarrative *Zangezi* are in accord with the concepts of the history of philosophy of some works by the reviewer himself. (Н. Пунин – Е. Полетаев, *Против цивилизации*, Петроград, 1918.)

10 Khlebnikov's so-called 'laws of time' present a mathematized philosophy of history, its mytho-poetic interpretation. (В. Хлебников, 'Наша основа', in: *В. Хлебников*, op. cit., vol. V, pp. 237–42; В. Хлебников, *Доски судьбы*, Петроград, 1922–3.) Khlebnikov was trying to bring about 'a revolution in the understanding of time encompassing the sphere of several sciences' and advocated the right to 'prophesy', to make a historical 'forecast'. (On the new interpretation of time in Khlebnikov *see* В.В. Иванов, 'Категория времени в искусстве и культуре XX века', in: *Ритм, пространство и время в литературе и искусстве*, Ленинград, 1977, pp. 45–49.) Khlebnikov's attempts to comprehend nature in its dynamic, rhythmic aspect and discover a mathematical expression of that regularity unexpectedly harmonized with the works on the theory of biorhythms by his contemporary N.Ia. Pern, a physiologist. (Н.Я. Перн, *Ритм жизни и творчества*, Ленинград – Москва, 1925.) However, Khlebnikov was apparently unfamiliar with those works of Pern that made a significant contribution to the science of chronobiology.

11 This principle of Tatlin's stage direction (*see* 'On "Zangezi"', p. 248) has its origin in the basic principle of construction in Khlebnikov's supernarrative discussed by the author in his foreword to *Zangezi*: 'The narrative is made out of words as units of construction in a building. A minor stone of words of equal size serves as the basic unit. A supernarrative, or trans-narrative (*zapovest'*), is made up from independent fragments each with a unique God, unique faith and unique regulations... The narrative of the first order is the unit of construction, the stone of the supernarrative.' (V. Khlebnikov, op.cit., vol. III, p. 317.)

12 *See* 'On Zangezi', p. 248.

13 In 1935 when Tatlin could resume his work only as an artist-stage designer, *Literaturnaia Gazeta* published an interview with him ('Tatlin in the Theatre') in which an anonymous author renders the artist's own account of a curious fact concerning the production of *Zangezi*: 'Both the performance and its creator had a sensational success; Tatlin received many congratulations from directors but not a single offer of work.' ('Tatlin in the Theatre,' p. 315)

14 Punin is mistaken in naming the Hungarian mathematician Bolyai as the addressee of Gauss's letter of 28 November 1846; it was to the Danish astronomer G.H. Schumacher that Gauss wrote on that date describing Lobachevskii's work 'On the Foundations of Geometry' as 'masterfully written in the spirit of pure geometry'. In his declaration 'The Trumpet of the Martians' (1916) Khlebnikov, who divided the whole of mankind into inventors and acquisitors, calls Gauss 'the first inventor'. (V. Khlebnikov, op. cit., vol. V, p. 153.)

15 As Tatlin and Punin point out in their articles, the stage version of *Zangezi* was performed by non-professional actors.

16 *See* 'The Initiative Individual', p. 237.

17 The actors' factory, FEKS, eccentrics – the author means a Petrograd drama studio, The Factory of the Eccentric Actor (1921–24), the first public debates of its founders, the eccentric theatre's performance of *The Marriage* (1922), which caused a scandal, and a collection of articles (Г. Козинцев, Л. Трауберг, Г. Крыжицкий, С. Юткевич, *Эксцентризм*, Петроград, 1922) by Kozintsev, Trauberg, Kryzhitskii and Iutkevich.

18 The Museum of Artistic Culture was situated in the house of the Miatlev family (9 Isaakievskaia Square).

19 The author means the dead 'classical' repertoire, stagnation in production techniques and the kind of stage design that would not go beyond a two-dimensional decorative style typical of the following academic theatres: the Theatre of Opera and Ballet (former Marynskii), the Dramatic Theatre (former Alexandrinskii) and the Opera House (former Mikhailovskii).

20 The FEKS raised the banner of 'Americanization', 'mechanization' and 'electrification' of art, proclaiming a new eccentric theatricality ('life as a stunt'), trying to create a 'topsy-turvy theatre' and orienting their work towards 'lower' genres (music-hall, circus, street show, cinema, variety show, poster). (*See* n17) In their spiteful declarations they engaged in polemics with and negation of all preceding 'left' movements in art, including Constructivism (*see* the attacks on Tatlin by Iutkevich and Trauberg, ibid.). Notwithstanding their polemics and escapades, one of the eccentrics' declarations appealed to the reputation of the Constructivists, while the list of proposed instructors for the Eccentric Theatre Studio (ibid.) mentioned Tatlin and Punin. While Tatlin was working on the production of *Zangezi* the eccentrics were in the process of preparing a second performance-stunt, *Foreign Trade Ministry On the Eiffel Tower*. This was staged after *Zangezi*, in June 1923, but the first advertisement for that 'Americanized performance' appeared in the papers earlier. The very title of the play had a transparently polemical allusion (by contrast or comparison) to the title of the project for the Monument to the Third International. Iutkevich, one of the founders of the Eccentric Theatre, rejected the innovative tendencies of Tatlin's production and severely criticized Punin's enthusiastic article as well as 'defending' theatre as such (*see* Bibliog.: Iutkevich, 1923). Tatlin's experimental production has become a significant event in theatrical Constructivism and now occupies an indisputable place in the history of Soviet theatre.

21 *See* n18.

22 *See* n17, 19.

Text and notes prepared by Aleksandr Efimovich Parnis

A.V. Tufanov, On the Stage Production of the Poem 'Zangezi' by Velemir Khlebnikov

On 11 and 13 of May in the Museum of Artistic Culture the artist Tatlin staged V. Khlebnikov's poem 'Zangezi'.

216–222

When reviewing theatre productions one can apply one of two approaches.

The common approach involves: 1) piling up special theatrical terminology: coloratura, ensemble, stunt, 'firm breasts' (Volinskii)[1] and so on, and so forth – that can be absorbed with some benefit, and 2) describing the reviewer's subjective impressions: good, bad, vague, clear, unintelligible, etc., about which the reader could not care less.

Such evaluations are written by *established* persons, with a 'world-wide reputation' and 'of considerable talent', so that thighs and breasts are specified for everyone to remember.

While all of us – to repeat it once more – are 'students', i.e. someone who studies, learns, becomes, *evolves* within a living creative current flowing toward irresistible freedom. Where the means of production for material life are unchanged we are the fluid *stanovliane*[2] [the evolving ones] leaning according to the angle of a certain existence.

For that reason we shall approach the production of the poem 'Zangezi' as directly perceived by the whole audience, i.e. we shall provide *an outline of the general sediment of the immediate reaction* and let every reader make his own individual evaluation.

So, the poem 'Zangezi' was produced on stage under the direction of the artist Tatlin, Punin and others, performed by the students of higher educational establishments (Academy of Arts, Technological Institute and the University).

213–215   On the stage there are machines, a stage-light and a tower for the hero of the poem 'Zangezi'. In the middle of the stage there is a board inscribed 'people', while at the far end of the hall above the audience similar boards say 'birds' and 'gods'.[3]

The performance opens with a choral song of the birds in which consonants predominate and a song of the gods in which vowels prevail, thus, out of the two trans-rational 'unintelligible' languages, that of the gods is less perfect since there exist only five vowel phonemes. Even in ancient languages, as, for instance, the Semitic ones (Arabic, Hebrew), vowel alternation had, according to comparative linguistics, a purely formal significance, and not a material one. The light from the stage points to the objects frozen in man's spatial perception.

N.N. Punin explains from the podium the mathematical laws of time perception, illustrating them by means of the relation between the powers of 2 and of 3, and historical events according to Khlebnikov.[4]

Then comes the unfolding of the 'descent' of the 'astral songs'[5] towards the 'boards', i.e. the people who, although they occasionally rebel and demand 'entertainment', nevertheless huddle together and recite in a chorus a monologue on the *omnipotence* of Zangezi, the verse being based on the consonant sound G:

Иди, могатырь, ...
Могей, мое я и т.д.[6]   [untranslatable play on words]

Zangezi himself recites from his tower the words of the hymn to the consonant sounds —(G), (L), (R), (M) and others, transporting his achievements in the form of written characters[7] down to the ground where they are explained with the help of drawings, and a lecture is given on the wealth of speech units in the poem, on the combination of various artistic devices, and, predominantly, on trans-sense.[8]

Above the machines, and opposite the gods and the birds, *Repentance* and *Death*[9] appear – not as boards, for some reason, but as living specific figures that provide plastic reinforcement for spatial perception.   221, 222

It would have been better to hang the boards with their respective inscriptions and to erase the latter by rotating the boards, which would be in accord with Khlebnikov's desire to destroy a spatial perception of death.

At the end, one of the boards declares:

Зангези умер...   Zangezi died...
Зарезался бритвой,   Killed himself with a razor
Оставив записку.   Leaving a note.[10]

One of the performers recites these words from among the audience but then Zangezi appears on the stage and the news of death is denied. A canvas unfolds above the stage with the inscription: '28 June 1922: the date of Velemir Khlebnikov's death.'[11]

General 'meditations at the main entrance'[12] fall into two groups:
1) If all living objects (linguistic phenomena) unfold on stage *in the process of evolution*, then how can a connection between an intuitive juxtaposition of words with altered root consonants (*mogei, ia mogeiu, mogatyr'*, etc.) and geometrical drawings of a surface crossed by a line, of rotating movement, etc., have the power of a convincing law?
2) Why are ideas (God, repentance, death) conveyed by means of both boards and living beings? Would it not have been better to place the performers behind the boards inscribed 'repentance' and 'death'? Doesn't the appearance of a psychotic violate the general style of the increasing construction of the 'astral songs' (trans-sense)? Has he not been borrowed from the theatre of the past? And why are the songs *astral*? In 'trans-sense' a spontaneous lyricism is closest to the unthinking nature, the soil.

А.В. Туфанов, 'К постановке поэмы "Зангези" Велемира Хлебникова', Красный студент,1923, по. 7–8, рр. 29–30.

A.V. Tufanov's **article** forms the second part of his 'Review of Artistic Life' published under the pen-name 'Silentium'. In the above-mentioned magazine the article was accompanied by a drawing of the *mise en scène* made by a stage artist Popov-Voronezhskii (*see* Ill. 215). Like Punin, the author of this article regarded Tatlin's production as 'an extremely valuable event in the artistic sense' (ibid., p. 28).

Tufanov, Aleksandr Vasil'evich (1877–1941), a transrational poet, who in 1925–27 was the leader of the 'Left' group within the Leningrad division of the Poets' Union. The members of the group (Kharms, Vvedenskii and others) subsequently separated (*Золова арфа*, Петроград, 1917) to found an independent Oberiu group. In the early 1930s Tufanov joined Zorved, a left-wing group of artists (Matiushin, Ender, Grinberg and others), and became an art theorist. Tufanov started as an epigone of the Symbolist and Acmeist tradition, but left it in the early 1920s and subsequently gravitated towards early Futurist poetics, predominantly in the sphere of trans-sense (*see 'К Зауми'* [Стихи и исследования о функциях согласных фонем]. Петроград, 1924; *'Ушкуйники'*, Ленинград, 1927).

Regarding himself as a follower of the Khlebnikov school, Tufanov used to sign his declarations somewhat pretentiously 'Chairman of the Trans-Rational Globe'. In his theoretical works he advocated verse without words ('I cannot retain the word and the "objectness" as art material' – from *К Zaumi*, p. 9) and elaborated semantization of individual phonemes continuing Khlebnikov's experiments: 'When approaching unthinking nature after the death of Velemir Khlebnikov I reached the most elementary material of art. The material of my art is the articulatory-auditory units of language, phonemes...' (Ibid.).

For more on Tufanov and his role in the Oberiu group *see* Л. Флейшман, 'Маргиналии к истории русского авангарда', in: *Н.М. Олейников, Стихотворения,* 1975, рр. 4–6. (И.Бахтерев, 'Когда мы были молодыми', in: *Воспоминания о Заболоцком,* Москва, 1977, рр. 64–6, 75).

Notes

1 A. L. Volinskii (Fleksner) (1863–1926) was a well-known art historian and critic, the author of numerous monographic studies on literature, painting, theatre and music.

2 *Stanovliane* [the evolving ones] was a word coined by Tufanov by analogy with Khlebnikov's neologisms *budetliane* [the future ones] and *tvoriane* [the creative ones] (the latter from the poem 'Ladomir']. Interestingly enough, Tufanov associated his neologism with the poetics of the early Cubo-Futurists, to whom he traced back his genealogy: 'Our predecessors Elena Guro, Kruchenykh and Khlebnikov were moving towards trans-sense via the "resurrection of the word" [Shklovskii's term – A.P.], that is why they are *stanovliane* [the evolving ones], rather than *budetliane* [the future ones]. They were evolving, turning into transrational poets but did not manage to cope with the "scum of our mother tongue" to use Khlebnikov's expression' (*see К Zaumi*, p. 9).

3 The stage solution of the first episode by Tatlin is a realization of one of his major orientations declared in his article 'On "Zangezi"': (*see* p. 248): 'The "Song of the Astral Language" and in general everything Zangezi says is a slowly moving ray, as it were, from the thinker to the uncomprehending crowd. This contact is established by means of a specially designed apparatus.' The most detailed, if sarcastic, description of that episode was given by B. Kazanskii in his review of the production: 'Tatlin kindly agreed to perform the main role, although it meant sitting just below the ceiling – as befits the hero of a play these days – repeating the words of the text after the prompter who was sitting next to him (both definitely rose to the occasion) or dropping posters with words too difficult or impossible to pronounce, while a group of young people on the stage were reading them out loud syllable by syllable.' (Б. Казанский, Хлебников в постановке Татлина.) Compare also Iutkevich's ironic remark: 'The poster declared: people, objects, lights are involved in the action... Only one stage light was wandering dejectedly across the clever "counter-relief" by Tatlin and the crudely painted boards with Khlebnikov's trans-sense descending down the rope were not coming to life ...' (*see* Bibliog.: Iutkevich, 1923, p.181).

4 (On the content of Punin's talk *see* p. 398, n3) The numerical nature of time was formulated by Khlebnikov in his letter of 14 March 1922 to the artist Miturich: 'My principal law of time is as follows: a negative shift in time takes place in 3^n days while a positive one in 2^n days.' (В. Хлебников, op. cit., vol. V, p. 324). This means that in 2^n days an event is on the rise but in 3^n days it turns into an anti-event. The 'law of time' discovered by the author of *Zangezi* inspired Miturich's drawing on the cover of *Velemir Khlebnikov's Herald,* (*see* Вестник Велемира Хлебникова, no. 2, Москва, 1922).

5 The 'astral language's' theory is a component part of the 'new world language', the creation of which was proclaimed by Khlebnikov in his theoretical papers and developed in his poetic works (В. Хлебников, 'Наша основа', op. cit., vol. V, pp. 228, 243). To use V.P. Grigor'ev's definition, 'the poet's astral language is far from being valid in a scientific and philosophical sense but, as a supplementary means of poetic discovery and reinforcement of semantic associations, it produced in Khlebnikov's best works some impressive samples of an aesthetic attitude towards language' (*see* Григорьев, 'Ономастика Велемира Хлебникова', in: *Ономастика и норма,* Москва, 1976, p. 189).

6. В. Хлебников, op. cit. vol. IV, p. 337. In 'plane 10' of *Zangezi* Khlebnikov gives neologisms based on the word *mogu* (I can).

7 Compare quotations from the articles by Kazanskii and Iutkevich (note 3).

8 The author means a talk by Professor Iakubinskii (see notes 3 and 5 on pp. 398, 399).

9 Here and later in the text of the article one of the characters of *Zangezi* is mistakenly identified as Death instead of Laughter: in 'plane 10' Repentance and Laughter appear.

10 An inaccurate quotation from the finale of *Zangezi* (vol. III, pp. 367–68). The finale of that supernarrative, like that of his other play *Death's Error*, which used the same device of resurrecting the hero (Death), is directly related to one of the first Futurist plays: the opera *Victory over the Sun* (1913) by Kruchenykh and Matiushin, in which a slain pilot is 'resurrected' in the finale. The very last phrase of that opera ('The world will perish but we shall know no end!') was particularly singled out by Khlebnikov, who attached to it an ideological meaning important to the *budetliane*.

11 By introducing these words on a canvas Tatlin identified, as it were, Khlebnikov the author with the protagonist of the supernarrative, the poet-prophet Zangezi. In a letter to Miturich (*see* p. 245), Tatlin wrote about using posters with the same text announcing the death of the poet at the exhibition of the Union of New Tendencies in Art (Museum of Artistic Culture, July 1922), which turned into a kind of summary exhibition dedicated to the leader of the artistic left of the 1910–1920s, Khlebnikov. The two or three performances of *Zangezi* directed by Tatlin took place on the eve of the anniversary of Khlebnikov's death and were the first among a number of memorial functions dedicated to the poet. In the Museum of Artistic Culture the first commission was formed (including the artists Tatlin, Matiushin, Lapshin and Taran) to study the poet's creative work and collect biographical material; on 28 June 1923 an exhibition was opened there dedicated to Khlebnikov's memory, in which the central place was occupied by Miturich's works, including two posthumous portraits of Khlebnikov, while Tatlin exhibited the maquette, drawings for the stage designs and costumes of *Zangezi*, and Bruni showed his designs for the unrealized production of *Death's Error*. (For more detail on this *see* Н. Пунин, 'Выставка памяти Хлебникова', *Жизнь искусства*, 3 July 1923; Н. Лапшин, 'Хлебников – Митурич', *Русское искусство*, 1923, no. 2–3, pp. 99–101.)

12 'Meditations at the Main Entrance' is the title of a well-known poem by Nekrasov (1858).

Text and notes prepared by Aleksandr Efimovich Parnis

N. Punin, Routine and Tatlin

Engel'meier said: 'Routine is inconceivable without creativity, just as creativity is inconceiv- 239
able without routine.' Yet we still continue habitually to oppose a genius to his environment,
and if anyone is endowed with a great power he must definitely 'take arms against a sea of
troubles'; all the romanticism about 'the great man' is based on such a 'rebellion'. Romanti- 247–251
cism symbolizes the best in mankind, but romanticism itself can be different.   245, 246

Tatlin, as many people know, has lately been working on designs for a stove, clothes, a
bed; I am going to discuss only the stove, Tatlin's stove, since it has caused the greatest
bewilderment.

First of all, what is it – that notorious stove which causes fear in some people, and laughter,
irony and ridicule in others? I shall describe it briefly: from the outside it presents a parallelepiped made of tiles without any decorations and of strictly prescribed proportions; thus
one can speak of the form of the stove only as of something secondary, a direct consequence
of the construction itself. Tatlin's stove consists of a furnace with complicated and adjustable
passages which make it possible to heat all of it or only its central part – the air chamber.
The latter is so designed that it also serves as a range or, to put it more simply, it is a range
covered with an air box; there is a small glass window in one of the sides to peer into the
chamber; the chimneys have hooks inside for smoking food, etc; other details are outside the
scope of the present discussion. The meaning of this stove is in the fact that it can simul-
taneously heat the room, preserve the heat within itself, i.e. in the oven, for a relatively long
period of time like any other tiled stove, thus making warm food (water) always available,
and, finally, serve as a range. There is no other possible meaning than this for the stove, and
it can probably be made by any good stove-man.

Why then are people talking so much about a common, simple and useful stove? Why has
it stirred so much controversy and even anger? And there is a lot of talk and argument going
on – I have witnessed so much of it that it has made me sick and tired of the whole thing,
so much so that I decided to write an article about it all.

They are talking about it mainly because the stove was made by Tatlin, an artist, the most gifted, spontaneously gifted man. Nobody seems to doubt that Tatlin is, indeed, the most gifted artist of our generation. I am an exception only in that for me Tatlin is a matter of pride; I am proud of his name and of his presence on our earth at the time when I am destined to live... but that may be bias and hyperbole, for which I shall probably have to answer.

They are arguing about it, i.e. about Tatlin's stove, because people cannot feel purely and think simply. They are angry because on top of everything else they are corrupted by silly romanticism and dead aestheticism, they are conservative and self-satisfied.

Tatlin made a stove and claims to be an artist interested only in art. Does it mean that a stove is a work of art and a stove-man is equal to an artist? Thus the bewildered professionals exclaim in horror and anger – and especially those for whom art is only what is contained in the Hermitage museum. I would neither proclaim nor disclaim the equality between a stove-man and an artist, between a stove and a work of art – it is a waste of time and effort; neither I nor those who regard as art only that which is confined within the Hermitage have in our pockets a decree or a letter from the rental office manager saying what is art and what is the artist's vocation, but if one talks sincerely and calmly (which I find difficult to do) with the same Hermitage enthusiasts one will discover that they, too, in any case agree to regard as art the activity or the result of activity engaged in by a person filled with a kind of creative elemental force (whether in painting and plastic arts or poetry and music) through which this person contemplates, reforms or builds the world; such inclusive understanding of art enables both Tatlin and his stove to be completely covered by the terms artist and a work of art. Indeed, while building his stove Tatlin builds life, and he is doing it with his own self, his own spirit, a consciousness which is sufficiently filled – as is known to those who are familiar with Tatlin's works – with the elemental force of painting and the plastic arts. Moreover, this consciousness is obsessed with this elemental force, obsessed to the point of passion, frenzy, brilliance. Hence, the question can only be whether that elemental force was indeed present – and in what degree – in the construction of the stove or, if you wish, whether it spilt over from Tatlin, the artist, into the creation of his hands, into his artifact. I shall try to answer this question in full.

First of all, we *do not know* how to define the instinctive force of painting and plastic arts, i.e. that aesthetic element which endows any material, say, a simple piece of canvas and simple oil paints, with artistic value; human thought in the course of its two hundred and fifty centuries of existence has not produced a definition of that aesthetic element. We do not know it but we feel it, so in future I am going to talk about feelings and sensations rather than knowledge. Neither do we know the source of the inexplicable pleasure we experience at the sight of Leonardo's 'Gioconda', that simple surface of canvas painted with oils; it is somewhere out there in space and material, in the reality we call 'Gioconda'. In a similar way, when listening to Tatlin and examining with him his stove I, too, experience an 'inexplicable pleasure' in front of that reality transversed by a simple, inventive and witty human thought, that passed through and assumed its form in material and space, i.e. those very elements that make up the most profound essence of the world of painting and the plastic arts. And if there is any difference between those two pleasures it consists in the fact that in the first example we enjoy an object designed for contemplation, while in the second case we enjoy a thing of utilitarian value, but that does not at all change the feeling itself defined by our inner experience as artistic-plastic, i.e. aesthetic pleasure. Do we deny the artistic value of a snuff-box, an amphora, a neolithic pot or a palaeolithic axe just because they are objects of utilitarian production? The extreme aesthetes do not dare to go that far, the most they can do is to avoid all mention of these objects in their 'art history'. So what kind of misunderstanding can there be and what argument is needed? A work of art is a reality evoking in us a certain feeling that we inwardly define for ourselves as the aesthetic feeling; very often, though probably not always, such a feeling is generated by what can best be described as the free play of the creative power. It seems to me that in everything Tatlin does there is a share of such play – a joyous, light play of a great creative power.

Yet I do not wish particularly to insist on the 'aesthetic' significance of Tatlin's stove or to identify its aesthetics with that of, say, that same 'Gioconda', and the only purpose in starting this discussion at all was to show that we have no formal reasons to deny Tatlin's stove the status of a work of art, i.e. in other words, there is no ground for denying its aesthetic value. So the best arrangement would seem to be as follows: let those whom I call today 'the Hermitage people' refrain from negating the aesthetic value of Tatlin's stove while I for my part shall refrain from insisting on its presence and we shall then discuss something else, which is of greater importance and interest to us, namely, the meaning of Tatlin's desire to make a stove, why an artist started making stoves. To confirm that this is, indeed, more important and, incidentally, to reinforce our agreement I shall say the following. It is certainly true that we do not really know what art is, but we have probably some reasons to claim that artifacts produced by human hands become 'art' (in the 'Hermitage' sense of the word) only after time has touched them, having made its frightening choice; so while these artifacts are still with us they are not objects of artistic value (dead values?) but the living participants in our existence and our passions, the implements of our will. That is why it is not so much their aesthetic significance that is important but rather their existential, everyday or, if you wish, symbolic meaning in our world, in that knot of struggling forces which is our life.

A year ago Tatlin threw in a slogan: 'Not to the left, not to the right, but to the necessary.' It is a simple and obvious slogan but it is worth thinking about. First of all, why did Tatlin have to repeat that truism about art which is necessary; has anyone ever denied the necessity of art, and are they not proclaiming louder than anything else nowadays the need (and a most extensive need at that) for art? Moreover, can anything unnecessary exist at all or perpetuate itself? Certainly not. When Tatlin talks about the necessary and denies the right and the left he is arguing that art which is created nowadays does not meet the needs of the epoch, that there is a chasm between life as Tatlin perceives it and art, and that this chasm cannot be justified by the artist's 'leftness' or 'rightness'. So what kind of life has been predicted by Tatlin and what kind of art does it need? Tatlin's answer to this main question was a stove. Such an answer meant first of all that the artist's attention is focused with particular interest on what is usually called everyday life, but not on its higher levels, not the surplus which crosses the borderlines of day-to-day existence and serves as its superstructure and embellishment, but on its lower levels of daily human needs. Indeed, what can be more common or, in other words, belonging to everyday existence than a stove, and what can be simpler than to make a stove designed for daily needs? In this case the heart of the matter lies in its simplicity and ability to meet the needs, as becomes evident from the fact that Tatlin produced neither an electric stove nor even a gas one – in a word, none of those American-ized stoves – but an ordinary wood stove to be used by anybody at all. 'The time for "Americanized" stoves in the conditions of our Russian way of life has not yet arrived,' says Tatlin. We need things as simple and primitive as our simple and primitive daily existence. I find this opinion especially remarkable. This is a mentality possible only in a person free from false and empty enthusiasm, in possession of consciousness and taste purified from the unhealthy romanticism of the aesthetic epigones of the nineteenth century.

In an epoch of such changes in social relations and such a downfall of old values as we are now experiencing, it is not merely tasteless but even criminal to walk on the stilts of aesthetic subtleties, oblivious of current developments, learning nothing and forgetting nothing.

Professionals are crying out about the growing crudity of art and its decline, but everything around us is crude and declining: the whole structure of Europe is crumbling down both in depth (its social system) and in width (its map). It is absurd to pretend that nothing is happening and to take on our shoulders the burden of emptiness, holding dead aesthetic values above our heads. The old world has collapsed and with it the artist's opportunity to do what he used to do, so he started doing what happened to be necessary in his environment, in his whole life. The aesthetes are still puzzled: a stove? – yes, a stove. But why should a stove be made by an artist rather than a stove-man? And what is an artist? Was it an artist who invented the first wheel on the principle of a rolling stone or a log? He was and he was not; he was an artist inasmuch as he gave form to his contemporary daily existence in material and space; he was not an artist since having made a useful thing for himself and his household he stopped at that point; he stopped because he had to stop in order to use that thing, reinforcing thereby the routine of his everyday existence. And this is normal, for an artist is not an abstraction or a creature from 'other worlds' but a human being, a living person leading an ordinary life, a man who has emerged from the earth and for the earth. Tatlin's strength lies in the fact that he is precisely such a man, with strong and deep roots; he is breathing with his soil and he shares the spirit of his century. This spirit is poor, its body is coarse, its culture is primitive; so what? – at least this spirit and this culture are living values.

It is nice when there is a surplus, when it is possible to indulge playfully in embellishment and prosperity; but when there is none of that, when we are paupers – should an artist stop existing or (at best) exhaust himself in a romantic struggle for the dead past? No, he should not. And Tatlin does not do that; he exists within the limits of his culture and is probably aware that he, Tatlin, and his culture represent a living creative value, a greater one than any museum possessions. This living value, this life should be cherished by us, his contemporaries, since we possess no other life that could help us to shape and strengthen our mode of life or, to speak more inclusively, the way of life of the age that arrived with us.

5 July 1924   N. Punin

Н. Пунин, Рутина и Татлин. Manuscript in the Punin family's archive, Leningrad.

The draft of the article was written in black ink in a ruled notebook (19 pages), signed and dated by the author. The draft version of the article is written almost as a final copy: without corrections, crossings out and alternative suggestions (Ill. 239). It was written on the spur of the moment, as it were, inspired by a personal impulse to defend Tatlin, for whom Punin had a particular predilection, as he himself admits. Since the spring of 1923 when his first clothes' designs (Ill. 247, 250–1) were exhibited, Tatlin's design work provoked a strongly negative response – both verbal and printed – from the majority of his contemporaries. Thus, for example, Miklashevskii ridicules Tatlin's dilettantism in clothes design: 'English companies produce coats presenting in this respect the result of a long practical experience and a high degree of perfection. With a hastily drawn sketch Tatlin, on the other hand, wants to do better than they and publicly exhibits drawings that, naturally, lack the skill. All that reveals the designers' view of themselves as priests by the grace of God.' (*See* Bibliog.: Miklashevskii, 1924, p. 61.)

'I regret that Tatlin descended into Constructivism, his talent is so great and so necessary – I regret that he is inventing and building economical stoves (I have seen them: they are, indeed, excellent stoves for winter and summer needs and have a small glass to peer through at what's cooking inside without opening the door); I regret that he is making designs and patterns for Constructivist caps, coats and trousers (narrowed at the cuffs to protect against the wind); I feel sorry that he is polishing and priming boards. He is subjectively happy – everyone saves himself in his own way – but art is unhappy, it still remembers Tatlin the artist, it could still regard as its own Tatlin the builder, the fantastic architect of the Tower of the Third International.' So wrote Efros in 1924. (*See* Bibliog.).

Punin's article, though similar in its tendencies to the views of the Productivist critics from the Moscow INKhUK and VKhUTEMAS, is at the same time distinguished by its emphatically aesthetic approach, an inclusive understanding of art as 'construction of life' incorporating both spiritual and material culture, both contemplation and reformation of the world. According to Punin, Tatlin designs objects not 'instead of' art but as its unique form, 'necessary' and indispensable for the contemporary historical period.

The very word routine, which has a derogatory connotation, sounds lofty and ennobled when Punin places it next to Tatlin. Punin's article is polemically directed against the elitist romanticizing of art, its alienation from life. Hence his emphatically broad interpretation of the sphere of art, his inclusion in it of palaeolithic implements, the Hermitage collection of paintings and Tatlin's contemporary activity of designing a stove.

Punin's emphasis on the uniqueness of Tatlin's talent and his place in Soviet art as well as his broad interpretation of artistic activity as a kind of synthesis of the arts, technology and the production process, link this article with his programmatic works on Tatlin of 1920–1 (*see* 'The Monument', p. 344; *Tatlin*, p. 347). In this sense the article contradicts his earlier work (*see* Bibliog.: Punin, 1923, pp. 19–21) in which Punin discusses Tatlin's path towards transcending Cubism as well as the work of a wide circle of contemporary Soviet artists. (*See Tatlin*, p. 347.) That was probably the reason why the article has never been published.

Engel'meier, Petr Klement'evich. The quotation opening Punin's article is taken from Engel'meier's book *Theory of Creativity* (П. Энгельмайер, *Теория творчества,* Санкт-Петербург, 1910, p. 15). One has to keep in mind that the notion of routine was used by Engel'meier as well as Punin without the negative connotation it has currently acquired. Engel'meier understands routine as a mass phenomenon of life activity according to established, deeply rooted laws, and it is precisely in this sense that it is contrasted with creativity.

Efros, Abram Markovich, an art critic.

The New Way of Life

While doing research in the area of new forms, the Section for Material Culture of the Museum of Artistic Culture (under Glavnauka) has set as one of its major tasks experiments leading to a reorganization of everyday life.

This work is based on drawing maximum attention to the simplest objects around us. An artist should participate in the creation of new things and not merely use the old ones. In this connection the Section has worked out projects and has already arrived at some samples: clothes, heating appliances, furniture, etc. We shall now describe some of these samples.

The coat reproduced in the picture has the following typical features. Its shape, wide in the shoulders and narrowing down towards the bottom, results in the following characteris- 245 tics: heat is not lost out of the bottom, the fabric does not cling to the body but retains a layer of air which, on the one hand, better preserves the heat (the principle of the double-glazed window) and, on the other, creates more hygienic conditions.

The coat is made in such a way as not to restrict movement and to enable the person wearing it to retain a natural posture: the pockets, for instance, are placed at arm's length (Fig. 1). Moreover, the coat has two removable linings – a flannelette one (for autumn) and a sheepskin one (for winter), which can be fastened to the soft waterproof outer part with a special fastening.

Since the coat consists of three separate parts put together when necessary, each of them can be replaced by a new one when the original part is worn out. The overall pattern of the suit is designed according to the same principle. The sleeves of the jacket and the trouser legs also narrow down towards the bottom. There is no vest. An attached collar can be buttoned all the way to the top. There are no trimmings at all. The coat and the suit have been produced in co-operation with the Leningrad Clothing Manufacturers' Trust.

Of the five samples of common stoves already made we shall discuss the one shown in Figure 3: this stove has an economical furnace producing a considerable heating effect with a small expenditure of wood (six logs). The stove is supplied with an oven and a large hermetically sealed chamber capable of keeping water and food hot for 28–30 hours; at the same time with only one furnace it can heat a room of $8 \times 6 \times 6$ arshins for 48 hours, maintaining a temperature of 14–16 degrees Réaumur.

Besides this, new designs for beds and other objects are being worked on. It is a collective effort by a group of workers including the artist Tatlin, who is at the same time the head of the above Section for Material Culture.

'Новый быт', Красная панорама, no. 23(41), 4 December 1924, anonymous.

The article. Tatlin himself probably participated in preparing the texts and the photographs for it. The article is accompanied by a series of illustrations (Ill. 245) with the following captions: 1–4 Design for a new type of coat: made so as to avoid restricting movement. The coat is serviceable both in summer and winter with a change of lining. 2 Head of the Section for Material Culture, the artist Tatlin. 3 A new type of stove providing a great amount of heat with a small expenditure of wood. The hot air chamber keeps food hot for 28–30 hours.

New Way of Life – montage. Tatlin found the article suitable for use in a montage *The New Way of Life* (Ill. 246) arranged according to the principle 'old – new', where Tatlin's hand-written observations comment on the printed text. The montage was probably made for an exhibition in the 'showroom' of the Section for Material Culture.

Tatlin's designs attracted a keen press coverage. His designs of clothes were evaluated first by Punin and Isakov in their articles on the Exhibition of Petrograd Artists of all Tendencies. (*Жизнь искусства*, no. 21 [396] 1923, pp. 14–15; no. 22 [397], pp. 1–2.)

Tatlin's designs (clothes, stoves) were also highly acclaimed in Isakov's article 'The New Way of Life and Tatlin's Work': 'The work of Tatlin and those young people who gather around him will play a significant role in the struggle against the old way of life, in that cultural struggle bequeathed to us by comrade Lenin.' (On Tatlin's stoves and clothes *see also* Bibliog.: Efros, 1924; Malevich, 1929.)

K. Artseulov, About 'Letatlin'

313–353   V.E. Tatlin's flying apparatus belongs to the type ornithopter: a flying machine with moving wings. This type reproduces the principle of bird's flight as precisely as possible. In the downward motion the wing bends and forms a screw-like surface which both supports the machine in the air and propels it forwards. In the upward motion the wings – owing to their resilience – assume a wide angle of contact and are lifted almost unaided by the pressure of the opposing air flow.

In the apparatus described both the mechanics of the wing action and the form themselves resulted from studying these organic forms (of the bird) whose quality we have often observed but have not taken the trouble to test.

To set the wings in motion the creator of the apparatus makes use of the muscle power of a flying man. Is that sufficient? To date all attempts to rise into the air using only human effort have been limited to 10m long jumps at the most. A calculation of the physical effort involved in flight also points to the almost insurmountable difficulty of solving this problem. It is enough, however, to observe a flying sea-gull, heron or crane to be struck by the extraordinary ease of their flight. And, indeed, they could not possibly fly for hours covering enormous distances if the physical effort involved were as great as theoreticians assume it to be. An important role in birds' flight belongs to the principles of oscillatory movement (resonance), undulatory movement and resilience. All that has been taken into consideration

319, 344   by the designer in his ornithopter. The arms of the wing spars are tightly bound by a rubber cord (a shock absorber) that performs the job of maintaining the wings in a horizontal position during the flight.

Tatlin's machine does not have such devices as an elevator and rudder-bars to control direction and transverse stability. Instead, there is a capacity to alter the angle of contact between the wings and move their ends forward and backward, which is supposed to achieve maximum stability during the list and the turn. Wing control is in the pilot's hands. The whole construction is based on the principle of elasticity, by which an effort that would destroy a rigid structure will only temporarily deform an elastic one – after which the construction will remain unchanged because of its resilience.

The most rigid part of the ornithopter, the fuselage, is based on the principle of a 'basket' made of bent elastic elements which enables it to take considerable blows without any damage. The wing spars (longerons) made of bentwood in the shape of a complicated figure of double eight, possess a high degree of resilience when twisted and bent. The wing ribs, glued in place with a strip of whalebone, are capable of bending considerably and straightening again without any residual deformation. The bentwood parts required a great number of special matrix-moulds into which previously steamed or soaked wood was squeezed and dried, subsequently retaining the exact shape of the matrix.

The whole structure was based on the principle of selecting the material according to its function and using it as well as possible. Thus wood, for instance, was not sawn but split into pieces of the required width to preserve the length of the fibres. Depending on the properties required from the materials, ash, linden, cane, cork, silk cord, Duralumin, steel rope, whalebone and even raw leather belt have been used in the construction. The moving parts are mounted on ball-bearings. The covering is made of silk. The designer paid special attention to the ratio of the weight of the wings to that of the whole body, which is 1 to 6 and is the same as the ratio found in most birds.

The total weight of the construction is 32 kg.

Surface area of the wings 12 m².

The weight per square metre is 8 kg.

We shall eagerly look forward to the test flights of these daringly designed and built human wings.

К. Арцеулов, 'О Летатлине', in: Выставка работ заслуженного деятеля искусств В.Е. Татлина. *Государ-ственный Музей изобразительных искусств, Москва – Ленинград,* 1932, pp. 9–11; Бригада художников, no. 6, 1932, pp. 17–18.

Artseulov, Konstantin Konstantinovich (born in 1891), is a grandson of the artist Aivazovskii. Since 1911 he was a sportsman-pilot; during the First World War he joined the air force. In 1916 he became the first man in the world to get out of the vertical spin. During the Civil War in Russia he was in charge of the flight unit at the Moscow flying school. He achieved the rank of brigade commander in the Red Army. In the 1920–30s he was attracted to gliding. While still in the army he did some volunteer work for the Society for the Promotion of Defence and Aero-Chemical Development (OSOAVIAKhIM), where he was head of the gliding section. In that capacity he became interested in Tatlin's idea and assisted in the construction of *Letatlin.* After leaving the air force in 1936 he worked as an artist, mainly illustrating books and the magazine *Tekhnika molodezhi.* He had four one-man shows and is a member of the Moscow Branch of the Union of Soviet Artists.

Another author, Zelinskii, regarded the flying machine as a purely technological invention, an escape from art into technology, and criticized Tatlin's designing activity from vulgarized sociological positions. (*See* К. Л. Зелин-ский, *Летатлин,* Вечерняя Москва, 6 April, 1932.)

J. Mácza, About the Artist Tatlin

Tatlin's name is widely known. It is known not only here, in the Soviet Union, but also in artistic circles in the West. This fame has passed through several stages. Initially, during the first years of the Revolution his name stood for some uncertain and for many people even totally incomprehensible notion of 'left-art', a 'revolutionary art' that breaks away from all tradition, experiments and invents. Then the same name turned into something frightening: it became the focus of everything negative in art. It was ideologically meaningless, non-representational, formalist and even 'eccentric'.

This 'progression' of Tatlin's fame increasingly obscured Tatlin himself: a real person, an artist living in our midst. His name has turned into an abstract notion. Tatlin has become 'counter-reliefs', the 'Tower of the Third International' (which was more often called 'Tatlin's tower'), 'Letatlin'. And yet it is not true. Or, rather, not quite true. We, who know by heart all Tatlin's nicknames that created both his reputation as the 'lion of the left' and, subsequently, his notorious fame, hardly know Tatlin. Or else we have forgotten what we used to know about him.

This becomes quite evident if one approaches Tatlin without any preconceived notions of him as a 'famous' or 'infamous' artist and talks to him 'heart to heart', so to speak, looking through the huge folders of his works hidden in the corners of his room, his little-known works.

And then the following will become clear:

This grim and seemingly unrefined person with a voice that would do for a regiment has the kind eyes of a child. But this is not enough. All types of people may have the eyes of a child. But this man who was demolishing art with his counter-reliefs, who was destroying it and who started doing 'eccentric' things in the sphere of aeronautics remote from art – this man loves art. Very much. This artist who was demolishing art and loving it at the same time has an enormous number of drawings, studies for paintings and sketches – at the sight of which some German 'leftist', who during the years of inflation proclaimed 'Tatlinism' as the highest form of non-representational Constructivism, would reject his idol, scoffing and spitting.

But the heart of the matter is not in the precocious 'Tatlinists' who actually failed to understand Tatlin altogether. Nor is it in the drawings, studies and sketches executed with great ease but also with great sophistication and confidence. The best among them will one day emerge from the dark corners of his studio and from under his couch to demonstrate the unfamiliar or little-known aspects of Tatlin. The heart of the matter is in the artist himself. Why was he doing those 'counter-reliefs' of his as well as the numerous stage designs and the sensational 'bicycle' for the enthusiasts of aeronautics? Why was he demolishing and recreating art?

This question has a very simple answer. He was creating and recreating that art day after day because he loved it and loves it still. He was rebelling, destroying and demolishing because he had not found in it what he used to love. Does this sound paradoxical? But Tatlin himself is quite paradoxical. He wished to reform, improve and create anew his mistress. But she was disobedient and capricious. So Tatlin rebelled. He rebelled because he was lost as thousands and thousands of his brethren were lost during the imperialist war and the period of the greatest socialist revolution. And having rebelled he, like many others, was temporarily disoriented, he lost his sense of proportion and embarked on the destruction of that which should not have been destroyed.

Dissatisfied with his 'beloved' and carried away by the desire to reform her, he was distracted from the whole and the living and started contemplating parts of the whole, 'correcting', reforming her piece by piece. Composition – separately. The texture of the material – separately. The colour combination – separately.

Tatlin was searching, experimenting, inventing. And in the process of experimentation he lost his integrity just as the petty bourgeois and philistine art of the imperialist period lost its perspective and its sense of integrity.

But this does not at all imply that there is no room for exploration, experimentation and inventiveness in art. Nor does it mean that everything Tatlin has produced is bad and irrelevant, even though he may have made quite a few mistakes!

164–206 Take, for example, his 'Tower of the Third International', that first particularly significant experiment of his. First of all it is good and heartening to see a 'passionate' artist being carried away not by some abstract or false idea but by the greatest idea of a revolutionary solidarity uniting workers of the whole world. Does it tell us anything? Yes, it does: it tells us first of all that the artist who was perplexed at the beginning of the revolutionary events was searching for and has found a firm foundation for his position, it tells us that, although in the years of the Civil War, ruin and technological backwardness that super-daring project of Tatlin might have struck many people as a groundless Utopia, it can hardly be described in those terms today. On the contrary, I believe that one can find in it much that is interesting and important, that will stimulate one's thinking, imagination and creative initiative. And I mean creative initiative not in the sense of creative experiments by an artist working in isolation as an independent artisan but as practised by an artist who is aware of the immense opportunities of our technological development and who does not withdraw from them into the picturesque world of the romantic 'studios'.

That yearning to discover new unique beauty in the technological advances of the day, to relate the notion of a 'standard object' to the notion of beauty – the beauty that used to belong exclusively to 'unique' works of art; the yearning to make man's victory over nature

313–352 not merely a great deed but a beautiful one as well – that yearning gave birth to 'Letatlin.' The same yearning stimulated Tatlin's creative thinking in his other, lesser experiments. To reduce all that to 'eccentricity', 'formalism devoid of ideological content' and nothing else is rather irresponsible, if not worse. Tatlin did suffer from the disease of formalism. He may not have completely recovered from it even now. But this is not the main thing. The main and decisive thing is the essence of his creative impulses. It is precisely the essence rather than the form of the results taken in isolation. And in this essence one can discover the way towards determining the greatest task: the task of comprehending the opportunities for socialist technology in art, and for socialist art in our advanced technology. And this task is our task.

To solve it we need experimenters and inventors. They exist. They will exist. Independent of the desires of both Tatlin and his critics. And for them Tatlin will be neither an idol nor an eccentric. He will be one of those who were groping for the new paths in art.

И. Маца, О художнике Татлине (manuscript).

The article: Judging from the author's comment in the Russian original of this article, dated 2 February 1934, Mácza, who visited Tatlin's studio in 1934, wrote it under the title 'Tatlin and "Letatlin"' for publication in the newspaper *Izvestiia*. His earlier writings show that he fully understood Tatlin's endeavours and in the 1930s, under new conditions, he felt duty bound to defend Tatlin. He could not have his article published, however. The article, which is highly telling of the 1930s, was first published in 1972 in Hungary: *Legendák és tények*. Corvina.

Mácza, János (1893–1974), a Hungarian, was a member of Lajos Kassák's Activist circle. Upon the fall of the Hungarian Republic of Councils in 1919 he emigrated to Vienna, where he worked for the reorganized journal *MA*. He published there his translation of an excerpt from Punin's pamphlet on the Monument to the Third International (p. 344) with a pencil sketch of the model. (*See* Strigalev, note 135, p. 43.)

In 1923 he moved to the Soviet Union where he was known as Ivan Matsa. He was head of the Fine Arts Section at the Communist Academy and taught at VKhUTEIN.

From 1929 to the end of his life he was a teacher, subsequently a professor with a Ph.D. in art criticism at the Moscow State University. He compiled the collection of articles entitled *15 Years of Soviet Art*, published in 1933, which became a standard work. (*Советское искусство за 15 лет*. Огиз-Изогиз, Москва–Ленинград, 1933.) He was the author of numerous books on Soviet and Western art. (Г.А. Недошивин, 'К восмидесятилетию И. Л. Маца', *Архитектура СССР*, no. 10, 1973, pp. 53–4.)

B. Alekseev, New Elements in the Art of V.E. Tatlin

V.E. Tatlin's stage designs for A.V. Sukhovo-Kobylin's drama 'The Affair' at the Red Army Theatre is one of several new stage versions of that extraordinary satirical drama.　369–370

The artist produced maquettes, drawings for stage designs and an enormous number of sketches and watercolours for costumes, make-up and character types. We are familiar with a number of previous designs for 'The Affair', usually executed in a stylized form or in a symbolist tradition, or else in a[n E.T.A.] Hoffmannesque style. Tatlin's approach to stage design is purely realistic. He has come to that interpretation of 'The Affair' as a result of a careful scrutiny of the author's plays and his epoch. As we know, the authorial comments on stage designs, costumes and characters in the play are extremely terse, expressed in two or three sharp, pointed, laconic words. The author seems to be consciously trying to conceal the visual image of his characters lest naturalistic descriptions should transform a profoundly realistic social satire into a situational drama. Tatlin, in our opinion, understood both the idea of the play and its structure. He tried to give a picture of the dark and cruel period of the 1850s in a realistic and intelligible manner. But he shows that epoch through only those elements that characterize its style and essence. In that respect the artist follows Sukhovo-Kobylin's method, conveying as tersely and sharply as possible only the most essential elements while discarding everything irrelevant and secondary: all kinds of superfluous decorative orna- mentation, embellishments and purely situational elements. It is worth mentioning that Tatlin does not simplify anything, he does not reduce stage designs to abstract surfaces or limit their role to that of a playground's walls. The lines of the stage designs and their execution are typical of the period, for the artist has found them in life itself, they are based on what the artist has studied, seen and observed. For that purpose the artist visited the premises of former ministries and government departments and temporarily resided in old mansions and apart- ments which had been made out of them and were inconvenient and accidental like those where the Muromskiis used to live. Tatlin's designs for the interiors are distinguished by a certain sharpness and cruelty of line, which is, however, in accord with the dry, sharp and pointed style of the play itself.

It should be mentioned that the artist handles very tactfully those visually unflattering conditions in which Sukhovo-Kobylin's characters lived. Thus, for instance, following strictly the text of the play, Tatlin creates the very architecture of the interior design already in the scene which traditionally used to focus exclusively on the poverty of the furnishing. Tatlin makes it into 'the Sahara desert' rather than a room. It is a strange, desolate, restructured apartment without a single comfortable little nook, it is a place where one does not feel at home, and it is obvious that the room has been partitioned and the tenants have been given the worst part. Logically developing the author's stage directions, the artist had to make door and window openings in the walls of the divided room and to put screens and hang curtains where they do not seem appropriate at first glance, since they do not make the room more beautiful. That logic based on a careful study of the text justifies not only the main lines of the stage designs executed by Tatlin firmly, forcefully and distinctly (though not at all graphically) but also those few details that the artist introduces into his work. The composition of the scene at the government department is reproduced by the artist predominantly by means of bookcases piled with files; those bookcases, however, are arranged so as to provide a large number of actors with a sufficiently spacious acting area. One may question the artist's exaggerated fascination with the *faktura* of the objects, the colour of polished wood which, according to Tatlin, is very typical of the period and serves as the main colour of the background, as it were, to the formal, drab suits of the civil servants.

The theatre hardly needs that natural beauty of objects, while the exploration of man is not helped by elevating to the status of an image the object itself which, in Tatlin's approach, begins to play the same role as the actor.

371–383 Besides sketches and maquettes for the stage design Tatlin produced a large number of drawings and watercolours for costumes and make-up. In those drawings and watercolours Tatlin was trying to convey above all the characters. He has been searching the individual features persistently for a long time. The proof of this lies in the numerous versions of the drawings, in which one can trace the vague, opaque and accidental traits of the image which gradually acquires distinction and precision as a result of that search.

We do not believe that the artist's desire to find visual forms of the image for the actor interferes with the latter's independence – something like putting one's sickle into another's harvest.

At first Tatlin approached his search for the type like a book illustrator trying to visualize a character's general appearance; he then started correcting his sketches following the fabric of the costumes and their colours in relation to the stage-setting; finally the last versions were made when the artist became personally acquainted with each actor, after which the drawings sufficiently corresponded to the facial features, figure and acting style of the real actors.

Such drawings transcend the role of mere projects for costumes and make-up and turn into the director's visual directions, helping actors in their work on the production.

Unfortunately, one should say that the theatre has in many respects failed to understand the artist's ideas. Thus, for example, the first scene suffered from excessive *mise en scène*, it was cluttered with all kinds of little tables and chairs, some with coloured kerchiefs on them, which made the room look inhabited, cosy and comfortable instead of desolate as it appears from the text of the play. The bookcases for the second scene were made by the theatre workshops incorrectly, without proper understanding and not from the material stipulated in the design. As a result, the artist had to compromise, to agree with what was contrary to his creative concept, to authorize the use of materials that were not suitable for his purpose.

The issue of the artist's role in the theatre is a very serious one and the Theatre Section of the Moscow Branch of the Union of Soviet Artists should discuss it.

Tatlin's work on designs for Sukhovo-Kobylin's 'The Affair' represents a new stage in his creative activity. The artist is giving up formalism and is beginning to form a realistic perception of reality.

Let us wish the artist to become firmly established in his new positions.

Б. Алексеев, 'Новое в творчестве В.Е. Татлина', Творчество, nо. 8, 1940, pp. 14–15, with 9 illustrations.

Alekseev, Boris Ivanovich: we have no information on his life or his work.

313 Belfry of the Novodevichii Convent in Moscow, 1690. Photograph, taken in 1930: Legacy L.A. Zhadova

314 Pavil'onov in 1930–1.
Photograph: Collection A.G. Sotnikov, Moscow
315 A.G. Sotnikov in 1930–1.
Photograph: Collection A.G. Sotnikov, Moscow
316 A.G. Sotnikov's sketch reconstruction of the entrance to the belfry of the Novodevichii Convent, with the 'Experimental Laboratory for Material Culture' plaque
317 A.G. Sotnikov and Pavil'onov during the construction of *Letatlin*, 1931–2.
Photograph: Collection A.G. Sotnikov, Moscow
318 Tatlin with the wing of *Letatlin* in the studio in the bell tower of the Convent, 1932, Cat. VI/5b
319 Tatlin with the main beam of the wing of *Letatlin* in the gallery of the bell tower of the Novodevichii Convent, 1932, Cat. VI/5a

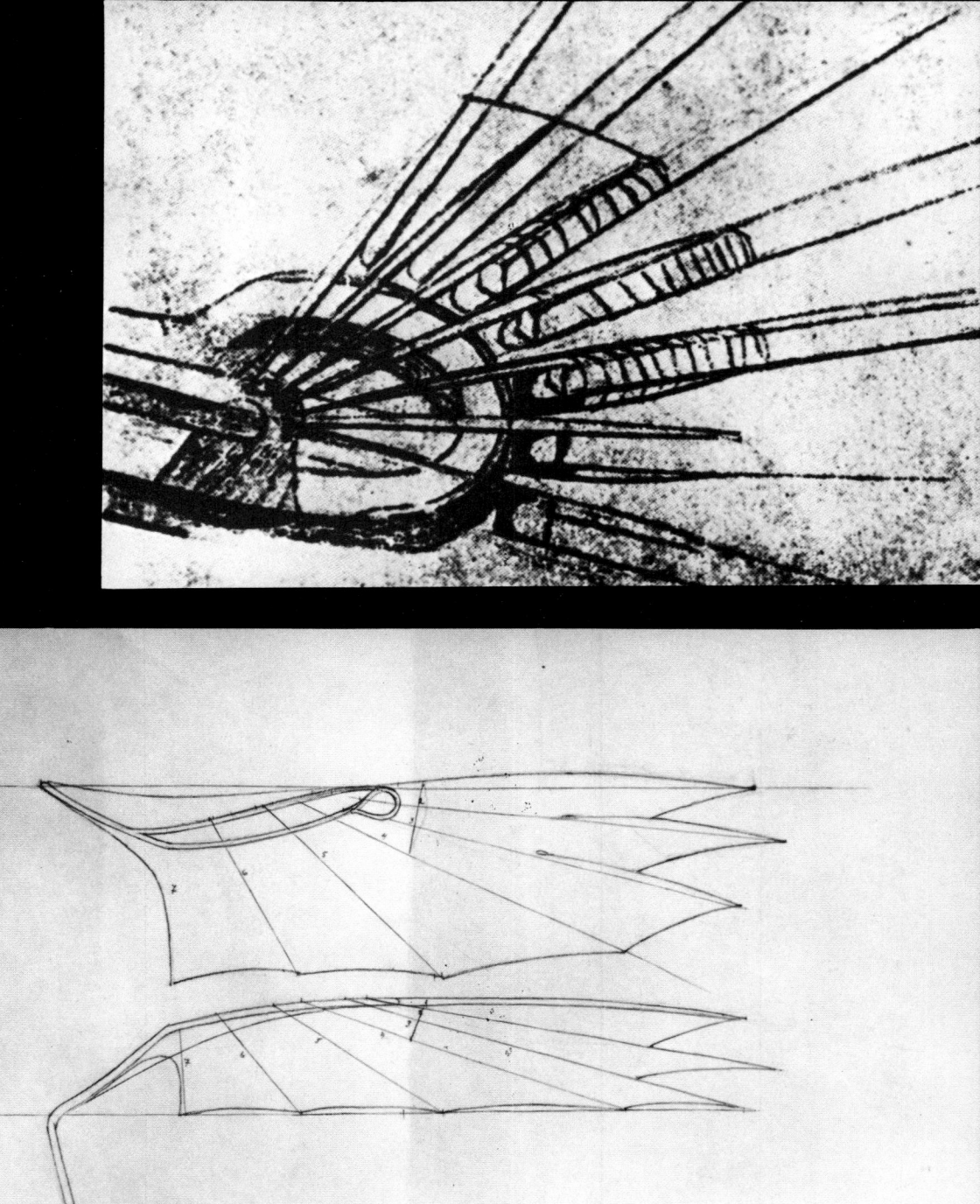

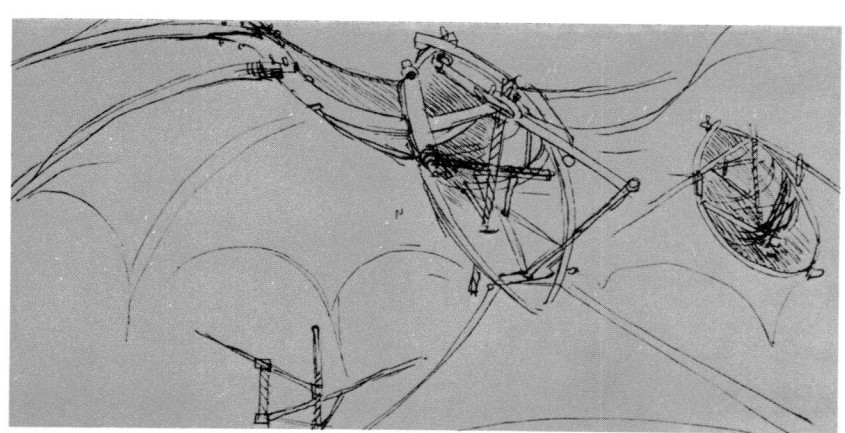

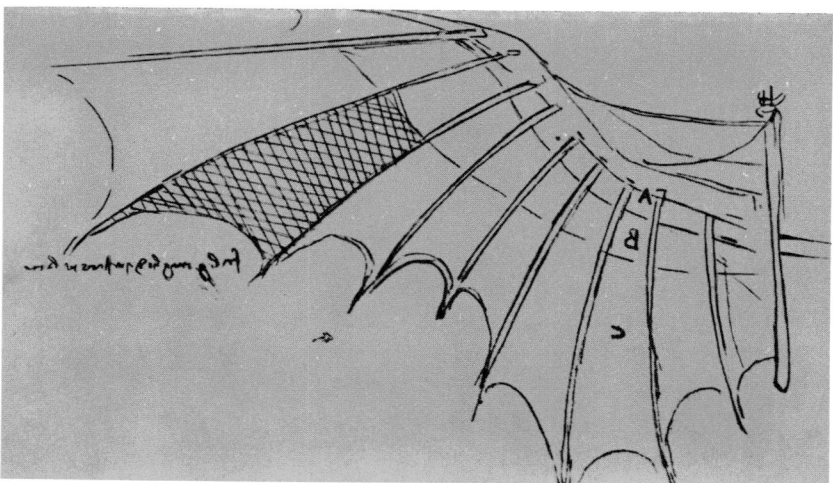

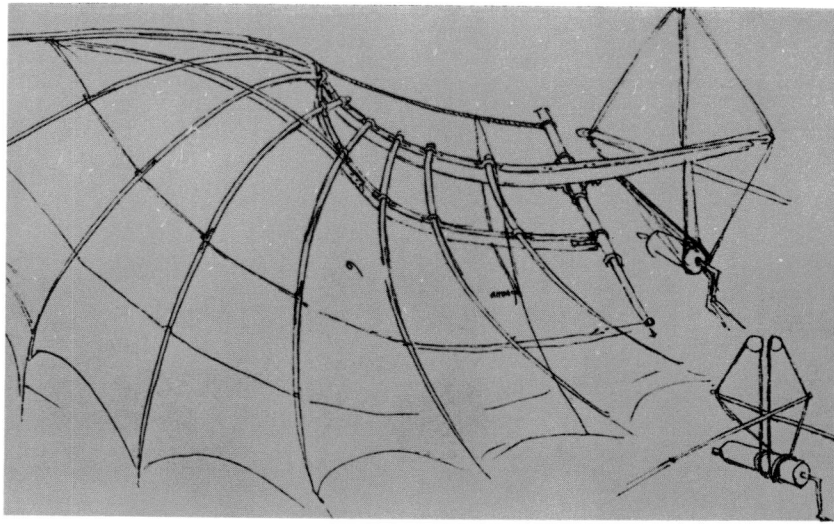

322–4 Design of Leonardo da Vinci's flying machine
325 Tatlin demonstrating the operation of *Letatlin*, Cat. VI/5g ▷

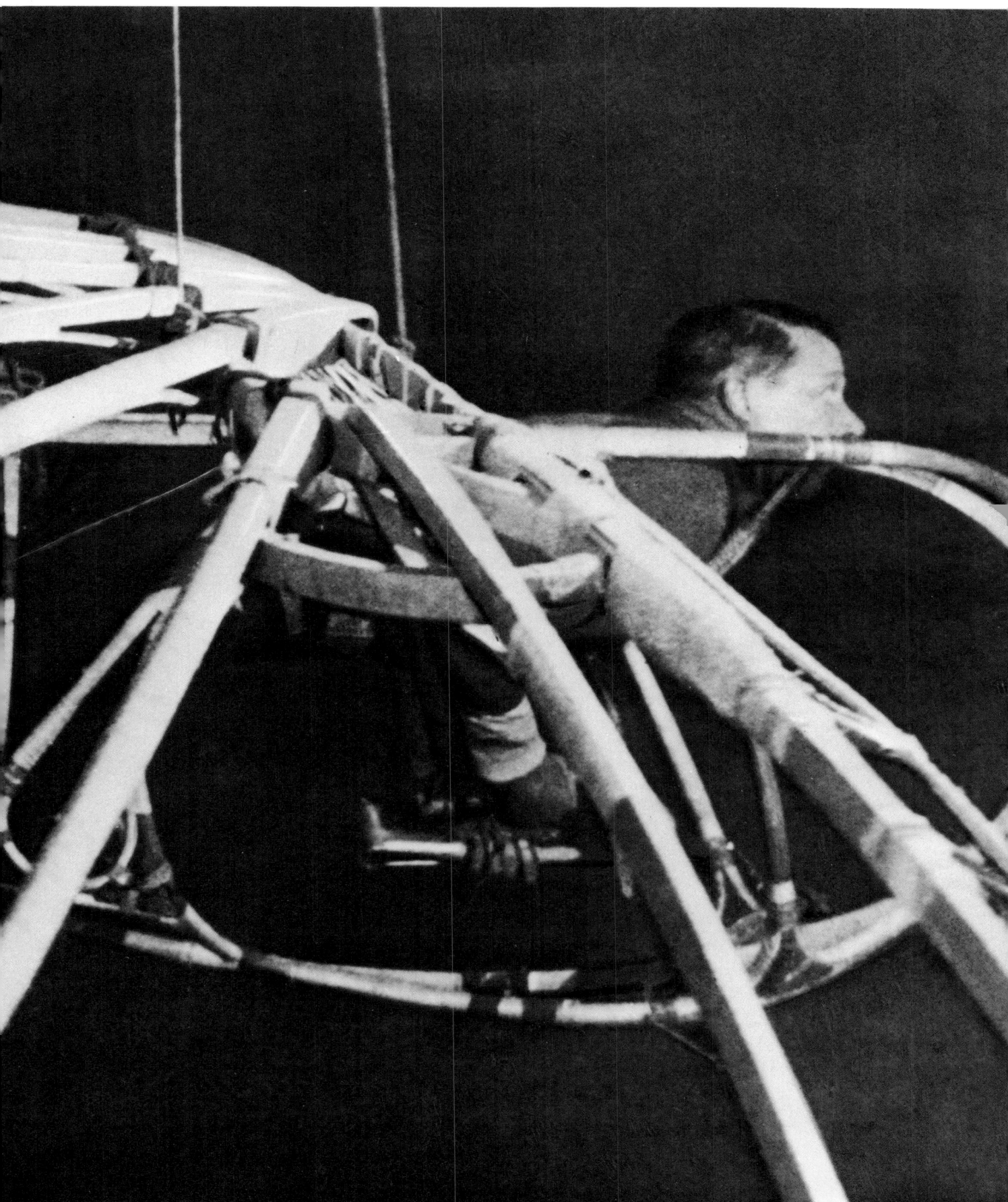

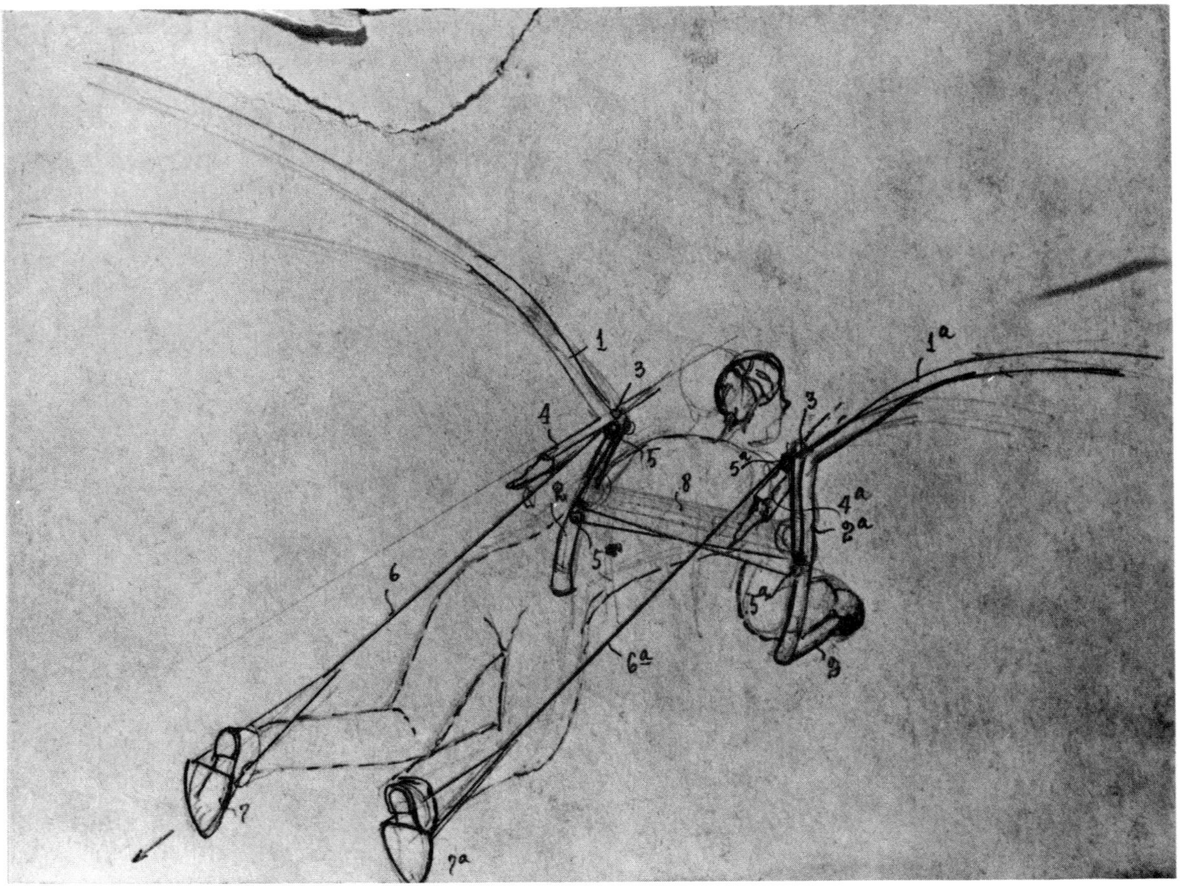

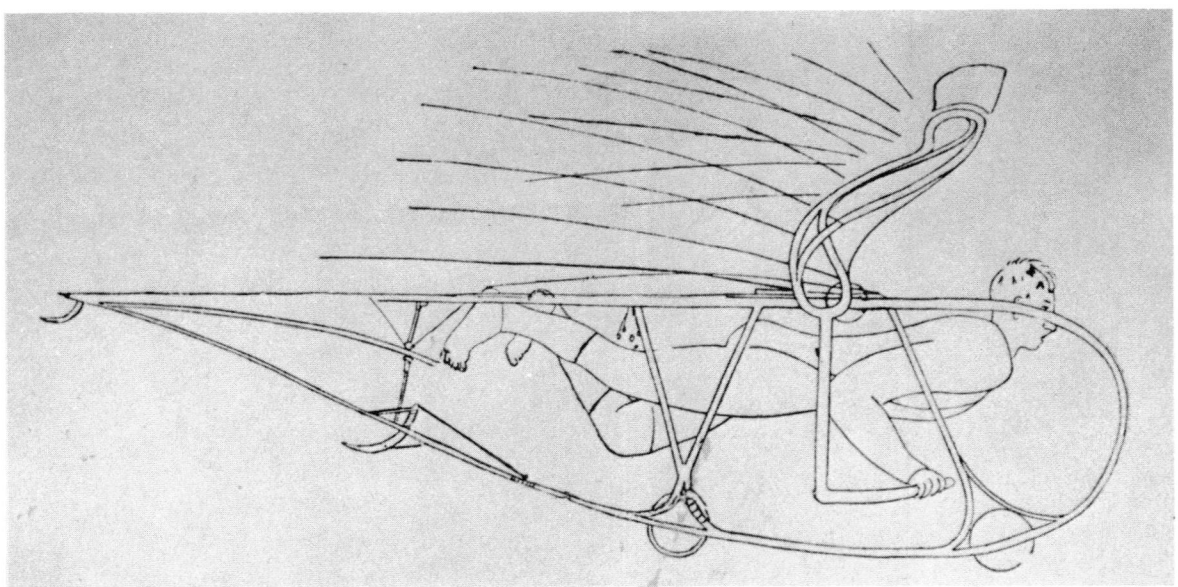

326 Description of body position during flight, Cat. VI/3
327 Description of body position during flight, Cat. VI/4

* **328** Model of *Letatlin* with wing-stiffening struts,
Cat. VI/5f
329 Pavil'onov and *Letatlin*, Cat. VI/5h

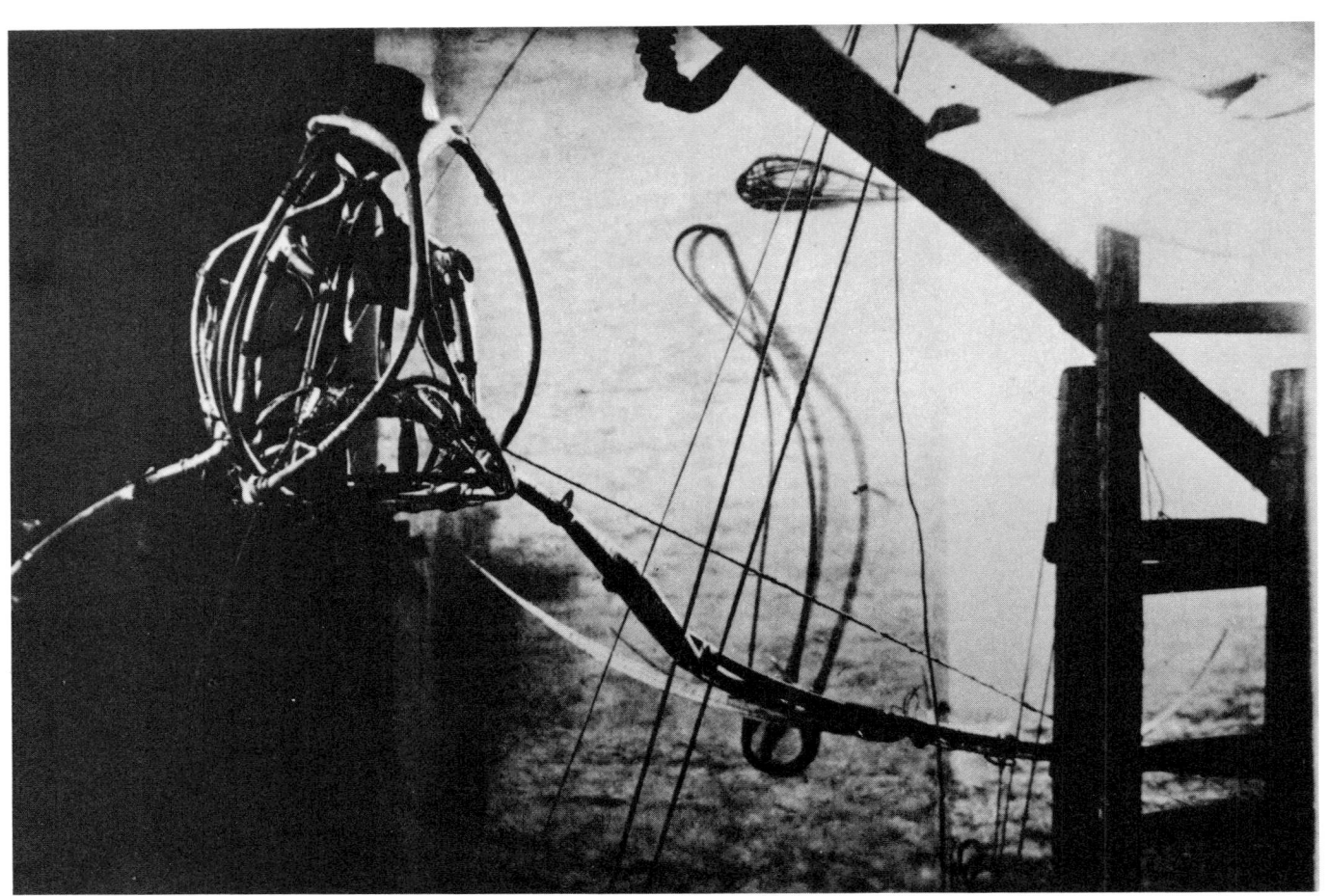

330 *Letatlin* without skin in the studio in the bell tower of the Novodevichii Convent, 1929–32, Cat. VI/5d
331 Fuselage of *Letatlin*, 1932, Cat. VI/5c

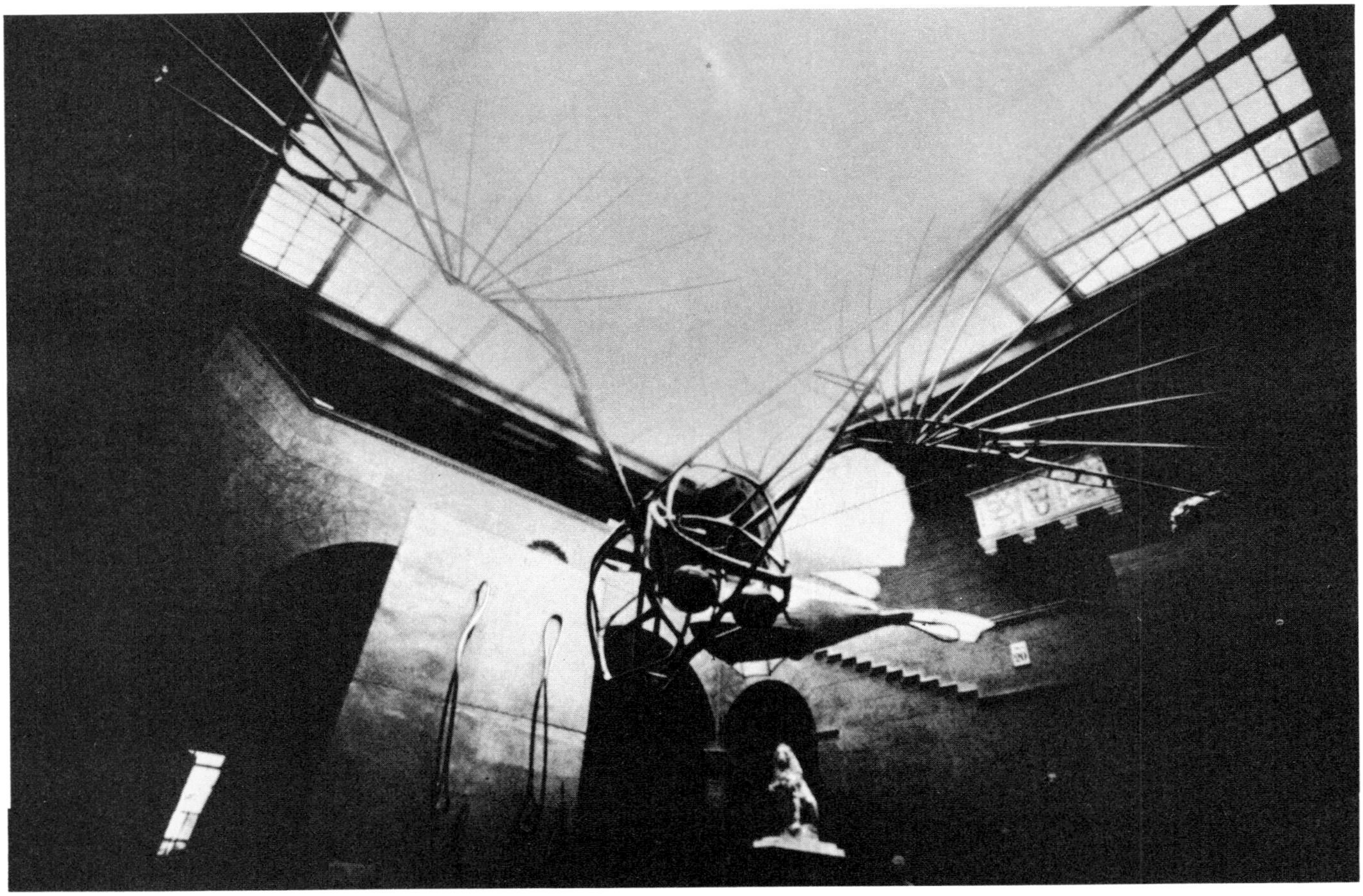

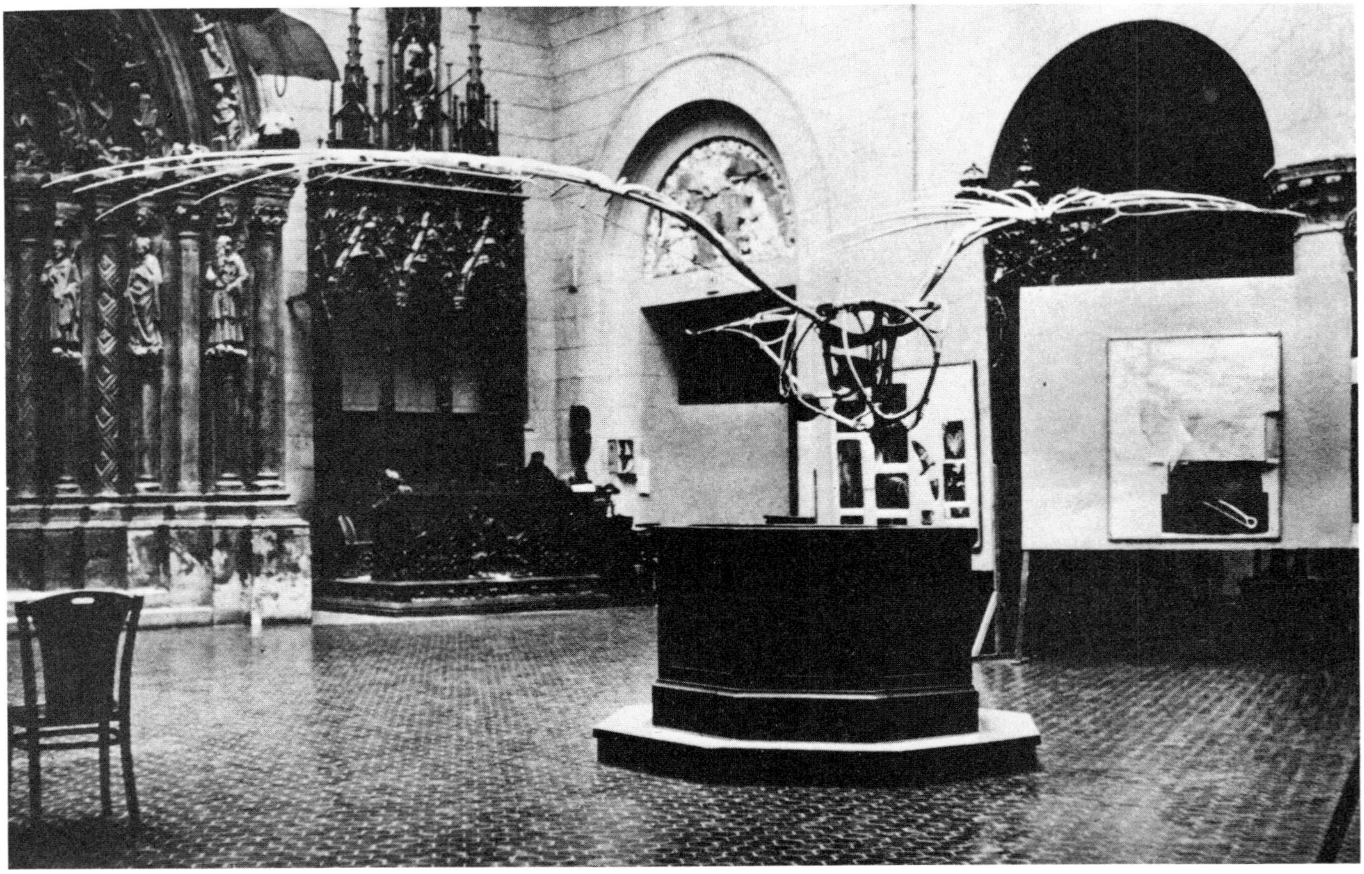

332–3 *Letatlin* without skin on display in the Italian Hall of the
Museum of Fine Arts, 1932, Cat. VI/5i, VI/5j
334 *Letatlin* without skin exhibited in the banquet hall of the Club
of the Union of Soviet Writers, 1932, Cat. VI/5l
335 Model of *Letatlin* with skin and wing supports in the Italian Hall
of the Museum of Fine Arts, 1932, Cat. VI/5k

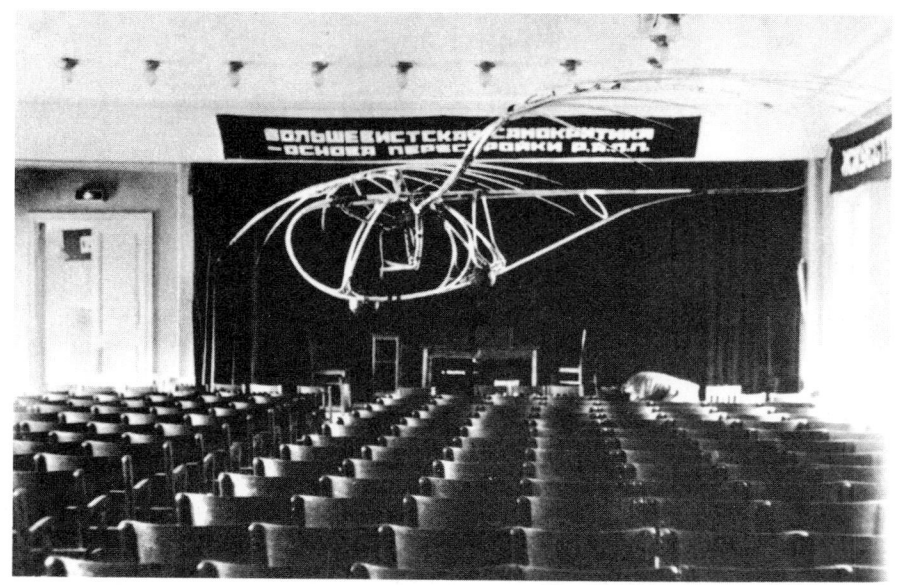

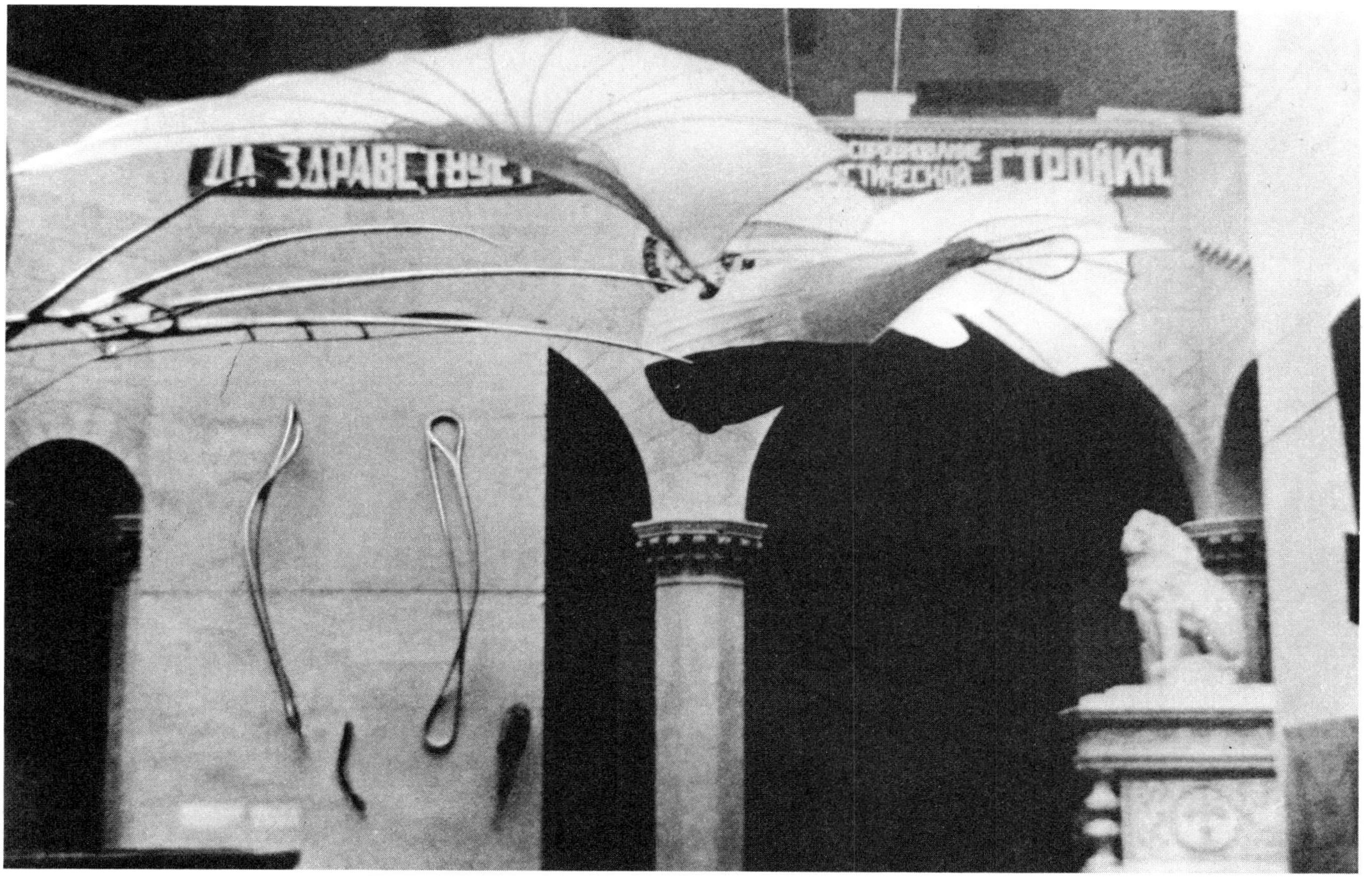

ГОСУДАРСТВЕННЫЙ МУЗЕЙ ИЗОБРАЗИТЕЛЬНЫХ ИСКУССТВ

ВЫСТАВКА РАБОТ

ЗАСЛУЖЕННОГО ДЕЯТЕЛЯ ИСКУССТВ

В. Е. ТАТЛИНА

ОГИЗ—ИЗОГИЗ
МОСКВА 1932 ЛЕНИНГРАД

Список экспонатов

1. Аппарат в обтяжке «Летатлен» № 1.
2. То же № 2.
3—4. Конструкция аппарата без обтяжки.
5. Модель фюзеляжа.
6. Модель сложного кривого лонжерона.
7. Нервюры.
8. Рисунки и чертежи аппарата.
9. Фото с аппарата «Летатлина».
10. Фото с монумета «Коминтерна».
11. Фото и брошюры различных работ.
12. Работы по оформлению быта.

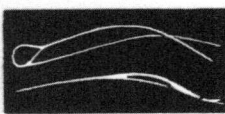

— Вид сверху

— Вид спереди

Сложный кривой лонжерон (рычаг, ясень, малье)

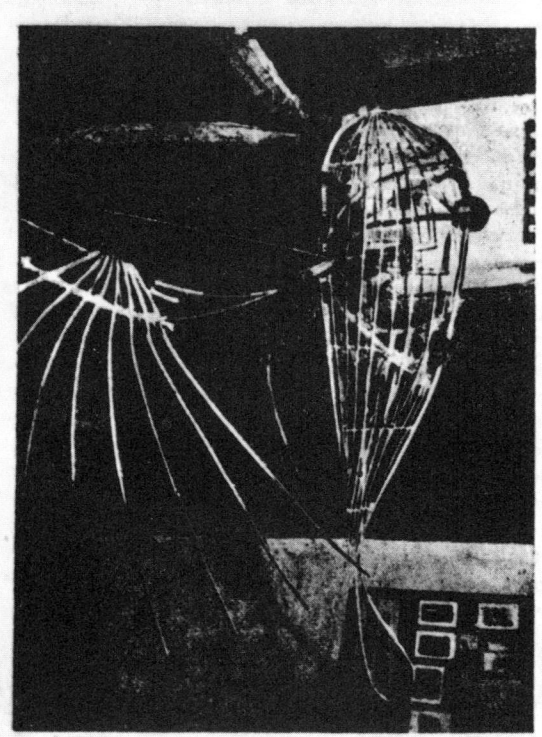

Конструкция «Летатлина» без обтяжки

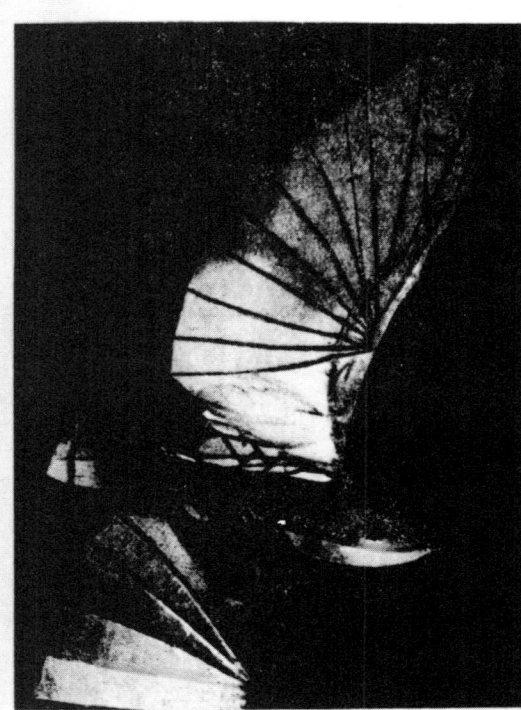

Общий вид аппарата «Летатлина» в обтяжке

336–8 Catalogue of the Exhibition by Honoured Art Worker of the RSFSR, Tatlin, Moscow and Leningrad, 1932, Cat. XII/24, VI/5e
339 I.A. Rakhtanov, '*Letatlin*. An Aerial Bicycle', interview, 1932, Cat. XII/25
* **340** 'The Inventor-Pioneer of Modern Technology in Defence of the Homeland', poster, 1934, Cat. XII/27

Летатлин-
ВОЗДУШНЫЙ ВЕЛОСИПЕД

Очерк И. Рахтанова

Высокий человек стоял на маленькой сцене. Зал был переполнен. Высокий человек не был актером, он не пел, не читал, не играл на скрипке. У него были красные руки мастерового.

Над публикой колыхалась широкая птица. Она простерла крылья над стульями, и было непонятно, как попала она сюда, как влетела она в этот тесный зал.

Но птица была не покрыта. Это был скелет, но скелет живой. Вероятно это было ископаемое.

Высокий человек на сцене говорил:

— Расчеты? Только пусть товарищи инженеры не обижаются на меня. Вы спрашивали ворону, по каким расчетам у нее крыло?

В зале засмеялись, кто-то хлопнул.

Уже к необыкновенным вертушкам привыкли. Ежегодно они появлялись на площадях больших городов.

А Татлин в это время работал. Он занимался необычным для художника делом — поставить кресло на крылья летающей птицы.

Человек в летатлине будет лежать в позе пловца. И управлять полетом. Он будет работать руками и ногами, как уже работает

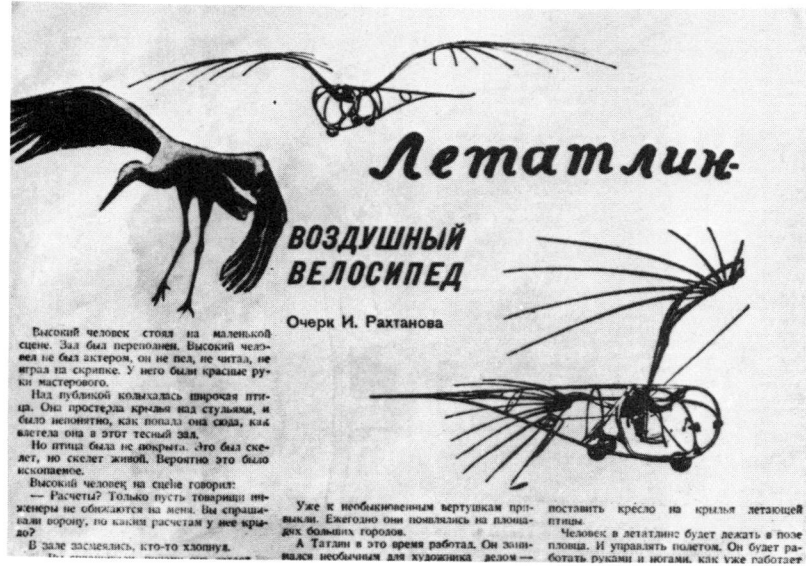

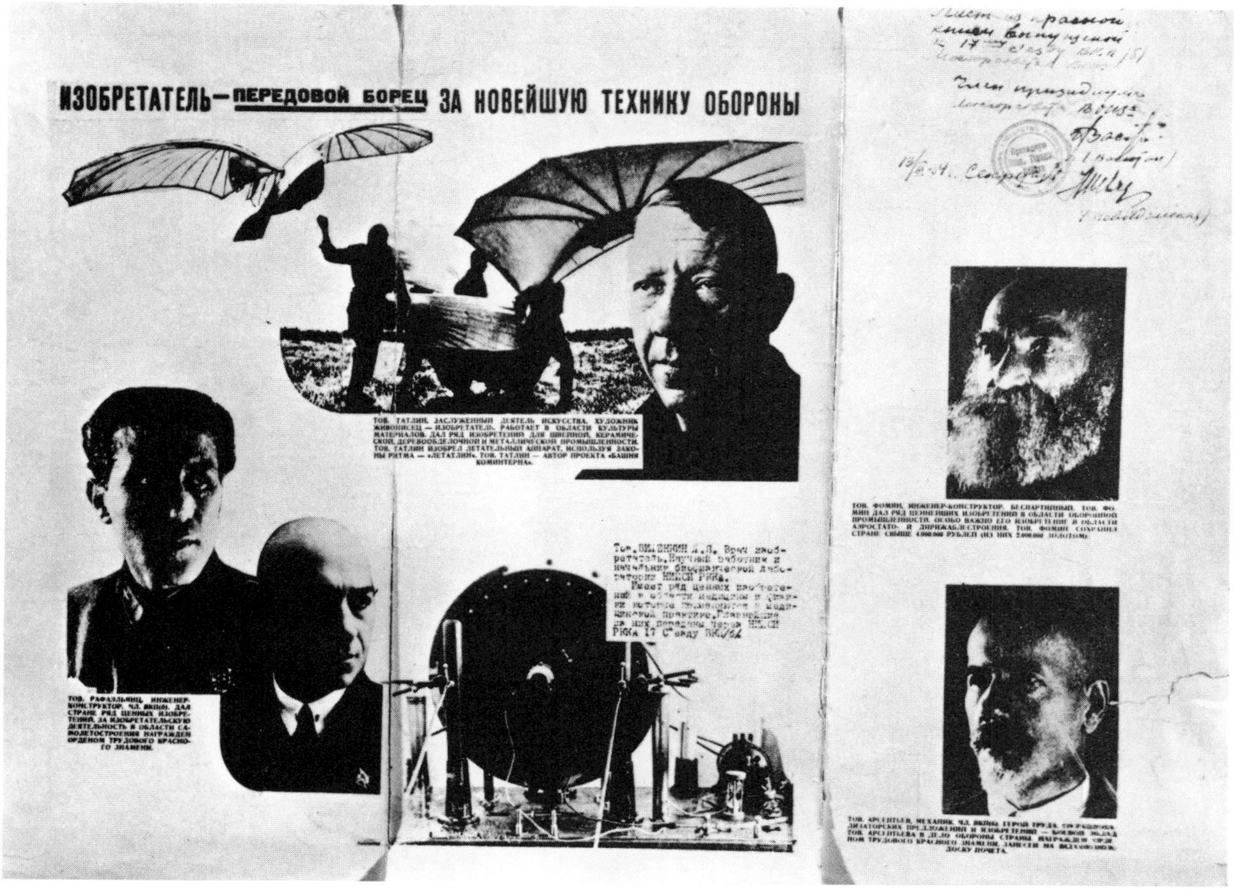

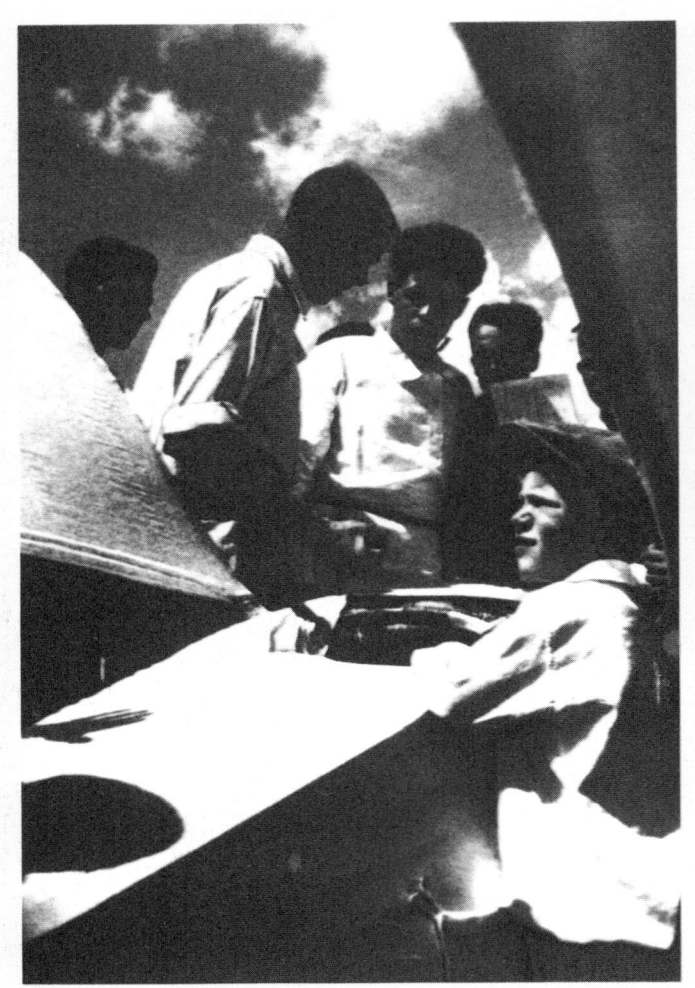

341–2 *Letatlin* at the review of Moscow and Moscow District sailplanes, 1933 (Tatlin is demonstrating the flying machine to pilots and sailplane pilots), Cat. VI/5n, VI/5o
343 The review, same location, Cat. VI/5m

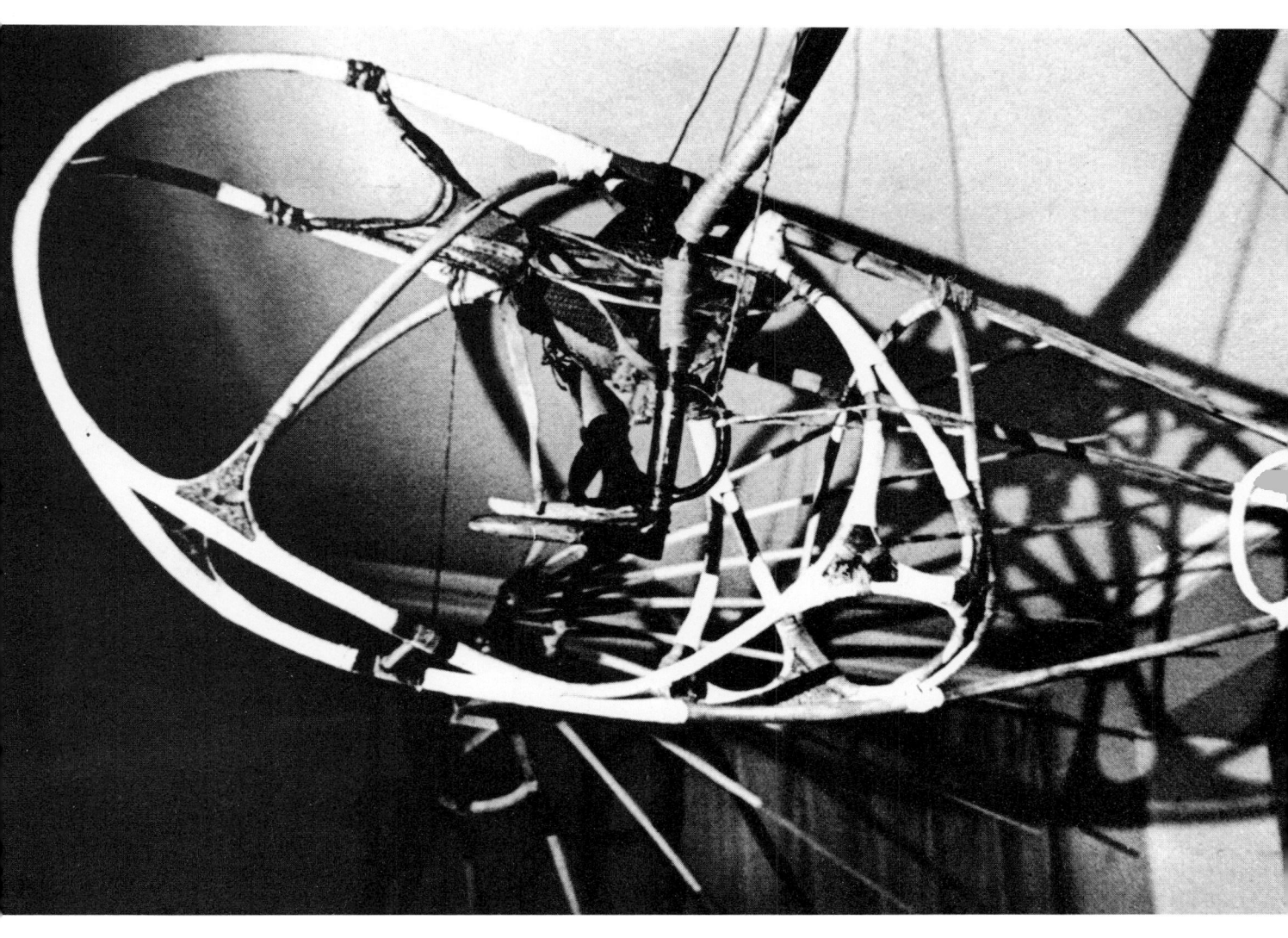

344 The main wing strut of *Letatlin* in the studio of the sculptor A.E. Zelenskii, 1950s, Cat. VI/5p
345–6 The parts of *Letatlin* at the Tatlin Exhibition held at the Moscow Headquarters of the Union of Writers, 1977, Cat. VI/6e, VI/6c

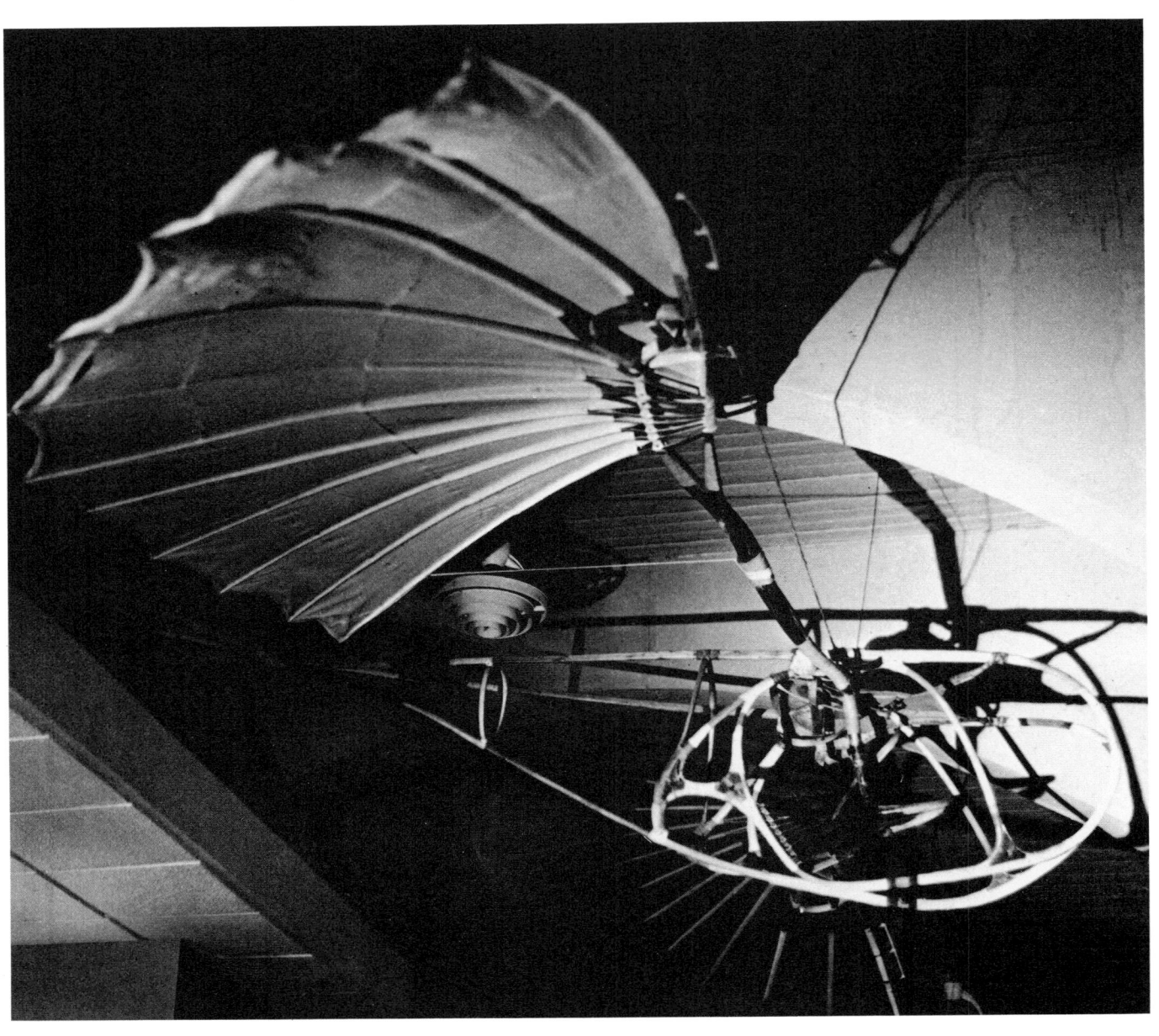

347 *Letatlin*. The model reconstructed from the original parts, 1960s, Cat. VI/6a
348–9 The parts of Letatlin at the Tatlin Exhibition held at the Moscow Headquarters of the Union of Writers, 1977, Cat. VI/6b, VI/6d

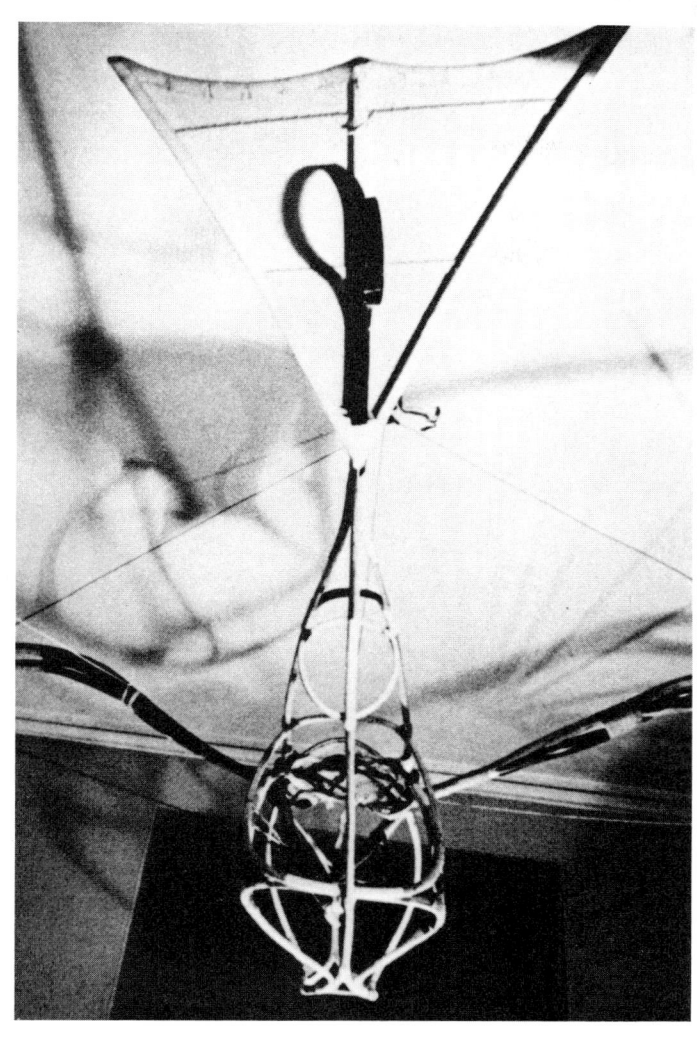

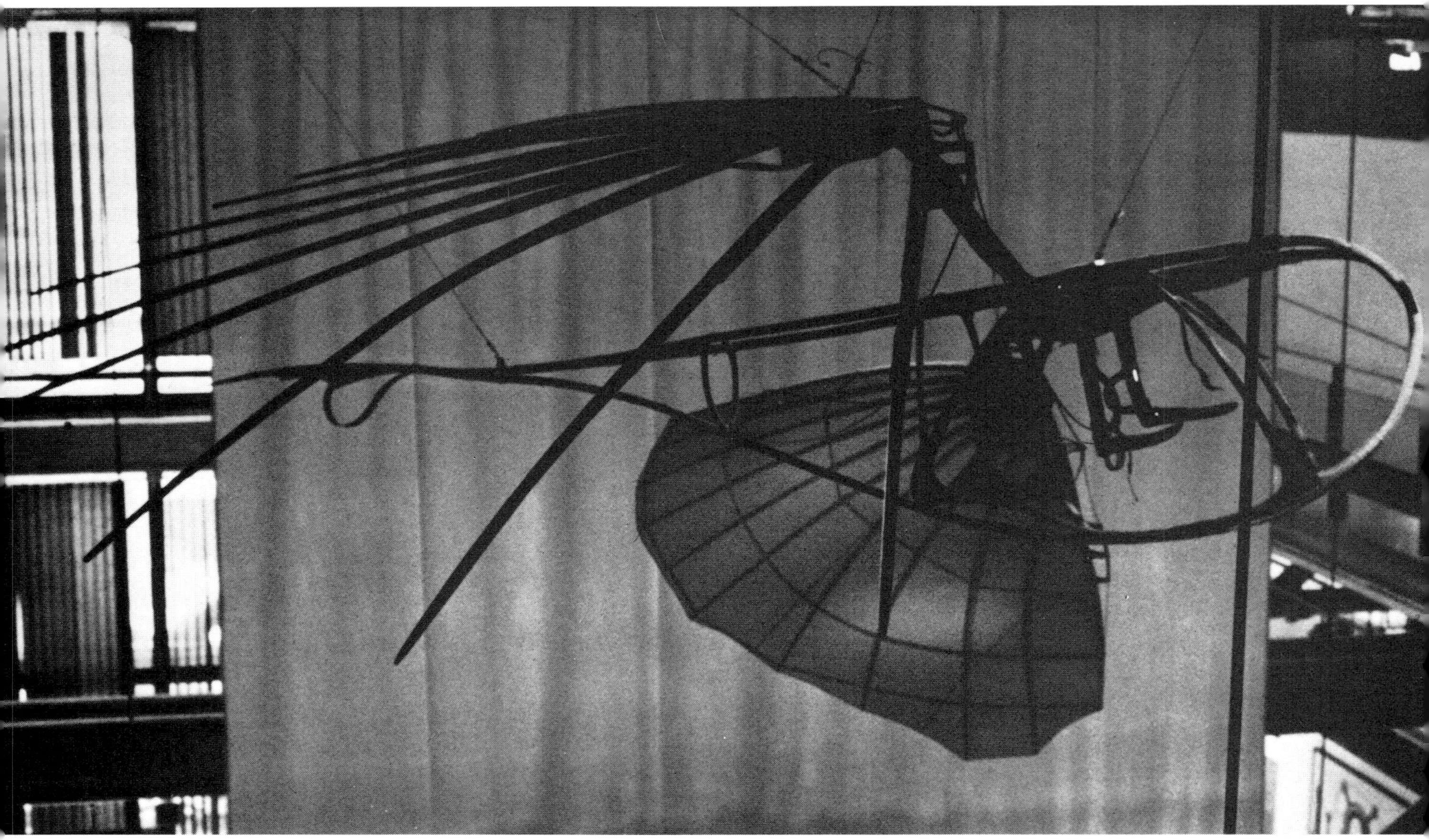

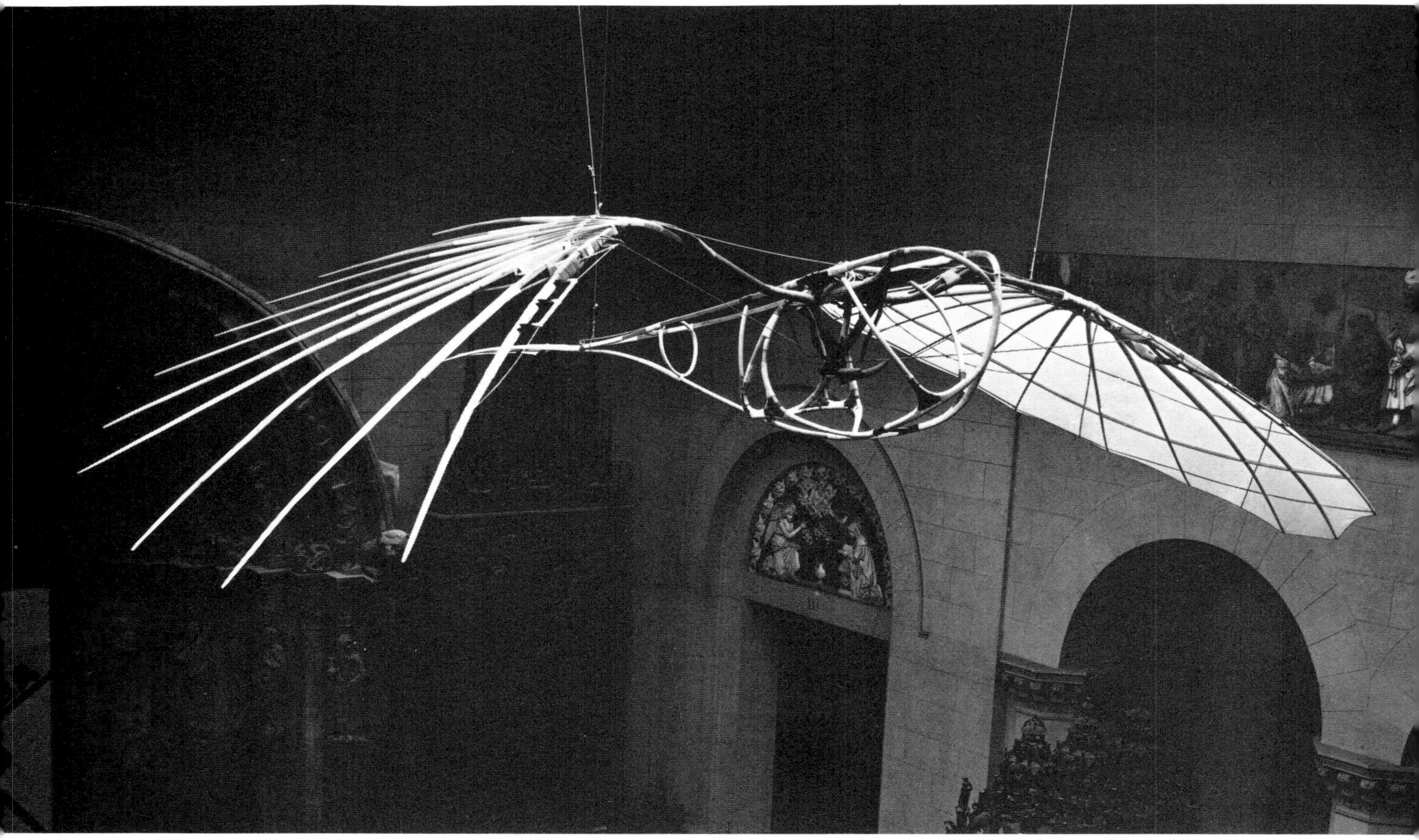

350 *Letatlin* at the Paris–Moscow Exhibition, Paris, 1979, Cat. VI/6f
351–3 *Letatlin* at the Moscow–Paris Exhibition, Moscow, 1981, Cat. VI/6g, VI/6h, VI/6i

Exhibition of Tatlin's Works in Moscow in 1977 and Related Materials

An exhibition of works by Tatlin, Honoured Art Worker of the RSFSR, was organized in February 1977 by the Writers' Union of the USSR, the Artists' Union of the USSR and TsGALI at the Fadeev Writers' Hall in Moscow. Works by Tatlin were provided for the exhibition by TsGALI, the State Tret'iakov Gallery, the Bakhrushin Museum, the Leningrad State Museum of Theatre History, the Soviet Air Force Museum and the Glinka Museum of Music History. The exhibition was designed and arranged by Rozenblium, and opened by Efimov. Its catalogue was compiled by Zhadova and Mellit, and designed by Mikhail Anikst. Such an exhibition had been a pressing issue for a long time. This is confirmed by the public interest in Tatlin reflected in several publications on his life and work, as well as in a number of articles that appeared in the Soviet press prior to the exhibition. Some examples follow here.

During the exhibition some visitors were interviewed for documentaries and television and those interviews have been preserved in shorthand records. Extracts also follow here.

Numerous visitors to the exhibition left their written comments on what they had seen, and these comments are now in the possession of TsGALI. The Archive also have a shorthand record of a closing discussion on 25 February 1977.

Articles

V.B. El'konin, What I Remember about Tatlin

I made Tatlin's acquaintance in 1928 at the home of Lev Aleksandrovich Bruni. L.A. Bruni was one of my professors at VKhUTEIN. I made friends with him while only a second-year student and he invited me to attend his 'Tuesdays'. The gifted and easy-going Levushka (as he was known) was a favourite of the Moscow intelligentsia. Every Tuesday artists, writers, poets and musicians used to gather at his place, all of them extremely different and extremely interesting people, among whom one might mention such artists as Tatlin, Favorskii, Istomin, the poets Sergei Gorodetskii and Marshak, the pianist Heinrich Neuhaus, the actor Dmitrii Zhuravlev, Punin visiting from Leningrad and many others, well-known and obscure.

Bruni lived in 21 Miasnitskaia Street (now Kirov Street) in Bazhenov's house, which used to belong to the College of Painting, Sculpture and Architecture, and which then accommodated part of VKhUTEMAS–VKhHUTEIN. There were also several apartments for professors. His was a communal apartment shared with the artists Os'merkin and Viktor Kiselev. Bruni occupied two small rooms there.

Tatlin lived in a two-storey brick house in the courtyard of the same building, and to visit Bruni all he had to do was to cross the courtyard. He regularly attended these Tuesdays. There was no dining-table, people used to sit at several small tables in the corners of the room engaged in group discussions, which at times would turn into a general conversation involving everybody. It was always very lively and interesting there; visitors were served tea and brown bread, and even those were in short supply. These were the late 1920s. The times were hard. And the host himself had a large family to support.

Tatlin did not talk much, never voiced his opinions on art, did not get involved in arguments, nor did he expound any theories. He listened to what others were saying; he had a subtle perception of humour and repeated some particularly witty jokes smiling to himself, as it were. Very seldom would he express any judgment of things and even when he did it would be as if in response to his own thoughts rather than in relation to the conversation. Those judgments were always very terse and original in a typical Tatlin fashion. I recall his remark about the artist Petr Miturich, who used to be a close friend of Khlebnikov and was married to his sister Vera Khlebnikova: 'I say, Miturich is an independent man.' By Tatlin's standards this meant a very high appreciation of the person.

Although Tatlin was in general quiet, he was nevertheless the life of the party for he had a very unusual, one can say unique, musical gift. Tatlin could sing and play a bandore ... He had made that bandore with his own hands and it was a work of art in itself. The varieties of wood were selected with great artistic intuition, the surfaces were made extremely beautifully and the whole instrument in its own way was probably on the same level as the violins of Stradivari. Tatlin's singing to the accompaniment of that bandore was staggering. Those who heard him could never forget it. He used to sing Ukrainian folk ballads; he

performed with great expression, rolling his eyes in such a way that his pupils became almost invisible, which would make his roughly cut features strongly resemble the faces of the blind bandore-players who used to sing at fairs (I remember seeing them as a child in Poltava at the Elijah's Day Fair). It even seemed that his face, too, was pock-marked, like the faces of those blind musicians (maybe it was, indeed, slightly pock-marked).

After the Ukrainian songs he would sing hymns ...

Another side of his talent consisted in his wonderful manner of reciting Khlebnikov, and for those who heard him it was unforgettable. He knew Khlebnikov by heart and recited to us an enormously long poem, 'A Night House-Search', from the first line to the last. His recitation of Khlebnikov was not merely artistic and beautiful, it was a revelation of the poet. Khlebnikov – then as now – was considered trans-rational and incomprehensible, or at best 'a poets' poet'; Tatlin's reading, however, revealed Khlebnikov's simplicity and clarity, it helped one to understand that remarkable poet whom Tatlin worshipped.

At first glance Tatlin did not look like an artist at all: he reminded one, rather, of a workman, a plumber sent by a house manager. He was thin and tall, his features were very large, as if carved with an axe; his thin hair was parted on one side. Under his unbuttoned jacket he used to wear a thick woollen vest that did not hide his sinewy neck. His manner was purposefully unpolished and he would use the familiar 'thou' instead of the formal 'you' when speaking to everybody, even to people he hardly knew. And yet on closer acquaintance every unbiased person would sense his significance and begin to realize that such an unpreprossessing appearance belonged to a great artist.

Tatlin had a remarkable eye for talent and for painting in general. To be praised by Tatlin was an unlikely possibility; even if he merely said that something was all right it used to be taken as a very high evaluation. But some of his comments which normally would not be considered judgmental meant high appreciation when spoken by him ...

When Tatlin began work on 'Letatlin' he started selecting assistants. I have no idea how it happened but from the huge sea of the VKhUTEMAS student body he chose four very different people: Shchipitsyn,

Pavil'onov, Zelenski and Sotnikov. Not only did they have different personalities but their professions differed too. Shchipitsyn was a painter, Zelenski a sculptor, Pavil'onov a monumentalist, and only Sotnikov was Tatlin's own student from the VKhUTEMAS ceramics department. So Tatlin did not merely bring together his own disciples, but formed a group of very different artists of different interests, temperaments and spirit, and managed to unite them in the process of work on his 'Letatlin', probably by taking from each whatever he was capable of contributing to the common effort. All those artists, whose individual lives followed difficult courses, had been the most talented among us and their later activity proved that Tatlin's choice had been correct and subtle.

'Letatlin' was being built in the tower of the Novodevichii Convent. Nobody was allowed into that tower; in general Tatlin was fond of making his work appear mysterious and secretive, which used to make people wonder what was going on in that tower. And when 'Letatlin' was ready it was exhibited in the Museum of Fine Arts on the Italian patio next to the copies of Michelangelo (David), Verocchio (Colleoni) and Donatello (Gattamelata). The impression his work made was striking. It was a work of art and one would forget that it was an apparatus designed for flying. Tatlin was striving to create an organic object according to the laws followed by nature in its own creativity. And that thing too was like a creation of nature. It was a bird, an unusual bird created, however, on the basis of studying the flight of a living bird. The function of flight stipulated the form, while the perfect form stipulated the function of flight. Two versions were suspended from the ceiling of the museum: one presented a skeleton of the apparatus, a harmoniously connected construction with wing-spars made of bentwood; the other was the finished apparatus upholstered with silk, so beautiful that one could admire it forever. And somehow it did not even occur to one to wonder whether the machine would fly or not. But actually all the calculations were correct and it could be used for flying. Although Pavil'onov's attempt to fly it failed and Pavil'onov fell down, everybody – both Tatlin and his assistants – thought that flying has to be learned: people learn to walk, then to swim. Flying is certainly no easier than swimming, so flying has to be learned too.

Tatlin had a difficult character: he was suspicious, distrustful, afraid of being robbed in a creative sense, i. e, of being robbed of the ideas he was working on. It was said that when he visited Picasso with his bandore he sang and played for him but did not admit to being an artist for fear that if Picasso found out that he was an artist he would not show him his most important things.

They say that when Tatlin participated in exhibitions he used to cover his works with a cloth, which he would remove only when the public was admitted. (I did not know about this, for by the time I knew him he had stopped exhibiting.) His relations with artists were very complicated: he had frequent conflicts with them; he would quarrel even with Bruni, whom he liked very much, and then make peace. His relations were complicated not only with Bruni, but probably with Malevich as well. I remember Bruni saying that in Leningrad Tatlin used to live one floor below Malevich's apartment, right under it, and when he heard Malevich's footsteps upstairs he would point his finger upwards and say: 'He walks!'

Tatlin certainly realized his own significance and behaved according to his understanding of how a major artist should behave. The following incident occurred in VKhUTEMAS once. Tatlin had to see the chairman of one of the departments to discuss some business. The latter was sitting at his desk looking through his papers and did not pay any attention to Tatlin's arrival. After waiting several minutes the artist said: 'I am Tatlin, while you without your desk are nothing but long johns.'

His relations with other artists were aggravated by Tatlin's ability to make cutting jokes. During my meetings with him at the Red Army Theatre, where he was working on the play 'The Affair' by Sukhovo-Kobylin, I happened to hear the following dialogue. An older stage-designer at the theatre, Ivan Sergeevich Fedotov, was working there, so Tatlin asks him: 'Listen, Vania, do they give money today?' Fedotov replies: 'How do I know, Vladimir Evgrafovich?' 'Well, you are employed here.' Such things certainly offended people and did not improve Tatlin's relationships with his colleagues.

At that time I was painting tapestries for the production of 'The Taming of the Shrew' in that same theatre at the request of the artist Shifrin. Tatlin met me at the staircase and said: 'Listen, paint some roses for me and I'll go and get you some kerosene' (typical of Tatlin's humour). – 'Which roses?' – 'I need a carpet for my play, something like those made in Kursk.' – 'Well, ask the production department and I'll paint them' (although I was afraid of painting for him). But he never discussed anything with the production department. His relations with it were rather strained. He used only wood for his productions, even the ornamental curtain was made of wood in the shape of a wooden curtain with a tie. His understanding of the true nature of the material permeated all his work but was not appreciated in the theatre and caused very serious conflicts. Experienced theatre professionals could not understand why it was necessary to make a curtain and other things out of wood when, in their opinion,

it would have been far simpler to use papier mâché as is normally done.

The very fact of Tatlin being offered a production at that time in one of the central Moscow theatres should be attributed to the civic courage of the chief artist of the theatre, Nisson Abramovich Shifrin, who had great respect for Tatlin, realized his importance and wanted to help him very much. But even Shifrin did not fully understand his ideas. He laughed when telling me how Tatlin described his maquette: 'These are doors, you see, for coming in and going out.' I laughed too, for it struck me then as attributing a non-existent significance to things. But afterwards, as I was thinking about Tatlin's words, I realized that he was right in a very profound sense, for the main goal of art is to see surrounding objects and phenomena as if for the very first time and to restore thereby their original meaning and significance, which is worn out in everyday use and no longer noticed.

Tatlin's activity during his last years was limited exclusively to the theatre. Besides 'The Affair' he designed, also in wood, the production of Ostrovskii's 'A Comic Actor of the 17th Century' for MKhAT-2, which, unfortunately, I did not see – I saw only its maquette. But I did see another production, totally forgotten nowadays, Faiko's play 'Captain Kostrov' in the Moscow Theatre of the Revolution. I do not remember at all what that play was about; I do not think it was an important phenomenon in dramaturgy. But it is impossible to forget what Tatlin did there: a large disc was rotating at an angle to the plane of the stage, which created a spatial arrangement such as I have never seen any artist reproduce. The first episode represented the Volga. The leaning disc was covered with sheets of white tin. On that tin there was a real tar-coated black boat, and on that boat there was a pole with a piece of faded red cloth tied to it. The backdrop of the stage design presented a semispherical grey horizon, without any modelling, without clouds. As the materials of the stage-setting could be distinguished clearly, a strikingly convincing poetic image of a Russian river was created. And it left an enormous impression by its simplicity, clarity and poetic quality. In other scenes turning the disc produced a gap between it and the stage. That gap was filled with carved wood, which created the effect of a sandy precipice; at the top of the precipice there was a wooden bench.

Tatlin's desire to convey the true nature of the material sometimes resulted in sad disappointments. In the Kamernyi Theatre he designed sets for the play about the Cheliuskin's expedition – I cannot recall its title. Tatlin insisted that the ice in that play should be made of glass. He must have had a hard time trying to get permission to do it; on that occasion, however, his suggestion was accepted. The 'ice' was brought from the factory and piled on the stage. Tatlin was fond of staying at night alone in the theatre. He would look at the stage from a spectator's seat contemplating his productions and how to do them. So one night in the theatre he suddenly heard a chinking sound, and then another and another. He rushed on stage to find that all his ice blocks were falling apart. The thing is that changes in temperature start certain processes within large blocks of glass of irregular shape and as a result the blocks disintegrate. Tatlin was talking about it with a rather black humour. I do not know how he found the way out of that problem.

Tatlin did not shun making speeches in public, he was a wonderful speaker and people used to listen to him with great concentration and involvement; his speeches were distinguished by a peculiar, typically Tatlinesque wittiness. I remember one of his speeches probably because it had some relation to myself. The artists' city committee arranged an exhibition of young artists with the purpose of admitting the best of them to the Moscow Union of Artists. There was a public discussion at the exhibition, after which the commission was to go through the exhibition and accept those it considered worthy. It was that discussion that Tatlin attended. It was a period of intensive industrialization, which found a wide expression in painting as 'the industrial theme'. However, this was mostly represented through numerous landscapes with smoking factory chimneys. So Pavil'onov and I, who participated in the exhibition, were accused of ignoring the industrial theme by the speakers during the discussion. Tatlin objected to that in his speech and said in his typical fashion: 'The Party is already choking from all that smoke.'

He was greatly concerned about the state of Soviet art. The general condition of the activity he regarded as his own worried him a great deal, probably more than the atmosphere of non-recognition surrounding him during his last years. When I met him in the Moscow Union of Artists he asked without any preamble as soon as he said hello: 'Do you think any of that will survive?'

He was concerned whether there was a meaningful grain in the process occurring in contemporary art, whether that grain would grow into anything valuable.

Tatlin's last years were difficult. The artist Aksel'rod and I happened to meet him in Maslovka Street near his studio (where he would not admit anyone) shortly before his death, and unexpectedly he invited us in: 'Let us go to my place!' We went to his studio. He played the bandore for us and sang, then started showing his paintings. During those last years he resumed his easel painting very intensively: it was quite different from his painting of the 1910–20s, from 'Fishmonger' and 'Sailor'. Tatlin painted

with oils on wood covered with a primer. He painted flowers, still-lifes (there was a beautiful still-life with a chunk of meat and a knife). I liked his paintings, they showed a sense of responsibility for each stroke of brush on the surface, and that was amazing and even strange. I told him that I liked it. He said: 'No, really? Are you serious about it?' I said: 'Why should I say it then, if I do not believe it?' 'But everybody here says it is rubbish.' He was told by everybody around him that what he was doing was rubbish. The end of his life was very hard. And when he died there were only about seven or eight of us at his funeral. These were Aleksandra Nikolaevna Korsakova, the architect Lev Rudnev, Favorskii, Sarra Lebedeva, the artists Sergei Sen'kin and Aksel'rod, my wife Nadezhda Mikhailovna El'konina and myself. That is about all. I may have forgotten somebody.

Rudnev and Favorskii made speeches at his coffin. Favorskii, who appeared to be incompatible with Tatlin at first glance, must have understood and highly valued him. I remember him saying: 'Tatlin loved material and material revealed to him its secrets.'

V. B. El'konin
'Что я помню о Татлине'

'... We are greatly indebted to the artist. His work has not been studied either in the field of material culture or in the sphere of pure art. We are thus, strictly speaking, impoverishing ourselves and discovering things that were discovered a long time ago...'

Abramova, 'Tatlin',
Декоративное искусство, no. 2, 1966

'... During the last period of his creative activity (1943–53) Tatlin produced twenty-six paintings. He had been preparing an exhibition of his works but death prevented him from realizing that dream.

Vladimir Evgrafovich was deprived of a deserved recognition in his own lifetime. But he had been working without rest in the name of the future until he breathed his last: "I see my Motherland as a treasure-house of great traditions. My contribution is there too".'

Begicheva's Reminiscences
Вітчизна, no. 2, 1969

'... Tatlin was the closest and most important teacher in my education... I very much liked his lectures, his views. Something in me must have appealed to him too. Once he invited me to his studio. It was set up inside the bell-tower of the Novodevichii Convent. As a rule, he never let any artist step inside. It was an unusual studio — a studio of an artist-constructor and an enthusiastic scientist ...'

Sotnikov's Reminiscences
Художники об искусстве керамики.
Искусство, Москва, 1971

'... The initial period of relations between Maiakovskii and Tatlin resulted in a creative co-operation that produced a collection of poems and drawings: "The Service-Book of the Three", published in March 1913 in Moscow. One of the poems in the collection, Maiakovskii's "Signboards", was illustrated by two autolithographs (India ink): still-lifes executed in a "shopsign" style. One of them was done by the author of the poem, the other by Tatlin. So Tatlin should be regarded as Maiakovskii's first illustrator.

Maiakovskii's list of "the first works of the October epoch" included only three works: the second place was given to Maiakovskii's "Mystery-Bouffe" directed by Meierkhol'd; the third place to V. Kamenskii's long poem "Sten'ka Razin", while the first place was given to the Monument to the Third International by Tatlin.'

Khardzhiev, Maiakovskii's First Illustrator
Московский художник, 18 December
1975

Interviews

It is good that all the works have come together now and we can easily leap from them — from drawings and paintings to this marvellous central object, the Tower of the Third International. You can observe in it that same, buoyant style of the paintings, ready to push something out into the future, forward into the depth — the same resistance to space ... He could do everything: he makes a bandore, he makes the Tower of the Third International — what an extraordinary range! One is taken from the past, the other from the future. And all that was done by one person. Incredible! An incredible person — a dreamer and so very Russian in his appearance, in his generous nature, his love for everything Russian ....

V.M. Goriaev
People's Artist of the RSFSR,
state prize laureate graphic artist

This artist together with other colleagues managed to show something totally unexpected and new, something that in architecture provided a basis for much of what has since been done all over the world. For myself, both the Tower and 'Letatlin', which will certainly never fly, have always remained a romantic leap into the future — a leap that should have been envied by everybody who was dreaming that the Revolution would bring along something unexpected and extraordinary. While we, the students, were trying to make that unexpected come true. The 1920s were extraordinary. Together with student architects we were making designs for the festive celebrations of May Day and 7 November: to cover the Red Square with some unusual glass structures, from the GUM department store to the Kremlin wall, so that under those structures the trees in blossom and totally unheard-of processions would pass by, which we would be able to decorate. Tatlin was a product of those times. And whenever I am told about 'Letatlin' I recall the flying peasant from the film 'Andrei Rublev'. What does it matter if it does not fly! Yet what was the main dream on which Tatlin based that construction? If the form is absolutely ideal and if the artist is able to discover this ideal form, it will fly by itself. What can be more beautiful than such a desire and such an idea?

A.D. Goncharov
Honoured Art Worker of the RSFSR,
professor, corresponding member
of the USSR Academy of Arts

I used to know Tatlin – a huge man who reminded me of a revolutionary sailor, with large hands, a fine singer who made his instruments himself and looked into the future with passion and calm. That life in the future, that creation of the day after tomorrow are indispensable, for it is impossible to ride into the future without going uphill. When trying to prove that the earth was a globe Strabo quoted Homer, who made his Odysseus see the shore only when he was raised by an enormous wave. And precisely that future emerging from the sea, an indubitable and beautiful future, was the task for the revolutionary artists.

V.B. Shklovskii
writer

By that time I was already a fairly experienced pilot and head of the flight unit at the Moscow Flying School.

One day the head of our sport section summoned me and said: 'Go to the Novodevichii Convent and there you will find the artist Tatlin, who has been building an airplane that looks like a bird. If it is indeed worthy of consideration we should help him.'

I went to the Novodevichii Convent, found the tower where Tatlin was working and entered a place that reminded me of the Renaissance: not only was it ancient itself but it was also crowded with all kinds of archaic contraptions, while from the ceiling of the tower the flying machine was suspended. It had already been finished and Tatlin with his assistants was working on the next one.

I was struck by the charm that man possessed, by his sturdy appearance which was also reminiscent of the Renaissance.

I introduced myself to Tatlin as a pilot as well as a gliding enthusiast, and he started explaining to me what he was doing ... A whale's whole jaw with whiskers was lying in the studio. The thing is that the edge of

the wing in a flying apparatus should be very resilient, and when made of wood would break very easily, but when made of steel it is too heavy. Whereas a whale's whisker is both supple and light.

Tatlin used to say that a resilient construction was more durable, it was not as subject to destruction as a rigid structure. 'I examined debris from your airplanes which break into smithereens when they crash,' he said. 'Whereas here we had an accident when a beam fell from under the roof of the tower onto the wing spar – and nothing happened: it bounced off the wing spar and the latter remained perfectly unharmed.' The lines of the apparatus designed by Tatlin were very beautiful.

I recall telling Tatlin during one of our discussions that scientists did not believe man to be capable of flying by means of his muscle power, and asking him: 'What do you think will happen to your apparatus?' He replied:

'I reared two cranes. I found them as nestlings. Later on, when their wings started growing, they found a place between the fence and the barn which, because of a strong draught, resembled a kind of aerodynamic tube. And in their air current the young cranes started unfolding their wings and leaping up. At first nothing happened, then gradually they began floating in the air, and finally they were flying – at first low, using the opposing air current, then higher. In the end I had to let them go. So shall I learn, just as they did.'

K.K. Artseulov
Honoured Pilot of the USSR,
glider pilot

...His beautiful model of an ornithopter evokes admiration for its aesthetic form, the simplicity of its construction and even for an apparent reliability. While looking at it I immediately imagined that the apparatus was flying at low speed, although for that kind of apparatus the problem consists precisely in flying at low speed safely and for long periods, without consuming too much of the energy man spends when moving ...

V.I. Sevast'ianov
pilot-astronaut,
twice Hero of the Soviet Union

Today, at this exhibition I saw for the first time Tatlin's famous tower. We saw it in textbooks many times, we knew it and seemed to imagine it very well. But when I saw it today in three dimensions it shook me. In a word, even today it strikes me as a project of the twenty-first century. Even nowadays our architecture and our technology are not prepared for tackling such a grand design... Those coils disappearing into the sky and that slant seemingly unjus-

tified from the viewpoint of construction create an internal construction that possesses a great deal of logic and, I would say, some inner mystery. Even when looking at the model I did not at once understand how those forms had been put together, built and conceived. But the visual impression is staggering! I cannot vouch for all of them but it seems to me that had an architect designed that tower he would have made it complete with a spire or some other form aiming at the sky. Here, however, everything is different: the coils in combination with horizontal lines and volumes create a unique emotional state within the lacework of those constructions.

I.A. Pokrovskii
architect, state prize
laureate

I recall 1948 and my début, in fact, in Moscow with Iroshnikova's play 'Somewhere in Siberia'. Prior to that the Art Theatre had produced a play 'Deep Reconnaissance' for which Vladimir Evgrafovich Tatlin had made stage designs. And he was the artist I invited. He seemed to be very close to the method of interpretation that I had in mind for that play.

Such was the beginning of our acquaintance. He was an illustrious master, an artist of world-wide fame, while I was a beginning young director.

The action in the play took place at a factory, in hostels, during the war on the home front; it was about young people. Together we visited a chemical plant near Moscow to get an idea of the real thing. He transformed it into a very interesting, totally theatrical mode. A huge sheet of white tin was made in which a huge rotating wheel was permanently reflected ....

My contact with the great artist gave me a great deal.

In the theatre his approach – which, to my mind, is only now being truly developed – was very significant. I shall never forget, for instance, the way he presented extreme heat in Azerbaijan in the play 'Deep Reconnaissance'. He put up real boards and brought from the film studio some huge stage lights which bombarded the boards with real light, thus revealing the texture and pattern of the wood. He then placed a basin filled with water in the centre of the stage and directed reflections off the water on to the boards. And the combination of those two things – the transparent wooden walls with reflections bouncing off the water in the basin – created a unique atmosphere.

G.A. Tovstonogov
People's Artist of the USSR,
Lenin Prize laureate, theatre director

Comments in the Visitors' Book

I got to know Tatlin in the 1930s during the preparations for testing his 'Letatlin'. I was asked to do the trial flights. I was then working as an instructor in gliding and was flying many kinds of gliders. When 'Letatlin' appeared in our school the event produced a sensation. There began a pilgrimage to the apparatus and it naturally stirred a tremendous amount of controversy. I discussed at length with Vladimir Evgrafovich the unusual control system of 'Letatlin'. Everything was unusual there: the pilot had to lie on a special couch and to hold on to the levers of the wings, altering their angle, while his legs worked like a cyclist and were supposed to flap the wings. That kind of control of the apparatus radically differed from the generally accepted way of controlling all types of gliders and airplanes.

It was decided to start training on the ground. I used to get into the pilot's workplace with only my head raised above the machine and tried to work with my arms and legs, trying to imagine I was flying. The take-off was supposed to be carried out with the help of a rubber cord – a shock-absorber. To my great regret I was not able to carry out the flight, for during my absence a colleague of mine, V.V. Nefedov, attempted to do it himself. However, when everything was ready for launching 'Letatlin' a sudden gust of wind turned it upside down and the pilot was jammed between the levers of the construction.

As a result of that accident, 'Letatlin' was badly damaged.

Many years have passed, the talented inventor V.E. Tatlin is no longer with us. But his work and ideas remain. It is very encouraging that there are some thoughtful people who have managed to collect V.E. Tatlin's creative legacy and present it to our contemporaries.

V.F. Khapov
Honoured Test Pilot
of the USSR

I would like to express my deep gratitude to the Writers' Union for organizing Tatlin's exhibition.

Vladimir Evgrafovich Tatlin was my immediate teacher. In the Faculty of Wood- and Metalworking of VKhUTEMAS he taught a subject that even today would seem innovative: Material Culture.

A.I. Damskii
architect

The exhibition is very interesting and it enables us to get a feeling of the artist's personality, to realize that he was a revolution-ary artist – an artist of the Revolution, the sixtieth anniversary of which is celebrated this year.

I was acquainted with Tatlin. He used to read poetry to me (mainly Khlebnikov's) and to sing (I remember two songs).

We used to discuss the art of the new age at length (or, rather, he did the talking while I listened).

Tatlin is still waiting to be discovered.

An album of his works should be published.

Lev Ozerov
poet

The exhibition is most necessary but rather limited in size. I smelled the air of the early republic and experienced Tatlin's elevation as part of the general upsurge of that time. One would like to see a more detailed exhibition transcending the limits of what was done exclusively by Tatlin; more informational and factual material both on Tatlin and his time as well as on the art of that period.

We probably need a museum of Tatlin's works, books about him and, certainly, permanent exhibitions in the existing museums.

L. Kol'berg
Producer of popular science films
(Leningrad)

Nowadays, from the vantage point of the [19]70s of this same twentieth century, 'Letatlin', the chair and other works are perceived differently.

It seems to me that, among those who were fascinated with new form at the turn of this century, this artist was less than any other a prisoner of that form. Tatlin's form is truly indispensable and unnoticeable as well as non-dominating. So it seems nowadays.

M. Liubich
college student

The exhibition of Tatlin's works seems to me a major event reminiscent of the best traditions of Soviet revolutionary art. These traditions and, first and foremost, the art of Tatlin himself, belong to the left, progressive culture of the whole world and occupy a leading place in it ... That is why it seems to me that the materials of this exhibition deserve to be widely popularized on the international level. In my opinion, one should give thought to the possibilities for their exhibition in other countries, where they would undoubtedly add more credit to the name of Soviet artistic culture.

E.A. Goldzamt
Doctor of Architecture,
professor

Press Reaction

B. Galanov, 'Tatlin, a Visionary of the Blades'

In the Central Writers' Hall an exhibition has opened of works by Vladimir Evgrafovich Tatlin (1885–1953), a man of amazing, versatile talent who offered his creative work to the commune from the first days of the Revolution. At Tatlin's exhibition one is continually amazed when passing from one item to another, from one display to another, from still-lifes with bunches of red, blue, yellow and light-blue flowers to vivid landscapes, from the landscapes to portraits, from Tatlin the painter to Tatlin the graphic artist, book illustrator, original stage designer, the author of the once sensational project for the Monument-Tower of the Third International. Its rotating model is also on display at the exhibition. Tatlin, the designer, giving much thought to a new convenient appearance of things used in the everyday life of contemporary man, a designer of everyday clothes, kitchen-ware, furniture. Take a good look at these exhibits. Tatlin is interested in everything: in designing a chair for your room, a kettle, a sugar-bowl. And Tatlin the inventor of the flying apparatus 'Letatlin', which today is soaring under the ceiling at the entrance to the exhibition hall, its wings casting a shadow over the visitors.

I first heard Tatlin's name when I was a child, a schoolboy, on the day of Maiakovskii's funeral, when I saw the poet's coffin on the truck made by Tatlin into a kind of pedestal for a future monument to Maiakovskii. A few years later I had the good fortune to meet the artist himself. At that time he was fascinated by the idea of creating an original flying apparatus with flapping wings. I was then working as a reporter and wrote a short article for *Vecherniaia Moskva* about the planned trial flights of 'Letatlin'. First one. Then another. From that time on I started visiting the artist. He used to stay up with me until very late in a rather empty and somewhat desolate room. Its only decoration was a painting of a reclining woman or, as it seemed to me, a sculpture of a lying woman, for her forms were sculpted (definitely sculpted rather than painted) so palpably and boldly. Tatlin found a grateful listener in me and he contemplated with enthusiasm the future of his flying apparatus.

I realize now that having carefully studied the designs and descriptions of Leonardo's flying machines Tatlin religiously believed in his own idea. Even after the failure (or half success) of 'Letatlin's' trial flights Tatlin was convinced that man can take off into the air by means of his own muscle power. He used to say half-jokingly and half-seriously – and I used to believe him – that the apparatus with flapping wings would become a part of everyday life by 1950, and then one could easily fly from Potapovskii Lane, where my newspaper's editorial office was, to his Miasnitskaia Street.

'Letatlin' – and this is probably the main thing – was his favourite creation, his beloved child. Into it he poured his talent, skill, art, his notion of beauty and his dream of the 'bird-man'. Significantly, he himself used to say that people should not approach that work from a purely utilitarian point of view, for he had created it as an artist ...

It is good that the exhibition at the Central Writers' Hall, where many works by Tatlin have been thoughtfully collected and so carefully restored, where one can see some rare documents and photographs, reminds us of that generous master. Velemir Khlebnikov called Tatlin 'a visionary of the blades' and 'a stern bard of the propeller'. Well, the fruits of his labour and inspiration have survived. 'Letatlin' survives too – one of the beautiful incarnations of the daring thought of the artist-'sun-snarer'.

B. Galanov, 'Tainovidets lopastei',
Literaturnaia Gazeta,
23 February 1977

Ivan Rakhillo, On Eccentrics and Tatlin's Bandore

Tatlin spent his last years in Maslovka, a small community of artists, under the same roof with Fedor Reshetnikov. Vsevolod Vishnevskii helped to move him there.

'One should not just write about this man,' Vishnevskii used to exclaim, 'one should shout about him, ring all the bells!'
... Reshetnikov and I call on Tatlin. A huge empty room. A black-and-blue poster on the wall. Vladimir Evgrafovich forlornly sits on a stool. He holds a bandore in his arms but he is not playing it – just stroking the instrument gently with pensive fingers as if enjoying feeling the beauty of its polished surface. The bandore was made with his own hands. One could see the quiet, undisguised infatuation of an artist, a poet, a master with his creation. Tatlin's only son was killed during the Great Patriotic War; he had been attached to him. Now he is lonely and quiet.

'So, how are you doing?' asks Reshetnikov in Ukrainian, greeting him in a neighbourly fashion. 'Well, just sitting here, thinking, searching...' 'Searching!' – the whole of Tatlin was in that word. All his life he had been 'searching', he had always

been on the forward outposts of time. But after 'Letatlin' many people close to him regarded him as an eccentric. They could not comprehend how a talented artist with a name and a high status in art could 'dissipate' his talents and give up his positions by getting into unknown and totally hopeless inventions. The name of eccentric remained attached to him all through his last years.

'Yet he has a lively mind', Reshetnikov used to say. He cannot bear routine. In anything. The spirit of search is in his blood. He is constantly working on some problem. Now it is clothes. Now it is machines. Now it is furniture. He dreams of designing a chair for people engaged in intellectual pursuits that would make a person feel as if he were sitting 'on a cloud'. So that the body would relax by equally distributing its weight 'onto all points'. And a kind of electric cap would hang over one's head and by means of special 'magnetic rays' would absorb all tiredness from the person, leaving him refreshed, after which he would go back to work! 'I am thinking, I am searching. It is difficult. But I believe I shall cope with it.'

This time Vladimir Evgrafovich showed us a small still-life with white flowers, remarkable for its composition and unusual technique.

Then he and Reshetnikov started singing two-part Ukrainian songs to bandore accompaniment.

I was sitting there, listening and thinking about Russian eccentrics. Eccentrics have always been a phenomenon. And Tatlin's 'I am searching' has been the mainstay of their character. A tireless search. They were heralds of the new – those unselfish wanderers – 'Inhabitants of the Globe'. They are enthusiasts ready to serve their people. Aren't our 'great eccentrics' such as Tsiolkovskii, Fedorov, Tsander from the same source? Nesterov, Shaliapin, Konenkov? Maiakovskii, Chkalov, Esenin?... People with difficult and unusual destinies. Their names, illumined by light, are beloved by our people.

That is what I was thinking about to the sounds of Tatlin's many-stringed bandore...

I. Rakhillo, 'O chudakakh i tatlinskoi
bandure,' Literaturnaia Rossia,
18 March 1977

V. Logvinov, Like a Poem in Metal

The model of the Monument to the Third International is on display in the main hall of the No. 41 Trade and Technical School in Gor'kii. A lace structure is girdled by the spirals running towards each other ...

The model, commissioned by the Shchusev Museum of Architecture, has been executed by the instructors and students of the school at the Gor'kii Art Studios.

The fate of the model is interesting. In 1919, Leningrad artists V. Tatlin, I. Meerzon and T. Shapiro decided to participate in carrying out Lenin's plan of monumental propaganda. They set themselves the task of producing a monument to the Third International, a congress of which was held in Moscow in 1919 under the leadership of Lenin. According to the authors' original concept this was to be a palace 500 metres high in which international rallies of fighters for freedom would take place.

'We wanted to create a monument that would reflect the spirit of the times: dynamism, aspirations, enthusiasm', recollects T. Shapiro. 'We believed that the monumental image of the Revolution should become a grandiose construction – a poem in metal.'

The authors of the project were provided with studios at the Academy of Arts. They wanted to make the model in metal – a symbol of the new epoch. But where would one get it from? So they had to use wood, cardboard, veneer, tracing-paper. Even nails were impossible to obtain. Two thousand rivets had to be made from wire.

In a year's time the model was ready. It was transported to Moscow in a dismantled state and was mounted in the hall of columns at the House of Unions. Delegates to the Eighth Congress of Soviets were the first to see the structure.

'Lenin saw the model of the monument', T. Shapiro continues. 'Vladimir Il'ich asked us two questions: how much the construction would cost and whether it was feasible to build. Alas, we were not able to answer those questions ...'

In 1925 the model was sent to Paris to the International Exhibition of Modern Decorative Art, where it was awarded a gold medal. When the exhibition was over the model was presented to one of the French workers' clubs. It was destroyed during the German occupation of France.

The Monument, however, was not 'lost track of'. Publications dealing with Soviet art mentioned that gigantic 'Tower'. Now the model has been reconstructed. The reconstruction has been carried out under the guidance of the oldest Leningrad artist and architect, T. Shapiro. Dozens of buildings have been constructed according to his designs in Leningrad. He talks about the friends with whom he worked on the Monument fifty-six years ago...

Soon this model will be sent to the Shchusev Museum of Architecture as a sample of the art of those fiery years.

V. Logvinov, 'Kak poema v metalle',
Pravda,
22 May 1977

A Tower-Monument

Soon after the revolutionary events that shook the world the artist Tatlin was inspired by a recollection of an ancient Russian tradition to commemorate the steps of history not with sculpted figures but with buildings. In 1919 he began work on the project of a tower – an architectural monument in honour of the October Revolution. Subsequently the monument was related to another event: the organization of the Third International...

Unlike the static and symmetrical Eiffel Tower, 'Tatlin's Tower' expresses a dynamic impulse. The whole of it is like an upward thrust of the dialectical spiral of history conceived by the author as a symbol of revolutionary liberation...

The Fine Arts Department of the People's Commissariat of Education requested that drawings should be made for the project and also a model for the Eighth All-Russia Congress of Soviets. But those were the years of economic hardship, and plans for the electrification of the country were only in the initial stage of discussion; so naturally the tower seemed to be pure fantasy, although experts in architecture and engineering found it technically feasible. Fifty-eight years have passed and Tatlin's design does not seem unrealistic any more. The image he created is still astonishing and grandiose. It captivates by its synthesis of both the rebellious and the life-asserting spirit of the Revolution. The author produced several models of the monument. Besides the one built for the Eighth Congress there was a model made in 1925 for the international exhibition in Paris, where it was awarded a gold medal and where, unfortunately, it perished during the war. There are copies of the model in London and Stockholm.

Now that the model has again been reconstructed it will be possible to see it in Moscow, in the Shchusev Museum of Architecture.

Monument-bashnia
(Iz redaktsionnogo obzora:
Kamennaia letopis' istorii)
Literaturnaia gazeta,
7 November 1977

APPENDICES

Biographical Data

1885 Vladimir Evgrafovich Tatlin is born in Moscow on 16 December (28 December New Style). His father: Evgraf Nikiforovich Tatlin, a railway engineer; his mother: Nadezhda Nikolaevna Tatlina, née Bart, a poet.

1887 His mother dies and his father remarries a few years later. The family moves to Khar'kov.

1895(?)–1902 Attends a non-classical secondary school, but soon runs away to Odessa. Signs on a sailing ship as a ship's boy and his first trip abroad is to Bulgaria and Turkey. Finds a job in an icon-painting studio, where he works with two young artists, Levenets and Kharchenko. Considered these two as his first teachers.

1902–4 Studies painting at the Moscow College of Painting, Sculpture and Architecture. In 1903 he is expelled from the College because of 'lack of progress and objectionable behaviour'. In a surviving 'Petition' dated 1903, the artist's father requests the College to reinstate his son (TsGALI, fond 680, inventory 2, unit 1801).
According to the artist, he was a student at the College for the second time between 1909(?) and 1910 (see p. 262). His teachers were Korovin and Serov. He did not complete his studies. It is possible that he supported himself during these years by working as an assistant stage-hand in the scenery workshops of the Solodovnikov Opera.

1905–10 Is admitted to the I.D. Sileverstov College of Art in Penza. Passes his final examinations on 3 and 4 April 1910 and receives the 'Certificate of Professional Draughtsman', which entitles him to teach 'drawing, draughting and calligraphy at educational establishments at the secondary level'. The certificate is dated 30 June 1910 and is numbered 612. (Penza College of Art Archive, fond 120, file 28, pp. 102–115 – archival data courtesy of painter A. Stroev.) His teachers were Afanas'ev and Goriushkin-Sorokopudov, painters in the popular style, who were well acquainted with Russian folklore.

1909–10 Is placed under police surveillance as one of the most active student political activists at the Penza College, and, because of his revolutionary views, is held in growing suspicion by the authorities from the Revolution of 1905–7 onwards. (See documents of the Penza Provincial Police, TsGAOR, fond 63, inventory 28, unit 2245/920; fond 102, inventory 101, unit 4945–1909 – material located by V.V. Medvedev.)
During the summers he sails the Mediterranean on board the sailing ships the *Grand Duchess Mariia Nikolaevna* and the *Voronezh*, and on the steamer the *Evgeniia Ol'denburgskaia*; he reaches Asia Minor, Greece and colonies of Italy in Africa. During his wanderings through Russia he also works as a boxer in a circus. Copies old Russian church frescoes.

1908–11 Becomes a friend of Larionov. During the summer they paint together at Larionov's in Tiraspol'. He makes friends also with Sagaidachnyi, Le Dantiu, Fabri and the Burliuk brothers. During his stay in St Petersburg he, Le Dantiu, Lapshin and Lebedev attend Bernshtein's private school of drawing. Starts exhibiting works.

1910–11 Returns from Penza to Moscow, where he attends the Moscow College of Painting, Sculpture and Architecture. Studies painting at the studio of Mashkov and Mikhailovskii (see p. 332).
Designs scenery for the popular play, *Tsar Maximilian and his Disobedient Son, Adolf*, which is staged under the direction of Bonch-Tomashevskii at the Literary and Artistic Circle of Moscow.

1911–15 Participates in the activities of the artistic studio 'Tower', located on the Kuznetskii Most, which is frequented by theatrical specialists, poets and artists, such as Khlebnikov, Maiakovskii, Lentulov, Larionov, Goncharova, Le Dantiu, Fal'k, Popova. Paints and draws among his colleagues and students in a studio located at no. 37 Ostozhenka, now Metrostroevskaia Street. From time to time Aleksandr Vesnin, Udal'tsova, Popova, Khodasevich and Fal'k also participate in the work of the studio. Becomes a friend of Aleksandr Vesnin, who at that time was chiefly engaged in painting, and who was later to become one of the founders of Soviet Constructivism in architecture.
Becomes a friend of the painter Lebedev and his wife, Darmolatova (Lebedeva), a sculptor.
He also works at a studio where icons are painted.

1911–12 Takes part in the debates, social programmes and exhibitions of the young poets and artists and is included in their publications. Meets the poet Velemir Khlebnikov; their relationship is to deepen into a friendship which will influence the artist's entire career. Tatlin, Larionov and Goncharova become the poet's first illustrators.
Breaks off with Larionov.

1913 On 3 January he is accepted, along with Malevich, Morgunov, Bubnova and others, as a member of the Union of Youth.
As Maiakovskii's first illustrator he prepares drawings for the poem 'Signboards'.
He begins work on painterly reliefs, selections of materials and counter-reliefs. Coins the motto: 'Let us place the eye under the control of touch.'
Prepares stage and costume design for Glinka, *Ivan Susanin* (*A Life for the Tsar*) which is ultimately not performed.

1914 From February to April performs as a bandore player at the Russian exhibition of folk art in Berlin. With the money earned from this activity he is able to visit Paris (see p. 181), where he meets Picasso and studies the collections of the Louvre.
The First Exhibition of Painterly Reliefs runs from 10 to 14 May in the studio at no. 37 Ostozhenka Street.

1915 Shows painterly reliefs at the Tramway V exhibition, and centre and corner counter-reliefs at 0—10. The Last Futurist Exhibition in Petrograd. An illustrated booklet, *Vladimir Evgrafovich Tatlin*, dated 17 December 1915, is produced (see p. 331).
He and his new artist friends, Bruni, Miturich, Lebedev, Tyrsa, Punin and Isakov, found the society Apartment no. 5 in Petrograd. The first article to appear dealing exclusively with Tatlin analyses and praises his work (see p. 333).

1915–16 Designs the scenery and costumes for Wagner, *The Flying Dutchman*, which finally is not staged.

1916–20 Moves his studio to no. 33 Staro-Basmannaia Street.

1916 In March he organizes The Store exhibition in Moscow, where he shows selection of materials and counter-reliefs. He meets Khlebnikov and Petrovskii in Tsaritsyn, where he and the poets hold a cultural evening on 25 March at the House of Research and Art.
(Khlebnikov gives a lecture entitled 'Cast-Iron Wings'.)
Khlebnikov composes the poem 'Tatlin' (see p. 336)
Tatlin participates in an artistic evening at the apartment of N.N. Kulbin, where Maiakovskii reads selections from his poem 'War and peace'.

1917 After the February Revolution he joins the 'left wing' of the newly formed Union of Art Workers (SDI), which sends him from Petrograd to work in Moscow. In November he officially quits the Union when it opposes the October Socialist Revolution.
He is elected president of the 'Left-Wing Federation' of the Trade Union of Painters of Moscow, which had just been formed. On 21 November the Union sends him as a delegate to the Artistic Section of the Moscow Soviet of Workers' and Soldiers' Deputies (letter of commission no. 21).
During the summer and autumn he participates in the interior decoration of the Café Pittoresque as a member of an artists' collective under the direction of Iakulov.
During the autumn he works on the designs for a stage production of works by Khlebnikov, which he and the poet, artist and composer, Lur'e, intend to co-produce. However, the production does not take place. The designs for the scenery of the film *Spectral Charms*, on which he began to work on the advice of Meierkhol'd, also remain in the planning stage.

1917–18 During the winter and spring he is active in the Commission for Protecting Monuments of Art and Antiquity.

1918 On 11 April he is appointed a member of the Moscow Artistic Collegium of IZO Narkompros. He soon becomes the head of this collegium and retains the office until May 1919. At this time he becomes a member also of the Museums Collegium of the Narkompros.
He works both as director and as organizer within the areas of 'monumental propaganda', artistic education, museum affairs and book publishing.
On 18 June 1918 he forwards to the Sovnarkom the report of the Moscow Artistic Collegium on the erection in Moscow of fifty monuments 'to outstanding figures in the area of revolutionary and social activity, in philosophy, literature, sciences and the arts' (see p. 185).
On 10 July 1918 he and Lunacharskii sign the letter which reports to Lenin on the problems of organizing the 'monumental propaganda'.
During the autumn of 1919 he sends a letter to Lunacharskii on the situation of the monumental propaganda in Moscow. The people's commissar forwards it to Lenin (see p. 187).
Tatlin designs the cover of Petnikov's *Third Volume of Verses* for the publishing house Liven', but this is finally not published.

1918–19 Becomes a professor at the Moscow Free State Artistic Studios and also assumes the directorship of this institution's two teaching studios. During the same period, and probably as early as 1918, he also begins to plan the opening of a studio at the Petrograd Free State Artistic Teaching Studios (formerly known as the Academy of Arts). Becomes a member of a bureau set up to further the formation of an international federation of artists and, along with Lunacharskii, Khlebnikov, Kuznetsov, Malevich, Morgunov, Punin and others, is invited to the editorial board of a new periodical *Internatsional Iskusstv*, which was at that time in preparation. He writes an article entitled 'The Initiative Individual in the Creativity of the Collective' (see p. 237). Tatlin, Malevich and Morgunov write one of three appeals addressed to progressive Italian, American and French artists.
He joins the newly formed Artist-Inventors' Association. Among others, Malevich and Dymshits-Tolstaia also join.
He moves to Petrograd at the end of the summer or the beginning of autumn.

1919–22 He becomes a professor at the Studio of Materials, Volume and Construction of the Petrograd Free State Artistic Teaching Studios, known formerly as the Studio of Volume, Construction and Colours. He subsequently becomes the director of the Studio, which was operating in the mosaics wing of the Academy of Arts.

1919–20 He participates in the monumental propaganda campaign also as an artist, preparing designs for a memorial to the October Revolution. As the work progresses, he names it a *Monument to the Third International.*

1919 Begins working on the designs in Moscow in 1919, but continues in Petrograd.

1920 Completes the designs in 1920 and between March and November prepares a model of the tower with the help of his students and colleagues, Shapiro, Meerzon and Vinogradov.
It is during the planning stage that Punin's article 'Monument to the Third International' appears (see p. 344).
In the summer of 1920 Tatlin's scheme is provoking lively reaction abroad. Raoul Hausmann makes a collage of Tatlin, and at their exhibition in Berlin Dadaists describe him as their spiritual leader.
During the autumn of 1920 the works of the students of the Studio of Material, Volume and Construction are also shown at an exhibition of the achievements of the Petrograd Free State Artistic Teaching Studios.
Between 8 October and 1 December the model of the Monument to the Third International is shown in the mosaics hall of the Petrograd Free State Artistic Teaching Studios. A special poster commemorating the exhibition is released and an 'artistic and political conference' is organized concurrently.
In mid-December Tatlin gives a lecture, illustrated with photographs, on the project of the Monument to the Third International, in the Cézanne Club of the Moscow VKhUTEMAS. The lecture is followed by a rally, which is attended also by Maiakovskii.
The model is transported to Moscow in December 1920 and is shown at an exhibition set up in the House of Unions on

the occasion of the Eighth All-Russian Congress of Soviets. An article, entitled 'The Work Ahead of Us', signed by Tatlin, Shapiro, Meerzon and Vinogradov, is published (see p. 239).

1921–5 Becomes a member of the Permanent Museums Committee. Organizes and directs the section which will later function as the Section for Material Culture in the Petrograd Museum of Artistic Culture. The Museum is reorganized into the Institute of Artistic Culture during the autumn of 1923. Later it receives the name State Institute of Artistic Culture (GINKhUK). He becomes a corresponding member of the Moscow Institute of Artistic Culture (INKhUK) also.

1921 At the beginning of January the Academic Centre approves a study trip for Tatlin to the United States and Germany, without, however, financial assistance. He does not take advantage of this opportunity. (Information made public by the Committee for Study Trips Abroad attached to the Academic Centre, 4 Jan. 1923. TsGAOR, fond 2555, inventory 1, file 475, p. 24.)
Punin's monograph, *Tatlin* (*Against Cubism*) is published (see p. 347). Tatlin issues his slogan 'Through the discovery of material to the creation of a new object' (see p. 243).
Attempts to set up a design studio at the New Lessner Mechanical Engineers' Trust.
On 29 December he takes part in a unique evening of poetic recital organized in the Moscow VKhUTEMAS, in which Maiakovskii, Khlebnikov, Kamenskii and Kruchenykh all perform.

1921–2 Founds the Union of New Tendencies in Art in Petrograd. Takes part in the reorganization of the former Academy of Arts, that is, in the unification of the arts and crafts studios of the Academy and those of the former Baron Shtiglits Artistic College into Higher Artistic and Technical Studios (VKhUTEMAS). Strives to set up 'independent left-wing experimental studios' within the VKhUTEMAS (see p. 339).

1922 On 10 June in his capacity as president of the Petrograd Union of New Tendencies in Art, he opens a retrospective exhibition of the same name in the halls of the Museum of Artistic Culture. When he learns of Khlebnikov's death (28 June 1922) he organizes in the same place another exhibition in memory of the poet.
Tatlin's works are shown at the First Russian Exhibition of Fine Arts in the Galerie van Diemen in Berlin. In Berlin the journal *Veshch'-Objet-Gegenstand* begins publication in three languages. Its editors are El Lissitzky and Il'ia Ehrenburg. In the first issue the editorial article is entitled 'The Blockade of Russia is Over'. Contributors to the journal include Tatlin, Charlie Chaplin, Le Corbusier, Fernand Léger, Lajos Kassák, Béla Uitz, Maiakovskii, Malevich, Rodchenko and Shklovskii.
Punin's article, 'Tatlin's Tower', illustrated with photographs, appears in the first issue. El Lissitzky prepares a symbolical collage portrait of Tatlin.

1923 As both designer and director he stages Khlebnikov's dramatic 'sverkhpovest' (supernarrative), *Zangezi*. The performances take place on 11 and 13 June and, according to some accounts, on 30 June. Tatlin also acts in the play.

On 27 May he delivers a paper in the Museum of Artistic Culture, entitled 'Material Culture. Down with Tatlinism'. At the state-sponsored Exhibition of Petrograd Artists of All Tendencies he puts on show set and costume designs for *Zangezi,* drawings and sketches of novel clothes and the Monument to the Third International. His works are referred to as products of the collective work of the Central Group of the Union of New Tendencies in Art.
These works are shown within the context of the slogans 'Not to the left, not to the right, but to the necessary' and 'Not the old, not the new, but the necessary' (*see* p. 244).
On 28 June, the anniversary of Khlebnikov's death, a commemorative exhibition opens at the museum of Artistic Culture in Petrograd. The exhibition, originally organized in Moscow by Pavel Miturich, is taken to Petrograd and augmented on Tatlin's initiative. Maiakovskii describes Tatlin's designs for the *Monument to the Third International* as 'one of the first artistic creations of the October epoch'.

1923–5 Tatlin is experimenting with the design and manufacture of new types of furniture, radiators, clothing and dishes, at first within the group which he founded, and later in the Section for Material Culture of the State Institute of Artistic Culture. He strives to realize his ideas at the Leningrad Clothing Manufacturers' Trust. He also contacts the Low-voltage Electrical Factories Trust. At the Section for Material Culture the surgeon Geintse, Tatlin's wife, carries out the preparatory research for the creation of *Letatlin* (i.e. preparing birds and carrying out anatomical studies of their wings). From 15 March to 8 June there is an exhibition, 'Material Culture', forming a part of a larger GINKhUK demonstrational exhibition in the exhibition hall of the Section. During the spring and summer Tatlin energetically popularizes design, the newest area of artistic endeavour, among the engineers and managers of various industrial and manufacturing plants. Uses sample models to illustrate his lectures, which he entitles 'Material Culture and its Role in the Production and Life of the USSR'.

1924 In autumn he takes a trip to Barnaul and Biisk in Western Siberia.

1925 At the beginning of the year he is working at the Petrograd Institute of Applied Arts; it is probable that the second model of the *Monument to the Third International* is prepared in the workshops of this institution.
This model is shown in the Soviet Pavilion of the Paris International Exhibition of Modern Decorative and Industrial Arts. It wins a gold medal.
With Bruni, Kupriianov, Lebedev, L'vov, Miturich and Tyrsa he participates in an exhibition of drawings at the Tsvetkov Gallery in Moscow.

1925–7 He is a professor at the Faculty of Painting of the Kiev College of Art and director of the Department of Dramatic, Cinematic and Photographic Arts. In 1926–7 participates in Maiakovskii's recital evenings in Kiev.
In 1927 participates in the All-Ukrainian Anniversary Exhibition organized in Khar'kov to commemorate the tenth anniversary of the October Revolution.
Is commissioned to illustrate Bazhan, Semenko and Shkurupii, *Meeting at the Crossroads*.

The experiments leading to the first variants of the structure of *Letatlin* are begun. Tatlin's paintings are shown at the Exhibition of Newest Tendencies in Art, which opens on 1 October 1927 at the Leningrad State Russian Museum.

1927–30 He becomes an associate professor and then a professor at the Moscow VKhUTEMAS and, later, a professor at the Faculty of Wood and Metal Working, and the Faculty of Ceramics. (He continues teaching at the latter until 1933. In the meantime the Faculty is transferred to the Institute of Silicates and Building Materials.) His lectures are entitled 'Material Culture', and in his practical sessions he deals with the design of novel utilitarian objects.
In 1929 he prepares illustrations for Kharms, *Firstly and Secondly* and for Sergel' *On the Sailing-Ship*, working under the pseudonym of 'LOT'.

1929–32 Heads the Experimental Laboratory for Material Culture of the Narkompros. The Laboratory is in the belfry of the Novodevichii Convent. He works on *Letatlin* with his students Sotnikov and Pavil'onov at the Moscow Artistic and Technical Institute (VKhUTEIN). Geintse, Losev, Zelenskii and Shchipitsyn also take part in the work.

1930 With the help of his students at the VKhUTEIN he designs, constructs and mounts on the back of a truck the bier in which Maiakovskii's body is transported to the cemetery of the Novodevichii Convent after his civil obsequies.

1931 On 17 January he is granted the title Honoured Art Worker by Resolution no. 75 of the Soviet of People's Commissars of the RSFSR.
P.I. Novitskii, rector of VKhUTEIN, writes to the Central Committee of the Trade Union of Art Workers: 'Tatlin's significance to the history of the visual arts is immense. The great achievements in industrial design made in the Soviet Union after the October Revolution owe a great deal to Tatlin. We may be honouring him as the greatest exponent of the art of material design, as a person who today is world famous, but we do not rely on him as much as we should. Tatlin is an artist of great culture, a true master, who is a devoted worker for the proletarian revolution. He, before anyone else, deserves the title of Honoured Art Worker' (TsGALI, fond 681, inventory 31, unit 199, p. 28).

1932 Tatlin's model of *Letatlin* is shown on 5 April at the Moscow Writers' Club, and a literary evening is organized in Tatlin's honour.
Between 15 and 30 May an exhibition is held at the State Pushkin Museum of Fine Arts, where sketches, designs and constructions and three models of *Letatlin* are shown. Photographs of the designs for the *Monument to the Third International* and various other model designs by Tatlin are also exhibited. A pamphlet containing Tatlin's 'Art into Technology' (see p. 310) and an article by the test pilot K.A. Artseulov entitled 'On *Letatlin*' (see p. 408) are published. A suggestion is made that Tatlin should participate as designer and artist in the making of a film on robots called *R.I.R.* (based on a work by K. Čapek; script by G.N. Debner, directed by N. Andreevskii). According to Andreevskii, it was impossible to meet Tatlin's conditions and requirements. He asked for a movie camera instead of the usual honorarium, so Tatlin's student from Kiev, Kaplunovskii, became the artistic collaborator on the film. (The film was released in 1933 under the title *The Death of Sensation*.) Originally Andreevskii intended to invite the collaboration of Le Corbusier. Lunacharskii negotiated with him in Paris.

1933 On 25 May Tatlin, Gerasimov, Béla Uitz, and Pavel Kuznetsov and others make speeches (see p. 313) at the evening arranged in honour of Petrov-Vodkin at the Moscow Branch of the Union of Soviet Artists. (They are all members of the Moscow Branch since its foundation in 1932.)

1934 Tatlin makes a speech at the Conference on the Artistic Design of Porcelain, which coincided with an exhibition of products of the Porcelain Works of the Narkomestprom, the People's Commissariat of Local Industries.
Letatlin is shown in the Inventions section of the Polytechnical Museum.

1935 Designs stage settings and costumes for the production of *A Comic Actor of the 17th Century* and for the play *Let us not Surrender*.

1938 Directs the designing of the Pavilion of Animal Husbandry at the Agricultural Exhibition.

1940 Designs the Moscow edition of Khlebnikov, *Unpublished Works*. The dust-jacket, with its portrait of the poet, is Tatlin's work. The collection contains Khlebnikov's poem 'Tatlin – A Visionary of the Blades'.

1939–40 Designs scenery and costumes for Sukhovo-Kobylin, *The Affair*.

1940–3 Works with Kedrov on the production of the play *Deep Reconnaissance* at the Moscow Art Theatre.

1941–3 The period of Tatlin's evacuation to Sverdlovsk.

1943 His son dies on the front.

1943–53 The tempo of his theatrical work increases. During this period he prepares designs for fifteen productions. As a member of the Section of Theatre Arts he belongs also to the Moscow Branch of the Union of Soviet Artists.

1953 He prepares various relief models for the Geographical Museum of Moscow State University. Between 11 and 14 January he participates in a conference on non-rigid-wing flight at the Flying Club of the Zhukovskii Air Academy.

On 31 March Tatlin dies in Moscow.
He is followed to his final resting place by his companion, the artist Korsakova, the architect Rudnev, the painters Favorskii and Lebedeva, and S. Sen'kin, Aksel'rod, V.B. El'konin and N.M. El'konina. Rudnev and Favorskii make farewell speeches at the graveside. The urn is interred in the cemetery of the Novodevichii Convent.

354–68 Ostrovskii, *A Comic Actor of the 17th Century*, stage and costume designs, 1934–5
354 Model of stage setting, Cat. VIII/39
355 Model of stage setting, Cat. VIII/40

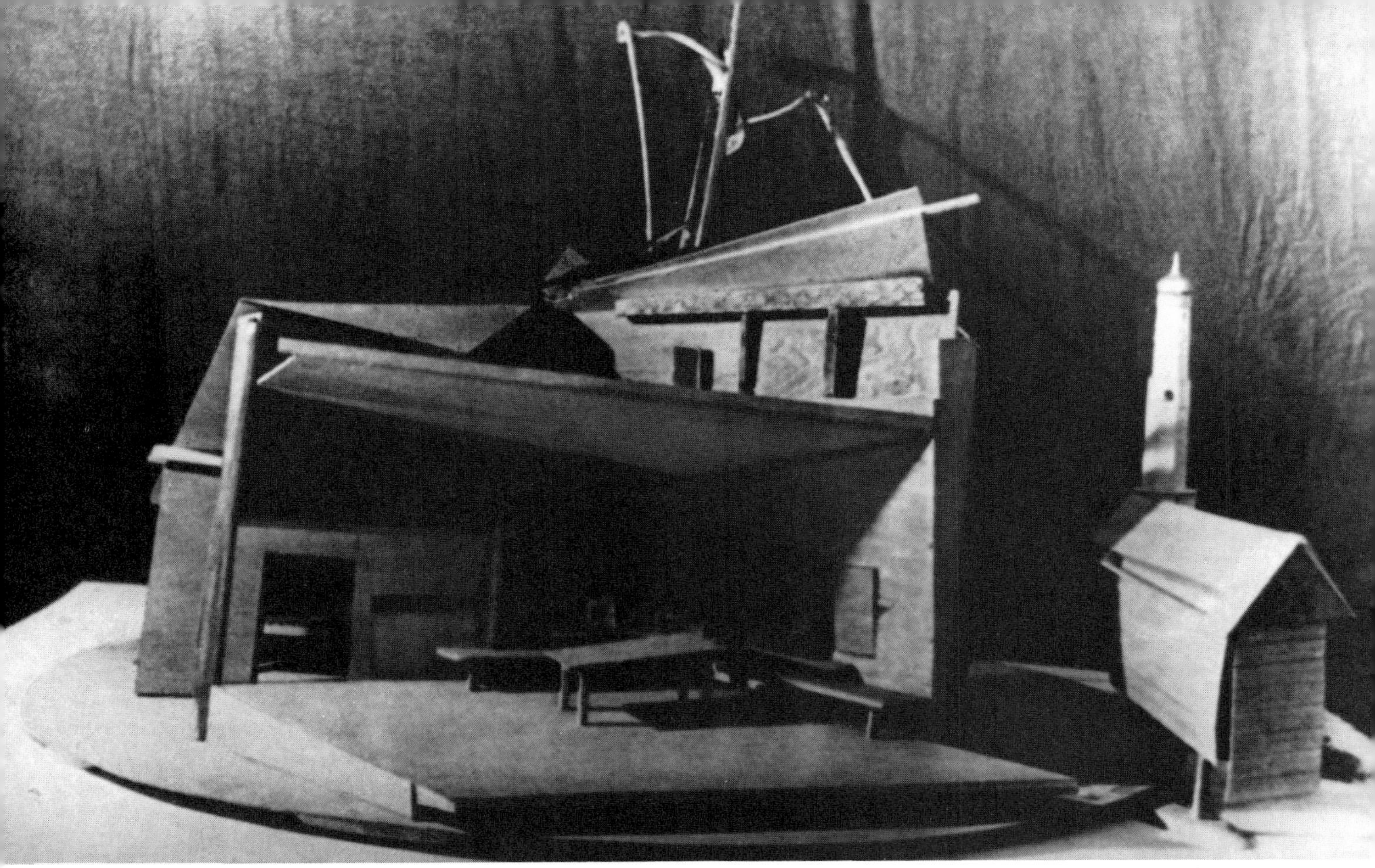

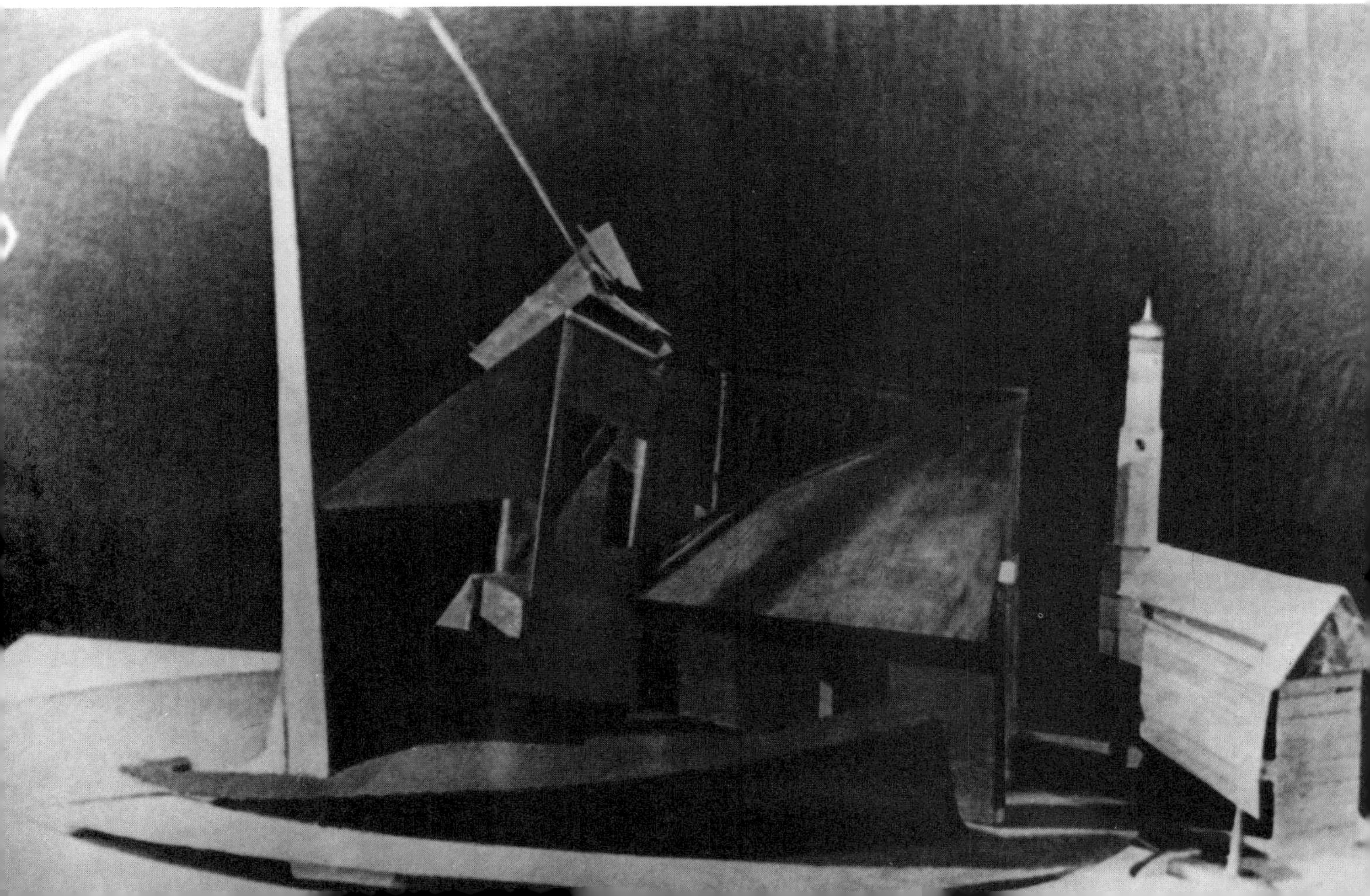

356–9 Pictures of the performance, MKhAT–2

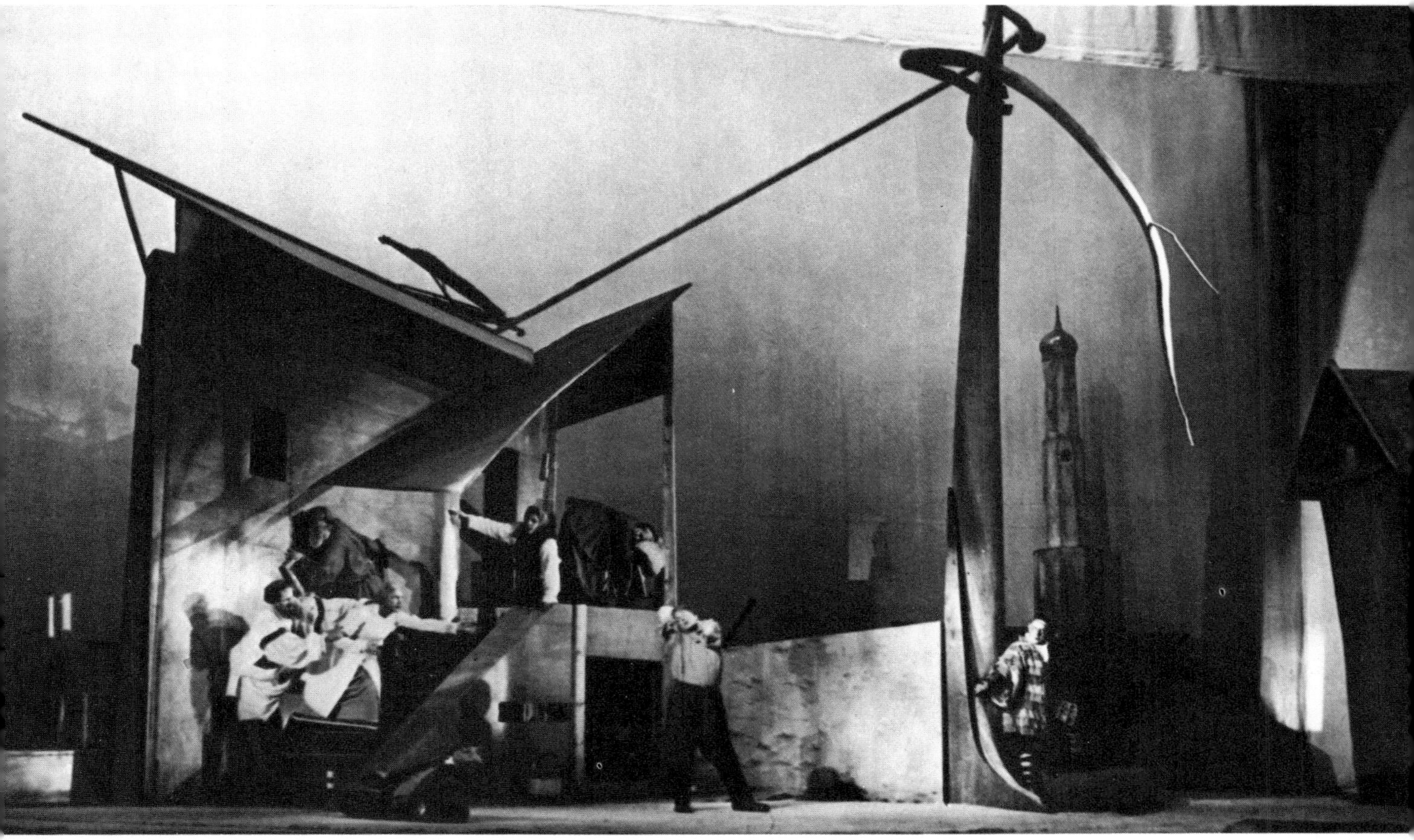

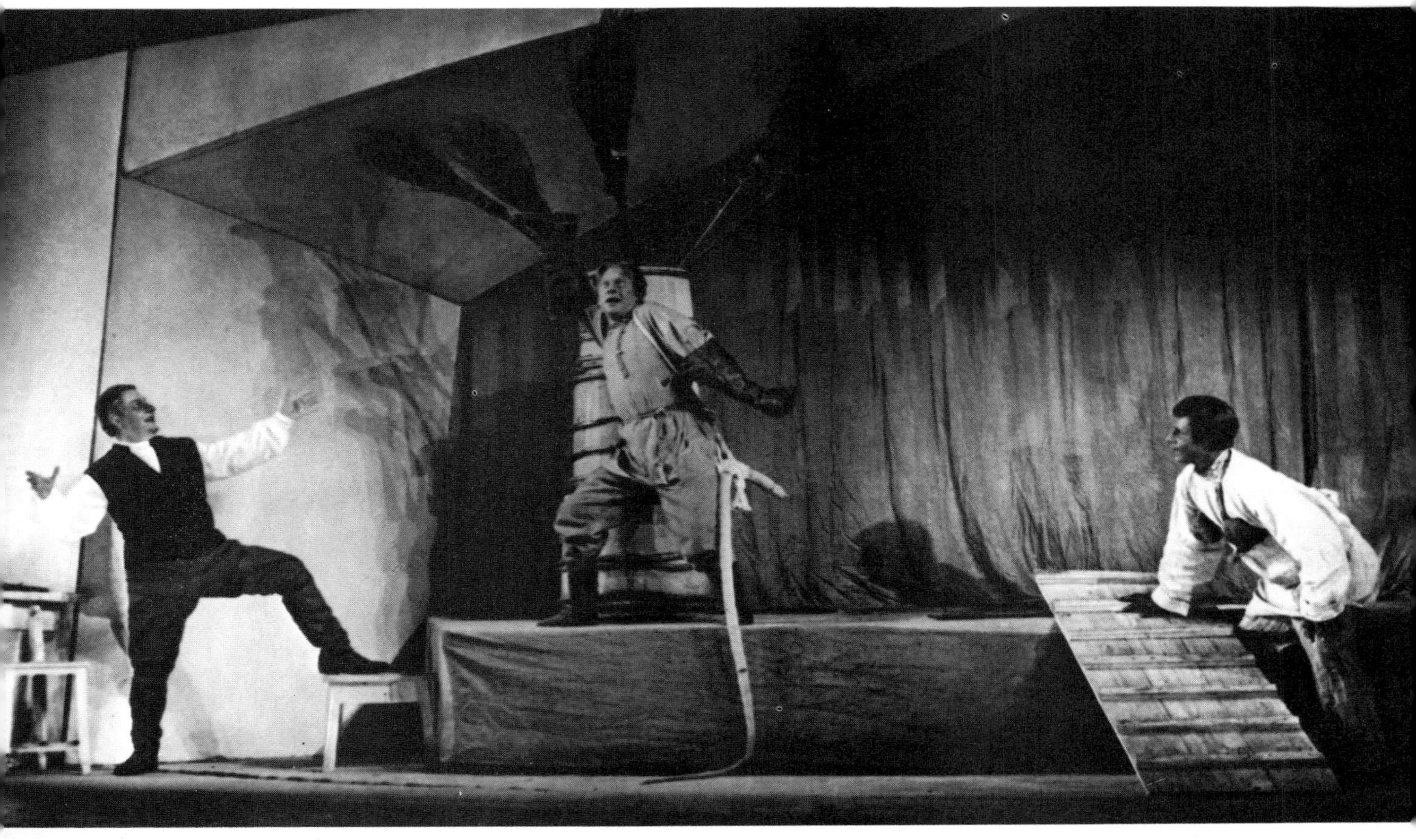

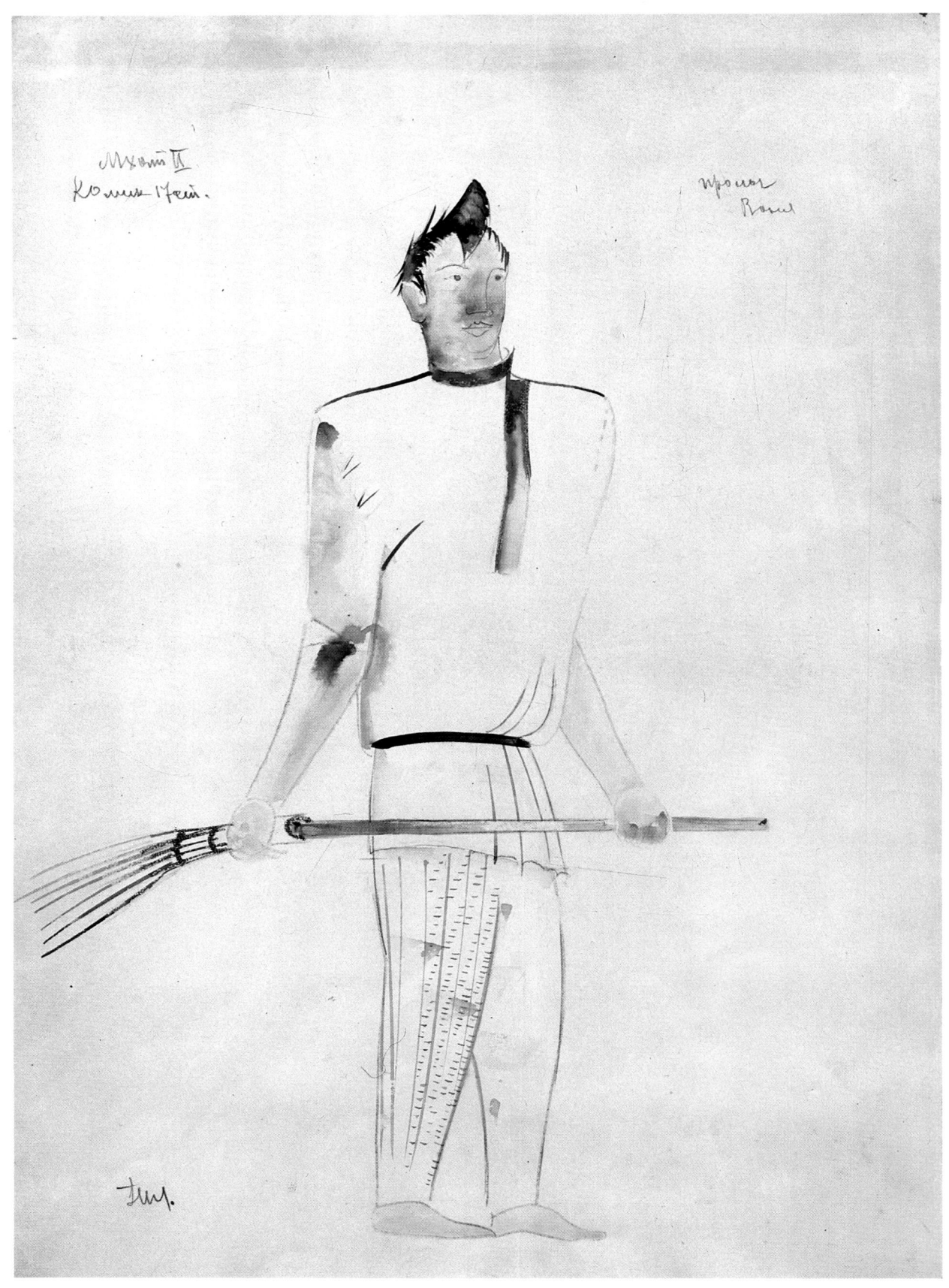

360 *Vania*, Cat. VIII/41
* **361** *Tat'iana*, Cat. VIII/42

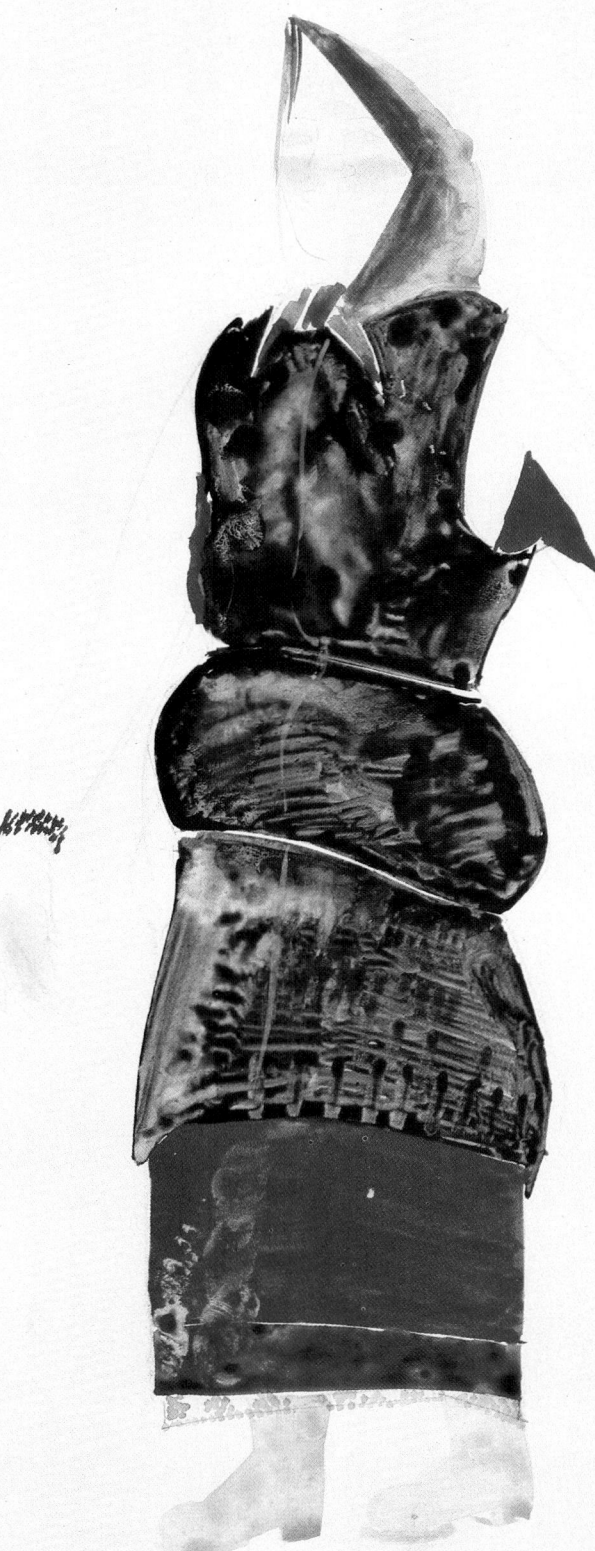

362 *God in Paradise*, Cat. VIII/47
363 *Adam*, Cat. VIII/49
364 *Boyars*, Cat. VIII/44
365 *The Babylonian Thief*, Cat. VIII/46
* **366** *The Drunken Kliushin*, Cat. VIII/43
367 *Fodiev*, Cat. VIII/45
* **368** *Eve*, Cat. VIII/48

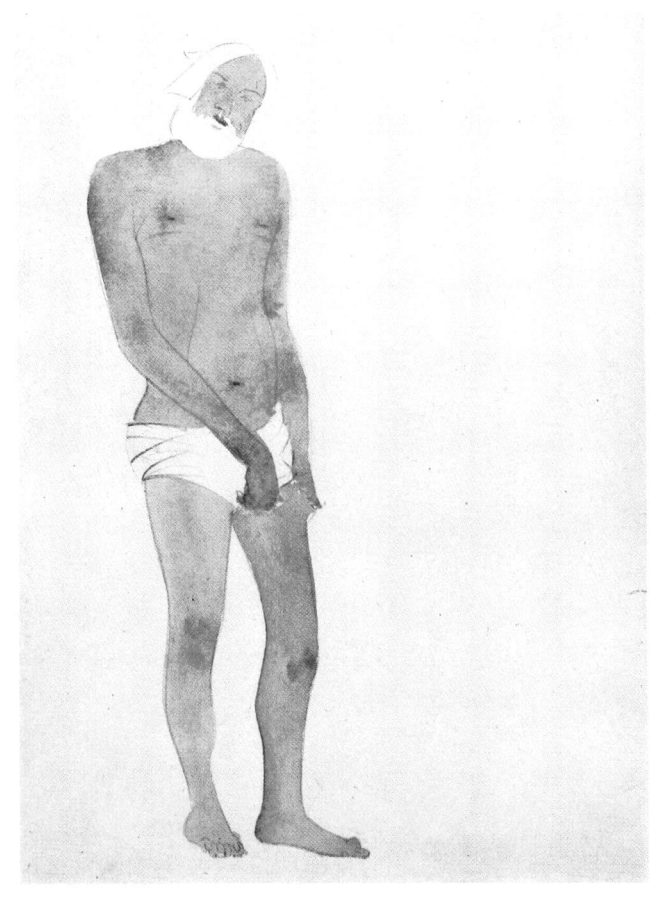

369–83 A. Sukhovo-Kobylin, *The Affair*, stage and costume designs, 1939–40

369 *Stage design*, Cat. VIII/50
* **370** *Office*, Cat. VIII/51

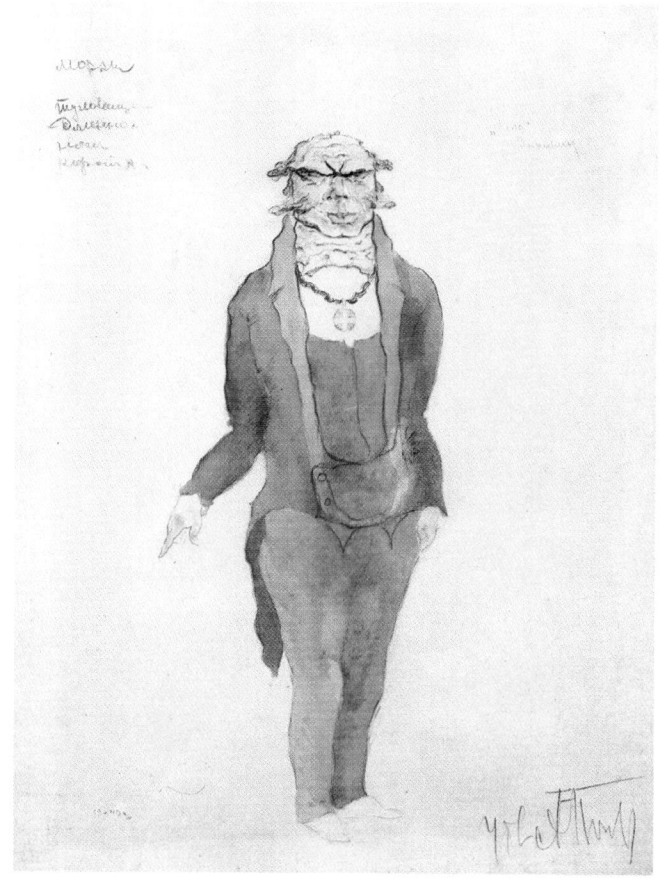

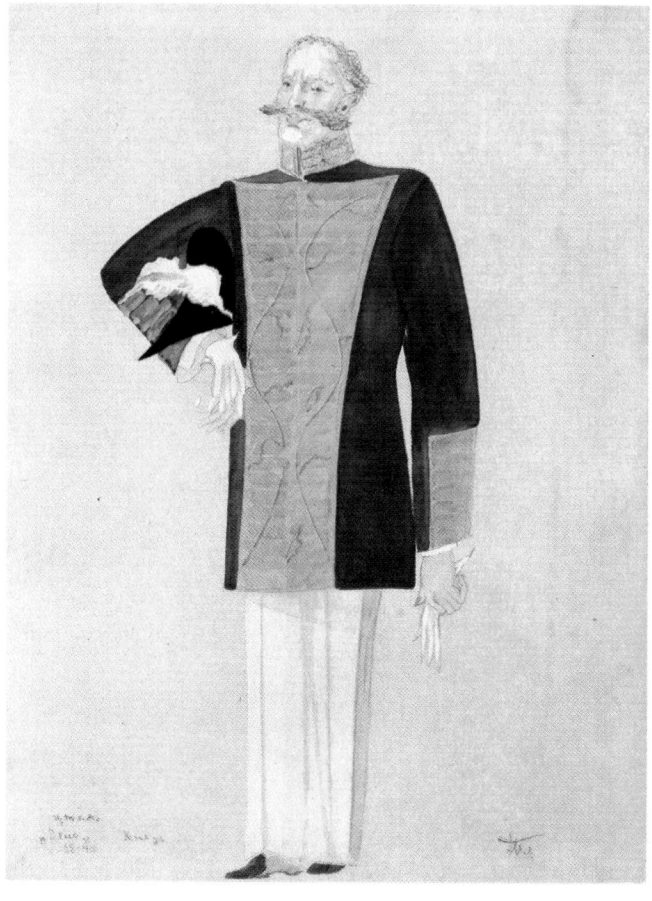

◁ **371** *Varravin*, Cat. VIII/54
◁ **372** *Zhivets*, Cat. VIII/59
◁ **373** *Tarelkin*, Cat. VIII/57   **375** *The Prince in a Cloak*, Cat. VIII/53
◁ **374** *The Prince in Dress Uniform*, Cat. VIII/52   **376** *Atueva*, Cat. VIII/61

377–9 *Lidochka*, Cat. VIII/62, 63, 64

380–1 *Ibisov*, Cat. VIII/55, 56
382 *Schmerz*, Cat. VIII/58
383 *Razuvaev*, Cat. VIII/60
384 A. Shtein: *Kronshtadt (Spring of '21)*
Poster for the performance at the Moscow Theatre of the
Lensoviet, 1940, Cat. XIII/28
385–91 A. Shtein, *Kronshtadt (Spring of '21)* stage and
costume designs, 1939–40

385 *Curtain*, Cat. VIII/65

* **386–7** *Stage Designs*, Cat. VIII/66

*   **388** *Lower Deck*, Cat. VIII/67   **389** *Prison Cell*, Cat. VIII/68

* **390** *Ramkov*, Cat. VIII/69
391 *Kudrin*, Cat. VIII/70
392–6 A. Kron, *Deep Reconnaissance*, stage and costume designs, 1940–3
* **392** *Square in front of the Barracks*, Cat. VIII/71
393 Photograph of the performance at the MKhAT, Act IV, TsGTM Photo Archive

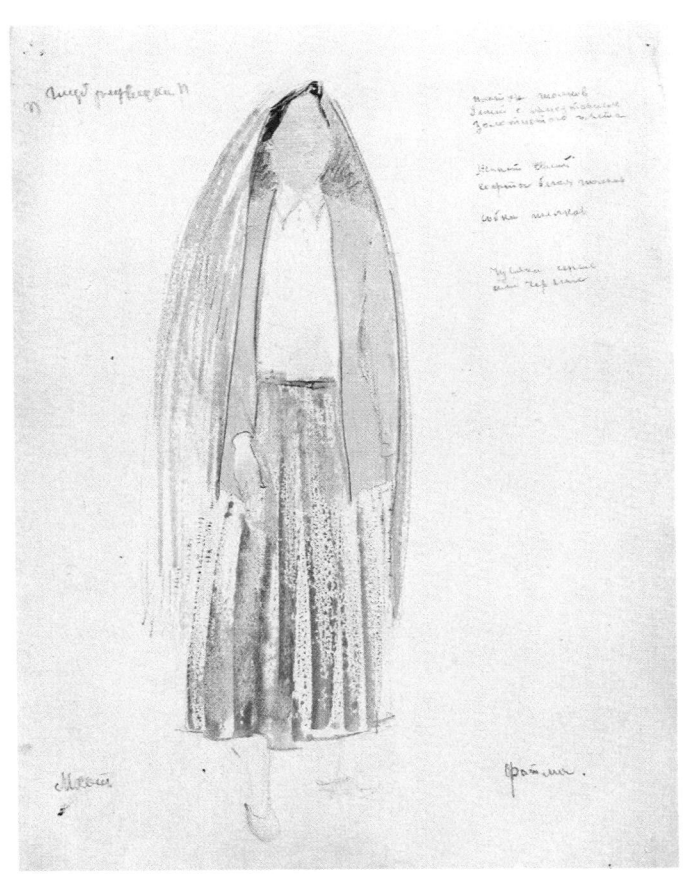

* **394** *Fatyma*, Cat. VIII/72
  395 *Man's Costume*, Cat. VIII/74
* **396** *Man's Costume*, Cat. VIII/73

* **397** E.L. Shvarts, *A Far Country*, stage design, 1944, Cat. VIII/76

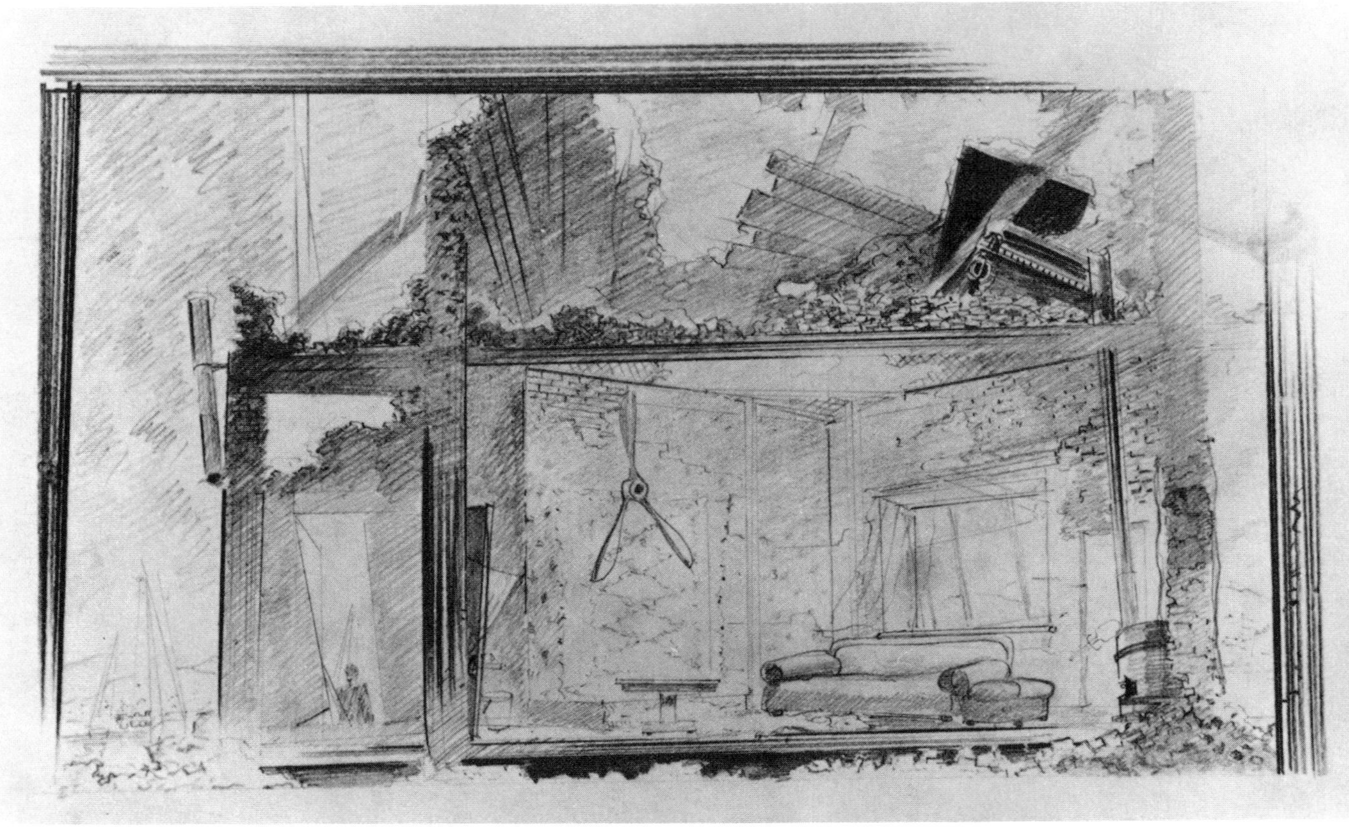

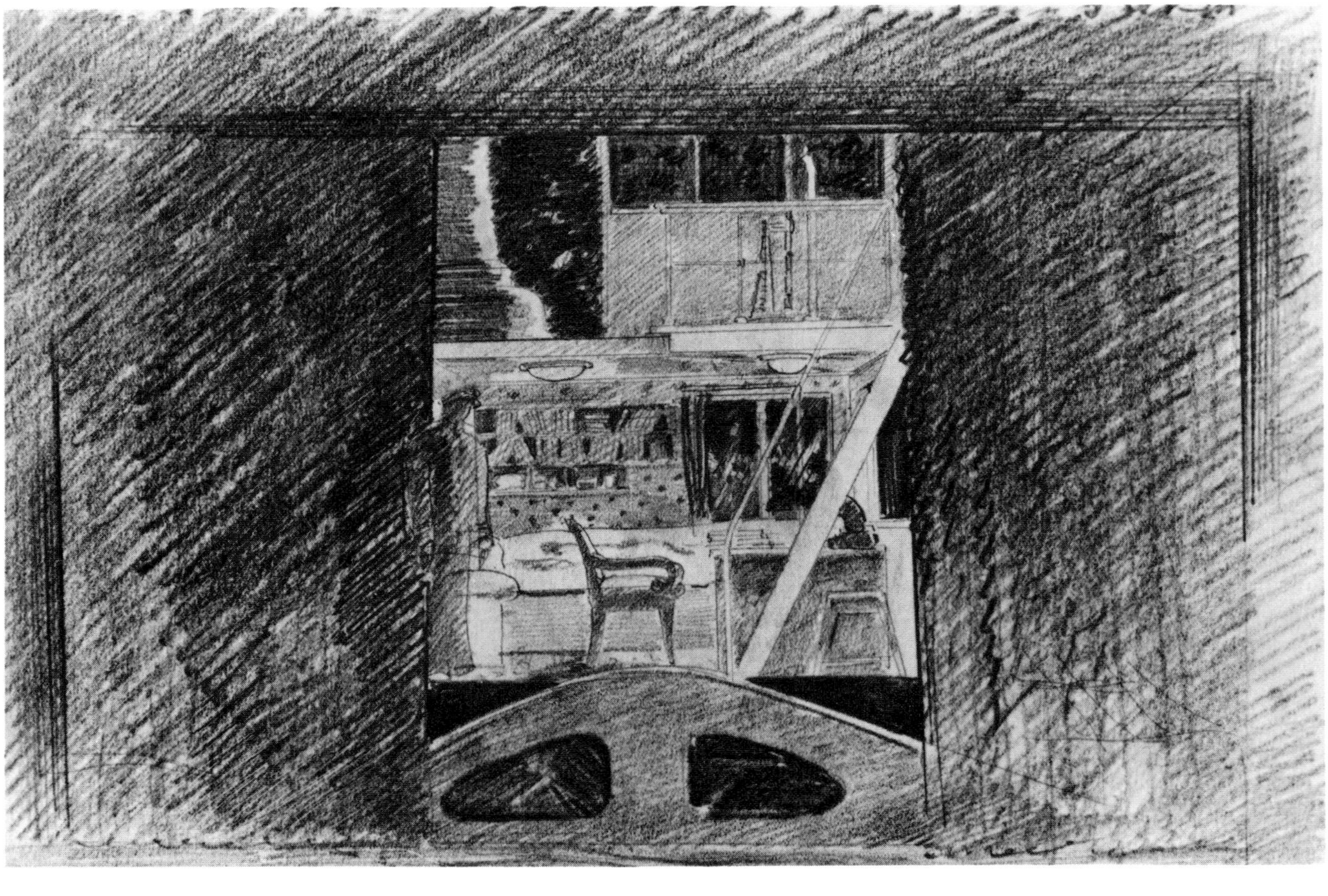

* **398** I.V. Shtok, *Fog over the Bay. The Bombed House*, stage design, 1945, Cat. VIII/77
* **399** A.M. Faiko, *Captain Kostrov. Stage Design*, 1946, Cat. VIII/78
  400 An unknown play, *Forest*, stage design, beginning of 1950s, Cat. VIII/79

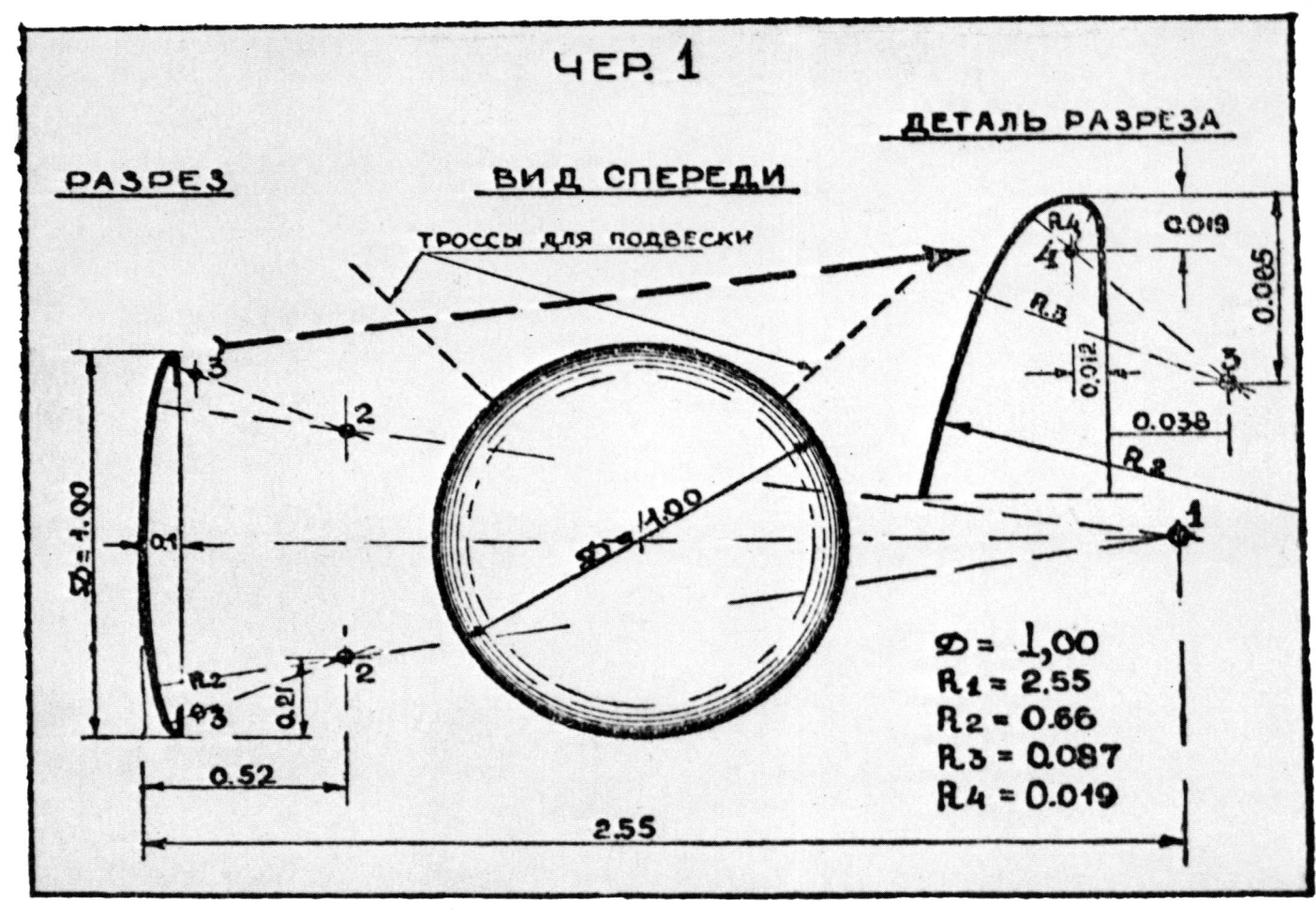

401 A. Kron, *Deep Reconnaissance. The Moon on Stage*, technical drawing, 1940–3. Cat. VIII/75

402–4 Interior of studio with the rack which Tatlin constructed especially to store paintings.
Photograph: Collection V.I. Kostin, Moscow
405 The block that housed Tatlin's studio, 1930–53, block no. 1, Artists' Colony, in Verkhnaia Maslovka. Recent photograph

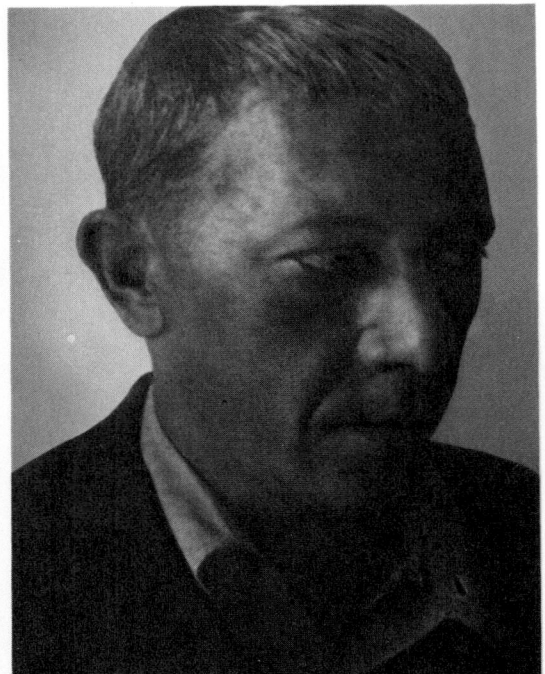

* **406** Tatlin, 1930s.
Photograph: TsGALI, Moscow
407 Tatlin at the beginning of the 1930s.
Photograph: TsGALI, Moscow
408 Tatlin in 1933.
Photograph TsGALI, Moscow
409 Tatlin with his bandore in the 1940s.
Photograph: TsGALI, Moscow

* **410** *Woman in Fur Coat*, 1930s, Cat. II/9
* **411** *Female Nude in front of Easel*, 1940s, Cat. II/11
* **412** *Woman Wearing a Hat*, 1940s. Cat. II/12
* **413** *Portrait of a Woman*, 1940s, Cat. II/10

414 *Female Bather*, 1930s. Cat. I/24

415 *Woman's Portrait*, 1933, Cat. I/23

416 *Clay Mug with Flowers*, 1930s, Cat. I/26
* **417** *Red Flowers*, 1930s, Cat. I/25

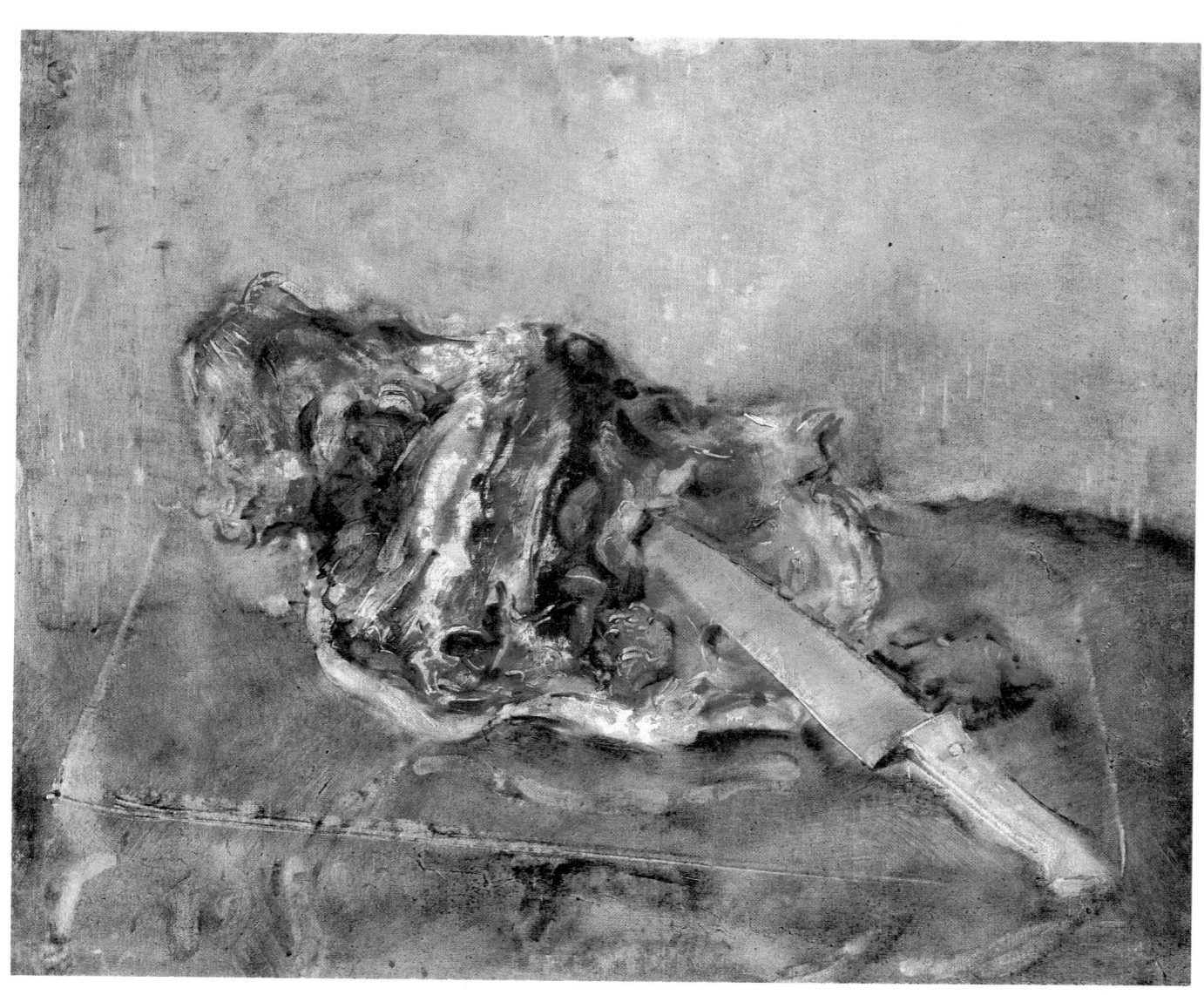

* **418** *Bouquet,* 1940, Cat. I/27
419 *Meat,* 1947, Cat. I/28

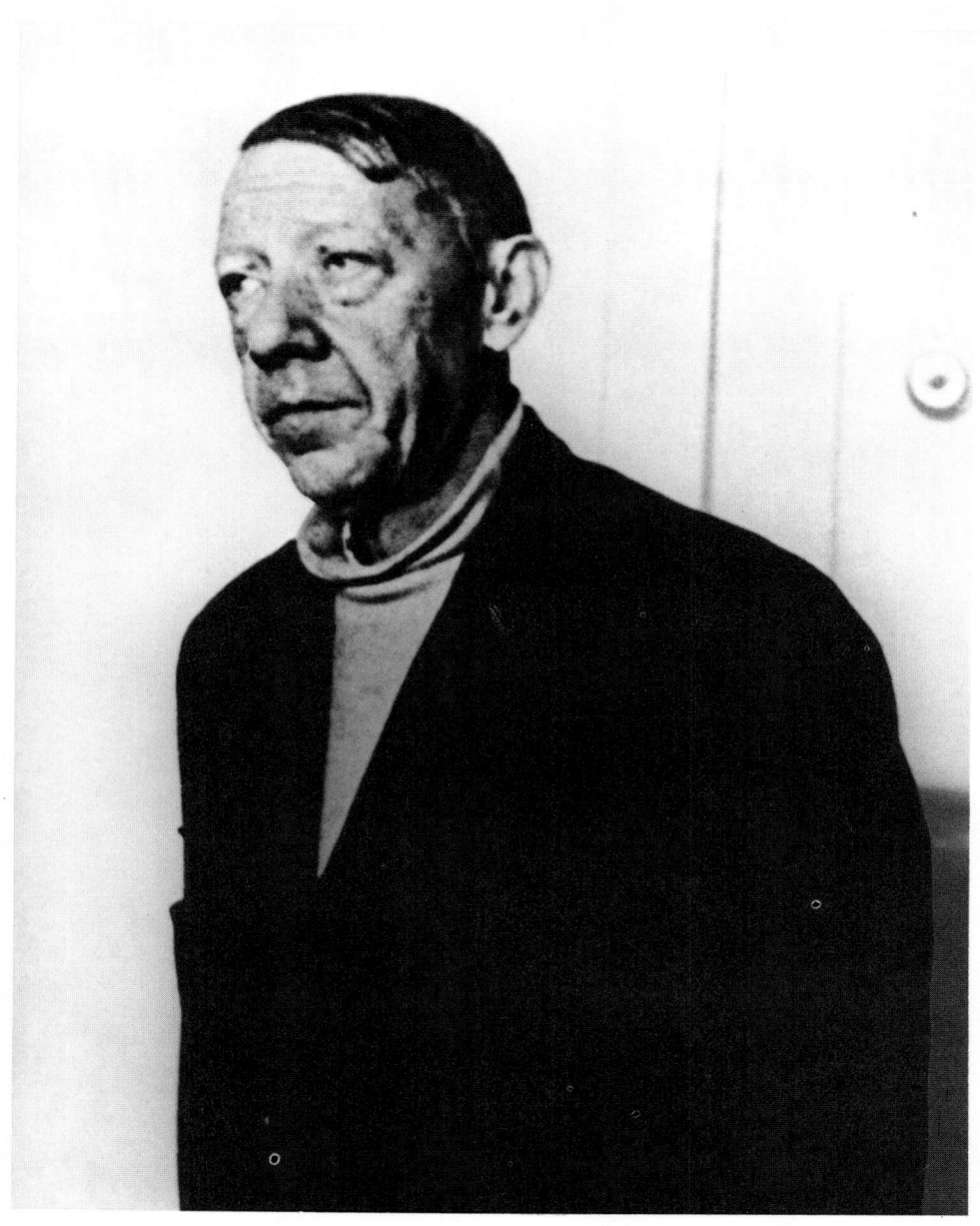

420 *Self-Portrait*, 1940s, Cat. II/13
421 Tatlin in his last years.
Photograph: TsGALI, Moscow

422 Tatlin's tomb in the wall of the cemetery of the Novodevichii Convent in Moscow.
Recent photograph
423 The bell tower of the Novodevichii Convent.
Recent photograph

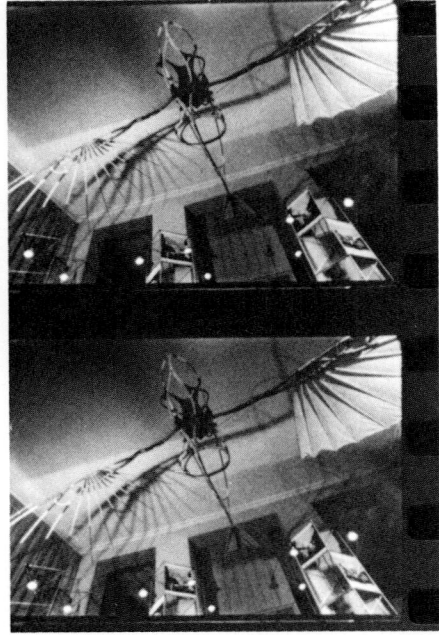

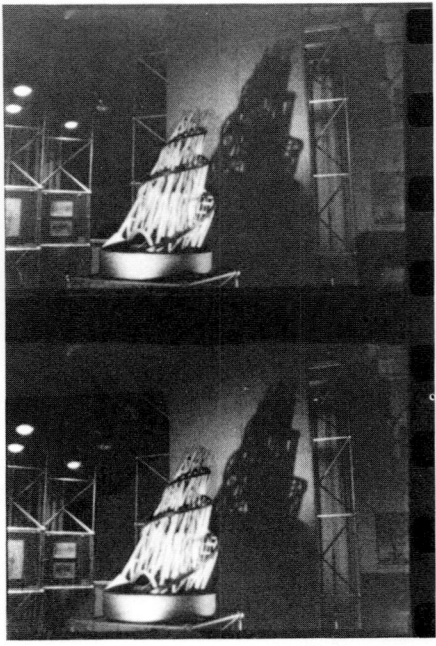

424–6 Stills from M.I. Goldovskaia, *An Extraordinary Man*, documentary film, Moscow State Television and Radio, 1977 (Director: D.N. Chukovskii)

Tatlin at Russian and Soviet Exhibitions

1910–11
Second Salon
344 *In the Garden*
345 *Sketch*
346 *Sketch*
347 *In Turkestan* (watercolour)
348 *Market-Place*
349 *Watercolour*
356 *Shop*
361 *In the Harbour*
362 *Watercolour*
Second *Salon*. Catalogue of the International Art Exhibition. Exhibition arranged and foreword written by V.A. Izdebskii. Odessa, 1910–11

Салон 2-й
344 В саду
345 Эскиз
346 Эскиз
347 В Туркестане (акварель)
348 Рынок
349 Акварель
356 Лавочка
361 В порту
362 Акварель
Салон 2-й. Каталог международной художественной выставки. Устроитель и автор предисловия В.А. Издебский. Одесса, 1910–1911

1911
Union of Youth
181 *Kitchen Garden*
182 *Female Nude*
183–191 *Drawings*
192 *Portrait*
Catalogue of the second exhibition of the Union of Youth, St Petersburg, 1911

Союз Молодежи
181 Огород
182 Натурщица
183–191 Рисунки
192 Портрет
Каталог 2-й выставки картин общества художников 'С.М.'. СПБ, 1911

1911–12
Union of Youth
84 *Sailor*
85 *Landscape*
86 *Landscape*
87 *Fishmonger*
88 *Drawing*
89 *Fisherman*
90 *Beggar*
91 *At the End of the Sailing Season*
Catalogue of the Union of Youth exhibition, St Petersburg, 1911–12
(Location: 73 Nevskii Prospekt, St Petersburg; date: 4 Dec. 1911 to 10 Jan. 1912)

Союз Молодежи
84 Матрос
85 Пейзаж
86 Пейзаж
87 Продавец рыбы
88 Рисунок
89 Рыбак
90 Нищий
91 К закрытию навигации
Каталог выставки картин общества художников 'С.М.'. СПБ, 1911–1912

1912
Union of Youth
131–2 *Fishmonger*
133 24 stage and costume designs for the Moscow performance of *Tsar Maximilian*. Collection L.I. Zheverzheev
Catalogue of the third exhibition of the Union of Youth, St Petersburg, 1912
(Location: 73 Nevskii Prospekt, St Petersburg. The exhibition was arranged by the artists of the Union of Youth together with the Donkey's Tail, a new Moscow group to which Tatlin also belonged. The group's name did not appear on the cover; however, next to the name of the members appeared the identification: Moscow, Donkey's Tail. An unidentified entry in the catalogue – '139 30 draft costume designs for the St Petersburg performance in January 1912 of Tsar Maxem'ian*, Collection L.I. Zheverzheev' – is also attributed to Tatlin, with the remark that the sketches in question were executed by M. Le Dantiu. There is no mention of Tatlin's participation in the St Petersburg production in any other publication.)*

Союз Молодежи
131–132. Продавец рыбы
133 24 Декорации и костюмы к постановке 'Царь Максемьян' в Москве. Собр. Л.И. Жевержеева
Каталог 3-й выставки картин общества художников 'С.М.'. СПБ, 1912

1912
Donkey's Tail

220–43 Costume designs for the performance of the popular play *Tsar Maximilian*. Collection L.I. Zheverzheev
244 *In the Garden*
245 *Sketch*
246 *Sketch*
247 *In Turkestan*
248 *The Harbour Market*
249 *Watercolour*
250 *Shop*
251 *In the Harbour*
252 *Watercolour*
253 *Repose*
254 *Fishmonger*
255 *Fishmonger*
256 *Self-Portrait*
   [The numbers between 256 and 265 are missing from the catalogue]
265 *Peaches* (study, 1909)
266 *The Garden* (study, 1909)
267 *Southern Street* (sketch, 1909)
267 *Carnations* (study, 1909)
268 *Cloth Merchant*
269 *Drawing in India Ink*
270 *The Beginning of the Sailing Season*
Catalogue of the exhibition of the Moscow group of artists, Donkey's Tail, Moscow, 1912
(Location: Moscow College of Painting, Sculpture and Architecture; date: March 1912. In the catalogue two pictures are erroneously numbered 267)

1912–13
Modern Painting

272 *Composition with Fishermen*
273 *Still Life*
274–6 *Drawing*
Exhibition of paintings, sculpture, graphics and handicrafts, entitled Modern Painting (Catalogue), Moscow, Free Art Society of Artists, 1912–13

1913
Jack of Diamonds

324 *Nude Composition*
325 *Boy*
326 *Portrait of the Painter*
327 *Composition with Fishermen,* 1912
328 *Flowers*
329 *Flowers,* 1911. Property of A.A. Vesnin
330 *Flowers*
331–2 1913
Catalogue of the Donkey's Tail exhibition, Moscow, 1913
(Date: 3–28 April 1913)

1913
World of Art

439 *The Spassky Gate*
440 *Domnino Village*   Stage designs for the opera,
441 *Forest*   *A Life for the Tsar*
442 *Ball*
443 *Strel'tsy*
444–6 Costume designs for the opera *A Life for the Tsar*

Ослиный хвост

220–243 Костюмы к постановке народной драмы 'Царь Максимилиан'. Собрание Л.И. Жевержеева
244 В саду
245 Эскиз
246 Эскиз
247 В Туркестане
248 Порт-базар
249 Акварель
250 Лавочка
251 В порту
252 Акварель
253 Отдых
254 Продавец рыбы
255 Продавец рыбы
256 Автопортрет

265 Персики (Этюд 1909 г.)
266 Сад (Этюд 1909 г.)
267 Южная улица (Эскиз 1909 г.)
267 Гвоздики (Этюд 1909 г.)
268 Продавец сукна
269 Рисунок тушью
270 К открытию навигации
Каталог выставки картин московской группы художников 'Ослиный хвост'. Москва, 1912

Современная живопись

272 'Композиция из рыбаков'
273 Натюрморт
274–276 Рисунок
Выставка картин, скульптуры, графики, индустрии 'Современная живопись' (Каталог). Общество художников 'Свободное искусство'. Москва, 1912–1913

Бубновый валет

324 Композиция из обнаженной натуры
325 Мальчик
326 Портрет художника
327 Композиция из рыбаков. 1912 г.
328 Цветы
329 Цветы. 1911 г. Собств. А.А. Веснина
330 Цветы
331–332 1913 г.
Каталог выставки картин общества художников 'Бубновый валет'. Москва, 1913

Мир искусства

439 Спасские ворота
440 Домнино   Эскизы декораций
441 Лес   к опере 'Жизнь за царя'
442 Бал
443 Стрельцы
444–466 Костюмы к опере 'Жизнь за царя'

466a The same (Property of F.F. Notgaft)
Catalogue of the exhibition of the World of Art group of artists, Moscow, 1913
(Location: 11 Bol'shaia Dmitrovka, Moscow)

1913
World of Art
334 *The Spassky Gate*   Sketches for the opera
335 *Domnino Village*   *A Life for the Tsar*
336 (Omission)
337 *Strel'tsy*
338–43   Costume designs for the
343a–o   opera *A Life for the Tsar*
Catalogue of the exhibition of the World of Art, 1st ed., St Petersburg, 1913
(Location: 3 Koniushennyi Pereulok, St Petersburg)

1913–14
Modern Painting
246 *Lute Player*
247 *Explanatory Drawing*
Catalogue of the Second Modern Painting exhibition of paintings, sculpture, graphics and industrial art. Free Art Society of Artists, Moscow, 1913–14

1913–14
Union of Youth
127 *Composition-Analysis* (oil)
128–30 *Drawing in India Ink*
Catalogue of the Union of Youth exhibition, St Petersburg, 10 Oct. 1913 to 10 Jan. 1914
(Location: 73 Nevskii Prospekt, St Petersburg; date: 10 Nov. 1913 to 10 Jan. 1914)

1914
First Exhibition of Painterly Reliefs
(No catalogue was prepared for this exhibition. Location: The artist's studio at 37 Ostozhenka Street, Moscow; date: 10–14 May 1914)

1914–15
Moscow Artists in Aid of Victims of the War
505 *Painterly Relief* (wood, border-stone, wire, iron, paper, enamel)
506 Scenery and costume designs for the opera *A Life for the Tsar*
Catalogue of the exhibition of paintings and sculpture, Moscow Artists in Aid of Victims of the War, organized by the Moscow Provincial Committee of the All-Russian Zemstvo Association to Aid the Wounded and by the Central Bureau of the Metropolitan Municipality, Moscow, 1914–15
(Location: Lianozov House, 3 Kantsergerskii Pereulok, Moscow)

1915
Tramway V. The First Futurist Exhibition
64–9 *Painterly Relief,* 1914
70 1915
Catalogue of Tramway V. The First Futurist Exhibition, Petrograd, 1915
(Location: The Small Hall of the Imperial Circle of the Friends of Art; date of opening: 3 March 1915. The proceeds from the exhibition were donated to the Artistic Workers' Hospital for Soldiers.)

466a То же (Собств. Ф.Ф. Нотгафт)
Каталог выставки картин 'Мир искусства'. Москва, 1913

Мир искусства
334 Спасские ворота
335 Домнино   Эскизы к опере
336 [Отсутств.]   'Жизнь за царя'
337 Стрельцы
338–343   Костюмы к опере
343a–o   'Жизнь за царя'
Каталог выставки картин 'Мир искусства', 1-е издание. СПБ, 1913

Современная живопись
246 Кобзарь
247 Пояснительный рисунок
Каталог 2-й выставки картин, скульптуры, графики, индустрии 'Современная живопись'. Общество художников 'Свободное искусство'. Москва, 1913–1914

Союз Молодежи
127 Композиционный анализ (масло)
128–130 Тушь
Каталог выставки картин общества художников 'С.М.'. СПБ, 1913–1914

Первая выставка живописных рельефов

Художники Москвы – жертвам войны
505 Живописный рельеф (дерево, кордон, проволока, железо, бумага, эмаль)
506 Эскизы декораций и рисунки костюмов к опере 'Жизнь за царя'
Каталог выставки картин и скульптуры 'Художники Москвы — жертвам войны', организованной Московским губернским комитетом Всероссийского земского Союза помощи раненым и центральным бюро при городской управе. Москва, 1914–1915

1-я футуристическая выставка картин 'Трамвай В'
64–69 Живописный рельеф. 1914 г.
70 1915 г.
Каталог 1-й футуристической выставки картин 'Трамвай В'. Петроград, 1915

1915
Mementos of the Russian Theatre
1194 *Stage Design*
1195 *Costume Design. Pagan Venus*
1196 Same. *Tsar*
1197 Same. *Senator*
1198 Same. *Ambassador Mohamed*
1199 Same. *Warrior Anika*
1200 Same. *Rooster*
1201 Same. *Page*
1202 Same. *Royal Courtier*
1203 Same. *Grave-Digger's Wife*
1204 Same. *Blacksmith*
1205 Same. *Piper*
1206 Same. *Seductive Venus*
1207 Same. *Death*
1208 Same. *Courier*
1202 [1209!] Same. *Western Man*
1211 Same. *Grave-Digger*
1212 Same. *Adol'fa* [popular form of Adolf]
Tsar Maxem'ian and his Disobedient Son Adolf, Moscow, 6
Nov. 1911. Produced by M.M. [Bonch-] Tomashevskii
Mementos of the Russian Theatre. Collection L.I. Zheverzheev (Catalogue). List of an exhibition organized for the
benefit of the Field Hospital of the School of Folk Art. Foreword by N.N. Everinov. Moscow, 1915, pp. 74–5

1914–15
Women Artists in Aid of Victims of the War
Catalogue of the exhibition of the Moscow Society of
Women Artists, Moscow, 1914–15
*(Among the works of the women artists are listed also works
by Malevich, Mashkov, Pasternak, Iakovlev and others. Tatlin is remembered to have said that he also took part in the
exhibition but he was not included in the catalogue.)*

1915
Exhibition of Paintings of the Year 1915
Catalogue of the Exhibition of Paintings of the Year 1915,
Moscow, 1915
*(The works of Tatlin and his colleagues, Maiakovskii,
Malevich and Morgunov, are not included in the catalogue.
In all probability, the eccentricity of their works and some
unfavourable audience reaction caused Kandaurov, the or-
ganizer of the exhibition, to exclude their names from the
catalogue. They attracted, however, keen critical attention:
Golos Moskvy, 25 March 1915; Russkie vedomosti, 28
March 1915; Kievskaia mysl', 6 May 1915. Tatlin exhibited
'selections of materials'.)*
(Location: Salon of Art, 11 Bol'shaia Dmitrovka, Moscow)

1915–16
0—10. The Last Futurist Exhibition
132–43 Works from 1915
144 Works from 1913–14
Catalogue of 0—10. The Last Futurist Exhibition, Petrograd,
1915
*(The exhibition was organized by Puni. Location: 7 Field of
Mars, Artistic Bureau; date: 17 Dec. 1915 to 19 Jan. 1916)*

1916
The Store
Futurist Exhibition

Выставка памятников русского театра
1194 Эскиз декорации
1195 Эскиз костюма. Венера Кумерская
1196 То же. Царь
1197 То же. Сенатор
1198 То же. Магомет, посол
1199 То же. Аника, воин
1200 То же. Петух
1201 То же. Паж
1202 То же. Царедворец
1203 То же. Жена гробокопателя
1204 То же. Кузнец
1205 То же. Дудильщик
1206 То же. Венерина Прелестница
1207 То же. Смерть
1208 То же. Скороход
1202 То же. Западный
1211 То же. Гробокопатель
1212 То же. Адольфа
'Царь Максемьян и его непокорный сын Адольф', Москва,
6 ноября 1911 г. Пост. М.М. [Бонч] Томашевского.
Каталог: 'Опись выставленных в пользу лазарета Школы на-
родного искусства... памятников русского театра из собрания
Л.И. Жевержеева'. Вступительная статья Н.Н. Евреинова. Петроград, 1915, 74–75

Художницы – жертвам войны
Каталог выставки картин 'Московского общества художниц'.
Москва, 1914–1915 гг.

Выставка живописи – 1915 год
Каталог Выставки живописи – 1915 год. Москва, 1915

Последняя футуристическая выставка 0–10
132–143 Работы 1915 года
144 Работы 1913–1914 годов
Каталог 'Последней футуристической выставки 0–10'.
Петроград, 1915

Магазин
Футуристическая выставка

66–7 *Corner Counter-Reliefs,* 1914–15
68–71 *Reliefs,* 1913–14
72 *Relief,* 1915
Catalogue of The Store, a Futurist exhibition, Moscow, 1916
(The exhibition was organized by V.E. Tatlin. Date: March 1916)

66–67 Угловые контррельефы 1914–1915 гг.
66–71 Рельефы 1913–1914 годов
72 Рельеф 1915 года
Каталог футуристической выставки 'Магазин'. Москва, 1916

1918
Exhibition of Paintings and Drawings by the Moscow Futurists
130 *Harbour* (drawing)
Catalogue of the Exhibition of Paintings and Drawings by the Moscow Futurists, Tiflis, 1918
(The exhibition was organized by editors of the journal ARS. Artisterium, third [exhibitions] section. Location: 9 Golovinskii Prospekt, Tiflis)

Выставка картин и рисунков московских футуристов

130 Рисунок 'Пристань'
Каталог 'Выставки картин и рисунков московских футуристов'. Тифлис, 1918

1920
Exhibition of the Monument to the Third International
(No catalogue was prepared for the exhibition. Location: Mosaics Studio of the former Academy of Arts, Petrograd; date: 8 Nov. to 1 Dec. 1920. A special poster was issued for the event.)

Выставка модели проекта памятника III Интернационала

1920–1
Model of the Monument to the Third International
Exhibition organized on the occasion of the Eighth Congress of Soviets
(No catalogue was prepared for the exhibition. Location: foreground of the Colonnade of the House of Unions, Moscow; date: end of December, 1920 to beginning of January, 1921)

Модель проекта памятника III Интернационала
Выставка к VIII съезду Советов

1922
Survey of New Tendencies in Art
(No catalogue was prepared for the exhibition. We have no definite data; however, judging from the reviews, Tatlin showed several items representing some of the most important stages in the development of his career. Again without specific data, he showed some nudes, one corner counter-relief, and Pink Board, *a study in colour and glazing with paint, which was representative of some of the experiments conducted in his studio.)*
(Location: Museum of Artistic Culture – Miatlev House – Petrograd; date of opening: 15 June 1922)

Обзор новых течений искусства

1922
First Russian Exhibition of Fine Arts
506 *Sailor,* tempera
507 *Forest,* stage design
569 *Counter-Relief*
Erste Russische Kunstausstellung (Catalogue), Berlin, 1922 (Includes reproductions of the works numbered 507 and 569)
(Location: Galerie van Diemen & Co., 21 Unter den Linden, Berlin)

1922
First Russian Exhibition
(Location: Amsterdam. The Berlin exhibition was transferred in its entirety, and the catalogue is identical.)

1922
Exhibition of stage designs and studio works prepared at the Institute, 1918–22
249 Décor for *Tsar Maxem'ian*
Catalogue of the Exhibition of stage designs and studio works prepared at the Institute 1918–22, Petrograd, 1922. Introductory articles by L.I. Zheverzheev, N.N. Punin and G. Stebnitskii
(Location: Central Institute of Applied Arts of the Academy, Petrograd; date of opening: November 1922)

1923
Exhibition of Petrograd Artists of all Tendencies

1444–1503 Collection of flat surfaces for the performance of Khlebnikov, *Zangezi*, 1923
1504a, b Costumes for the performance of Khlebnikov, *Zangezi*, 1923
1505–6 Designs for the backdrops of Khlebnikov, *Zangezi*
1507–8 Sketches of a model of the Monument to the Third International, 1919
1509–10 Designs for clothes (drawing)
1511 'Iverni-Viverni' (machinery for *Zangezi*)
Catalogue of the Exhibition of Petrograd Artists of all Tendencies, 1918–22, Petrograd, Sorabis (Trade Union of Art Workers), 1923
(Location: Academy of Arts, Petrograd; date of opening: 15 May 1923. On all Tatlin's works shown at this exhibition a round stamp with the words 'Tatlin's studio' appears instead of the artist's signature. At the exhibition Tatlin led the Central Group of the Union of New Tendencies in Art. Co-exhibitors were Lebedev, Dymshits-Tolstaia, Lapshin, Pchel'nikova, Taran, Uspenskii, Pessiatii and Enei, Tyrsa, Bruni, Miturich, Lebedeva, Pakulin, Nemenova, Dubinskaia, Popov-Voronezhskii, Pakhomov and Isakov.)

1923
Exhibition In Memoriam Khlebnikov
(No catalogue was made for the exhibition. Tatlin showed models of stage and costume designs prepared for Khlebnikov, Zangezi. Location: The White Hall of the Museum of Artistic Culture [Miatlev House], Petrograd; date of opening: 28 June 1923. The exhibition was originally organized by Miturich in Moscow. Later, on the first anniversary of the poet's death, the exhibition was transported to Petrograd, and a few new items were added.)

1925
GINKhUK Exhibition of Examination Materials
(No catalogue was prepared for the exhibition. Tatlin organized the exhibition of his Section for Material Culture in its own lecture hall. Combinations of colours [colour norms], clothing designs and models, and three variants of a novel stove were shown.)
(Location: State Institute of Artistic Culture [Miatlev House], Petrograd; date: 15 May to 8 June 1925. The Section for Theoretical Analysis of Form directed by Malevich, the Section for Organic Culture directed by Matiushin, and Mansurov's Experimental Section also took part in the exhibition.)

1925
Soviet Section at the International Exhibition of Modern Decorative and Industrial Arts

Выставка эскизов театральных декораций и работ мастерских института за 1918–1922 гг.
249 Эскиз убранства сценической площадки для спектакля 'Царь Максемьян'
Каталог выставки эскизов театральных декораций и работ мастерских института за 1918–1922 гг. Петроград, 1922 г. Вступительные статьи Л.И. Жевержеева, Н.Н. Пунина и Г. Стебницкого

Выставка картин петроградских художников всех направлений
1444–1503 Колода плоскостей к постановке 'Зангези' В. Хлебникова. 1923
1504а-б. Костюмы к 'Зангези' В. Хлебникова. 1923
1505–1506 Проекты материальных фонов в 'Зангези' В. Хлебникова
1507–1508 Рисунки-чертежи модели памятника III Интернационала. 1919
1509–1510 Нормали одежды (рисунки). 1923
1511 'Иверни-выверни' Зангези (машина)
Каталог выставки картин художников Петрограда всех направлений 1918–1923 гг. Сорабис. Петроград, 1923

Выставка, посвященная памяти В.В. Хлебникова

Отчетная выставка ГИНХУКа

Model of the Monument to the Third International, Section URSS. Exposition Internationale des Arts Décoratifs et Industriels Modernes. Union des Républiques Soviétiques Socialistes, (Catalogue), Paris, 1925 (Illustration on p.171) *(Location: Octagonal Hall, Grand Palais, Paris. The second version of the model of the Monument to the Third International, which was prepared specially for this exhibition, was shown in the architectural section of the Soviet Section.)*

1925
Group Exhibition of Drawings by L.A. Bruni, N.N. Kupriianov, V.V. Lebedev, P.I. L'vov, P.V. Miturich, V.E. Tatlin, N.A. Tyrsa

110 *Laughter*, sketch for the performance of *Zangezi*, 1923. 55.5 × 37.5; charcoal on p[aper]
111 *Repentance*, sketch for the performance of *Zangezi*, 1923. 56 × 37.5; charcoal on p[aper]
Group Exhibition of Drawings by L.A. Bruni, N.N. Kupriianov, V.V. Lebedev, P.I. L'vov, P.V. Miturich, V.E. Tatlin, N.A. Tyrsa (Catalogue), Moscow, 1925
(Location: State Tsvetkov Gallery, Moscow)

1927
New Tendencies in Art
(No catalogue was prepared for the exhibition. A photo of the exhibition shows that the following works of Tatlin were shown: Carnation, *1908;* Sailor, *1911;* Bouquet, *1912;* Nude, *1913)*
(Location: State Russian Museum, Leningrad)

1927
All-Ukrainian Anniversary Exhibition
Department of Dramatic, Cinematic and Photographic Arts of the Kiev College of Art
Artistic directors: Prof. V.E. Tatlin, Prof. N.I. Triaskin.
First-year students. Scenery models. Works by the students Varpekhovskii, Borisovets, Rogochii, Zlochevskii, Grigorovich, Kaplunovskii, Sokol-Chernilovskii, Khomaza and Shvets
1–6 Panorama (1st assignment)
7–9 Service pavilion (2nd assignment)
10–12 Model sketches (3rd assignment)
13–14 Compositional sketches for the 1st assignment
15–17 Clothing designs (costumes) for the 2nd assignment
18–22 Sketches for the 3rd assignment
23–4 Sketches for the 1st film assignment
25 Costumes for the performance of Ostrovskii, *The Barbarians* and *The Storm* (student Semenko)
26–30 Models for the 1st film assignment
31–4 Models for the 2nd film assignment
Selection of Materials. (Study assignments for the representation of the material environment)
35–7 Models (students Umanskii, Shumanskii and Pavlov)
38 Model of a stage for a workers' club (fourth-year student P.V. Stovbunenko)
39–68 Settings for films on slides
69–103 Photographs of film and stage scenery
105–51 Photographs
The work of students L.S. Baianov, D.S. Bochak, V.I. Gorbovets, A.A. Kaleshits, G.S. Loiko, M. Varpekhovskii, V.A. Naumets, O.E. Pashnitskii, A.N. Prakhov and P. Redchits.
Catalogue of the All-Ukrainian Anniversary Exhibition Commemorating the Tenth Anniversary of the October Rev-

Выставка рисунков группы художников: Бруни Л.А., Куприянова Н.Н., Лебедева В.В., Львова П.И., Митурича П.В., Татлина В.Е., Тырсы Н.А.
110 'Смех'. Эскиз для постановки 'Зангези', 1923, 55,5 × 37,5, б., уголь
111 'Горе'. Эскиз для постановки 'Зангези', 1923, 56 × 37,5, б., уголь
Каталог выставки рисунков группы художников: Бруни Л.А., Куприянова Н.Н., Лебедева В.В., Львова П.И., Митурича П.В., Татлина В.Е., Тырсы Н.А. Москва, 1925

Выставка новых течений в искусстве

Всеукраинская юбилейная выставка
Киевский художественный институт,
Отдел тео-кино-фото.
Руководители: пр. В.Е. Татлин, пр. Н.И. (А) Тряскин.
1-й курс. Тео-макеты. Работы студентов.: Варпе(а)ховский, Борисовец, Рогочий, Злочевский, Григорович, Каплуновский, Сокол-Черниловский, Хомаза, Швец.
1–6 Панорама (1-е задание)
7–9 Бытовой павильон (2-е задание)
10–12 Эскизы макетов (3-е задание)
13–14 Эскизы композиции к 1-му заданию
15–17 Эскизы одежды (костюмы) ко 2-му заданию
18–22 Эскизы к 3-му заданию
23–24 Эскизы к 1-му кинозаданию
25 Костюмы (для постановок) 'Варвары', 'Гроза' Островского (студент Семенко)
26–30 Макеты (1-е кинозадание)
31–34 Макеты (2-е кинозадание)
Материальный подбор (учебные задания на выявление материального окружения).
35–37 Макеты (ст. Уманский, Шуманский, Павлов)
38 Макет сцены рабочего клуба (ст. IV курса Стовбуненко П.В.)
39–68 Диапозитивы макетов кино
69–103 Фотографии макетов кино и тео
105–151 Фотографии. Работы студентов: Баянов Л.С., Бочак Д.С., Горбовец В.И., Калешиц А.А., Лойко Г.С., Варпеховский М., Наумец В.А., Пашницкий О.Ю., Прахов А.Н., Редчиц П.
'Каталог Всеукраїнскої юбілейної виставки 10 років Жовтня 1917–1927. Живопись, скульптура, архитектура, фото-, кино, керамика, текстиль'. Харьків, Киів, Одесса, 1927

olution. Painting, sculpture, architecture, photography, film, ceramics, textiles. Khar'kov–Kiev–Odessa, 1927
(Tatlin participated in this exhibition as the professor directing the work of the students.)

1928
Exhibition of New Acquisitions by the State Art Foundation
242 *The Flying Dutchman. Helmsman*, charcoal on paper, 76 × 54
243 *The Flying Dutchman. Woman*, charcoal on paper, 76 × 50
244 *The Flying Dutchman. Ship's Captain*, charcoal on paper, 76 × 51
245 *The Flying Dutchman. Spinner*, charcoal on paper, 71.5 × 51
Catalogue of the Exhibition of New Acquisitions by the State Art Foundation, Moscow, 1928. With an introduction by A.A. Fedorov-Davydov

1929
Exhibition of Contemporary Art of Soviet Russia
94 *Helmsman* (drawing)
123 *Nude* (1913, State Tret'iakov Gallery)
277 Costume for *Zangezi*
Exhibition of Contemporary Art of Soviet Russia (Catalogue), Grand Central Plaza, New York, 1929
(It is probable that the same exhibition was shown in Detroit and Boston.)

1930
Exhibition of New Acquisitions by the State Art Foundation, 1928–9
213 *Picking up Matches,* ink, 25.3 × 18
214 *Child Loafing on the Boulevard*, ink, 18 × 25.5
Catalogue of the Exhibition of New Acquisitions by the State Art Foundation, 1928–9, Moscow, 1930

1930
War and Art
'... on the high pedestal, where the map of the various periods of the Civil War can be seen, there stands also V.E. Tatlin's creation, a model of the Monument to the Third International. ...The model was constructed for the first time in 1919 (the model which is on display here is the second version of the work) ...'
War and Art (Guide), Leningrad, GRM (State Russian Museum), 1930, p. 14

1932
Exhibition by Honoured Art Worker V.E. Tatlin
1 *Letatlin* no. 1, flying machine with covered fuselage
2 No. 2, the same
3–4 The machine with uncovered fuselage
5 Model of the fuselage
6 Model of the curved main beam
7 The ribs
8 Drawings and blueprints of the machine
9 Photograph of *Letatlin*
10 Photograph of the Monument to the Comintern
11 Photographs and brochures of various works
12 Designs of utilitarian objects

Выставка приобретений государственного художественного фонда
242 Летучий голландец. Рулевой. Уголь, бум., 76 × 54
243 Летучий голландец. Женщина. Уголь, бум., 76 × 50
244 Летучий голландец. Капитан. Уголь, бум., 76 × 51
245 Летучий голландец. Пряха. Уголь, бум., 71,5 × 51
Каталог Выставки приобретений гос. художественного фонда. Москва, 1928. Вступит. статья А.А. Федорова-Давыдова

Выставка приобретений государственного художественного фонда за 1928–1929 гг.
213 Человек, поднимающий спички. Тушь, 25,3 × 18
214 Беспризорник на бульваре. Тушь, 18 × 25,5
Каталог Выставки приобретений государственного художественного фонда за 1928–1929 гг. Москва, 1930

Война и искусство
'...На высоком постаменте, по которому размещаются карты разных моментов гражданской войны, высится памятник III Интернационала – модель работы худ. В.Е. Татлина... Модель исполнена в первый раз в 1919 г. (настоящая модель – и второй вариант) ...'
Путеводитель состоявшейся в ГРМ выставки 'Война и искусство'. Изд. ГРМ. Ленинград, 1930, с. 14

Выставка работ заслуженного деятеля искусств В.Е. Татлина
1 Аппарат в обтяжке. 'Летатлин' № 1
2 То (же). № 2
3–4 Конструкция аппарата без обтяжки
5 Модель фюзеляжа
6 Модель сложного кривого лонжерона
7 Нервюры
8 Рисунки и чертежи аппарата
9 Фото с аппарата 'Летатлин'
10 Фото с монумента Коминтерна
11 Фото и брошюры различных работ
12 Работы по оформлению быта

Catalogue of the Exhibition by Honoured Art Worker V.E. Tatlin, Moscow and Leningrad, 1932 (with an article each by Tatlin and Artseulov)
(Location: Italian Hall of the State Museum of Fine Arts, Moscow)

'Выставка работ заслуженного деятеля искусств В.Е. Татлина' (Каталог). Москва – Ленинград, 1932. В каталог-буклет включены статьи Татлина и К. Арцеулова

1932
Exhibition of Fifteen Years' Work by Artists of the RSFSR

155 *Tsarevich*, ornamental plate, 1922. Executor: S. Chekhonin

Exhibition of Fifteen Years' Work by Artists of the RSFSR (Catalogue), Leningrad, 1932
(Location: State Russian Museum, Leningrad; date of opening: 11 November 1932)
(Paintings, graphics and statues were shown at the anniversary exhibition)

Художники РСФСР за 15 лет

155 Тарелка 'Царский сын', 1922 г. Исполн. С. Чехонин.
Каталог выставки 'Художники РСФСР за 15 лет'. Ленинград, 1932

1933
Exhibition of Fifteen Years' Work by Artists of the RSFSR

783 *Board No. 1*, 1917
784 *Selection of Materials*, 1917, wood, tin
989 The *Letatlin* flying machine

Exhibition of Fifteen Years' Work by Artists of the Russian Soviet Federated Socialist Republic (Catalogue), Moscow, 1933
(The Moscow exhibition was arranged with materials from the Leningrad anniversary exhibition, and was completed by additional materials from Moscow museums and works from the artists' studios.)

Художники РСФСР за 15 лет

783 Доска № 1, 1917 г.
784 Материальный подбор, 1917 г. Дерево, жесть
989 Летательный аппарат 'Летатлин'
Каталог выставки 'Художники РСФСР за 15 лет'. Москва, 1933

1934
Exhibition of Letatlin in the Inventions Section of the Polytechnical Museum
(No catalogue was prepared for the exhibition. Location: Moscow; date: spring 1934)

Выставка, посвященная летательному аппарату 'Летатлин', в Отделе изобретений Политехнического музея

1936
Exhibition Commemorating the Fiftieth Anniversary of the Death of A.N. Ostrovskii

MKhAT–2: *A Comic Actor of the 17th Century*. Stage and costume design by Tatlin
1037 One model
1038–46 9 photographs of sets
1047–73 26 photographs of actors

Exhibition Commemorating the Fiftieth Anniversary of the Death of the Great Russian Dramatist, A.N. Ostrovskii (Catalogue), Moscow, 1936

Выставка А.Н. Островского в связи с 50-летием со дня смерти

МХАТ—II. Комик XVII столетия — художник Татлин

1037 1 макет
1038–1046 9 фото сцен
1047–1073 26 фото персонажей
Каталог выставки, посвященной творчеству великого русского драматурга А.Н. Островского, в связи с 50-летием со дня смерти. Москва, 1936

1939
Exhibition of Works by Moscow Stage and Costume Designers
(No catalogue was prepared for the exhibition. Critiques of the exhibition: Tvorchestvo, *no. 9, 1939;* Sovetskoe iskusstvo, *21 May 1939)*
(Location: Art Workers' Hall, Moscow)

Выставка театральных художников

1945
Works for the Theatre by Moscow Artists, 1941–5

Московские художники в спектаклях 1941–1945 гг.

(No catalogue was prepared for the exhibition. Critiques of the exhibition: Sovetskoe iskusstvo, *12 Oct. 1945;* Izvestiia, *17 Oct. 1945)*
(Location: vestibule of the Actors' Hall, Moscow; date: October 1945)

1954–7
Soviet Porcelain Art. Exhibition of Products from the Lomonosov Porcelain Factory
Tsarevich Maximilian, decorative plate, Leningrad Porcelain Factory, no. 3047
Soviet Porcelain Art (Catalogue of the Exhibition of Products from the Lomonosov Porcelain Factory), Leningrad, 1961
(Location: State Russian Museum, Leningrad. Coloured over-glaze painting, depicting Tsarevich Maximilian, the hero of an old Russian play. Prepared from a design by V.E. Tatlin)

Советский художественный фарфор завода им. Ломоносова
Тарелка, изображающая царевича Максимилиана. Л.Ф.З., № 3047
Каталог выставки 'Советский художественный фарфор'. Ленинград, 1961

1962
Maiakovskii's Illustrators and Book Designers
(No catalogue was prepared for the exhibition.)
(Location: State Maiakovskii Library and Museum, Moscow; date: 19–21 April 1962. Invitation cards were printed for the exhibition.)

Художники-оформители произведений В. Маяковского

1966
Memorial Evening and Exhibition in Honour of Tatlin's Eightieth Anniversary
No catalogue was prepared for the exhibition. More than ten paintings were shown: Portrait of a Woman, *1933;* Meat, *1947; several landscapes and still-lifes – flowers, poplar branches, etc. – from the years between 1930 and 1950; the India ink drawing entitled* Fisherman *from the 1910s; photographs of other works from the same decade and documentary photographs.)*
(Location: House of Architects, Moscow; date of opening: 26 April 1966)
(A printed invitation was prepared for the exhibition.)

Вечер-выставка, посвященный 80-летию со дня рождения художника Татлина

1966
Paintings, Drawings and Sketches by Russian Artists from the First Third of the Twentieth Century
Collection Ia.E. Rubinshtein
Theatrical Setting, 1913, tempera on c[ardboard], 34 × 45
Fisherman, 1920s, India ink on paper, 24 × 14.5
Paintings, Drawings and Sketches by Russian Artists from the First Third of the Twentieth Century. Collection Ia.E. Rubinshtein (Catalogue), Tallinn, 1966
(Location: Tallinn, Estonian Museum of Arts)

Картины, рисунки и акварели русских художников из собрания Я.Е. Рубинштейна – первая треть XX века

Театральная декорация. 1913 г. Темп., 34 × 45
Рыбак. 1920-е гг., б., тушь, 24 × 14,5
Картины, рисунки и акварели русских художников из собрания Я.Е. Рубинштейна (первая треть XX века). Каталог. Таллин, 1966

1967
National Exhibition of Works by Designers of Scenery and Costumes for the Theatre, Cinema and Television
Costume designs for A.N. Ostrovskii, *A Comic Actor of the 17th Century:*
Piper, watercolour on paper, 44 × 29
Eve, watercolour on paper, 44 × 30
Gregorii, watercolour on paper, 44.4 × 31.8
Kochetov, watercolour on paper, 45 × 30
Klushin, watercolour on paper, 45 × 32

Всесоюзная выставка работ художников театра, кино, телевидения

Эскизы костюмов к комедии А. Островского 'Комик XVII столетия':
Трубач-дуда – б., акв., 44 × 29
Ева – б., акв. 44 × 30
Грегори – б., акв., 44,4 × 31,8
Кочетов – б., акв., 45 × 30
Клушин – б., акв., 45 × 32

Vania, watercolour on paper, 45 × 32
Second Moscow Art Theatre, 1935
Costume designs for A. Sukhovo-Kobylin, *The Affair*:
Muromskii, pencil and watercolour on paper, 44 × 31.8
Atueva, pencil and watercolour on paper, 44 × 32
Lidochka, pencil and watercolour on paper, 44 × 32.2
Prince, pencil and watercolour on paper, 44 × 33
Tarelkin, pencil and watercolour on paper, 44 × 28.2
Varravin, pencil and watercolour on paper, 43 × 33.3
Ibisov, pencil and watercolour on paper, 43.5 × 32.8
Central Theatre of the Red Army, Moscow, 1940
Model for A. Kron, *Deep Reconnaissance*, Gor'kii Moscow
Art Theatre, 1943
National Exhibition of Works by Designers of Scenery and
Costumes for the Theatre, Cinema and Television (Catalogue), Moscow, 1967

Ваня – б., акв., 45 × 32
МХАТ–II–1935.
Эскизы костюмов к драме А. Сухово-Кобылина 'Дело':
Муромский – б., кар., акв., 44 × 31,8
Атуева – б., кар., акв., 44 × 32
Лидочка – б., кар., акв., 44 × 32,2
Князь – б., кар., акв., 44 × 33
Тарелкин – б., кар., акв., 44 × 28,2
Варравин – б., кар., акв 43 × 33,3
Ибисов – б., кар., акв., 43,5 × 32,8
ЦТКА, Москва, 1940.
Макет декорации к пьесе А. Крона 'Глубокая разведка'.
МХАТ им. Горького, 1943
Каталог Всесоюзной выставки работ художников театра, кино, телевидения. Москва, 1967

1967
Russian Prints at the Turn of the Century
Still-Life with Fish, 1913, lithograph, 19.5 × 14.7
Underneath on the left side: Tatlin
Painter, 1913, lithograph, 17.7 × 16.5
Underneath on the right side: Tatlin
Russian Prints at the Turn of the Century (Catalogue), Leningrad, 1967. The introduction was written by the organizer of the exhibition, E.F. Kovtun. (With one black-and-white illustration: *Painter*, p. 13)

Русский эстамп конца XIX—начала XX века
Натюрморт с рыбой, 1913 г. Литография. 19,5 × 14,7
Внизу слева: Татлин
Маляр, 1913 г. Литография. 17,71 × 6,5
Внизу справа: Татлин
Каталог выставки 'Русский эстамп конца XIX—начала XX вв.
Ленинград, 1967. Автор вступительной статьи и составитель
Е.Ф. Ковтун. Одна черно-белая иллюстрация: Маляр, с. 13

1967
Russian Art from the Scythians to the Present
500 Costume design for Glinka's opera *Ivan Susanin*, 1913, watercolour, 31.5 × 45, Bakhrushin Central State Museum of Theatre History, Moscow, inventory number: 6662
501 Costume design for *Ivan Susanin*. *Boyar*, watercolour, 50 × 32.5, Bakhrushin Museum, inventory number: 26421/17
502 Stage design for *Ivan Susanin*. *Forest*, watercolour, 54.4 × 95.5. State Tret'iakov Gallery, Moscow, inventory number: 9299
L'art russe des Scythes à nos jours. Trésors des musées soviétiques (Catalogue), Paris, 1967
(Location: Grand Palais, Paris)

1969
Russian and Soviet Still-Lifes
Carnation, 1908, oil on canvas, 73.5 × 66.5. On the verso of the canvas: 'V.E. Tatlin, *Carnation*, Moscow, 1908', inventory number: 1626.
Flowers, 1912, oil on canvas, 71.5 × 71.5. On the verso of the canvas: '*Nature Morte*, V.E. Tatlin, [1]912' inventory number: 1541
Russian and Soviet Still-Lifes (Catalogue), Leningrad, GRM (State Russian Museum), 1969
(The following works, although not listed in the catalogue, were also shown at the exhibition: Bouquet, 1911–12, oil on canvas, 93 × 48, and Branches, 1946, oil on canvas, 80 × 70.)
(Location: State Russian Museum, Leningrad)

Русский и советский натюрморт
Гвоздика, 1908 г. х., м., 73,5 × 66,5. На обороте холста: 'В.Е.
Татлин: "Гвоздика". Москва 1908'. Инв. № 1626

Цветы, 1912 г., х., м., 71,5 × 71,5. На обороте холста надпись:
'"Натуре морте" В.Е. Татлин. 912'. Инв. № 1541
Каталог выставки 'Русский и советский натюрморт', ГРМ. Ленинград, 1969

1971
Art in Revolution
Joint Exhibition by the Ministry of Culture of the USSR and the Arts Council of Great Britain

Model of the 1,200 ft high Monument to the Third International, 1919–20, which, according to some accounts, was originally to be erected on the banks of the Neva in Petrograd. (The reconstruction was the work of Christopher Cross, Jeremy Dickson, Swan Rindell, Peter Watson and Christopher Woodward. Scale: 1:50. It was shown on the Sculpture Terrace overlooking the Thames.)
Corner Relief, 1915. Reconstruction; wood, metal and cable 31 × 38 × 28 in. (79.5 × 26 × 71 cm.) Prepared by Martyn Chalk, 1966–70
Combined Counter-Relief, 1915. Reconstruction; iron, zinc, aluminium, etc., 31 × 60 × 30 in. (79 × 151 × 75.5 cm) Prepared by Martyn Chalk, 1966–70
Chair made from curved metal tubing, with a moulded rubber seat, 1927. Reconstruction by the Enterprise Metal Company
Art in Revolution. Soviet Art and Design since 1917 (Catalogue), London, 1971. Illustrations: the Tatlin-Rogozhin chair and the Monument to the Third International
(Location: Hayward Gallery, London; date: 26 February to 18 April 1971)
(The reconstruction of the model of the Monument to the Third International was based on surviving blueprints and photographs and detailed information from A.A. Strigalev.)

1973
Exhibition of Book Illustrations from Private Collections in Moscow

Illustration for Maiakovskii's poem 'Signboards', 1913, lithograph, 19.5 × 15.2. Collection Iu.A. Molok
Exhibition of Book Illustrations from Private Collections in Moscow (Catalogue), Moscow, Union of Artists of the RSFSR, 1973
(Location: Art Collectors' Club, Headquarters of the Union of Art Workers, Moscow)

1976
Children's Books by Leningrad Artists Exhibition to Commemorate the Fortieth Anniversary of the Detgiz Publishing House

(No catalogue was prepared for the exhibition. Tatlin's illustrations for Kharms, Firstly and Secondly, *Moscow and Leningrad, 1929, were shown.)*
(Location: Artists' Club of the Moscow Branch of the Union of Artists of the RSFSR, Moscow; date: July 1976)

1977
Russian Painting 1890–1917
Pictures from the Museums of the USSR

63 *Still-Life. Flowers*, 1912. oil on canvas, 71.5 × 71.5. On the verso: *'Nature Morte*, V.E. Tatlin. 12'
64 *Forest*, 1913, tempera on pasteboard, 54.4 × 95.5 cm State Tret'iakov Gallery, inventory number: 9299. Stage design for the opera *Ivan Susanin*
Russische Malerei 1890–1917. Bilder aus Museen der UdSSR. München, 1977 (Illustrated with pictures no. 63 and 64)
(Date: 19 January to 6 March 1977)

1977
Russian and Soviet Painting
Fishmonger, 1911
Russian and Soviet Painting. New York and San Francisco, 1977. With an introduction by D. Sarab'ianov

Книжная графика московских собирателей изобразительного искусства
Стихотворение В. Маяковского 'Вывескам' (Иллюстрация Т. 1913 г. Литография, 19,5 × 15,2. Собр. Ю.А. Молока).
Каталог выставки 'Книжная графика московских собирателей изобразительного искусства', Союз художников РСФСР. Москва, 1973

Ленинградские художники детской книги (к 40-летию ДЕТГИЗа)

1977

V.E. Tatlin, Honoured Art Worker of the RSFSR

1 Photographs of the blueprints of the Monument to the Third International (1919), and of the Monument's first and second versions (1920 and 1925); the 1975 reconstruction of the model

2–29 Paintings from the period 1910–40 TsGALI, State Tret'iakov Gallery

30 *Man's Portrait*, gouache, 1909, TsGALI

31 Nine drawings from an album from 1912–14, TsGALI

32 Six drawings from a 1914 album, TsGALI

33 *Portrait of Tatlin's Son* [?], 1930s, TsGALI

34 *Self-Portrait*, 1940s, Bakhrushin Museum

35–41a Illustrations

42–96 Stage and costume designs, 1910–1940s. Bakhrushin Museum, Leningrad Museum of Theatre History, State Tret'iakov Gallery

97 Model of *Letatlin* from the Zhukovskii Central State Air and Astronautical Museum

98 *Selection of Materials*, State Tret'iakov Gallery

99–101 Photographs of the design for the 'economical stove', suits and coats, 1923

102–107 Designs for dishes, 1923, drawing, Bakhrushin Museum

108 Design of model chair, 1927, photograph of the original work and the reconstructed model, 1976

V.E. Tatlin, Honoured Art Worker of the RSFSR, 1885–1953 (Catalogue), Moscow, 1977. Arr.: L.A. Zhadova, Z.P. Mellit (drawing)

(Location: Fadeev Writers' Hall; date: 17–28 February 1977)

1977

Book Covers by Russian Artists from the Beginning of the Twentieth Century

230 *Vladimir Evgrafovich Tatlin*, Petrograd. A publication of *Novyi zhurnal dlia vsekh*, 1915. 37.5 × 27, Collection A.S. Lado, Leningrad

231 D.I. Kharms, *Firstly and Secondly*, Moscow and Leningrad, GIZ, 1929, 26.5 × 20, Collection of E.P. Podvolotskaia, Leningrad

Book Covers by Russian Artists from the Beginning of the Twentieth Century, Leningrad, 1977. The introduction written by the compiler of the catalogue, I.V. Kovtun

(Location: State Russian Museum, Leningrad; date: Summer 1977)

1977

Restoration of Works of Art in the Soviet Union

Nude, 1916. oil on canvas, 106 × 142.5. On the verso: *Still-Life*. TsGALI. Restorer: A. Makarov (1976)

Restoration of Works of Art in the Soviet Union (Catalogue), Moscow, Ministry of Culture of the USSR, 1977)

(Location: Academy of Arts: Moscow)

1978

Exhibition of New Acquisitions. Soviet Painting

Flowers, 1940, oil on wood, 75.5 × 67.5, inventory number: 8350

Exhibition of New Acquisitions. Soviet Painting (Catalogue), Leningrad, 1978

(Location: State Russian Museum, Leningrad; date: 22 March to 6 July 1978)

В.Е. Татлин – заслуженный деятель искусств РСФСР

1. Фотографии эскизов, чертежей проекта Памятника III Интернационала (1919), 1-го и 2-го вариантов модели его (1920 и 1925 г.), а также модель-реконструкция 1975 г.

2–29 Живопись 1910-х и 1940-х гг. ЦГАЛИ и ГТГ

30 Портрет мужчины. Гуашь. 1909 г. ЦГАЛИ

31 9 рисунков из альбома. 1912–1914 гг. ЦГАЛИ

32 6 рисунков из альбома. 1914 г. ЦГАЛИ

33 Портрет сына (?). 1930-е гг. ЦГАЛИ

34 Автопортрет. 1940-е гг. ЦГТМ

35–41а Иллюстрации

42–96 Эскизы театральных декораций и костюмов. 1910-е – 1940-е гг., из ЦГТМ, ЛГТМ, ГТГ

97 Модель 'Летатлина' из Центрального государственного музея авиации и космонавтики им. Н.Е. Жуковского

98 Материальный подбор. ГТГ

99–101 Фотографии проекта 'экономической печи' и моделей костюма и пальто. 1923 г.

102–107 Проекты посуды, 1923 г., рис. ЦГТМ

108 Стул – проект-модель 1927 г., фотография оригинала, а также модель-реконструкция 1976 г.

Каталог выставки 'В.Е. Татлин – заслуженный деятель искусств РСФСР. 1885–1953'. Москва, 1977

Книжные обложки русских художников начала XX века

230 'Владимир Евграфович Татлин'. Пг., изд. Нового журнала для всех. 1915 г. Цинкография, 37,5 × 27. Собрание А.С. Ладо, Ленинград

231 Хармс Д.И. 'Во-первых и во-вторых'. М.-Л., ГИЗ, 1929. Цинкография, 26,5 × 20. Собрание Е.П. Подволоцкой, Ленинград

Каталог выставки 'Книжные обложки русских художников начала XX века'. Ленинград, 1977. Автор вступит. статьи и составитель каталога Е.В. Ковтун.

Реставрация музейных ценностей в СССР

'Обнаженная'. 1916 г. х., м., 106 × 142,5. На обороте: 'Натюрморт'. ЦГАЛИ, реставратор А. Макаров. (1976)

Каталог выставки 'Реставрация музейных ценностей в СССР', Министерство культуры СССР. Москва, 1977

Выставка новых поступлений. Советская живопись

'Цветы'. 1940 г. Дерево, масло, 75,5 × 67,5. Инв. № 8350. Каталог 'Выставки новых поступлений. Советская живопись'. Ленинград, 1978

1978
Creations in Russian Stage Design in the Collections of I.V. Kachurin and Ia.E. Rubinshtein
Stage design for Glinka, *A Life for the Tsar* (*Ivan Susanin*), 1913, gouache on paper, 33.5 × 45.5
Design for Dance-Frock, 1920s, coloured paper glued to pasteboard, 36 × 27.5, Collection I.V. Kachurin
Creations in Russian Stage Design in the Collections of I.V. Kachurin and Ia.E. Rubinshtein (Catalogue), Tallinn, 1978
(Location: State Museum of the Estonian SSR, Tallinn)

1978
Russian and Soviet Art of the First Third of the Twentieth Century
Stage design for Glinka *A Life for the Tsar* (*Ivan Susanin*), 1913, gouache on paper, 33.5 × 45.5
Russian and Soviet Art of the First Third of the Twentieth Century (Catalogue), Iaroslavl', 1978
(Location: District Museum of Art, Iaroslavl')

1979
Paris-Moscow, 1900–1930

1981
Moscow-Paris, 1900–1930
Fishmonger, 1911. Gum paint on canvas, 77 × 90 cm, Tret'iakov Gallery, Moscow
Self-Portrait (*Sailor*), 1911, oil on canvas, 71.5 × 71.5 cm, Russian Museum, Leningrad
Nude, 1913, oil on canvas, 143 × 108 cm, Tret'iakov Gallery, Moscow
Nude, 1913, oil on canvas, 104.5 × 130.5 cm, Russian Museum, Leningrad
Selection of Materials, 1916. Counter-relief made of wood and iron, Tret'iakov Gallery, Moscow
Letatlin, model of the flying machine, Museum of Aviation, Moscow
Technical illustration of human body position in *Letatlin*, pencil on paper, 26.5 × 21 cm, Bakhrushin Museum
Models of clothing, two sketches, pencil on paper, 62 × 39.5 cm, 56.8 × 77 cm, Bakhrushin Museum
Pavel Kozhin, 'Egg', tea pot, 1929 (prepared under Tatlin's guidance), porcelain with spray-painted glaze, Sample, Museum of Ceramic Art, Kuskovo, Moscow
Rogozhin, Chair, Tatlin's studio, reconstructed by V. Sokolov and V. Pavlov, 1976, metal and leather, Collection L. Zhadova, Moscow
Aleksei Sotnikov, Wicker tray with compartments for children's nursing vessels (made under Tatlin's guidance), porcelain, straw, steel. Reconstruction (1979). Collection A. Sotnikov.
Model of the Monument to the Third International (1919). The reconstruction was based on blueprints owned by the State Shchusev Research Museum of Architecture and prepared at the Longépé firm in Paris. Centre Georges Pompidou, Paris
A Life for the Tsar (*Ivan Susanin*), 1913, Glinka's opera. The production did not take place
Forest, stage design, glue-water on cardboard, 54.4 × 95.5 cm, Tret'iakov Gallery, Moscow
Polish Ball, stage design, gum paint, pencil, gouache on cardboard, 55.5 × 93.2 cm. Tret'iakov Gallery, Moscow

Русское театрально–декорационное искусство из собраний И.В. Качурина и Я. Е. Рубинштейна
Эскиз театральной декорации для постановки оперы М.И. Глинки 'Жизнь за царя'. 1913 г., б., гуашь, 33,5 × 45,5. Эскиз костюма для танцев. 1920-е гг. К., аппликация из цветной бумаги, 36 × 27,5. Собрание И.В. Качурина.
Каталог выставки 'Русское театрально-декорационное искусство из собраний И.В. Качурина и Я.Е. Рубинштейна'. Таллин, 1978

Русское и советское искусство первой трети XX века
Эскиз театральной декорации для постановки оперы М.И. Глинки 'Жизнь за царя'. 1913 г., бгуашь, 33,5 × 45,5
Каталог выставки 'Русское и советское искусство первой трети XX века'. Ярославль, 1978

Москва–Париж. 1900–1930
Продавец рыбы. 1911 г. Клеевые краски, холст, 77 × 90 см. Москва, Третьяковская галерея
Автопортрет в образе Матроса. 1911 г. Масло, холст, 71,5 × 71,5 см. Ленинград, Русский музей
Натурщица. 1913 г. Масло, холст, 143 × 108 см. Москва, Третьяковская галерея
Натурщица. 1913 г. Масло, холст, 104,5 × 130,5 см. Ленинград, Русский музей
Материальный подбор. 1916 г. Контррельеф на дереве, железо. Москва, Третьяковская галерея
'Летатлин'–модель летательного аппарата. Москва, Музей авиации
Рисунок (технический) фиксации положения тела в полете на 'Летатлине'. Бумага, карандаш, 26,5 × 21 см. Москва, ГЦТМ
Проект мужского и женского костюма. Два эскиза. Бумага, карандаш, 62 × 39,5 см и 56,8 × 77 см. Москва, ГЦТМ
Кожин, Павел: Чайник 'Яйцо'. 1929 г. [Под руководством Татлина.] Фарфор глазурованный, трафарет, аэрография. Кусково (Москва), Музей керамики
Рогожин: Стул. Мастерская В. Татлина. Реконструкция: В. Соколов и В. Павлов. 1976 г. Металл, кожа. Москва, колл. Л. Жадовой
Сотников, Алексей: Кассета поильников для детей. [Под руководством Татлина.] Фарфор, солома, сталь. Реконструкция 1979 г. Колл. А. Сотникова
Модель 'Памятника III Интернационалу'. 1919 г. Реконструкция по чертежам Государственного научно-исследовательского института им. А. Щусева. Исполнение: Париж, фирма 'Лонгепе'. Париж, Центр Жоржа Помпиду.
'Жизнь за царя'. 1913 г. Музыка М. Глинки. Спектакль не осуществлен
'Лес', илл. с. 381. Эскиз декорации. Клеевые краски, картон, 54,4 × 95,5 см. Москва, Третьяковская галерея
'Польский бал'. Эскиз декорации. Клеевые краски, карандаш, гуашь на картоне, 55,5 × 93,2 см. Москва, Третьяковская галерея

Spassky Gate (did not appear in the exhibition.) Stage design. Oil on cardboard, 54.5 × 98.2 cm, Tret'iakov Gallery, Moscow Master Tatlin's bandore, 1920s, length: 114 cm, width: 59 cm, depth: 9 cm
The Service-Book of the Three (in Russian), Moscow, published by Kuzmin and Dolinskii, 1913 (Museum of Literature, Moscow). In addition to the works of the three chief authors of the text and drawings, Khlebnikov, Maiakovskii and David Burliuk, the works of Nikolai and Vladimir Burliuk, and Tatlin, are also there in the volume.
Paris-Moscow, 1900–1930. Arts plastiques, arts appliqués et objets utilitaires, architecture-urbanisme, agitprop, affiche, théâtre-ballet, littérature, musique, cinéma, photo créative, Paris, 1979
(Location: Georges Pompidou National Arts and Culture Centre, Paris; date: 31 May to 5 Nov. 1979
Illustrations on pp. 107–9, 261 and 381)
The following works were shown only at the Moscow–Paris exhibition:
Tsarevich, 1922, by S.V. Chekhonin, decorative plate, based on a costume design, over-glaze painting, Leningrad Porcelain Factory
Design for a set of dishes, 1923, two sheets, pencil on paper, 19.1 × 22.3 cm; 23 × 21.7 cm, Bakhrushin Museum
Wing of *Letatlin*, variant, pencil on paper, 32.2 × 54.8, Bakhrushin Museum
Man's suit, 1923, reconstruction (1981)
Design of the Monument to the Third International, 1919, façade, photograph
Zangezi, Khlebnikov's heroic poem, directed by Tatlin
Repentance, costume design, charcoal on paper mounted on cardboard, 55.2 × 38, Bakhrushin Museum
Laughter, costume design, charcoal on paper mounted on cardboard, 56 × 38, Bakhrushin Museum
Moscow–Paris, 1900–1930. Fine Arts, Industrial Arts, Architecture and Urbanism, Agitprop, Poster, Theatre, Literature, Music, Film, Photography. Moscow, Sovetskii khudozhnik, 1981
(Location: Pushkin State Museum of Fine Arts, Moscow; date: 3 June to 4 October 1981)

Спасские ворота. Эскиз декорации. Масло, картон, 54,5 × 98,2 см. Москва, Третьяковская галерея
Бандура мастера Татлина. 20-е гг. Длина 11,4 см, ширина 59 см, глубина 9 см
Требник троих. Сборник на русском языке. Москва, изд. Кузмин и Долинский. 1913 г. (Литературный музей, Москва) К трем главным авторам текстов и рисунков этого сборника: Хлебникову, Маяковскому и Давиду Бурлюку присоединились Николай и Владимир Бурлюк и художник Владимир Татлин.

Тарелка 'Царевич'. 1922 г. Роспись по эскизу театрального костюма выполнена С.В. Чехониным. Фарфор, надглазурная роспись. Ленинград, Музей ЛФЗ
Эскизы сервиза. 1923 г. Два листа. Бумага, карандаш, 19,1 × 22,3 см; 23 × 21,7 см. Москва, ГЦТМ
Крыло 'Летатлина'. Вариант. Бумага, карандаш, 32,2 × 54,8 см. Москва, ГЦТМ
Мужской костюм. 1923 г. Реконструкция 1981 г.
Проект памятника III Интернационала. 1919 г. Фасад. Фото
'Зангези'. Героическая поэма В. Хлебникова. 1923 г. Режиссер В. Татлин [. . .]
Горе. Эскиз костюма. Бумага на картоне, уголь, 55,2 × 38 см. Москва, ГЦТМ
Смех. Эскиз костюма. Бумага на картоне, уголь, 56 × 38. Москва, ГЦТМ
Москва—Париж. 1900—1930. Изобразительное искусство; Прикладное и промышленное искусство; Архитектура и градостроительство; Агитационно-массовое искусство; Плакат; Театр; Литература; Музыка; Кино; Художественная фотография. 'Советский художник', Москва, 1981.

List of Tatlin's Works for the Theatre

1911 *Tsar Maximilian and his Disobedient Son, Adolf* [Действо о царе Максимилиане и его непокорном сыне Адольфе]. Popular comedy. Produced in Moscow by the Literary and Artistic Circle, and in (St) Petersburg by the Union of Youth. Directed by M.M. Bonch-Tomashevskii. The sketches are preserved in the Bakhrushin Central State Museum of Theatre History, Moscow, and in the Leningrad State Museum of Theatre History.

1913–14 M.I. Glinka, *Ivan Susanin (A Life for the Tsar)* [Иван Сусанин. (Жизнь за царя)].This opera was not staged. The sketches are preserved in the State Tret'iakov Gallery, Moscow, the Bakhrushin Museum and the Leningrad Museum of Theatre History.

1915–18 Richard Wagner, *The Flying Dutchman* [Летучий голландец].This opera was not staged. The sketches are preserved in the Bakhrushin Museum.

1917 V.V. Khlebnikov, *Death's Error; Thirteen in the Air* [Ошибка барышни Смерти; 13 в воздухе]. Directed by V.V. Khlebnikov. The location of the sketches is not known.

1923 V.V. Khlebnikov, *Zangezi* [Зангези]. Produced by an amateur company of the Experimental Theatre of the Museum of Artistic Culture on Isaakievskaia Square in Petrograd. Directed by V.E. Tatlin, who also played the principal role. The sketches are preserved in the Bakhrushin Museum.

1925 Jules Romains, *Cromedeyre-le-Vieil*. Produced by the Gor'kii Dramatic Theatre in Leningrad. The location of the sketches is not known.

1926 V.Z. Gzhitskii, *At Dawn (In the Footsteps of the Stars)* [По зоре. (За звездами)].Produced by the Kiev State Children's Theatre. Directed by I.S. Deeva. The location of the sketches is not known.

1926 Andersen, *Bum and Iula* [Бум и Юла]. Produced by the Kiev State Children's Theatre. Directed by V.P. Kozhich. The location of the sketches is not known.

1934–5 A.N. Ostrovskii, *A Comic Actor of the 17th Century* [Комик XVII столетия]. Produced by the Moscow Art Theatre II. Directed by A. Gurov and P.D. Ermilov. The sketches are preserved in the Bakhrushin Museum.

1935 S.A. Semenov, *Let us not Surrender* [Не сдадимся]. Produced by the Moscow Kamernyi Theatre. Directed by A.I. Tairov. The sketches are preserved in the Bakhrushin Museum.

1939(?) A.P. Globa, *Pushkin* [Пушкин]. Produced by the Sverdlovsk State Dramatic Theatre. The director is not known. The location of the sketches is not known.

1939–40 A.P. Shtein, *Kronshtadt (Spring of '21)* [Кроншатдт. (Весна 21-го)]. Produced by the Moscow Theatre of the Lensoviet. Directed by A.K. Plotnikov. The sketches are preserved in the Bakhrushin Museum.

1940 A.V. Sukhovo-Kobylin, *The Affair* [Дело]. Produced by the Central Theatre of the Red Army. Directed by A.D. Popov. Some of the sketches are preserved in the Bakhrushin Museum.

1940–43 A.A. Kron, *Deep Reconnaissance* [Глубокая разведка]. Produced by the Moscow Arts Academic Theatre. Directed by M.N. Kedrov. Some of the models and sketches are preserved in the Museum of the Moscow Arts Academic Theatre, and the rest of the sketches are in the Bakhrushin Museum.

1940s V.P. Kataev, *The Blue Kerchief* [Синий платочек]. No information is available on the performance or on the location of the sketches.

1940s V.S. Mikhalkov, *Missing without News (Natasha Moskvina)* [Пропавший без вести (Наташа Москвина)]. Produced by the Stanislavskii State Opera and Dramatic Studio. Some of the sketches are preserved in the Bakhrushin Museum.

1944 E.L. Shvarts, *A Far Country* [Далекий край]. Directors: A.Z. Okunchikov, S.Kh. Gushanskii. Central Children's Theatre. Some sketches in the Bakhrushin Museum.

1945 I.V. Shtok, *Fog over the Bay* [Туман над заливом]. No information is available on the performance. The sketches are preserved in the Bakhrushin Museum.

1946 A.M. Faiko, *Captain Kostrov* [Капитан Костров]. Produced by the Moscow Theatre of Drama (today known as the Maiakovskii Moscow Academic Theatre). Directed by E.I. Stradomskaia. Some of the sketches are preserved in the Bakhrushin Museum.

1946 S.I. Marshak, *Twelve Months* [Двенадцать месяцев]. Produced by the Central House of Young Talents. The name of the director and the location of the sketches are not known.

1947 V.A. Lavrenev, *For Those at Sea* [За тех, кто в море]. Produced by the Moscow Theatre of the Lenin Komsomol. Directed by I.N. Bersenev. Some of the sketches are preserved in the Bakhrushin Museum.

1947 A.A. Surov, *Secretary of the Regional Committee* [Секретарь райкома]. Produced by the Theatre of the Moscow Soviet. Directed by V.V. Vanin. The location of the sketches is not known.

1948(?) B.A. Lavrenev, *For Those at Sea* [За тех, кто в море]. Produced by the State Theatre of the Cinema Actor. Directed by N.S. Plotnikov. Some of the sketches are preserved in the Bakhrushin Museum.

1948 A.A. Surov, *Offence (Great Fortune)* [Обида (Большая судьба)]. Produced by the Theatre of the Moscow Soviet. Directed by V.V. Vanin. The sketches are preserved in the Bakhrushin Museum.

1948 A.N. Ostrovskii: *Enough Simplicity in Every Wise Man* [На всякого мудреца довольно простоты]. Produced by the Moscow Realistic Dramatic Theatre. The sketches are preserved in the Bakhrushin Museum.

1949 I.I. Iroshnikova, *Somewhere in Siberia* [Где-то в Сибири]. Produced by the Central Children's Theatre. Directed by G.A. Tovstonogov. Some of the sketches are preserved in the Bakhrushin Museum.

1949 P.G. Malerevskii, *The Wonderful Treasure* [Чудесный клад]. Produced by the Moscow State Youth Variety Theatre. Directed by M.I. Lishin. Costumes designed by A.N. Korsakova. Two of the sketches are preserved in the Bakhrushin Museum. The location of the remainder is not known.

1950 N.G. Vinnikov, *Cup of Joy* [Чаша радости]. Produced by the Theatre of the Moscow Soviet. Directed by B.V. Kolesaev. Costumes designed by A.N. Korsakova. The sketches are preserved in the Bakhrushin Museum.

1951 S.P. Antonov, *The Emissary of Peace (Ekaterina Nikanorova)* [Посланец мира (Екатерина Никанорова)]. Produced by the Moscow Literary and Dramatic Theatre of the All-Russian Theatre Company. Directed by K.V. Vakhterov. Costumes designed by A.N. Korsakova. The location of the sketches is not known.

1950s Berezin, *The Truth about his Father* [Правда о его отце]. Produced by the Moscow Literary and Dramatic Theatre of the All-Russian Theatre Company. Directed by V.M. Bebutov. Some of the sketches are preserved in the Bakhrushin Museum.

1952 I.L. Selvinskii, *The Battle of Grunwald (From Poltava to Hanko)* [Битва при Грюнвальде (От Полтавы до Гангута)]. Directed by V.S. Kantsel. This play was not staged. Some of the sketches are preserved in the Bakhrushin Museum.

Catalogue of Tatlin's Works Reproduced in this Book

An asterisk (*) preceding the title of a work denotes that in the original Hungarian edition of this book it was published for the first time. The number in bold-face following a work denotes the serial number of its reproduction in this book.

I Paintings and Sketches

* **1** *Apostle on the Cupola of the Church of St George, Staraia Ladoga* (12th cent.), copy, 1905–10
Watercolour and white paint on tracing paper glued to paper, 24 × 15.5 cm
(The fresco reproductions were made by a group of students in the Penza College of Art, among them Tatlin, under the direction of Afanas'ev.) TsGALI, Moscow **(11)**
2 *Carnation*, 1908
Oil on canvas, 73.5 × 66.6 cm
State Russian Museum, Leningrad **(13)**
* **3** *Twilight*, late 1900s
Oil on canvas, 50 × 57.5 cm
TsGALI, Moscow **(14)**
* **4** *Summer*, late 1900s
Oil on canvas, 53 × 66 cm
TsGALI, Moscow **(15)**
* **5** *Sitting Male Figure*, 1909
Watercolour and gouache on paper, 260 × 220 mm
TsGALI, Moscow **(18)**
* **6** *Man's Portrait*, 1909 (?)
Oil on canvas, 71.5 × 72.5 cm
TsGALI, Moscow **(16)**
7 *Vendor of Sailor Uniforms*, 1910
Watercolour, gouache, ink on cardboard, 32 × 20 cm
State Radishchev Museum, Saratov **(25)**
* **8** *Sailor Uniforms*, beginning of 1910s
Watercolour and gouache on paper, 65.5 × 53 cm
(Verso of next painting)
Bakhrushin Museum **(26)**
* **9** *Fishmonger's Trade*, beginning of 1910s
Watercolour and gouache on paper, 65.5 × 53 cm
(Verso of previous painting)
Bakhrushin Museum **(27)**
* **10** *Portrait of the Painter*, beginning of 1910s
Oil on canvas, 104 × 88 cm
Kostroma District Museum of Fine Arts **(35)**
11 *Fishmonger*, 1911
Gum paint on canvas, 76 × 98 cm
State Tret'iakov Gallery, Moscow **(31)**
12 *Bouquet*, 1911–12
Oil on canvas, 93 × 48 cm
State Tret'iakov Gallery, Moscow **(74)**
13 *Still-Life* (Flowers), 1912
Oil on canvas, 71.5 × 61.5 cm
State Russian Museum, Leningrad **(75)**
14 *Sailor*, 1911
Tempera on canvas, 71.5 × 71.5 cm
State Russian Museum, Leningrad **(34)**
15 *Fisher Lad*, c. 1912
India ink on paper, 38 × 28 cm
Collection G. Costakis **(30)**
* **16** *Sailor (Self-Portrait)*, 1912
Lithograph, 14 × 9.3 cm
Collection D.V. Sarab'ianov, Moscow **(19)**

17 *Fishmonger*, 1912
Lithograph, 14 × 9.3 cm
Collection D.V. Sarab'ianov, Moscow **(28)**
* **18** *Nude*, 1912–13
Whereabouts unknown
Photograph: Collection V.P. Smirnov, Moscow **(76)**
19 *Nude*, 1912–13
Oil on canvas, 106 × 142 cm
(Verso of item 26 below)
TsGALI, Moscow **(77)**
20 *Nude*, 1913
Oil on canvas, 104.5 × 130 cm
State Russian Museum, Leningrad **(78)**
21 *Nude*, 1913
Oil on canvas, 143 × 108 cm
State Tret'iakov Gallery, Moscow **(79)**
* **22** *Composition-Analysis*, sketch, 1913
Lead pencil, gouache and watercolour on paper, 490 × 330 cm
Collection A.A. Kapitsa, Moscow **(103)**
23 *Woman's Portrait*, 1933
Oil on wood, 55 × 46.7 cm
State Tret'iakov Gallery, Moscow **(415)**
24 *Female Bather*, 1930s
Oil on canvas, 75.5 × 50.5 cm
TsGALI, Moscow **(414)**
* **25** *Red Flowers*, 1930s
Oil on canvas, 80 × 53.5 cm
TsGALI, Moscow **(417)**
26 *Clay Mug with Flowers*, 1930s
Oil on canvas, 106 × 142 cm
(Verso of item 19 above)
TsGALI, Moscow **(416)**
* **27** *Bouquet*, 1940
Oil on wood, 26 × 19 cm
Collection M.V. Alpatov, Moscow **(418)**
28 *Meat*, 1947
Oil on canvas with cardboard backing, 63 × 71.5 cm
State Tret'iakov Gallery, Moscow **(419)**

II Drawings

* **1** *Male Nude*, study, 1910
Pencil on paper, with signature 'Vl. Tatlin. 1910 II 3'
Archive of the Penza Savitskii School of Art **(42)**
2 Drawings from the two Ostozhenka Studio Albums, 1911–14
Graphite, pencil, India ink, pen on cream-coloured paper, 430 × 260 mm
TsGALI, Moscow
* (a) p. 80 *Female Nude with Slightly Raised Arm* **(49)**
* (b) verso of p. 70 *Seated Female Nude in Profile* **(43)**
 (c) p. 62 *Oval Shaped Nude* **(50)**
 (d) p. 70 *Standing Nude, Front View* **(51)**

* (e) p. 82 *Nude with Arms Crossed* (**44**)
* (f) p. 38 *Standing Woman* (**45**)
  (g) verso of p. 25 *Female Nude, Rear View* (**48**)
* (h) p. 49 *Female Nude, Three-Quarter View* (**46**)
* (i) p. 40 *Woman, Rear View* (**47**)
* (j) p. 10 *Female Nude, Rear View, with Raised Arm* (**52**)
* (k) p. 20 *Female Nude, Turning About* (**57**)
  (l) p. 23 *Sketch of a Seated Figure* (**56**)
* (m) p. 91 *Female Nude* (**53**)
* (n) p. 73 *Seated Woman, Front View* (**54**)
* (o) p. 76 *Structure of the Front View of a Seated Figure* (**55**)
* (p) p. 95 *Three-Quarter View of the Structure of a Seated Figure* (**62**)
* (q) p. 79 *Seated Male Nude* (**58**)
* **3** *Female Nude with Elbow on Knee*, 1912–14
  Lead pencil on paper, 420 × 260 mm
  Collection D.V. Sarab'ianov, Moscow (**64**)
* **4** *Seated Female Nude*, 1913
  Lead pencil on paper, 420 × 260 mm
  (Notation on verso: 6 November 1913, Mlle Karelika)
  Collection D.V. Sarab'ianov, Moscow (**63**)
* **5** *Male Nude, Rear View*, 1913
  Lead pencil on paper, 420 × 260 mm
  Collection D.V. Sarab'ianov, Moscow (**65**)
* **6** *Seated Female Nude, Front View*, 1913
  Lead pencil on paper, 420 × 260 mm
  Collection D.V. Sarab'ianov, Moscow (**66**)
* **7** *Sketch of Standing Figure* , 1913
  Lead pencil on paper, 420 × 260 mm
  Collection D.V. Sarab'ianov, Moscow (**67**)
  8 *Fisherman*, early 1910s
  India ink on paper 240 × 130 mm
  Collection D.V. Sarab'ianov, Moscow (**29**)
* **9** *Woman in Fur Coat*, 1930s
  Pencil on paper, 440 × 320 mm
  Collection M.V. Alpatov, Moscow (**410**)
* **10** *Portrait of a Woman*, 1940s
  Pencil on paper, 410 × 300 mm
  Collection M.V. Alpatov, Moscow (**413**)
* **11** *Female Nude in front of Easel*, 1940s
  Pencil on paper, 411 × 300 mm
  TsGALI, Moscow (**411**)
* **12** *Woman Wearing a Hat*, 1940s
  Pencil on paper, 432 × 320 mm
  TsGALI, Moscow (**412**)
  13 *Self-Portrait*, 1940s
  Pencil on dark blue paper, 450 × 320 mm
  Bakhrushin Museum (**420**)

III Book Illustrations

1 Illustration for Khlebnikov's poem 'Let us be as Merciless as Ostranitsa' ('Будем грозны, как Остраница'), 1912
Lithograph
А. Крученых, В. Хлебников, *Мирсконца* (*Worldbackwards*), Москва, 1912 (**73**)
2 Illustration for Maiakovskii's poem 'Signboards' ('Вывескам'), 1913
Lithograph

В. Маяковский, *Требник троих* (*The Service-Book of the Three*), Москва,1913 (**71**)
3 *Portrait of Vladimir Burliuk*, 1913
Lithograph
Ibid. (**72**)
4 Illustration for Vladimir Burliuk's poem 'Twilight: the Painter with his Wide Brush…', 1913
Lithograph
Ibid. (**70**)
5 Cover of the booklet *Vladimir Evgrafovich Tatlin*, 1915
Zincotype
Владимир Евграфович Татлин, Изд. Новый журнал для всех, Петроград, 1915 (**124**)
6 Punin, *The Monument to the Third International*, brochure
Н. Пунин, *Памятник III Интернационала*, Москва, 1920
(a) Dust-jacket, 1920
   Zincotype (**182**)
(b) Illustration, 1920
   Zincotype (**183**)
7 Cover of Bazhan, Shkurupii, Semenko, Tatlin, *Meeting at the Crossroads*, 1927
Zincotype
Бажан, Шкурупій, Семенко, Татлін, *Зустріч на перехресті*, Київ, 1927(**293**)
8 Illustrations for S. Sergel', *On the Sailing-Ship*, 1929
(Under the pseudonym LOT)
С. Сергель, *На парусном судне*,1929 (**294–7**)
(a) Cover
   Zincotype (**294**)
(b) *The Sailing-Ship Chernomor* (p. 8)
   Zincotype (**295**)
* (c) *The Crew at Lunch*, sketch
   Pencil on paper, 264 × 203 and 198 × 163 mm
   Bakhrushin Museum (**296**)
* (d) *Storm*, sketch
   Pencil on paper, 269 × 230 mm and 138 × 164 mm
   Bakhrushin Museum (**297**)
  9 Illustrations for D. Kharms, *Firstly and Secondly*, 1929
  Д. Хармс, *Во-первых и во-вторых*, М.-Л., ГИЗ,1929
  (a) Cover, zincotype (**298**)
  (b) Title-page, zincotype (**299**)
* (c) *For the Third Time*, sketch
   Pencil on paper, 269 × 366 and 269 × 300 mm
   Bakhrushin Museum (**304**)
  (d) *For the Third Time* (p. 7), zincotype (**308**)
* (e) *For the Fourth Time*, sketch
   Pencil on paper, 360 × 297 and 360 × 240 mm
   Bakhrushin Museum (**305**)
  (f) *For the Fourth Time* (p. 9), zincotype (**309**)
  (g) *For the Fourth Time*, 2nd. ill. (p. 11) zincotype (**300**)
* (h) *For the Fifth Time*, sketch
   Pencil on paper, 386 × 251 and 311 × 251 mm
   Bakhrushin Museum (**303**)
  (i) *For the Fifth Time* (p. 13), zincotype (**307**)
  (j) *For the Sixth Time* (p. 15), zincotype (**302**)
  (k) *For the Seventh Time* (p. 17), zincotype (**301**)
* (l) *For the Eighth Time*, sketch
   Pencil on paper, 360 × 297 and 360 × 240 mm
   Bakhrushin Museum (**306**)
  (m) *For the Eighth Time* (p. 19), zincotype (**310**)
* (n) *For the Ninth Time*, sketch

Pencil on paper, 362 × 270 mm
on the right – 328 mm, on the left – 333 × 275 mm
Bakhrushin Museum **(311)**
10 The graphic design of V. Khlebnikov's *Unpublished Works*, 1940
В. Хлебников, *Неизданные произведения*, Москва,1940
(a) Cover **(233)**
(b) *Khlebnikov's Portrait*, zincotype **(232)**

IV Constructions and Experiments with Materials

1. *Bottle (painterly relief)*, 1913
Tin, cardboard, netting, wall paper
Whereabouts unknown
Photograph: Collection D.V. Sarab'ianov, Moscow **(111)**
2 *Painterly Relief*, 1913–14
Wood, oil, metal foil, 63 × 53 cm
(damaged)
State Tret'iakov Gallery (from the former Costakis Collection), Moscow **(108)**
3 *Painterly Relief*, 1913–14
Wood, iron
(Formerly owned by I.A. Puni)
Whereabouts unknown
Reproduction: *Владимир Евграфович Татлин*, Изд. Новый журнал для всех, Петроград, 1915 **(125)**
4 *Painterly Relief*, 1913–14
Wood, cardboard, metal
(Formerly owned by A.A. Exter)
Whereabouts unknown
Reproduction: Ibid. **(125)**
5 *Selection of Materials*, 1914
(a) Iron, plaster, glass, tar
Whereabouts unknown
Reproduction: Н.Н. Пунин, *Татлин (Против кубизма)*, Петроград, 1921 **(115)**
(b) The same, from a different perspective.
Reproduction: *Изобразительное искусство*, no. 1, 1919, p. 11 **(116)**
6 *Corner Counter-Relief*, 1914–15
(a) Metal, wood, wire
(restoration under way)
State Russian Museum, Leningrad
Reproduction: *Владимир Евграфович Татлин*, Изд. Новый журнал для всех, Петроград,1915 **(126)**
(b) The same, detail **(124)**
7 *Composition* (The Month of May), 1916
Wood, tempera, various techniques
Privately owned, Federal Republic of Germany **(105)**
8 *Board No. 1 Staro-Basman* (Old Basmannaia Street), 1917
Wood, egg tempera, primer, bronze, 105 × 57 cm
State Tret'iakov Gallery, Moscow **(104)**
9 *Selection of Materials*, 1917
Varnished mahogany, rosewood, pine, galvanized roofing tin, 100 × 64 cm
State Tret'iakov Gallery, Moscow **(110)**
10 *Selection of Materials*, 1917

(Unfinished; final version: IV/9)
Iron, rosewood, pine, 100 × 64 cm
Whereabouts unknown
Reproduction: Н.Н. Пунин, *Татлин (Против кубизма)*, Петроград, 1921 **(109)**
11 *Painterly Relief*, 1917
Whereabouts unknown
Reproduction: Vytvarné' umeni, no 7–8, 1967, p. 413 **(112)**
12 *Counter-Relief*, late 1910s
Whereabouts unknown
Reproduction: *Das Kunstblatt*, no. 11, 1922, p. 496 **(118)**
13 *Corner Counter-Relief* (Higher-type corner relief; selection of materials), 1915
(a) Iron, aluminium, primer
Reproduction: Н.Н. Пунин, *Татлин* (Против кубизма), Петроград, 1921 **(119)**
(b) The same, from a different viewpoint
Reproduction: *Владимир Евграфович Татлин*, Изд. Новый журнал для всех, Петроград, 1915 **(125)**
(c) The same. At the Last Futurist Exhibition, 0—10, 1915
Photograph: State Film, Photographic and Sound Archive, Leningrad **(121)**
14 *Counter-Relief*, late 1910s
Whereabouts unknown
Photograph: State Russian Museum, Leningrad, photo no. B-33355 **(114)**
15 *Counter-Relief*, late 1910s
Whereabouts unknown
Reproduction: Erste Russische Kunstausstellung, Berlin, 1922
Based on the catalogue **(117)**
16 *Counter-Relief*, late 1910s
Whereabouts unknown
Reproduction: Camilla Gray, *The Russian Experiment in Art*, Thames & Hudson **(113)**

V The Monument to the Third International

1. Sketch of the vertical view, 1919
Whereabouts unknown
Photograph: Bakhrushin Museum **(171)**
2 Sketch of the view of the inclined axis, 1919
Whereabouts unknown
Photograph: Bakhrushin Museum **(170)**
3 First model of the Monument to the Third International, 1920
Wood, cardboard, wire, metal, oil paper, *c.* 500 cm (The model was constructed by a collective composed of Shapiro, Meerzon and Vinogradov under Tatlin's direction)
(a) The construction of the model, 1920 (From left to right: Dymshits-Tolstaia, Tatlin, Shapiro, Meerzon)
Photograph: Bakhrushin Museum **(173)**
(b) The same, from a different viewpoint
Photograph: Bakhrushin Museum **(172)**
(c) The model in the Studio of Materials, Volume and Construction, in the Mosaics Studio of the former Academy of Arts, Petrograd, November 1920
(Tatlin, second from left)

Photograph: Bakhrushin Museum **(174)**
(d) The same, from a different viewpoint
Reproduction: Н.Н. Пунин, *Памятник III Интернационала* (проект художника В.Е. Татлина), Петроград, 1920 **(175)**
(e) The Tatlin Studio Collective in front of the model. Same location (Tatlin third, Shapiro fourth from left).
Photograph: Bakhrushin Museum **(178)**
(f) The same, from above
Reproduction: Н.Н. Пунин, *Памятник III Интернационала* (проект художника В.Е. Татлина), Петроград, 1920 **(177)**
(g) The model at the Exhibition in Honour of the Eighth Congress of Soviets, in the foreground of the colonnade of the House of Unions, Moscow, late 1920, early 1921
Photograph: Troels Andersen **(181)**

4 Second model of the Monument to the Third International, 1925
(a) The model at the Paris International Exhibition of Decorative and Industrial Arts in the Octagonal Hall of the Grand Palais, 1925
Photograph by Aleksandr Rodchenko
Photograph: Collection V.A. Rodchenko, Moscow **(186)**
(b) Detail of the exhibition
Photograph by Aleksandr Rodchenko
Photograph: Collection V.A. Rodchenko, Moscow **(187)**

5 Simplified version of the model constructed on the back of a truck, at the Leningrad May Day parade, 1926
Reproduction: *Vladimir Tatlin* (Catalogue), Moderna Museet, Stockholm, 1968 **(164)**

VI Letatlin

The model of the flapping-wing flying machine based on the flight of birds, which Tatlin worked out with the advice of the surgeon, Geintse, and the flight instructor, Losev. Originally, Tatlin prepared three versions of the model with the co-operation of his colleagues Sotnikov and Pavil'onov, and with the help of Zelenskii and Shchipitsyn. 1929–32

1 Sketch of the wing
Pencil on paper, 322 × 548 mm
Bakhrushin Museum **(321)**
2 Sketch of the wing
Whereabouts unknown
Reproduction: *Бригада художников,* no. 6, 1932 **(320)**
3 Description of body position during flight
Pencil on paper, 210 × 265 mm
Bakhrushin Museum **(326)**
4 Description of body position during flight
Whereabouts unknown
Reproduction: *Бригада художников* no. 6, 1932 **(327)**
5 The original models and their parts, 1929–32
(a) Tatlin with the main beam of the wing in the gallery of the bell tower of the Novodevichii Convent, 1932
Photograph: TsGALI, Moscow **(319)**
(b) Tatlin with the wing of *Letatlin* in the studio in the bell tower of the Novodevichii Convent.
Photograph: TsGALI, Moscow **(318)**
(c) Fuselage of *Letatlin,* 1932
Photograph: TsGALI, Moscow **(331)**
(d) *Letatlin* without skin in the studio in the bell tower of the Novodevichii Convent, 1929–32
Photograph: Collection A.G. Sotnikov, Moscow **(330)**
(e) *Letatlin* without skin and with skin. Same location, 1929–32
Reproduction: 'Honoured Art Worker of the RSFSR V.E. Tatlin, Exhibition' (Catalogue), Moscow–Leningrad, 1932 **(338)**
* (f) Model of *Letatlin* with wing-stiffening struts, same location
Photograph: Collection A.G. Sotnikov, Moscow **(328)**
(g) Tatlin demonstrating the operation of *Letatlin*
Photograph: TsGALI, Moscow **(325)**
(h) Pavil'onov and *Letatlin*
Photograph: Sotnikov Collection, Moscow **(329)**
(i) *Letatlin* without skin in the Italian Hall of Museum of Fine Arts, Moscow, 1932 (Detail of the exhibition)
Photograph: Е. Кронман, 'Уход в техкнику Татлина и Летатлин', Бригада художников, no. 6, 1932 **(332)**
(j) *Letatlin* without skin, same location, 1932 (Detail of the exhibition)
Photograph: ibid. **(333)**
(k) Model of *Letatlin* with skin and wing supports Same location, 1932
(Detail of the exhibition)
Reproduction: Е. Кронман, 'Уход в технику Татлина и Летатлин', Бригада художников, no. 6, 1932 **(335)**
(l) *Letatlin* without skin in the banquet hall of the Club of the Union of Soviet Writers, 1932
Photograph: Collection A.G. Sotnikov, Moscow **(334)**
(m) *Letatlin* at the review of Moscow and Moscow district sailplanes. At the sailplane field by the Pervomaiskaia Station near Moscow, 1933
Photograph by Aleksandr Rodchenko, Collection V.A. Rodchenko, Moscow **(343)**
(n) Tatlin demonstrating the flying machine to pilots and sailplaners, 1933, same location
Photograph by Aleksandr Rodchenko, Collection V.A. Rodchenko, Moscow **(341)**
(o) The same, from a different viewpoint
Photograph by Aleksandr Rodchenko, Collection V.A. Rodchenko, Moscow **(342)**
(p) The main wing strut of *Letatlin* in the studio of the sculptor, A.E. Zelenskii, 1950s. State Tret'iakov Gallery, Moscow
Photograph: Collection V.I. Kostin **(344)**

6 Reconstructed model of *Letatlin*
Of the three original models of *Letatlin* only one has been preserved. It was reconstructed during the 1960s from the surviving original parts by Gen. L. Reino and test pilots A. Sheukov, K. Artseulov and M. Shishkin.
Wood, cork, Duralumin, silk cord, steel wire mesh, whalebone, hide rope. Wingspan: 8 m, length: 5 m

Aeronautical and Astronautical Museum, Monino
(a) The model reconstructed from the surviving original parts as an exhibit at the Aeronautical and Astronautical Museum (347)
(b) The parts of *Letatlin* at the Tatlin exhibition held at the Moscow Headquarters of the Union of Writers, 1977 (349)
(c) The same, from a different viewpoint (346)
(d) The same, from below (348)
(e) Detail of wing. Same location (345)
(f) *Letatlin* at the Paris–Moscow Exhibition, 1979 Centre Georges Pompidou, Paris (350)
(g) *Letatlin* at the Moscow–Paris Exhibition, 1981 State Pushkin Museum, Moscow (351)
(h) The same, from a different viewpoint(352)
(i) The same, from a different viewpoint (353)

VII Industrial Arts

* **1** Bench, late 1910s
(Executed by Tatlin himself)
N.A. Bruni, Moscow (253)
2 Novel heater, one of five designs of the economical stove, 1923
Reproduction: 'New Life-Styles in Photomontage' ('Новый быт', *Красная панорама*, 4 Dec. 1924, p. 17)
(In the same picture Tatlin also models a new type of suit and short overcoat.)(245)
3 Design for model chair, 1927
Curved maple, textile
(Made by Rogozhin, a student at the Faculty of Woodworking of VKhUTEIN, under Tatlin's guidance)
Photograph by Aleksandr Rodchenko, Collection V.A. Rodchenko, Moscow (255)
4 Sledge frame, late 1920s
Bent maple
(Made at the Woodworking Faculty of the VKhUTEIN under Tatlin's direction)
Whereabouts unknown
Reproduction: 'Художник – организатор быта', *Рабис*, 25 November 1929, p. 4 (254)
5 Design for man's coat, 1923
Pencil on paper, 620 × 395 mm
Bakhrushin Museum (250)
* **6** Design for man's coat ('Utility clothing'), 1923
Charcoal on tracing paper 1,077 × 715 mm
Bakhrushin Museum (247)
7 Design for woman's clothing, 1923
Pencil on paper, 568 × 770 mm
Bakhrushin Museum (251)
8 Novel street clothing, pattern, 1923–4
(a) Model from the front
(b) Model from the rear
Whereabouts of sketches unknown
Photograph: Bakhrushin Museum (248–9)
9 *New Way of Life*, montage illustrating the work of the Section for Material Culture in the design of a new type of clothing, 1923–4

Paper, photographs, newspaper clippings
TsGALI, Moscow (246)
10 *Tsarevich*, 1922
Painted plate
(a) Painted on glaze
Painted by Chekhonin from Tatlin's sketch
Museum of the Leningrad Porcelain Works (263)
(b) Signature and stamp on the bottom of the plate (264)
11 Design for milk-jug, 1923
Pencil on paper, 210 × 266 mm
With stamp of Tatlin's studio
Bakhrushin Museum (269)
12 Milk-jug viewed from above, 1923
Pencil on paper, 190 × 223 mm
With stamp of Tatlin's studio,
Bakhrushin Museum (271)
13 Design for teapot, 1923
Pencil on paper, 191 × 223 mm
With stamp of Tatlin's studio
Bakhrushin Museum (266)
* **14** Design for teacup, 1923
Pencil on paper, 184 × 183 mm
With stamp of Tatlin's studio
Bakhrushin Museum (267)
* **15** Design for dish, 1923
Pencil on paper, 230 × 204 mm
With stamp of Tatlin's studio
Bakhrushin Museum (270)
16 Design for sugar-bowl, 1923
Pencil on paper, 230 × 217 mm
With stamp of Tatlin's studio
Bakhrushin Museum (268)
17 Design for multi-purpose metal dish: pot + teapot + frying pan, 1923
Pencil on paper, 568 × 770 mm
(Reverse of item no. 7)
Bakhrushin Museum (265)

VIII Theatre

Tsar Maximilian and his Disobedient Son, Adolf
Stage and costume designs, 1911
1 *Panel Sketch*
Watercolour and pencil on paper, 500 × 680 mm
Leningrad Museum of Theatre History(38)
2 *Rowdy Son of Venus*, costume design
Watercolour on paper, 240 × 170 mm
Bakhrushin Museum(41)
3 *Pagan Venus*, costume design
Watercolour on paper, 240 × 133 mm
Bakhrushin Museum(40)
4 *Tsar Maximilian*, costume design
Watercolour on blue paper, 229 × 170 mm
Bakhrushin Museum (39)

Glinka, Ivan Susanin (A Life for the Tsar) (Opera)
Scene and costume designs, 1913–14
* **5** *Domnino Village* (Act I), stage design
Watercolour, gouache, shellac, India ink on cardboard, 475 × 962 mm
Bakhrushin Museum (137)

6 *King Sigismund's Throne Room* (Act II), stage design
Watercolour, glue-water, pencil, India ink and shellac on
cardboard, 544 × 955 mm
State Tret'iakov Gallery, Moscow**(138)**

7 *The Forest* (Act IV), stage design
Glue-water on cardboard, 544 × 955 mm
State Tret'iakov Gallery, Moscow**(139)**

8 *At the Spassky Gate* (Epilogue), stage design
Oil on canvas, 54,5 × 98,2 cm
State Tret'iakov Gallery, Moscow**(140)**

* **9** *Vania* (Act I, Domnino Village), costume design
Watercolour, pencil, gouache on cardboard,
462 × 322 mm
Bakhrushin Museum**(146)**

* **10** *Russian Woman's National Costume* (Act I, Domnino
Village), costume design
Watercolour, pencil, gouache, India ink, brush on card-
board, 462 × 314 mm
Bakhrushin Museum**(150)**

* **11** *Russian Woman's National Costume* (At the Spassky
Gate), costume design
Pencil, watercolour, gouache, India ink, brush on paper,
461 × 322 mm
Bakhrushin Museum**(147)**

* **12** *Russian Woman's National Costume* (At the Spassky
Gate), costume design
Pencil, watercolour, gouache on paper, 472 × 318 mm
Bakhrushin Museum **(148)**

* **13** *Russian Woman's National Costume* (At the Spassky
Gate), costume design
Pencil, watercolour, gouache, brush on cardboard,
495 × 324 mm
Bakhrushin Museum **(142)**

* **14** *Russian Woman's National Costume* (At the Spassky
Gate), costume design
Pencil, watercolour, gouache, India ink, brush on paper
glued to cardboard, 462 × 324 mm
Bakhrushin Museum **(151)**

15 *Russian Woman's National Costume* (At the Spassky
Gate), costume design
Watercolour, gouache, pencil, India ink, brush on paper
glued to cardboard, 443 × 311 mm
Bakhrushin Museum**(143)**

* **16** *Antonida* (At the Spassky Gate), costume design
Pencil, watercolour, India ink, gouache, brush on paper
glued to cardboard, 469 × 320 mm
Bakhrushin Museum **(145)**

* **17** *Boyar Girl* (At the Spassky Gate), costume design
Pencil, watercolour, gouache, India ink, brush on paper,
498 × 324 mm
Bakhrushin Museum **(144)**

* **18** *Boyar* (At the Spassky Gate), costume design
Pencil, watercolour, gouache, India ink, brush, shellac
on paper, 489 × 322 mm
Bakhrushin Museum **(149)**

* **19** *Embellishment to the Scenery* (At the Spassky Gate)
Pencil on tracing paper, 201 × 266 mm
Bakhrushin Museum
(On the verso of the sketch there is a note, or perhaps the
first lines of his letter to Sarra Dmitrievna Lebedeva. See
'Letter to Anna Darmalatova' p. 184)**(155)**

* **20** *Burkevich's Runner*, costume design

Pencil, watercolour, gouache, India ink, brush on paper,
460 × 321 mm
Bakhrushin Museum **(153)**

* **21** *Imperial Guardsman*, costume design
Pencil, watercolour, gouache on paper, 479 × 318 mm
Bakhrushin Museum **(152)**

22 *Strel'tsy* (Scene), costume design
Watercolour, brush on paper mounted on cardboard.
485 × 646 mm
Bakhrushin Museum **(141)**

23 *Antonida and Vania*, costume design
Pencil on tracing paper, 195 × 183 mm
Bakhrushin Museum **(154)**

**Richard Wagner, The Flying Dutchman (Opera)
Stage and costume designs, 1915–18**

* **24** *Ship's Deck*, stage design
Oil on canvas, 87 × 156 cm
Bakhrushin Museum**(157)**

* **25** *Ship's Deck,* stage design
Charcoal on paper, 900 × 720 mm
Bakhrushin Museum **(156)**

* **26** *Mast,* stage design
Charcoal on paper, 735 × 510 mm
Bakhrushin Museum **(163)**

* **27** *Helmsman*, costume design
Pencil, gouache, India ink on paper, 636 × 479 mm
Bakhrushin Museum **(161)**

* **28** *Helmsman* (variant), costume design
Pencil on tracing paper on paper, 636 × 371 mm
Bakhrushin Museum **(158)**

29 *Sailor*, costume design
Charcoal on paper, 770 × 514 mm
Bakhrushin Museum **(160)**

* **30** *Nun*, costume design
Pencil on paper, 705 × 504 mm
Bakhrushin Museum **(159)**

* **31** *Woman's Costume*, costume design
Pencil, watercolour, India ink, gouache on paper,
170 × 514 mm
Bakhrushin Museum **(162)**

**Velemir Khlebnikov, Zangezi
Stage and costume designs, 1923**

* **32** *Stage Design*
Charcoal on paper, 550 × 760 mm
With stamp of Tatlin's studio
State Russian Museum, Leningrad **(218)**

* **33** *Stage Design*
Charcoal on paper, 550 × 760 mm
With stamp of Tatlin's studio
State Russian Museum, Leningrad **(217)**

* **34** *Stage Design*
Pencil, India ink on paper. 249 × 310 mm
Bakhrushin Museum**(219)**

35 *Stage Design* (Person with bird-cage)
Pencil on paper, 345 × 508 mm
Bakhrushin Museum **(220)**

36 Model of stage setting
Whereabouts unknown
Reproduction: Русское искусство, no. 1, 1923 **(216)**

37 *Laughter,* costume design
Charcoal on paper mounted on cardboard,
546 × 376 mm
Bakhrushin Museum (**222**)
38 *Repentance,* costume design
Coal on paper mounted on cardboard, 546 × 376 mm
Bakhrushin Museum (**221**)

Ostrovskii, A Comic Actor of the 17th Century
Stage and costume designs, 1934–5
39 Model of stage setting
Whereabouts unknown
Photograph: Bakhrushin Museum (**354**)
40 Model of stage setting
Whereabouts unknown
Photograph: Bakhrushin Museum (**355**)
41 *Vania,* (Prologue), costume design
Pencil, watercolour on paper, 450 × 320 mm
Bakhrushin Museum (**360**)
* 42 *Tat'iana,* costume design
Watercolour, gouache on paper, 439 × 291 mm
Bakhrushin Museum (**361**)
* 43 *The Drunken Kliushin,* costume design
Pencil, watercolour on paper, 420 × 285 mm
Bakhrushin Museum (**366**)
44 *Boyars. Lopukhin and Matveev,* costume design
Pencil drawing copied on tracing paper, 415 × 280 mm
Bakhrushin Museum (**364**)
45 *Fodiev,* costume design
Pencil, watercolour on paper, 340 × 240 mm
Bakhrushin Museum (**367**)
46 *The Babylonian Thief* (entr'acte), costume design
Pencil, watercolour, gouache on paper, 410 × 282 mm
Bakhrushin Museum (**365**)
47 *God in Paradise,* costume design
Pencil, watercolour on paper, 418 × 280 mm
Bakhrushin Museum (**362**)
* 48 *Eve,* costume design
Pencil, watercolour, gouache on paper, 440 × 300 mm
Bakhrushin Museum (**368**)
49 *Adam,* costume design
Pencil, watercolour on paper, 440 × 300 mm
Bakhrushin Museum (**363**)

Sukhovo-Kobylin, The Affair
Stage and costume designs, 1939–40
50 *Stage Design* (Act II)
Pencil on paper, 175 × 315 mm
Bakhrushin Museum (**369**)
* 51 *Office,* stage design
Pencil on paper, 174 × 300 mm
Bakhrushin Museum (**370**)
52 *The Prince in Dress Uniform,* costume design
Pencil, watercolour, white lead paint, India ink on paper
mounted on plywood, 440 × 315 mm
Bakhrushin Museum (**374**)
53 *The Prince in a Cloak,* costume design
Pencil, watercolour on paper mounted on plywood,
440 × 315 mm
Bakhrushin Museum (**375**)

54 *Varravin,* costume design
Pencil, watercolour on paper mounted on plywood,
430 × 332 mm
Bakhrushin Museum (**371**)
55 *Ibisov,* costume design
Pencil on paper, 428 × 310 mm
Bakhrushin Museum (**380**)
56 *Ibisov,* costume design
Pencil, watercolour on paper mounted on plywood,
435 × 366 mm
Bakhrushin Museum (**381**)
57 *Tarelkin,* costume design
Pencil, watercolour on paper mounted on plywood,
440 × 282 mm
Bakhrushin Museum (**373**)
58 *Schmerz,* costume design
Pencil, watercolour on paper mounted on plywood
440 × 320 mm
Bakhrushin Museum (**382**)
59 *Zhivets,* costume design
Pencil, watercolour on paper mounted on plywood,
440 × 320 mm
Bakhrushin Museum (**372**)
60 *Razuvaev,* costume design
Pencil, watercolour on paper mounted on plywood,
440 × 320 mm
Bakhrushin Museum (**383**)
61 *Atueva,* costume design
Pencil, watercolour on paper mounted on plywood,
440 × 320 mm
Bakhrushin Museum (**376**)
62 *Lidochka,* costume design
Pencil on paper, 437 × 314 mm
Bakhrushin Museum (**377**)
63 *Lidochka* (variant), costume design
Pencil on paper, 438 × 310 mm
Bakhrushin Museum (**378**)
64 *Lidochka,* costume design
Paper mounted on plywood, 440 × 322 mm
Bakhrushin Museum (**379**)

A. Shtein, Kronshtadt (Spring of '21)
Stage and costume designs, 1939–40
65 *Curtain,* stage design
Pencil, watercolour on paper, 200 × 322 mm
Bakhrushin Museum (**385**)
* 66 *Stage Designs* (Acts I and III)
Pencil on paper, 217 × 316 mm
Bakhrushin Museum (**386–7**)
* 67 *Lower Deck,* stage design
Pencil on paper mounted on cardboard, 235 × 318 mm
Bakhrushin Museum (**388**)
68 *Prison Cell* (Act II), stage design
Pencil on paper mounted on cardboard, 207 × 314 mm
Bakhrushin Museum (**389**)
* 69 *Ramkov,* costume design
Pencil on paper, 470 × 305 mm
Bakhrushin Museum (**390**)
70 *Kudrin (Self-Portrait),* costume design
Pencil on paper, 465 × 306 mm
Bakhrushin Museum (**391**)

A. Kron, Deep Reconnaissance
Stage and costume designs, 1940–3
* **71** *Square in front of the Barracks* (Act II), stage design
Pencil on paper, 307 × 439 mm
Bakhrushin Museum **(392)**
* **72** *Fatyma*, costume design
Pencil, watercolour on paper, 317 × 240 mm
Bakhrushin Museum **(394)**
* **73** *Man's Costume*, costume design
Pencil, watercolour on paper, 310 × 220 mm
Bakhrushin Museum **(396)**
74 *Man's Costume*, costume design
Pencil, watercolour on paper, 310 × 220 mm
Bakhrushin Museum **(395)**
75 *The Moon on Stage*, technical drawing
Whereabouts unknown
Reproduction: Луна на сцене, Москва, 1944 **(401)**

E.L. Shvarts, A Far Country
* **76** *Stage Design*, 1944
Pencil on paper, 215 × 288 mm
Bakhrushin Museum **(397)**

I. Shtok, Fog over the Bay
* **77** *The Bombed House*, stage design, 1945
Pencil on paper, 214 × 323 mm
Bakhrushin Museum **(398)**

A. Faiko, Captain Kostrov
* **78** *Stage Design*, 1946
Pencil on paper, 208 × 300 mm
Bakhrushin Museum **(399)**

An unknown play
79 *Forest*, stage design, beginning of 1950s
Canvas mounted on wood, 373 × 568 mm
Bakhrushin Museum **(400)**

IX Decoration

1 Interior of the Café Pittoresque, Moscow, 1917–18
(The interior decoration is the work of a group of artists
led by Iakulov: Rodchenko, Udal'tsova, Pestel', Bromir-
skii and Tatlin.)**(132–3)**
2 Maiakovskii's catafalque and funeral procession, 1930
(Constructed of iron plates on the back of a truck by
Tatlin and his students at VKhUTEIN.) Photographs of
the funeral, 19 April 1930
TsGALI, Moscow **(290–2)**
* **3** Window-display design for the bookshop of the State
Publishing House (GIZ), 1930s
Charcoal, collage on paper, 708 × 935 mm
Bakhrushin Museum **(289)**

X Reconstructions of Tatlin's Works

(approved by this book's authors)
1 *Corner Counter-Relief*
Wood, metal, wire, 66.6 × 83.2 × 78.7
Reconstruction by Martyn Chalk, 1966–70 **(120)**

2 Model of the Monument to the Third International
Wood, metal, 4–5 m
Reconstruction by Arne Holm, Eslie Nandurs, Henrik
Ösdberg, 1968
(a) Moderna Museet, Stockholm **(202)**
(b) The same. Venice Biennale, 1970 **(203)**
3 The same
Reconstruction by Christopher Cross, Jeremy Dickson,
Swan Rindell, Peter Watson and Christopher Wood-
ward, 1971
(Soviet materials were used for this reconstruction sent
by A.A. Strigalev with the permission of the Cultural
Ministry of the USSR.)
Hayward Gallery, London**(204)**
4 The same
Reconstruction by T.M. Shapiro, 1976
Legacy L.A. Zhadova, Moscow**(205)**
5 The same
Reconstruction based on the sketches in the Shchusev
Museum, 1979
Centre Georges Pompidou, Paris **(206)**
6 Model of the Tatlin-Rogozhin chair
Metal, leather, 80 × 65 cm
Reconstruction by the graduating artist V.G. Solopov
and the locksmith V.I. Pavlov, 1976
Legacy L.A. Zhadova, Moscow **(256–8)**

XI Works by Tatlin's Students Prepared under his Direction

SVOMAS, Petrograd
Studio of Materials, Volume and Construction
1 Work by students: *Painterly Relief*, 1921
Whereabouts unknown
Reproduction: Н.Н. Пунин, *Татлин (Против кубизма)*,
Петроград, 1921. 16th ill. **(128)**

Kiev College of Art
**Department of Dramatic, Cinematic and Photo-
graphic Arts**
2 Work by students: *Composition* on the theme 'The
Selection of Materials', 1926–7
Whereabouts unknown
Reproduction: *Новая генерация*, no. 7, 1928 **(129)**
3 Work by students: *Composition* on the theme 'The
Selection of Materials', 1927
Whereabouts unknown
Reproduction: ibid. **(130)**

VKhUTEIN, Moscow
Faculty of Metalworking
4 A.I. Damskii, *Composition* on the theme 'The Selection
of Materials', end of 1920s
Whereabouts unknown
Photograph: Property of the artist **(131)**

VKhUTEIN, Moscow
Department of Ceramics
5 A.G. Sotnikov, Child's nursing vessel (First version),
1930

(a) Glazed tile, ⌀ 7.5 cm, volume: 27 cm³
Legacy L.A. Zhadova, Moscow (278–9)
(b) Child's nursing vessel with casting mould
Legacy L.A. Zhadova, Moscow (284)
6 A.G. Sotnikov, Child's nursing vessel (Final version), 1930
Glazed tile, ⌀ 8 cm, volume: 24 cm³
Collection E.M. Ginstling, Moscow (280–1)
7 A.G. Sotnikov, Teapot, 1930
Glazed porcelain
Whereabouts unknown
(The teapot is in Tatlin's hand in the photograph.)
Photograph: TsGALI, Moscow (275)
8 E.M. Ginstling, Twin vases ('Flight'), Work for the diploma, 1931
Glazed porcelain
Property of the artist (285)

Reconstructions

We include in this list only those pieces that have been approved by the authors of the studies in the first section of this book.
9 A.G. Sotnikov, Wicker tray with compartments for ten children's nursing vessels, 1930
(a) Sketch for the reconstruction
Pencil on paper
Legacy L.A. Zhadova, Moscow (282)
(b) The artist's own reconstruction, 1978–9
Porcelain, metal, straw
Kuskovo Museum of Ceramic Art (283)
10 P.M. Kozhin, Teapot, ('Egg'), 1930
Glazed porcelain
Reconstruction, early 1970s
Kuskovo Museum of Ceramic Art (288)
11 V.V. Borkin, Pepper shaker, 1930
Porcelain
Reconstruction, 1976
Kuskovo Museum of Ceramic Art (287)
12 A.G. Sotnikov, Teapot, 1930
Porcelain
The artist's own reconstruction, early 1970s
Kuskovo Museum of Ceramic Art (276–7)
13 V.V. Borkin, Shaving kit, 1930
Porcelain
Reconstruction, 1976
Kuskovo Museum of Ceramic Art (286)

XII Photographs of Written Documents Relating to Tatlin's Work

* **1** Documents from the dossier of the Penza Provincial Police, containing the entries regarding the surveillance of students of the Penza College of Art – Kriukov, Subbotin, Tatlin and others – during the years 1909–11.
(Tatlin's cover name in the dossier is 'Pochard'.)
TsGAOR, Leningrad (7–10)
* **2** Graduation certificate from the Penza College of Art.
Dated 30 June 1910, Moscow
TsGALI, Moscow (6)

3 Ticket to the opening of the Donkey's Tail exhibition, 11 March 1912, Moscow
TsGALI, Moscow (84)
4 Poster for the Jack of Diamonds exhibition, 3–28 April 1913, Moscow
TsGALI, Moscow (85)
* **5** Manuscript of the booklet *Vladimir Evgrafovich Tatlin*, which was prepared by N.A. Udal'tsova based on Tatlin's own words in his notebook of artistic correspondence and notes, October 1915
Collection I.A. Drevina, Moscow (122–3)
6 The booklet *Vladimir Evgrafovich Tatlin* (Владимир Евграфович Татлин), 1915 (124–6)
7 *Novyi zhurnal dlia vsekh* (Новый журнал для всех),12 Dec. 1915, cover
(It was in this issue that Isakov's article, the first published mention of Tatlin's Counter-Reliefs, appeared.)(127)
8 Khlebnikov, 'Architecture of the Future' (Sketches), 1915–16
India ink, pen on paper, 80 × 120 mm
Institute of Russian Literature, Leningrad, (Pushkinskii dom) (224)
* **9** Khlebnikov: 'Architecture of the Future' Sketches in the manuscript of the utopia in prose, 'Houses and Us' – Мы и дома,1915–16
India ink, pen on paper
Collection A.I. Parnis, Moscow (225)
* **10** Khlebnikov, *Portrait of Tatlin*, 1915–16
Pencil on paper, 225 × 360 mm
Collection M.V. Miturich, Moscow (223)
11 Catalogue of The Store exhibition
Moscow, March 1916 (86–8)
* **12** Typewritten copy of Khlebnikov's poem 'Tatlin', 1916
(Prepared at Tatlin's request by V.P. Smirnov from Khlebnikov's manuscript, which was lost during the printing of the 'Неизданные произведения'.)
Collection V.P. Smirnov, Moscow (231)
* **13** Poster of the 'Cast-Iron Wings' (Чугунные крылья) Futurist lecture
House of Science and Art, Tsaritsyn, 25 May 1916
Collection A.I. Parnis, Moscow (89)
* **14** Contract for the staging of Khlebnikov's *Selection of Objects* (Комплект вещей), signed by Tatlin, Khlebnikov and A.S. Lur'e, 2 November 1917
India ink on paper. 535 × 390 mm
Bakhrushin Museum (207)
15 Title-page of *Vremennik* (Временник), issue no. 2, Moscow, 1917
(V. Kamenskii, F. Petnikov, V. Khlebnikov) The 'Tatlin's studio' stamp relates to the fact that there was a small library at the Section for Material Culture of GINKhUK, where Khlebnikov's works were also collected (238)
* **16** Tatlin's certificate of membership of the Museums Committee of the People's Commissariat of Education, bearing the signature of Lunacharskii, the People's Commissar of Education.
Issued May 30, 1918
TsGALI, Moscow (168)
* **17** Detail from the manuscript of Khlebnikov's article 'Artists of the World' ('Художники мира'),with drawings by the author, 1919
Collection A.I. Parnis, Moscow (227)

18 Poster for the exhibition of the model of the Monument to the Third International, held in the Mosaics Studio of the former Petrograd Academy of Art, 1920
TsGALI, Moscow **(179)**

19 Cover of N.N. Punin's monograph *Tatlin*, Petrograd, 1921. (This copy was given by Tatlin to Aleksandr Vesnin, a leading figure of Russian architectural Constructivism, and bears Tatlin's inscription: 'For the dear Vesnin Family, in token of our lasting friendship.' 30 Mar. 1921) **(184)**

20 Poster for Tatlin's lecture 'Material Culture', 27 May 1923, Museum of Artistic Culture
India ink on paper
Bakhrushin Museum **(243)**

* **21** Poster with Tatlin's slogan 'Not the old, not the new, but the necessary'.
India ink on paper
(Used at the Exhibition of Petrograd Artists of All Tendencies, May–June 1923.)
Bakhrushin Museum **(234)**

* **22** Page from the manuscript of Punin, 'Routine and Tatlin', 1924
Private collection of N.N. Punin's family, Leningrad **(239)**

23 Poster for the stage production of Khlebnikov, *Zangezi* (White Hall of Miatlev House – Petrograd Museum of Artistic Culture)
The performances took place on 10 and 11 May 1923, and, judging from the announcement, presumably on 30 May 1923.
India ink on paper
Bakhrushin Museum **(211)**

24 Exhibition by Honoured Art Worker of the RSFSR Tatlin, catalogue, Moscow–Leningrad, 1932 **(336–8)**

25 N. Rakhtanov's interview '*Letatlin*. An Aerial Bicycle'.
Пионер, no. 9, 1932 **(339)**

* **26** Tatlin's inscription in the three-volume set of Khlebnikov's *Collected Works* presented to Smirnov on 6 July 1933. (See p. 338 for translation.)
Collection V.P. Smirnov, Moscow **(228–30)**

* **27** 'The Inventor – Pioneer of Modern Technology in Defence of the Homeland', poster, 1934
TsGALI, Moscow **(340)**

28 Poster for the performance of A. Shtein, *Kronshtadt (Spring of '21)* at the Moscow Theatre of the Lensoviet, 1940
Bakhrushin Museum **(384)**

Selected Bibliography

The writings published in this book are not listed here; see the beginning of the commentaries on them for their bibliographic details.

General Works

Большая Советская Энциклопедия [Great Soviet Encyclopaedia], 3rd ed., vol. XXV, Москва, Советская энциклопедия, 1976, p. 298

Всеобщая история искусств [Universal History of Arts], vol. VI, Москва, 1966, pp. 213, 214

Выставки советского изобразительного искусства (Справочник) [Soviet Art Exhibitions (Guide)], vol. I: 1917–1932, Москва, 1966, pp. 97, 98, 107, 118, 217, 237, 258, 335, 341, 348, 412

Государственный Русский музей. Живопись. XVIII—начало XX века [State Russian Museum. Painting from the 18th to the Beginning of the 20th Century. Catalogue], (Ленинград), 1980, p. 317

Искусство стран и народов мира. Краткая художественная энциклопедия [Art of the Countries and Peoples of the World. A Short Encyclopaedia of Arts], Москва, Советская энциклопедия, 1971, p. 735

История русского искусства [History of Russian Art], vol. XI, Москва, 1957, p. 135

История советской архитектуры, 1917—1958 [History of Soviet Architecture, 1917–1958], Москва, 1962, pp. 13–15

50 лет советского искусства. Художники театра (Альбом) [Fifty Years of Soviet Art. Artists of the Theatre. (Album)], Москва, 1969, pp. 12, 142, 145

Театральная энциклопедия [Encyclopaedia of the Theatre], vol. V, Москва, 1967, p. 81

Writings on Tatlin

'Московские художники в спектаклях 1941—1945 гг.' [Moscow Artists' Contribution to Theatrical Productions, 1941–45], Советское искусство (Москва), 12 Oct. 1945

'Об учебной жизни в реформированной Академии художеств' [On Academic Life at the Reorganized Academy of Arts], Искусство коммуны, 7 Dec. 1918

'Художник В.Е. Татлин оформляет пьесу "Кромдейр-старый" в Ленинграде в Большом драматическом театре' [The Artist V.E. Tatlin Designs Cromedeyre-le-Vieil for the Great Theatre of Drama in Leningrad], Вечерняя

Красная газета (Ленинград), 6 Jan. 1925

'Художники об искусстве керамики [Artists on Ceramics], **Искусство**, (Москва), 1971, p. 241

(Abramova, A.—Antonov, R.) А. Абрамова — Р. Антонов, 'Летатлин' [*Letatlin*], **Советская культура**, 18 Маr. 1967

Annenkov, G., **Tatlin och konstruktivismen** (Catalogue), Moderna Museet, Stockholm, 1961

(Annenkov, Iu.) Ю. Анненков, **Дневник моих встреч. Цикл трагедий** [Diary of my Meetings. Cycle of Tragedy], vol. II, New York, 1966, pp. 237–53

(Arkin, D.) Д. Аркин, 'Татлин и Летатлин' [Tatlin and *Letatlin*], **Советское искусство**, (Москва) 9 Apr. 1932, p. 4

(Beskin, E.) Эм. Бескин, 'Комик XVII столетия в МХАТ–II' [A Comic Actor of the 17th Century at the Second Moscow Arts Academic Theatre] **Экономическая жизнь**, (Москва), 30 Oct. 1935

(Botsianovskii, VI.) Вл. Боцяновский, 'Что сделали художники' [What the Artists Did] **Жизнь искусства**, (Петроград), 3 Jan. 1922, p. 3

(Chekrygin, V.N.) 'Из писем В.Н. Чекрыгина Н.Н. Пунину'. Публикация Ю.А. Молока, В.И. Костина 'Об одной идее будущего синтеза живых искусств' [V.N. Chekrygin's letters to N.N. Punin. Iu. A. Molok's and V.I. Kostin's publication 'About an Idea for the Future Synthesis of the Living Arts'] in: **Советское искусствознание 76**, vol. II, Москва, 1977. pp. 291, 301, 303, 304, 323, 325, 329

(Chernevich, E.V.) Е.В. Черневич, 'О каталоге выставки "В.Е. Татлин"' [About the Catalogue of the Exhibition 'V.E. Tatlin'], **Техническая эстетика**, no. 6, 1977, p. 30

(Danin, D.) Д. Данин, 'Улетавль' [The Flying Machine], **Дружба народов**, no. 2, 1979, pp. 220–36

(Donets, L.) Л. Донец, 'Портрет мастера' [Portrait of the Master], **Телевидение-Радиовещание**, no. 1, 1978, pp. 32–4

(Efros, A.) А. Эфрос, 'Живопись театра' [Theatrical Painting], **Аполлон** (Петроград), no. 10, 1914

——, 'Восстание зрителя' [Revolt of the Spectator], **Русский современник**, (Москва—Ленинград), no 1, 1924, p. 276

(Ehrenburg, I.G.) И.Г. Эренбург, **А все-таки она вертится…** [For all that, it turns…] Берлин, 1922, pp. 18–21, 26, 90

——, 'Ein Entwurf Tatlins', **Frühlicht** (Magdeburg), no. 3, 1922, pp. 92–3

(Eisenstein, S.) С. Эйзенштейн, **Избранные произведения в шести томах** [Selected Works in Six Volumes], vol. III, Москва, 1964. pp. 630; vol. IV, Москва, 1966, pp. 139, 760

(Ermilov, P.D.) П.Д. Ермилов, 'Талант, рожденный революцией' [A Talent Born of the Revolution], **Мичуринская правда**, 4 Aug. 1977

(Fevral'skii, A.) А. Февральский, 'Комик XVII столетия' [A Comic Actor of the 17th Century], **Литературная газета**, (Москва), 9 Oct. 1935

——, **Первая советская пьеса 'Мистерия-буфф' В.В. Маяковского** [The First Soviet Play – Maiakovskii's *Mystery-Bouffe*], Москва, 1971, pp. 84, 127

——, **Пути к синтезу. Мейерхольд и кино** [The Roads to a Synthesis. Meierkhol'd and the Cinema], Москва, 1978. pp. 62–5

(Gollerbakh, E.) Э. Голлербах, **Пути новейшего искусства на Западе и у нас** [Directions in New Art in the West and in our Country], Ленинград, 1930, pp. 6, 17, 18,

(Grossman, L.) Л. Гроссман, **Театр Сухово-Кобылина** [The Theatre of Sukhovo-Kobylin], Москва—Ленинград, 1940, pp. 119, 120

(Isakov, S.K.) С.К. Исаков, 'Новый быт и работа Татлина' [The New Way of Life and Tatlin's Work], **Ленинградская правда**, 15 June 1923, p. 7

——, 'Художники и революция' [The Artists and the Revolution], **Жизнь искусства**, 5 June 1926, p. 1

(Iutkevich, S.I.) С.И. Юткевич, 'Сухарная столица' [Biscuit Capital], **ЛЕФ**, (Москва), no. 3, 1923, pp. 181–2

(Khan-Magomedov, S.O.) С.О. Хан-Магомедов, 'У истоков советского дизайна' [At the Roots of Soviet Design], **Техническая эстетика**, no. 4–5, 1977, pp. 32–43

(Khardzhiev, N.) Н. Харджиев, 'Маяковский и живопись', in: Н. Харджиев — В. Тренин, **Поэтическая культура Маяковского.** [Maiakovskii and Painting in: N. Khardzhiev—V. Trenin: *Maiakovskii's Poetic Culture*], Москва, 1970, pp. 9–50

——, 'Первый иллюстратор Маяковского. К 90-летию со дня рождения Татлина' [Maiakovskii's First Illustrator. In Honour of the Ninetieth Anniversary of Tatlin's Birth], **Московский художник**, 18 Dec. 1975, no. 51

(Khlebnikov, V.) В. Хлебников, **Неизданные произведения** [Unpublished Works]. (The poems were edited and commented on by N. Khardzhiev and the prose works by T. Grits.) Москва, 1940

(Khodasevich, V.) В. Ходасевич, **Было** [This is the Way it Was], (Manuscript), 1957–70, A.A. Kapitsa's Collection, Moscow

——, 'Татлин' [Tatlin], **Декоративное искусство**, no. 3, 1980, pp. 40–2

(Kiriushina, L.) Л. Кирюшина, 'Тысячи стрел в будущее' [Thousands of Arrows into the Future], **Архитектура**, 30 May 1978

(Komardenkov, V.) В. Комарденков, **Дни минувшие (Из воспоминаний художника)** [Days Gone by. Reminiscences of an Artist], Москва, 1972, pp. 46, 55, 56, 62

(Kronman, E.) Е. Кронман, 'Уход в технику. Татлин и Летатлин' [Departing into Technology. Tatlin and *Letatlin*], **Бригада художников**, (Москва), no. 6, 1932, pp. 19–23

(Labas, A.) А. Лабас, 'Размышления и воспоминания' [Thoughts and Memories] in: Э. Буторин, **Александр Лабас** (E. Butorin, *Aleksandr Labas*), Москва, 1979

(Lapshin, N.I.) Н.И. Лапшин, 'Обзор новых течений искусства' [Survey of New Tendencies in Art], **Жизнь искусства**, 11 July 1922, p. 3

——, 'Хлебников-Митурич' (Khlebnikov-Miturich), **Русское искусство**, (Москва-Ленинград), no. 2–3, 1923, p. 101

——, 'Художественная жизнь Москвы и Петрограда в Октябре-декабре 1917 г.' [Artistic Life in Moscow and Petrograd from October to December 1917], **Советское искусствознание**, 1977, (Москва), vol. I, 1978, pp. 296, 298

Larionov, M., 'Malevitch, Souvenirs de Michel Larionov', **Aujourd'hui**, no. 15, 1957

(Lissitzky, El) Член, 'Выставки в России' [Exhibitions in Russia], **Вещь** (Берлин), No. 1–2, 1922, p. 19

Lissitzky, El, **Maler, Architekt, Typograph, Fotograf**, Dresden, VEB Verlag der Kunst, 1967, pp. 16, 21, 38, 45, 47, 76, 94, 333–5, 338–9, 347, 351, 353, 367

(Lobov) Лобов, 'Мебель факультета по обработке дерева и металла ВХУТЕИНа ' [Wood and Metal Furniture Made at VKhUTEIN] **Архитектура и строительство Москвы**, no. 7, 1929, pp. 9–11

(Lunacharskii, A.V.) А.В. Луначарский, **Собрание сочинений** [Collected Works] Москва, 1964–7. vol. II, pp. 230, 336, 639; vol. III, p. 124; vol. IV, p. 370; vol. V, pp. 42, 44, 694; vol. VII, pp. 263, 264, 664, 665

(Lupandina, A.)А. Лупандина, 'Комик XVII столетия' [A Comic Actor of the 17th Century], in: **Художник, сцена, экран**, Москва, 1975, pp. 145–9

(Mácza, J., ed.) И.Л. Маца, **Советское искусство за 15 лет. Материалы и документация** [Fifteen Years of Soviet Art. Materials and Documents], Москва–Ленинград, 1933. pp. 44–5, 95, 125, 141, 150, 151, 153, 334, 663

(Maiakovskii, V.) В. Маяковский, **Полное собрание сочинений в 13 томах** [Collected Works in Thirteen Volumes], Москва, 1957–64, vol. IV, pp. 212, 246; vol. V, p. 161; vol. XII, pp. 17, 42; vol. XIII, pp. 118, 405

(Malevich, K.S.) К.С. Малевич, 'Конструктивная живопись русских художников и конструктивизм' [Constructivist Painting by Russian Artists and Constructivism], **Новая генерация** (Харьков), no. 8, 1929, pp. 47–54

(Meierkhol'd, V.E.) В.Э. Мейерхольд, **Статьи, письма, речи, беседы, 1917—1939** [Articles, Letters, Speeches, Interviews, 1917–39], part II, Москва, 1968, pp. 16, 22, 523, 608

——, **Переписка. 1986—1939** [Correspondence, 1896–1939] Москва, 1976, pp. 187, 188, 286

(Miklashevskii, K.) К. Миклашевский, **Гипертрофия искусства** [Hypertrophy in Art], Петроград, 1924, pp. 60–1, 64–7

(Molchanovskii) Молчановский, 'О Летатлине' [On *Letatlin*], **Самолет**, (Москва), no. 10–11, 1932

(Morev, N.) Н. Морев, 'Каменная летопись истории' [Chronicles of History Etched in Stone], **Литературная газета**, 7 Feb. 1977

(Nikol'skaia, S.) С. Никольская, 'Башня-памятник'[Tower Monument], **Вечерняя Москва**, 23 Sept. 1977

(Parnis, A.I.) А.И. Парнис, 'Хлебников, сотрудник "Красного воина"' [Khlebnikov, Co-Worker at 'Krasnyi Voin'], **Литературное обозрение**, no. 2, 1980, p. 112

(Petrovskii, D.) Дм. Петровский, 'Воспоминания о Велемире Хлебникове'[Reminiscences of Velemir Khlebnikov], **ЛЕФ**, (Москва), no. 1, 1923, pp. 143–181

(Punin, N.N.) Н.Н. Пунин, 'Разорванное сознание'[Muddled Consciousness], **Искусство коммуны**, (Петроград), 19 Jan. 1919, p. 2; 26 Jan. 1919, p. 1

——, 'Мера искусства' [The Standard in Art] **Искусство коммуны** (Петроград) 2 Feb. 1919, p. 2.

——, 'В Москве' (письмо)[In Moscow (a letter)], **Искусство коммуны**, 9 Feb. 1919, p. 2

——, 'О памятниках нового типа' [On Monuments in the New Style], **Искусство коммуны**, 9 Mar. 1919, pp. 2–3

——, 'Татлинова башня.Tour de Tatline', **Вещь**, no. 1–2, 1922, p. 22

——, 'Новое искусство и его критики' [The New Art and its Critics], **Жизнь искусства**, 11 July 1922, p. 3

——, 'Обзор новых течений в искусстве Петрограда'[Review of New Tendencies in the Art of Petrograd], **Русское искусство**, no. 1, 1923, pp. 18–21

——, 'Памятник III Интернационала'[The Monument to the Third International] **Горе пахаря**, (Владивосток), 25 Feb. 1923, (Republished in no. 26)

——, 'Государственная выставка. О левых' [State Exhibition. On Artists of the Left] **Жизнь искусства**, 29 May 1923, pp. 14–15

——, 'Выставка памяти Хлебникова' [An Exhibition in Khlebnikov's Memory], **Жизнь искусства**, 3 July 1923, p. 14

——, 'Новейшие течения в русском искусстве.' Лекция I-я [The Newest Tendencies in Russian Art. First lecture] A publication of the State Russian Museum, p. 8

(Radlov, N.E.) Н.Э. Радлов, **О футуризме** [On Futurism], Петроград, 1923, pp. 42–3, 48

(Red'ko, Kliment) Климент Редько, **Дневники, воспоминания, статьи** [Diaries, Reminiscences, Articles] Москва, 1974, pp. 10, 63, 64

Rodchenko, Alexandre: 'Vladimir Tatlin', **Opus Internazional,** no. 4, 1967, pp. 15–18

(Rylov, A.A.) А.А. Рылов, **Воспоминания** [Reminiscences], Ленинград, 1940, pp. 174–8

(Segal, S.)С. Сегаль, **Новая живопись в ее истоках и развитии** [The Origins and Development of New Painting], Берлин, 1923, pp. 60, 62–3

(Shapiro, T.M.) Т.М. Шапиро, 'Манифест революционной романтики. К возможности воссоздания модели башни В.Е. Татлина' [Manifesto of Revolutionary Romanticism. On the Possibility of Reconstructing V.E. Tatlin's Tower], **Строительство и архитектура Ленинграда**, no. 11, 1976, pp. 43–5

(Shneiderman, I.) И. Шнейдерман, 'Художник читает пьесу' [The Artist Reads a Play], **Советское искусство**, 31 Aug. 1940

(Simonov, K.) К. Симонов, 'Летатлин' [Letatlin], **Воздушный транспорт**, 30 Mar. 1978

(Sokolova, N.) Н. Соколова, 'Опыт оформления спектакля' [The Experience of Stage and Costume Design], **Советское искусство**, 14 Mar. 1947

(Strigalev, A.) А. Стригалев, 'Кому пролетариат ставит памятники?' [To whom does the Proletariat Erect Monuments?] **Декоративное искусство СССР**, no. 144, 1969, pp. 1–2, 27, 52

——, 'О проекте Памятника III Интернационала художника В.Е. Татлина' [On Tatlin's Project The Monument to the Third International], in: **Вопросы советского изобразительного искусства и архитектуры,** [Москва], 1973, pp. 408–52

——, 'Участие В.Е. Татлина в организации и проведении монументальной пропаганды' [V.E. Tatlin's Role in the Organization and Implementation of the Monumental

Propaganda], in: **Проблемы истории советской ар-хитектуры**, (Москва), 1975, pp. 51–67

——,'О некоторых новых терминах в русском искусстве XX в.' [On some New Terms in Twentieth Century Russian Art], in: **Проблемы истории советской архитектуры**, (Москва), no. 2, 1976, pp. 66–71

——, 'Об одной концепции дизайна в архитектуре' [On a Conception of Design in Architecture], in: **Проблемы истории советской архитектуры**, no. 4, 1978, pp. 28–31

——, 'Бионические основы творческой концепции В. Е. Тат-лина' [Bionic Bases of Tatlin's Creative Conception], in: **Проблемы формообразования в советской архитек-туре**, (Москва), no. 4, 1978, pp. 29–32

(Stupin, V.) В. Ступин, 'Пути монументальной пропаган-ды'[Paths of the Monumental Propaganda], **Советская культура**, 13 May 1977

(Syrkina, F.Ia. – E.M. Kostina) Ф.Я. Сыркина – Е.М. Костина, **Русское театрально-декорационное искусство** [Rus-sian Stage Design], Москва, 1978, pp. 178, 193

Vladimir Tatlin (Catalogue), Compiled by Troels An-dersen, Moderna Museet, Stockholm, 1968, pp. 80, 92

(Tatlin, V.E.) В.Е. Татлин, 'О памятниках нового типа, 1919'[On the New Type of Monuments 1919], in: **Мас-тера советской архитектуры об архитектуре** [Edited with foreword and commentaries by A. A. Strigalev), vol. II, Искусство, Москва, 1975

——, **В.Е. Татлин. Заслуженный деятель искусств РСФСР. 1885–1953** [V.E. Tatlin. Honoured Art Worker of the RSFSR. 1885–1953] (Catalogue and collection of studies, edited by L.A. Zhadova) Советский художник, Москва,1977, 68 pp., 50 illustrations

——, (Kostin. V.I.) В.И. Костин, 'Рисунки В.Е. Татлина 1912–1914 годов'[V.E. Tatlin's Drawings in 1912–1914], pp. 34–40

——, (Rakhtanov, I.A.) И.А. Рахтанов, 'Спираль худож-ника'[The Artist's Spiral], pp. 59–61

——, (Strigalev, A.A.) А.А. Стригалев, 'Проект памятника

III Интернационалу' [The Plan of the Monument to the Third International], pp. 16–19

——, (Syrkina, F.Ia.) Ф.Я. Сыркина, 'Театр Татлина'[Tatlin's Theatre], pp. 43–57

Umansky, K.: **Neue Kunst in Russland. 1914–1919** Potsdam–München, 1920, pp. 19–20, 35

——, 'Neue Kunstrichtungen in Rußland' I. Der Tatlinis-mus oder die Maschinenkunst. II. Die neue Monumen-talskulptur in Rußland. In: **Der Ararat,** no. 4, 1920, p. 12; no. 5–6, p. 32

(Voinov, Vs.) Вс. Воинов, 'Юбилейная Выставка в Октябрь-ские дни в Ленинграде и Москве'[The October Jubilee Exhibition in Leningrad and Moscow], **Красная пано-рама**, (Ленинград), 3 Dec. 1927

(Zhadova, L.A.) Л.А. Жадова, 'Советский отдел на меж-дународной выставке декоративного искусства и промыш-ленности в Париже в 1925-м году'[The Soviet Section at the 1925 Paris International Exhibition of Decorative and Industrial Arts], **Творчество**, no. 11, 1967

——, 'О теории советского дизайна 20-Х годов'[On the Theory of Soviet Design in the 1920s], **Вопросы тех-нической эстетики** (Москва),vol. I, 1968, pp. 84, 86, 88, 93

——, 'Толпа прозрачно-чистых сот...'[A Transparently Clean Honeycomb] **Наука и жизнь**, no. 9, 1976, pp. 102, 104

——, 'К выставке В.Е. Татлина – одного из основополож-ников советской школы дизайна'[For the Exhibition by V.E. Tatlin, One of the Founders of Soviet Design], **Тех-ническая эстетика**, no. 6, 1977, pp. 24–29

——, 'Первая посуда для детей'[The First Dish for Child-ren], **Декоративное искусство**, no. 11, 1979, p. 16

——, 'Татлин, проектировщик материальной культуры'[Tat-lin, a Planner of Material Culture], **Советское декора-тивное искусство**, 1977–8, Москва, 1980

(Znamenskii, S.) С. Знаменский, '"Чаша радости" – пьеса Н. Винникова в Театре им. Моссовета'['Cup of Joy', Vin-nikov's Play in the Theatre of the Moscow Soviet], **Советское искусство**, no. 11, 1979, p. 16

Picture Credits

Alinari, Florence **195, 198**
Andersen, Troels **181**
Artek, Helsinki **259**
Arts Council of Great Britain, London **204**
Bak, Imre **120**
Bauhaus-Archiv (Museum für Gestaltung, West Berlin) **261, 262, 273**
Centre National d'Art et de Culture Georges Pompidou, Paris **33, 79, 206**
Corvina, archive of **101, 102**
Hajnóczy, Gyula **194**
Heartfield, Gertrud **136**
Károly, Attila **117, 322–324**
Kostin, V.I. **402–404**
Kunsthistorisches Museum, Vienna **193**
Lavrentev, A. **95, 187, 244**
Maurer, Dóra **260, 350**
Moderna Museet, Stockholm
  Photograph: Hans Hammerskjöld **135, 202**
Museum Bellerive, Sammlung des Kunstgewerbemuseums, Zurich
  Photograph: Marlen Parez **201**
The Museum of Modern Art, New York **17, 200**
Nasjongalleriet, Oslo **107**
Nationalgalerie Staatliche Museen Preussischer Kulturbesitz, West Berlin **105**

Photographie Giraudon, Paris **188**
The Solomon R. Guggenheim Museum, New York
  Photograph: E. Mates **199**
Sarab'ianov, D. V. **12, 111**
Szelényi, Károly **30, 36, 38, 68–73, 86–88, 109, 112, 115, 116, 119, 124–128, 132, 133, 165, 173–176, 180, 182–185, 189, 205, 209, 210, 216, 227, 231–233, 237, 238, 240–242, 252–254, 256–258, 274, 276–279, 282, 284, 293, 294, 299, 314, 317, 318, 327–331, 334, 336–339, 345, 348, 349, 401, 405, 422, 423**
Szerencsés, János **118, 190, 316**
VAAP (Vsesoiuznoe agentstvo po avtorskim pravam, Moscow) **1–11, 13–16, 18–29, 31, 34, 35, 37, 39–67, 74–78, 80–85, 89–94, 97, 98, 100, 104, 106, 108, 110, 114, 121–123, 129–131, 134, 137–163, 167–172, 177–179, 186, 191, 196, 207, 208, 211–213, 215, 217–226, 228–230, 234–236, 243, 245–251, 263–272, 275, 280, 281, 283, 286–292, 296–298, 300–313, 315, 319–321, 325, 326, 332, 333, 335, 340–343, 351–400, 407–421, 424–426**
Wittelsbacher Ausgleichfond, Munich **99**
Zhadova, L.A. **96, 103, 113, 164, 166, 192, 197, 203, 214, 239, 255, 285, 344, 347, 406**

Acknowledgments

The authors of this book thank the members of the staffs of IRLI, LGALI, the Research and Bibliographic Archive of the Academy of Arts, the State Russian Museum, the State Tret'iakov Gallery, TsGALI, TsGAOR and TsGTM for their assistance, and the persons who enabled us to reproduce documents and works of arts in their property.

Abbreviations

FEKS	Factory of the Eccentric Actor
GINKhUK	State Institute of Artistic Culture
Glavnauka	Main Directorate of Scientific Institutions
GSKhM	Free State Artistic Studios
INKhUK	Institute of Artistic Culture
IRLI	Institute of Russian Literature
IZO Narkompros	Fine Arts Department of the People's Commissariat of Education
LEF	Left Front of the Arts
LGALI	Leningrad State Archive of Literature and Art
Mastfor	Foregger's Studio
MKhAT	Moscow Art Academic Theatre
MKhAT-2	Second Moscow Art Academic Theatre
MOSSKh	Moscow Branch of the Union of Soviet Artists
MUZhVZ	Moscow College of Painting, Sculpture and Architecture
n	note
Narkompros	People's Commissariat of Education
O—10	Last Futurist Exhibition
Oberiu	Society for Realistic Art
OPOIaZ	Society for the Study of Poetic Language
OSA	Union of Contemporary Architects
OSOAVIAKhIM	Society for the Promotion of Defence and Aero-Chemical Development
OST	Society of Easel Painters
PGSKhUM	Petrograd Free State Teaching Studios
Proletkul't	Organization for Proletarian Culture
PUNU	Petrograd Directorate of Scientific Institutions
Rabis–Sorabis	Trade Union of Art Workers
SDI	Union of Art Workers
Sovnarkom	Soviet of People's Commissars
SVOMAS	Free Artistic Studios
TsGALI	Central State Archive of Literature and Art
TsGAOR	Central State Archive of the October Revolution
TsGIAL	Central State Historical Archive, Leningrad
TsGTM	Bakhrushin Central State Museum of Theatre History
VKhUTEIN	Higher Artistic and Technical Institute
VKhUTEMAS	Higher Artistic and Technical Studios

Subject Index

Numbers in italics refer to illustrations and those in bold-face to annotations

Academy of Arts, *see* Free Artistic Studios

Apartment no. 5	Квартира № 5	**335,** 338, 342, 346, 445

Artistic Collegium (of Narkompros), *see* People's Commissariat of Education

Artistic Section of the Moscow Soviet of Workers' and Soldiers' Deputies	Художественная секция Московского Совета рабочих и солдатских депутатов	23, 266, 323, 446
Bakhrushin Central State Museum of Theatre History (TsGTM), Moscow	Государственный Центральный театральный музей имени Бахрушина	151, 177, 178, 179, 320, 325, 437, 499, 501, 503, 504, 506, 507, 508, 509, 510, 511, 512, 513, 514, *37, 393*
Bauhaus		142, 153, 265, **266,** 340, *261*
Bernshtein's private school of drawing, St. Petersburg	Частная художественная студия Бернштейна	17, 68, 332, 445
Bestuzhev courses	Бестужевские курсы	170, 179, 321, **326**
Blue Rose	Голубая роза	57, 62
Central Children's Theatre	Центральный театр для детей	175, 179, 320, 324, 504
Central State Archive of Literature and Art (TsGALI), Moscow	Центральный государственный Архив литературы и искусства (ЦГАЛИ)	41, 61, 72, 133, 151, 152, 183, 184, 186, 237, 238, 245, 259, 260, 261, 266, 318, 319, 328, 329, 397, 437, 445, 448, 501, 505, 509, 512, 513, 514, *4, 5, 20, 21, 22, 23, 24, 90, 91, 92, 93, 94, 212, 236, 406, 407, 408, 409, 421*
Central State Archive of the October Revolution (TsGAOR), Leningrad	Центральный государственный Архив Октябрьской революции (ЦГАОР)	41, 152, 251, 252, 253, 255, 256, 257, 258, 259, 260, 399, 445, 447, 513
Commissariat of Properties of the Republic	Народный комиссариат имуществ Республики	188

Commission for Protecting Monuments of Art and Antiquity, *see* Artistic Section of the Moscow Soviet of Workers' and Soldiers Deputies

Dobychina's Artistic Bureau (Dobychina's Gallery)	Художественное бюро (галерея) Добычиной	165, 178, 492
Donkey's Tail	Ослиный хвост	40, 44, 45, 53, 61, 62, 262, **263,** 331, 332, 489, 490, 513, *84*
Exhibition of Pictures of Petrograd Artists of all Tendencies	Выставка петроградских художников всех направлений	134, 244, 251, 254, 399, 407, 447, 494, 514

Exhibition of Paintings of the Year 1915	1915 год	331, 492
Experimental Laboratory for Material Culture, see People's Commissariat of Education		
Experimental Section, see State Institute of Artistic Culture		
Fadeev Writers' Hall, Moscow	Центральный московский Дом литераторов имени А.А. Фадеева	154, 437, *345, 346, 348, 349*
FEKS (Factory of the Eccentric Actor)	ФЭКС (Фабрика эксцентрического актера)	396, **400**
Fine Arts Department (IZO Narkompros), see People's Commissariat of Education		
First Exhibition of Painterly Reliefs	Первая выставка живописных рельефов	326, 331, 332, 445, 491
First Russian Exhibition of Fine Arts, Berlin		43, 394, 447, 493
Foregger's Studio (Mastfor)	Мастерская Фореггера (Мастфор)	243
The Four	«4»	40
Free Artistic Studios (SVOMAS), Petrograd (also known as the Petrograd Free State Artistic Teaching Studios [PGSKhUM]; the former Academy of Arts)	Свободные художественные мастерские (СВОМАС) (Петроградские государственные художественно-учебные мастерские [ПГСХУМ]; Академия художеств)	24, 25, 30, 31, 42, 134, 135, 151, 152, 154, 163, 240, 244, 247, 248, 249, 250, 252, 261, 263, 265, 266, 321, 322, 323, 327, 328, 335, 338, 339, 340, 346, 393, 395, 400, 442, 446, 447, 493, 494, 507, 514, *165, 174, 176, 179, 180*
Studio of Materials, Volume and Construction (formerly the Studio of Volume, Construction and Colours)		24, 135, 151, 250, 251, 265, 266, 328, 338, 339, 340, 393, 399, 446, 507, 508, 512, *174*
Free State Artistic Studios, Moscow	Государственные свободные художественные мастерские	24, 25, 42, 240, 261, 264, 328, 333, 339, 346, 446
Golden Fleece	Золотое руно	40, 262, **263,** 264, 322, 327, 331
Group for Material Culture, see State Institute of Artistic Culture		
Higher Artistic and Technical Institute, see VKhUTEIN		
Higher Artistic and Technical Studios, see VKhUTEMAS		
House of Unions, Moscow	Дом Союзов	10, 31, 34, 240, 244, 245, 246, 265, 325, 442, 446, 493, 508, *166, 181*
Institute of Applied Arts, Petrograd and Leningrad	Институт художественной культуры (ИНХУК) (Музей живописной культуры; Музей художественной культуры)	142, 153, 447, 494
Institute of Artistic Culture (INKhUK), Moscow (formerly the Museum of Painterly Culture or Museum of Artistic Culture)	Декоративный институт	34, 41, 43, 133, 143, 152, 162, 240, 241, **242,** 258, 323, 346, 406, 447

Institute of Russian Literature (IRLI) (also known as Pushkin House)	Институт русской литературы (Пушкинский дом)	247, 513
Institute of Silicates and Building Materials, Moscow	Институт силикатов и стройматериалов	10, 153, 323, 325, 326, 328, 448
Jack of Diamonds	Бубновый валет	17, 18, 45, 52, 53, 57, 58, 61, 62, 182, 183, 262, **263,** 322, 326, 327, 331, 332, 390, 490, 513, *85*
Kamernyi Theatre, *see* Moscow Kamernyi Theatre		
Kiev College of Art	Киевский художественный институт	130, 135, 165, 254, 260, **261,** 264, 265, 266, 323, 325, 328, 398, 447, 495, 512, *235*
Knave of Diamonds, *see* Jack of Diamonds		
Last Futurist Exhibition, 0—10	Последняя футуристическая выставка, 0–10	19, 41, 150, 178, 331, 333, 335, 337, 445, 492, 507
LEF (Journal of the Left Front of the Arts)	ЛЕФ	249, 264, 312, 394
Leningrad Clothing Manufacturers' Trust	Ленинградодежда	137, 144, 153, 251, **252,** 255, 257, 265, 407, 447
Leningrad Museum of Theatre History	Ленинградский государственный театральный музей	177, 437, 501, 503, 509
Leningrad State Archive of Literature and Art (LGALI)	Ленинградский государственный Архив литературы и искусства (ЛГАЛИ)	41, 43, 152, 243, 247, 249, 254
Literary and Artistic Circle	Литературно-художественный кружок	155, 181, 314, 324, 445, 503
Main Directorate of Scientific Institutions (museums, research and artistic institutions [Glavnauka])	Главное управление научными (музейными и научно-художест-венными) учреждениями (Главнаука)	153, 250, 251, 252, 257, 258, 407
Mir Iskusstva *see* World of Art		
Modern Painting	Современная живопись	62, 326, 331, 490, 491
Moscow Art Academic Theatre (MKhAT)	Московский художественный академический театр (МХАТ)	11, 153, 155, 172, 173, 174, 177, 179, 317, 318, 320, 324, 325, 328, 338, 440, 448, 497, 504, *393*
Moscow Artistic Collegium (of IZO Narkompros), *see* People's Commissariat of Education		
Moscow Artistic Department (of Narkompros), *see* People's Commissariat of Education		
Moscow College of Painting, Sculpture and Architecture (MUZhV)	Московское училище живописи, ваяния и зодчества	17, 24, 45, 46, 69, 129, 143, 152, 261, **262,** 263, 264, 321, 322, 326, 327, 445, 490
Moscow Kamernyi Theatre	Московский камерный театр	157, 159, 167, **316,** 324, 328, 438, 504

Moscow Trade Union of Artists and Painters	Московский профессиональный союз художников-живописцев	23, 264, 266, 446
Museum of Artistic Culture, Moscow, *see* Institute of Artistic Culture		
Museum of Artistic Culture, Petrograd, *see* State Institute of Artistic Culture		
Museum of Contemporary Art	Музей современного искусства	**237,** 242, 266
Museum of Painterly Culture, Moscow, *see* Institute of Artistic Culture		
Museum of Painterly Culture, Petrograd, *see* State Institute of Artistic Culture		
Museums Collegium (of Narkompros), *see* People's Commissariat of Education		
Museums Department (of Narkompros), *see* People's Commissariat Education		
Oberiu (Society for Realistic Art)	Обьединение реального искусства (Обериу)	133, 398, 402
OPOIaZ (Society for the Study of Poetic Language)	ОПОЯЗ (Общество изучения поэтического языка)	26, 249, 342, 398, 399
Paris International Exhibition of Modern Decorative and Industrial Arts		10, 32, 259, 260, 325, 394, 442, 447, 494, 508, *186*
Penza Sileverstov College of Art	Пензенское художественное училище имени Н.Д. Силеверстова	17, 22, 41, 44, 47, 67, 68, **262,** 263, 264, 321, 322, 326, 327, 332, 445, 505, 513, *6*
People's Commissariat of Education (Narkompros)	Народный комиссариат по делам просвещения (Наркомпрос)	23, 30, 178, 187, 188, 264, 265, 323, 325, 448
Artistic Collegium	Художественная коллегия	23, 185, 186, 188, 237, 243, 266, 338
Experimental Laboratory for Material Culture	Экспериментальная научно-исследовательская лаборатория культуры материалов	135, 136, 153, 311, 448, *316*
Fine Arts Department (IZO Narkompros)	Отдел изобраизтельного искусства (ИЗО Наркомпроса)	10, 23, 25, 29, 30, 41, 42, 151, 153, 182, 184, 185, 187, 188, 260, 261, 264, 266, 323, 344, 346, 347, 392, 443
Moscow Artistic Collegium (of IZO Narkompros)	Московская художественная коллегия (ИЗО Наркомпроса)	23, 41, 185, 186, 187, 188, 237, 243, 264, 333, 446
Moscow Artistic Department (of Narkompros)	Московский отдел изобразительных искусств при Наркомпросе	23, 30, 41, 185, 188, 327
Museums Collegium (of Narkompros)	Музейная коллегиця Наркомпроса	23, 237, 242, 266, 446, 513
Museums Department (of Narkompros)	Музейный отдел при Наркомпросе	239, 242, 264, 327
Peredvizhniki, *see* Society of Itinerant Exhibitions		
Petrograd Directorate of Scientific Institutions (PUNU)	Петроградское управление научными учреждениями (ПУНУ)	250, 252, 257

Petrograd Directorate of the Institutions of the Academic Centre	Петроградское управление учреждениями академического центра	241, 242, 251, 340, 447
Petrograd Free State Artistic Teaching Studios, *see* Free Artistic Studios		
Proletkul't (Organization for Proletarian Culture)	Пролеткульт	253
Research and Bibliographic Archive of the Academy of Arts	Научно-библиографический архив Академии искусств	342
ROSTA (Russian Telegraphic Agency)	РОСТА	**343**
St. Petersburg Practical Technological Institute	Петербургский практический технологический институт	14, 163, 321, **326**
Second Moscow Art Academic Theatre (MKhAT-2)	Московский художественный академический театр-II (МХАТ-II)	164, 177, 178, 314, **315,** 316, 324, 438, 497, 504, *356, 357, 358, 359, 393*
Section for Material Culture, *see* State Institute of Artistic Culture		
Section for Organic Culture, *see* State Institute of Artistic Culture		
Section for Theoretical Analysis of Form, *see* State Institute of Artistic Culture		
(Baron) Shtiglits Artistic College, Petrograd	Училище Штиглица	31, 258, 340, 447
Society for Realistic Art, *see* Oberiu		
Society for the Encouragement of the Arts	Общество поощрения художеств	258
Society for the Promotion of Defence and Aero-Chemical Development (OSOAVIAKhIM)	Общество содействия обороне, авиации и химическому строительству (ОСОАВИАХИМ)	147, 148, **154,** 409
Society for the Study of Poetic Language, *see* OPOIaZ		
Society of Easel Painters (OST)	Общество станковистов (ОСТ)	164, **178**
Society of Itinerant Exhibitions (Wanderers)	Товарищество передвижных выставок (передвижники)	23, 44, 244, 263, 327, 331, 341, 342, 391
Society of Women		331
Solodovnikov Opera, Moscow	Солодовниковская опера	14, 155, 312, **313,** 445
Soviet of People's Commissars (Sovnarkom)	Совет Народных Комиссаров (Совнарком)	41, 185, 186, 187, 188, 320, 326, 340, 343, 446, 448
State Institute of Art Study	Государственный институт изучения искусств	41, 335

State Institute of Artistic Culture (GINKhUK), Petrograd and Leningrad (It was founded in 1924 as the successor of the Museum of Artistic Culture, which was also called the Museum of Painterly Culture, the Institute's earliest name.) | Государственный институт художественной культуры (ГИНХУК) (Музей художественной культуры; Музей живописной культуры) | 14, 24, 34, 41, 42, 43, 133, 134, 135, 140, 142, 151, 152, 153, 162, 163, 237, 240, **242,** 243, 244, 245, 246, 247, 248, 249, 250, 251, 252, 253, 255, 257, 258, 259, 260, 262, 265, 266, 314, 315, 324, 328, 340, 346, 396, 397, 398, 400, 403, 447, 493, 494, 503, 514, *82, 214, 237*

   Experimental Section | | 257, 258, 494

   Group (later Section) for Material Culture | | 14, 41, 134, 135, 136, 140, 142, 143, 145, 151, 152, 153, 242, 245, 247, 249, 250, 251, 252, 253, 254, 255, 256, 257, 258, 265, 328, 407, 447, 494, 513, *237, 246*

   Section for Organic Culture | | 243, 494

   Section for the Theoretical Analysis of Form | | 258, 494

State Museum of Fine Arts, Moscow (today Pushkin Museum) | Государственный музей изобразительных искусств (Государственный музей изящных искусств; Государственный музей изобразительных искусств имени Пушкина) | 10, 11, 148, 313, 438, 448, 496, 503, 508, *106, 332, 333, 335*

State Russian Museum, Leningrad | Государственный Русский музей (ГРМ) | 40, 43, 61, 62, 178, 182, 187, 239, 242, 246, 247, 253, 260, 262, 265, 314, 320, 324, 325, 335, 339, 448, 495, 496, 497, 498, 499, 501, 502, 505, 507, 510, *82*

State Shchusev Museum and Institute of Building Science and Research | Государственный научно-исследовательский музей архитектуры имени Щусева | 240, 442, 502, 512

State Tret'iakov Gallery, Moscow | Государственная Третьяковская галерея (ГТГ) | 43, 61, 62, 237, 239, 240, 246, 262, 265, 320, 322, 324, 325, 437, 499, 500, 501, 502, 503, 505, 507, 508, 510, *12, 97, 98*

The Store | Магазин | 41, 150, 264, **266,** 332, 337, 446, 492, 513, *86, 87, 88*

Stroganov College of Applied Arts | Строгановское художественно-промышленное училище | 24, 261

Studio of Materials, Volume and Construction, *see* Free Artistic Studios | |

Studio of Ritual Theatre | Мастерская обрядового театра | 243

Studio of Volume, Construction and Colours, *see* Free Artistic Studios | |

Survey of New Tendencies in Art | Обзор новых течений в искусстве | 33, 242, **243,** 245, 248, 251, 254, 264, 493, *82*

Target | Мишень | 40, 61

Theatre of Antiquity	Старинный театр	155, **177**
Theatre of Popular Comedy	Театр народной комедии	243
Tower	Башня	445
Trade Union of Art Workers (Rabis–Sorabis)	Профессиональный союз работников искусств (Рабис-Сорабис)	247, 250, 251, 264, 323, **327,** 494
Tragical Popular Farce	Трагический балаган	155, 156, 181
Tramway V	Трамвай В	41, 331, 332, 334, 445, 491
Tsionglinskii's studio	Студия Ционглинского	332
Union of Art Workers (SDI)	Союз деятелей искусств (СДИ)	23, 41, 264, **266,** 446
Union of Contemporary Architects (OSA)	Общество Современных Архитекторов (ОСА)	312
Union of New Tendencies in Art	Объединение новых течений в искусстве	241, 242, 243, 246, 247, 264, 340, 397, 403, 447, 494,
Union of Russian Artists	Союз русских художников	263, 322, 324, **327,** 328
Union of Soviet Artists	Союз советских художников	72, 178, 314, 437
Moscow Branch (MOSSKh)		314, 318, 320, 409, 412, 439, 448
Union of Youth	Союз молодежи	15, 17, 40, 57, 61, 62, 149, 177, 182, 183, 184, 253, 262, **263,** 322, 326, 327, 331, 332, 445, 489, 491, 503
VKhUTEIN (Higher Artistic and Technical Institute), Moscow	ВХУТЕИН (Высший художественно-технический институт	135, 136, 137, 140, 141, 145, 148, 151, 152, 153, 154, 252, 254, 261, 264, 265, 268, 312, 323, 325, 328, 394, 411, 437, 448, 509, 512, *240, 241, 242, 244, 272*
VKhUTEMAS (Higher Artistic and Technical Studios), Moscow	ВХУТЕМАС (Высшие художественно-технические мастерские)	25, 145, 151, 240, 251, **261,** 323, 328, 333, 340, 394, 398, 406, 437, 438, 441, 446, 447, 448, *240, 241, 242*
Wanderers, *see* Society of Itinerant Exhibitions		
World of Art	Мир искусства	155, 156, 182, **183,** 262, 263, 322, 324, 326, 327, 328, 331, 332, 490, 491
0—10 (Exhibition Zero-Ten), *see* Last Futurist Exhibition		
Zorved	Зорвед	402

Index of Names

Numbers in italics refer to illustrations and those in bold-face to biographical sketches

Aalto, Alvar 140, 142, 153, *259*
Abramova, Alina Vasil'evna 263, 439
Afanas'ev, Aleksei Fedorovich 16, 17, 41, 44, 45, 67, 262, **263,** 322, 326, 332, 445, 505
Agin, Aleksandr Alekseevich 169, **179**
Aksel'rod, Vsevolod B. 439, 448
Aksenov, Ivan Aleksandrovich 62
Aleksandrov, A. A. 133
Alekseev, Boris Ivanovich 411
Tsar Aleksei Mikhailovich 178
Alpatov, Mikhail V. 505, 506
Al'tman, Natan Isaevich 39, 242, 335, 339, 341, **342**
Altukhov, Iov Kornilovich 321, **326**
Andersen, Hans Christian 164, 504
Andersen, Troels 43, 508
Andreets 339
Andreevskii, A. N. 448
Antonov, S.P. 504
Archipenko, Aleksander 58
Artseulov, Konstantin Konstantinovich 11, 147, 148, 154, 312, 408, **409,** 440, 448, 497, 508
Arkin, David Efimovich **260**
Arvatov, Boris Ignat'evich 40, 151, 152, 394
Aseev, Nikolai Nikolaevich 337, 394

Bader, Mikhail Khristoforovich **253**
Baianov, L.S. 495
Bakharev, O. *192*
Bakhterev, Igor Vladimirovich 398, 402
Baranov-Rossine, Vladimir Davidovich 339
Bart, Viktor Sergeevich 263
Bart, Nadezhda Nikolaevna (Tatlina) 326, 445, *2*
Bazhan, Nikolai Platonovich 130, 133, 149, 154, 447, 506, *293*
Bebutov, Valerii Mikhailovich 324, 395, 504
Bebutova, Elena Mikhailovna 320
Beethoven, Ludwig van 160
Begicheva, Anna Alekseevna 149, 154, 398, 439
Beliaev 339
Belogrud, Andrei Evgen'evich 340
Benois, Alexandre 156, 182, **183,** 316, 327, 332, 333, 335, 339
Berezin 324, 504
Bernard, Émile 390, 393
Bernshtein, Mikhail Davidovich 17, 68, 332, 445
Bersenev, Ivan Nikolaevich (Pavlishchev) 11, 164, 165, 167, 175, 176, 315, 324, **328,** 504
Bespalova, G. M. 329
Bestuzhev-Riumin, Konstantin Nikolaevich 170
Białostocki, Jan 66
Bilibin, Ivan Iakovlevich 177
Boccioni, Umberto 29, *200*
Bochak, D.S. 495
Bogomazov, Sergei Mikhailovich 179

Boguslavskaia, Ksenia L. 331
Bolotina, Irina S. 332
Bol'shakov, Konstantin 394
Bolyai, János 396, 399
Bonch-Tomashevskii, Mikhail Mikhailovich 155, 156, **181,** 445, 492, 503
Borisovets 495
Borkin, Vasilii Vasil'evich 147, **154,** 513, *286, 287*
Borromini, Francesco 29, *198*
Bowlt, John E. 62
Brandt, Marianne *273*
Braque, Georges 18, 263
Breuer, Marcel 141
Brik, Osip Maksimovich 394
Bromirskii, Petr Ignat'evich 185, 512
Brueghel, Pieter 29, *193*
Bruni, Lev Aleksandrovich 145, 150, 266, 335, 337, 393, 398, 403, 437, 438, 445, 447, 494, 495, 509
Bubnova 445
Bulgakov, Mikhail Afanas'evich 177
Bur, Gilles de 153
Burliuk, Vladimir Davidovich 47, 52, 129, 262, 332, 337, 503, 506, *17, 70, 72*
Burliuk brothers 67, 263, 332, 445, 503

Cander 442
Čapek, Karel 448
Cézanne, Paul 16, 45, 46, 51, 57, 69, 334, 389, 390, 393, 394
Chagall, Marc 42, 45
Chalk, Martyn 500, 512
Chaplin, Charlie 447
Chekhonin, Sergei Vasil'evich 136, 181, **182,** 503, 509
Chekhov, Anton Pavlovich 178
Chekrygin, Vasilii Nikolaevich 41, 45, 129
Chkalov, Valerii Pavlovich 442
Chukovskii, D. N. *424, 425, 426*
Chukovskii, Kornei Ivanovich 247
Chuzhak, Nikolai Fedorovich 394
Costakis, George 505, 507
Courbet, Gustave 23
Cranach, Lucas 56, 63, 64, 65, 66, *99, 101, 102*
Cross, Christopher 500, 512

Damskii, Abram Isaakovich 441, 512, *131*
Danin, Daniil Semenovich 131, 132, 133, 159, 160, 169, 178, 337
Darkin 153
Darmolatova, Anna Dmitrievna (Radlova) **184**
Darmolatova, Sarra Dmitrievna (Lebedeva) 40, **184,** 439, 445, 448, 494, 510
David, Jacques Louis 23
Davidova, Mariia Vladimirovna 177
Debner, G.N. 448

de Bur, Gilles, *see* Bur, Gilles de
Deeva, I.S. 503
Degas, Edgar 69
Deineka, Aleksandr Aleksandrovich 315
Delaunay, Robert *199*
Derain, André 18, 263
Derunov, Vladimir Ivanovich 147, 151, 153, **154**
Desiderio da Settignano 64
Diaghilev, Serge 155, 156, 177, 183
Dickson, Jeremy 500, 512
Dmitriev, Vladimir Vladimirovich 170, 172, 179, 396
Dobuzhinskii, Mstislav Valerianovich 177
Dobychina, Nadezhda Evseevna 165, 178, 239
Donatello 438
Dormidontov, Nikolai Ivanovich 43
Dorofeev, V.G. *272*
Dostoievskii, Fedor Mikhailovich 170
Dovzhenko, Aleksandr Petrovich 38
Drevin, Aleksandr Davidovich 185
Drevin, Andrei Aleksandrovich 335, *60, 61, 83*
Drevina, Ekaterina Andreevna 332, 513
Drizen, Nikolai Vasil'evich 158, 177
Druskin, Mikhail Semenovich 164, 397
Dubinetskii 339
Dubinskaia 494
Duchamp, Marcel 44
Dudin, I.O. 184
Dupré, Dominique 153
Dymshits-Tolstaia, Sof'ia Isaakovna 17, 24, 40, 41, 42, 43, 186, **187,** 188, 237, 238, 263, 266, 339, 446, 494, 507, *173*

Efimov, Boris Efimovich 437
Efros, Abram Markovich 43, 158, 159, 178, 406, **407**
Ehrenburg, Il'ia Grigor'evich 43, 339, 447, *134, 185*
Eikhenbaum, Boris Mikhailovich 342
Einstein, Albert 15
Eisenstein, Sergei Mikhailovich 38, 327
El Lissitzky, *see* Lissitzky
El'konin, V.B. 263, 333, 338, 437, 439, 448
El'konina, Nadezhda Mikhailovna 439, 448
El'skii, Vsevolod Osipovich 181
Ender, Boris Vladimirovich **243,** 402
Enei 494
Engel'meier, Petr Klement'evich 403, **406**
Erdman, Boris Robertovich 318, 320
Erlich, Viktor 339
Ermilov, P.D. 164, 504
Ershov, Petr Pavlovich 263
Esenin, Sergei Aleksandrovich 10, 442
Evreinov, Nikolai Nikolaevich 177, 492
Evseev, M. I. 43
Exter, Alexandra A. 40, 58, 64, 66, 157, 159, 250, 263, 266, 507

Fabri, M. 445
Faiko, Aleksei Mikhailovich 324, 438, 504, 512, *399*
Fal'k' Robert Rafailovich 17, 41, 45, 68, 263, 266, 445
Favorskii, Vladimir Andreevich 154, 437, 439, 448
Fedorov, Nikolai Fedorovich 442
Fedorov-Davydov, Aleksei Aleksandrovich 496
Fedotov, Ivan Sergeevich 438

Fidler, Ivan Ivanovich 41
Filonov, Pavel Nikolaevich 44, 57, 58, 133, 178, **258,** 263, 332, 398
Fleishman, Lazar Solomonovich 402
Fomin, Ivan Aleksandrovich 250, 339
Fonvizin, Artur Vladimirovich 50, 263
Forreger von Greifenturn, Nikolai Mikhailovich **243**
Franketti, V. 41
Friedländer, Max 66

Gabo, Naum (Neemiia Abramovich Pevsner) 27
Galaktionov, P. 268
Galanov, Boris Efimovich 441
Gastev, Aleksei Kapitonovich 21
Gauss, Karl Friedrich 396, 399
Geintse, Mariia Andreevna 149, 255, **256,** 257, 261, 262, 311, 312, 447, 448, 508
Gerasimov, Sergei Vasil'evich 314, 448
Gessen, Iakov Matveeich **260**
Ginstling, Esfir' Mikhailovna 147, 151, **153,** 513, *285*
Ginzburg, Moisei Iakovlevich 250, 339
Gladkov, Evgenii Konstantinovich 154
Gladkov, Fedor Vasil'evich 147
Gleizes, Albert 263, 347, 348, 389, 390, 391, 393,
Glinka, Mikhail Ivanovich 63, 66, 71, 156, 183, 240, 265, 324, 445, 499, 502, 503, 509, *137–155*
Globa, Andrei Pavlovich 172, 324, 504
Gogol', Nikolai Vasil'evich 169, 172, 179
Goldovskaia, M.I. *424, 425, 426*
Goldzamt, Edmund A. 441
Goncharov, Andrei Dmitrievich 314, 439, 440
Goncharova, Natalia Sergeevna 44, 45, 50, 53, 58, 156, 176, 178, 263, 445, *37*
Gorbovets, V.I. 495
Goriaev, Vitalii Nikolaevich 439
Goriushkin-Sorokopudov, Ivan Silych 44, 322, **327,** 332, 445
Gornfel'd, Arkadii Georgievich 341, **342**
Gorodetskii, Sergei Mitrofanovich 437
Grabar', Igor Emanuilovich 41, 42, 46
Grashchenkov 63, 64
Gray, Camilla 62, 507
Gregori, Johann Gottfried 164, 178, 179
Gremislavskii, Ivan Iakovlevich 172, 173, 174, 176
Grigor'ev, Viktor Petrovich 133, 402
Grigorovich 495
Grinberg, Nikolai Ivanovich 402
Grishchenko, A.B. 263
Gropius, Walter 266
Grossman, Leonid Petrovich 171, 179
Grosz, George 35, 43, *136*
Guminer, A. 340
Guro, Elena Genrikhovna 340, 402
Gurov, Evgenii Alekseevich 164, 504
Gushanskii, S.Kh. 504
Gustomesov, Leonid Vasil'evich **329**
Gzhitskii, Vladimir Zenonovich 164, 503

Hansen-Löwe, A. 399
Hausmann, Raoul 35, 446, *135*
Heartfield, John 35, *136*
Heartfield, Gertrud *136*

Hoffmann, E. T. A. 411
Holm, Arne 512
Homer 440

Iakovlev, Vasilii Nikolaevich 492
Iakubinskii, Lev Petrovich 248, **249,** 342, 395, 398, 399, 403
Iakulov, Georgii Bogdanovich 16, 23, 24, 52, 57, 185, 446, 512
Il'in, Lev Aleksandrovich 250, 339
Iroshnikova, Irina Ivanovna 175, 440, 504
Isakov, Sergei Konstantinovich 15, 19, 37, 40, 43, 153, 244, 245, 253, 259, **260,** 333, **335,** 393, 407, 445, 494
Istomin, Konstantin Nikolaevich 437
Tsar Ivan IV, the Terrible 178
Ivanov, Pavel Ivanovich 24, 41, 321
Ivanov, Viacheslav Vsevolodovich 399
Iurtsev, A. 147
Iustitskii, Valentin Mikhailovich 266
Iutkevich, Sergei Osipovich 164, 178, 397, 400, 402
Izdebskii, Vladimir Alekseevich 61, 489

Jivelegov, Aleksei Karpovich 66

Kachurin, I. V. 502
Kaleshits, A.A. 495
Kamenskii, Vasilii Vasil'evich 21, 164, 315, 322, **327,** 394, 395, 439, 447, 513
Kantsel, V.S. 504
Kandaurov 492
Kandinsky, Wassily (Vasil'evich) 24, 41, 44, 57, 58
Kapeliush, Bella Naumovna 340
Kapitsa, Anna Aleksandrovna 66, 505
Kaplunovskii, Vladimir Pavlovich 325, **328,** 448, 495
Karev, 339
Kardovskii, Dmitrii Nikolaevich 339
Kasatkin, Nikolai Alekseevich 322, **327**
Kassák, Lajos 447
Kataev, Valentin Petrovich 504
Kazanskii, Boris Vasil'evich 397, 402
Kedrov, Mikhail Nikolaevich 11, 172, 173, 176, 324, **328,** 448, 504
Khan-Magomedov, Selim Omarovich 43, 152, 267
Khapaev, Nikolai Alekseevich 43, 153, 250, **252,** 255, 256, 257, 399
Khapov, Vladimir F. 147, 154, 441
Kharchenko 17, 321, 445
Khardzhiev, Nikolai Ivanovich 129, 133, 154, 160, 337, 439
Kharms, Daniel Ivanovich (Iuvachev) 130, 131, 132, **133,** 168, 398, 402, 448, 500, 501, 506, *298–312*
Khlebnikov, Velemir (Velimir, Viktor) Vladimirovich (pen-names: Lunev and Vekha) 10, 13, 15, 16, 17, 18, 20, 21, 22, 23, 31, 37, 40, 43, 47, 69, 70, 71, 129, 130, 131, 132, 133, 134, 135, 136, 137, 142, 146, 147, 149, 150, 152, 154, 160, 161, 162, 163, 164, 178, **238,** 243, 245, 248, 249, 251, 263, 312, 314, 315, 322, 324, 327, 332, 335, 336, 337, 338, 393, 395, 396, 397, 398, 399, 400, 401, 402, 403, 437, 442, 445, 446, 447, 448, 494, 503, 506, 507, 510, 513, 514, *73, 207, 208, 211, 215, 216–225, 227–233*
Khlebnikova, Vera Vladimirovna 245, 437

Khodasevich, Valentina Mikhailovna 17, 40, 56, 61, 62, 63, 64, 66, 68, 72, 149, 152, 154, 266, 445
Kholodnaia, M.P. 398
Kholodov 153, 250, 255, **256,** 257
Kholopov 250
Khomaza 495
Khrakovskii, Vladimir L'vovich 42
Khrenikova, Ol'ga Nesterovna (Maks Li) 177, 181
Khvoinik, I. 130, 133
Kiselev, Viktor 437
Kliuev, Nikolai Alekseevich 335
Kliun, Ivan Vasil'evich (Klinkov) 58, 266, 331, 335, *96*
Klutsis, Gustav Gustavovich 152
Kobelev 153, 250, 255, **256,** 257
Koepplin, Dieter 66
Kol'berg, L. 441
Kolesaev, V.S. 504
Konchalovskii, Petr Petrovich 52, 263, 393
Konenkov, Sergei Timofeevich 41, 42, 186, 188, 442
Koonen, Alisa Georgievna 328
Korolev, Boris Danilovich 41, 186, 188
Korotkov 153, 250
Korovin, Konstantin Alekseevich 45, 46, 159, 262, **263,** 322, 326, 445
Korsakova, Aleksandra Nikolaevna *see* Rudovich, A.N.
Kosiakov, Georgii Antonovich 339
Kostin, Vladimir Ivanovich 8, 40, 41, 45, 48, 61, 62, 67, 178, 266, 508, *402–404*
Kovtun, Evgenii Fedorovich 331, 337, 499, 501
Kozhich, Vladimir Platonovich 164, 504
Kozhin, Pavel Mikhailovich 146, 147, **153,** 325, 328, 502, 513, *288*
Kozintsev, Grigorii Mikhailovich 400
Kozlinskii, Vladimir Ivanovich 68, 320
Kozlov, Aleksei Nikolaevich 172, 179
Kramarenko, L. A. 153
Kristi, Mikhail Petrovich 246, 247, 252, 253, 255, 258, 260
Kriukov, M. 41, 513
Kron, Aleksandr Aleksandrovich 172, 173, 179, 324, 499, 504, 512, *392–396, 401*
Kronman, Evgenii 43, 245, 312, 313, 508
Kruchenykh, Aleksei Eliseevich 58, 61, 178, 338, 394, 397, 402, 403, 447, 506
Krupskaia, Nadezhda Konstantinovna 323, **327**
Kryzhitskii, Georgii Konstantinovich 400
Kubin, Al'fred 263
Kulbin, Nikolai N. 446
Kuprianov, N. N. 447, 495
Kuprin, Aleksandr Vasil'evich 263
Kurbas-Les', Aleksandr Stepanovich 398
Kushner, Boris 152, 394
Kut, A. *see* Kutuzov, A.V.
Kutuzov, A.V. 43, 62, 151, 249, 312, **313**
Kuznetsov, Pavel Varfolomeevich 41, 45, 57, 145, 238, 314, 446, 448

Labas, Aleksandr Arkad'evich 151
Lado, A.S. 501
Lamanova, Nadezhda Petrovna 144, **153,** *252*
Lamtsov, Ivan Vasil'evich 152
Lang, Lothar 340

Lapshin, Nikolai Fedorovich 40, 43, 68, 151, 162, 242, 243, 246, **247,** 251, 263, 332, 393, 398, 403, 445, 494, *213*

Larionov, Mikhail Fedorovich 16, 17, 22, 40, 44, 45, 46, 47, 49, 50, 51, 52, 53, 57, 58, 61, 65, 67, 183, 262, **263,** 332, 333, 445, *12, 17, 32, 33*

Lassalle, Ferdinand 345, 347

Lavinskii, Anton Mikhailovich 394

Lavrenev, Boris Andreevich 175, 324, 504

Lebedev, Vladimir Vasil'evich 31, 39, 68, 143, 184, 340, 393, 445, 446, 447, 494, 495

Lebedeva, *see* Darmolatova, Sarra

Leblanc, Mikhail Varfolomeevich 184

Le Corbusier (Jeanneret, Charles Éduard) 44, 141, 447, 448

Le Dantiu, Mikhail Vasil'evich 16, 17, 68, 177, 181, 263, 445, 489

Le Fauconnier, Henri 262, 263, 332

Léger, Ferdinand 447

Lenin, Vladimir Il'ich 41, 185, 187, 188, 250, 327, 407, 442, 446

Lentulov, Aristarkh Vasil'evich 53, 184, 263, 314, 445

Leonardo da Vinci 39, 63, 64, 66, 149, 404, 441, *100, 322, 323, 324*

Leonidov, Ivan Il'ich 38

Levenets 17, 321, 445

Levitan, Isaak Il'ich 238, 239, 322, **327**

Lilienthal, Otto 39

Lindinger, H. 153

Lishev 339

Lishin, Mikhail Efimovich 324, 504

Lissitzky, El (Lazar' Markovich) 35, 43, 44, 339, 447, *134*

Liubich, M. 441

Liubimova, Valentina Aleksandrovna 179

Lobachevskii, Nikolai Ivanovich 15, 396, 399

Lobov, M.P. 152

Logvinov, V. 442

Loiko, G.S. 495

Lopatin, N. 177

Losev, A.V. 149, 311, **312,** 448, 508

Lunacharskii, Anatolii Vasil'evich 23, 41, 42, 185, 187, 188, 238, 251, 260, 323, 327, 394, 396, 397, 398, 446, 448, 513

Lunev, *see* Khlebnikov, Velemir

Lur'e, Artur Sergeevich 178, 335, 337, 396, 446, 513

L'vov, Petr I. 335, 447, 495

Lysenko 321

Mácza, János (Matsa, Ivan Liudvigovich) 409, 411

Maiakovskii, Vladimir Vladimirovich 10, 21, 22, 37, 38, 40, 41, 45, 70, 129, 131, 133, 147, 153, 177, 178, 185, 187, 244, 245, **246,** 247, 260, 263, 314, 315, 322, 326, 327, 335, 337, 343, 393, 394, 395, 397, 398, 439, 441, 442, 445, 446, 447, 448, 492, 498, 500, 503, 506, 512, *71, 290, 291, 292*

Makarov, A. 501

Maks Li, *see* Khrenikova, Ol'ga

Malerevskii, P.G. 504

Malevich, Kazimir Severinovich 17, 21, 22, 26, 27, 38, 41, 42, 44, 45, 50, 57, 58, 60, 65, 133, 151, 152, 153, 178, 238, 242, 253, 255, **258,** 259, 263, 266, 331, 332, 333, 339, 397, 398, 438, 445, 446, 447, 492, 494, *96*

Malinovskii, Pavel Petrovich 187, **188**

Mamontov, Savva Ivanovich 158

Mandel'shtam, Osip Emil'evich 335

Manet, Édouard 348, 389

Mansurov, Pavel Aleksandrovich 40, 257, **258,** 259, 494

Mariengof, Anatolii Borisovich 40

Marinetti, Filippo Tommaso 15

Markish, Perets Davidovich 174

Markov, *see* Matvei

Marquet, Albert 18, 263

Marshak, Samuel Iakovlevich 324, 437, 504

Martynov, Leonid Nikolaevich 253

Mashkov, Il'ia Ivanovich 41, 45, 52, 53, 263, 332, 445, 492

Matiushin, Mikhail Vasil'evich 178, **243,** 247, 248, 255, 331, 340, 393, 397, 402, 403, 494

Matveev, Alexandr Terent'evich 339

Matvei, V. 263

Medvedev, V.V. 445

Medvedeva, Galina Valerianovna 177, 178

Meerzon, Iosif Aizikovich 30, 31, 42, 43, 239, **240,** 340, 344, 442, 446, 447, 507, *173*

Meierkhol'd' Vsevolod Emil'evich (Meyerhold) 21, 23, 38, 40, 159; 187, 244, 312, **313,** 314, 315, 327, 393, 394, 395, 396, 397, 398, 399, 439, 446

Mellit, Zinaida Pavlovna 151, 437, 501

Mel'nikov, Konstantin Stepanovich 38

Mendeleev, Dmitrii Ivanovich 15

Men'kov, Mikhail Ivanovich 58, 331

Metzinger, Jean 262, **263,** 332, 347, 348, 389, 390, 391, 393

Meyerhold, *see* Meierkhol'd

Michelangelo Buonarroti 68, 438

Mies van der Rohe, Ludwig 141, 142, *262*

Mikhailovskii, Aleksandr Nikolaevich 332, 445

Mikhalkov, Sergei Vladimirovich 324, 504

Miklashevskii, Konstantin Mikhailovich 151, 152, 154, 245, 397, 406

Minkel'dei 41

Miturich, Mai Petrovich 513

Miturich, Petr Vasil'evich 133, **245,** 335, **338,** 393, 402, 437, 445, 447, 494, 495

Moholy-Nagy, László 44

Molok, Iurii Aleksandrovich 41, 500

Mondrian, Piet 22, 44

Monet, Claude 389

Morgunov, Aleksei Alekseevich 41, 56, 263, 266, 445, 446, 492

Morozov, Mikhail Vladimirovich 18, 45, 174, 179, 263

Morris, William 333, **335**

Moskvichev 41

Mukhina, Vera Ignat'evna 42

Müller, Vladimir Nikolaevich 165, 166, 178, 179

Munts 339

Nandurs, Eslie 512

Naumets, V.A. 495

Nefedov, V.V. 148, 154, 441

Nekrasov, Evgenii Nikolaevich 153, 250, 255, **256,** 257

Nekrasov, Nikolai Alekseevich 321, **326,** 403

Nemenova 494

Neradovskii, Petr Ivanovich 238, **239,** 260, 261, 262

Nesterov, Mikhail Vasil'evich 442

Neuhaus, Heinrich 437
Neznamov, Petr Vasil'evich 394
Tsar Nicholas I 169
Nikol'skii, Aleksandr Sergeevich 38
Nivinskii, Ignatii Ignat'evich 250
Norbert, Edgar Ivanovich 250
Notgaft, F.F. 491
Novitskii, Pavel Ivanovich 40, 41, 260, **261,** 312, 448

Obrist, Hermann 29, *201*
Okhlopkov, Nikolai Pavlovich 324
Okunchikov, A.Z. 504
Oleinikov, Nikolai Makarovich 402
Ösdberg, Henrik 512
Os'merkin, Aleksandr Aleksandrovich 437
Ostrovskii, Aleksandr Nikolaevich 71, 164, 165, 171, 174, 314, 315, 324, 325, 438, 497, 498, 504, 511, *354–368*
Ovid 343
Ozerov, Lev Adol'fovich 441

Pakhomov, Aleksei Fedorovich 40, 43, 494
Pakulin 494
Parnis, Aleksandr Efimovich 8, 151, 154, 177, 178, 332, 337, 400, 403, 513, 514
Pashnitskii, O.E. 495
Pasternak, Boris Leonidovich 40, 394
Pasternak, Leonid Osipovich 322, **327,** 492
Pavil'onov, Georgii (Iurii) Sergeevich 39, 148, **154,** 311, **312,** 438, 439, 448, 508, *314, 317, 329*
Pavlenko, Oksana Trofimovna 145
Pavlishchev, Ivan, *see* Bersenev, Ivan
Pavlov, V.Ia. 152, 502, 512
Pavlovskii, Serafim Aleksandrovich 398
Pchel'nikova, O. 43, 494
Pern, N. Ia. 399
Perov'skaia, Sof'ia L'vovna *169*
Pessiatii 494
Pestel', Vera Efimovna 58, 183, 266, 512, *83*
Tsar Peter I, the Great 143, 155, 178, 181
Petnikov, Grigorii Nikolaevich 446, 513
Petrova, Marina Vladimirovna 151, 177
Petrovskii, Dmitrii Vasil'evich 154, 337, 338, 446
Petrov-Vodkin, Kuz'ma Sergeevich 39, 45, 313, **314,** 339, 448
Pevsner, Natan Abramovich 27
Pevsner, Naum, *see* Gabo, Naum
Picasso, Pablo 16, 17, 18, 20, 262, **263,** 332, 334, 348, 389, 390, 391, 392, 393, 394, 395, 438, 445, *106, 107*
Pimenov, Iurii Ivanovich 178
Piscator (Visscher Claes Jans) 29
Plamen', Baian 185
Plotnikov, Aleksandr Konstantinovich 168, 176, 324, 504
Podvolotskaia, E.P. 501
Pokhomov 30
Pokrovskii, Igor Aleksandrovich 440
Pokrovskii, Mikhail Nikolaevich 41, 188
Poletaev, Evgenii Aleksandrovich 399
Polonskii, Iakov Petrovich, 321, **326**
Popov 339
Popov, Aleksei Dmitrievich 169, 171, 324, 504
Popov, P. 62
Popov, V.A. 317, 324

Popova, Liubov Sergeevna 17, 44, 54, 55, 56, 57, 58, 62, 64, 68, 143, 266, 394, 445, *59*
Popov-Voronezhskii, Ivan Nikoforovich 402, 494, *215*
Prakhov, A. N. 495
Prichard, G. Izdebski 61
Prutkovskaia *83*
Puni, Ivan Al'bertovich 58, 331, 335, 339, 492, 507
Punin, Nikolai Nikolaevich 13, 16, 18, 19, 29, 30, 34, 40, 41, 42, 43, 45, 46, 48, 52, 61, 62, 129, 130, 138, 139, 140, 144, 151, 152, 153, 163, 164, 167, 237, 238, 239, 241, 242, **243,** 244, 246, **247,** 248, 255, **258,** 260, 263, 335, 339, 340, 344, **346,** 347, 392, 393, 394, 395, 396, 397, 398, 399, 400, 401, 402, 403, 406, 407, 437, 445, 446, 447, 494, 506, 507, 508, 514, *182, 183, 184, 212, 213, 239*
Punina, Irina Nikolaevna 151
Pushkin, Aleksandr Sergeevich 132, 178, 263, 316, 395

Rabinovich, Miron Il'ich (Roslavlev) 174, **183,** 250, 320
Radlov, Nikolai Ernestovich 21, 40, 41, 42, 243
Radlov, Sergei Ernestovich **243,** 397
Radlova, *see* Darmolatova, Anna
Raikhenshtein, Anna Moiseevna 237
Rakhillo, Ivan Spiridonovich 442
Rakhtanov, Isar Arkad'evich 267, 309, **310,** 514, *339*
Redchits, P. 495
Red'ko, Aleksandr Mefodievich 397
Red'ko, Kliment 394
Reino, L. 508
Repin, Il'ia Efimovich 327, 341, **342**
Rerikh, Nikolai Konstantinovich 177
Reshetnikov, Fedor Pavlovich 442
Riabushkin, Andrei Petrovich 16, 322, **327**
Riemann, Georg Friedrich 15
Rimskii-Korsakov, Nikolai Andreevich 156, 158, 178
Rindell, Swan 500, 512
Ripellino, Angelo Maria 398
Robbia, Luca della 64
Rodchenko, Aleksandr Mikhailovich 41, 44, 60, 140, 143, 144, 145, 152, 185, 266, 268, 394, 447, 508, 509, 512, *95, 244*
Rodchenko, Varvara Aleksandrovna 246, 508, 509, *95, 244*
Rodin, Auguste 29, 334
Rogochii 495
Rogozhin, N.N. 140, 152, 267, 500, 502, 509
Rohe, Mies van der, *see* Mies van der Rohe, Ludwig
Romains, Jules 164, 503
Romanovich, Sergei Mikhailovich 45
Röntgen, Wilhelm Conrad 15
Rosenberg, Jakob 66
Roslavlev, *see* Rabinovich, Miron I.
Rostislavov, Aleksandr Aleksandrovich 250
Rozanova, Ol'ga Vladimirovna 58, 178, 263, 334, 335
Rozenblium, Evgenii Abramovich 437
Rozhdestvenskii, Vasilii Vasil'evich 68, 263
Rubinshtein, Ia. E. 498, 502
Rublev, Andrei 53
Rudnev, Lev Vladimirovich 39, 339, 439, 448
Rudovich, Aleksandra Nikolaevna (Korsakova) 151, 153, 177, 178, 241, **329,** 439, 448
Ruskin, John 333, **335**
Rybakov, 321

Rylov, Arkadii Aleksandrovich 339
Ryndin, Vadim Fedorovich 167, 177, 316

Sagaidachnyi, Evgenii Iakovlevich 69, 176, 177, 181, 262, 263, 445
Sakovich 153, 250
Sanin, Aleksandr Akimovich 177
Sarab'ianov, Dmitrii Vladimirovich 8, 40, 42, 44, 62, 63, 64, 66, 72, 133, 178, 184, 258, 263, 500, 505, 506, 507, *59*
Sarian, Martinos Sergeevich 45, 57
Savinskii 339
Savitskii, Konstantin Apollonovich 44
Schade, Werner 66
Schuchardt, Christian 64, 66
Schumacher, Heinrich Christian 399
Schwitters, Kurt 44
Segonzac, André Dunoyer de 332
Selvinskii, Il'ia L'vovich 504
Semenko, Mikhail Vasil'evich 130, **133,** 154, 447, 495, 506, *293*
Semenov, Sergei Aleksandrovich 167, 504
Sen'kin, Sergei 439, 448
Sergel', S. 40, 130, 131, 448, 506, *294–297*
Serov, Valentin Aleksandrovich 45, 52, 67, 69, 262, **263,** 322, 326, 445
Severianin, Igor (Lotarev) 40
Sevast'ianov, V. I. 440
Shaliapin, Fedor Ivanovich 442
Shamurin, Iurii 42
Shapiro, Tevel' Markovich 30, 31, 42, 43, 239, **240,** 340, 344, 442, 446, 447, 507, 508, 512, *173, 178*
Shchipitsyn, Aleksandr Vasil'evich 61, 148, 312, 437, 438, 448, 508
Shchukin, Sergei Ivanovich 18, 45, 47, 263
Shchuko, Vladimir Alekseevich 250
Shchusev, Aleksei Viktorovich 250
Shekhtel', Fedor Osipovich 240
Shemshin, V. 62
Shervud, Leonid Vladimirovich 68, 339
Sheukov, A. 508
Shevchenko, Aleksandr Vasil'evich 41, 61, 263
Shifrin, Nisson Abramovich 178, 318, 319, **320,** 438
Shima, I. 61
Shishkin, M. 508
Shklovskii, Viktor Borisovich 21, 26, 41, 42, 151, 341, **342,** 343, 402, 440, 447
Shkol'nik, Iosif Solomonovich 17, 178, **182,** 237, 263
Shkurupii, G. 130, 133, 154, 447, 506, *293*
Schmidt, Otto Iul'evich **316**
Shneiderman, Isaak Izrailevich 179, 315
Shtal'berg, Ernest Iakovlevich 339
Shtein, Aleksandr Petrovich 168, 504, 511, *384–391*
Shterenberg, David Petrovich 21, 41, 145, 238, 259, **260,** 339
Shtiglits, Aleksandr Ludvigovich 258
Shtoffer, Iakov Zakharovich 325, **328**
Shtok, Isidor Vladimirovich 174, 179, 504, 512, *398*
Shukhaev, Vasilii Ivanovich 339
Shukhov, Vladimir Grigor'evich *189, 191*
Shumanskii 495
Shvarts, Evgenii L'vovich 176, 324, 504, 512, *397*
Shvets 495

Signac, Paul 263
Sileverstov, I.D. 17, 262, 445
Simonov, Konstantin Mikhailovich 9, 11
Sinaiskii, Viktor Aleksandrovich 347
Smirnov, Vasilii Petrovich 147, 336, 337, 338, 505, 513, 514, *226, 228–230*
Sokol-Chernilovskii 495
Sokolova, Natalia Ivanovna 175, 179
Sologub, Fedor *see* Teternikov F. K.
Solopov, Vladimir G. 152, 502, 512
Sotnikov, Aleksei Georgievich 39, 136, 145, 146, 148, 151, **153,** 154, 246, 252, 311, 312, 325, 328, 438, 439, 448, 502, 512, 513, *275–284, 315, 316, 317*
Spandikov, Eduard Karlovich 177, 181, **253,** 263
Spasovskii, M. 340
Stakanov 43
Stalin, Iosif Vissarionovich 310
Stam, Mart 141, 142, *261*
Stebnitskii, G. 494
Stenberg, Georgii Augustovich 40
Stenberg, Vladimir Augustovich 40
Stepanova, Varvara Fedorovna 143, 144, 394
Stovbunenko, P.V. 495
Strabo 440
Stradomskaia, E.I. 504
Stravinsky, Igor Fedorovich 156
Strigalev, Anatolii Anatol'evich 8, 13, 41, 42, 43, 44, 61, 62, 72, 133, 151, 152, 154, 178, 183, 188, 238, 240, 243, 258, 263, 266, 312, 339, 500, 512
Strizhenova, Tat'iana A. 153
Strizhiminskii, Vladislav M. 41
Stroev, A. 445
Subbotin 41, 513
Sukhovo-Kobylin, Aleksandr Vasil'evich 41, 71, 169, 170, 171, 172, 179, 324, 325, 328, 411, 412, 438, 448, 499, 504, 511, *369–383*
Surov, A.A. 324, 504
Suvorova, O.A. 153
Syrkina, Flora Iakovlevna 8, 40, 43, 62, 66, 72, 133, 151, 152, 154, 155, 181, 238, 315, 396

Tairov, Aleksandr Iakovlevich 167, 316, 324, **328,** 504
Taran, Andrei Ivanovich 41, 43, 242, 246, **247,** 262, 403, 494
Tatlin, Evgraf Nikoforovich 14, 40, 321, 326, 445, *1*
Tatlin, F. 14, 40
Tatlin, Semen Semenovich 139, 151, 152, 162, *1, 2, 3*
Tatlin, Vladimir Vladimirovich (Volodia) 149, 173, 262, 448, *236*
Tatlina, Nadezhda, *see* Bart, N.N.
Terlitskii 43
Ternovets, Boris Nikolaevich 186
Teternikov, Fedor Kuz'mich (Sologub) 159, 312, **313**
Theophanes the Greek 66, *97, 98*
Tikhanova, V.A. 153
Tolstaia, Sof'ia Isaakovna, *see* Dymshits-Tolstaia
Tolstoi, Aleksei Konstantinovich 263
Tolstoi, Lev Nikolaevich 172
Tovstonogov, Georgii Aleksandrovich 11, 175, 176, 324, 328, 440, 504
Traskunov, Aron Borisovich 147, 154
Trauberg, Leonid Zakharovich 400

Tret'iakov, Sergei Mikhailovich 394
Triaskin, N. I. 495
Tsiolkovskii, Konstantin Edvardovich 442
Tsionglinskii, Ian Frantsevich 68, 332
Tuberovskii, M.D. 243
Tufanov, Aleksandr Vasil'evich 162, 163, 164, 178, 397, 398, 400, **402,** *215*
Tugendkhol'd, Iakov Aleksandrovich 43, 244, **250,** 260
Tynianov, Iurii Nikolaevich 137, 152, 342
Tyrsa, Nikolai Andreevich 39, 151, 335, 340, 393, 445, 447, 494, 495
Tyshler, Aleksandr Grigor'evich 174, 178, 320

Udal'tsova, Nadezhda Andreevna, 17, 41, 58, 68, 70, 185, 266, 331, **332,** 333, 335, 445, 512, 513, *60, 61*
Uitz, Béla 314, 447, 448
Ul'ianov, Nikolai Pavlovich 45
Umanskii, Morits Borisovich 325, **328,** 495
Umansky, Konstantin 35, 37, 43
Uspenskii 494

Vakhtangov, Sergei Evgenevich 315
Vakhterov, K.V. 504
Vallotton, Felix 263
Van Dongen, Kees 18, 263
Van Gogh, Vincent 46, 47
Vanin, V.V. 504
Varpekhovskii, M. 495
Vasil'eva, Zoia Vasil'evna 147, 153, **154,** 266
Vasnetsov, Viktor Mikhailovich 158
Vekha, *see* Khlebnikov
Verlaine, Paul 348
Verne, Jules 341
Verocchio, Andrea del 438
Vesnin, Aleksandr Aleksandrovich 17, 38, 54, 55, 61, 62, 68, 70, 143, **182,** 250, 266, 322, 323, 328, 445, 514, *80, 81*
Vesnin, Leonid Aleksandrovich 38, 182, 250
Vil'iams, Petr Vladimirovich 173, 178

Vinogradov, Nikolai Dmitrievich 187, **188**
Vinogradov, Pavel Mikhailovich 30, 42, 239, **240,** 255, **256,** 325, **328,** 344, 347, 446, 447, 507
Vinnikov, Nikolai Georgievich 179, 504
Vishnevskii, Vsevolod Vital'evich 147, 167, 442
Vlaminck, Maurice 263
Volinskii, Akim L'vovich (Fleksner) 400, **402**
Volkov, Aleksandr Nikolaevich 178, 320
Vvedenskii, Aleksandr Nikolaevich 398, 402
Vysheslavtseva, Sof'ia Grigor'evna 397

Wagenfeld, Wilhelm *274*
Wagner, Richard 160, 183, 240, 324, 325, 445, 503, 510, *156–163*
Watson, Peter 500, 512
Wingler, Hans Maria 340
Woodward, Christopher 500, 512

Zabolotskii, Nikolai Alekseevich 398
Zaitsev, Nikolai Semenovich 321
Zalaman 339
Zalka, Máté 147
Zaporozhets 188
Zavadskii, Iurii Aleksandrovich 324
Zdanevich, Kirill Mikhailovich 61, 62, 263
Zelenskii, Aleksei Evgen'evich 148, 171, 312, 438, 508, *344*
Zelinskii, Kornelii Liutsianovich 250, 267, **309,** 336, 409, 448
Zhadova, Larissa Alekseevna 8, 9, 40, 43, 62, 63, 66, 72, 129, 133, 134, 154, 177, 178, 179, 184, 238, 242, 251, 257, 266, 267, 399, 501, 512, 513, *166, 235, 313, 316*
Zhegin, Lev Fedorovich 45
Zheltikov 153, 250
Zheverzheev, Levkii Ivanovich 17, 181, 183, 263, 489, 490, 492, 494
Zhirmunskii, Viktor Maksimovich 42, 342
Zlochevskii 495
Zolotnitskii, D. 398

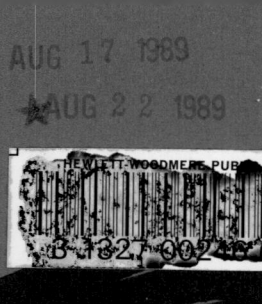